Foundations of Communication

W9-CMO-470

Skill	Use	Procedure	Example
Making a verbal statement that reflects your understanding of another person's behavior.	To enable you to test the accuracy of your perceptions.	1. Describe the behaviors of the other that have led to your perception. 2. Add your interpretation of the behavior to your statement.	After taking a phone call, Shimika comes into the room with a completely blank expression and neither speaks to Donnell nor acknowledges that he is in the room. Donnell says, "Shimika, from your blank look, I get the feeling that you're in a state of shock. Has something happened?"

Using Specific Language (page 65)

Skill	Use	Procedure	Example
Clarify meaning by narrowing what is understood from a general category to a particular group within that category, by appealing to the senses, by choosing words that symbolize exact thoughts and feelings, or by using concrete details or examples.	To help the listener picture thoughts analogous to the speaker's.	1. Assess whether the word or phrase to be used is less specific (or concrete or precise) than it can be. 2. Pause to consider alternatives. 3. Select a more specific (or concrete or precise) word, or give an example or add details.	Instead of saying, "Bring the stuff for the audit," say, "Bring the records and receipts from the last year for the audit." Or, instead of saying, "Make sure you improve your grades," say, "This term, we want to see a B in Spanish and at least a C in Algebra."

Communication Skills

PULL OUT SECTION☞

Group Communication

Brainstorming (page 241)

Skill	Use	Procedure	Example
An uncritical, nonevaluative process of generating associated ideas.	To generate a list of potential solutions to a problem.	1. Verbalize ideas as they come to mind. 2. Refrain from evaluating the merits of ideas. 3. Encourage outrageous and unique ideas. 4. Build on or modify the ideas of others. 5. Use extended effort to generate more ideas. 6. Record the ideas.	Problem: "What should we do to raise money to help a child who needs a liver transplant?" Ideas: sell cookies, sell candy, sell wrapping paper; wrap packages at a mall for donations; find corporate sponsors; have a corporate golf outing, a youth golf outing, a tennis tournament, a bowling tournament, a paintball tournament; auction donated paintings; or do odd jobs for money.

Problem Solving in Groups (page 243)

Skill

Using a systematic, six-step process to work out difficulties or resolve issues.

Use

A guide for groups to follow in arriving at conclusions to fact or value questions.

Procedure

1. Define the problem in specific and precise language as a question of fact, value, or policy containing one central idea. The question is: "What textbook should we adopt for the required Human Communication course?"
2. Analyze the problem using the experiences of group members, information obtained from public sources, and through interviews with other knowledgeable people.
3. Determine the solution criteria.
4. Identify possible solutions through brainstorming.
5. Evaluate the solutions by comparing them to the criteria.
6. Decide using expert opinion, average group opinion, majority, unanimity, or consensus method.

Example

The question is: "What textbook should we adopt for the required Human Communication course?" Members who have taught the course before recount their experiences with various texts. We read the publishers' information packets, and we talk to the sales reps. The criteria we will use are coverage, writing style, web support, and cost.
We identify six books that might work.

We compare the books to each other using our criteria.

We adopt a consensus method for deciding.

Public Speaking

Crafting a Specific Speech Goal
That Meets Audience Needs (page 291)

Skill

The process of identifying a speech purpose that draws on the speaker's knowledge and interests and is adapted to a specific audience and setting.

Use

To identify a speaking goal where speaker interest and expertise, audience needs and interests, and setting overlap.

Procedure

1. Identify topics within subject areas in which you have interest and expertise.
2. Analyze your audience's demographic characteristics, interests, and attitudes toward your subject.
3. Understand the occasion and the location for the speech.
4. Select a topic that will meet the interests and needs of your audience and setting.
5. Write a specific speech goal that clearly states the exact response you want from your audience.

Example

Ken first writes, "I want my audience to know what to look for in buying a dog." As he revises, he writes, "I want my audience to understand four important considerations in buying the perfect dog." Once Ken has a goal with a single focus and a clearly specified, desired audience reaction, he tests his first version by writing two differently worded versions.

Communication Skills

Assertiveness (page 187)

Skill	Use	Procedure	Example
Standing up for yourself and doing so in interpersonally effective ways that describe your feelings honestly and exercise your personal rights while respecting the rights of others.	To show clearly what you think or feel.	1. Identify what you are thinking or feeling. 2. Analyze the cause of these feelings. 3. Identify what your real preferences and rights are. 4. Use describing feelings and describing behavior skills to make "I" statements that politely explain your position.	When Gavin believes he is being unjustly charged, he says, "I have never been charged for a refill on iced tea before—has there been a change in policy?"

Organizing the Speech (page 331)

Skill	Use	Procedure	Example
The process of identifying main points, constructing a thesis statement, outlining the body of the speech, developing section transitions, creating an introduction, crafting a conclusion, and cataloguing a list of sources.	To create a hierarchy and sequence of ideas that help a particular audience to easily understand the speaker's ideas and the goal of the speech.	1. Identify your main ideas. 2. Write a thesis statement. 3. Outline the body of the speech by carefully wording main points, selecting an organizational pattern, selecting and organizing support, and preparing section transitions. 4. Create introductions and select the best one. 5. Create conclusions and select the best one. 6. List sources.	The three aspects of romantic love are passion, intimacy, and commitment. I. Passion is the first aspect of romantic love to develop. II. Intimacy is the second. III. Commitment is the third. Example for "passion": A. Passion is a compelling feeling of love. B. (Focus on function.) C. (Discuss maintenance.) Transition from I to II: Although passion is essential to a relationship, passion without intimacy is just sex. Possible introduction: What does it mean to say "I'm in love"? And how can you know whether what you are experiencing is not just a crush? Possible conclusion: Developing romantic love involves passion, intimacy, and commitment. Sample entry: Strenberg, Robert J. and Michael L. Barnes, eds. *The Psychology of Love.* New Haven, CT: Yale University Press, 1988.

Interpersonal Communication

Paraphrasing (page 151)

Skill	Use	Procedure	Example
A response that conveys your understanding of another person's message.	To increase listening efficiency; to avoid message confusion; to discover the speaker's motivation.	1. Listen carefully to the message. 2. Notice what images and feelings you have experienced from this message. 3. Determine what the message means to you. 4. Create a message that conveys these images or feelings.	Grace says, "At two minutes to five, the boss gave me three letters that had to be in the mail that evening!" Bonita replies, "If I understand, you were really resentful that your boss dumped important work on you right before quitting time when she knows you have to pick up the baby at day care."

Describing Feelings (page 179)

Skill	Use	Procedure	Example
Putting an emotional state into words.	For self-disclosure; to teach people how to treat you.	1. Identify the behavior that has triggered the feeling. 2. Identify the specific emotion you are experiencing as a result of the behavior. Anger? Joy? Be specific. 3. Frame your response as an "I" statement. "I feel _____." 4. Verbalize the specific feeling.	"I just heard I didn't get the job, and I feel cheated and bitter" or "Because of the way you defended me when I was being belittled by Leah, I feel both grateful and humbled."

RUDOLPH F. VERDERBER
Distinguished Teaching Professor of Communication
University of Cincinnati

KATHLEEN S. VERDERBER
Northern Kentucky University

with
CYNTHIA BERRYMAN-FINK
University of Cincinnati

THOMSON
WADSWORTH

Australia • Brazil • Canada • Mexico • Singapore • Spain • United Kingdom • United States

THOMSON

WADSWORTH

Communicate! **Twelfth Edition**
Verderber and Verderber

Acquistions Editor: Jaime Perkins

Senior Development Editor: Greer Lleuad

Assistant Editor: John Gahbauer

Editorial Assistant: Kimberly Gengler

Technology Project Manager: Lucinda Bingham

Marketing Manager: Erin Mitchell

Marketing Assistant: Mary Anne Payumo

Marketing Communications Manager: Jessica Perry

Project Manager, Editorial Production: Matt Ballantyne

Creative Director: Rob Hugel

Art Director: Maria Epes

Print Buyer: Doreen Suruki

Permissions Editor: Sarah D'Stair

Production Service: Newgen–Austin

Text Designer: Lisa Delgado

Photo Researcher: Rebecca Seggel

Copy Editor: Joan Harris

Illustrator: Newgen–Austin

Cover Designer: Lisa Delgado

Compositor: Newgen

Text and Cover Printer: RR Donnelley–Willard

Library of Congress Control Number: 2006933091

ISBN-13: 978-0-495-09583-5
ISBN-10: 0-495-09583-4

Thomson Higher Education
10 Davis Drive
Belmont, CA 94002-3098
USA

For more information about our products, contact us at:
Thomson Learning Academic Resource Center
1-800-423-0563

For permission to use material from this text or product, submit a request online at **http://www.thomsonrights.com**. Any additional questions about permissions can be submitted by e-mail to **thomsonrights@thomson.com**.

BRIEF CONTENTS

CONTENTS

PREFACE

1 t is with great excitement that we present you with the twelfth edition of *Communicate!*, a text that remains a market leader because of our commitment to helping students master the concepts, theories, and skills that careful research and scholarship demonstrate are essential for effective human communication.

When we begin a revision, we carefully consider feedback from instructors across the country that informs us about the changing needs of their students. We review the latest scholarship to see how concepts and theories of communication have been refined, and we then update the text so that what students learn represents the best and latest thinking. Additionally, we revise our examples and illustrations so they correspond to changes in theory and practice and reflect the changing social and cultural landscapes to which students are exposed. Finally, we continue to ensure that we are at the forefront of integrating computer-mediated resources into the text so that students are encouraged to be interactive learners, adept at utilizing the vast resources available on the World Wide Web.

This new edition of *Communicate!* continues to combine theory, skills practice, and competency evaluation so that students (1) understand the major concepts from communication theory and research, (2) recognize how these concepts and theories provide a basis for applying communication skills, (3) develop a range of communication skills, and (4) begin to apply what they learn in class to real-life situations, resulting in increased communication competence in all settings.

Strengths of the Text

A major challenge with any revision is to be sensitive to the burgeoning research in communication while still providing a manageable, coherent introduction to the field that makes a real difference to the development of students' skills. This edition, like previous editions, overcomes this challenge by clearly describing well-accepted scholarship that is specifically related to understanding and practicing communication competence. We work hard to accurately translate scholarship into language that is easily understood by introductory students. This revision continues to employ what previous users have said is a reliable learning model. This model has six integrated steps:

1. **Theoretical understanding** of communication theories that provide the foundation for specific skills

2. **Examples** that enable students to identify effective skill usage

3. **Steps** involved in the performance of skills

4. **Practice** in using skills

5. **Self-assessment–based learning goals** that encourage students to assess their current skill levels and to write specific goals that will help them master key skills

6. **Review**

New to This Edition

This new edition incorporates many conceptual and pedagogical changes, including the following significant chapter-by-chapter revisions.

- Chapter 5, "Communicating across Cultures," a **new chapter on intercultural communication,** highlights the increased coverage of diversity throughout the book, making this a text that will reflect any classroom's cultural needs.

- An **updated chapter on relationships,** Chapter 8, "Communicating in Relationships," emphasizes the types of relationships students experience in college and includes an expanded section on communication during the beginning, maintenance, and disintegration stages of relationships.

- **Integrated discussions of cyber-relationships and technology** throughout the book reflect the interpersonal, group, and public speaking situations students experience on a daily basis.

- **Communicate on Your Feet speech assignment boxes** appear throughout the book. In Parts I and II, these assignments encourage students to begin building their public speaking skills immediately while also addressing the needs of instructors who assign prepared speeches throughout the course. In Part IV, these assignments correspond to the speech types discussed in Chapters 15–17.

- **Chapter 12, "Developing Your Topic and Doing Your Research,"** is a new, condensed chapter, formerly Chapters 12 and 13. This chapter provides not only streamlined coverage of these important steps in preparing a speech but also faster entry for students to the speech-making process.

- **Chapter 16, "Informative Speaking,"** has been substantially revised to focus on methods of informing.

- **Chapter 17, "Persuasive Speaking,"** uses the Elaboration Likelihood Model (ELM) to help students understand how to make the best use of reasoning, emotion, and speaker credibility when preparing effective persuasive speeches.

- **All-new student sample speeches and analyses** are featured in Chapter 15, "Overcoming Speech Apprehension by Preparing Delivery," in Chapter 16, "Informative Speaking," and in Chapter 17, "Persuasive Speaking."

In addition, the twelfth edition includes the following new and updated technological features, all highlighted at the end of each chapter in the *Communicate!* Online section:

- The *Communicate!* **online textbook resources,** which provide students with one-stop access to all the integrated technology resources that accompany the book. These resources include the ThomsonNOW™ for *Communicate!* online study system, chapter-by-chapter resources at the *Communicate!* premium book companion website, the *Communicate!* interactive video communication scenarios and speeches, InfoTrac® College Edition, and Speech Builder Express™. All of these resources are referenced in the text and highlighted with an icon. Integrated throughout the chapters—and expanded upon at the ends of chapters in the *Communicate!* Online section—these references direct students to numerous online activities while reinforcing and enriching the concepts presented. **Note to faculty:** If you want your students to have access to the online textbook resources, please be sure to order them for your course. The content in these resources can be bundled at no additional charge to your students with every new copy of the text. If you do not order them, your students will not have access to these online resources. *Contact your local Thomson Wadsworth sales representative for more details.*

- The **ThomsonNOW™ for *Communicate!*,** available to students when instructors order this online textbook resource packaged with the text. Using chapter-by-chapter diagnostic pre-tests that identify concepts students don't fully understand, this online system creates a personalized study plan for each chapter. Each plan directs students to specific resources designed to improve their understanding, including pages from the text in e-book format. Chapter post-tests give them an opportunity to measure how much they've learned and let them know if they are ready for graded quizzes and exams. For instructors, ThomsonNOW is available on WebCT and Blackboard, allowing them to provide virtual office hours, post syllabi, set up threaded discussions, and track student progress.

- The revised *Communicate!* **premium book companion website,** available to students at no additional charge when instructors order this online textbook resource packaged with the book. This website provides students with a multitude of text-specific learning aids, including interactive electronic versions of all text exercises. From the website students can download worksheets, data collection sheets, and speech checklists as well as complete activities online, e-mail them to their instructors if requested, and compare their responses to activities with models provided by the authors. The website also features study aids such as chapter outlines, flash cards and other resources for mastering glossary terms, continually updated web links, and chapter quizzes that help students check their understanding of key concepts.

- The ***Communicate!* interactive video activities,** available to students at no additional charge when instructors order this online textbook resource packaged with the book. This resource features the Conversation & Analysis communication scenario clips presented in Chapters 6–9 and 11 of the text so students can see and hear how the skills they are studying can be used to create effective conversations in various circumstances. It also features all-new Speech & Analysis clips that allow students to watch and analyze the new sample informative and persuasive student speeches included in Chapters 15–17.

- **Web Resource web links** and **InfoTrac College Edition activities,** available to students at no additional charge when instructors order this online textbook resource packaged with the book. These links and activities have been integrated into the text to expand skills practice and learning online. Highlighted in the text with colored text and icons, they are easily accessed from the *Communicate!* online textbook resources. All the web links and InfoTrac College Edition articles are monitored to ensure that they remain active.

- Many of the Speech Plan Action Steps can be completed with **Speech Builder Express organization and outlining program,** available to students at no additional charge when instructors order this online textbook resource packaged with the book. This interactive web-based tool coaches students through the speech organization and outlining process. By completing interactive sessions based on the in-text Speech Plan Action Steps, students can prepare and save their outlines—including a plan for visual aids and a works cited section—formatted according to the principles presented in the text. Both text and video models reinforce students' interactive practice.

Revised Features

- **Communication Skill** and **Skill Building** boxes visually reinforce learning of many specific skills described and exemplified in the text. Each Communication Skill box (formerly the Skill Builder boxes) includes the definition of the skill, a brief description of its use, the steps for enacting the skill, and an example that illustrates the skill. A convenient tear-out chart at the beginning of the book provides a summary of all the Communication Skill boxes. The Skill Building boxes (formerly the Test Your Competence boxes) follow up on the Communication Skill boxes, providing activities that allow students to use the skills they are learning and to make the connection between theory and practice. Students can complete these activities online and then compare their answers with models provided by the authors.

■ **Observe and Analyze** activities require students to observe a specific event or series of events related to concepts they are learning. They are then asked to analyze what happened using the theories and concepts from the chapter. With this edition, many new Observe and Analyze activities give students an opportunity to critically evaluate communication scenarios drawn from popular culture. Students are able to complete these activities online; download worksheets and data collection forms; and write, edit, and (if requested) e-mail reports of their findings to their instructors.

■ Online **Test Your Competence** activities allow students to practice the skills they are learning and then compare their answers with models provided by the authors.

■ **Speech Plan Action Steps** in Chapters 12–15 guide students through a step-by-step preparation process that results in significantly better speeches. These Action Step activities are supplemented by online examples of each activity prepared by other students.

■ **Self-Review** quizzes appear at the end of each part. In accord with the findings of learning motivation research, students are encouraged to set specific goals for skill improvement by writing skills improvement plans for interpersonal, group, and public settings. Students are able to complete these quizzes online and, if requested, e-mail them to their instructors.

■ **Diverse Voices** are excerpts of longer, previously published articles that give voice to the communication experiences of people from a wide range of social and cultural backgrounds. These excerpts, several of which are new to this edition, highlight the personal thoughts and experiences of the individuals featured on topics related to concepts discussed in the chapter, helping students to understand and appreciate how culture affects communication.

■ **What Would You Do? A Question of Ethics** boxes are short case studies that appear toward the end of chapters. These cases, several of which are new to this edition, present ethical challenges and require students to think critically, sorting through a variety of ethical dilemmas faced by communicators. Conceptual material presented in Chapter 1 lays groundwork for the criteria on which students may make their assessments. But in each case the dilemma posed focuses on issues raised in the specific chapter.

■ **Spotlight on Scholars** boxes feature the work of eight eminent communication scholars. Based on interviews with the scholars, these short articles put a face on scholarship by telling each scholar's "story," including a description of what motivated the scholar to follow the line of research discussed in the text. This unique and highly praised feature helps students understand the research and theory-building process by providing a glimpse of some of the people who have been especially influential in developing communication theories. Chapter 10 features a new spotlight on Randy Hirokawa, who specializes in small-group communication and decision-making effectiveness.

Supplementary Materials

In addition to the *Communicate!* online textbook resources described previously, the twelfth edition can be packaged with a suite of integrated resources for students and instructors.

Student Resources

InfoTrac College Edition An easy-to-use online library, available to students for four months at no additional charge when instructors order this online textbook resource packaged with the book. This extensive, easy-to-use database of more than 18 million reliable, full-length articles (not abstracts) from 5,000 top academic journals and popular sources is ideal for helping students master online research and is especially useful when students are preparing speeches.

vMentor™ Live one-on-one tutoring, available to students at no additional charge when instructors order this online textbook resource packaged with the book. vMentor gives your students access to virtual office hours—one-on-one online tutoring help from a subject-area expert at no additional cost. In vMentor's virtual classroom, students interact with the tutor and other students using two-way audio, an interactive whiteboard for illustrating the problem, and instant messaging. To ask a question, students simply click to raise a "hand." *For proprietary college and university adopters only. For additional information, please contact your Thomson Wadsworth sales representative.*

Student Workbook *by Brian L. Heisterkamp, California State University, San Bernardino.* The student workbook offers chapter-by-chapter skill-building exercises, vocabulary lists, quizzes, and copies of the worksheets, data collection sheets, and speech checklists featured in the text.

Service Learning in Communication Studies: A Handbook *by Rick Isaacson, Bruce Dorries, and Kevin Brown.* This handbook is an invaluable resource for students in a basic course that integrates or is planning to integrate a service learning component. The handbook provides guidelines for connecting service learning work with classroom concepts as well as advice for working effectively with agencies and organizations. The handbook also provides model forms and reports and a directory of online resources.

A Guide to the Basic Course for ESL Students *by Esther Yook, Mary Washington College.* This guide assists the non-native speaker. It features FAQs, helpful URLs, and strategies for accent management and overcoming speech apprehension.

Instructor Resources

Instructor's Resource Manual with Test Bank *by Lisa Heller Boragine, Cape Cod Community College.* This indispensable manual features changes from the eleventh edition to the twelfth edition, sample syllabi, chapter-by-chapter outlines, summaries, vocabulary lists, suggested lecture and discussion topics, classroom exercises, assignments, and a comprehensive test bank with answer key and rejoinders.

Instructor's Resource CD-ROM *by Amber Finn, Texas Christian University.* This CD-ROM contains an electronic version of the Instructor's Resource Manual, ExamView® Computerized Testing, and pre-designed Microsoft® PowerPoint® presentations. The PowerPoint presentations contain text and images, and they can be used as is or customized to suit your course needs.

Student Speeches for Critique and Analysis This multivolume video series offers both imperfect and award-winning sample student speeches. The speeches presented in *Communicate!* are available in this series.

Communication Scenarios for Critique and Analysis This video series provides faculty and students with real-life contexts of interpersonal communication in action. A great tool for helping students learn to critique and analyze interpersonal communication skills, this video features scripted, videotaped scenarios including the conversations featured in *Communicate!*

Media Guide for Interpersonal Communication *by Charles G. Apple, University of Michigan–Flint.* This guide provides faculty with media resource listings focused on general interpersonal communication topics. Each listing provides compelling examples of how interpersonal communication concepts are illustrated in particular films, books, plays, websites, or journal articles. Discussion questions are provided.

The Teaching Assistant's Guide to the Basic Course *by Katherine G. Hendrix, University of Memphis.* Based on leading communication teacher training programs, this guide covers general teaching and course management topics as well as specific strategies for communication instruction—for example, providing effective feedback on performance, managing sensitive class discussions, and conducting mock interviews.

Acknowledgments

First, we want to thank Cynthia Berryman-Fink, who joined us in authoring this edition. Her work on the first three sections of the book has enabled this edition to reflect current theory and scholarship, and her ability to consistently meet very demanding deadlines allowed the project to remain on schedule. Although we have known her for a long time, we continue to be impressed with her professionalism and feel fortunate to have her as a friend.

The twelfth edition could not have been completed without the help of many people. Most important are the reviewers, whose insights, candor, and suggestions for refining the book were invaluable: Christy Barns, Jacksonville State University; Lisa Heller Boragine, Cape Cod Community College; Christopher J. Miller, College of DuPage; Ethan Russell, Keiser College, Melbourne; Clifford Ruth, Pima Community College; and Karen Wolf, Suffolk Community College. Many of these reviewers have been faithful adopters of *Communicate!*. We are grateful for their support.

We would also like to express our gratitude to the Thomson Wadsworth Communication Studies team: Lyn Uhl, publisher; Jaime Perkins, acquisitions editor; Lucinda Bingham, technology project manager; Matthew Ballantyne, content production manager; John Gahbauer, assistant editor; Kim Gengler, editorial assistant; Erin Mitchell, marketing manager; and Mary Anne Payumo, marketing assistant. Others at Wadsworth, including Michael Burggren, senior production manager, and Jessica Perry, advertising project manager, have offered their support and expertise. Jamie Armstrong of Newgen–Austin oversaw the production of this book, and we have valued her ability to keep our book on schedule. A special word of appreciation goes to Greer Lleuad, senior developmental editor, a truly remarkable professional who oversaw all of the work on this revision. Her kindness, wisdom, patience, guidance, expertise, and eye for detail nurtured us through this revision and the preparation of the materials for the website. She was always "home" when we needed counsel. We also want to note the contributions of Kim Russell, former marketing manager for the Communication Studies team, who for the past several years has kept us up to date on emerging trends in the market and so has helped us better serve students. Finally, we want to thank students who have used the text and who have communicated their ideas about how we can make the book better. We encourage you to follow their example and to use the *Communicate!* website to contact us with questions, ideas, and suggestions. We only hope that you will find this book to be one that not only stimulates your intellect but also improves your ability to understand and be understood by others.

Rudy and Kathie Verderber

Communicate!

OBJECTIVES

After you have read this chapter, you should be able to answer these questions:

- What is the definition of communication?
- How does the communication process work?
- Why do we communicate?
- What characterizes each of the communication settings you will study in this course?
- What are seven basic principles of communication?
- Why should a communicator be concerned about culture?
- What major ethical issues face communicators?
- What is communication competence?
- How can you improve your communication skills?

1

Communication Perspectives

Mimi and Marcus finished interviewing the fifth life insurance agent.

"From what I could understand, most of the basic policies are about the same," said Mimi. "So, for me, it comes down to who we'd feel most comfortable with."

"Yeah, that's pretty much the way I see it. And from that standpoint, I'd pick Carrie's policy," Marcus responded.

"She really seemed nice, didn't she?" asked Mimi. "She seemed friendly, approachable, and—unlike Paul—she talked to both of us, not just you."

Marcus replied, "I noticed that she presented a policy that was tailored to our specific needs, unlike Dempsey who spent most of his time talking about a plan that really didn't relate to our needs."

Mimi added, "Yeah, and Gloria was so disorganized . . . "

"And she was so engrossed in the PowerPoint presentation that she didn't even notice when you tried to ask a question!" Marcus interjected.

"I sort of liked Steve," Mimi continued, "but when we suggested that the rates he was quoting were just out of our budget, he didn't offer much help. Once he got off his 'script,' he seemed lost."

"Well," Marcus replied, "not only did Carrie offer a policy I could understand, she also led me to believe that we could call her about other types of insurance and financial advice."

"OK," Mimi said as she nodded. "So we agree; Carrie gets our insurance business!"

hy was Carrie successful? Was it her insurance policy? Her specialized expertise in the insurance business? Not necessarily. From this conversation, it appears that Carrie's success was due to her ability to communicate with Mimi and Marcus. Carrie's success is not unusual. Studies done over the years have concluded that, for almost any job, two of the most important skills sought by employers are oral communication skills and interpersonal abilities (Goleman, 1998, pp. 12–13). Even in fields not usually thought of as requiring strong communication skills, employers look for competence. For instance, an article on the role of communication in the workplace found that in engineering, a highly technical field, 72 percent of the employers surveyed indicated that speaking skills were very important (Darling & Dannels, 2003, p. 12). A survey by the National Association of Colleges and Employers (Koncz, 2006) reported the top 10 personal qualities and skills that employers seek from college graduates. The number one skill was communication, including both speaking and writing, and the seventh item was interpersonal skills. So this course can significantly increase your ability to get a job and to be successful in your chosen career.

How effective you are in your communication with others is important to your career, but it is also the foundation for all of your personal relationships. Your ability to make and keep friends, to be a good family member, to have satisfying intimate relationships, to participate in or lead groups, and to prepare and present speeches depends on your communication skills. During this course, you will learn about the communication process and have an opportunity to practice basic communication skills that will help you improve your relationships.

In this first chapter, we explain the basic communication process, provide an overview of the functions communication serves, and explore the settings in which our communications occur. Then we describe the major principles of communication. Finally, we discuss communication competence and a process you can use for improving your communication skills.

The Communication Process

communication
the process of creating or sharing meaning in informal conversation, group interaction, or public speaking.

Communication is the process of creating or sharing meaning in informal conversation, group interaction, or public speaking. To understand how this process works, we begin by describing its essential elements: participants (who), messages (what), context (where), channels (how), presence or absence of noise (distractions), and feedback (reaction).

Participants

participants
individuals who assume the roles of senders and receivers during an interaction.

The **participants** are the individuals who assume the roles of senders and receivers during an interaction. As senders, participants form and transmit messages using verbal symbols and nonverbal behavior. As receivers, they interpret the messages and behaviors that have been transmitted to them.

Messages

Messages are the verbal utterances and nonverbal behaviors to which meaning is attributed during communication. To understand how messages are created and received, we need to understand meanings, symbols, encoding and decoding, and form or organization.

messages
verbal utterances and nonverbal behaviors to which meaning is attributed during communication.

Meanings   **Meanings** include the thoughts in one person's mind as well as interpretations one makes of another's message. Meanings refer to the ways that communicators make sense of messages. It is important to realize that meanings are not transferred from one person to another, but are created together in an exchange. Some communication settings enable participants to verify that they have shared meanings; in other settings this is more difficult. For instance, if Sarah describes to Tiffany that her cat is old and fat, through the exchange of messages, they can together come to some degree of understanding of what "old" and "fat" mean. But if Tiffany is in an audience of 200 people listening to a speech Sarah is giving about cats, her ability to question Sarah and negotiate a mutual meaning is limited.

meaning
thoughts in our minds and interpretations of others' messages.

Symbols   To express yourself, you form messages comprising verbal symbols and nonverbal behaviors. **Symbols** are words, sounds, and actions that seek to represent specific ideas and feelings. As you speak, you choose word symbols to express your meaning. At the same time, facial expressions, eye contact, gestures, and tone of voice—all symbolic, nonverbal cues—accompany your words in an attempt to express your meaning. As a listener, you make interpretations or attribute meaning to the message you heard.

symbols
words, sounds, and actions that are generally understood to represent ideas and feelings.

Encoding and decoding   **Encoding** is the process of putting our thoughts and feelings into words and nonverbal cues. **Decoding** is the process of interpreting another's message. Ordinarily you do not consciously think about either the encoding or the decoding process. Only when there is a difficulty, such as speaking in a second language or having to use an easier vocabulary with children, do you become aware of encoding. You may not think about decoding until someone seems to speak in circles or uses unfamiliar technical words and you have difficulty interpreting or understanding what is being said.

encoding
the process of putting our thoughts and feelings into words and nonverbal cues.

decoding
the process of interpreting another's message.

Form or organization   When the meaning we wish to share is complex, we may need to organize it in sections or in a certain order. Message form is especially important when one person talks without interruption for a relatively long time, such as in a public speech or when reporting an event to a colleague at work.

Contexts

contexts
the settings in which communication occurs, including what precedes and follows what is said.

Context is the setting in which a communication encounter occurs, including what precedes and follows what is said. The context affects the expectations of the participants, the meaning these participants derive, and their subsequent behavior. Context includes the (1) physical, (2) social, (3) historical, (4) psychological, and (5) cultural circumstances that surround a communication episode.

physical context
its location, the environmental conditions (temperature, lighting, noise level), the distance between communicators, seating arrangements, and time of day.

Physical context The **physical context** includes its location, the environmental conditions (temperature, lighting, and noise level), the distance between communicators, seating arrangements, and time of day. Each of these factors can affect the communication. For instance, the meaning shared in a conversation may be affected by whether it is held in a crowded company cafeteria, an elegant candlelit restaurant, over the telephone, or on the Internet.

social context
the nature of the relationship that exists between the participants.

Social context The **social context** is the nature of relationship that may already exist between the participants. Whether communication takes place among family members, friends, acquaintances, work associates, or strangers influences what and how messages are formed, shared, and interpreted. For instance, most people change how they interact when talking with their parents or siblings as compared to how they interact when talking with their friends.

historical context
the background provided by previous communication episodes between the participants that influence understandings in the current encounter.

Historical context The **historical context** is the background provided by previous communication episodes between the participants. It influences understandings in the current encounter. For instance, suppose one morning Chad tells Shelby that he will get the draft of the report that they had left for their boss to read. As Shelby enters the office that afternoon, she sees Chad and says, "Did you get it?" Another person listening to the conversation would have no idea what the "it" is to which Shelby is referring. Yet Chad may well reply, "It's on my desk." Shelby and Chad would understand each other because of the contents of their earlier exchange.

psychological context
the mood and feelings each person brings to the conversation.

Psychological context The **psychological context** includes the moods and feelings each person brings to the interpersonal encounter. For instance, suppose Corinne is under a lot of stress. While she is studying for an exam, a friend stops by and pleads with her to take a break and go to the gym with her. Corinne, who is normally good-natured, may explode with an angry tirade. Why? Because her stress level provides the psychological context within which she hears this message and it affects how she responds.

cultural context
the values, attitudes, beliefs, orientations, and underlying assumptions prevalent among people in a society.

Cultural context The **cultural context** includes the values, attitudes, beliefs, orientations, and underlying assumptions prevalent among people in a society (Samovar, Porter, & McDaniel, 2007, p. 20). Culture penetrates

Karen Kapoor/Getty Images

How might the conversation of these people differ if they were in the library working on a class project?

into every aspect of our lives, affecting how we think, talk, and behave. Everyone is a part of one or more ethnic cultures, though we may differ in how much we identify with our ethnic cultures. When two people from different cultures interact, misunderstandings may occur because of the cultural variation between them. For example, the role of student in Asian cultures may mean being very quiet, respectful, and never challenging others' views, while the student role in U.S. classrooms may mean being talkative, assertive, and debating the views of others.

Channels

Channels are both the route traveled by the message and the means of transportation. Messages are transmitted through sensory channels. Face-to-face communication has two basic channels: verbal symbols and nonverbal cues. Online communication uses these same two channels, though some of the nonverbal cues like movements, touch, and gestures may be missing. Many aspects of the nonverbal channel such as facial expressions, aspects of voice, and use of time do occur online, however. We will explain more of these concepts in Chapter 4, "Communicating through Nonverbal Behaviors."

channel
both the route traveled by the message and the means of transportation.

Noise

noise
any stimulus that interferes with the process of sharing meaning.

physical noise
sights, sounds, and other stimuli in the environment that draw people's attention away from intended meaning.

psychological noise
internal distractions based on thoughts, feelings, or emotional reactions to symbols.

internal noise
thoughts and feelings that compete for attention and interfere with the communication process.

semantic noise
distractions aroused by certain symbols that take our attention away from the main message.

Noise is any stimulus that interferes with the process of sharing meaning. Noise can be physical (based on external sounds) or it can be psychological (based on internal distractions).

Physical noise includes the sights, sounds, and other stimuli in the environment that draw people's attention away from intended meaning. For instance, while a friend is giving you directions on how to work the new MP3 player, your attention may be drawn away by the external noise of your favorite TV show, which is on in the next room. External noise does not have to be a sound, however. Perhaps, while the person gives the directions, your attention is drawn momentarily to an attractive man or woman. Such visual distractions are also physical noise.

Psychological noise includes internal distractions based on thoughts, feelings, or emotional reactions to symbols and can fall into two categories: internal noise and semantic noise. **Internal noise** refers to the thoughts and feelings that compete for attention and interfere with the communication process. If you have tuned out the lecture your professor is giving in class and tuned into a daydream or a past conversation, then you have experienced internal noise.

Semantic noise refers to the distractions aroused by certain symbols that take our attention away from the main message. If a friend describes a 40-year-old secretary as "the girl in the office," and you think "girl" is an odd and condescending term for a 40-year-old woman, you might not even hear the rest of what your friend has to say. Whenever we react emotionally to a word or a behavior, we are experiencing semantic noise.

Feedback

feedback
reactions and responses to messages.

Feedback refers to the reactions and responses to messages that indicate to the sender whether and how that message was heard, seen, and interpreted. We can express feedback verbally through words or nonverbally through body language. We continuously give feedback when we are listening to another, if only by paying attention, giving a confused look, or showing signs of boredom. Or we may be very direct with feedback by saying, "I don't understand the point you are making," or "That's a great comment you just made."

A Model of the Basic Communication Process

Figure 1.1 illustrates the communication process between two people. In the minds of these people are meanings, thoughts, or feelings that they intend to share. The nature of those thoughts or feelings is created, shaped, and affected by their total field of experience, including such factors as values, culture, environment, experiences, occupation, sex, interests, knowledge, and attitudes. To communicate a message, the sender encodes thoughts or feelings into a message that is sent using one or more channels.

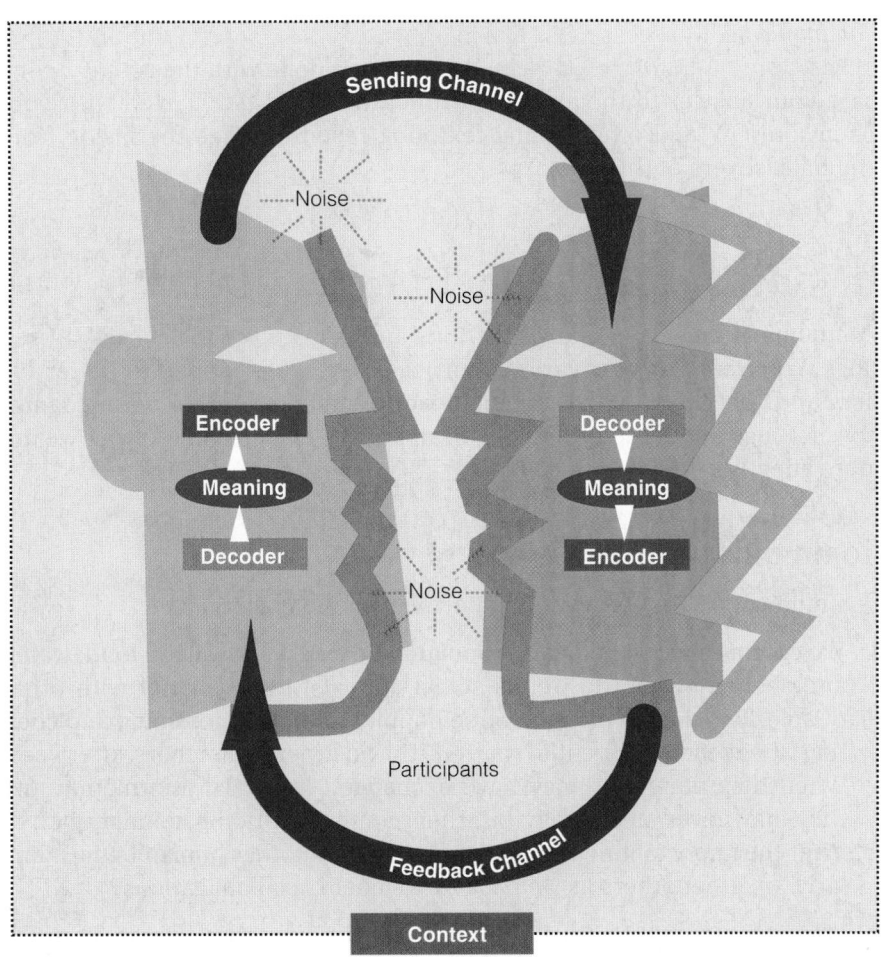

Figure 1.1
A model of communication between two individuals

The receiver decodes or interprets the symbols in an attempt to understand the speaker's meaning. This decoding process is affected by the
receiver's total field of experience—that is, by all the same factors that
shape the encoding process. Feedback messages complete the process so
that the sender and receiver can arrive at a similar understanding of the
message.

The model depicts the context as the area around the participants. The
physical, social, psychological, and cultural contexts permeate all parts of
the process. Similarly, the model shows that during conversation physical
and psychological noise, including internal and semantic distractions, may
occur at various points and therefore affect the people's ability to arrive at
similar meanings. As you might imagine, the process becomes much more
complex when more than two people are conversing or when someone is
speaking to a large and diverse audience.

To complete an activity that will help you identify elements of the communication process in a hypothetical conversation, go to ThomsonNOW for

Communicate! to access **Skill Learning Activity 1.1: Identifying Elements of the Communication Process**. When you're done with the activity, compare your answer to the authors'. (To learn how to get started with your ThomsonNOW and other online textbook resources, see the inside front and back covers of this book.)

Communication Functions and Settings

Communication serves many functions and takes place in a variety of settings. When we know its various purposes, we are equipped to better understand the goals of the communication situation. When we recognize how settings affect the process, we can adapt our behavior so that we are more effective.

Communication Functions

Communication serves several important functions for us.

1. **We communicate to meet our social needs.** Just as we need food, water, and shelter, so too do we, as social animals, need contact with other people. Two people may converse happily for hours, gossiping and chatting about inconsequential matters that neither remembers afterward. When they part, they may have exchanged little real information and they may never meet again, but their communication has functioned to meet the important need simply to talk with another human being. Similarly, we greet others as we pass by to meet social obligations.

2. **We communicate to develop and maintain our sense of self.** Through our interactions, we learn who we are, what we are good at, and how people react to how we behave. We explore this important function of communication in detail in Chapter 2, "Perception of Self and Others."

3. **We communicate to develop relationships.** Not only do we get to know others through our communication with them but, more importantly, we develop relationships with them—relationships that grow and deepen or stagnate and wither away. We discuss how communication creates and maintains relationships in Chapter 6, "Communicating in Relationships."

4. **We communicate to exchange information.** Some information we get through observation, some through reading, some through media, and a great deal through direct communication with others either face-to-face or online. Whether we are trying to decide how warmly to dress or whom to vote for in the next presidential election, all of us have countless exchanges that involve sending and receiving information. We discuss communication as information exchange in Chapter 10, "Participating in Group Communication," and Chapter 16, "Informative Speaking."

5. **We communicate to influence others.** It is doubtful that a day goes by in which you don't engage in behavior such as trying to convince your friends to go to a particular restaurant or to see a certain movie, to persuade your supervisor to alter your schedule, or to convince an instructor to change your course grade. We discuss the role of influencing others in Chapter 11, "Member Roles and Leadership in Groups," and in Chapter 17, "Persuasive Speaking."

Communication Settings

While the basic communication process describes how meanings are shared, various communication skills can be learned so that you are effective across a variety of settings. In this book, you will be introduced to skills that will help you achieve communication competence in interpersonal, problem-solving group, public speaking, and electronically mediated settings.

Interpersonal communication settings Most of our communication takes place in **interpersonal communication settings,** which are characterized by informal interaction among a small number of people who have relationships with each other. Talking to a group of classmates on campus, chatting on the phone with your mother, arguing the merits of a movie with your brother, instant messaging with several friends, and comforting someone who has suffered a loss are all examples of interpersonal communication.

Our study of interpersonal communication begins by exploring how we develop, maintain, improve, or end our relationships with others. Then we will study the theory and skills of listening and responding empathically, sharing personal information, and self-disclosure and feedback. We will also discuss talking with people online and describe the skills you will need to be effective in interviews.

interpersonal communication settings *interactions among a small number of people who have relationships with each other.*

Problem-solving group settings **Problem-solving group settings** are characterized by participants who come together for the specific purpose of solving a problem or arriving at a decision. Much of this kind of communication takes place in formal or informal meetings.

Our study of problem-solving group settings includes a discussion of the characteristics of effective groups, the stages of group development, problem solving and decision making, and the roles participants play, including leadership.

problem-solving group settings *participants come together for the specific purpose of solving a problem or arriving at a decision.*

Public speaking settings **Public speaking settings** are characterized by one or more participants, the speakers, who deliver a prepared message to a group or audience who has assembled to hear the speakers.

Our discussion of public speaking settings focuses on the skills associated with effective speech preparation and delivery, including determining

public speaking settings *one participant, the speaker, delivers a prepared message to a group or audience who has assembled to hear the speaker.*

speaking goals, gathering and evaluating material, organizing and developing material, adapting material to a specific audience, and presenting the speech, as well as variations in procedure for information exchange and persuasion.

Electronically mediated communication (EMC) settings Today interpersonal communication, group discussion, and public speaking can all take place in **electronically mediated communication settings,** which are characterized by participants who do not share a physical context but communicate through the use of technology. Electronically mediated communication (EMC) can occur in real time or in delayed time, can involve as few as two people or as many as millions of people, and can use one or multiple channels (written, voice, images).

Interpersonally, we may keep in touch with family and friends through e-mail, instant messaging, or text messaging. **E-mail** involves electronic correspondence conducted between two or more users on a network where the communication does not appear in real time. There is a delay between the sending and receiving of messages. **Instant messaging (IM)** involves electronic communication through maintaining a list of people that you can interact with in real time when they are online, with people that you have agreed to interact with by adding them to your IM list. **Text messaging** involves the sending of short, written messages between mobile phones and other handheld electronic devices. Messages may be exchanged in real time between phone users, or messages may be stored for later retrieval.

Group communication may occur through some of these types of EMC and through other types of online communication including Listservs, chat rooms, weblogs, or interactive games. **Listservs** are electronic mailing lists sent through e-mail; they allow for widespread distribution of information to many Internet users. Any message sent to the Listserv goes to all users, so online discussions can occur in a delayed time format. **Chat rooms** are web-based forums designed for interactive message exchange between two or more people who are logged into the room, where they exchange multiple messages in real time. **Weblogs** or **blogs** are online journals housed on a website. They include short, frequently updated postings arranged chronologically. They may be private and restricted to

electronically mediated communication settings
involves participants who do not share a physical context but communicate through the use of technology.

e-mail
electronic correspondence conducted between two or more users on a network where the communication does not occur in real time.

instant messaging
communication through maintaining a list of people that you can interact with in real time when they are online.

text messaging
short, written messages between mobile phones and other handheld electronic devices, exchanged in real time or stored for later retrieval.

Listservs
electronic mailing lists through the use of e-mail that allow for widespread distribution of information to many Internet users, so online discussions can occur in a delayed time format.

chat rooms
interactive message exchange between two or more people where multiple messages are exchanged in real time.

weblogs or blogs
online journals housed on a website.

E-mail has taken the place of letter writing in most settings.

© Bob Daemmrich/PhotoEdit

certain users who can read each other's blogs; or, they may be public, allowing any Internet user to read the messages. **Online games** are web-based sites where a group of people interact in real time to play common board games, games of chance, or fantasy role-playing games. Electronically mediated communication is particularly useful for conveying messages to a large public audience. The Internet has become the medium for posting job ads and résumés, for advertising and buying products, for political speechmaking and activism, for sharing social information widely and establishing relationships, and for sending and retrieving information of all types.

Communication Principles

Principles are general truths. Understanding the principles of communication is important as you begin your study. In this section, we discuss seven principles: communication has purpose, communication is continuous, communication messages vary in conscious thought, communication is relational, communication is guided by culture, communication has ethical implications, and communication is learned.

Communication Has Purpose

When people communicate with each other, they have a purpose for doing so. The purpose of a given transaction may be either serious or trivial. One way to evaluate the success of the communication is to ask whether it achieved its purpose. When Beth calls Leah to ask whether she'd like to join her for lunch to discuss a project they are working on, her purpose may be to resolve a misunderstanding they've had. Speakers may not always be aware of their purpose. For instance, when Jamal passes Tony on the street and says lightly, "Tony, what's happening?" Jamal probably doesn't consciously think, "Tony's an acquaintance and I want him to understand that I see him and consider him worth recognizing." In this case, the social obligation to recognize Tony is met spontaneously with the first acceptable expression that comes to Jamal's mind. Regardless of whether Jamal consciously thinks about the purpose, it still motivates his behavior. In this case, Jamal will have achieved his goal if Tony responds with an equally casual greeting.

Communication Is Continuous

Because communication is nonverbal as well as verbal, we are always sending behavioral messages from which others draw inferences or meaning. Even silence or absence is communication behavior if another person infers meaning from it. Why? It is because your nonverbal behavior represents reactions to your environment and to the people around you. If you are cold, you shiver; if you are hot or nervous, you perspire; if you are

online games
interaction among a group of people in real time to play common board games or fantasy role-playing games.

bored, happy, or confused, your face or body language probably will show it. As skilled communicators, we need to be aware of the explicit and implicit messages we are constantly sending to others.

Communication Messages Vary in Conscious Thought

As we discussed earlier in this chapter, sharing meaning with another person involves presenting verbal and nonverbal messages. Our messages may (1) occur spontaneously, (2) be based on a "script" we have learned or rehearsed, or (3) be carefully constructed based on our understanding of the unique situation in which we find ourselves.

spontaneous expressions
spoken without much conscious thought.

Many of our messages are **spontaneous expressions,** spoken without much conscious thought. For example, when you burn your finger, you may blurt out "Ouch." When something goes right, you may break into a broad smile.

scripted messages
phrasings learned from past encounters that we judge to be appropriate to the present situation.

At other times, our messages are **scripted,** phrasings that we have learned from our past encounters and judge to be appropriate to the present situation. Many of these scripts are learned in childhood. For example, when you want the sugar bowl but cannot reach it, you may say, "Please pass the sugar," followed by "Thank you" when someone complies. This conversational sequence comes from your "table manners script," which may have been drilled into you at home. Scripts enable us to use messages that are appropriate to the situation and are likely to increase the effectiveness of our communication. One goal of this text is to acquaint you with general scripts (or skills) that can be adapted for use in your communication encounters across a variety of relationships, situations, and cultures.

constructed messages
messages put together with careful thought when we recognize that our known scripts are inadequate for the situation.

Finally, our messages may be carefully constructed to meet the unique requirements of a particular situation. **Constructed messages** are those that we put together with careful thought when we recognize that our known scripts are inadequate for the situation.

Communication Is Relational

Saying that communication is relational means that in any communication setting, in addition to sharing content meaning, our messages also reflect two important aspects of our relationships: immediacy and control (dominance/submissiveness).

immediacy
the degree of liking or attractiveness in a relationship.

Immediacy is the degree of liking or attractiveness in a relationship. For instance, when José passes by Hal on campus he may say, "Hal, good to see you" (a verbal expression of friendliness); the nonverbal behavior that accompanies the words may show Hal whether José is genuinely happy to see him or is only expressing recognition. For instance, if José smiles, has a sincere sound to his voice, looks Hal in the eye, and perhaps pats him on the back or shakes hands firmly, then Hal will recognize these signs of friendliness. If, however, José speaks quickly with no vocal inflection and with a deadpan facial expression, Hal will perceive the comment as solely meeting some social expectation.

© Michael Keller/CORBIS

What messages about affect and control do wedding couples send as they feed each other cake? Power in relationships is influenced by both verbal and nonverbal messages.

Control is the degree to which one participant is perceived to be more dominant or powerful. Thus, when Tom says to Sue, "I know you're concerned about the budget, but I'll see to it that we have money to cover everything," his words and the sound of his voice may be saying that he is "in charge" of finances—that he is in control. How Sue responds to Tom determines whether, on this issue, she submits to his perception of control. If Sue says, "Thanks, I know you have a better handle on finances than I do," then she accepts that on this issue, she is willing to submit to Tom at this time. A few days later, if Tom says to Sue, "I think we need to cut back on credit card expenses for a couple of months," and Sue responds, "No way! I need a new suit for work, the car needs new tires, and you promised we could replace the couch," then the nature of the relationship will require further discussion.

control
the degree to which one participant is perceived to be more dominant or powerful.

Communication Is Guided by Culture

Culture may be defined as systems of knowledge shared by a relatively large group of people. It includes a system of shared beliefs, values, symbols, and behaviors. How messages are formed and interpreted depends on the cultural background of the participants. We need to look carefully at ourselves and our communication behavior; as we interact with others whose cultural backgrounds differ from our own, we may unintentionally communicate in ways that are culturally inappropriate or insensitive and thereby undermine our relationships.

culture
systems of knowledge shared by a relatively large group of people.

We must also be sensitive to how differences among people based on sex, age, class, physical characteristics, and sexual orientation affect communication. Failure to take those differences into account when we interact can also lead us to behave insensitively.

Throughout the history of the United States, we've experienced huge migrations of people from different parts of the world. According to the

DIVERSE VOICES

Lessons from American Experience

by Harland Cleveland

Harland Cleveland, former president of the University of Hawaii, is president of the World Academy of Art and Science. In this selection, Cleveland explains how Hawaii, the most diverse of our 50 states, achieves ethnic and racial peace. He argues that the Hawaiian experience is no different from the experience of immigrants to the mainland; the ability to tolerate diversity is not unique in the world.

We Americans have learned, in our short but intensive 200-plus years of history as a nation, a first lesson about diversity: that it cannot be governed by drowning it in "integration."

I came face-to-face with this truth when, just a quarter of a century ago, I became president of the University of Hawaii. Everyone who lives in Hawaii, or even visits there, is impressed by its residents' comparative tolerance toward each other. On closer inspection, paradise seems based on paradox: Everybody's a minority. The tolerance is not despite the diversity but because of it.

It is not through the disappearance of ethnic distinctions that the people of Hawaii achieved a level of racial peace that has few parallels around our discriminatory globe. Quite the contrary. The glory is that Hawaii's main ethnic groups managed to establish the right to be separate. The group separateness, in turn, helped establish the rights of individuals in each group to equality with individuals of different racial aspect, ethnic origin, and cultural heritage.

Hawaii's experience is not so foreign to the transatlantic migrations of the various more-or-less white Caucasians. On arrival in New York (passing that inscription on the Statue of Liberty, "Send these, the homeless, tempest-tossed, to me"), the European immigrants did not melt into the open arms of the white Anglo Saxon Protestants who preceded them. The reverse was true. The new arrivals stayed close to their own kind; shared religion, language, humor, and discriminatory treatment with their soul brothers and sisters; and gravitated at first into occupations that did not too seriously threaten the earlier arrivals.

The waves of new Americans learned to tolerate each other—first as groups, only thereafter as individuals. Rubbing up against each other in an urbanizing America, they discovered not just the old Christian lesson that all men are brothers, but the hard, new, multicultural lesson that all brothers are different. Equality is not the product of similarity; it is the cheerful acknowledgement of difference.

What's so special about our experience is the assumption that people of many kinds and colors can together govern themselves without deciding in advance which kinds of people (male or female, black, brown, yellow, red, white, or any mix of these) may hold any particular public office in the pantheon of political power.

For the twenty-first century, this "cheerful acknowledgement of difference" is the alternative to a global spread of ethnic cleansing and religious rivalry. The challenge is great, for ethnic cleansing and religious rivalry are traditions as contemporary as Bosnia and Rwanda in the 1990s and as ancient as the Assyrians.

In too many countries, there is still a basic (if often unspoken) assumption that one kind of people is anointed to be in general charge. Try to imagine a Turkish chancellor of Germany, an Algerian president of France, a Pakistani prime minister of Britain, a Christian president of Egypt, an Arab prime minister of Israel, a Jewish president of Syria, a Tibetan ruler of Beijing, anyone but a Japanese in power in Tokyo. Yet in the United States during the twentieth century, we have already elected an Irish Catholic as president, chosen several Jewish Supreme Court justices, and racially integrated the armed forces right up to the chairman of the Joint Chiefs of Staff . . . .

I wouldn't dream of arguing that we Americans have found the Holy Grail of cultural diversity when, in fact, we're still searching for it. We have to think hard about our growing pluralism. It's useful, I believe, to dissect in the open our thinking about it, to see whether the lessons we are trying to learn

might stimulate some useful thinking elsewhere. We still do not quite know how to create "wholeness incorporating diversity," but we owe it to the world, as well as to ourselves, to keep trying.

Excerpted from Harland Cleveland, "The Limits to Cultural Diversity," in Intercultural Communication: A Reader *(11th ed.), eds. Larry A. Samovar, Richard E. Porter, and Erwin R. McDaniel (Belmont, CA: Wadsworth, 2006), pp. 405–408. Reprinted by permission of the World Future Society.*

New York Times Almanac (Wright, 2002), the 2000 census shows that today, the largest number of new immigrants is from Latin America and Asia. At the end of the twentieth century, people of Latin and Asian descent constituted 12.5 percent and 3.8 percent, respectively, of the total U.S. population. About 2.4 percent of the population regards itself as multiracial. Combined with the approximately 13 percent of our population that is of African descent, these four groups account for nearly 32 percent of the total population. According to the U.S. Census Bureau, within the next 45 years, this figure is predicted to rise to nearly 50 percent. To read more about the U.S. foreign-born population, go to your ThomsonNOW for *Communicate!* to access **Web Resource 1.1: Profile of Foreign-Born Population**. (To learn how to get started with your ThomsonNOW and other online textbook resources, see the inside front and back covers of this book.)

According to Samovar, Porter, & McDaniel (2007) "three cultural elements have the potential to affect situations in which people from different backgrounds come together: (1) perception, (2) verbal processes, and (3) nonverbal processes" (p. 11). Because cultural concerns permeate all of communication, in each chapter of this book we will point out when the concepts and skills you are learning are viewed differently by other cultural groups. In addition, the Diverse Voices feature found in many chapters presents excerpts from articles whose authors explain how they or their culture views a concept presented in the text. In this chapter, Harlan Cleveland describes how the diverse peoples in the United States have learned to live together.

Communication Has Ethical Implications

In any encounter, we choose whether or not we will communicate ethically. **Ethics** is a set of moral principles that may be held by a society, a group, or an individual. Although what is considered ethical is a matter of personal judgment, various groups still expect members to uphold certain stan-

ethics
a set of moral principles that may be held by a society, a group, or an individual.

dards. These standards influence the personal decisions we make. When we choose to violate the standards that are expected, we are viewed to be unethical. Here are five ethical standards that influence our communication and guide our behavior.

truthfulness and honesty
refraining from lying, cheating, stealing, or deception.

1. **Truthfulness and honesty** mean refraining from lying, cheating, stealing, or deception. "An honest person is widely regarded as a moral person, and honesty is a central concept to ethics as the foundation for a moral life" (Terkel & Duval, 1999, p. 122). Although most people accept truthfulness and honesty as a standard, they still confess to lying on occasion. We are most likely to lie when we are caught in a **moral dilemma,** a choice involving an unsatisfactory alternative. An example of a moral dilemma would be a boss asking us if our coworker arrived to work late today and knowing that telling the truth would get the coworker fired. To understand more about how and why people lie, read the article "Lying and Deception," available through InfoTrac College Edition—go to your ThomsonNOW for *Communicate!* to access **Web Resource 1.2: Lying and Deception.** (To learn how to get started with your Thomson-NOW and other online textbook resources, see the inside front and back covers of this book.)

moral dilemma
a choice involving an unsatisfactory alternative.

integrity
maintaining a consistency of belief and action (keeping promises).

2. **Integrity** means maintaining a consistency of belief and action (keeping promises). Terkel and Duval (1999) say, "A person who has integrity is someone who has strong moral principles and will successfully resist the temptation to compromise those principles" (p. 135). Integrity, then, is the opposite of hypocrisy. A person who had promised to help a friend study for the upcoming exam would live up to this promise even when another friend offered a free ticket to a sold-out concert for the same night.

fairness
achieving the right balance of interests without regard to one's own feelings and without showing favor to any side in a conflict.

3. **Fairness** means achieving the right balance of interests without regard to one's own feelings and without showing favor to any side in a conflict. Fairness implies impartiality or lack of bias. To be fair to someone is to listen with an open mind, to gather all the relevant facts, consider only circumstances relevant to the decision at hand, and not let prejudice or irrelevancies affect how you treat others. For example, if two of her children are fighting, a mom is exercising fairness if she listens openly as the children explain "their side" before she decides what to do.

respect
showing regard or consideration for others and their ideas, even if we don't agree with them.

4. **Respect** means showing regard or consideration for others and their ideas, even if we don't agree with them. Respect is not based on someone's affluence, job status, or ethnic background. In a classroom, students show respect for others by attentively listening to another student's speech with a main point that violates their political or religious position.

responsibility
being accountable for one's actions and what one says.

5. **Responsibility** means being accountable for one's actions and what one says. Responsible communicators recognize the power of words. Mes-

sages can hurt and messages can soothe. Information is accurate or it may be faulty. A responsible communicator would not spread a false rumor about another friend.

To learn more about ethics, check out the website for the Markkula Center for Applied Ethics at Santa Clara University. Go to your Thomson-NOW for *Communicate!* to access **Web Resource 1.3: Ethics Connection**. (To learn how to get started with your ThomsonNOW and other online textbook resources, see the inside front and back covers of this book.)

In our daily lives, we often face ethical dilemmas and must sort out what is more or less right or wrong. In making these decisions, we usually reveal our ethical standards. At the end of each chapter of this book, the feature What Would You Do? A Question of Ethics will ask you to think about and resolve an ethical dilemma that relates to that chapter's content. Your instructor may use these as a vehicle for class discussions, or you may be asked to prepare a written report.

Communication Is Learned

Just as you learned to walk, so too you learned to communicate. But talking is a complex undertaking. You may not yet have learned all of the skills you will need to develop healthy relationships. Because communication is learned, you can improve your ability. Throughout this text, we identify interpersonal, group, and public speaking skills that can help you become a more competent communicator.

© George Simian/CORBIS

Just as children learn how to behave from their parents, so too do they learn to communicate. What specific communication behaviors can you identify that you learned at home?

Increasing Our Communication Competence

Communication competence is the impression that communicative behavior is both appropriate and effective in a given situation (Spitzberg, 2000, p. 375). Communication is *effective* when it achieves its goals; it is *appropriate* when it conforms to what is expected in a situation. We create the perception that we are competent communicators through the verbal mes-

communication competence
the impression that communicative behavior is both appropriate and effective in a given situation.

sages we send and the nonverbal behaviors that accompany them. Competence is an impression or judgment that people make about others. Because communication is at the heart of how we relate to each other, one of your goals in this course will be to learn strategies to increase the likelihood that others will view you as competent. In the Spotlight on Scholars, we feature Brian Spitzberg on Interpersonal Communication Competence. Spitzberg believes perceptions of competence depend, in part, on personal motivation, knowledge, and skills (2000, p. 377).

Motivation is important because we will only be able to improve our communication if we are *motivated*—that is, if we want to. People are likely to be more motivated if they are confident and if they see potential rewards.

Knowledge is important because we must know what is involved in increasing competence. The more knowledge people have about how to behave in a given situation, the more likely they are to be able to develop competence.

skills
goal-oriented actions or action sequences that we can master and repeat in appropriate situations.

Skill is important because we must know how to act in ways that are consistent with our communication knowledge. **Skills** are goal-oriented actions or action sequences that we can master and repeat in appropriate situations. The more skills you have, the more likely you are to be able to structure your messages effectively and appropriately.

credibility
a perception of a speaker's knowledge, trustworthiness, and warmth.

social ease
communicating without anxiety or nervousness.

In addition to motivation, knowledge, and skills, credibility and social ease are important components of communication competence. **Credibility** is a perception of a speaker's knowledge, trustworthiness, and warmth. Listeners are more likely to be attentive to and influenced by speakers they see as credible. **Social ease** means communicating without anxiety or nervousness. To be seen as a competent communicator, it is important that you can speak in a style that conveys confidence and poise. Communicators that are apprehensive or anxious are not likely to be regarded as competent, despite their motivation or knowledge.

The combination of our motivation, knowledge, skills, credibility, and social ease leads us to perform effectively in our encounters with others. The rest of this book is aimed at helping you increase the likelihood that you will be perceived as competent. In the pages that follow, you will learn about theories of interpersonal, group, and public speaking that can increase your knowledge and your motivation. You will also learn how to perform specific skills, and you will be provided with opportunities to practice them. Through this practice, you can increase the likelihood that you will be able to perform these skills when needed.

Develop Communication Skill Improvement Goals

To get the most from this course, we suggest that you write personal goals to improve specific skills in your own interpersonal, group, and public communication repertoire.

Although Brian Spitzberg has made many contributions to our understanding of interpersonal communication, he is best known for his work in interpersonal communication competence. This interest in competence began at the University of Southern California. For an interpersonal communication seminar assignment, he read the available research on interpersonal competence and found that the conclusions went in different directions. Spitzberg believed the time was ripe for someone to synthesize these perspectives into a comprehensive theory of competence. His final paper for the seminar was his first effort toward constructing a competence theory.

Today, the model of interpersonal communication competence Spitzberg formulated guides most of our thinking and research in this area. He views competence neither as a trait nor as a set of behaviors. Rather, Spitzberg says that interpersonal communication competence is a perception people have about themselves or another person. If competence is a perception, then it follows that your perception of your interpersonal communication competence or that of your relationship partner would affect how you feel about that relationship. So people are more likely to be satisfied in a relationship when they perceive themselves and the other person as competent. According to Spitzberg, we make these competence judgments based on how each of us acts when we talk together. But what determines how we act in a particular conversation?

As Spitzberg was trying to organize his thinking about competence, he was taking another course in which he became acquainted with theories of dramatic acting. These theories held that an actor's performance depended on the actor's motivation, knowledge of the script, and acting skills. Spitzberg found that these same variables could be applied to communication competence, and he incorporated them into his theory. How we behave in a conversation depends first on how personally motivated we are to have the conversation;

second, on how personally knowledgeable we are about what behavior is appropriate in such situations; and third, on how personally skilled we are at actually using the appropriate behaviors during the conversation.

In addition, Spitzberg's theory suggests that context variables, such as those previously discussed in this chapter, also affect how we choose to act in a conversation and the perceptions of competence that they create.

Spitzberg formed most of these ideas while he was still in graduate school, but he and others have spent more than 20 years refining the theory, conducting programs of research based on his theory, and measuring the effectiveness of the theory.

The research has fleshed out parts of the theory and provided some evidence of the theory's accuracy. Over the years, Spitzberg has developed about a dozen specific instruments to measure parts of the theory. One of these measures, the Conversational Skills Rating Scale, has been adopted as the standard measure of interpersonal communication skills by the National Communication Association (a leading national organization of communication scholars, teachers, and practitioners). His most recent work involves translating the model and measures of competence into the computer-mediated context. To what extent are the skills we use in face-to-face communication similar to those we use in computer-based interaction? Several research projects are currently investigating this question.

Whether the situation is a first date or a job interview, a conflict with a roommate or an intimate discussion of your feelings, Spitzberg believes it is important that others perceive you to be competent. For a list of a few of Spitzberg's publications on competence, see the References section at the end of this book.

For more information about Brian Spitzberg, log on to http://www-rohan.sdsu.edu/dept/schlcomm/public_html/facultybios/spitzberg.html.

Courtesy Brian Spitzberg

Before you can write a goal statement, you must first analyze your current communication skills repertoire. After you read each chapter and practice the skills described, select one or two skills to work on. Then write down your goal statement in four parts.

1. **State the problem.** Start by stating a communication problem that you have. For example: "Problem: Even though some of my group members in a team-based class project have not produced the work they promised, I haven't spoken up because I'm not very good at describing my feelings."

2. **State the specific goal.** A goal is specific if it is measurable and you know when you have achieved it. For example, to deal with the problem stated above, you might write, "Goal: To describe my disappointment to other group members about their failure to meet deadlines."

3. **Outline a specific procedure for reaching the goal.** To develop a plan for reaching your goal, first consult the chapter that covers the skill you wish to hone (for instance, Describing Feelings in Chapter 8). Then translate the general steps recommended in the chapter to your specific situation. For example: "Procedure: I will practice the steps of describing feelings. (1) I will identify the specific feeling I am experiencing. (2) I will encode the emotion I am feeling accurately. (3) I will include what has triggered the feeling. (4) I will own the feeling as mine. (5) I will then put that procedure into operation when I am talking with my group members."

4. **Devise a method of determining when the goal has been reached.** A good goal is measurable, and the fourth part of your goal-setting effort is to determine your minimum requirements for knowing when you have achieved a given goal. For example: "Test of Achieving Goal: This goal will be considered achieved when I have described my disappointment to my group members about missed deadlines."

At the end of each section, you will be challenged to develop a goal statement related to the material presented. Figure 1.2 provides another example of a communication improvement plan, this one relating to a public speaking problem.

Problem: When I speak in class or in the student senate, I often find myself burying my head in my notes or looking at the ceiling or walls.

Goal: To look at people more directly when I'm giving a speech.

Procedure: I will take the time to practice oral presentations aloud in my room. (1) I will stand up just as I do in class. (2) I will pretend various objects in the room are people, and I will consciously attempt to look at those objects as I am talking. (3) In giving a speech, I will try to be aware of when I am looking at my audience and when I am not.

Test of Achieving Goal: This goal will be considered achieved when I am maintaining eye contact with my audience most of the time.

Figure 1.2
Communication improvement plan

What Would You Do?

Molly has just been accepted at Stanford University and calls her friend Terri to tell her the good news.

MOLLY: Hi Terri! Guess what? I just got accepted to Stanford Law School!

TERRI [*Surprised and disappointed*]: Oh, cool.

MOLLY: Thanks—you sound so enthusiastic!

TERRI: Oh, I am. Listen, I have to go—I'm late for class.

MOLLY: Oh, OK. See you.

The women hang up, and Terri immediately calls her friend Monica.

TERRI: Monica, it's Terri.

MONICA: Hey, Terri. What's up?

TERRI: I just got some terrible news—Molly got into Stanford!

MONICA: So, what's wrong with that? I think it's great. Aren't you happy for her?

TERRI: No, not at all. I didn't get in, and I have better grades and a higher LSAT score.

MONICA: Maybe Molly had a better application.

TERRI: Or maybe it was what was on her application.

MONICA: What do you mean?

TERRI: You know what I mean. Molly's black.

MONICA: Yes, and . . . ?

TERRI: Don't you see? It's called affirmative action.

MONICA: Terri, give it a rest!

TERRI: Oh, please. You know it, and I know it. She only got in because of her race and because she's poor. Her GPA is really low and so is her LSAT.

MONICA: Did you ever stop to think that maybe she wrote an outstanding essay? Or that they thought the time she spent volunteering in that free legal clinic in her neighborhood was good background?

TERRI: Yes, but we've both read some of her papers, and we know she can't write. Listen, Monica, if you're black, Asian, Native American, Latino, or any other minority and poor, you've got it made. You can be as stupid as Forrest Gump and get into any law school you want. It's just not fair at all.

MONICA [*Angrily*]: No, you know what isn't fair? I'm sitting here listening to my so-called friend insult my intelligence and my ethnic background. How dare you tell me that the only reason I'll ever get into a good medical school is because I'm Latino. Listen, honey, I'll get into medical school just the same way that Molly got into law school—because of my brains, my accomplishments, and my ethical standards. And based on this conversation, it's clear that Molly and I are way ahead of you.

Describe how well each of these women followed the ethical standards for communication discussed in this chapter.

Adapted from "Racism," a case study posted on the website of the Ethics Connection, Markkula Center for Applied Ethics, Santa Clara University. http://www.scu.edu/ethics/ practicing/focusareas/education/racism.html. Used with permission.

Summary

We have defined communication as the process of creating or sharing meaning, whether the context is informal conversation, group interaction, or public speaking.

The elements of the communication process are participants, messages, context, channels, noise, and feedback.

Communication plays a role in all aspects of our lives. First, communication serves many important functions. People communicate to meet needs, to develop and maintain a sense of self, to develop relationships, to fulfill social obligations, to exchange information, and to influence others. Second, communication occurs in interpersonal, group, public speaking and electronically mediated settings.

Our communication is guided by at least seven principles. First, communication is purposeful. Second, interpersonal communication is continuous. Third, interpersonal communication messages vary in degree of conscious encoding. Messages may be spontaneous, scripted, or constructed. Fourth, interpersonal communication is relational, defining the power and affection between people. Fifth, communication is guided by culture. Sixth, communication has ethical implications. Ethical standards that influence our communication include truthfulness, integrity, fairness, respect, and responsibility. And seventh, interpersonal communication is learned.

A primary issue in this course is competence—we all strive to become better communicators. Competence is the perception by others that our communication behavior is appropriate as well as effective. It involves a desire to improve our communication, increasing our knowledge of communication, identifying and attaining goals, being able to use various skills, and presenting ourselves as credible and confident communicators. Skills can be learned, developed, and improved, and you can enhance your learning this term by writing goal statements to systematically improve your own skill repertoire.

Thomson™
NOW!

Communicate! Online

N ow that you have read Chapter 1, use your ThomsonNOW for *Communicate!* for quick access to the electronic resources that accompany this text. Your ThomsonNOW gives you access to the Web Resources and Skill Learning Activities featured in this chapter, InfoTrac College Edition, and online study aids such as a digital glossary and review quizzes. *To learn how to get started with your ThomsonNOW and other online textbook resources, see the inside front and back covers of this book.*

Your *Communicate!* ThomsonNOW is an online study system that helps you identify concepts you don't fully understand, allowing you to put your study time to the best use. Using chapter-by-chapter diagnostic pre-tests, the system creates a personalized study plan for each chapter. Each plan directs you to specific resources designed to improve your understanding, including pages from the text in e-book format. Chapter post-tests give you an opportunity to measure how much you've learned and let you know if you are ready for graded quizzes and exams.

Key Terms

Go to your ThomsonNOW for *Communicate!* to access your online glossary for Chapter 1. Print a copy of the glossary for this chapter and test yourself with the electronic flash cards or complete the crossword puzzle to help you master these key terms:

channel (7)
chat rooms (12)
communication (4)
communication competence (19)
constructed messages (14)
contexts (6)
control (15)
credibility (20)
cultural context (6)
culture (15)
decoding (5)
electronically mediated communication settings (12)
e-mail (12)
encoding (5)
ethics (17)

fairness (18)
feedback (8)
historical context (6)
immediacy (14)
instant messaging (12)
integrity (18)
internal noise (8)
interpersonal communication settings (11)
Listserv (12)
meaning (5)
messages (5)
moral dilemma (18)
noise (8)
online games (13)
participants (4)
physical context (6)
physical noise (8)

problem-solving group settings (11)
psychological context (6)
psychological noise (8)
public speaking settings (11)
respect (18)
responsibility (18)
scripted messages (14)
semantic noise (8)
skills (20)
social context (6)
social ease (20)
spontaneous expression (14)
symbols (5)
text messaging (12)
truthfulness and honesty (18)
weblogs or blogs (12)

Review Quiz

Test your knowledge of the concepts in this chapter by taking the online review quiz for Chapter 1. Go to your ThomsonNOW for *Communicate!* to access the quiz. When you have completed the quiz, submit it for scoring.

Skill Learning Activities

Go to the ThomsonNOW for *Communicate!* to complete the Observe & Analyze and Test Your Competence activities for Chapter 1. You can submit your Observe & Analyze answers to your instructor, and you can compare your Test Your Competence answers to those provided by the authors.

1.1: Test Your Competence: Identifying Elements of the Communication Process (10)

1.2: Observe & Analyze: Communication Functions (10)

1.3: Observe & Analyze: Communication over the Internet (13)

Web Resources

Go to your ThomsonNOW for *Communicate!* to access the Web Resources for this chapter.

1.1: Profile of Foreign-Born Population (17)

1.2: Lying and Deception (18)

1.3: Ethics Connection (19)

OBJECTIVES

After you have read this chapter, you should be able to answer these questions:

- What is perception?

- How does your mind select, organize, and interpret information?

- What is the self-concept, and how is it formed?

- What is self-esteem, and how is it developed?

- How do self-concept and self-esteem affect our communication with others?

- What affects how accurately we perceive others?

- What are some methods for improving the accuracy of your social perception?

2

Perception of Self and Others

As Dwayne and Miguel leave their Spanish Literature class on the first day of the semester, Dwayne comments: "I give up! This course is going to be impossible—I don't want to take it."

"Really?" replies Miguel. "I thought the course sounded interesting. The professor was funny, and I really liked how we could choose our own paper topic."

"But did you see what we're reading?" asks Dwayne. "We've got four books to read—with a test over each book, and then we're supposed to write a paper!"

"But the books look pretty interesting," replies Miguel. "They're novels and some even have movies based on the book. And because the professor seems to know what he's talking about—I mean he was born and educated in Spain—he'll probably be able to tell us a lot about Spain."

"Right," says Dwayne, "but I'm taking four other courses that look pretty tough. I like Spanish, but four books and a paper!"

H ave you had this kind of disagreement with a friend after a first day of class? How do we come to have different takes on the same event? As we analyze this conversation, we can see that Dwayne focuses on the time requirements and workload in the class whereas Miguel focuses on what he can learn. They attended the same class but carried away different perceptions. Because much of the meaning we share with others is based on our perceptions, our study of communication begins with understanding the general perceptual process and the social perceptions that affect how we view others.

In this chapter, we discuss the perception process, perceptions of self including self-concept and self-esteem, and perceptions of others. We offer suggestions for improving the accuracy of your perceptions.

The Perception Process

perception
the process of selectively attending to information and assigning meaning to it.

Perception is the process of selectively attending to information and assigning meaning to it. At times, our perceptions of the world, other people, and ourselves agree with the perceptions of others. At other times, our perceptions are significantly different from the perceptions of other people. For each person, perception becomes reality. What one person sees, hears, and interprets is real and considered true to that person. Another person who may see, hear, and interpret something entirely different from the same situation will regard that different perception as real and true. So when our perceptions are different from those with whom we interact, sharing meaning becomes more challenging.

Your brain selects the information it receives from your senses, organizes the information, and then interprets it.

Attention and Selection

Although we are subject to a constant barrage of sensory stimuli, we focus attention on relatively little of it. How we choose depends in part on our needs, interests, and expectations.

Needs We are likely to pay attention to information that meets our biological and psychological needs. When you go to class, how well in tune you are to what is being discussed is likely to depend on whether you believe the information is important to you—that is, does it meet a personal need?

Interests We are likely to pay attention to information that pertains to our interests. For instance, you may not even recognize that music is playing in the background until you find yourself suddenly listening to some old favorite. Similarly, when you are really attracted to a person, you are more likely to pay attention to what that person is saying.

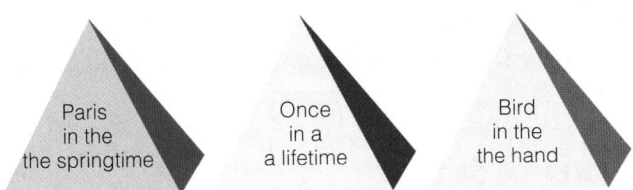

Figure 2.1
A sensory test of expectation

Expectations Finally, we are likely to see what we expect to see and to miss information that violates our expectations. Take a quick look at the phrases in the triangles in Figure 2.1. If you have never seen these triangles, you probably read "Paris in the springtime," "Once in a lifetime," and "Bird in the hand." But if you re-examine the words, you will see that what you perceived was not exactly what is written. Do you now see the repeated words? It is easy to miss the repeated word because we don't *expect* to see the word repeated.

Organization of Stimuli

Even though our attention and selection process limits the stimuli our brain must process, the absolute number of discrete stimuli we attend to at any one moment is still substantial. Our brains follow certain organizing principles to arrange these stimuli so that they make sense. Two common principles we use are simplicity and pattern.

Simplicity If the stimuli we attend to are very complex, the brain simplifies the stimuli into some commonly recognized form. Based on a quick look at what someone is wearing, how she is standing, and the expression on her face, we may perceive her as a successful businesswoman, a doctor, or a soccer mom. Similarly, we simplify the verbal messages we receive. So, for example, Tony might walk out of an hour-long performance review meeting with his boss in which the boss described four of Tony's strengths and three areas for improvement and say to Jerry, his coworker, "Well, I better shape up or I'm going to get fired!"

Pattern A second principle the brain uses when organizing information is to find patterns. A **pattern** is a set of characteristics used to differentiate some things from others. A pattern makes it easy to interpret stimuli. For example, when you see a crowd of people, instead of perceiving each individual, you may focus on a characteristic of sex and "see" men and women, or you may focus on age and "see" children, teens, adults, and seniors. In our interactions with others, we try to find patterns that will enable us to interpret and respond to their behavior. For example, each time Jason and Bill encounter Sara, she hurries over to them and begins an animated conversation. Yet when Jason is alone and runs into Sara, she barely says "Hi." After a while Jason may detect a pattern to Sara's behavior. She is warm

pattern
a set of characteristics used to differentiate some things from others.

and friendly when Bill is around and not so friendly when Bill is absent. Based on this pattern, Jason may interpret Sara's friendly behavior as flirting with Bill.

Interpretation of Stimuli

interpret
assigning meaning to information.

As the brain selects and organizes the information it receives from the senses, it also **interprets** the information by assigning meaning to it. Look at these three sets of numbers. What do you make of them?

A. 631 7348

B. 285 37 5632

C. 4632 7364 2596 2174

In each of these sets, your mind looked for clues to give meaning to the numbers. Because you use similar patterns of numbers every day, you probably interpret A as a telephone number. How about B? A likely interpretation is a Social Security number. And C? People who use credit cards may interpret this set as a credit card number.

Our interpretation of others' behavior in conversation affects how we interact with them. If Jason believes that Sara is only interested in Bill, he may not participate in conversations that she initiates.

In the remainder of this chapter, we will apply this basic information about perception to the study of perceptions of self and others in our communication.

Perceptions of Self: Self-Concept and Self-Esteem

self-concept
your self-identity.

self-esteem
your overall evaluation of your competence and personal worthiness.

Self-concept and self-esteem are the two self-perceptions that have the greatest impact on how we communicate. **Self-concept** is your self-identity (Baron, Byrne, & Brascombe, 2006). It is the idea or mental image that you have about your skills, your abilities, your knowledge, your competencies, and your personality. **Self-esteem** is your overall evaluation of your competence and personal worthiness (based on Mruk, 1999, p. 26). In this section, we describe how you come to understand who you are and how you evaluate yourself. Then we examine what determines how well these self-perceptions match others' perceptions of you. Finally, we discuss the role self-perceptions play when you communicate with others.

Forming and Maintaining a Self-Concept

How do we learn what our skills, abilities, knowledge, competencies, and personality are? Our self-concept comes from the unique interpretations about ourselves that we have made based on our experience and from others' reactions and responses to us.

Self-perception We form impressions about ourselves based on our own perceptions. Through our experiences, we develop our own sense of our skills, our abilities, our knowledge, our competencies, and our personality. For example, if you perceive that it is easy for you to talk in front of a group of people, you may conclude that you are a "natural" as a public speaker.

We place a great deal of emphasis on the first experience we have with a particular phenomenon. For instance, someone who is rejected in his first try at dating may perceive himself to be unattractive to the opposite sex. If additional experiences produce results similar to the first experience, this first perception will be strengthened. Even if the first experience is not immediately repeated, it is likely to take more than one contradictory experience to change the original negative perception.

When we have positive experiences, we are likely to believe we possess the personal characteristics that we associate with that experience, and these characteristics become part of our picture of who we are. So if Sonya quickly debugs a computer program that Jackie has struggled with, she is more likely to incorporate "competent problem solver" into her self-concept. Her positive experience confirms that she has that skill, so it is reinforced as part of her self-concept.

Reactions and responses of others In addition to our self-perceptions, our self-concept is formed and maintained by how others react and respond to us (Rayner, 2001, p. 43). We use other people's comments as a check on our own self-descriptions. They serve to validate, reinforce, or alter our perception of who and what we are. For example, if during a brainstorming session at work, one of your coworkers tells you, "You're really a creative thinker," you may decide that this comment fits your image of who you are. Such comments are especially powerful in affecting your self-perception if you respect the person making the comment. And the power of such comments is increased when the praise is immediate rather than delayed (Hattie, 1992, p. 251).

Some people have very strong self-concepts; they can describe numerous skills, abilities, knowledge, competencies, and personality characteristics that they possess. They think positively about themselves. Others have weak self-concepts; they cannot describe the skills, abilities, knowledge, competencies, or the personality characteristics that they have. They think negatively about themselves.

Our self-concept begins to form early in life, and information we receive from our families shapes our self-concept (Demo, 1987). One of the major responsibilities that family members have is to talk and act in ways that will help develop accurate and strong self-concepts in other family members. For example, the mom who says, "Roberto, your room looks very neat. You are very organized," or the brother who comments, "Kisha, lending Tomika 20 dollars really helped her out. You are very generous," is helping Roberto or Kisha to recognize important parts of their personalities.

Unfortunately, in some families, members do not fulfill these responsibilities. Sometimes family members actually do real damage to each

© David Young-Wolff/PhotoEdit

Our family members shape our self-concept. Can you recall a time when someone in your family praised you for something you had done? Is that something you still consider yourself to be good at?

other's self-image, especially to the developing self-images of children. Communicating blame, name-calling, and repeatedly pointing out another's shortcomings are particularly damaging.

Developing and Maintaining Self-Esteem

You'll recall that our self-esteem is our overall evaluation of our competence and personal worthiness—it is our positive or negative evaluation of our self-concept. Our evaluation of our personal worthiness is rooted in our values and develops over time as a result of our experiences. As Mruk (1999) points out, self-esteem is not just how well or poorly we do things (self-concept) but the importance or value we place on what we do well or poorly (p. 27). For instance, as part of Chad's self-concept, he believes he is physically strong. But if he doesn't believe that physical strength or other characteristics he possesses are worthwhile or valuable to have, then he will not have high self-esteem. Mruk explains that it takes both the perception of having a characteristic and a personal belief that the characteristic is of positive value to produce high self-esteem.

When we successfully use our skills, abilities, or knowledge in worthwhile endeavors, we raise our self-esteem. When we are unsuccessful in using our skills and abilities, or when we use them in unworthy endeavors, we lower our self-esteem.

Social construction of self We create multiple selves in an ongoing manner through our relationships with many different people. All people progressively modify and reinvent their public personas. We create different characters to respond to different situations and change ourselves in the process. We socially construct ourselves through the roles we enact.

role
a pattern of learned behaviors that people use to meet the perceived demands of a particular context.

A **role** is a pattern of learned behaviors that people use to meet the perceived demands of a particular context. For instance, during the day you may enact the roles of student, brother/sister, and salesclerk. Let's look at all the different personas or selves that one person may create and present across a few days. Ashley presents certain aspects of herself at work as a restaurant server. There she is very polite, helpful, agreeable, and attentive to others. She does not talk about herself much or use cusswords. She is confident, moves quickly, and cares about being efficient and productive. When Ashley goes out with her friends after work, she is more casual and less concerned about time. Perhaps she is louder and more boisterous. She may talk about herself more, cuss occasionally, and get into heated debates of issues and ideas. When Ashley visits her grandmother, she may act more childlike, she may be cautious not to mention topics that may offend her grandmother, and she may listen more than she talks. Ashley will enact other selves at school, as a babysitter of young children, on a date, or with her siblings. Which is Ashley's real self? They all are. We are not unitary beings. Our sense of self is the total of all the selves we play and how others react to those selves. Ashley and society will create and recreate her sense of self continuously throughout her life.

With the advent of the Internet and the anonymity it affords, we can now create roles that are quite different from our offline roles. To read about navigating who we are in cyberspace, use your ThomsonNOW for *Communicate!* to access **Web Resource 2.1: Identity in Cyberspace**. (To learn how to get started with your ThomsonNOW and other online textbook resources, see the inside front and back covers of this book.)

Self-monitoring In any situation that we face, we can choose how we present ourselves to others. **Self-monitoring** is the internal process of observing and regulating your own behavior based on your analysis of the situation and others' responses to you. Because self-monitoring goes on inside your head, others don't know if or when you are doing it. Some people are very aware of other people's responses to their behavior. They notice people's expressions and reactions and use this feedback to adjust their own behavior so that they leave the impression they wish to leave. Other people are less aware of the impression they are making. As a result, they

self-monitoring
the internal process of observing and regulating your own behavior based on your analysis of the situation and others' responses to you.

BSIP Agency/Jupiterimages

How do you suppose this dentist's behavior changes when she goes on a vacation with her brothers and sisters?

tend to do and say things that may be viewed as inappropriate or lead others to have an inaccurate impression of them.

We are more likely to self-monitor when we are in new situations. When we don't know what is expected, we look to others for cues to see if we are behaving appropriately and we are likely to adjust our behavior accordingly. So when Mia, who is visiting her friend at another college, finds herself at a party with a bunch of strangers, she may want to show her sophisticated side so she can fit in. As a result, she may find her self-talk filled with self-monitoring statements like, "Why did I just make that comment—it sounded so lame?" or "Well, I sure scored points there; now I've got their attention." Being aware of and attentive to other's feedback is an important part of self-monitoring.

Accuracy of Self-Concept and Self-Esteem

The accuracy of our self-concept and self-esteem depends on the accuracy of our own perceptions and how we process others' perceptions of us. All of us experience success and failure, and all of us hear praise and criticism. If we are overly attentive to successful experiences and positive responses, our self-concept may become overdeveloped and our self-esteem inflated. If, however, we perceive and dwell on failures and give little value to our successes, or if we only remember the criticism we receive, our self-image may be underdeveloped and our self-esteem low. In neither case does our self-concept or self-esteem accurately reflect who we are.

incongruence
the gap between our inaccurate self-perceptions and reality.

Incongruence, the gap between our inaccurate self-perceptions and reality, is a problem because our perceptions of self are more likely than our true abilities to affect our behavior (Weiten, 1998, p. 491). For example, Raul may actually possess all the skills, abilities, knowledge, competencies, and personality characteristics for effective leadership, but if he doesn't perceive that he has these characteristics, he won't step forward when leadership is needed. Unfortunately, individuals tend to reinforce their self-perceptions by adjusting their behavior to conform with their perceived self-conceptions. That is, people with high self-esteem tend to behave in ways that lead to more affirmation, whereas people with low self-esteem tend to act in ways that confirm the low esteem in which they hold themselves. The inaccuracy of a distorted picture of oneself is magnified through self-fulfilling prophecies and by filtering messages.

self-fulfilling prophecies
events that happen as the result of being foretold, expected, or talked about.

Self-fulfilling prophecies **Self-fulfilling prophecies** are events that happen as the result of being foretold, expected, or talked about. They may be self-created or other-imposed.

Self-created prophecies are those predictions you make about yourself. We often talk ourselves into success or failure. For example, researchers have found that when people expect rejection, they are more likely to behave in ways that lead others to reject them (Downey, Freitas, Michaelis, &

Khouri, 2004, p. 437). So Aaron, who sees himself as unskilled in establishing new relationships; says to himself, "I doubt I'll know hardly anyone at the party—I'm going to have a miserable time." Because he fears encountering strangers, he feels awkward about introducing himself and, just as he predicted, spends much of his time standing around alone thinking about when he can leave. In contrast, Stefan sees himself as quite social and able to get to know people easily. As a result of his positive self-esteem and prophecy, he looks forward to the party and, just as he predicted, makes several new acquaintances and enjoys himself.

Self-esteem has an important effect on the prophecies people make. For instance, people with positive self-esteem view success positively and confidently prophesy that they can repeat successes; people with low self-esteem attribute their successes to luck, and so prophesy that they will not repeat them (Hattie, 1992, p. 253).

The prophecies others make about you also affect your performance and self-image. For example, when teachers act as if their students are bright, students "buy into" this expectation and learn. Likewise, when teachers act as if students are not bright, students may live "down" to these imposed prophecies and fail to achieve. So how we talk to ourselves and how we treat others affects self-concepts and self-esteem.

Filtering messages A second way that our self-perceptions can become distorted is through the way we filter what others say to us. We are prone to pay attention to messages that reinforce our current self-image, whereas messages that contradict this image may not "register" or may be downplayed. For example, suppose you prepare an agenda for your study group. Someone comments that you're a good organizer. If you spent your childhood hearing how disorganized you were, you may not really hear this comment, or you may downplay it. If, however, you think you are good at organizing, you will pay attention to the compliment and may even reinforce it by responding, "Thanks, I'm a pretty organized person. I've learned it from my boss at work."

Changing self-concepts and self-esteem Self-concept and self-esteem are enduring characteristics, but they can be changed. At times, comments that contradict your current self-concept and self-esteem are absorbed and lead you to slowly change your self-image. Certain situations seem to expedite this process. When you experience a profound change in your social environment, you are likely to be amenable to incorporating new information into your self-image. When children begin school or go to sleep-away camp; when teens start part-time jobs; when young adults go to college; or when people begin or end jobs or relationships, become parents, or grieve the loss of someone they love, they are more likely to absorb messages that are at odds with their current self-images.

Therapy and self-help techniques can assist us when we want to alter our self-concept and improve our self-esteem. In his analysis of numerous research studies, Christopher Mruk (1999, p. 112) found that self-esteem is increased through "hard work and practice, practice, practice—there is simply no escaping this basic existential fact."

So why is this important to communication? Because our self-esteem affects with whom we choose to form relationships, how we interact with them, how we participate when we are in small groups, and how comfortable we feel when we are called on to present a speech. Researchers have found that "people with high self-esteem are more committed to partners who perceive them very favorably, while people with low self-esteem are more committed to partners who perceive them less favorably" (Leary, 2002, p. 130).

Many books have been written to help people raise their self-esteem, and there are rich sources of information available on the World Wide Web. To check out one such source, Coping.org's Model of Self-Esteem program, go to your ThomsonNOW for *Communicate!* to access **Web Resource 2.2: Self-Esteem Model.** (To learn how to get started with your ThomsonNOW and other online textbook resources, see the inside front and back covers of this book.)

In this book, we consider many specific communication behaviors that are designed to increase your communication competence. As you begin to practice and to perfect these skills, you may begin to receive positive responses to your behavior. If you continue to work on these skills, the positive responses you receive will help improve your self-concept and increase your self-esteem.

Self-Concept, Self-Esteem, and Communication

Just as our self-concept and self-esteem affect how accurately we perceive ourselves, so too do they influence our communication by moderating competing internal messages in our self-talk and influencing our personal communication style.

self-talk
the internal conversations we have with ourselves.

Self-perceptions moderate how we talk to ourselves. Self-talk is the internal conversations we have with ourselves. A lot of this conversation is also about ourselves. People who have high self-esteem are likely to engage in positive self-talk, such as "I know I can do it" or "I did really well on that test." They are also more likely to have self-talk that is more accurate. People with negative self-esteem are likely to overemphasize negative self-talk or, ironically, they may overinflate their sense of self-worth to compensate. So they may tell themselves that they are good at everything they do.

Self-perception influences how we talk about ourselves with others. If we feel good about ourselves, we are likely to communicate positively. For instance, people with a strong self-concept and higher self-esteem usually take credit for their successes. Likewise, people with healthy self-perceptions are inclined to defend their views even in the face of opposing arguments. If we feel bad about ourselves, we are likely to communicate negatively by downplaying our accomplishments.

Why do some people put themselves down regardless of what they have done? People who have low self-esteem are likely to be unsure of the value of their contributions and expect others to view them negatively. As a result, people with a poor self-concept or low self-esteem may find it less painful to put themselves down than to hear the criticism of others. Thus, to preempt the likelihood that others will comment on their unworthiness, they do it first.

Cultural and Gender Influences

A person's culture has a strong influence on the self-perception process (Samovar, Porter, & McDaniel, 2007, p. 130). In some cultures, described as individualistic, people stress the self and personal achievement. In these cultures, the individual is treated as the most important element in a social setting. In individualistic cultures, people care about self-concept, self-esteem and self-image. The United States is considered an individualistic culture. In fact, all the information thus far in this chapter reflects an individualistic cultural perspective on perception and the self-concept. Other cultures are considered collectivist and they tend to downplay the individual. Groups and social norms are more important in collectivist cultures. People are expected to be interdependent and to see themselves in terms of the group. Notions of self-concept and self-esteem have little meaning in collectivist cultures. In an individualistic culture, you would think only of what is best for yourself when making a decision, such as taking a new job. You might move far away from family for the job. At work, you would want to be paid, judged, and promoted on your own work rather than how the group is performing. In a collectivist culture, your decision about taking a new job would be made collectively by your family and you would be expected to live nearby the family. Your salary, performance evaluations, and promotions would naturally be based on how well the entire group, team, or department was functioning.

Similarly, men and women are socialized to view themselves differently and to value who they are based on whether their behavior corresponds to or challenges the behavior expected of their sex in their culture. There are norms of what it means to be feminine and what it means to be masculine in our society. Gender expectations in a society inevitably influence our perceptions, sense of self, and social construction of self. Generally in the United States, males are taught to base their self-esteem on their achievements, status, and income, while females are taught that their self-esteem derives from their appearance and their relationships (Wood, 2007). Thus, it is difficult to understand the process of social perception without taking into consideration the influences of culture and gender. The Diverse Voices box in this chapter by Dolores V. Tanno describes the influence of gender and culture on perceptions of self and others. It also describes how our sense of self is socially constructed through the many roles we play or are expected to play.

DIVERSE VOICES

I Am . . .

by Dolores V. Tanno

Dolores V. Tanno, University of Nevada, Las Vegas, describes how her self-concept and self-esteem are shaped by labels others use to describe her and the multiples roles she plays related to gender and culture.

O ver the course of my life, one question has been consistently asked of me: *"What are you?"* I used to reply that I was American, but it quickly became clear this was unacceptable because what came next was, "No, really what are you?" In my more perverse moments I responded, "I am human." I stopped when I realized that people's feelings were hurt. Ironic? Yes, but the motive behind the question often justified hurt feelings. I became aware of this only after asking a question of my own: "Why do you ask?"

Confronting the motives of people has forced me to examine who I am. In the process I have had to critically examine my own choices, in different times and contexts, of the names by which I am placed in society. The names are "Spanish," "Mexican American," "Latina," and "Chicana."

"I am Spanish." Behind this label is the story of my childhood in northern New Mexico. New Mexico was the first permanent Spanish settlement in the Southwest, and New Mexicans have characterized themselves as Spanish for centuries. My parents, grandparents, and great-grandparents consider themselves Spanish; wrongly or rightly they attribute their customs, habits, and language to their Spanish heritage, and I followed suit. In my young mind, the story of being Spanish did not include concepts of racial purity or assimilation; what it did do was allow me to begin my life with a clearly defined identity and a place in the world. For me, the story of being Spanish incorporates into its plot the innocence of youth, before the reality of discrimination became an inherent part of the knowledge of who I am.

"I am Mexican American." When I left New Mexico, my sense of belonging did not follow me across the state border. When I responded to the question, "What are you?" by saying, "I am Spanish," people corrected me: "You mean Mexican, don't you?" My initial reaction was anger; how could they know better than I who I was? But soon my reaction was one of puzzlement, and I wondered just why there was such insistence that I be Mexican. Reading and studying led me to understand that the difference between Spanish and Mexican could be found in the legacy of colonization. Thus behind the name "Mexican American" is the story of classic colonization that allows for prior existence and that also communicates duality. As Richard A. Garcia argues: "Mexican in culture and social activity, American in philosophy and politics." As native-born Mexican Americans, we also have dual visions: the achievement of the American Dream and the preservation of cultural identity.

"I am Latina." If the story behind the name Mexican American is grounded in duality, the story behind the name "Latina" is grounded in cultural connectedness. The Spaniards proclaimed vast territories of North and South American as their own. They intermarried in all the regions in which they settled. These marriages yielded offspring who named themselves variously as Cubans, Puerto Ricans, Colombians, Mexicans, and so forth, but they connect culturally with each other when they name each other Latinas. To use the name *Latina* is to communicate acceptance and belonging in a broad cultural community.

"I am Chicana." This name suggests a smaller community, a special kind of Mexican American awareness that does not involve others (Cubans, Puerto Ricans, and so on). The name was the primary political as well as rhetorical strategy of the Chicano movement of the 1960s. Mirande and Enriquez argue that the dominant characteristic of the name "Chicana" is that it admits a "sense of marginality." There is a political tone and character to "Chicana" that signifies a story of self-determination and empowerment. As such, the name denotes a kind of political becoming. At the same time, however, the name communicates the idea of being American, not in a "melting pot" sense that presupposes assimilation, but rather in a pluralistic sense that acknowledges the inalienable right of existence for different peoples.

What, then, am I? The truth is I am all of these. Each name reveals a different facet of identity that allows symbolic, historical, cultural, and political connectedness. These names are no different than other multiple labels we take on. For example, to be mother, wife, sister, and daughter, is to admit to the complexity of being female. Each name implies a narrative of experiences gained in responding to circumstances, time, and place and motivated by a need to belong.

In my case, I resort to being Spanish and all it implies whenever I return to my birthplace, in much the same way that we often resort to being children again in the presence of our parents. But I am also Mexican American when I balance the two important cultures that define me: Latina when I wish to emphasize cultural and historical connectedness with others, and Chicana whenever opportunities arise to promote political empowerment and assert political pride.

It is sometimes difficult for people to understand the "both/and" mentality that results from this simultaneity of existence. We are indeed enriched by belonging to two cultures. We are made richer still by having at our disposal several names by which to identify ourselves. Singly the names Spanish, Mexican American, Latina, and Chicana communicate a part of a life story. Together they weave a rhetorically powerful narrative of ethnic identity that combines biographical, historical, cultural, and political experiences.

Excerpted from D. V. Tanno, "Names, Narratives, and the Evolution of Ethnic Identity," in Our Voices: Essays in Cultural Ethnicity and Communication (3rd ed.), *eds. A. Gonzalez, M. Houston, and V. Chen (Los Angeles, CA: Roxbury Publishing Company, 2001), pp. 25–28.*

The Internet offers a variety of sources on the topics of self-concept and self-esteem. Many of them offer suggestions that people have found useful. You can use a search engine like Google to find and view such sites. To read a particularly provocative article about self-esteem, Dr. Richard O'Connor's "Self-Esteem: In a Culture Where Winning Is Everything and Losing Is Shameful," go to your ThomsonNOW for *Communicate!* to access **Web Resource 2.3: Real Self-Esteem?** (To learn how to get started with your ThomsonNOW and other online textbook resources, see the inside front and back covers of this book.) What points does O'Connor make? How does his conclusion coincide with what you have observed?

Perception of Others

As we encounter others, we are faced with a number of questions: Do we have anything in common? Will others accept and value us? Will we be able to get along? Because this uncertainty makes us uneasy, we try to alleviate it. Charles Berger describes the process we use to overcome our discomfort as **uncertainty reduction,** the process of monitoring the social environment to learn more about self and others (Littlejohn & Foss, 2005). As

uncertainty reduction
the process of monitoring the social environment to learn more about self and others.

implicit personality theories

assumptions people have developed about which physical characteristics and personality traits or behaviors are associated with another.

people interact, they gain information and form impressions of others. For example, when Nicole and Justin meet for the first time at a party, they probably pay much attention to how each other looks, because that's the only source of information they have about each other at first. Then, they ask each other questions about their majors, jobs, hobbies, interests, and people they may know in common. This small talk helps them gain information so that they can find things they have in common. The more they learn about each other and find commonalities, the less uncertain they are about each other. These perceptions will be reinforced, intensified, or changed as their relationship develops. The factors likely to influence perceptions of others include their physical characteristics and social behaviors, their messages, your use of stereotyping, and your emotional state.

Observing Physical Characteristics and Social Behaviors

Social perceptions, especially first impressions, are often made on the basis of physical characteristics and social behaviors. On the basis of people's physical attractiveness (facial characteristics, height, weight, grooming, dress, sound of voice), we are likely to categorize people as friendly, trendy, intelligent, cool, or their opposites (Aronson, 1999, p. 380). In one study, professional women dressed in jackets were assessed as more powerful than professional women dressed in other clothing (Temple & Loewen, 1993, p. 345). Show a friend a picture of your child, uncle, or grandmother, and your friend may well form impressions of your relative's personality on the basis of that photo alone!

Early impressions are also made on the basis of a person's social behaviors. If, on the first day of class, a fellow student strikes up conversations with strangers sitting near him, makes humorous remarks in class, and gives the best self-introduction in a class activity, you are likely to form the impression that he is confident, extroverted, and friendly.

First impressions are formed not only in face-to-face communication, but in online interaction as well. People care about creating the right impression online through the timeliness of their responses, the use of chat room nicknames, and their use of vocabulary, grammar, and manners (sometimes called netiquette). Initial interaction online often begins with the question A/S/L?, which asks for someone's age, sex, and location. This is a get-to-know-you question, which allows someone to reduce uncertainty about the other person. Creating personal homepages also relates to self-identity and first impressions. Creating a personal homepage is an opportunity for people to reflect upon themselves and to think about how they want to represent themselves to the world. It is an attempt to influence others' first impressions of you (Thurlow, Lengel, & Tomic, 2004).

Some judgments of other people are based on **implicit personality theories,** which are assumptions people have developed about which physical characteristics and personality traits or behaviors are associated with another (Michener & DeLamater, 1999, p. 106). Because your own implicit personality theory says that certain traits go together, you are likely to generalize and perceive that a person has a whole set of characteristics when you have actually observed only one characteristic, trait, or behavior. When you do this, your perception is exhibiting what is known as the **halo effect.** For instance, Heather sees Martina personally greeting and welcoming every person who arrives at the meeting. Heather's implicit personality theory views this behavior as a sign of the characteristic of warmth. She further associates warmth with goodness, and goodness with honesty. As a result, she perceives that Martina is good and honest as well as warm.

In reality, Martina may be a con artist who uses her warmth to lure people into a false sense of trust. This example demonstrates a "positive halo" (Heather assigned Martina positive characteristics), but we also use implicit personality theory to inaccurately impute bad characteristics. Given limited amounts of information, then, we fill in details. This tendency to fill in details leads to a second factor that explains social perception, stereotyping.

halo effect
to generalize and perceive that a person has a whole set of characteristics when you have actually observed only one characteristic, trait, or behavior.

Using Stereotypes

Perhaps the most commonly known factor that influences our perception of others is stereotyping. **Stereotypes** are "attributions that cover up individual differences and ascribe certain characteristics to an entire group of people" (Hall, 2002, p. 198). So, when we find out that someone is Hispanic or Muslim, a skateboarder, a chess player, an elementary school teacher, or a nurse—in short, any "identifiable group"—we use this information to attribute to the person a host of characteristics. These perceived group characteristics, taken as a whole, may be positive or negative, and they may be accurate or inaccurate (Jussim, McCauley, & Lee, 1995, p. 6).

stereotypes
attributions that cover up individual differences and ascribe certain characteristics to an entire group of people.

We are likely to develop generalized perceptions about any group we come in contact with. Subsequently, any number of perceptual cues—skin color, style of dress, a religious medal, gray hair, a loud voice, an expensive car, and so on—can lead us to stereotype our generalizations onto a specific individual. A professor may see a student's purple spiked hair and numerous tattoos and assume the student defies authority, does not take school seriously, and seeks attention. In reality, this person may be a quiet, serious honor student who obeys rules and aspires to graduate school. A customer may generalize that her bank teller is professional and competent because the teller is wearing a business suit and speaks with proper grammar, while, in reality, the bank teller makes frequent mistakes and is about to be fired. According to B. J. Hall (2002, p. 201), we don't form most of the stereotypes we use from our personal experience. Instead we learn them from family, friends, coworkers, and the mass media. So we adopt stereotypes before we have any personal "proof." And because stereotypes guide what we perceive, they can lead us to attend to information that confirms them and to overlook information that contradicts them.

Stereotyping can lead to prejudice and discrimination. According to B. J. Hall (2002), **prejudice** is "a rigid attitude that is based on group mem-

prejudice
a rigid attitude that is based on group membership and predisposes an individual to feel, think, or act in a negative way toward another person or group.

bership and predisposes an individual to feel, think, or act in a negative way toward another person or group" (p. 208). Notice the distinction between a stereotype and a prejudice. Whereas a stereotype is a set of beliefs or expectations, a prejudice is a positive or negative attitude; both relate to group membership. Stereotypes and prejudice are cognitive—that is, things we think.

discrimination
a negative action toward a social group or its members on account of group membership.

Discrimination, on the other hand, is a negative action toward a social group or its members on account of group membership (Jones, 2002, p. 8). Whereas prejudice and stereotype deal with attitudes, discrimination involves negative action. For instance, when Laura discovers that Wasif, a man she has just met, is a Muslim, she may stereotype him as a chauvinist. If she is a feminist, she may use this stereotype to prejudge him and assume that he will expect women to be subservient. Thus she holds a prejudice about him. If she acts on her prejudice, she may discriminate against him by refusing to partner with him on a class project. So, without really having gotten to know Wasif, Laura uses her stereotype to prejudge him and discriminate. In this case, Wasif may never get the chance to be known for who he really is, and Laura may have lost an opportunity to get to work with the best student in class.

Thomson™
NOW!

To read about balancing actions you can take to counteract stereotypes, go to your ThomsonNOW for *Communicate!* to access **Web Resource 2.4: Fighting Words with Words.** To read more about stereotyping, read the article "You May Be Stereotyping Your Co-Workers, and That Hurts All of Us," available through InfoTrac College Edition—go to your ThomsonNOW for *Communicate!* to access **Web Resource 2.5: Stereotyping at Work.** (To learn how to get started with your ThomsonNOW and other online textbook resources, see the inside front and back covers of this book.)

What is the relationship between these colleagues? How did stereotyping influence your perception?

© G. Baden/zefa/Corbis

Emotional States

A final factor that affects how accurately we perceive others is our emotional state at the time of the interaction. Based on his research, Joseph Forgas (1991) has concluded that "there is a broad and pervasive tendency for people to perceive and interpret others in terms of their (own) feelings at the time" (p. 288). If, for example, you received the internship you had applied for, your good mood is likely to spill over so that you perceive other things and other people more positively than you might under different circumstances. If, however, you just learned that your car needs $1,500 in repairs, your perceptions of people around you are likely to be colored by your negative mood and anxiety about paying this bill.

Our emotions also cause us to engage in selective perceptions, ignoring inconsistent information. For instance, if Nick is physically attracted to Jessica, he is likely to focus on the positive aspects of Jessica's personality and may overlook or ignore the negative ones that are apparent to others.

Our emotional state also affects our attributions (Forgas, 2000, p. 397). **Attributions** are reasons we give for others' behavior. In making judgments about people, we attempt to construct reasons to explain why people behave as they do. According to attribution theory, what we determine—rightly or wrongly—to be the causes of others' behavior has a direct impact on our perceptions of them. For instance, suppose a coworker with whom you had made a noon lunch date has not arrived by 12:20 p.m. If you like and respect your coworker, you may attribute his lateness to something out of his control: an important phone call at the last minute, the need to finish a job before lunch, or some accident that may have occurred. If you are not particularly fond of your coworker, you are more likely to attribute his lateness to something in his control: forgetfulness, inconsiderateness, or malicious intent. In either case, your attribution will affect your perception of him and probably how you treat him.

Like prejudices, the attributions we make can be so strong that we ignore contrary evidence. If you are not particularly close to your coworker, when he does arrive and explains that he had an emergency long-distance phone call, you may believe he is lying or discount the urgency of the call.

Understanding that our physical characteristics and social behaviors, stereotyping, and emotional states affect our perceptions of others is a first step in improving our perceptual accuracy. Now we want to describe three guidelines and a communication skill you can use to improve the accuracy of your social perceptions of others.

attributions
reasons we give for others' behavior.

Improving Social Perception

Because distortions in perception are common and because they influence how we communicate, improving perceptual accuracy is an important first step in becoming a competent communicator. The following guidelines can aid you in constructing accurate impression of others and assessing your own perceptions of others' messages.

1. **Question the accuracy of your perceptions.** Questioning accuracy begins by saying, "I know what I think I saw, heard, tasted, smelled, or felt, but I could be wrong. What other information should I be aware of?" By accepting the possibility that you have overlooked something, you will become interested in increasing your accuracy.

2. **Seek more information to verify perceptions.** If your perception is based on only one or two pieces of information, try to collect further information so that your perceptions are better grounded. Note that your perception is tentative—that is, subject to change.

   The best way to get additional information about people is to talk with them. It's OK to be unsure about how to treat someone from another group. But rather than letting your uncertainty cause you to make mistakes, talk with the person and ask for the information you need to become more comfortable.

3. **Realize that your perceptions of a person will change over time.** People often base their behavior on perceptions that are old or based on incomplete information. So when you encounter someone you haven't seen for a while, you will want to become reacquainted and let the person's current behavior rather than their past actions or reputation inform your perceptions. A former classmate who was "wild" in high school may well have changed and become a mature, responsible adult.

To complete an activity that will help you examine how culture affects your perceptions of other people, go to your ThomsonNOW for *Communicate!* to access **Skill Learning Activity 2.4: Culture and Perception.** (To learn how to get started with your ThomsonNOW and other online textbook resources, see the inside front and back covers of this book.)

Perception of Messages

In the first chapter, we discussed how the communication process worked and explained that conversational partners or speakers and audiences use messages as the vehicle through which they attempt to create shared meanings. Their success at sharing meaning depends on the encoding and decoding processes, which, in turn, depend on how the messages are perceived. Although many things can affect the message perception process, three important factors are the context, the extent to which the participants share a common language and nonverbal code, and the skillfulness the message sender uses in preparing the message.

Context rules! The most important factor in determining how a message will be understood by the receiver is the context in which it is sent and received. We use contextual cues to help us understand the content and the intent of the speaker in sending the message. For example, several years ago at a family dinner Jeorge's dad, who dislikes conflict, sought to distract family members from a quarrel that had begun between two aunts by look-

▶ Speech Assignment: Communicate on Your Feet

Presenting Others: Conversation and Speech of Introduction

The Assignment

Following your instructor's directions, pair with someone in class. You are to spend some time talking with this person in class, getting to know them, so that next class period you can give a short 2-minute speech introducing this classmate to the rest of the class.

Speeches of Introduction

A speech of introduction is given to acquaint a group with someone they have not met. We make short "speeches" of introduction all the time. When a high school friend comes to visit for a weekend, you will introduce her to your friends. Not only will you tell them her name, but you will probably mention other things about her that will make it easy for your friends to talk with her. Likewise, a store manager may call the sales associates together in order to introduce a new hire. The manager might mention the new team member's previous experience, interests, and other items of information that will make it easy for the team to respect, help, and become acquainted with the new employee.

Speeches of introduction often precede formal addresses. The goal of the introducer is to establish the credibility of the main speaker by letting the audience know the education, background, and experiences of the speaker that are related to the topic of the speech and to build audience interest in listening to the address.

The beginning of a speech of introduction should raise the audience's interest so that they want to learn more about the person. The main part of the speech of introduction should focus on three or four things about the person you are introducing that are interesting and important for the audience to understand so that they will want to get to know the person better or listen to what the person will say in a speech. When the person being introduced is not scheduled to present a speech (like in the assignment or when introducing a friend or coworker) you might end your introduction with a creative statement that peaks audience interest in getting to know the person you have introduced. When you introduce a main speaker, you conclude by briefly identifying the speaker's topic or the title of the speech. Remember that your goal is not to embarrass the person you are introducing, so avoid statements that while playful, may be misconstrued.

ing up at the elaborate crystal chandelier hanging above the table and asking, "How do you suppose they clean that chandelier?" Now, because the aunts were aware that Jeorge's dad hated conflict, they immediately understood "the message" and discontinued their argument. Thereafter, regardless of the situation, when anyone in the family wanted to avoid a brewing conflict, they would simply say, "How about that chandelier?" and the potential conflict would usually be diffused. Obviously, people who had not been present at the initial dinner would not have understood the historical context of this message and would likely be confused by what was said.

Obviously the better we know someone, the more likely we are to share an understanding of the context in which our messages are sent and received. When we don't know someone well or when we are speaking with several people or a large audience, there are expanded opportunities for messages to be perceived differently.

perception check
a message that reflects your understanding of the meaning of another person's nonverbal behavior.

Shared language It is obvious that for people to be able to decode messages, they need to be able to understand the language in which they were encoded. But because of the nature of language and nonverbal symbols, it is possible for receivers to understand the language in which a message is encoded and yet misperceive the meaning of the sender. This can occur because the sender is using a word with which the receiver is unfamiliar, using a word that has multiple meanings in an ambiguous way, misusing a symbol, or using a personal and idiosyncratic definition of a word. So when Justin tells his wife that he's "going out with the guys for an hour or so," she may expect him home in 60–90 minutes. When he shows up 5 hours later, she will probably be distraught. Justin may have figured that his "or so" would cover any additional time he was away, while his wife viewed it as something less than 2 hours. In this case, while the message was sent in a language that both "understood," they did not share meaning because they perceived the message to mean different lengths of time.

Skillfulness in encoding and decoding messages Although a multitude of factors can conspire to make accurately perceiving and decoding the messages of others difficult, we can help each other as we strive to share meaning when we thoughtfully construct the messages we send. This means that we need to choose specific, concrete, and precise words as we form our messages. We need to provide details and use examples. We must be careful to adapt our language to the specific listener or group of listeners so that the words we use are likely to be perceived as we intended. When we are giving a speech to an audience where the likelihood of misperception is greatest, we need to make our messages vivid, using similes and metaphors to help our audience "picture" what we are hoping to convey. In addition, we need to help our audience perceive what is important by giving parts of our speech messages more emphasis through the proportion of time spent discussing an idea, repetition, and the use of guiding transitional phrases. We will discuss each of these techniques in depth in Chapter 3.

Perception Checking

Whether we are trying to accurately perceive ourselves, others, or messages that we receive, one way to assess the accuracy of a perception is to verbalize it and see whether others agree with what you see, hear, and interpret. A **perception check** is a message that reflects your understanding of the meaning of another person's nonverbal behavior. It is a process of describing what you have seen and heard and asking for feedback from the other person. Perception checking calls for you to (1) watch the behavior of the other person, (2) ask yourself "What does that behavior mean to me?" and (3) describe the behavior and put your interpretation into words to verify your perception.

The following examples illustrate the use of perception checking. In each of the examples, the final sentence is a perception check. Notice that

Communication Skill <u>Perception Checking</u>

Skill	Use	Procedure	Example
Making a verbal statement that reflects your understanding of another person's behavior.	To enable you to test the accuracy of your perceptions.	1. Describe the behaviors of the other that have led to your perception. 2. Add your interpretation of the behavior to your statement.	After taking a phone call, Shimika comes into the room with a completely blank expression and neither speaks to Donnell nor acknowledges that he is in the room. Donnell says, "Shimika, from your blank look, I get the feeling that you're in a state of shock. Has something happened?"

Skill Building <u>Perception Checking</u>

For each of the following situations, write a well-phrased perception check.

1. When Franco comes home from the doctor's office, you notice that he looks pale and his shoulders are slumped. Glancing at you with a sad look, he shrugs his shoulders.
   You say:

2. As you return the basketball you borrowed from Liam, you smile and say, "Thanks, here's your ball." You notice Liam stiffen, grab the ball, and, turning abruptly, walk away.
   You say:

3. Natalie, who has been waiting to hear about a scholarship, dances into the room with a huge grin on her face.
   You say:

4. You see your adviser in the hall and ask her if she can meet with you on Wednesday afternoon to discuss your schedule of classes for next term. You notice that she pauses, frowns, sighs, turns slowly, and says, "I guess so."
   You say:

Compare your written responses to the guidelines for effective perception checking discussed earlier. Edit your responses where necessary to improve them. Now say them aloud. Do they sound "natural"? If not, revise them until they do.

Thomson NOW! You can complete this activity online and compare your answers to the authors'. Go to your Thomson-NOW for *Communicate!* to access **Skill Learning Activity 2.6**. (To learn how to get started with your ThomsonNOW and other online textbook resources, see the inside front and back covers of this book.)

What Would You Do?

U niConCo, a multinational construction company, successfully bid to build a new minor league stadium in a Midwestern city that had very little diversity. Miguel Hernandez was assigned to be the Assistant Project Manager, and he moved his family of seven to town. He quickly joined the local Chamber of Commerce, affiliated with the local Rotary group, and was feeling the first signs of acceptance. One day Mr. Hernandez was working at his desk when he accidentally overheard a group of local Anglo construction workers who were on the project talking about their Mexican American coworkers. Miguel was discouraged to hear the negative stereotypes that were being used. The degree of hatred expressed was clearly beyond what he was used to, and he was further upset when he recognized several of the voices as belonging to men he had fought to hire.

A bit shaken, Mr. Hernandez returned to his office. He had a problem. He recognized his workers' prejudices, but he wasn't sure how to change them. Moreover, he wanted to establish good work relationships with his Anglo workers for the sake of the company, but he also wanted to create a good working atmosphere for the other Latino workers who would soon be moving to town to work on the project. What could Mr. Hernandez do?

Devise a plan for Mr. Hernandez. How could he use his social perceptions to address the problem in a way that is within ethical, interpersonal communication guidelines?

the perception-checking statements do not express approval or disapproval of what is being received—they are purely descriptive statements of the perceptions.

> Valerie walks into the room with a completely blank expression. She does not speak to Ann or even acknowledge that Ann is in the room. Valerie sits down on the edge of the bed and stares into space. Ann says, "Valerie, did something happen? You look like you're in a state of shock. Am I right? Is there something I can do?"

> While Marsha is telling Jenny about the difficulty of her midterm exam in chemistry class, she notices Jenny smiling. She says to Jenny, "You're smiling. I'm not sure how to interpret it. What's up?" Jenny may respond that she's smiling because the story reminded her of something funny or because she had the same chemistry teacher last year and he purposely gave an extremely difficult midterm to motivate students, but then he graded them on a really favorable curve.

> Cesar, speaking in short, precise sentences with a sharp tone of voice, gives Bill his day's assignment. Bill says, "From the sound of your voice, Cesar, I get the impression that you're upset with me. Are you?"

So when we use the skill of perception checking, we encode the meaning that we have perceived from someone's behavior and feed it back so that it can be verified or corrected. For instance, when Bill says, "I can't help but get the impression that you're upset with me. Are you?" Cesar may say: (1) "No, whatever gave you that impression?" in which case Bill can further describe the cues that he received; (2) "Yes, I am," in which case Bill can get Cesar to specify what has caused the feelings; or (3) "No, it's not you, it's just that three of my team members didn't show up for this shift." If Cesar is not upset with him, Bill can examine what caused him to misinterpret Cesar's feelings; if Cesar is upset with him, Bill has the opportunity to change the behavior that caused Cesar to be upset.

Summary

Perception is the process of selectively attending to information and assigning meaning to it. Our perceptions are a result of our selection, organization, and interpretation of sensory information. Self-concept is our self-identity, the idea or mental image that we have about our skills, abilities, knowledge, competencies, and personality. Self-esteem is our overall evaluation of our competence and personal worthiness. Self-concepts come from interpretations of self based on our own experience and on the reactions and responses of others. The inaccuracy of a distorted picture of oneself becomes magnified through self-fulfilling prophecies and filtering messages. Our self-concept and self-esteem moderate competing internal messages in our self-talk, influence our perception of others, and influence our personal communication style. Our self-concept is socially constructed by us and by others, and the different roles we play in various situations create our multiple selves.

Perception plays an important role in forming impressions of others. We form these impressions based on others' physical characteristics and social behaviors, our stereotyping, and our emotional states. Your communication will be most successful if you do not rely entirely on your own interpretation to determine how another person feels, what that person is really like, or what you think the person means by a certain message. You can learn to improve perception if you actively question the accuracy of your perceptions, seek more information to verify perceptions, talk with the people about whom you are forming perceptions, and realize that perceptions of people need to change over time.

In addition to perceiving ourself and others, we also use perception to decode and understand the messages that we receive. As we perceive messages, the three important factors that affect our perception are the context in which we receive the message, the language and nonverbal behavior that form the message, and the skillfulness with which the message was formed.

Perception checking is a communication skill that can help us increase the likelihood that we will share meaning with others. It can help us increase the accuracy of our self-perceptions, our perceptions of others' behavior, and our perceptions of the nonverbal parts of the messages that we receive.

Thomson NOW!

Communicate! Online

Now that you have read Chapter 2, use your ThomsonNOW for *Communicate!* for quick access to the electronic resources that accompany this text. Your ThomsonNOW gives you access to the Web Resources and Skill Learning Activities featured in this chapter, InfoTrac College Edition, and online study aids such as a digital glossary and review quizzes. *To learn how to get started with your ThomsonNOW and other online textbook resources, see the inside front and back covers of this book.*

Your *Communicate!* ThomsonNOW is an online study system that helps you identify concepts you don't fully understand, allowing you to put your study time to the best use. Using chapter-by-chapter diagnostic pre-tests, the system creates a personalized study plan for each chapter. Each plan directs you to specific resources designed to improve your understanding, including pages from the text in e-book format. Chapter post-tests give you an opportunity to measure how much you've learned and let you know if you are ready for graded quizzes and exams.

Key Terms

Go to your ThomsonNOW for *Communicate!* to access your online glossary for Chapter 2. Print a copy of the glossary for this chapter and test yourself with the electronic flash cards or complete the crossword puzzle to help you master these key terms:

attributions (45)
discrimination (44)
halo effect (43)
implicit personality theories (42)
incongruence (36)
interpret (32)

pattern (31)
perception (30)
perception check (48)
prejudice (43)
role (34)
self-concept (32)
self-esteem (32)

self-fulfilling prophecies (36)
self-monitoring (35)
self-talk (38)
stereotypes (43)
uncertainty reduction (41)

Review Quiz

Test your knowledge of the concepts in this chapter by taking the online review quiz for Chapter 2. Go to your ThomsonNOW for *Communicate!* to access the quiz. When you have completed the quiz, submit it for scoring.

Skill Learning Activities

Go to your ThomsonNOW for *Communicate!* to complete the Observe & Analyze and Skill Building activities for Chapter 2. You can submit your Observe & Analyze answers to your instructor, and you can compare your Skill Building answers to those provided by the authors.

2.1: Observe & Analyze: Who Am I? (37)
2.2: Observe & Analyze: Monitor Your Enacted Roles (42)
2.3: Observe & Analyze: Stereotypes and Media (46)
2.4: Culture and Perception (46)

Web Resources

Go to your ThomsonNOW for *Communicate!* to access the Web Resources for this chapter.

Activity 2.5

Title: **The Speech of Introduction about You**

Instructions: Listen to the speech of introduction that a classmate gives about you.

Questions and Answers
Answer the following questions in the fields below.

Question 1: Did anything the speaker said embarrass you?

Question 2: How do you feel about what was said?

Question 3: On a scale of 1 to 10, rate how pleased you were to be introduced as you were.

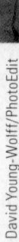

The chalkboard shows:

Swahili = English
mtoto = a child
mwanadamu = a man
mwanamke = a woman
toto mchanga = baby
jamaa = famil

OBJECTIVES

After you have read this chapter, you should be able to answer these questions:

- What is language?
- What is a speech community?
- How does language shape perception?
- What factors influence the meaning of language?
- What is the difference between denotative and connotative meaning?
- How do culture and gender affect language use?
- How can you improve your language usage so that it is more specific?
- How can you make your messages vivid?
- How can you emphasize parts of your message?
- How can you use the skills of dating and indexing generalizations?
- How can you phrase messages so that they are perceived as appropriate for the situation?

3

Communicating Verbally

D onna approached her friend, May, and said, "Ed and I are having a really tough time."

"I'm sorry to hear that," replied Mary. "What's happening?"

"Well, you know, it's just the way he acts."

"Is he being abusive?"

"Uh, no—it's not that. I just can't seem to figure him out."

"Well, is it what he says?"

"No, it's more what he doesn't say."

"What do you mean 'what he doesn't say'?"

"You know, he comes home and I ask him where he's been."

"And . . . ?"

"He says he was working overtime."

"And you don't believe him?"

"No, I believe him. It's just that he's working so much; I'm starting to feel lonely."

"Have you talked with him about this?"

"No, I don't know how to say it, and I don't think he'd understand me."

G iven what Donna has said and the way she has said it, would you understand? Sometimes, for a variety of reasons, the way we form our messages makes it difficult for others to understand. Sometimes the problem is what we say; other times it's how we say it.

As Thomas Holtgraves (2002), a leading scholar in language use reminds us, "Language is one of those things that we often take for granted" (p. 8). Yet we could all improve our use of language. In this chapter, we discuss the nature and use of language and improving our verbal language skills.

The Nature and Use of Language

language
a body of symbols (most commonly words) and the systems for their use in messages that are common to the people of the same speech community.

Language is both a body of symbols (most commonly words) and the systems for their use in messages that are common to the people of the same speech community.

speech community
a group of people who speak the same language (also called a language community).

A **speech community,** also called a language community, is a group of people who speak the same language. There are between 3,000 and 4,000 speech communities in the world, with the number of native speakers in a community ranging from a hundred million or more to communities with only a few remaining native speakers. Around 60 percent of the world's speech communities have fewer than 10,000 speakers. The five largest speech communities in order are Mandarin Chinese, English, Spanish, Arabic, and Hindi (Encyclopedia.com, 2002).

words
symbols used by a speech community to represent objects, ideas, and feelings.

Words are symbols used by a speech community to represent objects, ideas, and feelings. While the exact word used to represent the object or idea is arbitrary, for a word to be a symbol it must be recognized by members of the speech community as standing for a particular object, idea, or feeling. So different speech communities use different word symbols for the same phenomenon. For example, the season for planting is called *spring* in English-speaking communities but *printemps* in French-speaking communities.

Speech communities vary in the words that they use, and they also vary in how words are put together to form messages. The structure a message takes depends on the rules of grammar and syntax that have evolved in a particular speech community. For example, in English a sentence must have at least a subject (a noun or pronoun) and a predicate (a verb). To make a statement in English, the subject is placed before the predicate.

Sapir–Whorf hypothesis
a theory claiming that language influences perception.

Language affects how people think and what they pay attention to. This concept is called the **Sapir–Whorf hypothesis,** named after two theorists, Edward Sapir and Benjamin Lee Whorf (Littlejohn & Foss, 2005). Language allows us to perceive certain aspects of the world by naming them and allows us to ignore other parts of the world by not naming them. For instance, if you work in a job such as fashion or interior design that deals with many different words for color distinctions, you will be able to perceive finer differences in color. Knowing various words for shades of white, such as ecru, eggshell, cream, ivory, pearl, bone china white, or antique white actually helps you see differences in shades of white. Similarly, there are concepts that people and society did not fully perceive until a word was coined to describe that concept. Think of the relatively new words added to American English vocabulary in the last few decades such as *date rape* or *male bashing*. Whatever behaviors to which those words refer certainly existed before the terms were coined. But as a society, we did not collectively perceive these behaviors until language allowed us to name them.

Uses of Language

Although language communities vary in the words that they use and in their grammar and syntax systems, all languages serve the same purposes.

1. **We use language to designate, label, define, and limit.** So, when we identify music as "techno," we are differentiating it from other music labeled rap, punk, pop, goth, or grunge.

2. **We use language to evaluate.** Through language we convey positive or negative attitudes toward our subject. For instance, if you see Hal taking more time than others to make a decision, you could describe Hal positively as "thoughtful" or negatively as "dawdling." Kenneth Burke, a prominent language theorist, describes this as the power of language to emphasize hierarchy and control (1968). Because language allows us to compare things, we tend to judge those things as better or worse, which leads to social hierarchy or a pecking order.

3. **We use language to discuss things outside our immediate experience.** Language enables us to talk about ourselves, discuss things outside our immediate experience, speak hypothetically, talk about past and future events, and communicate about people and things that are not present. Through language, we can discuss where we hope to be in five years, analyze a conversation two acquaintances had last week, or learn about the history that shapes the world we live in. Language enables us to learn from others' experiences, to share a common heritage, and to develop a shared vision for the future.

4. **We can use language to talk about language.** We can use language to discuss how someone phrased a statement and whether different wording would have had a better outcome or a more positive response. Think of the power of language when we can communicate about how we are communicating. For instance, if your friend said she would see you "this afternoon," but she didn't arrive until 5 o'clock, and you ask her where she's been, the two of you are likely to discuss your communication and the different interpretations you each bring to the words "this afternoon."

Language and Meaning

On the surface, the relationship between language and meaning seems perfectly clear: We select the correct words, structure them using the rules of syntax and grammar agreed upon by our speech community, and people will interpret our meanings correctly. In fact, the relationship between language and meaning is not nearly so simple for several reasons.

One reason is that the meaning of words is in people, not in the words themselves. If Juan describes to Julia that the restaurant is expensive, each of them probably has a different meaning of the word expensive in this context. Maybe Julia thinks one meal will cost $40, while, for Juan, expensive might mean a $20 meal. All words, especially abstract ones, have multiple meanings depending on who is using them and who is hearing them. Think of all the variations of meaning that people bring to words such as responsibility, freedom, and love.

denotation
the direct, explicit meaning a speech community formally gives a word.

A second factor complicating language and meaning is the fact that words have two levels of meaning: denotation and connotation. **Denotation** is the direct, explicit meaning a speech community formally gives a word—it is the meaning found in a dictionary. Different dictionaries may define words in slightly different ways. For instance, whereas the *Encarta World English Dictionary* defines "bawdy" as "ribald in a frank, humorous often crude way," the *Cambridge American English Dictionary* defines "bawdy" as "containing humorous remarks about sex." Similar? Yes, but not the same. Second, for many words there are multiple definitions. For instance, the *Random House Dictionary of the English Language* lists 23 definitions for the word "great." **Connotation,** the feelings or evaluations we associate with a word, may be even more important to our understanding of meaning than denotation. C. K. Ogden and I. A. Richards (1923) were among the first scholars to consider the misunderstandings resulting from the failure of communicators to realize that their subjective reactions to words are based on their life experiences. For instance, when Tina says, "We bought an SUV; I think it's the biggest one Chevy makes," Kim might think "Why in the world would anyone want one of those gas guzzlers that take up so much space to park?" and Lexia might say, "Oh, I envy you. I'd love to afford a vehicle that has so much power and sits so high on the road." Word denotation and connotation are important because the only message that counts is the message that is understood, regardless of whether it is the one you intended.

connotation
the feelings or evaluations we associate with a word.

syntactic context
the position of a word in a sentence and the other words around it.

A third complication of language and meaning is that meaning may vary depending on the **syntactic context** (the position of a word in a sentence and the other words around it) in which the word is used. For instance, in the same sentence a person might say, "I love to vacation in the mountains where it's really cool in mornings and when you hike you're likely to see some really cool animals." Most listeners would understand that "mornings are really cool" refers to temperature and "see some really cool animals" refers to animals that are uncommon or special.

A fourth factor affecting language meaning is that the language used by any speech community will change over time. Language changes in many ways, including the creation of new words, the abandonment of old words, changed word meanings developed by segments of society, and the influx of words from the mixing of cultures. For instance, the latest edition of *Merriam-Webster's Collegiate Dictionary* contains ten thousand new words and usages.

New words are created to express new ideas. For example, younger generations, business people, and scientists, among others, will invent new words or assign different meanings to the words they learn to better express the changing realities of their world. For example, *bling bling* is used to describe flashy jewelry and decorations, *e-tailing* is Internet retail selling, and *bioinformatics* is a field of study concerned with the creation and maintenance of databases of biological information. In the past 20 years, entire vocabularies have been invented to allow us to communicate about the explosion of new technologies. So we *google* to get information, use the *wi-fi* on our *laptop,* and *listen* to a *pod cast* while we write our *blog.* Words frequently used by older generations may fade as they no longer describe current realities or are replaced by newer words. *Cellophane* was the word used years ago for what we call plastic wrap today. We once used a *mimeograph* but now we use a *copy machine.* In addition, some members of the speech community will invent new meanings for old words to differentiate themselves from other subgroups of the language community. For instance, in some parts of the country, teenagers use *stupid* to mean *cool,* as in "That's a really stupid shirt" and *played to* mean *tiresome* or *boring,* as in "This party is played; let's go."

As a society absorbs immigrants who speak different languages and becomes more multicultural, the language gradually adopts some words from the native language of the immigrants. So in English we now use and understand what were once foreign words, such as *petite, siesta, mench, kindergarten,* and *ciao,* among thousands of others. Similarly, the slang or jargon used by a subgroup may also eventually be appropriated by the larger speech community. So the African American slang term for athletic shoes, *kicks,* is now used and understood by a more diverse group of American speakers.

Cultural and Gender Influences on Language Usage

Culture and gender both influence how words are used and interpreted. Cultures vary in how much meaning is embedded in the language itself and how much meaning is interpreted from the context in which the communication occurs. In **low-context cultures,** like the United States and most northern European countries, messages are direct and language is very specific. Speakers say exactly what they mean and the verbal messages are very explicit, with lots of details provided. In low-context cultures, what the speaker intends the message to mean is not heavily influenced by the

low-context cultures *cultures in which messages are direct, specific, and detailed.*

high-context cultures
cultures in which messages are indirect, general, and ambiguous.

setting or context; rather, it is embedded in the verbal message. In **high-context cultures,** like Latin American, Asian, and Native American, what a speaker really means you to understand from the verbal message depends heavily on the setting or context in which it is sent. So verbal messages in high-context cultures may be indirect, using more general and ambiguous language. Receivers in high-context cultures, then, rely on contextual cues to help them understand the speaker's meaning (Chen & Starosta, 1998).

When people from low-context cultures interact with others from high-context cultures, problems of understanding often occur. Imagine that Isaac from a German company and Zhao from a Chinese company are trying to conduct business.

ISAAC: "Let's get right down to it. We're hoping that you can provide 100,000 parts per month according to our six manufacturing specifications spelled out in the engineering contract I sent you. If quality control finds more than a 2-percent error, we will have to terminate the contract. Can you agree to these terms?"

ZHAO: "We are very pleased to be doing business with you. We produce the highest quality products and will be honored to meet your needs."

ISAAC: "But can you supply that exact quantity? Can you meet all of our engineering specifications? Will you consistently have less than a 2-percent error?"

ZHAO: "We are an excellent, trustworthy company that will send you the highest quality parts."

Isaac is probably frustrated with what he perceives as general, evasive language used by Zhao, while Zhao may be offended by the direct questions, specific language, and perceived threat in the message. Global migration, business, and travel are increasing the interactions that occur between people accustomed to high- or low-context expectations. As this happens, the likelihood of misunderstanding increases. So to be a competent communicator, you will need to be aware of, compensate for, or adapt to the cultural expectations of your conversational partner.

Societal expectations for masculinity and femininity influence language use. According to Wood (2007), **feminine styles of language** typically use words of empathy and support, emphasize concrete and personal language, and show politeness and tentativeness in speaking. **Masculine styles of language** often use words of status and problem solving, emphasize abstract and general language, and show assertiveness and control in speaking.

Feminine language often includes empathic phrases like, "I can understand how you feel," or "I've had a similar experience, so I can sense what you are going through." Likewise, feminine language often includes language of support such as, "I'm so sorry that you are having difficulty," or "please let me know if I can help you in any way." Feminine language often goes into detail by giving specific examples and personal disclosures.

feminine styles of language
use words of empathy and support, emphasize concrete and personal language, and show politeness and tentativeness in speaking.

masculine styles of language
use words of status and problem solving, emphasize abstract and general language, and show assertiveness and control in speaking.

To appear feminine is to speak politely by focusing on others and by not being too forceful with language. Words and phrases like "I may be wrong but . . . it's just my opinion . . . maybe . . . perhaps . . . I don't want to step on anyone's toes here . . . " are associated with feminine styles of speaking.

By contract, masculine styles of speaking often emphasize status through phrases like "I know that . . . my experience tells me . . . " and communicates problem solving or advice giving through such language as "I would . . . you should . . . the way you should handle this is . . ." Masculine styles of communication may favor theoretical or general discussions and avoid giving personal information about oneself. To appear masculine, one's language must be forceful, direct, and in control through such phrases as "definitely, I have no doubt, it is clear to me, I am sure that . . . "

Women and men can use both masculine and feminine language, though, generally, society expects women to use feminine language and men to use masculine language. One style is not inherently better than another, but each may be better suited to certain communication situations.

Improving Language Skills

Regardless of whether we are conversing with a friend, working on a task force, or giving a speech, we should strive to use language in our messages that accurately conveys our meanings. We can improve our messages by choosing specific language, developing verbal vividness and emphasis, providing details and examples, dating information, and indexing generalizations.

Choose Specific Language

When we speak in specific language, we help listeners assign meaning to our words similar to what we intended. Compare these two descriptions of a near miss in a car: "Some nut almost got me a while ago" versus "An hour ago, an older man in a banged-up Honda Civic ran the light at Calhoun and Clifton and almost hit me broadside while I was in the intersection waiting to turn left at the cross street." In the second example, the message used language that was much more specific, so both parties are likely to have a more similar perception of the situation than would be possible with the first description.

Often as we try to express our thoughts, the first words that come to mind are general in nature. **Specific words** clear up confusion caused by general words by narrowing what is understood from a general category to a particular group within that category. Specific words are more concrete and precise than general words. What can we do to speak more specifically?

We speak more clearly when we select a word that most accurately or correctly captures the sense of what we are saying. At first I might say,

specific words
words that clarify meaning by narrowing what is understood from a general category to a particular item or group within that category.

DIVERSE VOICES

The Language of the Frontier

by Gloría Anzaldúa

The late Gloría Anzaldúa was a writer, poet, activist, and instructor of Chicano studies, women's studies, and creative writing at the University of California at Santa Cruz. The selection below is from her book Borderlands/La Frontera. *In this excerpt, Anzaldúa embraces the use of multiple English and Spanish dialects to express the many cultural and social influences in her life.*

"Pocho, cultural traitor, you're speaking the oppressor's language by speaking English, you're ruining the Spanish language." I have been accused by various Latinos and Latinas. Chicano Spanish is considered by the purist and by most Latinos deficient, a mutilation of Spanish.

But Chicano Spanish is a border tongue which developed naturally. Change, *evolución, enriquecimiento de palabras nuevas por invención or adopción* have created variants of Chicano Spanish, *un Nuevo lenguaje. Un lenguaje que corresponde a un modo de vivir.* Chicano Spanish is not incorrect, it is a living language.

For people who are neither Spanish nor live in a country in which Spanish is the first language; for a people who live in a country in which English is the reigning tongue but who are not Anglo; for a people who cannot entirely identify with either standard (formal, Castilian) Spanish nor standard English, what recourse is left to them but to create their own language? A language which they can connect their identity to, one capable of communicating the realities and values true to themselves—a language with the terms that are neither *español ni ingles,* but both. We speak a patois, a forked tongue, a variation of two languages.

Chicano Spanish sprang out of the Chicanos' need to identify ourselves as a distinct people. We needed a language with which we could communicate with ourselves, a secret language. For some of us, language is a homeland closer than the Southwest—for many Chicanos today live in the Midwest and the East. And because we are a complex, heterogeneous people, we speak many languages. Some of the languages we speak are

1. Standard English
2. Working-class and slang English
3. Standard Spanish
4. Standard Mexican Spanish
5. North Mexican Spanish dialect
6. Chicano Spanish (Texas, New Mexico, Arizona, and California have regional variations)
7. Tex-Mex
8. *Pachuco* (called *caló*)

My "home" tongues are the languages I speak with my sister and brothers, with my friends. They are the last five listed, with 6 and 7 being the closest to my heart. From school, the media, and job situations, I've picked up standard and working class English. From Mamagrande Locha and from reading Spanish and Mexican literature, I've picked up Standard Spanish and Standard Mexican Spanish. From *los recién llegados,* Mexican immigrants, and *braceros,* I have learned the North Mexican dialect. From my parents and Chicanos living in the Valley, I picked up Chicano Texas Spanish, and I speak it with my mom, younger brother (who married a Mexican and who rarely mixes Spanish with English), aunts, and older relatives.

With Chicanas from *Nuevo México* or Arizona I will speak Chicano Spanish a little, but often they don't understand what I'm saying. With most California Chicanas I speak entirely in English (unless I forget). When I first moved to San Francisco, I'd rattle off something in Spanish, unintentionally embarrassing them. Often it is only with another Chicana *tejano* that I can talk freely.

Words distorted by English are known as anglicisms or *pochismos.* The *pocho* is an anglicized Mexican or American of Mexican origin who speaks Spanish with an accent characteristic of North Americans and who distorts and reconstructs the language according to the influence of English. Tex-Mex, or Spanglish, comes most naturally to me. I may switch back and forth from English to Spanish in the same sentence or in the same word. With my sister and my brother Nune and with Chicano tejano contemporaries I speak in Tex-Mex.

From kids and people my own age I picked up *Pachuco. Pachuco* (the language of the zoot suiters) is a language of rebellion, both against Standard Spanish and Standard English. It is a secret language. Adults of the culture and outsiders cannot understand it. It is made up of slang words from both English and Spanish. *Ruca* means girl or woman, *vato* means guy or dude, *chale* means no, *simón* means yes, *churro* is sure, talk is *periquiar, pigionear* means petting, *que gacho* means how nerdy, *ponte águila* means watch out, death is called *la pelona.* Through lack of practice and not having others who can speak it, I've lost most of the *Pachuco* tongue.

Excerpted from Gloría Anzaldúa, Borderlands/La Frontera: The New Mestiza. *(San Francisco, CA: Aunt Lute Books, 1987, 1999). Reprinted by permission of Aunt Lute Books.*

"Waylon was angry at the meeting today." Then I might think, "Was he really showing anger?" So I say, "To be more accurate, he wasn't really angry. Perhaps he was more frustrated or impatient with what he sees as lack of progress by our group." What is the difference between the two statements in terms of words? By carefully choosing words, you can show shades of meaning. Others may respond quite differently to your description of a group member showing anger, frustration, or impatience. The interpretation others get of Waylon's behavior is very much dependent on the word or words you select. Specific language is achieved when words are concrete or precise or when details or examples are used.

Concrete words are words that appeal to our senses. Consider the word *speak.* This is an abstract word—that is, we can speak in many different ways. So instead of saying that Jill *speaks in a peculiar way,* we might be more specific by saying that Jill *mumbles, whispers, blusters,* or *drones.* Each of these words creates a clearer sense of the sound of her voice.

concrete words
words that appeal to the senses and help us see, hear, smell, taste, or touch.

We speak more specifically when we use **precise words,** narrowing a larger category to a smaller group within that category. For instance, if Nevah says that Ruben is a "blue-collar worker," she has named a general category; you might picture an unlimited number of occupations that fall within this broad category. If, instead, she is more precise and says he's a "construction worker," the number of possible images you can picture is reduced; now you can only select your image from the specific subcategory of construction worker. So your meaning is likely to be closer to the one she intended. To be even more precise, she may identify Ruben as "a bulldozer operator"; this further limits your choice of images and is likely to align with the one she intended you to have.

precise words
words that narrow a larger category.

Choosing specific language is easier when we have a large working vocabulary. One way to increase your vocabulary is to study vocabulary-

Frank and Ernest

COMMUNICATION WORKSHOP
———
SOMETIME TONIGHT IN A ROOM UPSTAIRS

Frank & Ernest reprinted by permission of Tom Thaves

building books, which are available in most libraries and bookstores. A second way is to use a dictionary to look up the meanings of words that you read or hear that you do not understand and add them to a vocabulary list that you keep and study. A third way to increase your vocabulary is to use a thesaurus (a list of words and their synonyms) to identify related words that are more concrete and precise than the ones you use most frequently. An easy way to consult a thesaurus is to access Merriam-Webster's online Collegiate Thesaurus—go to your ThomsonNOW for *Communicate!* to access **Web Resource 3.1: Merriam-Webster Online**.

Develop Verbal Vividness and Emphasis

Because your listeners cannot simply re-read what you have said, effective verbal messages use vivid wording and appropriate emphasis to help listeners understand and remember the message.

Vivid wording is full of life, vigorous, bright, and intense. For example, a novice baseball announcer might say, "Jackson made a great catch," but a more experienced commentator's vivid account would be, "Jackson leaped and made a spectacular one-handed catch just as he crashed into the center field wall." The words *spectacular, leaped, one-handed catch,* and *crashed* paint an intense verbal picture of the action. Vivid messages begin with vivid thoughts. You are much more likely to *express* yourself vividly when you have physically or psychologically *sensed* the meanings you are trying to convey.

Vividness can be achieved quickly through using similes and metaphors. A **simile** is a direct comparison of dissimilar things and is usually expressed with the words *like* or *as.* Clichés such as "She walks like a duck." And "She sings like a nightingale" are both similes. A **metaphor** is a comparison that establishes a figurative identity between objects being compared. Instead of saying that one thing is like another, a metaphor says that one thing *is* another. Thus, problem cars are "lemons" and a team's porous infield is a "sieve." As you think about and try to develop similes and metaphors, stay away from trite clichés. Although we use similes and metaphors frequently in conversations, they are an especially powerful

vivid wording
wording that is full of life, vigorous, bright, and intense.

simile
a direct comparison of dissimilar things.

metaphor
a comparison that establishes a figurative identity between objects being compared.

Communication Skill Using Specific Language

Skill	Use	Procedure	Example
Clarify meaning by narrowing what is understood from a general category to a particular group within that category, by appealing to the senses, by choosing words that symbolize exact thoughts and feelings, or by using concrete details or examples.	To help the listener picture thoughts analogous to the speaker's.	1. Assess whether the word or phrase to be used is less specific (or concrete or precise) than it can be. 2. Pause to consider alternatives. 3. Select a more specific (or concrete or precise) word, or give an example or add details.	Instead of saying, "Bring the stuff for the audit," say, "Bring the records and receipts from the last year for the audit." Or, instead of saying, "Make sure you improve your grades," say, "This term, we want to see a B in Spanish and at least a C in Algebra."

Skill Building Clarifying General Statements

Rewrite each of these statements to make it more specific by making general and abstract words more concrete and precise. Add details and examples.

1. My neighbor has a lot of animals that she keeps in her yard.
2. When I was a little girl, we lived in a big house in the Midwest.
3. My husband works for a large newspaper.
4. She got up late and had to rush to get to school. But she was late anyway.
5. Where'd you find that thing?
6. I really liked going to that concert. The music was great.
7. I really respect her.
8. My boyfriend looks like a hippie.
9. She was wearing a very trendy outfit.
10. We need to have more freedom to choose our courses.

Thomson NOW! You can complete this activity online and compare your answers to the authors'. Go to your Thomson-NOW for *Communicate!* to access **Skill Learning Activity 3.2**.

way to develop vividness when we are giving a speech. Try developing and practicing one or two different original metaphors or similes when you rehearse a speech to see which works best. To complete an activity that will help you identify vivid similes and metaphors that you hear in everyday conversation, go to your ThomsonNOW for *Communicate!* to access **Skill Learning Activity 3.3: Similes and Metaphors**.

Finally, while your goal is to be vivid, make sure that you use words that are understood by all your listeners. Novice speakers can mistakenly believe they will be more impressive if they use a large vocabulary, but using "big" words can be off-putting to the audience and make the speaker seem pompous, affected, or stilted. When you have a choice between a common vivid word or image and one that is more obscure, choose the more common.

emphasis
*the weight or importance
given to certain words or
ideas.*

Emphasis is the weight or importance given to certain words or ideas. Emphasis tells the audience what it should seriously pay attention to. Ideas are emphasized through proportion, repetition, and use of transitions. You emphasize an idea by the proportion of time you spend discussing it. Ideas to which you devote more time are perceived by listeners to be more important, whereas ideas that are quickly mentioned are perceived to be less important. Emphasizing by repeating means saying important words or ideas more than once. You can either repeat the exact words, "A ring-shaped coral island almost or completely surrounding a lagoon is called an atoll—an atoll," or you can restate the idea in different language, "The test will comprise about four essay questions; that is, all the questions on the test will be the kind that require you to discuss material in some detail." Emphasizing through transitions means using words that show the relationship between your ideas. Some transitions summarize, some clarify, and others forecast. Simple word transitions add material *(also, and, likewise, again, in addition, moreover, similarly, further);* add up, show consequences, summarize, or show results *(therefore, and so, so, finally, all in all, on the whole, in short, thus, as a result);* indicate changes in direction or provide contrasts *(but, however, on the other hand, still, although, while, no doubt);* indicate reasons *(because, for);* show causal or time relationship *(then, since, as);* or explain, exemplify, or limit—in other words *(in fact, for example, that is to say, more specifically).*

Provide Details and Examples

Sometimes clarity can be achieved by adding detail or examples. For instance, Linda says, "Rashad is very loyal." The meaning of "loyal" (faithful to an idea, person, company, and so on) is abstract, so to avoid ambiguity and confusion, Linda might add, "He defended Gerry when Sara was gossiping about her." By following up her use of the abstract concept of loyalty with a concrete example, Linda makes it easier for her listeners to "ground" their idea of this personal quality in a concrete or "real" experience. Likewise by providing details, we clarify our messages. Saying, "He lives in a really big house," can be clarified by adding details: "He lives in a 14-room Tudor mansion on a 6-acre estate."

Date Information

dating information
*specifying the time or time
period that a fact was true or
known to be true.*

Dating information means to specify the time or time period that a fact was true or known to be true. Because nearly everything changes with time, not dating our statements can lead someone to conclude that what we are saying is current, when it is not. For instance, Parker says, "I'm going to be transferred to Henderson City." Laura replies, "Good luck—they've had some real trouble with their schools." On the basis of Laura's statement, Parker may worry about the effect his move will have on his children. What he doesn't know is that Laura's information about this problem in Hender-

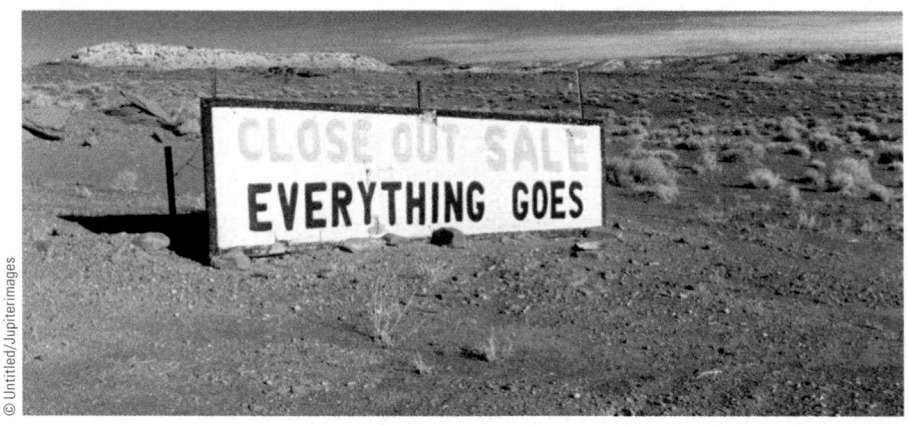

© Untitled/Jupiterimages

Have you ever been inconvenienced by information that was out of date? As you form messages, the skill of dating can help you be more accurate with the information you share.

son City is over five years old! Henderson City still may have problems, but again, the situation may have changed. Had Laura replied, "Five years ago, I know they had some real trouble with their schools. I'm not sure what the situation is now, but you may want to check," Parker would look at the information differently.

Here are two additional examples:

Undated: Professor Powell is really enthusiastic when she lectures.

Dated: Professor Powell is really enthusiastic when she lectures— at least she was *last quarter* in communication theory.

Undated: You think Mary's depressed? I'm surprised. She seemed her regular, high-spirited self when I talked with her.

Dated: You think Mary's depressed? I'm surprised. She seemed her regular, high-spirited self when I talked with her *last month.*

To date information, before you make a statement, (1) consider or find out when the information was true and (2) verbally acknowledge the date or time period when the information was true. When we date our statements, we increase the effectiveness of our messages and enhance our own credibility.

Index Generalizations

Indexing generalizations is the mental and verbal practice of acknowledging the presence of individual differences when voicing generalizations. While we might generally think that people who buy a Mercedes are rich, that may not be true for all Mercedes buyers. Thus, just because we learn that Brent has bought a top-of-the-line, very expensive Mercedes, it does not mean that Brent is rich. So, if we were to say, "Brent bought a Mercedes; he must be rich," we should add, "of course not all people who buy Mercedes are rich."

indexing generalizations the mental and verbal practice of acknowledging the presence of individual differences when voicing generalizations.

Let's consider another example:

Generalization: Your Toyota should go 50,000 miles before you need a brake job; Jerry's did.

Indexed Statement: Your Toyota may well go 50,000 miles before you need a brake job; Jerry's did, *but of course, all Toyotas aren't the same.*

To index, consider whether what you are about to say applies a generalization to a specific person, place, or thing. If so, qualify it appropriately so that your assertion does not go beyond the evidence that supports it. To practice adjusting messages so that they are dated or indexed, go to your ThomsonNOW for *Communicate!* to access **Skill Learning Activity 3.4: Dating and Indexing Messages.**

Speaking Appropriately

speaking appropriately
choosing language and symbols that are adapted to the needs, interests, knowledge, and attitudes of the listeners and avoiding language that alienates them.

Speaking appropriately means choosing language and symbols that are adapted to the needs, interests, knowledge, and attitudes of the listeners and avoiding language that alienates them. Through appropriate language, we communicate our respect and acceptance of those who are different from us. There are times when we use words that our listeners do not understand or that offend others. Some words are so familiar to us that we forget that others are unaware of their meaning. It is also important that we consider the effect that our words may have on others. When we speak appropriately, we: (1) use vocabulary the listener understands; (2) use jargon sparingly; (3) use slang appropriate to the situation; (4) use inclusive language; and (5) use nonoffensive language.

Use Vocabulary the Listener Understands

People vary in the extent to which they know and use a large variety of words. If you have made a conscious effort to expand your vocabulary, are an avid reader, or have spent time conversing with others who use a large and varied selection of words, then you probably have a large vocabulary. As a speaker, the larger your vocabulary, the more choices you have from which to select the words you want. Having a larger vocabulary, however, can present challenges when communicating with people whose vocabulary is more limited. As a speaker, you must try to adapt your vocabulary to the level of your listener so that your words will be understood. One strategy for assessing another's vocabulary level is to listen to the types and complexity of words the other person uses and to take your signal from your communication partner. When you have determined that your vocabulary exceeds that of your partner, you can use simpler synonyms for your words or use word phrases composed of more familiar terms. Adjusting your vocabulary to others does not mean talking down to them. It is merely polite behavior and effective communication to try to select words that others understand.

Use Jargon Sparingly

Jargon refers to technical terms whose meanings are understood only by a select group of people based on their shared activity or interests. We may form a special speech community, which develops a common language (jargon) based on a hobby or occupation. Medical practitioners speak a language of their own, which people in the medical field understand and those outside of the medical field do not. The same is true of lawyers, engineers, educators, and virtually all occupations. If you are an avid computer user, you may know many terms that non-computer users do not. Likewise, there is a lingo associated with sports, theatre, wine tasting, and science fiction, to name just a few interest groups. The key to effective use of jargon is to employ it only with other people who speak the same jargon. When people understand the same jargon, then its use facilitates communication. If you must use jargon with people who are not members of the occupation or special interest group, remember to explain the terms you are using. Without explanation to outsiders, jargon becomes a type of foreign language.

jargon
technical terms understood only by select groups.

Use Slang Appropriate to the Situation

Slang refers to informal vocabulary developed and used by particular groups in society. It is casual and sometimes playful language that is deliberately used in place of standard terms. Slang is a type of alternative vocabulary that performs an important social function. Slang bonds those in an inner circle who use the same words to emphasize a shared experience. But slang simultaneously excludes others who don't share the terminology. The simultaneous inclusion of some and exclusion of others is what makes slang popular with youth and marginalized people in all cultures. Slang may emerge from teenagers, urban life, college life, gangs, or other contexts. A teenager might say, "My bad" for "I made a mistake." That's "tight" could be translated, as "That's great, fine, or excellent." You can even find slang dictionaries online. Go to your ThomsonNOW for *Communicate!* to access **Web Resource 3.2: Slang Dictionary**. This link will direct you to a slang dictionary maintained by California State University at Pomona. Using slang appropriately means using it in situations where people understand the slang but avoiding it with people who do not share the slang terminology.

slang
informal vocabulary used by particular groups in society.

Thomson
NOW!

There is a new type of slang developing with digital and Internet technology. Experts in computer-mediated communication (Thurlow, Lengel, & Tomic, 2004) explain the unique features of this language, which goes by various names including Weblish, netlingo, e-talk, techspeak, wired style, or netspeak. Because of the need for speed in instant messaging, for example, many of the rules of grammar, style, and spelling are broken. Many people adopt a phonetic type of spelling, which increasingly is understandable to this speech community, but may not be understandable to others. Consider the language used in cyberspace versus traditional wording for the following question: wen wud u b hm (When would you be home?). New abbreviations have emerged such as jk (just kidding), bbl (be back later), and lol (laugh out loud). Some communication experts who emphasize traditional styles of communication regard this new language of cyberspace as incorrect, deficient, or inferior. While it is natural that people in cyberspace would develop their own alternative, using these terms in other settings is problematic.

Demonstrate Linguistic Sensitivity

You demonstrate linguistic sensitivity when you choose language that respects others and avoid usages that others perceive as offensive because they are sexist, racist, or otherwise biased. Generic and nonparallel languages are common types of insensitive language that can be easily corrected.

generic language
using words that may apply only to one sex, race, or other group as though they represent everyone.

Generic language **Generic language** uses words that may apply only to one sex, race, or other group as though they represent everyone. This usage is a problem because it linguistically excludes a portion of the population it ostensibly includes. The following paragraphs contain some examples of generic language.

Traditionally, English grammar called for the use of the masculine pronoun, *he,* to stand for the entire class of humans regardless of gender. Using this rule, we would say, "When a person shops, he should have a clear idea of what he wants to buy." Despite traditional usage, it is hard to picture people of both sexes when we hear the masculine pronoun "he."

You can avoid generic language in one of two ways. First, use plurals. For instance, instead of saying, "Because a doctor has high status, his views may be believed regardless of the topic," you could say, "Because doctors have high status, their views may be believed regardless of the topic." Secondly, you can use both male and female pronouns: "Because a doctor has high status, his or her views may be believed regardless of the topic." Stewart, Cooper, Stewart, and Friedley (1998, p. 63) cite research to show that when speakers refer to people using "he and she," and to a lesser extent "they," listeners often visualize *both* women and men. Thus, when speakers avoid generic language, it's more likely that listeners will perceive a message that is more gender balanced.

Another problem results from the traditional use of the generic word *man* when referring to all humans. Many of the words that have become a common part of our language are inherently sexist in that they refer to only one gender. Consider the term *man-made*. What this really means is that a product was produced by human beings, but its underlying connotation is that a male human being made the item. Research has demonstrated that people usually visualize men (not women) when they read or hear these words. Moreover, when job titles end in "man," their occupants are assumed to have stereotypically masculine personality traits (Gmelch, 1998, p. 51).

For most sex-biased expressions, you can use or create suitable alternatives. For instance, use police officer instead of policeman and substitute synthetic for man-made. Instead of saying mankind, change the construction—for example, from "All of mankind benefits" to "All the people in the world benefit."

Nonparallel language **Nonparallel language** is language in which terms are changed because of the sex, race, or other characteristic of the individual. Because it treats groups of people differently, nonparallel language is also belittling. Two types of nonparallel language are marking and unnecessary association.

nonparallel language
terms are changed because of the sex, race, or other characteristic of the individual.

Marking is the addition of sex, race, age, or other designations to a description. For instance, a doctor is a person with a medical degree who is licensed to practice medicine. Notice the difference between the following two sentences:

marking
the addition of sex, race, age, or other designations to a description.

Jones is a good doctor.

Jones is a good black doctor.

In the second sentence, use of the marker "black" is offensive; it has nothing to do with doctoring. Marking is inappropriate because you trivialize the person's role by introducing an irrelevant characteristic. The speaker may be intending to praise Jones, but listeners may interpret the sentence as saying that Jones is a good doctor "for a black person" (or woman, or old person, and so on) but not that Jones is as good as a white doctor (or a male, or young person, and so forth).

A second form of nonparallel language is emphasizing one person's relationship to another when that relationship is irrelevant. Introducing a speaker as "Gladys Thompson, whose husband is CEO of Acme Inc., is the chairperson for this year's United Way campaign," for example, is inappropriate. Using her husband's status implies that Gladys Thompson is chairperson because of her husband's accomplishments, not her own.

By monitoring yourself, you can become more inclusive in your language choices. How can you speak more appropriately? (1) Use vocabulary the listener understands, (2) use jargon sparingly, (3) use slang situationally, (4) and demonstrate linguistic sensitivity by avoiding generic and nonparallel language.

What Would You Do?

One day Heather, Terry, Paul, and Martha stopped at the Student Union Grill before their next class. After they had talked about their class for a few minutes, the conversation shifted to students who were taking the class.

"By the way," Paul said, "do any of you know Fatso?"

"Who?" the group responded in unison.

"The really fat guy who was sitting a couple of seats from me. We've been in a couple of classes together—he's a pretty nice guy."

"What's his name?" Heather asked.

"Carl—but he'll always be Fatso to me."

"Do you call him that to his face?" Terry asked.

"Aw, I'd never say anything like that to him—I wouldn't want to hurt his feelings."

"Well," Martha chimed in, "I'd sure hate to think that you'd call me 'skinny' or 'the bitch,' when I wasn't around."

"Come on—what's with you guys?" Paul retorted. "You trying to tell me that you never talk about another person that way when they aren't around?"

"Well," said Terry, "maybe a couple of times—but I've never talked like that about someone I really like."

"Someone you like?" queried Heather. "Why does that make a difference? Do you mean it's OK to trash-talk someone so long as you don't like the person?"

1. Sort out the ethical issues in this case. How ethical is it to call a person you supposedly like by an unflattering name that you would never use if that person were in your presence?

2. From an ethical standpoint, is whether you like a person or not what determines when such name-calling is OK?

Summary

Language is a body of symbols and the systems for their use in messages that are common to the people of the same language community. Language allows us to perceive the world around us. Through language we designate, label, and define; we evaluate; discuss things outside our immediate experience; and talk about language.

The relationship between language and meaning is complex because the meaning of words varies with people, people interpret words differently based on both denotative and connotative meanings, the context in which words are used affects meaning, and word meanings change over time.

Culture and gender influence how words are used and how we interpret others' words. In low-context cultures, messages are direct and language is specific. In high-context cultures, messages are indirect, general, and ambiguous. Societal expectations of masculinity and femininity influence language.

We can increase language skills by using specific, concrete, and precise language; by developing verbal vividness and emphasis; and by providing details and examples, dating information, and indexing generalizations. We can speak more appropriately by choosing vocabulary the listener understands, using jargon sparingly, using slang situationally, and demonstrating linguistic sensitivity.

Thomson NOW!
Communicate! Online

Now that you have read Chapter 3, use your ThomsonNOW for *Communicate!* for quick access to the electronic resources that accompany this text. Your ThomsonNOW gives you access to the Web Resources and Skill Learning Activities featured in this chapter, InfoTrac College Edition, and online study aids such as a digital glossary and review quizzes.

Your *Communicate!* ThomsonNOW is an online study system that helps you identify concepts you don't fully understand, allowing you to put your study time to the best use. Using chapter-by-chapter diagnostic pre-tests, the system creates a personalized study plan for each chapter. Each plan directs you to specific resources designed to improve your understanding, including pages from the text in e-book format. Chapter post-tests give you an opportunity to measure how much you've learned and let you know if you are ready for graded quizzes and exams.

Key Terms

Go to your ThomsonNOW for *Communicate!* to access your online glossary for Chapter 3. Print a copy of the glossary for this chapter and test yourself with the electronic flash cards or complete the crossword puzzle to help you master these key terms:

concrete words (63)
connotation (58)
dating information (66)
denotation (58)
emphasis (66)
feminine styles of language
  (60)
generic language (70)
high-context cultures (60)
indexing generalizations (67)

jargon (69)
language (56)
low-context cultures (59)
marking (71)
masculine styles of language
  (60)
metaphor (64)
nonparallel language (71)
precise words (63)
Sapir–Whorf hypothesis (56)

simile (64)
slang (69)
speaking appropriately (68)
specific words (61)
speech community (56)
syntactic context (58)
vivid wording (64)
words (56)

Review Quiz

Test your knowledge of the concepts in this chapter by taking the online review quiz for Chapter 3. Go to your ThomsonNOW for *Communicate!* to access the quiz. When you have completed the quiz, submit it for scoring.

Skill Learning Activities

Go to your ThomsonNOW for *Communicate!* to complete the Observe & Analyze, Skill Building, and Test Your Competence activities for Chapter 3. You can submit your Observe & Analyze answers to your instructor, and you can compare your Skill Building and Test Your Competence answers to those provided by the authors.

3.1: Observe & Analyze: Identifying Specific Language (61)

3.2: Skill Building: Clarifying General Statements (65)

3.3: Similes and Metaphors (65)

3.4: Test Your Competence: Dating and Indexing Messages (68)

Web Resources

Go to your ThomsonNOW for *Communicate!* to access the Web Resources for this chapter.

3.1: Merriam-Webster Online (64)

3.2: Slang Dictionary (69)

Activity 3.2
Test Your Competence: Dating and Indexing Messages

1. After writing your first draft, check to make sure that your revision is more concrete, precise, and provides examples and details.
2. Edit your response as needed.
3. Now read your response aloud. Does it sound "natural"? If not, revise it until it does.
4. Submit your response and compare it to the response supplied by the authors. Your answer need not be exactly the same as the authors' to be correct.

If you'd like to review the skill of dating and indexing before you begin, click on Skill Builders under the Book Resources menu at the Verderber & Verderber Communicate! home page, then click on the link "Dating or Indexing".

Chapter 3 Case Questions

1. Oh, Jamie's an accounting major, so I'm sure she keeps her checkbook balanced.

2. Forget taking statistics; it's an impossible course.

3. Never trying talking to Jim in the morning; he's always grouchy.

OBJECTIVES

After you have read this chapter, you should be able to answer these questions:

- What are the characteristics of nonverbal communication?
- What do body motions communicate?
- How does our voice communicate?
- What does our use of space communicate?
- What do our self-presentation cues communicate?
- What are the most significant cultural and gender differences in nonverbal communication?
- What guidelines can help you to interpret the nonverbal messages you receive and to send nonverbal messages?

4

Communicating through Nonverbal Behaviors

"You don't want me to buy that denim jacket we looked at this morning, do you?" Clay asked.

"What do you mean 'I don't want you to'?" Maya replied.

"You've got that look on your face."

"What look?"

"You know the look—the one you always get on your face when you don't want me to do something I want to do. But I'm going to get that jacket anyway."

"I don't know what you're talking about, Clay."

"Sure you do. You know how I can tell? Because now you're embarrassed that I know and so you're acting weird."

"I'm not acting weird."

"Oh yes you are."

"Clay, you're making me angry."

"You're just saying that because I know you too well and it bothers you."

"Know me too well? I really don't care whether you get that jacket or not."

"Of course you do. You don't have to tell me in words."

"Clay, it's your decision. If you want to get the jacket, get it."

"Well, I don't think I want to—but don't think you changed my mind."

We've all heard—and said—"actions speak louder than words." Actions are so important to our communication that researchers have estimated that in face-to-face communication as much as 60 percent of the social meaning is a result of nonverbal behavior (Burgoon & Bacue, 2003, p. 179). In other words, the meaning we assign to any communication is based on both the content of the verbal message and our interpretation of the nonverbal behavior that accompanies and surrounds the verbal message. And, as Clay found out, interpreting these nonverbal actions is not always the easiest thing to do.

We begin this chapter by briefly identifying the characteristics of nonverbal communication. Next, we describe the sources of nonverbal information that we use when we interpret and assign meaning to the behavior of others: body language (kinesics), nonsymbolic vocal sounds (paralanguage), our use of space (proxemics), and self-presentation cues. Then we explore how the meaning of nonverbal communication may vary based on culture, sex, and gender. Finally, we offer suggestions to help you improve your accuracy at interpreting nonverbal messages and for increasing the likelihood that others are able to accurately interpret your behavior.

In the broadest sense, the term *nonverbal communication* is commonly used to describe all human communication events that transcend spoken or written words (Knapp & Hall, 2006). Specifically, **nonverbal communication behaviors** are those bodily actions and vocal qualities that typically accompany a verbal message. The behaviors are usually interpreted as intentional and have agreed-upon interpretations in a particular culture or speech community (Burgoon & Hoobler, 2002, p. 244).

nonverbal communication behaviors
bodily actions and vocal qualities that typically accompany a verbal message.

Characteristics of Nonverbal Communication

Nonverbal communication is distinct from verbal communication in that it is continuous and multichanneled. It may be unintentional and ambiguous. The nonverbal part of the message is the primary conveyer of emotion.

First, nonverbal communication is *continuous*. Although you can choose to form and send a verbal message, you do not control whether your nonverbal behavior is interpreted as a communication message. As long as you are in the presence of someone else, that person may perceive your behavior as communication. When Austin yawns and stares off into the distance during a meeting at work, his coworkers will notice this behavior and assign meaning to it. One coworker may interpret it as a sign of boredom, another might see it as a sign of fatigue, and yet another may view it as a message of disrespect. Meanwhile, Austin is oblivious to all of the messages that his behavior is sending.

Second, nonverbal communication is *multichanneled*. We perceive meaning from a variety of nonverbal behaviors including posture, gestures, body movements, body appearance, non-language vocal mannerisms, and so on. When we interpret nonverbal behavior, we usually base our perception on a combination of these behaviors. So, Anna observes Mimi's failure to sustain eye contact, her bowed head, and her repetitive toe stubbing in the dirt, as cues that mean her daughter is lying about not hitting her brother.

Third, nonverbal communication can be *intentional* or *unintentional*. Although we can carefully control the verbal messages we send, because nonverbal behavior is continuous, we often display behaviors that we are not controlling. For example, President George W. Bush's noted "smirk," a nonverbal facial mannerism, may be an intentional message conveying contempt for another's opinion, or it may be an unintentional nervous reaction to speaking in public. Whether the smirk is intentional or unintentional, however, when we see it, we interpret and assign it meaning. Because nonverbal behavior is not easily controlled, it is perceived to be more accurate than verbal communication. So when your nonverbal behavior contradicts your verbal message, people are more likely to believe the nonverbal communication they perceive.

Fourth, the meaning of a particular nonverbal communication can be *ambiguous.* Any particular behavior can have many meanings. So regardless of what President Bush intends, the smirk is an ambiguous message and may be interpreted differently by different audience members.

Finally, nonverbal communication is the *primary conveyor of our emotions.* When we listen to others, we base our interpretation of their feelings and emotions almost totally on their nonverbal behavior. In fact, about 93 percent of the emotional meaning of messages is conveyed nonverbally. (Mehrabian, 1972). So, when Janelle says, "I'm really fine, but thanks for asking," her sister Renee will understand the real message based on the nonverbal behaviors that accompany it. For example, if Janelle uses a sarcastic tone, Renee will understand that Janelle is angry about something. If Janelle sighs, averts her eyes, tears up, and almost whispers her message, Renee will understand that Janelle is really sad and emotionally upset.

Sources of Nonverbal Communication

There are a variety of sources or channels for the nonverbal messages that we interpret from others and display ourselves. These include the use of the body (kinesics), the use of the voice (vocalics/paralanguage), the use of space (proxemics) and self-presentation.

Use of Body: Kinesics

Of all the research on nonverbal behavior, you are probably most familiar with **kinesics,** the technical name for the interpretation of body motions as communications (Wikipedia, 2006). Body motions are the movement of your body or body parts that others interpret and assign meaning. These include your gestures, eye contact, facial expression, posture, and your use of touch.

kinesics
the interpretation of body motions used in communication.

Gestures **Gestures** are the movements of your hands, arms, and fingers that you use to describe or to emphasize. People vary, however, in the amount of gesturing that accompanies their spoken messages; for example, some people "talk with their hands" far more than others. Some gestures, called **illustrators,** augment the verbal message. So when you say "about this high" or "nearly this round," we expect to see a gesture accompany your verbal description. One type of gesture, called **emblems,** can stand alone and substitute completely for words. When you raise your finger and place it vertically across your lips, it signifies "Quiet". Emblems have automatic agreed-upon meanings in a particular culture, but the specific meaning assigned to a specific gesture can vary greatly across cultures. For example, the American hand sign for "OK" has an obscene sexual meaning in some European countries. Gestures called **adaptors** occur unconsciously as a response to a physical need. For example, you may scratch an itch, adjust your glasses, or rub your hands together when they are cold. You do not mean to communicate a message with these gestures, but others do notice them and attach meaning to them.

gestures
movements of our hands, arms, and fingers that we use to describe or to emphasize.

illustrators
gestures that augment a verbal message.

emblems
gestures can substitute for words.

adaptors
gestures that respond to a physical need.

Eye contact **Eye contact,** also referred to as **gaze,** is how and how much we look at others when we are communicating. Although the amount of eye contact differs from person to person and from situation to situation, studies show that talkers hold eye contact about 40 percent of the time and listeners nearly 70 percent of the time (Knapp & Hall, 2006).

eye contact or gaze
how and how much we look at people with whom we are communicating.

Through our eye contact, we both express our emotions and we monitor what is occurring in the interaction. How we look at a person can convey a range of emotions such as anger, fear, or affection. Shakespeare acknowledged how powerfully we express emotions through eye contact when he said, "The eyes are the windows of the soul." With eye contact, you can tell when or whether a person or audience is paying attention to you, whether a person or audience is involved in what you are saying, and the reaction a person or audience is having to your comments.

Although the use and meaning of eye contact varies from one cultural group to another, in the United States, effective public speakers not only use direct eye contact with audience members to monitor how their speech is being received, but also to establish rapport and demonstrate their sincerity. Speakers who fail to maintain eye contact with audience members are perceived as ill at ease and often as insincere or dishonest (Burgoon, Coker, & Coker, 1986).

Facial expression **Facial expression** is the arrangement of facial muscles to communicate emotional states or reactions to messages. Our facial expressions are especially important in conveying the six basic human emotions of happiness, sadness, surprise, fear, anger, and disgust. It appears that the particular facial expression for each of these emotions is universal and does not vary by culture. But we can consciously choose to mask the feeling expressed by our face or to feign feelings that we do not have (Ekman, 1999).

Facial expressions are so important to communicating the emotional part of a message that people have invented **emoticons,** a system of typed symbols to convey facial expressions online. For example, :-) conveys a smile, while : -(conveys a frown (Walther & Parks, 2002).

facial expression
the arrangement of facial muscles to communicate emotional states or reactions to messages.

emoticons
typed symbols that convey emotional aspects of an on-line message.

posture
the position and movement of the body.

body orientation
posture in relation to another person.

haptics
the interpretation of touch.

Our facial expressions are especially important in conveying emotions. What is the message on this face?

Posture **Posture** is the position and movement of your body. From your posture, others interpret how attentive, respectful, and dominant you are. **Body orientation** refers to your posture in relation to another person. If you face another person squarely, this is called direct body orientation. When two people's postures are at angles to each other, this is called indirect body orientation. In many situations, direct body orientation signals attentiveness and respect, while indirect body orientation shows non-attentiveness and disrespect. Think of how you would sit in a job interview. You are likely to sit up straight and face the interviewer directly because you want to communicate your interest and respect. Interviewers tend to interpret a slouched posture and indirect body orientation as inattentiveness and disrespect. Yet, in other situations, such as talking with friends, a slouched posture and indirect body orientation may be appropriate and may not carry messages about attention or respect. When you are making a speech, an upright stance and squared shoulders will help your audience perceive you as poised and self-confident. So when you are giving a speech, be sure to distribute your weight equally on both feet so that you maintain a confident bearing.

Haptics **Haptics** is the interpretation of touch. Touching behavior is a fundamental aspect of nonverbal communication. We use our hands, our arms, and other body parts to pat, hug, slap, kiss, pinch, stroke, hold, embrace, and tickle others. Through touch we communicate a variety of emo-

OBSERVE & ANALYZE
Journal Activity
Body Motions

Find a public setting (for example, a restaurant) where you can observe two people having a conversation. They should be close enough to you so that you can observe their eye contact, facial expression, and gestures, but not close enough that you can hear what they are saying.

Carefully observe the interaction, with the goal of answering the following questions: What is their relationship? What seemed to be the nature of the conversation (social chitchat, plan making, problem solving, argument, intimate discussion)? How did each person feel about the conversation? Did feelings change over the course of the conversation? Was one person more dominant? Take note of the specific nonverbal behaviors that led you to each conclusion, and write a paragraph describing this experience and what you have learned.

You can use your Student Workbook to complete this activity, *(continued on page 82)* (*continued from page 81*) or you can complete it online, download an observation sheet to use during your data collection, and, if requested, e-mail

Thomson NOW!

your work to your instructor. Go to your ThomsonNOW for *Communicate!* to access **Skill Learning Activity 4.1**.

tions and messages. In Western culture, we shake hands to be sociable and polite, we pat a person on the back for encouragement, we hug a person to show love, and we clasp raised hands to demonstrate solidarity.

Because of individual preference, family background, or culture, people differ in their use of touching behavior and their reactions to unsolicited touch from others. Some people like to touch others and be touched; other people do not. Although American culture is relatively non-contact oriented, the kinds and amounts of touching behavior within our society vary widely. Touching behavior that seems appropriate to one person may be perceived as overly intimate or threatening by another. Moreover, the perceived appropriateness of touch differs with the context. Touch that is considered appropriate in private may embarrass a person when done in public or with a large group of people. To learn more about touch, read the article "Just the Right Touch," available through InfoTrac College Edition. Go to your ThomsonNOW for *Communicate!* to access **Web Resource 4.1: Just the Right Touch**.

Use of Voice: Vocalics

vocalics
the interpretation of the message based on the paralinguistic features.

paralanguage
the voiced but not verbal part of a spoken message.

The interpretation of a verbal message based on the paralinguistic features is called **vocalics. Paralanguage** is the voiced but not verbal part of a spoken message. Six vocal characteristics that comprise paralanguage are pitch, volume, rate, quality, intonation, and vocalized pauses.

pitch
the highness or lowness of vocal tone.

Pitch **Pitch** is the highness or lowness of vocal tone. People raise and lower vocal pitch and change volume to emphasize ideas, indicate questions, and show nervousness. They may also raise the pitch when they are nervous or lower the pitch when they are trying to be forceful. Lower pitch voices tend to convey more believability and credibility.

volume
the loudness or softness of tone.

Volume **Volume** is the loudness or softness of tone. Whereas some people have booming voices that carry long distances, others are normally soft-spoken. Regardless of their normal volume level, however, people do vary their volume depending on the situation and topic of discussion. For example, people talk loudly when they wish to be heard in noisy settings. They may vary their volume when they are angry, or they may speak more softly when they are being romantic or loving.

rate
the speed at which a person speaks.

Rate **Rate** is the speed at which a person speaks. People tend to talk more rapidly when they are happy, frightened, nervous, or excited and more slowly when they are problem solving out loud or are trying to emphasize a point.

quality
the sound of a person's voice.

Quality **Quality** is the sound of a person's voice. Each human voice has a distinct tone. Some voices are raspy, some smoky, some have bell-like qualities, while others are throaty or nasal.

Intonation **Intonation** is the variety, melody, or inflection in one's voice. Some voices have little intonation and sound monotone. Other voices have a great deal of melody and may have a childlike quality to them. People prefer to listen to voices with a moderate amount of intonation.

intonation
the variety, melody, or inflection in one's voice.

Vocalized pauses **Vocalized pauses** are extraneous sounds or words that interrupt fluent speech. The most common vocalized pauses that creep into our speech include "uh," "um," "er," "well," "OK," and those nearly universal interrupters of American conversations, "you know" and "like." At times we may use vocal pauses to hold our turn when we momentarily search for the right word or idea. Because they are not part of the intended message, occasional vocalized pauses are generally ignored by those who are interpreting the message. However, when you begin to use them to excess, others will perceive you as nervous or unsure of what you are saying. As your use increases, people will be less able to understand what you are saying and they may perceive you as confused and your ideas as not well thought out. For some people, the use of vocalized pauses presents interferences that are so pervasive that listeners are unable to concentrate on the meaning of the message.

vocalized pauses
extraneous sounds or words that interrupt fluent speech.

We can interpret the paralinguistic part of a message as complementing, supplementing, or contradicting the meaning conveyed by verbal message. So when Joan says, "Well, isn't that an interesting story." How we interpret her meaning will depend on the paralanguage that accompanies it. If she alters her normal voice so that the "Well" is varied both in pitch and tone while the rest of her words are spoken in a staccato monotone, we might interpret the vocalics as contradicting the words and perceive her message as sarcasm. But if her voice pitch rises with each word, we might perceive the vocalics as supplementing the message and understand that she is asking a question.

Use of Space: Proxemics

Have you ever been in the midst of a conversation with someone that you felt was "standoffish" or "pushy"? If you had analyzed your feeling, you might have discovered that your impression of the person or what was being said stemmed from how far the person chose to stand from you. If the person seemed to be farther away than you are accustomed to, you might have interpreted the distance as aloofness. If the distance was less than you would have expected, you might have felt uncomfortable and perceived the person as being overly familiar or pushy. **Proxemics** is the formal term for the interpretation someone makes of your use of space. People will interpret how you use the personal space around you, the physical spaces that you control and occupy, and the artifacts that you choose to decorate your space.

proxemics
the interpretation of a person's use of space.

personal space
the distance you try to maintain when you interact with other people.

Personal space **Personal space** is the distance you try to maintain when you interact with other people. Our need for and use of personal space stems from our biological territorial natures, which view space as a protective mechanism. How much space you need or view as appropriate depends on your individual preference, the nature of your relationship to the other person or people, and your culture. While the absolute amount of space varies from person to person, message to message, and from culture to culture, in general the amount of personal space we view as appropriate decreases as the intimacy of our relationship increases. For example, in the dominant U.S. culture, four distinct distances are generally perceived as appropriate and comfortable, depending on the nature of the conversation. *Intimate distance* is defined as up to 18 inches and is appropriate for private conversations between close, intimate friends. *Personal distance,* from 18 inches to 4 feet, is the space in which casual conversation occurs. *Social distance,* from 4 to 12 feet, is where impersonal business such as a job interview is conducted. *Public distance* is anything more than 12 feet (Hall, 1969).

Of greatest concern to us is the intimate distance—that which we regard as appropriate for intimate conversation with close friends, parents, and younger children. People usually become uncomfortable when "outsiders" violate this intimate distance. For instance, in a movie theater that is less than one-quarter full, people will tend to leave one or more seats empty between themselves and others whom they do not know. If a stranger sits right next to you in such a setting, you are likely to feel uncomfortable or threatened and may even move away. Intrusions into our intimate space are acceptable only in certain settings and then only when all involved follow the unwritten rules. For instance, people will tolerate being packed into a crowded elevator or subway and even touching others they do not know, provided that the others follow the "rules." The rules may include standing rigidly, looking at the floor or the indicator above the door, but not making eye contact with others. The rules also include ignoring or pretending that they are not touching.

physical space
the physical environment over which you exert control.

Physical space **Physical space** is the part of the physical environment over which you exert control. Our territorial natures not only lead us to maintain personal distance, but also lead us to assert ownership claims to parts of the physical space that we occupy. Sometimes we do not realize the ways that we claim space as our own; in other instances, we go to great lengths to visibly "mark" our territory. For example, Ramon arrives early for the first day of class, finds an empty desk, and puts his backpack next to it on the floor and his coat on the seat. He then makes a quick trip to the restroom. If someone comes along while Ramon is gone, moves his backpack and coat, and sits down at the desk, that person is violating what Ramon has "marked" as his territory. If you regularly take the same seat in a class, that habit becomes a type of marker, signaling to others that a particular seat location is yours. Other students will often leave that seat empty because they have perceived it as yours. Not only can we interpret someone's ownership of space by their markers, but we also can understand a person's status in a group by noting where the person sits and the amount of space over which ownership is claimed. In a well-established group, people with differing opinions will often choose to sit on opposite sides of the table, while allies will sit in adjacent spots. So if you are observant, you can tell where people stand on an issue by noticing where they have chosen to sit. There are many other meanings that can be discerned from how people use physical space.

Artifacts **Artifacts** are the objects and possessions we use to decorate the physical space we control. When others enter our homes, our offices, or our dorm rooms, they look around and notice what objects we have chosen to place in the space and how we have arranged them. Then they assign meaning to what they see. For example, when Katie visited her boyfriend Peter at school, the first thing she noticed was a picture hanging on his bulletin board of him hugging a really cute woman that she did not recognize. The second thing she noticed was that the framed picture she had given him of her before he left for school was nowhere to be found. From this, she concluded that Peter wasn't honoring his promise not to see anyone at school.

artifacts
objects and possessions we use to decorate the physical space we control.

The way that we arrange the artifacts in our space also can nonverbally communicate to others. Professors and businesspeople have learned that by choosing and arranging the artifacts in their space, they can influence interactions. We once knew a professor who was a real soft touch. So when he had to handle the students who were petitioning to enter closed classes, he turned his desk, which normally faced out the window, so that it was directly in front of the door. That way, the students couldn't get into his office, sit down, and break his resolve with their sad stories. Instead, they had to plead their case standing in the very public hall. In this case, his desk served as a barrier and protected him from his softhearted self.

People choose artifacts not just for the function of the object, but also for the message that the object conveys about them. So when Lee, the baby of his family, got his first job, the first items he purchased for his new apartment were a large, flat-screen TV and a stuffed leather couch and chair. He chose these primarily to impress his older and already successful brother. Whether the artifacts you choose are conscious attempts to impress or whether they simply reflect your taste or income, when others enter your space, they will notice the artifacts and draw conclusions.

Self-Presentation Cues

People learn a lot about us based on how we look. This includes our physical appearance, our clothing and grooming, and our use of time.

I'm Not Fat, I'm Latina

by Christy Haubegger

"Beauty is in the eye of the beholder." But when you are a "large" person, whether your size enhances or detracts from your own or others' perceptions of your beauty may depend on your cultural group.

1 recently read a newspaper article that reported that nearly 40 percent of Hispanic and African American women are overweight. At least I'm in good company. Because according to even the most generous height and weight charts at the doctor's office, I'm a good 25 pounds overweight. And I'm still looking for the panty-hose chart that has me on it (according to Hanes™, I don't exist). But I'm happy to report that in the Latino community, my community, I fit right in.

Latinas in this country live in two worlds. People who don't know us may think we're fat. At home, we're called *bien cuidadas* (well cared for). I love to go dancing at Cesar's Latin Palace here in the Mission District of San Francisco. At this hot all-night salsa club, it's the curvier bodies like mine that turn heads. I'm the one on the dance floor all night while some of my thinner friends spend more time waiting along the walls. Come to think of it, I wouldn't trade my body for any of theirs.

But I didn't always feel this way. I remember being in high school and noticing that none of the magazines showed models in bathing suits with bodies like mine. Handsome movie heroes were never hoping to find a chubby damsel in distress. The fact that I had plenty of attention from Latino boys wasn't enough. Real self-esteem cannot come from male attention alone.

My turning point came a few years later. When I was in college, I made a trip to Mexico, and I brought back much more than sterling-silver bargains and colorful blankets.

I remember hiking through the awesome ruins of the Mayan and Aztec civilizations, which created pyramids as large as the ones in Egypt. I loved walking through the temple doorways, whose clearance was only 2 inches above my head, and I realized that I must be a direct descendant of those ancient priestesses for whom those doorways had originally been built.

For the first time in my life, I was in a place where people like me were the beautiful ones. And I began to accept, and even like, the body that I have.

I know that medical experts say that Latinas are twice as likely as the rest of the population to be overweight. And yes, I know about the health problems that often accompany severe weight problems. But most of us are not in the danger zone; we're just *bien cuidadas*. Even the researchers who found that nearly 40 percent of us are overweight noted that there is a greater "cultural acceptance" of being overweight within Hispanic communities. But the article also commented on the cultural-acceptance factor as if it were something unfortunate, because it keeps Hispanic women from becoming healthier. I'm not so convinced that we're the ones with the problem.

If the medical experts were to try to get to the root of this so-called problem, they would probably find that it's part genetics, part enchiladas. Whether we're Cuban American, Mexican American, Puerto Rican, or Dominican, food is a central part of Hispanic culture. While our food varies from fried plantains to tamales, what doesn't change is its role in our lives.

You feed people you care for, and so if you're well cared for, *bien cuidada,* you have been fed well. I remember when I used to be envious of a Latina friend of mine who had always been on the skinny side. When I confided this to her a while ago, she laughed. It turns out that when she was growing up, she had always wanted to look more like me.

She had trouble getting dates with Latinos in high school, the same boys I dated. When she was little, the other kids in the neighborhood had even given her a cruel nickname: *la seca,* "the dry one." I'm glad I never had any of those problems.

Our community has always been accepting of us well-cared-for women. So why don't we feel beautiful? You only have to flip through a magazine or watch a movie to realize that beautiful for most of this country still means tall, blond, and underfed. But now we know it's the magazines that are wrong. I, for one, am going to do what I can to make sure that *mis hijas,* my daughters, won't feel the way I did.

Reprinted from Christy Haubegger, "I'm Not Fat, I'm Latina," in Readings for Diversity and Social Justice: An Anthology on Racism, Anti-Semitism, Sexism, Heterosexism, Ableism, and Classism, *eds. M. Adams, W. J. Blumenfeld, R. Castañeda, H. W. Hackman, M. L. Peters, & X. Zúñiga (New York: Routledge, 2000), pp. 242–243.*

Physical Appearance

People make judgments about others based on how they look. We can control our physique to some extent through exercise, diet, cosmetic surgery, and so on. But we also inherit much of our physical appearance, including our body type, and physical features such as hair and eyes. Our body is one of the first things that others notice about us and there are culture-based stereotypes associated with each of the three general body shapes. **Endomorphs,** who are shaped round and heavy, are stereotyped as kind, gentle, and jovial. **Mesomorphs,** who are muscular and strong, are believed to be energetic, outgoing, and confident. **Ectomorphs,** whose bodies are lean and have little muscle development, are stereotyped as brainy, anxious, and cautious. While not everyone fits perfectly into one of these categories, each person tends toward one body type. Even though these stereotypes are far from accurate, these is ample antidotal evidence to suggest that many of us form our first impression of someone using body type stereotypes. Yet, the messages we infer from body type also vary by culture, as Christy Haubegger explains in the Diverse Voices feature, "I'm Not Fat, I'm Latina."

endomorph
round and heavy body type.

mesomorph
muscular and athletic body type.

ectomorph
lean and little muscle development.

Clothing and Grooming

Your clothing and personal grooming communicate a message about you. Today, more than ever, people use clothing choices, body art, and other personal grooming to communicate who they are and what they stand for. Likewise, when we meet someone, we are likely to form our impression of them from how they are dressed and groomed. Because we can alter our clothing and grooming to suit the occasion, others rely heavily on these nonverbal cues to help them understand who we are and how to treat us. As a result, you can change how people perceive you by altering your clothing and grooming. For example, a successful sales representative may wear an oversize white T-shirt, baggy shorts, and a backward ball cap when

© Matthew McKee; Eye Ubiquitous/CORBIS

What three adjectives would you use to describe the personality of each of these people? What about their clothing and personal appearance led you to draw these conclusions?

hanging with his friends; put on khakis and a golf shirt to go to the office; and dress in a formal blue suit to make a major presentation to a potential client group. In each case, he uses what he is wearing to communicate who he is and how others should treat him.

Use of Time

chronemics
the interpretation of a person's use of time.

monochronic time orientation
a time orientation that emphasizes doing one thing at a time.

polychronic time orientation
a time orientation that emphasizes doing multiple things at once.

Chronemics is the way others interpret your use of time. Cultures differ in how they view time (Hall, E. T., 1959). Some of us have a **monochronic time orientation,** or a "one thing at a time" approach to time. We concentrate our efforts on one task, and only when it is finished or when the time we have allotted to it is complete, do we move on to another task. If we are monochronic, we see time as "real" and think about "spending time," "losing time," and so on. As a result, we subordinate our interpersonal relationships to our schedule (Dahl, 2004, p. 11). So when Margarite's sister, who is excited to share some good news, comes into the room and interrupts her "study time," Margarite, who is monochronic, screams, "Get out! Can't you see I'm studying!" Others of us have a **polychronic time orientation** and tackle multiple tasks at once. We see time as flexible and fluid. So we view appointment times and schedules as variable and subordinate to our interpersonal relationships, and we easily alter or adapt our schedule to meet the needs of our relationships (Dahl, 2004, p. 11). For example, George, who is polychronic, shows up for a noon lunch with Raoul at 12:47 p.m. because as he was leaving his office, his coworker stopped him to ask for help on a problem.

How Margarite's sister or Raoul interpreted the time behavior they experienced depends on their own time orientation. If Margarite's sister is also monochronic, she probably apologized, perceiving her own behavior to have been at fault. If Raoul is polychronic, he will not be offended by

George's arrival time because he will have viewed George's delay as understandable. We tend to view other's use of time through the lens of the culture from which we come. So if we are monochronic in our orientation to time, we will view the polychronic time behavior of someone else as being "rude" and vice versa.

Cultural and Gender Variations in Nonverbal Communication

Culture and gender often play a role in how we communicate nonverbally. Cultural and gender variations are seen in the use of kinesics, paralanguage, proxemics and territory, artifacts and physical appearance, and chronemics.

Kinesics

As we have said, the use of kinesics, or body motions and the meanings they convey, differs among cultures. Several cultural differences in body motions are well documented.

Eye contact A majority of people in the United States and other Western cultures expect those with whom they are communicating to "look them in the eye." Samovar, Porter, and McDaniel (2007) explain, however, that direct eye contact is not a custom throughout the world (p. 210). For instance, in Japan, prolonged eye contact is considered rude, disrespectful, and threatening. People from Latin America, Caribbean cultures, and Africa tend to avoid eye contact as a sign of respect.

In the United States, women tend to have more frequent eye contact during conversations than men do (Cegala & Sillars, 1989). Moreover, women tend to hold eye contact longer than men, regardless of the sex of the person they are interacting with (Wood, 2007). It is important to note that these differences, which we have described according to biological sex, are also related to notions of gender and standpoint in society. In other words, people (male or female) will give more eye contact when they are displaying feminine-type behaviors than when they are displaying masculine-type behaviors.

Facial expression and gestures Studies show that there are many similarities in nonverbal communication across cultures, especially in facial expressions. For instance, several facial expressions seem to be universal, including a slight raising of the eyebrow to communicate recognition, wriggling one's nose, and a disgusted facial look to show social repulsion (Martin & Nakayama, 2000, pp. 183–184).

Across cultures, people also show considerable differences in the meaning of gestures. For instance, the forming of a circle with the thumb and forefinger signifies the OK sign in the United States, but means zero or worthless in France, is a symbol for money in Japan, and is a vulgar gesture in Germany and Brazil (Axtell, 1999, pp. 44, 143, 212). Check out some common Brazilian gestures by going to your ThomsonNOW for *Communicate!* to access **Web Resource 4.2: Maria Brazil**.

Thomson
NOW!

Displays of emotion may also vary. For instance, in some Eastern cultures, people have been socialized to downplay emotional behavior cues, whereas members of other cultures have been socialized to amplify their displays of emotion. Research has shown some sex and gender effects in facial expressions and gestures. Women and men using a feminine style of communication tend to smile frequently. Gender differences in the use of gestures are so profound that people have attributed masculinity or femininity on the basis of gesture style alone (Pearson, West, & Turner, 1995, p. 126). For instance, women are more likely to keep their arms close to the body, are less likely to lean forward with the body, play more often with their hair or clothing, and tap their fingers more often than men.

Haptics According to Samovar, Porter, and McDaniel (2007), touching behavior is closely linked to culture. In some cultures, lots of contact and touching is normal behavior, while in other cultures, individual space is respected and frequent touching is not encouraged. According to Neuliep (2006), some cultures such as South and Central American countries, as well as many southern European countries, encourage contact and engage in frequent touching. By contrast, many northern European cultures are medium to low in contact, and Asian cultures are mainly low-contact cultures. The United States, which is a country of immigrants, is generally perceived to be medium in contact, though there are wide differences between individual Americans due to variations in family heritage.

Women tend to touch others less than men do, but women value touching more than men do. Women view touch as an expressive behavior that demonstrates warmth and affiliation, whereas men view touch as instrumental behavior, so that touching females is considered as leading to sexual activity (Pearson, West, & Turner, 1995, p. 142).

Paralanguage

There are a few cultural and gender variations in the use of paralanguage. It is in the use of volume where cultural differences are most apparent (Samovar, Porter, & McDaniel, 2007). Arabs speak with a great deal of volume to convey strength and sincerity, while soft voices are preferred in Britain, Japan, and Thailand.

In the United States, there are stereotypes about what are considered to be masculine and feminine voices. Masculine voices are expected to be low-pitched and loud, with moderate to low intonation; feminine voices are expected to be higher-pitched, softer in volume, and more expressive. The voice characteristic of breathiness is associated with femininity. Although both sexes have the option to portray a range of masculine and feminine paralanguage, most people probably conform to the expectations for their sex (Wood, 2007).

Proxemics and Territory

As is the case with most forms of nonverbal communication, one's use of space and territory is associated with culture (Samovar, Porter, & McDaniel, 2007). Recall our discussion of individualistic and collectivist cultures in Chapter 2. Cultures that stress individualism generally demand more space than do collectivist cultures and will defend space more closely (p. 217). Seating and furniture placement may also vary by cultural expectations. For example, Americans in groups tend to talk to those seated opposite them, but Chinese prefer to talk to those seated next to them. Furniture arrangement in the United States and Germany often emphasizes privacy. In France or Japan, furniture is arranged for group conversation or participation (pp. 218–219).

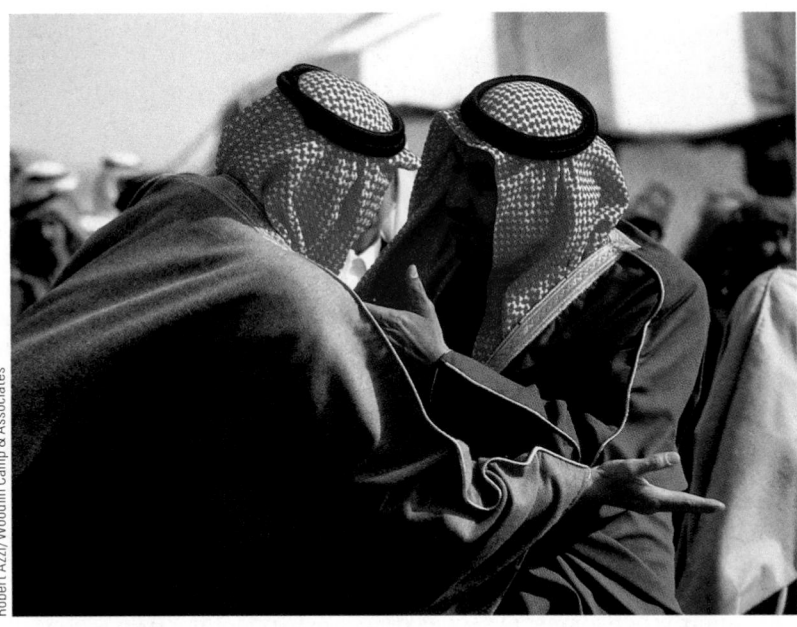

Robert Azzi/Woodfin Camp & Associates

People have differing concepts of personal space. Although you might find it rude for nonintimates to get this close to you in conversation, these men would find it rude if you backed away.

Artifacts and Physical Appearance

There are cultural and gender influences regarding artifacts and physical appearance. Different clothing styles signify masculinity and femininity within a culture. In the United States, women's and feminine clothing is more decorative, while men's and masculine clothing is more functional (Wood, 2007).

Chronemics

As you probably recognize, the dominant U.S. culture has a monochronic time orientation; Swiss and German cultures are even more oriented in this way. On the other hand, many Latin American and Arab cultures have polychronic orientation. The large-scale immigration that is occurring across the globe is leading to an influx of Arab workers into northern Europe and Latin American workers into the U.S. As a result, it is likely that you will encounter people whose use of time is different from your own.

Spotlight on Scholars | Judee K. Burgoon | Professor of Communication, University of Arizona, on Nonverbal Expectancy Violation Theory

With seven books and more than 150 articles and book chapters to her credit, Judee K. Burgoon is a leading scholar in nonverbal communication. Her fascination with nonverbal behavior dates back to graduate school at the University of West Virginia, where she was assigned to do research on *proxemics,* the study of space. From that assignment, she says, "I just got hooked. Nonverbal is more elusive and difficult to study, and I've always enjoyed a challenge!"

At the time, scholars believed the road to interpersonal success lay in conforming one's behaviors to social norms about the distances that are appropriate for certain types of interactions and the types of touch that are appropriate for individuals in different kinds of relationships. Thus, people would be successful in their interactions as long as they behaved in accord with these norms.

Encouraged by one of her professors to "look for the counterintuitive," Burgoon's research uncovered situations where violations of these norms resulted in positive, rather than negative, consequences. For example, in settings where two people were not well acquainted and one of them began "flirting" by moving closer to the other, thus "violating" that person's space, the other person did not always react by moving away from the violator as expected. In fact, at times the person seemed to welcome the violation, and at times may even have moved closer. Similarly, Burgoon noticed that touching behavior that violated social norms was sometimes rejected and at other times accepted.

To explain these observations, Burgoon developed what she named "expectancy violation theory," which is based on the premise that we have strong expectations about how people ought to behave when they interact with us. Whether people meet our expectations affects not only how

Courtesy Judee K. Burgoon

we interact with them, but also such outcomes as how competent, credible, and influential we perceive them to be and what we think of our relationship with them. She found that how we interpret a violation depends on how we feel about the person who committed the violation. If we like the person, we are likely to read the nonverbal violation as positive ("Gee, she put her arm around me—that means she's really interested in me"). If we don't like the person, we are likely to read the same nonverbal violation as negative ("He better take his arm off of me; this is a clear case of harassment"). And, because we have become sensitized to the situation, the violations will be subject to strong evaluations ("Wow, I really like the feel of her arm around my waist" versus "He's making me feel really uncomfortable").

Burgoon's scholarship has developed like a river. Her first work was a narrow stream with a focus on proxemics, which grew with expectancy violation theory to include all of nonverbal behavior, and it continues to branch. Presently, in one stream of work, she is studying what determines how people adapt their behavior when they experience any type of communication violation. Why and when do people reciprocate the violation (for example, if someone shouts, you shout back) or compensate for it (for example, if someone comes too close to you, you step back)? In a second stream, Burgoon is focusing on a specific type of expectancy violation: deception. She is trying to sort out the role nonverbal behavior plays in deceitful interactions. Whatever branch her research takes, Judee Burgoon brings the same readiness to challenge the current thinking that has been the hallmark of her work.

To learn more about Judee Burgoon's work, log on to her home page at www.u.arizona.edu/~judee.

Guidelines for Improving Nonverbal Communication

Because nonverbal messages are inherently continuous, ambiguous, multi-channeled, and sometimes unintentional, it can be tricky to accurately de-code them. Add to this the fact that the meaning for any nonverbal behavior can vary by situation, culture, and gender, and you begin to understand why we so often "misread" the behavior of others. The following guidelines can help you improve the likelihood that you will make accurate interpretations of others' behavior, and that your own behavior will lead others to perceive your nonverbal messages correctly.

Interpreting Nonverbal Messages

1. **When interpreting others' nonverbal cues, do not automatically assume that a particular behavior means a certain thing.** Except for the category of emblems, there is no automatic meaning of nonverbal behavior. And even the meaning of emblems varies culturally. There is much room for error when people make quick interpretations or draw rapid conclusions about an aspect of nonverbal behavior. Instead of making automatic interpretations of nonverbal cues, we should consider cultural, gender, and individual influences on nonverbal behavior.

2. **Consider cultural, gender, and individual influences when interpreting nonverbal cues.** We have shown how nonverbal behavior varies widely based on culture or expectations of masculinity and femininity. Note also that some people are totally unique in their display of nonverbal behavior. You may have learned over time that your friend grinds her teeth when she is excited. You may never encounter another person who uses this behavior in this way.

3. **Pay attention to multiple aspects of nonverbal communication and their relationship to verbal communication.** You should not take nonverbal cues out of context. In any one interaction, you are likely to get simultaneous messages from a person's eyes, face, gestures, posture, voice, and use of space and touch. Even in electronic communication, where much of the nonverbal communication is absent, there can be facial expression and touch communicated through emoticons, paralanguage through capitalization of words, and chronemics through the timing and length of an electronic message. By taking into consideration all aspects of communication, you will be more effective in interpreting others' messages.

4. **Use perception checking.** As we discussed in Chapter 2, the skill of perception checking lets you see if your interpretation of another person's message is accurate or not. By describing the nonverbal behavior you have noticed and tentatively sharing your interpretation of it, you can

get confirmation or correction of your interpretation. It may be helpful to use perception checking when faced with gender or cultural variations in nonverbal behavior.

Sending Nonverbal Messages

1. **Be conscious of the nonverbal behavior you are displaying.** Remember that you are always communicating nonverbally. Some nonverbal cues will always be out of your level of consciousness, but you should work to bring more of your nonverbal behavior into your conscious awareness. It is a matter of just paying attention to what you are doing with your body, voice, space, and self-presentation cues. If you initially have difficulty paying attention to your nonverbal behavior, ask a friend to point out the nonverbal cues you are displaying.

2. **Be purposeful or strategic in your use of nonverbal communication.** Sometimes, it is important to control what you are communicating nonverbally. For instance, if you want to be persuasive, you should use nonverbal cues that demonstrate confidence and credibility. These may include direct eye contact, a serious facial expression, a relaxed posture, a loud and low-pitched voice with no vocal interferences, and a professional style of clothing and grooming. While there are no absolute prescriptions for communicating nonverbally, there are strategic choices we can make to convey the message we desire.

3. **Make sure that your nonverbal cues do not distract from your message.** Sometimes, when we are not aware of what nonverbal cues we are displaying or when we are anxious, certain nonverbal behaviors will hinder our communication. Fidgeting, tapping your fingers on a table, pacing, mumbling, using vocal interferences, and using adaptors can hinder the other person's interpretation of your message. It is especially important to use nonverbal behaviors than enhance rather than distract from your message during a formal speech.

4. **Make your nonverbal communication match your verbal communication.** When nonverbal messages contradict verbal messages, people are more likely to believe the nonverbal, so it is important to have your verbal and nonverbal communication match. In addition, the various sources of nonverbal communication behavior should match each other. If you are feeling sad, your voice should be softer and less expressive, and you should avoid letting your face contradict your voice by smiling. People get confused and frustrated when receiving inconsistent messages.

5. **Adapt your nonverbal behavior to the situation.** Situations vary in their formality, familiarity among the people, and purpose. Just like you would select different language for different situations, you should adapt your nonverbal messages to the situation. Assess what the situ-

What Would You Do?

After the intramural, mixed-doubles tennis matches on Tuesday evening, most of the players adjourned to the campus grill for a drink and a chat. Marquez and Lisa sat down with Barry and Elana, the couple they had lost a match to that night largely because of Elana's improved play. Although Marquez and Lisa were only tennis friends, Barry and Elana had been going out together for much of the season.

After some general conversation about the tournament, Marquez said, "Elana, your serve today was the best I've seen it this year."

"Yeah, I was really impressed. And as you saw, I had trouble handling it," Lisa added.

"And you're getting to the net a lot better too," Marquez added.

"Thanks, guys," Elana said in a tone of gratitude, "I've really been working on it."

"Well, aren't we getting the compliments today," sneered Barry in a sarcastic tone. Then after a pause, he said, "Oh, Elana, would you get my sweater—I left it on that chair by the other table."

"Come on, Barry; you're closer than I am," Elana replied.

Barry got a cold look on his face, moved slightly closer to Elana, and said emphatically, "Get my sweater for me, Elana—now."

Elana quickly backed away from Barry as she said, "OK, Barry—it's cool," and she then quickly got the sweater for him.

"Gee, isn't she sweet," Barry said to Marquez and Lisa as he grabbed the sweater from Elana.

Lisa and Marquez both looked down at the floor. Then Lisa glanced at Marquez and said, "Well, I'm out of here—I've got a lot to do this evening."

"Let me walk you to your car," Marquez said as he stood up.

"See you next week," they both said in unison as they hurried out the door, leaving Barry and Elana alone at the table.

1. Analyze Barry's nonverbal behavior. What was he attempting to achieve?

2. How do you interpret Lisa's and Marquez's nonverbal reactions to Barry?

3. Was Barry's behavior ethically acceptable? Explain.

ation calls for in terms of body motions, paralanguage, proxemics and territory, artifacts, physical appearance, and use of time. Of course, you already do some situational adapting with nonverbal communication. You do not dress the same way for a wedding as you would to walk the dog. You would not treat your brother's space and territory the same way you would treat your doctor's space and territory. But the more you can consciously adapt your nonverbal behavior to what seems appropriate to the situation, the more effective you will be as a communicator.

Summary

Nonverbal communication refers to the interpretations that are made of bodily actions, vocal qualities, use of space, and self-presentation cues. Nonverbal communication is continuous, multichanneled, intentional or unintentional, possibly ambiguous, and the primary means by which we convey our emotions. The sources of nonverbal messages include use of body motions (kinesics: gestures, eye contact, facial expression, posture, and touch); use of voice (vocalics: pitch, volume, rate, quality and intonation, vocalized pauses); use of space (proxemics: personal space, physical space, use of artifacts); and our self-presentation cues (physical appearance, clothing and grooming, and use of time).

The nonverbal behaviors that we enact and how we interpret the nonverbal messages of others depends on our culture and gender. Regardless of our cultural background or gender, however, we can become more adept at interpreting others' nonverbal messages we receive by not jumping to conclusions, by considering cultural and gender differences, by paying attention to all aspects of nonverbal communication and their relationship to verbal communication, and by perception checking. We can improve our encoding of nonverbal communication by being conscious of the nonverbal behavior we are displaying, by being purposeful or strategic in its use, by making sure that our nonverbal cues do not distract from our message, by making our nonverbal communication match our verbal messages, and by adapting our nonverbal behavior to the situation.

Thomson™
NOW!

Communicate! Online

ow that you have read Chapter 4, use your ThomsonNOW for *Communicate!* for quick access to the electronic resources that accompany this text. Your ThomsonNOW gives you access to the Web Resources and Skill Learning Activities featured in this chapter, InfoTrac College Edition, and online study aids such as a digital glossary and review quizzes.

Your *Communicate!* ThomsonNOW is an online study system that helps you identify concepts you don't fully understand, allowing you to put your study time to the best use. Using chapter-by-chapter diagnostic pre-tests, the system creates a personalized study plan for each chapter. Each plan directs you to specific resources designed to improve your understanding, including pages from the text in e-book format. Chapter post-tests give you an opportunity to measure how much you've learned and let you know if you are ready for graded quizzes and exams.

Key Terms

Go to your ThomsonNOW for *Communicate!* to access your online glossary for Chapter 4. Print a copy of the glossary for this chapter and test yourself with the electronic flash cards or complete the crossword puzzle to help you master these key terms:

adaptors (80)
artifacts (85)
body orientation (81)
chronemics (88)
ectomorph (87)
emblems (80)
emoticons (81)
endomorph (87)
eye contact or gaze (80)
facial expression (81)
gestures (80)

haptics (81)
illustrators (80)
intonation (83)
kinesics (80)
mesomorph (87)
monochronic time orientation (88)
nonverbal communication behaviors (78)
paralanguage (82)
personal space (84)

physical space (84)
pitch (82)
polychronic time orientation (88)
posture (81)
proxemics (83)
quality (82)
rate (82)
vocalics (82)
vocalized pauses (83)
volume (82)

Review Quiz

Test your knowledge of the concepts in this chapter by taking the online review quiz for Chapter 4. Go to your ThomsonNOW for *Communicate!* to access the quiz. When you have completed the quiz, submit it for scoring.

Skill Learning Activities

Go to your ThomsonNOW for *Communicate!* to complete the Observe & Analyze activities for Chapter 4. You can submit your Observe & Analyze answers to your instructor.

4.1: Observe & Analyze: Body Motions (82)
4.2: Observe & Analyze: Vocal Characteristics (83)
4.3: Observe & Analyze: Violating Intimate Space Norms (84)
4.4: Observe & Analyze: Self-Presentation Audit (89)

Web Resources

Go to your ThomsonNOW for *Communicate!* to access the Web Resources for this chapter.

4.1: Just the Right Touch (82)
4.2: Maria Brazil (90)

Activity 4.1

Title: **Activity 4.1: Observe and Analyze: Body Motions**

Instructions: Find a public setting, such as a restaurant, where you can observe two people having a conversation. They should be close enough to you so that you can observe their eye contact, facial expressions, and gestures, but not close enough that you can hear what they are saying.

Carefully observe their interaction with the goal of answering the following questions: What is their relationship? What seemed to be the nature of the conversation (social chit-chat, plan making, problem solving, argument, intimate discussion)? How did each person feel about the conversation? Did feelings change over the course of the conversation? Was one person more dominant? To help you note the specific nonverbal behavior that led you to your conclusions, click on the "Media" button below and print out the Observation Form: Body Motions.

When the conversation has ended (and if it seems appropriate), approach the people, introduce yourself, explain that you have been observing them as part of a class assignment, and if they are willing, ask them to verify the accuracy of your analysis.

When you've collected your data, write a paragraph describing this experience and what you have learned.

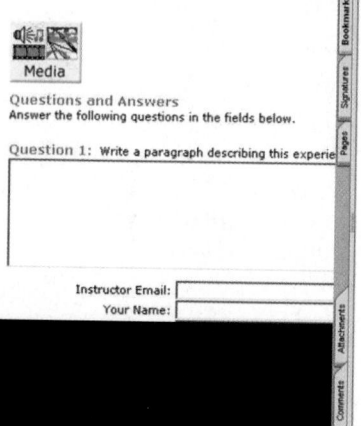

Media

Questions and Answers
Answer the following questions in the fields below.

Question 1: Write a paragraph describing this experie

Instructor Email:
Your Name:

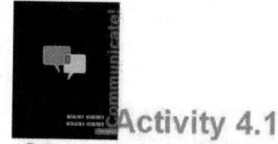

Activity 4.1

Observe and Analyze: Body Motions

Observation Form: Body Motions

	Participant 1			Participant 2		
Behavior	*Frequency of behavior*			*Frequency of behavior*		
Makes eye contact	High	Med	Low	High	Med	Low
Smiles	High	Med	Low	High	Med	Low
Leans body forward	High	Med	Low	High	Med	Low
Touches or plays with hair	High	Med	Low	High	Med	Low
Touches or plays with clothes	High	Med	Low	High	Med	Low

Establishing a Communication Foundation
from Chapters 2 through 4

What kind of a communicator are you? This review looks at 10 specifics that are basic to effective communicators. On the line provided for each statement, indicate the response that best captures your behavior: 1, almost always; 2, often; 3, sometimes; 4, rarely; 5, never.

_____ When I speak, I tend to present a positive image of myself. (Chapter 2)

_____ In my behavior toward others, I look for more information to confirm or negate my first impressions. (Chapter 2)

_____ Before I act on perceptions drawn from people's nonverbal cues, I seek verbal verification of their accuracy. (Chapter 2)

_____ I use specific language when I speak, avoiding generalizations that could be misinterpreted. (Chapter 3)

_____ I speak clearly, using words that people readily understand. (Chapter 3)

_____ When I am speaking with people of different cultures or of the opposite sex, I am careful to monitor my word choices. (Chapter 3)

_____ I tend to look at people when I talk with them. (Chapter 4)

_____ Most of my sentences are free from such expressions as "uh," "well," "like," and "you know." (Chapter 4)

_____ I consider the effect of my dress on others. (Chapter 4)

_____ I try to make sure that my nonverbal messages match my verbal messages. (Chapter 4)

Based on your responses, select the communication behavior you would most like to change. Write a communication improvement goal statement similar to the sample improvement plan in Chapter 1 (page 22). If you would like verification of your self-analysis before you write a goal, have a friend or fellow worker complete this same analysis for you.

Thomson NOW! You can complete this Self-Review online and, if requested, e-mail it to your instructor. Go to your ThomsonNOW for *Communicate!* to access Part I Self-Review.

OBJECTIVES

After you have read this chapter, you should be able to answer these questions:

- What is culture shock?
- What is intercultural communication?
- What is a dominant culture?
- What is a co-culture?
- What are the major bases of co-cultures?
- What four dimensions can help identify the similarities and differences between cultures?
- How does the communication of people from individualistic cultures differ from that of people in collectivist cultures?
- How does the communication of people from high uncertainty-avoidance cultures differ from that of people from low uncertainty-avoidance cultures?
- How does the communication of people from high power-distance cultures differ from that of the people from low power-distance cultures?
- How does the communication of people from masculine cultures differ from that of people from feminine cultures?
- What barriers do we face when communicating interculturally?
- How can you improve your intercultural communication?

5
Communicating across Cultures

"Jack, I don't think we should take this flight," Alicia said. "Why don't we wait and take the next one?"

"What are you talking about?" Jack replied. "Our reservations are confirmed, our bags are probably on board by now, and why would we want to sit around here for hours?"

"But Jack, over there," Alicia muttered behind her hand while nodding to her far right.

Jack turned his head. There on the end of the long bench sat a large bearded man in a turban.

"Jack, I'm afraid," Alicia whispered urgently. "He could be a terrorist."

"Relax, Alicia," Jack said. "He's a Sikh, not a Muslim. There is nothing to worry about. Anyway, what makes you think that all Muslims are terrorists?"

H ow could we evaluate Alicia's assumptions in this situation? Are the inferences underlying Jack's responses more accurate or well founded? In both cases, their judgments are based on their perceptions of people who are culturally different from themselves.

Because culture has a profound impact on not only our perceptions but also our communication behavior, in this chapter we are going to study how culture affects our communication behavior and how it influences our perception of the communication we receive from others. We begin by taking a look at some basic concepts of culture, identifying important values and norms that set cultures apart. Then we discuss the barriers that arise from cultural difference and offer strategies for improving intercultural communication competence.

Culture and Communication

How often have we heard people observe that the world is getting smaller and smaller and the people in it increasingly similar? Today, through the globalization of trade, the Internet and the World Wide Web, our lives are affected by the decisions and actions of people in other parts of the world and we can make instant personal contact with people around the globe through the click of a mouse. Some people celebrate this trend as a step toward world unity, while others mourn the loss of local cultures, traditions, and control and feel overwhelmed by the pervasiveness of communication.

You will recall from Chapter 1, that we defined *culture* as the values, attitudes, beliefs, orientations, and underlying assumptions prevalent among people in a society (Samovar, Porter, & McDaniel, 2007, p. 20). Yet, we do not have to journey to other countries to discover people of different cultures. As a nation of immigrants, the United States is defined as a multicultural society. Our population not only includes recent immigrants from Asia, Latin America, Eastern Europe, and other countries, but also the descendents of earlier immigrants, the descendents of Africans brought here against their will, and native peoples. So understanding how cultural groups vary in their approach to communication can help us as we interact with the people we meet each day.

Intercultural Communication

People are so familiar with their own language, gestures, facial expressions, conversational customs, and norms that they may experience anxiety when these familiar aspects of communication are disrupted. Yet, this occurs frequently when we interact with people from different cultures. **Culture shock** is the psychological discomfort you may feel when you attempt to adjust to a new cultural situation (Klyukanov, 2005, p. 33). Because culture shock is caused by an absence of shared meaning, you are likely to

culture shock
the psychological discomfort of adjusting to a new cultural situation.

feel it most profoundly when you are thrust into another culture through travel, business, or when studying abroad. But it can also occur when you have contact with people from other cultures within your home country. For example, Brittney, who is from a small town in Minnesota, may experience culture shock when she visits Miami for the first time. She may be overwhelmed by the distinct Hispanic flavor of the city, by hearing Spanish spoken among people on the street, the prevalence of Latin beat music, the prominence of outdoor advertisements written in Spanish, and the ways people look and are dressed. Not only is Brittney likely to be disoriented because of the prominence of Spanish, but also because the values, attitudes, beliefs, and behaviors of the people she encounters might seem quite foreign to her.

Intercultural communication refers to interactions that occur between people whose cultural assumptions are so different that the communication between them is altered (Samovar, Porter, & McDaniel, 2007, p. 10). In other words, when communicating with people whose attitudes, values, beliefs, customs, and behaviors are culturally different from ours, we are communicating across cultural boundaries, which can lead to misunderstandings that would not commonly occur between people who are culturally similar. It is important to recognize that not every exchange between persons of different cultures exemplifies intercultural communication. For example, when Brittney is on the beach in Miami and joins a group of Hispanics in a friendly game of beach volleyball, the cultural differences between her and the others are unlikely to affect their game-related exchanges. However, should Brittney decide to join the group for a night of club hopping, she is likely to experience conversations in which cultural differences lead to difficulty in understanding or interpreting what is said.

intercultural communication *interaction between people whose cultural assumptions are distinct enough to alter the communication event.*

Dominant Cultures and Co-Cultures

Although the United States is a multicultural society, there are many attitudes, values, beliefs, and customs that a majority of people hold in common. This shared system of meaning comprises our **dominant culture,** and like the dominant culture of any country, ours has evolved over time. The dominant culture of the United States once reflected the values of white, western European, English-speaking, Protestant, heterosexual men. But as we have recognized our diversity, the dominate culture has evolved and incorporated aspects of other cultural groups.. The result is a dominant culture that better reflects the diversity of the people in the United States.

dominant culture *the attitudes, values, beliefs, and customs that the majority of people in a society hold in common.*

In the United States, however, there are people who strongly identify with cultural groups whose values, attitudes, beliefs, and customs differ from the dominant culture. These groups, called **co-cultures,** exhibit communication that is sufficiently different to distinguish them from the dominant culture.

The following are some of the major contributors to co-cultures in United States society today:

co-cultures *groups of people living within a dominant culture but exhibiting communication that is sufficiently different to distinguish them from the dominant culture.*

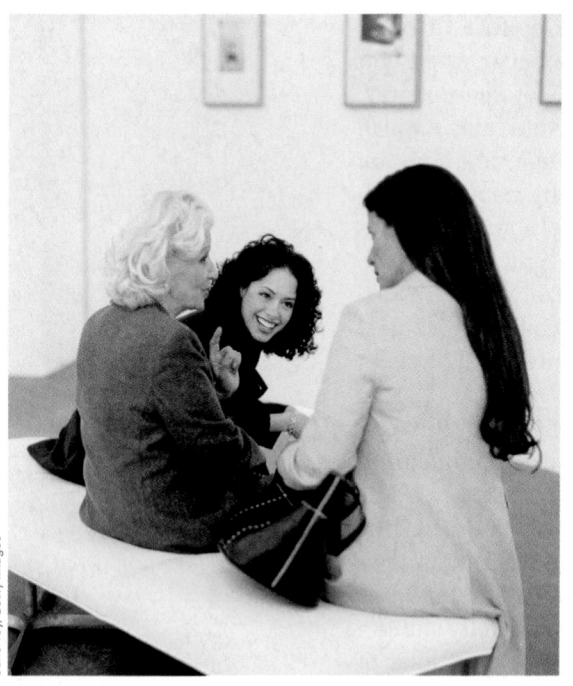

Julie Toy/Getty Images

Women and men tend to communicate differently because of their cultural differences: women often focus on feelings, whereas men often focus on outcomes. What about you? Do you communicate as women tend to do, as men tend to do, or do you communicate in different ways depending on the situation?

ethnicity
a classification of people based on combinations of shared characteristics such as nationality, geographic origin, language, religion, ancestral customs, and tradition.

Gender Men and women have different cultural identities because they are biologically different and because they are differently socialized throughout their lives (through clothes, games, toys, education, roles, and so on). Women and men communicate differently in a number of ways because of these cultural differences. For instance, research shows that women are primarily concerned with personal relationships when they communicate. They talk more about relationships and feelings, tend to include others in conversations, and actively respond to others. Men more often focus on tasks or outcomes when they communicate. They talk more about content and problem solving, tend to emphasize control and status, and are less responsive to others (Wood, 2007).

Race Traditionally, the term race has been used to classify people in terms of biological characteristics, such a skin and eye color, hair texture, and body shape. However, scientific justifications for such divisions have proven elusive, and the classification system itself has changed drastically over time (Hotz, 1995). Despite the difficulty of scientifically defining race, people have experienced the social effects of perceived race, and have formed communities and cultures based on racialized experiences. So race is an important cultural signifier for many people and racial identity can influence communication in a number of ways. The book, *African American Identities and Communication,* edited by Ronald Jackson (2004), describes linguistic and nonverbal patterns of African Americans who may switch from the communication styles of the dominant culture to communication forms unique to their race, depending on attitude, topics, or co-participants (Bonvillain, 2003). Other co-cultures based on gender, ethnicity, or social class may also change their communication from time to time, to be more similar to that of the dominant culture.

Ethnicity Like race, ethnicity is an inexact distinction. **Ethnicity** refers to a classification of people based on combinations of shared characteristics such as nationality, geographic origin, language, religion, ancestral customs, and tradition. People vary greatly in terms of the importance they attach to their ethnic heritage and the degree to which it affects their attitudes, values, and behavior. You may descend from an Italian heritage and this may affect your closeness to family, your religion, the foods you eat, and many other aspects of your identity. Your roommate may also have Italian ancestors but may not identify herself as Italian and may not follow any family traditions based on this ethnicity.

Language or mother tongue is an obvious influence of ethnicity on communication. Immigrants bring with them the language of their original country and they may or may not speak English when they arrive. Even after they learn English, many immigrants choose to speak their mother language at home, intentionally live in close proximity to other people from their home country, and interact with those people in their mother language. Although the United States is an English-speaking country, it now has the third largest Spanish-speaking population of any country in the world; furthermore, 70 percent of Hispanics in the United States mainly speak Spanish at home (Carlo-Casellas, 2002).

Sexual orientation In the United States, the dominant culture values heterosexuality. So, for example, most Americans are not offended when they see a man and a woman holding hands or kissing in public. Displays of affection between gay or lesbian couples may not be met with such tolerance. While the dominant culture has modified some of its most homophobic beliefs, people of other sexual orientations still face discrimination. So many gay, lesbian, bisexual, and transgender people participate in and identify with nonheterosexual communities whose distinct attitudes, values, customs, rites, rituals, and language markers provide social support that is absent in the dominant culture.

Religion A **religion** is a system of beliefs that is shared by a group and that supplies the group with an object (or objects) for devotion, rituals for worshipping the object of devotion, and a code of ethics. Although the dominant culture of the United States values religious freedom and diversity, historically it has reflected Judeo-Christian values and practices. All observant practitioners of a religion participate in co-culture. Those who strongly identify with a religious group that is outside the Judeo-Christian tradition will have different orientations that shape their relationships and their communication behavior. For example, Buddhism advises individuals to embrace rather than to resist personal conflict. Adversity, emotional upheaval, and conflict are seen as natural parts of life (Chuang, 2004). So a Buddhist is apt to communicate openly and calmly during an interpersonal conflict and embrace the positive aspects of conflict in strengthening interpersonal ties.

Social class **Social class** is a level in the power hierarchy of a society. Membership in each social class is determined by income, education, occupation, and social habits. The dominant culture of the United States reflects the culture of the middle class. Because social class often determines where people live, people of the same social class often establish communities where they develop and reinforce co-cultures with distinct values, rituals, and communication practices. For example, lower-class parents tend to emphasize obedience, acceptance of what others think, and hesitancy

---

OBSERVE & ANALYZE

Journal Activity

Race and Ethnicity

What is the difference between race and ethnicity? Can you think of examples of people who are ethnically different but racially the same? Racially different but ethnically the same? Can you think of anyone for whom both designations might be identical? For whom the two designations might be contradictory? What does this analysis suggest about the accuracy and legitimacy of such classification systems?

Thomson NOW! You can complete this activity online and, if requested, e-mail it to your professor. Go to your Thomson-NOW for *Communicate!* to access **Skill Learning Activity 5.1**.

religion
a system of beliefs shared by a group with objects for devotion, rituals for worship, and a code of ethics.

social class
an indicator of a person's position in a social hierarchy, as determined by income, education, occupation, and social habits.

in expressing desires to authority figures, while middle-class parents more often emphasize self-control, self-direction, and intellectual curiosity. Such differences in values based on social class may lead those from middle-class backgrounds to speak more directly and assertively than do people from working-class backgrounds (Gilbert & Kahl, 1982).

Age The time period in which we are born and raised can have a strong formative influence on us. People of the same generation form a cultural cohort group whose personal values, beliefs, and behaviors have been influenced by the common life experiences and events they encountered as they aged. People who grew up influenced by the Great Depression tend to be frugal; those alive during World War II value sacrifice of self for cause and country; those who came of age during the counterculture sixties are likely to question authority; and those we call Generation X, who experienced latchkey childhoods and the consequences of widespread divorce, value self-sufficiency.

Whether in family relationships or in the workplace, when people from different generations interact, their co-cultural orientations can create communication difficulties. For example, when members of different generational cohorts work together, miscommunication, misunderstandings, and conflict are likely to occur more than when people work with others of their same generation. Generally, people from earlier generations are less likely to question authority figures like parents, teachers, religious leaders, or bosses. They demonstrate their respect by using formal terms of address, such as referring to people by Mr., Ms., Dr., sir, and so on. People who came of age in the 1960s or later, on the other hand, tend to be more skeptical of authority and less formal in dealing with authorities. They are more likely to question their managers and to openly disagree with decisions that are made by those in authority (Zempke, Raines, & Filipczak, 2000).

Cultural Identity

As we saw in Chapter 2, our self-concept is the mental image that we have of ourselves, and that image is negotiated and reinforced through our communication with others. Membership in the cultural groups described above can contribute to our cultural identity, but it need not do so. Someone may greatly identify with their religion, ethnicity, or generation, while another person may scarcely think about those cultural groupings of which they are a part. Research has shown that cultural identity is determined by the importance that we assign to our membership in those cultural groups (Ting-Toomey

Hassidic reggae singer Matisyahu displays an interesting blend of cultural identities. He wears clothing that signifies how important his Jewish faith is to him. At the same time, he performs reggae music, inspired by the reggae culture's sense of optimism and emphasis on social reform.

et al., 2000). Shauna is a devoutly religious 20-year-old who attends prayer group every morning and is a leader in her church youth group. She is a counselor at her church summer camp, dates men of her same religion only, and listens exclusively to Christian music. Religion would be a large part of Shauna's cultural identity, guiding how she sees herself and her actions. For her coworker, Nicole, who practices religion only during major religious holidays, her cultural identity would not be shaped by her religion.

Identifying Cultural Norms and Values

Some aspects that identify the member of a culture may be easy to spot. We may be able to figure out someone's cultural background by the language spoken, their dress, or artifacts such as religious markers worn as jewelry or placed in the home. For example, when people meet Shimon, from his sidecurls, his yarmulke, and his black clothes, they can quickly discern that he is a Hassidic Jew. But beyond how one dresses, what does it really mean to be a Hassidic Jew? How do Hassidic Jews differ from the dominant culture and from other cultural groups? What are the other cultural groups to which they are similar? The work of Geert Hofstede gives us a way to understand how cultures are similar and different from one another and to understand how that variation affects communication.

Geert Hofstede (1980) identifies four major dimensions of culture that affect communication: individualism–collectivism, uncertainty avoidance, power distance, and masculinity–femininity. Table 5.1 (page 110) shows where the United States falls on each of these dimensions. For more detail about how the United States compares with the rest of the world in terms of these dimensions, use your ThomsonNOW for *Communicate!* to access **Web Resource 5.1: Hofstede's Cultural Dimensions.**

Individualism–Collectivism

In Chapter 2 we briefly discussed individualism and collectivism's effects on our self-perceptions. So you will recall that individualistic cultures are those in which people place primary value on the self and personal achievement. In an individualistic society, people consider the interests of others only in relationship to how they affect the interest of the self. If you come from an individualistic culture, you may consider your family and close friends when you act, but only because your interests and theirs align. People in individualistic cultures view competition between people as desirable and useful. Because of this, **individualistic cultures** emphasize personal rights and responsibilities, privacy, voicing one's opinion, freedom, innovation, and self-expression (Andersen, Hecht, Hoobler, & Smallwood, 2003).

In contrast, collectivist cultures place primary value on the interests of the group and group harmony. In a collectivist society, an individual's

individualistic culture *emphasizes personal rights and responsibilities, privacy, voicing one's opinion, freedom, innovation, and self-expression.*

decision is shaped by what is best for the group whether it serves the individual's interests or not. Collectivist societies are highly integrated and maintaining harmony and cooperation are valued over competitiveness and personal achievement. As a result, members of collectivist societies will probably have stronger bonds within the groups to which they belong (family, workplace, and community). **Collectivist cultures** emphasize community, collaboration, shared interest, harmony, the public good, and maintaining the avoidance of embarrassment (Andersen, Hecht, Hoobler, & Smallwood, 2003). According to Hofstede (1997), individualistic cultures include the United States, Australia, Great Britain, Canada, and northern and eastern European countries. Collectivist cultures are found in South and Central America, east and southeast Asia, and Africa.

collectivist culture emphasizes community, collaboration, shared interest, harmony, the public good, and avoiding embarrassment.

Notions of individualism and collectivism influence many aspects of communication, including most notably our self-concept formation, assertiveness behavior, and group communication (Samovar, Porter, & McDaniel, 2007). In individualistic cultures, people stress the self and personal achievement, and the individual is treated as the most important element in a social setting. In individualist cultures like the United States, our self-concept and self-esteem are rooted in how successfully we have advanced our own interests without respect to how our actions have affected others. In a collectivist culture, what affects self-concept and self-esteem is not individual achievement; rather, it is whether the group thrives and how people's actions have contributed to their group's success. So if Marie is raised in an individualist culture and she is the highest scoring player on her basketball team, she will feel good about herself and identify herself as a "winner" even if her team has a losing season. But if Marie is from a collectivist culture, the fact that she is the highest scoring player will have little effect on her self esteem, but the fact that her team had a losing season will likely cause her to feel less personal esteem.

People coming from each of these cultural perspectives also view conflict differently. The emphasis that is placed on the individual leads members of individualistic cultures to value and practice assertiveness and confrontational argument, while members of collectivist cultures value accord and harmony and so practice tentativeness and collaboration or avoidance in arguments. In the United States, we teach assertiveness and argumentation as useful skills and expect them to be used in interpersonal and work relationships, politics, consumerism, and other aspects of civic life. By contrast, to maintain harmony and avoid interpersonal clashes, Japanese business has evolved an elaborate process called "nemawashii," a term that also means binding the roots of a plant before pulling it out. In Japan, any subject that might cause conflict at a meeting should be discussed in advance, so that the interaction at the meeting will not seem rude or impolite (Samovar & Porter, 2001). In collectivist societies, a style of communication that respects the relationship is more important than the information exchanged (Jandt, 2001). In collectivist societies, group harmony, sparing others embarrassment, and a modest presentation of oneself are important ways to show respect. A person does not speak directly if it might hurt others in the group.

How people work in groups also depends on the type of culture they come from. Because members of collectivist cultures see group harmony and the welfare of the group to be of primary importance, they strive for consensus on group goals and may, at times, sacrifice optimal outcomes for the sake of group accord. Your cultural assumptions affect how you work to establish group goals, how you interact with other group members, and how willing you are to sacrifice for the sake of the group. Groups whose members come from both individualistic and collectivist cultures may experience difficulties due to their varying cultural assumptions. To read an article about how individualism and collectivism affect groups in school settings, go to your ThomsonNOW for *Communicate!* and access **Web Resource 5.2: Individualism and Collectivism**.

Uncertainty Avoidance

Cultures differ in how their members feel about and deal with unpredictable people, relationships, or events. **Low uncertainty-avoidance cultures** (such as the United States, Sweden, and Denmark) are more tolerant of uncertainty in how people behave, in relationships, and in events, and so put little cultural emphasis on reducing unpredictability. People from cultures with low uncertainty avoidance more easily accept the unpredictability and ambiguity in life. They tend to be tolerant of the unusual, prize initiative, take risks, and think that there should be as few rules as possible. People who come from **high uncertainty-avoidance cultures** have a lower tolerance for unpredictable people, relationships, and events. These cultures create systems of formal rules and believe in absolute truth as the way to provide more security and reduce the risk. They also tend to be less tolerant of people or groups with deviant ideas or behavior. Because their culture emphasizes the importance of avoiding uncertainty, they often view life as hazardous and experience anxiety and stress when confronted with unpredictable people, relationships, or situations. Nations whose cultures are marked by high uncertainty avoidance include Japan, Portugal, Greece, Peru, and Belgium (Samovar, Porter, & McDaniel, 2007).

How our culture has taught us to view uncertainty affects our communication with others. It shapes how we use language, develop relationships, and negotiate with others. People from high uncertainty-avoidance cultures use and value specific and precise language because they believe that through careful word choice, we can be more certain of what a person's message means. Imagine a teacher declaring to a class that "the paper must be well researched, with evidence cited, and professional in format and appearance." Students from high uncertainty-avoidance cultures would find the teacher's remarks to be too general and vague. They would most likely experience anxiety and ask a lot of questions about what kind of research is appropriate, how to cite evidence, how much evidence

low uncertainty-avoidance cultures
cultures characterized by greater acceptance of, and less need to control, unpredictable people, relationships, or events.

high uncertainty-avoidance cultures
cultures characterized by a low tolerance for, and a high need to control, unpredictable people, relationships, or events.

Table 5.1 U.S. Ranking among 53 Countries/Regions

Individualism	High uncertainty avoidance	High power distance	Masculinity
✓ (1st)			
			✓ (15th)
		✓ (38th)	
	✓ (43rd)		
Collectivism	Low uncertainty avoidance	Low power distance	Femininity

is needed, what writing style to use, and the length of the paper in order to reduce their uncertainty. These students would welcome a specific check-list or rubric that enumerated the exact criteria by which the paper would be graded. By contrast, students from a low uncertainty-avoidance cultural background would be annoyed by an overly specific list of rules and guide-lines, viewing it as a barrier to creativity and initiative. As you can imagine, a teacher with students from both of these backgrounds faces a difficult challenge when trying to explain an assignment.

How people approach new relationships and how they communicate in developing relationships is also affected by their culture's view of un-certainty. As you would expect, people from high uncertainty-avoidance cultures are wary of strangers and may not seek out new relationships or relationships with others they perceive as different (unpredictable). They generally prefer meeting people through friends and family and refrain from being alone with strangers. When developing relationships, people from high uncertainty-avoidance cultures tend to guard their privacy, re-frain from self-disclosure early in a relationship, and proceed more slowly through relationship development. Members of low uncertainty-avoidance cultures, on the other hand, are likely to initiate new relationships with people who differ from them, and enjoy the excitement of disclosing per-sonal information in earlier stages of relationship development.

Power Distance

high power distance
the cultural belief that in-equalities in power, status, and rank are "natural" and that these differences should be acknowledged and accentuated.

Cultures differ in how accepting they are of wide differences in power held by different groups of people in the culture and how people of unequal power expect to be treated. In cultures characterized as having **high power distance,** inequalities in power, status, and rank are viewed as "natural" and these differences are acknowledged and accentuated by all members of the culture. These cultures believe that everyone in the culture has a rightful "place" and that members who have higher power, status, and rank should be deferred to by those having less power, status, and rank. High power-distance cultures include most Arab countries of the Middle East, Malaysia, Guatemala, Venezuela, and Singapore, among other countries.

In cultures characterized as having **low power distance,** inequalities in power, status, and rank are underplayed and muted. People know that some individuals have more clout, authority, and influence, but lower ranking people are not in awe of, are not more respectful toward, and do not fear higher power people. Even though power differences exist, these cultures value democracy and egalitarian behavior. Austria, Finland, Denmark, Norway, the United States, New Zealand, and Israel are examples of countries whose dominant cultures are characterized by low power distance.

low power distance
the cultural belief that inequalities in power, status, and rank should be underplayed and muted.

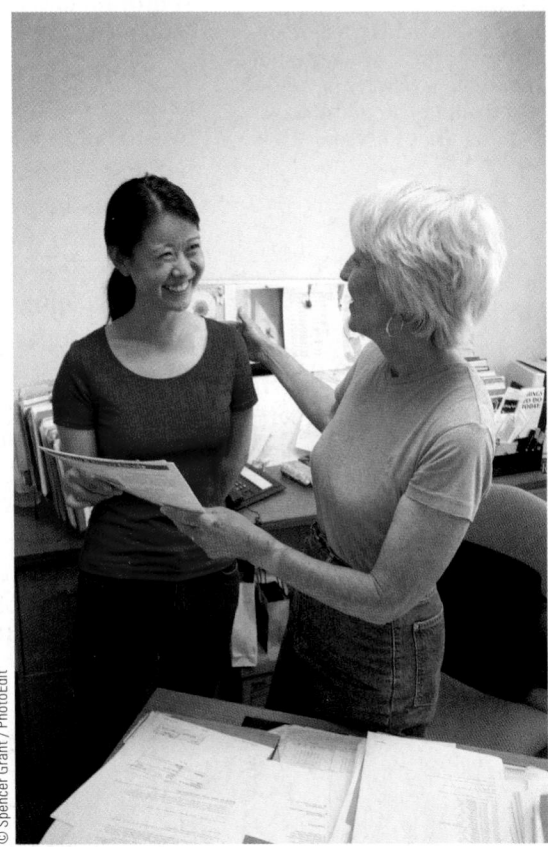

© Spencer Grant / PhotoEdit

Our cultural beliefs about power distance affect how we interact with others, including how we communicate with authority figures, our language use, and our nonverbal behavior. If you are a student, unskilled worker, or average citizen in a high power-distance culture you would not challenge a person in authority, because you would expect to be punished for doing so. You would expect the more powerful person to control the interaction and would listen to what that person said and do what was ordered without question. When talking with a more powerful person, you would address them formally by using their title as a sign of respect. Formal terms of address like Mr. or Mrs., proper and polite forms of language, as well as nonverbal signals of your status differences would be evident in the exchange. If you come from a low power-distance culture, because differences in status are muted, you are more comfortable challenging those in authority. When interacting with a higher-power person, you will feel comfortable directing the course of the conversation and will question or confront the powerbroker if you need to. You would not feel compelled to use formal titles when addressing the more powerful member.

Masculinity–Femininity

Cultures differ in how strongly they value traditional sex role distinctions. Cultures that Hofstede called **masculine cultures** expect people to maintain traditional sex roles and maintain different standards of behavior for men and women. Hofstede called these cultures "masculine" because, for the most part, groups that maintain distinct sex-based roles also value masculine roles more highly than feminine ones. If you come from a masculine culture like the ones that are dominant in Mexico, Italy, and Japan, you are likely to value men when they are assertive and dominant and to value women when they are nurturing, caring, and service oriented. When

In the United States, a low power-distance culture, employers and employees often interact informally in many work settings. How have you interacted with your bosses or employees? Has it varied from workplace to workplace?

masculine culture
a culture in which people are expected to adhere to traditional sex roles.

you encounter people who don't meet these expectations, you are likely to be uncomfortable. Overall, however, if you come from a masculine culture regardless of your sex, you will see masculine behaviors to be more worthwhile, so you are likely to value the masculine characteristics of performance, ambition, assertiveness, competitiveness, and material success more than you value traditionally feminine traits such as service, nurturing, investment in relationships, and helping behaviors (Hofstede, 2000). **Feminine cultures** expect that people, regardless of sex, will assume a variety of roles depending on the circumstances and their own choices, rather than any sex-role expectations. If you are from a feminine culture, like the national cultures of Sweden, Norway, and Denmark, not only will you feel free to act in ways that are not traditionally assigned to people of your sex, but you will also value those traits that have traditionally been associated with feminine roles (Hofstede, 1998).

feminine culture
a culture in which people, regardless of sex, are expected to assume a variety of roles based on the circumstances and their own choices.

Whether you come from a masculine or a feminine culture has a significant effect on how much behavioral flexibility you demonstrate. People from masculine cultures have strict definitions of appropriate behavior for people of a particular sex. As a result, they learn and are reinforced only for those behaviors that are seen to be appropriate for their sex. So men in these cultures are unprepared to engage in nurturing and caring behaviors, such as empathizing and comforting, and women are unprepared to be assertive and argue persuasively. Both men and women in feminine cultures learn and are reinforced for demonstrating both traditionally masculine and feminine behaviors. As a result, people from feminine cultures are more flexible in their communication behavior. Both men and women learn to nurture, empathize, assert, and argue, although any single individual may still lack skill in one or more behaviors.

Barriers to Effective Intercultural Communication

Now that we have developed an understanding of culture and the variations that can exist among cultures and co-cultures, we are in a better position to appreciate the specific barriers that cultural differences give rise to including anxiety, assumptions of similarity or difference, ethnocentrism, stereotypes and prejudice, incompatible communication codes, and incompatible norms and values.

Anxiety

It is normal to feel some level of discomfort or apprehension when we recognize that we are different from most everyone else or when we enter a cultural milieu that has unfamiliar customs. Most people experience fear, dislike, and distrust when first interacting with someone from a different culture (Luckmann, 1999). So when Marissa, who is from a barrio in Los Angeles, decided to attend a small, liberal arts college in New England, she was nervous and questioned if her decision to attend school in the northeast had been a good one. Sure, the other students had been friendly enough during orientation week, but it had become clear that she didn't really have much in common with them. While the others easily shared stories of spring-break trips they had taken with their families and joked about the cars they had wrecked, Marissa found she had little to add—her family always went to see her grandmother back in Mexico when her parents took time off from their jobs. She didn't even have a driver's license. When she hesitantly mentioned her quinceañera party, everyone turned and stared at her and one guy said, "What's a 'quicky hairy' party?" And all of the guys laughed. At first, the other women listened politely, but by that time Marissa was so nervous that she stumbled over her words and really didn't do a good job of explaining this coming-of-age tradition that was so important to her community. Most of us are like Marissa when we are anxious—we don't do a good job of sharing our ideas and feelings. So, our anxiety becomes a barrier to our communication.

Assuming Similarity or Difference

When people cross into an unfamiliar cultural environment, they often assume that the norms, values, and traditions that applied in their familiar situation match those that apply in the new one. When traveling internationally from the United States, for example, many people expect to eat their familiar hamburgers and fries, provided with rapid and efficient service. Likewise, they may be annoyed with shops and restaurants closing during midday in countries that observe the custom of siesta.

It can be just as great a mistake to assume that everything about an unfamiliar culture will be different. With time, Marissa is likely to find that the other students really aren't as different from her friends at home, and that school is still school even when there is snow on the ground. As she makes friends, she learns that although Rachel, who is Jewish, didn't have a quinceañera party, she did have a bat mitzvah celebration and Kate, who is Irish Catholic, had a big party when she made her confirmation. Because our assumptions guide our communication behavior, incorrectly assuming similarities that are not accurate or differences that do not exist can lead to miscommunication. The wisest way to overcome this barrier is not to assume anything, but to be aware of the feedback you receive, which provides cues to the real similarities and differences that exist between your cultural expectations and those of your interaction partners.

Ethnocentrism

Ethnocentrism is the belief that one's own culture is superior to others. The stereotype of the immigrant in the host country, loudly complaining of how much better everything is back home, is the classic example of ethnocentrism. In varying degrees, ethnocentrism is found in every culture (Haviland, 1993) and can occur in co-cultures as well. An ethnocentric view

OBSERVE & ANALYZE

Journal Activity

Similarities and Differences

Recall a time when you visited a place that was different from your usual social milieu: a different country, a different city, a different kind of club or market. Did you assume any similarities or differences? Were your assumptions correct? How did they affect your perception of the place? How did they affect your appreciation for, or enjoyment of, the place?

Thomson NOW! You can complete this activity online and, if requested, e-mail it to your professor. Go to your Thomson-NOW for *Communicate!* to access **Skill Learning Activity 5.2.**

ethnocentrism
the belief that one's own culture is superior to others.

of the world leads to attitudes of superiority and messages that are directly and subtly condescending in content and tone. As you would expect, these messages are offensive to receivers from other cultures or co-cultures.

Stereotypes and Prejudice

In Chapter 2, we defined stereotypes as attributions that cover up individual differences and ascribe certain characteristics to a group of people. Basing our interactions on stereotypes can lead to misunderstandings and can strain relationships. For example, when Laura anticipates meeting Joey, who she has heard is gay, she may expect him to be effeminate in his mannerisms and interested in fashion. So she embarrasses him and herself when, early in their conversation, she attempts to find common ground and asks him for advice on what type of cologne to buy her boyfriend—to which he replies, "What is your problem? I may be gay, but I'm not that Carson Kressley dude from *Queer Eye!*"

Also you will recall that in Chapter 2, we defined prejudice as a rigid attitude based on group membership that predisposes us to think, feel, or act in a negative way toward another person or group. Thinking that a Chinese student in your class will get the best grade in the course because all Chinese students excel intellectually, or assuming that Alberto, who is Mexican, is working in the United States as an illegal, undocumented worker, would be examples of prejudice. Colin is prejudiced and believes that all white people try to take advantage of people of color. So when his coworker John, who is white, offers to refer a client to Colin, Colin replies,

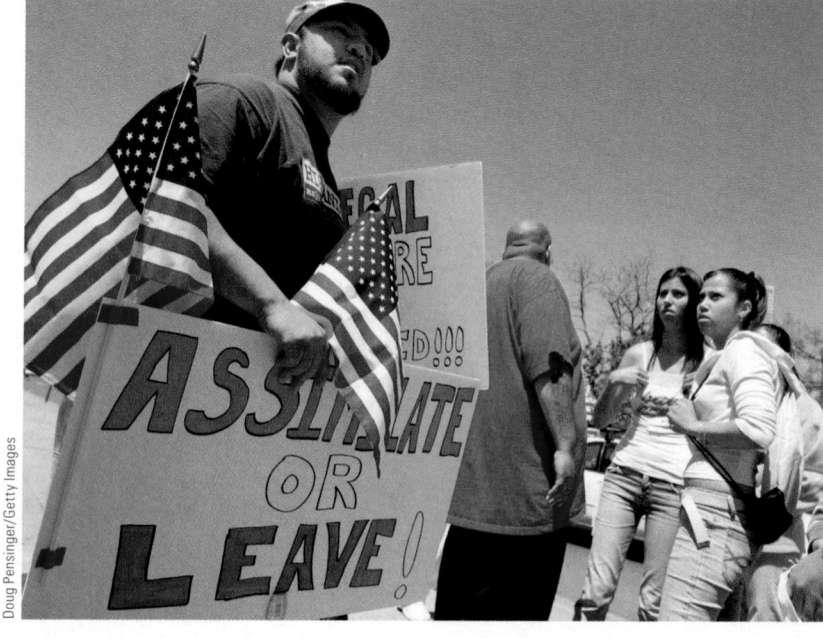

Prejudice and stereotypes can negatively affect not only our relationships with people we know personally, but also with our larger communities. How do you suppose this protester's sign will affect the young girls in the photo?

Doug Pensinger/Getty Images

"Forget it—you're not going to pawn off a deadbeat on me." When we interact based on stereotypes and prejudice, we risk creating messages that are inaccurate and damage our relationships; when we listen with our stereotypes and prejudices in mind, we may misperceive the intent of the person with whom we are talking.

Incompatible Communication Codes

Zeke could not understand why those Chinese guys always sat together in the dining hall. They were always fighting—screaming at each other and waving their arms. He had no idea what they were saying because he did not understand Mandarin, but he could tell that they were pretty angry. He was always expecting a fight to break out.

Zeke was judging the conversation of the Chinese students based on their use of paralanguage and body movement. He could not understand the words they used, but he interpreted their nonverbal communication as hostile and angry. Zeke did not understand that Mandarin is a tonal language. How the words are voiced affects their meaning. The great changes in pitch and volume that he heard did not represent the expression of strong emotion, but only the expression of different meanings.

When our conversational partners, people in our group, or audience members speak a different language, it is easy to see that we have incompatible communication codes, but even when people speak the same language, there will be cultural variations that result from the co-cultures to which they belong. For example, people from Great Britain take a "lift" to reach a higher floor, while Americans ride an elevator. Even within a national group, co-cultural use of the language can lead to incompatible communication codes. In fact, less powerful co-cultural groups will often purposefully develop "in group" codes that are easily understood by co-culture members but unintelligible to those from the outside. Just try to have a conversation about your computer problem with your friend Sam who is a "techno geek." As an insider, Sam is likely to talk in a vocabulary that is as foreign to you as if Sam were speaking Icelandic. People who speak different languages quickly comprehend their inability to communicate verbally, and invariably turn to some type of nonverbal signing in an effort to overcome the language barrier. As we have seen, however, there are also significant differences in the use and meaning of nonverbal behaviors. Not only do incompatible verbal communication codes create barriers to intercultural communication, so do our differences in how we use and interpret nonverbal behavior. For example, in some cultures, belching after eating signifies that the meal did not agree with the diner, while in other cultures it is a compliment to the cook. In some cultures, the gesture used in the United States to mean "OK" is obscene. Such differences in nonverbal behavior across cultures often account for misunderstandings or embarrassment when people from different cultures attempt to communicate with each other.

Incompatible Norms and Values

All cultures base their communication behaviors on cultural norms and rules and on personal values based on those cultural norms and rules. Sometimes the norms and values of two people of different cultures create barriers that make it difficult for them to understand each other. For example, Jeff and Tabito have been best friends since elementary school. They have shared everything: school work, summer vacations, sports, and camping trips. Now that they are in high school, their interests seem to be changing. One day Jeff tells Tabito that he has some pot and offers to share it with Tabito. Tabito simply says, "No," and offers no explanation. Jeff is confused by Tabito's behavior. To Jeff, a fourth-generation American whose family is individualistic in their cultural orientation, it's no big deal. He figures, "even if we get caught, it's not like we're selling and neither of us has ever been in trouble before, so all we'd get is a slap on the wrist." He doesn't consider how his arrest might affect his family and chides Tabito, saying, "Come on, don't wimp out on me now." What Jeff does not understand is that Tabito, coming from a first-generation Japanese American family, has the collectivist values of his parents. Being caught with drugs would bring great disgrace upon his whole family, and to him, the collectivist goal of maintaining the reputation of his family is much more important than having fun with a friend. But because Tabito and Jeff don't recognize that their cultural backgrounds have led them to have different expectations, they don't discuss it. But both feel the strain that it puts on their conversation and relationship.

Intercultural Communication Competence

Competent intercultural communicators overcome cultural barriers by adopting the correct attitudes toward other cultures, acquiring accurate information about other cultures' values and practices, and developing specific skills needed to be effective across cultures.

Adopt Correct Attitudes

The right attitudes for intercultural communication, according to Neuliep (2006) involve one's motivations and flexibility in interacting with others from different cultures. In other words, we must be willing to try and must have a desire to succeed when communicating interculturally. We must be willing to try new behaviors, rather than expecting the other person to adjust to our style of communicating. When we tolerate ambiguity, are open-minded, and act altruistically, these attitudes enable us to effectively communicate across cultural differences.

1. **Tolerate ambiguity.** Communicating with strangers creates uncertainty, and when we recognize that the stranger also comes from a different culture, we can become anxious about what they will expect of us. Peo-

ple beginning intercultural relationships must be prepared to tolerate a high degree of uncertainty about the other person and to tolerate it for a long period of time. If we enter an intercultural interaction with the belief that it is OK for us to be unsure about how to proceed, we are likely to pay closer attention to the feedback we receive from the other person and we can then work to adjust our behavior and messages so that together we can achieve understanding. Accepting the ambiguity in the interaction can help us work hard to make the conversation successful; we are much less apt to become frustrated or discouraged by the inevitable false starts and minor misunderstandings.

When Jerome read the Partner Assignment List posted on the bulletin board outside of the lab, he discovered that his lab partner had an Indian-sounding name, but he resolved to work hard to make the relationship a success. So when he met Meena in class and found that she was an exchange student from Mumbai, he worked hard to attune his ear to her accent and was pleased to discover that although her accent was at first difficult to understand, her command of English was as good as his. Over the semester, Jerome worked hard to understand Meena's English. He was rewarded, because she really had a much better grasp of chemistry than he did and was willing to tutor him as they worked on assignments.

2. **Be open-minded.** An open-minded person is someone who is willing to dispassionately receive the ideas and opinions of others. Open-minded people are aware of their own cultural values and recognize that other people's values are different. They resist the impulse to judge the values of other cultures in terms of those of their own culture. In other words, they resist ethnocentrism.

3. **Be altruistic. Altruism** is a display of genuine and unselfish concern for the welfare of others. The opposite of altruism is **egocentricity,** a selfish interest in one's own needs to the exclusion of everything else. Egocentric people are self-centered, while altruistic people are other-centered. Altruistic communicators do not neglect their own needs, but they recognize that for a conversation to be successful, both parties must be able to contribute what they want and take what they need from the exchange. In the Diverse Voices feature "What Do You Say?" June Lorenzo describes a painful conversation she once had regarding the word *squaw*. As you read the excerpt, try to imagine how the conversation might have differed had all of the participants acted altruistically.

altruism
a display of genuine and unselfish concern for the welfare of others.

egocentricity
a selfish interest in one's own needs, to the exclusion of everything else.

Acquire Knowledge about Other Cultures

The more we know about other cultures, the more likely we are to be competent intercultural communicators (Neuliep, 2006). There are various ways to learn about other cultures.

1. **Observe.** You can simply watch as members of another culture interact with each other. As you watch, you can notice how their values, rituals,

What Do You Say?

by June Lorenzo

ike our brothers and sisters in the African American, Hispanic, and Asian communities, Native Americans struggle with the "name game"—that those in power [get to] name and describe those who are not.

In December 1996 I learned that the Arizona legislature was considering legislation which would change the name of a local landmark because of its offensive meaning. At the time, I was at a gathering of Native American Christians in Phoenix. We gladly received this news as an indication that the Phoenix community was demonstrating some cultural sensitivity.

However, on my return to Washington, D.C., the following day, I overheard a conversation between two other Phoenix passengers as we waited for our luggage. The conversation went something like this:

"Did you hear that they're thinking of changing the name of Squaw Peak?"

"Yeah, it's supposed to be offensive or something."

"Yes, apparently the word *squaw* means 'woman' and that is offensive to some people" (chuckle chuckle). I don't know what the big deal is."

"Oh you never know how far they're going to go—the next thing you know they'll discover Indian burial grounds on my land, and then I'll have to move out of my home" (chuckle chuckle).

As I found myself in a dilemma, my blood rose. I had a thirty-second conversation with myself: "What do I say? Do I have a right to say anything? Who am I to say something to them? If I turn around and they see that I am a Native person, will they be embarrassed? Worse yet, what if they don't care? Will I be embarrassed? Will I even think of something intelligent to say? Shall I just say nothing? No—I can't just stand here and ignore these words! This is offensive to me!"

Before I lost my nerve, I turned around and faced an Anglo woman and an Anglo man. I decided that I'd first try to join their conversation: "Actually, the name used to be 'squaw tit' but that was

changed to its present name," I said, sharing information I had received in Phoenix. My intent was not to be funny, but their response was laughter. I decided to try again. "Actually the word means *vagina*. It was a French word used to describe Indian women, and I think it is offensive."

"Yes, but it just means woman, and I don't think it was French. And I don't think it was intended to be derogatory at the time," snapped the woman (as if she knew what the thinking of "the time" was).

I was unprepared for her indignation. Still, I opted to stick with my "be-patient-with-people-who-may-not-know" strategy and volunteered more information: "I believe it was a word used by the French to describe women in the upper Midwest," I continued, hoping I would appeal to her conscience. "There was a time when we did not think names like Black Sambo or the image of Aunt Jemima was offensive. If we can change these, then we surely can change names like Squaw Peak."

"Yeah—we should spend our tax dollars on things like that!" replied the man, sarcastically.

I began to wonder what I had gotten myself into. "Maybe, but hopefully it demonstrates more sensitivity."

"Maybe we're becoming too sensitive," he insisted. "Will this money will be spent on changing road signs," he said. The woman nodded in agreement.

I turned around to check for my luggage. I was fuming inside. I stood there for a moment, trying to calm down and asking myself whether I should say anything more. What do you say to words like these? Simply "these people don't get it" and dismiss it as ignorance? Rationalize that they are total strangers and therefore don't really matter? . . .

Regardless of the exact meaning of the word *squaw,* the point is that it is extremely offensive to Native women (at a minimum). That is sufficient. . . . If we inform people of how offensive *squaw* and other terms are, will it make a difference? Do those in power refrain from taking actions of support if they are not personally hurt? Because of cultural differences, how can they experience the hurt caused by the use of such derogatory terms?

Representative Jack Jackson, the Navajo sponsor of the bill, was criticized as "oversensitive" and "politically correct" . . . .

In the airport, I decided to say nothing more. But, if I could be honest about my feelings, what would I say? I would express to them how hurtful their comments and laughter were to me as a Native woman. I would tell them that every time I hear comments like theirs, I have to do battle inside myself, I have to tell myself, "No. This is not a truth about myself. It is a statement of their insensitivity."

As a member of a people who have struggled with genocide and systematic oppression in this country, as a person who inherited generations of self-hate from attempts to assimilate Indian people, I would tell them that it has taken years of work to say that I am a Native person and feel pride. I would say that I and my people are as fully human as they are and deserve respect.

But I would also say that despite the racism I experience in my life, I want to believe in the good of all people. This is what my people have taught me. I want to believe that the two people in the airport had no idea how hateful their words were.

Authors' note: It is a common misperception that the English word *squaw* was derived from the Iroquois or Mohawk language. Yet linguists, including specialists on Indian languages, agree that as early as 1624 the word was borrowed from the Algonquians who lived in the area of Massachusetts. In that language it simply meant "younger woman." Nevertheless, historically the word *squaw* has been used by whites as a derogatory reference to American Indian women and, as such, now has racist overtones. In his article "The Sociolinguistics of the 'S-word': 'Squaw' in American Placenames," William Bright, noted Professor Emeritus of Linguistics at UCLA, suggests that "we don't need sociolinguistic reasons to eliminate 'squaw' from official maps; simple courtesy is enough" (Bright, 2000). Although Ms. Lorenzo seems to couch some of her arguments in sociolinguistic terms, it is evident that her greatest concern is the racist connotations the term *squaw* embodies.

In April 2003, Arizona Governor Janet Napolitano used her leadership to change the name of Squaw Peak to Piestewa Peak in honor of Lori Peistewa, a member of the Hopi tribe who was killed in a battle in Iraq. Lori Peistewa is believed to be the first Native American woman to give her life in combat for the United States of America. Nevertheless, the battle over offensive place-names continues to this day.

Excerpted from June Lorenzo, "What Do You Say?" The Other Side, March–April 1998, vol. 34, no. 2, p. 48(2)

and communication styles are similar and different from your own and other cultures with which you are familiar. Passive observers study the communication behaviors that are used by members of a particular culture.

2. **Formally study.** You can learn about other cultures by reading accounts of cultural members such as ethnographic research studies, by taking courses, or by interviewing members of the culture about their values, rituals, and so on.

3. **Immerse yourself in the culture.** You can learn a great deal about another culture by actively participating in it. When you live or work with people whose cultural assumptions are different from yours, you not only acquire obvious cultural information, but you also learn the nuances that escape passive observers and are generally not accessible through formal study alone. One reason that study abroad programs often include home stays is to insure that students become immersed in

OBSERVE & ANALYZE

Journal Activity

Acquiring Correct Knowledge

For the next week, conduct research into a distinct culture with which you currently have little or no familiarity. This culture can be grounded in gender, race, religion, ethnicity, social class, sexual orientation, age, or some combination of these factors, but whatever culture you choose to study, be sure it is one that you can access locally. First, arrange to observe (continued on page 120) *(continued from page 119)* members of the culture engaged in a typical activity and note as many of their individual communication behaviors as you can. Be sure to take your notes respectfully, being careful not to offend those you observe. Next, spend some time formally researching the culture and its communication behaviors at a library or over the Internet, only consulting reputable sources for your information. Finally, observe members of the culture once more and then write a paragraph in which you answer these questions: What were your impressions of the culture's communication behaviors the first time you observed its members? How were these first impressions altered, if at all, by your formal research into the culture? How did your formal research affect your second observation of the culture?

You can use your Student Workbook to complete this activity, or you can complete it online, download a log to use, and, if requested, e-mail it to your instructor. Go to your ThomsonNOW for *Communicate!* Online Textbook Resources to access **Skill Learning Activity 5.3**.

intercultural empathy
imaginatively placing yourself in the dissimilar other person's cultural world to attempt to experience what he or she is experiencing.

flexibility
the ability to adjust your communication to fit the other person and the situation.

the culture of the host country. We hope that you will consider participating in a study abroad experience. The international or global studies office at your college or university can point you to a variety of study abroad opportunities and may even guide you to scholarships or grants to help pay your expenses.

Develop Culture-Specific Skills

To be effective in intercultural situations, you may need to adapt the communication skills that you will learn in this course to the demands of a particular culture. To this end, three of the specific skills that you will study that will be most useful are listening, empathy, and flexibility.

1. **Practice listening.** By carefully listening and demonstrating your listening, you can improve your communication with people from other cultures. Because language and nonverbal communication vary across cultures, it is vitally important that you focus closely on the other and listen attentively. In Chapter 7, you will learn the skills associated with active listening. It is important to note that there are cultural differences in how people engage in listening and the value that cultures place on listening. In the United States, we listen closely for concrete facts and information and often ask questions while listening. In other cultures, such as Japan, Finland, and Sweden, listeners are more reserved and do not ask as many questions (Samovar, Porter, & McDaniel, 2007). For many cultures in the Far East, listening is much more valued than speaking. Regardless of your cultural background, however, becoming a more skillful listener will help you in your intercultural encounters.

2. **Practice intercultural empathy. Intercultural empathy** means imaginatively placing yourself in the other person's cultural world to attempt to experience what he or she is experiencing (Ting-Toomey, 1999). The Native American saying, "Don't judge another person until you have walked two moons in his moccasins," captures this idea. By paying close attention to the other person and focusing on the emotions displayed, we can improve our empathic skills. We will elaborate on how to communicate empathy in Chapter 7.

3. **Develop flexibility.** We discussed the concept of flexibility as part of an appropriate attitude toward intercultural encounters, but we can also provide concrete strategies for becoming more flexible in your communication. **Flexibility** is the ability to adjust your communication to fit the other person and the situation. With flexibility, you can use a wide variety of communication skills during an interaction and modify your behavior within and across situations. Being flexible means analyzing a situation, making good decisions about how to communicate in that situation, and then modifying your communication when things are not going well.

For more on respecting cultural differences and learning how to enjoy successful multicultural collaboration, go to your ThomsonNOW for *Com-*

What Would You Do?

Tyler, Jeannie, Margeaux, and Madhukar were sitting around Margeaux's dining-room table working on a group marketing project. It was 2:00 a.m. They had been working since 6:00 p.m. and still had several hours' work remaining.

"Oh, the misery," groaned Tyler, pretending to slit his own throat with an Exacto knife. "If I never see another photo of a veggie burger it will be too soon. Why didn't we choose a more interesting product?"

"I think it had something to do with *someone* wanting to promote a healthy alternative to greasy hamburgers," Jeannie replied sarcastically.

"Right," said Tyler, "I don't know what I could have been thinking. Speaking of greasy hamburgers, is anyone else starving? Anybody want to order pizza or something?"

"No one will deliver up here this late," Margeaux replied, "but I have a quiche that I could heat up."

"Fancy," Tyler quipped.

"You wish," Margeaux said. "It came out of a box."

"Sure, that sounds great, thanks," Jeannie said. "I'm hungry too."

"It doesn't have any meat in it, does it?" asked Madhukar. "I don't eat meat."

"Nope, it's a cheese and spinach quiche," Margeaux said.

Tyler and Margeaux went off to the kitchen to prepare the food. Tyler took the quiche, still in its box, from the fridge. "Uh-oh," he said. "My roommate is a vegetarian, and he won't buy this brand because it has lard in the crust. Better warn Madhukar. He's a Hindu, so I imagine it's pretty important to him."

"Shhh!" said Margeaux, "I don't have anything else to offer him, and he'll never know the difference anyway. Just pretend you didn't notice that."

"Okay," Tyler said. "It's your kitchen."

1. What exactly are Margeaux's ethical obligations to Madhukar in this situation? Why?

2. Does the fact that Tyler is not the host relieve him of all ethical responsibility in this case?

---

municate! and access **Web Resource 5.3: Working on Common Cross-Cultural Communication Challenges**. And to read about intercultural competence in a particular setting, the workplace, go to your Thomson-NOW for *Communicate!* and access **Web Resource 5.4: Intercultural Communication in the Workplace**. This site defines problem areas in intercultural communication and offers tips for how to navigate them successfully.

 Thomson NOW!

Summary

Culture encompasses the values, attitudes, beliefs, orientations, and underlying assumptions prevalent among people in a society. Culture shock refers to the psychological discomfort people have when they attempt to adjust to a new cultural situation. Intercultural communication takes place when people's distinct cultural assumptions alter the communication event. A shared system of meaning exists within the dominant culture, but meanings can vary within co-cultures based on gender, race, ethnicity, sexual orientation, religion, social class, and age. Cultural norms and values vary in systematic ways, and we can understand how similar or different one culture is from others by understanding where the culture is on the dimensions of individualism–collectivism, uncertainty avoidance, power distance, and masculinity–femininity.

Barriers to intercultural communication include anxiety, assumptions about differences and similarities, ethnocentrism, stereotypes and prejudice, incompatible communication codes, and incompatible norms and values. To develop intercultural communication competence, we should learn to tolerate ambiguity, be open-minded, and be altruistic. We can acquire knowledge of other cultures by observing, through formal study, and through cultural immersion. Useful skills for intercultural communication competence are intercultural listening, empathy, and flexibility.

Communicate! Online

Now that you have read Chapter 5, use your ThomsonNOW for *Communicate!* for quick access to the electronic resources that accompany this text. Your ThomsonNOW gives you access to the Web Resources and Skill Learning Activities featured in this chapter, InfoTrac College Edition, and online study aids such as a digital glossary and review quizzes.

Your *Communicate!* ThomsonNOW is an online study system that helps you identify concepts you don't fully understand, allowing you to put your study time to the best use. Using chapter-by-chapter diagnostic pre-tests, the system creates a personalized study plan for each chapter. Each plan directs you to specific resources designed to improve your understanding, including pages from the text in e-book format. Chapter post-tests give you an opportunity to measure how much you've learned and let you know if you are ready for graded quizzes and exams.

Key Terms

Go to your ThomsonNOW for *Communicate!* to access your online glossary for Chapter 5. Print a copy of the glossary for this chapter and test yourself with the electronic flash cards or complete the crossword puzzle to help you master these key terms:

altruism (117)
co-culture (103)
collectivist culture (108)
culture shock (102)
dominant culture (103)
egocentricity (117)
ethnicity (104)
ethnocentrism (113)

feminine culture (112)
flexibility (120)
high power distance (110)
high uncertainty-avoidance
    cultures (109)
individualistic culture (107)
intercultural communication
    (103)

intercultural empathy (120)
low power distance (111)
low uncertainty-avoidance
    cultures (109)
masculine culture (111)
religion (105)
social class (105)

Review Quiz

Test your knowledge of the concepts in this chapter by taking the online review quiz for Chapter 5. Go to your ThomsonNOW for *Communicate!* to access the quiz. When you have completed the quiz, submit it for scoring.

Skill Learning Activities

Go to your ThomsonNOW for *Communicate!* to complete the Observe & Analyze activities for Chapter 5. You can submit your Observe & Analyze answers to your instructor.

5.1: Observe & Analyze: Race and Ethnicity (105)

5.2: Observe & Analyze: Similarities and Differences (113)

5.3: Observe & Analyze: Acquiring Correct Knowledge (119)

Web Resources

Go to your ThomsonNOW for *Communicate!* to access the Web Resources for this chapter.

5.1: Hofstede's Cultural Dimensions (107)

5.2: Individualism and Collectivism (109)

5.3: Working on Common Cross-Cultural Communication Challenges (121)

5.4: Intercultural Communication in the Workplace (121)

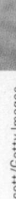

OBJECTIVES

After you have read this chapter, you should be able to answer these questions:

- What are the major types of relationships?
- What are guidelines for developing acquaintance, friendship, and intimate relationships?
- How does disclosure and feedback affect relationships?
- How do we begin a relationship?
- What strategies will maintain a relationship?
- How do we de-escalate or end a relationship?

6
Communicating in Relationships

It was Monday, between classes, and Jennifer had an hour before her next class. She decided to walk over to the bookstore. On the way, she looked up, spotted Maria, a woman in her accounting class, and asked, "Hey, how you doing?"

"OK," Maria replied. "What did you think of that test we had yesterday?"

"Not sure I want to think about it now," Jennifer replied with a little laugh.

"I know what you mean," Maria said. "I hope we get them back soon. See you in class tomorrow."

"Right," Jennifer replied as Maria made her way across the street.

A minute later, Jennifer was startled as she heard, "Hey beautiful, what are you doing here?"

"Greg!" Jennifer said with a big smile on her face. "You scared me. I thought you were working today!"

"Well," Greg replied, "as it turned out, my plans to work with Ken kind of fell through. Have you got time to get lunch?"

"You know I've always got time to spend with you."

"Like to decide what we're going to do this weekend?"

"Sounds good to me!"

relationships
sets of expectations two people have for their behavior based on the pattern of interaction between them.

good relationships
ones in which the interactions are satisfying to and healthy for those involved.

1 nterpersonal skills help you start, build, and maintain healthy **relationships,** sets of expectations two people have for their behavior based on the pattern of interaction between them (Littlejohn & Foss, 2005). Relationships run the gamut from acquaintances (like Maria and Jennifer) to intimate friends (like Greg and Jennifer). Regardless of the level of a relationship with a person, we seek **good relationships,** ones in which the interactions are satisfying to and healthy for those involved.

In this chapter, we describe three types of relationships and provide guidelines for developing acquaintance, friendship, and intimate relationships. Also, we examine disclosure and feedback in relationships and explain the stages that typical relationships go through.

Types of Relationships

We behave differently depending on whether our relationships are personal or impersonal. Moving on a continuum from impersonal to personal (Dindia & Timmerman, 2003, p. 687), we can classify our relationships as acquaintances, friendships, and close friends or intimates. There are specific communication competencies that help establish and maintain each type of relationship.

Acquaintances

acquaintances
people we know by name and talk with when the opportunity arises, but with whom our interactions are largely impersonal.

Acquaintances are people we know by name and talk with when the opportunity arises, but with whom our interactions are limited. Many acquaintance relationships grow out of a particular context. We become acquainted with those who live in our apartment building or dorm or in the house next door, who sit next to us in class, who go to our church, or belong to our club. Thus Melinda and Paige, who meet in biology class, may talk with each other about class-related issues, but they make no effort to share personal ideas or to see each other outside of class.

Acquaintanceship guidelines To meet other people and develop acquaintance relationships, it helps to be good at starting and developing conversations. The following guidelines can help you become more competent in conversing with others:

- Initiate conversations by introducing yourself, referring to the physical context, referring to your thoughts or feelings, referring to another person, or making a joke. For example, "Hi, I'm Kathie. Have you ever had this professor for a class before?"
- Develop an "other-centered" focus by asking questions, listening carefully, and following up on what has been said.
- Engage in appropriate turn-taking. Effective conversationalists balance talking with listening and do not interrupt the other. Not only

do we need to avoid dominating the conversation, but we also need to uphold our part by talking enough.

- Make your comments relevant to what has previously been said before you change subjects.

- Be polite. Consider how your conversational partner will feel about what you say and work to phrase your comments in a way that allows your partner to "save face."

You can learn more about holding effective conversations by reading the online *Communicate!* chapter, "Holding Effective Conversations." Go to your ThomsonNOW for *Communicate!* to access **Web Resource 6.1: Holding Effective Conversations**. To learn techniques you can use to begin conversations in large gatherings, read the article "How to Master Networking," available through InfoTrac College Edition—use your ThomsonNOW to access **Web Resource 6.2: Networking**.

Friends

Over time, some acquaintances become our friends. **Friends** are people with whom we have voluntarily negotiated more personal relationships (Patterson, Bettini, & Nussbaum, 1993, p. 145). As friendships develop, people move toward interactions that are less role bound and more interpersonally satisfying. For example, Melinda and Paige, who are acquaintances in biology class and have only talked about class-related subjects, may decide to get together after school to go to the gym. If they find that they enjoy each other's company, they may continue to meet outside of class and eventually become friends.

Some of our friendships are context bound. Thus, people often refer to their tennis friends, office friends, or neighborhood friends. These context friendships may fade if the context changes. For instance, your friendship with a person at the office may fade if you or your friend takes a job with a different company.

friends
people with whom we have negotiated more personal relationships that are voluntary.

Friendship guidelines For friendships to develop and continue, some key behaviors must occur. The following guidelines can help you develop and maintain your friendships. Samter (2003) explains five important competencies necessary to friendship relationships.

- **Initiation.** Be proactive in setting up times to spend together. One person must get in touch with the other and the interaction must be smooth, relaxed, and enjoyable. A friendship is not likely to form between people who rarely interact or who have unsatisfying interactions.

- **Responsiveness.** Each person must listen. Listen to others and respond to what they say. It is difficult to form friendships with people who focus only on themselves or their issues, and it is equally difficult to maintain relationships with someone who is uncommunica-

© Thomson Higher Education

How does race affect friendships? Do you have many friends of different races?

close friends or intimates
people with whom we share a high degree of commitment, trust, interdependence, and disclosure, and enjoyment.

platonic relationship
an intimate relationship in which the partners are not sexually attracted to each other or do not act on an attraction they feel.

romantic relationship
an intimate relationship in which the partners act on their sexual attraction.

trust
placing confidence in another in a way that almost always involves some risk.

tive. In Chapter 7 you will be introduced to skills that can help you be more effective in listening to others.

- **Self-disclosure.** Friends share feelings with each other. Although acquaintances can be maintained by conversations that discuss surface issues or abstract ideas, a friendship is based on the exchange of more personal and specific information including personal history, opinions, and feelings. In Chapter 8 you will learn the skills associated with effective disclosure and feedback.

- **Emotional support.** Provide comfort and support when needed. When we are emotionally or psychologically vulnerable, we expect to be helped by those we call friends. When your friends are hurting, they need you to support them by confirming their feelings and helping them work through making sense of what has happened. You will learn more about comforting and supporting in Chapter 7.

- **Conflict management.** Manage conflicts so that both parties' needs are met. It is inevitable that friends will disagree about ideas or behaviors. Friendship depends on successfully handling these disagreements. In fact, by competently managing conflict, people can strengthen their friendships. You will learn more about conflict management in Chapter 8.

Close Friends or Intimates

Close friends or **intimates** are those few people with whom we share close, caring, and trusting relationships characterized by a high degree of commitment, trust, interdependence, disclosure, and enjoyment. We may have countless acquaintances and many friends, but we are likely to have only a few truly intimate relationships. Intimacy is not synonymous with "love" or exclusivity, and both platonic and romantic relationships may become intimate. A **platonic relationship** is one in which the partners are not sexually attracted to each other or do not act on an attraction they feel. Conversely, a **romantic relationship** is one in which the partners act on their sexual attraction. One type of intimate relationship is a romantic relationship. To read an interesting article about the stages of romantic relationships, go to your ThomsonNOW for *Communicate!* to access **Web Resource 6.3: Stages in Romantic Relationships**.

Regardless of whether the relationship is platonic or romantic, for the relationship to remain intimate, both partners must continue to trust the other. **Trust** is placing confidence in another in a way that almost always involves some risk. As we disclose personal information, we monitor how well our partner keeps our confidence. Once we perceive our partner to be untrustworthy, we are likely to withdraw and not continue to disclose. As a result, over time the intimacy in the relationship will decrease. When there is a severe breach of our trust, we may even abruptly end the relationship. With close friends, we show commitment by pledging ourselves and our time to each other. We show trust by having positive expectations of the other person and believing that he or she will behave fairly and honestly. With our close friends, our lives are interdependent or intertwined. We rely upon each other. We are more likely to share personal, private information about ourselves to close friends. In close relationships, there is some fusion of the self and the other. The partner is perceived as part of yourself. In other words, you come to define who you are, in part, through your close relationships (Aron, Aron, Tudor, & Nelson, 2004).

Research shows that women and men tend to differ on the factors that lead to intimacy in relationships. This may be because society teaches women and men to behave differently, to follow norms of femininity and masculinity. Women tend to develop close relationships with others based on talking, opening up with the other, and sharing personal feelings. By gaining knowledge of the innermost being of their partner, women develop a sense of "we-ness" with others. Men tend to develop close friendships through joint activities, doing favors for each other, and being able to depend on one another. Men are less likely to define a close friend as someone with whom you can share feelings. For men, close friends are the people you can depend on to help you out of a jam and the people you regularly choose for pursuing enjoyable activities together (Wood & Inman, 1993). It is important to note that these differences are more pronounced in same-sex friendships. When men and women develop close friendships or intimate relationships with each other, these distinctions may not apply.

Intimacy guidelines Maintaining intimacy depends on developing and maintaining trust in your partner and commitment to your relationship. The following guidelines can help you establish and maintain trust (Boon, 1994, pp. 97–101).

- Be dependable so your partner knows they can rely on you at all times and under all circumstances.
- Be responsive in meeting your partner's needs. At times, this will require you to put their needs before your own.
- Be an effective partner in conflict by managing the conflict in a collaborative manner.
- Be faithful by maintaining your partner's confidential information and by abiding to sexual or other exclusivity agreements between you and your partner.
- Be transparent by honestly sharing your real ideas and feelings with your partner.
- Be willing to give up other activities or relationships to spend time with your partner.

OBSERVE & ANALYZE

Journal Activity

Distinguishing between Types of Relationships

1. List five people you have known for some time whom you consider to be acquaintances. Why do you consider these people to be acquaintances rather than friends? What do you talk about with each of these people? What subjects do you avoid? Do any of these relationships have the potential to become friendships? If so, what would you have to do to make that transition?

2. List five people you have known for some time whom you consider to be friends. Why do you consider each of these people to be a friend? How does your relationship with each differ from your relationships with your acquaintances? What do you talk about with each of these people? What subjects do you avoid? Do any of these relationships have the potential to become best friendships or intimate relationships? If so, what would you have to do to make the transition?

3. List one to three people you have known for some time whom you consider to be your best friends or your intimates. Why do you consider each of these people to be best friends or intimates? What do you talk about with each of these people? What subjects do you avoid? How does each of these relationships differ from those you have with your friends?

Write an essay in which you describe what you have learned about your relationships.

Thomson NOW! You can complete this activity online and, if requested, e-mail your essay to your instructor. Use your ThomsonNOW for *Communicate!* to access **Skill Learning Activity 6.1.**

Disclosure and Feedback Ratios in Relationships

As people interact in a relationship, they will engage in some degree of disclosure with each other and they will also give some amount of feedback to each other.

self-disclosure
sharing biographical data, personal ideas, and feelings that are unknown to the other person.

feedback
verbal and physical responses to people (and/or their messages) within the relationship.

Johari window
a tool for examining the relationship between disclosure and feedback in the relationship.

A healthy interpersonal relationship is marked by an appropriate balance of **self-disclosure** (sharing biographical data, personal ideas, and feelings that are unknown to the other person) and **feedback** (the verbal and physical responses to people and/or their messages) within the relationship. The **Johari window,** named after its two originators, Jo Luft and Harry Ingham, is a tool for examining the relationship between disclosure and feedback in the relationship (Luft, 1970). The window represents all of the information about you that can be known. You and your partner each may know some (but not all) of this information.

The window has four "panes" or quadrants, as shown in Figure 6.1. The first quadrant is called the "open" pane of the window because it represents the information about you that both you and your partner know. It includes information that you have disclosed and the observations about you that your partner has shared with you. It might include mundane information that you share with most people, such as your college major, but it also may include information that you disclose to relatively few people. Similarly, it could include simple observations that your partner has made, such as how cute you look when you wrinkle your nose, or more serious feedback you have received from your partner about your interpersonal style.

Figure 6.1
The Johari window

The second quadrant is called the "secret" pane. It contains all those things that you know about yourself but that your partner does not yet know about you. Secret information is made known through the process of self-disclosure. The information moves into the open pane of the window when you choose to share the information with your partner. For example, suppose that you had been engaged to be married, but on the day of the wedding your fiancé(e) had backed out. You may not want to share this part of your history with casual acquaintances, so it will be in the secret pane of your window in many of your relationships. But when you disclose this fact to a friend, it moves into the open part of your Johari window with this person. As you disclose information, the secret pane of the window becomes smaller and the open pane is enlarged.

The third quadrant is called the "blind" pane. This is the place for information that the other person knows about you, but about which you are unaware. Most people have blind spots—parts of their behavior or the effects of their behavior of which they are unaware. Information moves from the blind area of the window to the open area through feedback from others. When someone gives you an insight about yourself and you accept the feedback, then the information will move into the open pane of the Johari window you have with this person. Thus, like disclosure, feedback enlarges the open pane of the Johari window, but in this case, it is the blind pane that becomes smaller.

The fourth quadrant is called the "unknown" pane. It contains information about you that you don't know and neither does your partner. Obviously, you cannot develop a list of this information. So how do we know that it exists? Well, because periodically we "discover" it. If, for instance, you have never tried hang gliding, then neither you nor anyone else can really know how you will react at the point of takeoff. You might chicken out or follow through, do it well or crash, love every minute of it or be paralyzed with fear. But until you try it, all of this information is unknown. Once you try it, you gain information about yourself that becomes part of the secret pane, which you can move to the open pane through disclosure. Also, once you have tried it, others who observe your flight will have information about your performance that you may not know unless they give you feedback.

As you disclose and receive feedback, the sizes of the various window-panes change. These changes reflect the relationships. So the panes of the Johari window you have with different people will vary in size.

In Figure 6.2A we see an example of a relationship where there is little disclosure or feedback occurring. This person has not shared much information with the other, and has received little feedback from this partner as well. We would expect to see this pattern in a new relationship or one between casual acquaintances.

Figure 6.2B shows a relationship in which a person is disclosing to a partner, but the partner is providing little feedback. As you can see, the secret pane is smaller, but the hidden pane is unchanged. A window like this

Figure 6.2
Sample Johari windows:
(a) low disclosure, low feedback; (b) high disclosure, low feedback; (c) low disclosure, high feedback; (d) high disclosure, high feedback.

a   b   c   d

indicates that the individual is able to disclose information but the partner is unable or unwilling to give feedback (or, perhaps, that the individual refuses to accept the feedback that is being given). Because part of the way that we learn about who we are comes from the feedback we receive from others, relationships in which one partner does not provide feedback can become very unsatisfying to the other individual.

Figure 6.2C shows a relationship where a partner is good at providing feedback, but where the individual is not disclosing. Since most of us disclose only when we trust our partners, this pattern may be an indication that the individual does not have confidence in the relational partner.

Figure 6.2D shows a relationship in which the individual has disclosed information and received feedback. So the open pane of the window has enlarged as a result of both processes. Windows that look like this indicate that there is sufficient trust and interest in the relationship that both partners are willing to risk by disclosing and giving feedback.

Obviously, to get a complete "picture" of a relationship, each partner's Johari window would need to be examined. A healthy interpersonal relationship is marked by a balance of disclosure and feedback, so that both people are participating.

Communication in the Stages of Relationships

Regardless of whether a relationship is an acquaintanceship, a friendship, or an intimate relationship, every relationship develops and changes with time. Even though no two relationships develop in exactly the same manner, they tend to follow a "life cycle" that has three identifiable stages: beginning and developing, maintaining, and a deteriorating stage (Baxter, 1982; Duck, 1987; Knapp & Vangelisti, 2000; Taylor & Altman, 1987). How quickly any relationship moves through these stages depends on the interpersonal communication between the relationship partners. Relationships can alternate between maintenance, development (greater closeness), and deterioration (distancing) in almost imperceptible ways, so it may be difficult at any point in time to accurately label a stage of the relationship. At times, relationship stages may merge and at other times, they may be quite distinct. But if you are observant over time, you can detect which way the relationship is moving.

Beginning and Developing a Relationship

The early stage of a relationship depends on increasing your knowledge of the other person and beginning to feel relaxed and confirmed. As the relationship grows, there will be feelings of relaxation and confirmation, and more physical contact and psychological closeness will develop. As relationships develop, you will increase disclosure and support. The earliest communication in relationships focuses on learning about the other person so that uncertainty is reduced and you start to feel comfortable with each other (Littlejohn & Foss, 2005). As the relationship develops, there will be additional time spent together, with disclosures of a more personal nature. Both of you will experience a sense of support (Duck, 1999). As the relationship develops, partners will identify and capitalize on their similarities and tolerate or negotiate their differences.

As you know from your own experience, communication during the first earliest stage of a relationship, beginning and building relationships, is initially focused on getting information about the other person. We do this information exchanging as a way to reduce uncertainty (Berger & Bradac, 1982; Littlejohn & Foss, 2005). If we don't know anything about another person, we don't know how to act with them. Let's look at an example of two college roommates, Whitney and Madeline. During their first few conversations, they each are nervous, wondering if they will be compatible. To reduce this uncertainty, they will want to get to know each other. So they may talk about what they did in high school, what majors each is pursuing, what hobbies they like, and their favorite foods, movies, and music. As they learn more about each other, they find that although Whitney is majoring in fine arts and Madeline is in pre-med, they both are passionate environmentalists and vegetarians. As they learn more, they begin to relax and find that although they have many differences, they like and respect each other. Over the semester, they each find other friends that they socialize with alone, but they continue to have evening meals in the dining hall together. Life in the room they share begins to take on a predictable pattern. When Whitney is working on an art project for class, materials are strewn all over the room, so Madeline accommodates her by studying in the library. When Madeline is freaking out over her mid-term exam in chemistry, Whitney gets her a double latte from the coffee shop.

In the beginning stages of relationship formation, we also look for feelings of relaxation and confirmation. It should be more comfortable conversing with someone over time. We want conversation to flow smoothly and we want to feel enjoyment during the interaction. Each person wants the other to listen and to confirm one's sense of self and one's ideas. When relaxation and confirmation happen, we consider that we are connecting with the other person. Only when both parties experience relaxation and confirmation is the relationship likely to proceed to a deeper level.

If a relationship is growing deeper, then people perceive it to have closeness. They perceive that the relationship is developing to more interpersonally intimate levels. This also can happen via online relationships.

Some people report that they achieve more closeness in online relationships than in equivalent, offline relationships (Walther, 1996). Indeed, rapid and exaggerated intimacy can be part of the fun of online relationships (Rabby & Walther, 2003).

As the relationship escalates, it deepens and grows closer and partners tend to share greater physical contact. Physical contact may involve sitting closer together, leaning toward each other, more eye contact, and more touch. Such physical behaviors may or may not involve romantic feelings. Even friends increase physical contact with each other as the relationship develops, though females and males may differ in how they show physical contact in same- and opposite-sex friendships. Females may hold hands or hug other female friends, whereas males may slap hands in a high-five gesture or punch each other's arms as examples of physical contact in a developing relationship. Of course, cultural norms and age also affect how people engage in physical contact in relationships. Let's say the relationship between Whitney and Madeline is working out well. They spend time together, get to know each other well, and consider themselves to be close friends. By second semester, they hug each other when they return from spring break, share clothes, and do each other's hair, makeup, or nail polish.

Learning about another and developing a sense of relaxation and confirmation during interaction can occur in face-to-face or in online exchanges. Increasingly, the initial stage of relationship development may occur electronically (Ward & Tracy, 2004). Online communication may present a potentially less difficult way to meet and interact with others than traditional, face-to-face interactions. The initial interaction can occur in the comfort of your own home and at your own pace. You need not be concerned about physical aspects of the self or the other, and you can more

Many people enjoy the beginning stages of a relationship, when they're having fun getting to know another person.

© David Young-Wolff / PhotoEdit

precisely select what you are going to say (Ward & Tracy, 2004). For more on the differences between relationships in person and online, use your ThomsonNOW for *Communicate!* to access **Web Resources 6.5: In-Person versus Cyberspace Relationships**.

The need for physical contact seems to be an important aspect of relationship development, even for relationships that begin online. Two researchers of online relationships, James Katz and Philip Aspden (2004), have found that Internet relationships frequently lead to face-to-face meetings.

Many people who are escalating their relationship begin to share feelings and disclose more personal information, as well as depend upon each other for favors and support. At this stage, they are likely to seek each other out for help with a problem or talk for hours, sharing both the joys and the sorrows of their lives. Over time, Whitney and Madeline may share their innermost feelings with each other, cry on each others' shoulders during hard times, or lend each other money.

Maintaining a Relationship

Maintaining a relationship means that both people behave and communicate in ways that keep the relationship at a particular level of closeness or intimacy. Generally, the maintenance stage involves keeping the relationship from escalating to greater closeness or from moving to less closeness. Researchers have catalogued many strategies that people use to maintain relationships, including continuing to spend time with our partner, merging our social networks, and reciprocating unselfish acts (Rusbult, Olsen, Davis, & Hannon, 2004). Other ways that people maintain their relationships include continuing mutually acceptable levels of affection, self-disclosure, favors, and support.

maintaining a relationship behaving and communicating in ways that preserve a particular level of closeness or intimacy in a relationship.

You probably unconsciously use many of these techniques to maintain your relationships. In stable relationships, we choose to spend time with the other person. Most of the time, we do this in face-to-face conversations or on the phone, but increasingly, people are enjoying spending time in online interactions as well. We also maintain relationships by merging our social networks. As you become acquainted with other people who are important to your partner and your partner becomes acquainted with those you have relationships with, not only do you begin to appreciate your partner in a different context, but these mutual friends and relationships will act like a web that surrounds and supports your relationship with your partner. Finally, whatever type of relationship we are in (acquaintanceship, friendship, or intimacy), we will have established expectations for the kinds and frequency of unselfish acts that each of us will perform. Though individuals differ in the extent to which they will act selflessly, generally we are most likely to act selflessly with intimates, somewhat less willing with friends, and least willing with acquaintances.

Let's see how our roommates, Whitney and Madeline, use these strategies to maintain their friendship. Because they are both committed to the environment, they decide to join the campus chapter of the Student Environmental Action Coalition (SEAC), where they make a group of common friends. On parents' weekend they meet each other's parents, and when Whitney's best friend from high school visits, Madeline joins them at the gym and goes dancing with them in the evening. When Whitney falls and hurts her arm, perhaps Madeline breaks a date so that she can go with her to the emergency room.

De-Escalating and Ending a Relationship

Just as partners can develop their relationships to greater levels of intimacy and support, we can also behave in ways that weaken intimacy and support. Sometimes a relationship may become less satisfying to one or both relational partners. When this happens, one or both partners make a conscious decision to spend less time together, to develop more independence in social networks, and to engage in less selfless behavior. Other times, relationships deteriorate without either partner consciously feeling dissatisfied and deciding to change the relationship. Rather, deterioration occurs because the partners are not vigilant in doing those things necessary to maintain the relationship at its current level.

As your relationship becomes less intimate, it may devolve to a different level and stabilize there, or it may end. The communication in deteriorating relationships is marked by three phases: the recognition signs and hints of dissatisfaction, the process of disengaging behavior, and ending. Subtle signs of dissatisfaction include losing interest in the opinions and feelings of the other person, recognizing and emphasizing the other's faults while downplaying their virtues, and increasing the number of subjects that are off-limits or sources of conflict. As partners disengage, they become less willing to share ideas and feelings that were once commonly exchanged. They become more independent, less supportive, and indifferent to their partner.

Recognition of dissatisfaction The first sign that a relationship is de-escalating is a subtle indication of dissatisfaction. When one person begins to lose interest in the opinions and feelings of the other, the orientation of that person changes from *we* to *I*. The partners may begin to emphasize each other's faults and downplay virtues. Subjects that once yielded free and open discussion become off-limits or sources of conflict. As the relationship begins to be characterized by an increase in "touchy" subjects and more unresolved conflicts, partners become more defensive and less willing to foster a positive communication climate.

Disengaging If the relationship continues to be dissatisfying, people begin to drift apart. They become less willing to sacrifice for each other and they show less forgiveness. Their communication changes from deep sharing of ideas and feelings to small talk and other "safe" communication, to no significant communication at all. It may seem strange that people who had so much to share can find themselves with nothing to talk about. Not only are they no longer interested in exchanging significant ideas, they may begin to avoid each other altogether, seeking out other people with whom to share interests and activities. They depend less on each other and more upon other people for favors and support. Hostility need not be present; rather, this stage is likely to be marked by indifference.

So even though Whitney and Madeline have been very close during their first year at college, perhaps they develop new friendships and they each arrive at the separate decision that they want to room with someone different next year. As effective communicators, they would discuss their decisions with each other without blame or manipulation and acknowledge that their relationship is not as close as it once was. Over the summer, they may not interact and may drift apart. They move in with new roommates for the second year of college and see each other infrequently on campus. They talk at SEAC meetings and at a few parties, but they no longer have personal conversations, do not depend on each other for support, and do not have the same circle of friends. By the time they graduate, they have become so disengaged that there is little chance that they will continue to see each other.

Ending If the relationship can't be maintained at a less intimate level, it will end. A relationship has ended when the people no longer interact with each other. As Cupach and Metts (1986) show, people give many reasons for terminating relationships, including poor communication, lack of fulfillment, differing lifestyles and interests, rejection, outside interference, absence of rewards, and boredom.

At some point, one or both partners may decide that the relationship should end. Because many of us aren't skilled communicators, we may use manipulation ("This is

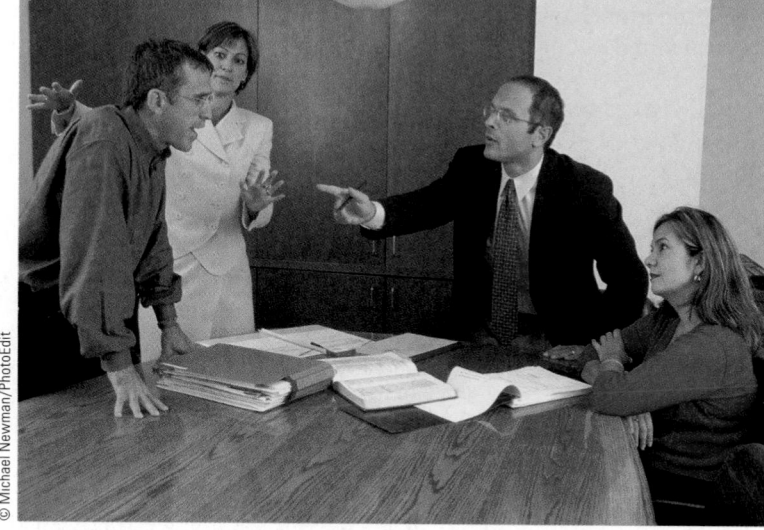

© Michael Newman/PhotoEdit

really the best thing for you"), withdrawal (spend less and less time together until you don't see each other at all), or avoidance (purposefully dodging the other) (Baxter, 1982). To end a deteriorating relationship, competent communicators should engage in a direct, open, and honest conversation. It is important to clearly state your wish to end the relationship, while being respectful of the other person and sensitive to the resulting emotions.

How relationships end depends on the interpersonal competence of both people. Do you know people who have amicable divorces? How do they differ from people who have hostile divorces?

What Would You Do?

Jeff and Magda, seniors at a small rural college, had been dating each other since they were freshmen. Jeff loved Magda and he planned to propose to her after they graduated in spring. At the same time, though, he reluctantly recognized that their relationship had fallen into a bit of a rut over the last six months or so, and he missed the excitement and romance of their first year together. Although he was troubled by these conflicting feelings, Jeff was unsure what to do about them.

One day while he was surfing MySpace.com, Jeff decided, on a whim, to create a fake user profile for the person he wanted to be in his fantasies. He spent quite a bit of time researching and designing the profile of his imaginary persona, a rap singer/flamenco guitarist/snowboarder/kung fu expert who went by the user name "MoonDog13." Jeff inserted photos of an obscure young Romanian actor he found online into MoonDog13's user profile. He posted lyrics to rap songs he wrote on MoonDog13's page and joined online user groups for those interested in flamenco guitar, snowboarding, and kung fu. In very little time, MoonDog13 had made a number of online friends, many of whom were admiring young women. MoonDog13 loved to flirt with these girls.

Jeff told Magda nothing about MoonDog13, even when the time he spent online managing the fictitious life of his alter ego began to interfere in his relationship with her. He justified this decision based on the belief that MoonDog13 was an imaginary figure who existed only in cyberspace. As long as fantasy didn't cross into reality, there was no reason Jeff had to feel guilty about anything MoonDog13 said or did.

1. How is Jeff acting ethically/unethically in this situation?

2. Like Jeff, people in general have a reputation of acting differently in cyberspace than they do in the real world. Are the ethics of cyberspace any different from those of the real world? What about fantasy—are the ethics of our private desires different from the real world? Are we ethically obliged to disclose our fantasies to our loved ones?

Conversation and Analysis

Go to your ThomsonNOW for *Communicate!* to access the video clip of Jan and Ken's conversation. (To learn how to access video via your ThomsonNOW, see the inside front and back covers of this book.) As you watch Jan and Ken talk, focus on how the nature of their relationship influences their interaction. What does each person do to help maintain the relationship? How does each person handle this conflict? How well does each person listen to the other? Are Jan and Ken appropriately assertive? Notice how well each provides feedback and describes feelings. You can respond to these analysis questions by clicking on "Analysis" in the menu bar at the top of the screen. When you've answered all the questions, click "Done" to compare your answers to those provided by the authors.

A transcript of the conversation is printed here. You can also find a copy of this transcript online, which allows you to take notes as you watch the video. Go to your ThomsonNOW for *Communicate!* to access **Skill Learning Activity 6.3**. When you have finished viewing the video and taking notes,

Thomson NOW!

click on "Authors' Model Analysis" to compare your notes to the detailed conversational analysis provided by the authors.

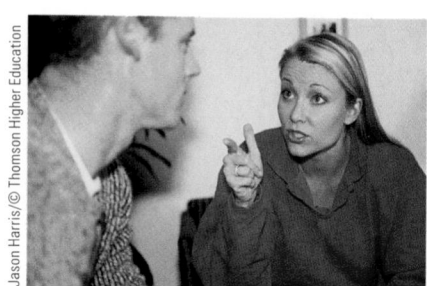

Jason Harris/© Thomson Higher Education

Jan and Ken are in their early to middle twenties. They meet at Jan's apartment. Jan and Ken have been good friends for most of their lives. But because of what she said last week, Ken believes Jan has betrayed their friendship.

Conversation

KEN: Jan, we need to talk. Why'd you tell Shannon about what happened between Katie and me? Now Shannon doesn't want to talk to me.

JAN [*Silent for a moment as she realizes that he knows*]: Ken, I'm sorry, I didn't mean to tell her. It just kind of slipped out when we were talking.

KEN: Sorry? Sorry is not enough. I told you that in private, and you promised that you'd keep it just between you and me.

JAN: Ken, I told her that long before the two of you started dating. You know, Shannon and I, we've been friends for a long time. We were just talking about guys and cheating and stuff. It wasn't about you specifically.

KEN: It wasn't about me? It was totally about me. You had no right to tell anyone that, under any circumstances. Now Shannon doesn't trust me. She thinks I'm a lowlife that sleeps around.

JAN: Well, I'm sorry, but the two of you weren't even dating yet.

KEN: Oh, that's irrelevant. You know, it would be irrelevant even if Shannon and I weren't dating. But, you know, the point is I thought I could trust you and tell you anything and that it would go no further.

JAN: Yeah, like the time I told you I was thinking about dropping out of school for a semester and you just happened to tell my dad?

KEN: Ah, that's not the same thing.

JAN: You know what? It's *exactly* the same. I trusted you and you squealed. My dad lit into me big-time. He should have never known I was thinking about that. I trusted you, and you betrayed me.

KEN: Well look, I was just trying to look out for you. I knew you were making a big mistake, and I was just trying to stop you. And besides, you know I was right! [*Gets discouraged*] Don't change the subject here. Are you saying that your telling Shannon is some sort of payback for me telling your dad?

JAN: No, I'm just trying to point out that you've got no right to throw stones!

KEN: You know what? Then maybe neither of us can trust the other. Maybe we just shouldn't tell each other anything that we don't want broadcast to the world, huh?

JAN: Don't be such a jerk. I'm sorry, OK?

KEN: Well, that's not good enough. You ruined any chance I had with her.

JAN: Are you saying that something I said about what you did a long time ago is ruining your chances?

KEN: Yeah, it might.

JAN: Ken, if she truly valued your friendship, something that you did a long time ago shouldn't matter.

KEN: Well, maybe you're right.

JAN: Look, I said I'm sorry, and I meant it. I'm also sorry about, you know, throwing in what you told my dad. I know that wasn't fair, but you know, you really hurt my feelings when you blew up at me like that.

KEN: Listen, listen, I shouldn't have, and I shouldn't have told your dad. I should have probably encouraged you to talk to him. We still friends?

Summary

Interpersonal communication helps develop and maintain relationships. A good relationship is any mutually satisfying interaction with another person. We have three types of relationships. Acquaintances are people we know by name and talk with, but with whom our interactions are limited in quality and quantity. Friendships are marked by degrees of warmth and affection, trust, self-disclosure, commitment, and expectation that the relationships will endure. Close or intimate friends are those with whom we share a high degree of commitment, trust, interdependence, disclosure, and enjoyment. A healthy relationship is marked by a balance of self-disclosure and feedback. The Johari window is a tool for analyzing this balance.

Relationships go through a life cycle that includes building and developing, maintaining, and perhaps de-escalating and ending. In the first stage of beginning and developing a relationship, we try to get to know each other to reduce uncertainty, we develop feelings of relaxation and confirmation, and we experience greater levels of disclosure and support. There are various ways to maintain a relationship including spending time together, merging social networks, doing unselfish acts, and exchanging affection, self-disclosure, favors, and support. When relationships start to deteriorate, we tend to recognize feelings of dissatisfaction, notice each other's faults, experience more conflict, discuss only safe topics, and spend less time together. Effective communicators consciously end relationships with direct, open, and honest communication rather than manipulation, withdrawal, or avoidance.

Thomson NOW!
Communicate! Online

Now that you have read Chapter 6, use your ThomsonNOW for *Communicate!* for quick access to the electronic resources that accompany this text. Your ThomsonNOW gives you access to the video of the conversation between Jan and Ken on pages 139–140, the Web Resources and Skill Learning Activities featured in this chapter, InfoTrac College Edition, and online study aids such as a digital glossary and review quizzes.

Your *Communicate!* ThomsonNOW is an online study system that helps you identify concepts you don't fully understand, allowing you to put your study time to the best use. Using chapter-by-chapter diagnostic pre-tests, the system creates a personalized study plan for each chapter. Each plan directs you to specific resources designed to improve your understanding, including pages from the text in e-book format. Chapter post-tests give you an opportunity to measure how much you've learned and let you know if you are ready for graded quizzes and exams.

Key Terms

Go to your ThomsonNOW for *Communicate!* to access your online glossary for Chapter 6. Print a copy of the glossary for this chapter and test yourself with the electronic flash cards or complete the crossword puzzle to help you master these key terms:

acquaintances (126)
close friends or intimates
    (128)
feedback (130)
friends (127)

good relationships (126)
Johari window (130)
maintaining a relationship
    (135)
platonic relationship (128)

relationships (126)
romantic relationship (128)
self-disclosure (130)
trust (128)

Review Quiz

Test your knowledge of the concepts in this chapter by taking the online review quiz for Chapter 6. Go to your ThomsonNOW for *Communicate!* to access the quiz. When you have completed the quiz, submit it for scoring.

Skill Learning Activities

Go to your ThomsonNOW for *Communicate!* to complete the Observe & Analyze and Conversation and Analysis activities for Chapter 6. You can submit your Observe & Analyze answers to your instructor. You can also submit your Conversation and Analysis answers to your instructor, as well as compare your answers to those provided by the authors.

6.1: Observe & Analyze: Distinguishing between Types of Relationships (129)
6.2: Observe & Analyze: Johari Window (132)
6.3: Conversation and Analysis: Jan and Ken (138)

Web Resources

Go to your ThomsonNOW for *Communicate!* to access the Web Resources for this chapter.

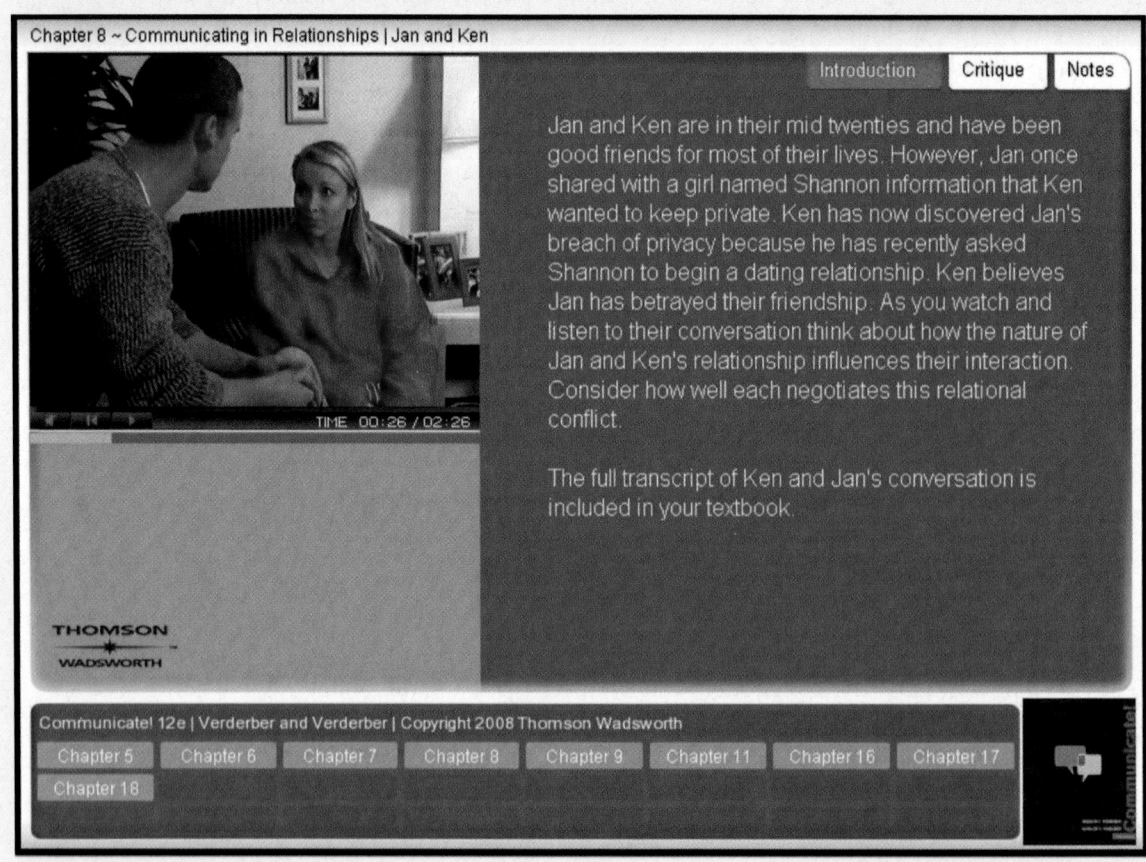

Chapter 8 ~ Communicating in Relationships | Jan and Ken

Introduction | Critique | Notes

Jan and Ken are in their mid twenties and have been good friends for most of their lives. However, Jan once shared with a girl named Shannon information that Ken wanted to keep private. Ken has now discovered Jan's breach of privacy because he has recently asked Shannon to begin a dating relationship. Ken believes Jan has betrayed their friendship. As you watch and listen to their conversation think about how the nature of Jan and Ken's relationship influences their interaction. Consider how well each negotiates this relational conflict.

The full transcript of Ken and Jan's conversation is included in your textbook.

TIME 00:26 / 02:26

THOMSON
WADSWORTH

Communicate! 12e | Verderber and Verderber | Copyright 2008 Thomson Wadsworth

Chapter 5 | Chapter 6 | Chapter 7 | Chapter 8 | Chapter 9 | Chapter 11 | Chapter 16 | Chapter 17 | Chapter 18

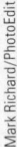

**After you have read this chapter, you should be able to answer
these questions:**

- What five processes are used during listening?
- How can you focus your attention?
- How can you increase your understanding?
- What is empathy?
- How can questioning increase understanding?
- What is paraphrasing?
- What are three tactics that can help you remember what you hear?
- How can you evaluate what you've heard?
- What characterizes support messages?
- What specific verbal messages provide comfort?

7

Listening and Responding

"Garson, do you have an extra key to the media cabinet? I misplaced mine, and I have to get into it right away."

"No, I don't have a key, but it doesn't matter because . . ."

"I can't believe it. When I left home this morning, I was sure I had it."

"Bart, it's OK . . ."

"I pulled out my keys—but I just had my car key and main door key."

"Bart, I've been trying to tell you, just try the . . ."

"It's just like me. I think I've got everything, but just before I check the last time, Sue will say something to me and I get sidetracked. Then I just take off."

"Bart, chill out. The door's . . ."

"Chill out?! If I can't get the DVD for the meeting, I'll get torn apart. We've got six advertising people coming from all over the city just to see the DVD. What am I supposed to say to them?"

"Bart, you don't have to say anything. I've been trying to . . ."

"Oh sure—I just go in there and say, 'By the way, the DVD of the new ad campaign is locked up in the cabinet and I left my key at home.' Come on, Garson—who's got the other key?"

"Bart, listen!!! I've been trying to tell you—Miller was in the cabinet and, knowing you'd be along in a minute, he left the door open."

"Well, why didn't you tell me?"

A re you a good listener when you are under pressure? Or, like Bart, do you occasionally find that your mind wanders when others are talking to you? Listening is a key communication skill, yet less than 2 percent of us have had any formal listening training (Listening Factoid, 2003). Most of us can improve our listening skills. We must not underestimate the importance of listening, which can provide clarification, connect us to others, build trust and empathy, help us learn and remember material, and improve our evaluation of information (Donoghue & Siegel, 2005).

Judi Brownell (2002) points out that members of the International Listening Association offer this definition of listening: "**Listening** is the process of receiving, constructing meaning from, and responding to spoken and/or nonverbal messages" (p. 48). Incorporated within this definition are the processes of attending, understanding, remembering, evaluating, and responding. You can begin your study of listening by completing an inventory of your listening skills. Use your ThomsonNOW for *Communicate!* to access **Web Resource 7.1: Listening Inventory**. The feedback from this inventory may help you pinpoint specific processes you need to improve.

listening
the process of receiving, constructing meaning from, and responding to spoken and/or nonverbal messages.

Attending

attending
the perceptual process of selecting and focusing on specific stimuli from the countless stimuli reaching the senses.

Attending is the perceptual process of selecting and focusing on specific stimuli from the countless stimuli reaching the senses. Recall from Chapter 2 that we attend to information that interests us and meets physical and psychological needs. But to be a good listener, we must train ourselves to attend to what people are saying regardless of our interest or needs. Let's consider four techniques for consciously focusing attention.

1. **Get physically and mentally ready to listen.** Physically, good listeners create a physical environment helpful for listening and adopt a listening posture. Creating a physical environment means eliminating distractions. If the music is playing so loudly that it competes with your roommate who is trying to talk with you, turn it down. The physical posture that is helpful when listening is one that moves the listener toward the speaker, allows direct eye contact and stimulates the senses. For instance, when the professor tells the class that the next bit of information will be on the test, effective listeners are likely to sit upright in their chairs, lean slightly forward, cease any extraneous physical movement, and look directly at the professor. Likewise, mentally they will focus their attention by blocking out miscellaneous thoughts.

2. **Make the shift from speaker to listener a complete one.** In conversation, we are called on to switch back and forth from speaker to listener so frequently that we may find it difficult at times to make these shifts completely. Instead of listening, it is easy to rehearse what you are going to say as soon as you have a chance. It is especially important when trying to be a good listener that you let the other person finish before you

take your turn to speak. Good listeners resist interrupting others. Especially when you are in a heated conversation or excited about what you just heard, you will consciously need to stop yourself from preparing a response or interrupting the speaker instead of listening completely.

3. **Hear a person out before you react.** Far too often, we stop listening before the person has finished speaking because we think we know what the person is going to say. Yet often we are wrong. In addition, we often stop listening to people because their mannerisms and words "turn us off." Think of the times you may have stopped listening to a professor's lecture and missed important information because of the teacher's accent or gestures. Most of us need to learn the value of patience and silence in freeing others to express themselves and helping us to listen closely and carefully.

4. **Observe nonverbal cues.** Listeners interpret messages more accurately when they observe the nonverbal behaviors accompanying the words. For instance, when Deborah says, "Don't worry about me. I'm fine, really," we must interpret cues such as tone of voice, body actions, and facial expression to tell whether she is really fine or whether she is upset but reluctant to tell you about it.

Understanding

Understanding is decoding a message accurately to reflect the meaning intended by the speaker. Sometimes we do not understand because the message is encoded in words that are not in our vocabulary, but most of our misunderstanding stems from passive listening. *Active listening* requires us to use empathy, questioning, and paraphrasing so that we understand both the message content and the speaker's intent.

understanding
decoding a message accurately to reflect the meaning intended by the speaker.

Empathy

Empathy is intellectually identifying with or vicariously experiencing the feelings or attitudes of another. Or, as Jon Hayes (2002) says, letting people "know that they have been understood from within their own frame of reference and that they can see the world as they see it while remaining separate from it" (p. 183). To empathize, we generally try to put aside our own feelings or attitudes about another. Three approaches people use when empathizing are empathic responsiveness, perspective taking, and sympathetic responsiveness (Weaver & Kirtley, 1995, p. 131).

empathy
intellectually identifying with or vicariously experiencing the feelings or attitudes of another.

Empathic responsiveness occurs when you experience an emotional response parallel to, and as a result of observing, another person's actual or anticipated display of emotion (Omdahl, 1995, p. 4; Stiff et al., 1988, p. 199). For instance, when Jackson tells James that he is in real trouble financially, and James senses the stress and anxiety that Jackson is feeling, we would say that James has experienced empathic responsiveness.

empathic responsiveness
experiencing an emotional response parallel to, and as a result observing, another person's actual or anticipated display of emotion.

perspective taking
imagining yourself in the place of another; the most common form of empathizing.

Perspective taking, imagining yourself in the place of another, is the most common form of empathizing. Although perspective taking is difficult for many of us (Holtgraves, 2002, p. 122), with conscious effort we can learn to imagine ourselves in the place of another. For example, if James personalizes the message by picturing himself in serious financial debt, anticipates the emotions he might experience, and then assumes that Jackson might be feeling the same way, then James is empathizing by perspective taking.

sympathetic responsiveness
feeling concern, compassion, or sorrow for another because of the other's situation or plight.

Sympathetic responsiveness is feeling concern, compassion, or sorrow for another because of the other's situation or plight. Having *sympathy* differs from the other two approaches. Rather than attempting to experience the feelings of the other, when you sympathize, you translate your intellectual understanding of what the speaker has experienced into your own feelings of concern, compassion, and sorrow for that person. In our previous example, James has sympathy for Jackson when he understands that Jackson is embarrassed and worried, but instead of trying to feel those same emotions, he feels concern and compassion for his friend. Because of this difference in perspective, many scholars differentiate sympathy from empathy.

"*Cheer up, Nicole! What does Princeton know? Say, you got any plans for that last bit of cobbler?*"

How well you empathize also depends on how observant you are of others' behavior and how clearly you "read" the nonverbal messages they are sending. To improve your observational skills, try this. When another person begins a conversation with you, develop the habit of silently posing two questions to yourself: (1) What emotions do I believe the person is experiencing right now? and (2) What cues is the person giving that I am using to draw this conclusion? Consciously asking these questions helps you focus your attention on the nonverbal aspects of messages, which convey most of the information on the person's emotional state.

To further increase the accuracy of reading emotions, we can use the skill of perception checking (introduced in Chapter 2). This is especially helpful when the other person's culture is different from our own. Let's consider an example. Suppose Jerry says that he feels embarrassed when people comment on how old he is to be wearing braces. His friend Mary might empathize by concentrating on the feelings he shows with both his verbal and nonverbal messages, and then she may show that she understands by saying, "I can understand your embarrassment—I might even be depressed if that kept happening to me." To explore additional suggestions for developing empathy, use your ThomsonNow for *Communicate!* to access **Web Resource 7.2: Listening and Empathy Responding**.

Thomson NOW!

Questioning

question
a statement designed to get further information or to clarify information already received.

Active listeners ask questions to get the information they need to understand. A **question** is a statement designed to get further information or to clarify information already received. Although you may have asked questions for as long as you can remember, you may notice that, at times, your questions don't get the information you want or irritate, fluster, or cause defensiveness. We can increase the chances that our questions will get us the information we want and reduce negative reactions if we observe these guidelines.

1. **Recognize the kind of information you need to increase your understanding.** Suppose Maria says to you, "I am totally frustrated. Would you stop at the store on the way home and buy me some more paper?" At this point, you may be a bit confused and need more information to understand. Yet if you simply respond "What do you mean?" Maria, who is already uptight may become defensive. To solicit the information you need, you might recognize one of the three types of information needs you have, and form a question to meet that need. You probably will not know precisely what you do not understand. To increase your understanding, you might ask Maria one of these three types of questions:

   ■ *Get details:* "What kind of paper would you like me to get, and how much will you need?"

   ■ *Clarify word meanings:* "Could you tell me what you mean by 'frustrated'?"

   ■ *Clarify feelings:* "What's frustrating you?"

2. **Monitor your nonverbal cues so that they convey genuine interest and concern.** Ask questions with a tone of voice that is sincere—not a tone that could be interpreted as bored, sarcastic, cutting, superior, dogmatic, or evaluative. We need to constantly remind ourselves that the way we speak may be even more important than the words we use. Sometimes, asking several questions in a row can seem like an interrogation. If you need to ask several questions, you might explain why you are asking them by saying something like, "I really want to understand what you are saying, so I need to ask a few questions. Is that OK?"

3. **Put the "burden of ignorance" on your own shoulders.** To minimize defensive reactions, especially when people are under stress, phrase your questions to put the burden of ignorance on your own shoulders. Preface your question with a short statement that suggests that any problem of misunderstanding may be the result of *your* listening skills. For instance, when Drew says "I've really had it with Malone screwing up all the time," you might say, "Drew, I'm sorry, I'm missing some details that would help me understand your feelings better—what kinds of things has Malone been doing?"

Here are two more examples that contrast inappropriate with more appropriate questioning responses.

TAMARA: They turned down my proposal again!

ART [*Inappropriate*]: Well, did you explain it the way you should have?

[*This question is a veiled attack on Tamara in question form.*]

OBSERVE & ANALYZE

Journal Activity

Empathizing Effectively

Write a paragraph describing a time when you effectively empathized with another person. What was the person's emotional state? How did you recognize it? What were the nonverbal cues? Verbal cues? What type of relationship did you have with this person? How similar were the two of you? What type of empathizing did you use? Why?

Thomson NOW! You can complete this activity online and, if requested, e-mail it to your instructor. Use your Thomson-NOW for *Communicate!* to access **Skill Learning Activity 7.1**.

paraphrasing
putting into words the ideas or feelings you have perceived from the message.

content paraphrase
one that focuses on the denotative meaning of the message.

feelings paraphrase
a response that captures the emotions attached to the content of the message.

remembering
being able to retain information and recall it when needed.

[*Appropriate*] Did they tell you why? [*This question is a sincere request for additional information.*]

RENEE: With all those executives at the party last night, I really felt strange.

JAVIER [*Inappropriate*]: Why? [*With this abrupt question, Javier is making no effort to be sensitive to Renee's feelings or to understand them.*]

[*Appropriate*] What is it about your bosses' presence that makes you feel strange? [*Here the question is phrased to elicit information that will help Javier understand, and it also may help Renee understand.*]

Paraphrasing

In addition to being skilled questioners, active listeners are also adept at **paraphrasing,** that is, putting into words the ideas or feelings you have perceived from the message. For example, during an argument with your sister, after she has stated her concern about your behavior, you might paraphrase what she has said as follows: "You say that you are tired of my talking about work and that you feel that I try to act better than you when I talk about my successes at work." Paraphrases may focus on content, on feelings underlying the content, or on both. A **content paraphrase** focuses on the denotative meaning of the message. The first part of the example above (You say that you are tired of my talking about work) is a content paraphrase. A **feelings paraphrase** is a response that captures the emotions attached to the content of the message. The second part of the example (you feel that I try to act better than you) is a feelings paraphrase.

By paraphrasing, you give the speaker a chance to verify your understanding. The longer and more complex the message, the more important it is to paraphrase. When the speaker appears to be emotional or when English is not the speaker's native language, paraphrasing is also important.

To paraphrase effectively, (1) listen carefully to the message, (2) notice what images and feelings you have experienced from the message, (3) determine what the message means to you, and (4) create a message that conveys these images or feelings.

Remembering: Retaining Information

Remembering is being able to retain information and recall it when needed. Too often, people forget almost immediately what they have heard. For instance, you can probably think of many times when you were unable to recall the name of a person to whom you were introduced just moments earlier. Think of how much the education system depends on listening and recalling information. Given the common use of lectures, class discussions, and other listening-based learning experiences, it is not surprising that research shows a link between effective listening and school success

Communication Skill <u>Paraphrasing</u>

Skill	Use	Procedure	Example
A response that conveys your understanding of another person's message.	To increase listening efficiency; to avoid message confusion; to discover the speaker's motivation.	1. Listen carefully to the message. 2. Notice what images and feelings you have experienced from this message. 3. Determine what the message means to you. 4. Create a message that conveys these images or feelings.	Grace says, "At two minutes to five, the boss gave me three letters that had to be in the mail that evening!" Bonita replies, "If I understand, you were really resentful that your boss dumped important work on you right before quitting time when she knows you have to pick up the baby at day care."

Skill Building <u>Questions and Paraphrases</u>

Provide an appropriate question and paraphrase for each of these statements. To get you started, look at this authors' model:

Example: "It's Dionne's birthday, and I've planned a *big* evening. Sometimes I think Dionne believes I take her for granted—well, after tonight she'll know I think she's something special!"

Question: "What specific things do you have planned?"

Paraphrase: "If I'm understanding you, you're really proud that you've planned a night that's going to be a lot more elaborate than what Dionne expects on her birthday."

1. Luis: "It was just another mind-numbing class. I keep thinking one of these days Professor Romero will get excited about something. He is a real bore!"

2. Angie: "Everyone seems to be raving about the new reality show on Channel 5 last night, but I didn't see it. You know, I don't watch the 'boob tube.'"

3. Kaelin: "I don't know if it's me or Mom, but lately she and I just aren't getting along."

4. Aileen: "I've got a report due at work and a paper due in management class. On top of that, it's my sister's birthday, and so far I haven't even had time to get her anything. Tomorrow's going to be a disaster."

Thomson NOW! You can complete this activity online and compare your answers to the authors'. Use your Thomson-NOW for *Communicate!* to access **Skill Learning Activity 7.2.**

(Bommelje, Houston, & Smither, 2003). Three techniques that can help you improve your ability to remember information are repeating, constructing mnemonics, and taking notes.

Repeat Information

Repetition—saying something two, three, or even four times—helps listeners store information in long-term memory by providing necessary reinforcement (Estes, 1989, p. 7). If information is not reinforced, it will be held in short-term memory for as little as 20 seconds and then forgotten. So, when you are introduced to a stranger named Jack McNeil, if you mentally say "Jack McNeil, Jack McNeil, Jack McNeil, Jack McNeil," you increase the chances that you will remember his name. Likewise, when you receive the directions "Go two blocks east, turn left, turn right at the next light, and it's in the next block," you can immediately repeat to yourself "two blocks east, turn left, turn right at light, next block—that's two blocks east, turn left, turn right at light, next block."

Construct Mnemonics

mnemonic device
any artificial technique used as a memory aid.

Constructing mnemonics helps listeners put information in forms that are more easily recalled. A **mnemonic device** is any artificial technique used as a memory aid. One of the most common ways of forming a mnemonic is to use the first letters of a list of items you are trying to remember to form a word. For example, an easy mnemonic for remembering the five Great Lakes is HOMES (*H*uron, *O*ntario, *M*ichigan, *E*rie, *S*uperior).

When you want to remember items in a sequence, you can form a sentence with the words themselves or assign words using the first letters of the words in sequence to form an easy-to-remember statement. For example, when you studied music the first time, you may have learned the notes on the lines of the treble clef (E, G, B, D, F) with the saying "*every good boy does fine*." (And for the notes on the treble clef spaces, F, A, C, E, you may have remembered the word *face*.) To practice creating mnemonics, go to your ThomsonNOW for *Communicate!* to access **Skill Learning Activity 7.3: Creating Mnemonics**. You can read more about mnemonic techniques at MindTools.com—use your ThomsonNOW for *Communicate!* to access **Web Resource 7.3: Mnemonics**.

Thomson™
NOW!

Take Notes

Although note taking would be inappropriate in the most casual interpersonal encounters, it represents a powerful tool for increasing your recall of information when you are involved in conversations where important information you need to remember is being shared. Note taking has been shown to be an important strategy for learners when they attempt to listen to and absorb information from lecture-type speech (Dunkel & Pialorsi, 2005). Note taking does more than provide a written record that you can go back to; it also allows you to take an active role in the listening process (Wolvin & Coakley, 1996, p. 239).

Useful notes may consist of a brief list of main points or key ideas, plus a few of the most significant details. Or they may be a short summary of the entire concept (a type of paraphrase) after the message is completed. For lengthy and rather detailed information, however, good notes likely will consist of a brief outline of what the speaker has said, including the overall idea, the main points of the message, and key developmental material.

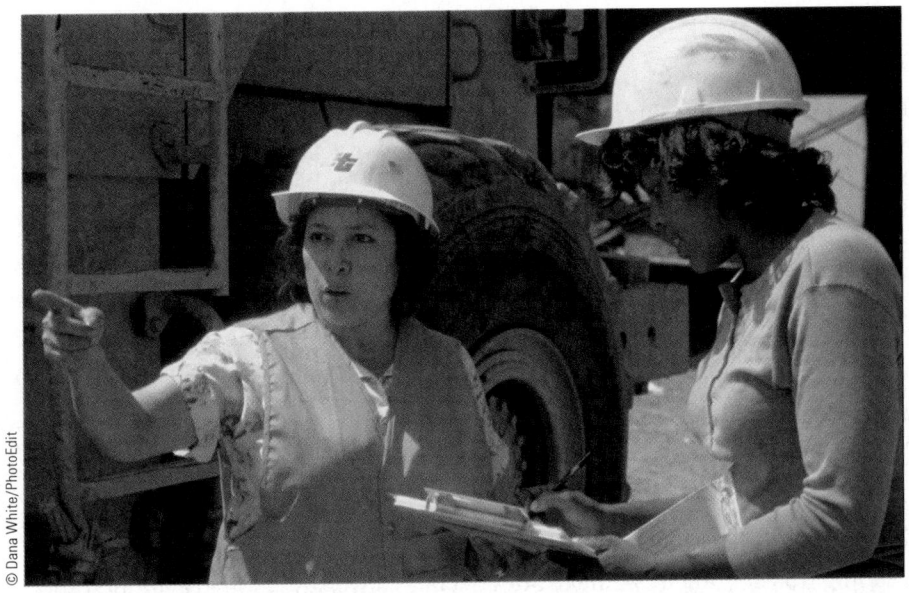

© Dana White/PhotoEdit

Effective managers understand the value of making notes about problems that employees point out. How can you use note taking at work to improve your performance?

Good notes are not necessarily very long. In fact, many classroom lectures can be reduced to a short outline of notes. Figure 7.1 is an example of this and is based on the material in this chapter. To complete an activity that will help you evaluate how well you remember what you hear, with or without notes, go to your ThomsonNOW for *Communicate!* to access **Skill Learning Activity 7.4: Listening to Remember.**

Thomson NOW!

Attend—focus
- Get ready (physically & mentally)
- Make complete shift (don't rehearse)
- Hear person out (don't check out or interrupt)

Understand—use active listening
- Empathize
- Ask questions (clarify words & feelings & get details)
- Paraphrase (content & feelings)

Remember
- Repeat info.
- Construct mnemonics (e.g., Great Lakes, HOMES)
- Take notes

Evaluate
- Separate facts from inferences

Respond supportively
- Supportive messages characteristics: aim to help, accept other, demonstrate concern, availability to listen, ally, acknowledge & validate feelings, encourage elaboration
- Supporting positive feelings
- Giving comfort: clarify intentions, politeness, other-centered messages, reframe, advice

Figure 7.1
Notes based on a lecture on listening

Evaluate or Critically Analyze

The fourth listening process is to critically analyze what has been said. **Critical analysis** is the process of evaluating what you have heard to determine its truthfulness. Critical listening is especially important when you are asked to believe, act on, or support what is being said. For instance, if a person is trying to convince you to vote for a particular candidate, or support efforts to legalize gay marriage, or buy an expensive gadget, you will want to listen critically so that you can evaluate the information and arguments presented. If you don't critically analyze what you hear, you risk going along with ideas or plans that may violate your values, are counterproductive to your interests, or mislead others (including the speaker) who value your judgment.

One important skill of critical analysis is to separate statements of fact from statements based on inference. **Factual statements** are those whose accuracy can be verified or proven. **Inferences** are statements made by the speaker that are based on facts or observations. If we comment, "You are reading this sentence" we have stated a fact. If we say, "You are understanding and enjoying what you are reading," we have made an inference.

Separating factual statements from inferences begins by recognizing whether what has been said is an established fact, or whether it is an opinion that may be related to a fact. If the statement is a fact, we need to determine if the fact that was stated is true because people sometimes make things up and pass them off as facts. If the statement is an inference, then we need to further evaluate it to see if the inference is valid. An inference may be false, even when it is based on observable facts. For instance, you are reading this sentence, you may even be nodding your head and smiling, but these facts do not alone provide proof of either your understanding or your enjoyment.

When we have determined that a statement is an inference, we need to test to see whether it is a valid inference. To do this we can ask ourselves (or the speaker) three questions: (1) What are the facts that support this inference? (2) Is this information really central to the inference? (3) Are there other facts or information that would contradict this inference? For example, when we hear "Better watch it—Katie's in one bad mood today. Did you catch the look on her face? That's one unhappy girl," we should stop and think, is Katie really in a bad mood? The fact that supports this is her facial expression. Is this fact accurate? Is Katie really looking unhappy or angry? Is the look on her face enough to conclude that she's in a bad mood? Or does Katie normally look unhappy? Is the look on her face really key to determining her mood? Or are there other cues that those of us who know her would expect to see? Is there anything else about Katie's behavior today that could lead us to believe that she's not in a bad mood? To practice evaluating inferences, go to your ThomsonNOW for *Communicate!* to access **Skill Learning Activity 7.5: Evaluating Inferences**.

OBSERVE & ANALYZE

Journal Activity

Critically Analyzing the Use of Facts and Inferences in the Media

Watch a political talk show and an infomercial on television. If possible, record the two programs so you can watch them more than once. While you are watching the programs, note as many individual factual statements and inferences in each program as you can. Next, write a paragraph in which you answer these questions: What was the ratio of factual statements to inferences in the two programs (for example, 1-to-1, 1-to-2, and so on)? Did these results surprise you? If so, how? Were the ratios different for the two programs? If so, how did the results conform to or deviate from your expectations? How

(continued on p. 155)

▶ Speech Assignment: Communicate on Your Feet

Critical Listening

Find and attend a formal public presentation that is being given on campus or in your community. Your goal is to listen so that you remember and can critically evaluate what you have heard. Be sure to take notes and record the main ideas the speaker presents. After you have heard the speech, analyze what you heard. You can use the following questions to guide your initial thinking:

■ What was the purpose of the speech? What was the speaker trying to explain to you or convince you about?

■ Was it easy or difficult to identify the speaker's main ideas? What did you notice about how the speaker developed each point she or he made?

■ Did the speaker use examples or tell stories to develop a point? If so, were these typical examples, or did the speaker choose examples that were unusual but seemed to "prove the point"?

■ Did the speaker use statistics to back up what was said? If so, did the speaker tell you where the statistics came from? Did the statistics surprise you? If so, what would you have needed to hear that would have helped you to accept them as accurate?

■ Do you think that the speaker did a good job? If so, why? If not, what should the speaker have done to be more effective?

When you have finished your analysis, follow your instructor's directions. You may be asked to write a short essay about the speech or to present what you learned to the class.

You are listening critically when you (1) separate facts from inferences, (2) analyze the "facts" to determine if they are true, and (3) test to see whether inferences are valid.

Responding Supportively to Give Comfort

Many times as we are listening, we recognize that the speaker is emotionally distressed and in need of comfort. We can respond supportively by confirming the speaker's feelings and providing emotional comfort. To **comfort** means to help people feel better about themselves and their behavior. Comforting occurs when one feels respected, understood, and confirmed.

Over the years, much of the groundbreaking scholarship on comforting has been done by Brant Burleson and his colleagues. Brant Burleson is featured in this chapter's Spotlight on Scholars.

Characteristics of Effective and Ineffective Emotional Support Messages

Supportive messages are comforting statements that have a goal to reassure, bolster, encourage, soothe, console, or cheer up. Supportive messages are helpful and provide comfort because they create a conversational environment that encourages the person needing support to talk about and

(continued from p. 154) did evaluating the inferences used in the two programs change your perception of their messages?

You can use your Student Workbook to complete this activity, or you can complete it online, download a log to use, and, if requested, email it to your instructor. Use your ThomsonNOW for *Communicate!* to access **Skill Learning Activity 7.6**.

---

comfort
to help people feel better about themselves and their behavior.

supportive messages
comforting statements that have a goal to reassure, bolster, encourage, soothe, console, or cheer up.

Spotlight on Scholars   Brant Burleson   Professor of Communication at Purdue University, on Comforting

Brant Burleson's interest in comforting behavior began during his undergraduate days at the University of Colorado at Boulder, where he was taught that all communication was persuasion. This proposition did not square with Burleson's own experiences. During the social turmoil of the 1960s, he had witnessed much hurt and conflict, but he had also seen people engaging in altruism and acts of comforting. These comforting acts, he reasoned, were not aimed at persuading anyone to change their opinion or behavior. They were simply done to help other people.

When Burleson entered graduate school at the University of Illinois, he began to formally study how individuals comfort others. He wanted to scientifically evaluate the social relevance of comforting messages.

In his research, Burleson has carefully defined comforting strategies as messages that have the goal of relieving or lessening the emotional distress of others. He has limited his work to looking at the verbal strategies people use to comfort others who are experiencing mild or moderate sadness or disappointment during everyday events. Burleson's care in defining the "domain" of his work is important. By carefully stating the type of emotional distress he is concerned with, and by clearly identifying the limits of his work, Burleson enables those who read his work to understand the types of situations to which his findings apply.

Burleson and others who study comforting seek to understanding the results of comforting. Previous research has judged comforting messages only on the extent to which they reduce the immediate distress a person is feeling. Burleson believes the effects of comforting extend beyond this effect. He theorizes that effective comforting should also help the person being comforted

Courtesy Brant Burleson

improve the quality of his or her relationship with the comforter, be able to cope better in the future, and possibly even improve his or her physical health. Skilled comforting should also benefit the comforter. When we effectively comfort others, Burleson believes we increase our own self-esteem. We also become better liked by the person we comfort and by those who see us effectively comfort others. Finally, Burleson believes those who are effective at comforting others are likely to have better long-term relationships. A growing list of research studies, some conducted by Burleson and his colleagues, provide support for his theory.

To better understand just why comforting messages help people feel better when other messages don't do anything—or even make people feel worse—Burleson has recently studied theories and research on emotion and factors that lead to emotional distress. This study of emotion dynamics has led to a new understanding of comforting as a conversational process that, at its best, helps distressed others make sense of what has happened to them, work through their feelings, and reappraise the upsetting situation. This view of the comforting process emphasizes the role of empathic listening and the importance of getting upset people to talk about their feelings and experiences in detail. People seem to make sense of their distressing experiences by expressing their thoughts and feelings in narratives or stories. Burleson and his graduate students are currently conducting several studies on sense-making narratives and how these narratives contribute to the reduction of emotional distress.

For more information on Burleson's research, consult the reference list at the back of the book and go to http://www.cla.purdue.edu/communication//html/people/pages/brantburleson.htm.

make sense of the situation that is causing distress. In recent studies, Burleson found that effective supportive messages had these characteristics (Burleson, 2003, pp. 565–568):

1. They clearly state that the speaker's aim is to help the other.
   Example: "I'd like to help you, what can I do?"

2. They express acceptance or affection for the other; they do not condemn or criticize.
   Example: "I understand that you just can't seem to accept this."

3. They demonstrate care, concern, and interest in the other's situation; they do not focus on a lengthy recount of a similar situation.
   Example: "What are you planning to do now?" Or "Gosh, tell me more; what happened then?"

4. They indicate that the speaker is available to listen and support the other without intruding.
   Example: "I know we've not been that close, but sometimes it helps to have someone to listen, and I'd like to do that for you."

5. They state that the speaker is an ally.
   Example: "I'm with you on this." Or "Well, I'm on your side; this isn't right."

6. They acknowledge the other's feelings and situation as well as express sincere sympathy; they do not condemn or criticize the other's behavior or feelings.
   Example: "I'm so sorry to see you feeling so bad; I can see that you're devastated by what has happened."

7. They assure the other that what he or she is feeling is legitimate; they do not tell the other how to feel or that the other should ignore his or her feelings.
   Example: "With what has happened to you, you have a right to be angry."

8. They encourage the other to elaborate on his or her story.
   Example: "Uh-huh," "yeah," or "I see. How did you feel about that?" or "Well, what happened before that, can you elaborate?"

Supporting does not mean making false statements or only telling someone what he or she wants to hear. Effective supporting responses are in touch with the facts but focus on how those facts can provide emotional support for the speaker.

Giving Comfort

Comforting is helping people feel better about themselves, their behavior, or the situation they are in by creating a safe conversational space where they can express their feelings and work out a plan for the future. Comfort-

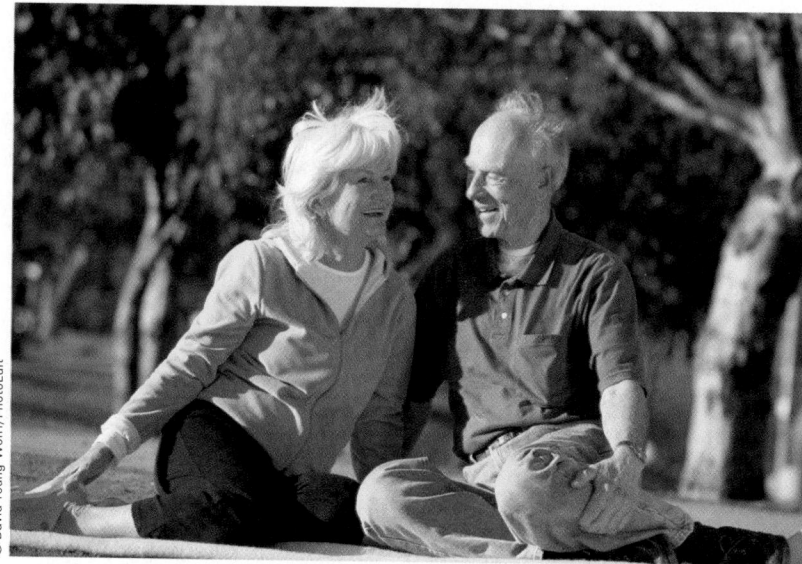

© David Young-Wolff/PhotoEdit

Recall an occasion when you were feeling especially happy and chose to share your feelings with someone. How did the person react? Was it what you hoped for? How did that person's reaction affect your feelings?

ing rarely happens in single statements. Instead, it usually occurs over several turns in a conversation or over several conversations that span weeks, months, and occasionally years. Supportive messages that comfort have the eight characteristics previously discussed, but they also draw from these five specific comforting message skills:

1. **Clarifying supportive intentions.** When people are experiencing turmoil, they may have trouble understanding the motives of those who want to help. You can **clarify your supportive intentions** by openly stating that your goal in the conversation is to help your partner. Notice how David does this in the following conversation:

   DAVID [*noticing Paul sitting in his cubicle with his head in his lap and his hands over his head*]: Paul, is everything OK?

   PAUL [*sitting up with a miserable but defiant look on his face*]: Like you should care. Yeah, everything is fine.

   DAVID: Paul, I do care. You've been working for me for five years; you're one of our best technicians. So if something is going on, I'd like to help, even if all I can do is listen. Now, what's up?

2. **Buffering face threats with politeness. Buffering** cushions the effect of messages by utilizing both positive and negative politeness skills. The very act of providing comfort can threaten the positive and negative face needs of your partner. (**Positive face needs** refer to the desire to be appreciated and approved, liked, and honored. **Negative face needs** refer to the desire to be free from imposition or intrusion.) On one hand, your partner can feel that you will respect, like, or value him less because of

clarify supportive intentions
openly stating that your goal in the conversation is to help your partner.

buffering
cushioning the effect of messages by utilizing both positive and negative politeness skills.

positive face needs
the desire to be appreciated and approved, liked, and honored.

negative face needs
the desire to be free from imposition or intrusion.

his situation. On the other hand, the very act of comforting suggests that the other person cannot independently handle the situation. So comforting messages are phrased very politely in ways that address the other person's face needs. Notice how David says to Paul, "You're one of our best technicians," which reaffirms his admiration for Paul's work. David also attends to Paul's need for independence by stating that maybe all he "can do is listen," which implies that Paul will be able to do the rest.

3. **Encouraging understanding through other-centered messages.** To reduce emotional distress, people need to make sense out of what has happened (Burleson & Goldsmith, 1998). People feel better if they can re-evaluate specific parts of the situation or change their opinion about what happened. An important way for people to do this is by repeatedly telling and elaborating on the story (what happened to them). We can help people do this by using **other-centered messages,** those that encourage our partners to talk about and elaborate on what happened and how they feel about it. Many of us find this difficult to do because we have been taught it is rude to pry or we are uncomfortable hearing someone's problems, so our gut reaction is to change the subject.

> **other-centered messages**
> *statements that encourage our partners to talk about and elaborate on what happened and how they feel about it.*

Other-centered messages may ask questions that allow the other to elaborate, they may simply be vocalized encouragement (um, uh-huh, wow, I see), they encourage the person to explore their feelings, and they demonstrate understanding and empathy.

4. **Reframing the situation.** When people are vulnerable and are in the midst of strong emotions, they are likely to perceive events in a limited way. At times, their limited vision prevents them from viewing the situation in ways that would enable them to re-evaluate the situation or their feelings. In these cases, it may be helpful for you to **reframe** the situation by offering ideas, observations, information, and alternative explanations that might help your partner understand the situation in a different light. For example, imagine that Travis returns from class and tells his roommate Abe, "Well, I'm flunking calculus. It doesn't matter how much I study or how many of the online problems I do, I just can't get it. This level of math is above me. I might as well just drop out of school before I flunk out completely. I can ask for a full-time schedule at work and not torture myself with school anymore." To reframe this situation, Abe might remind Travis that he has been putting in many hours at work and maybe his work schedule is interfering with his calculus grades. Or he might tell Travis that he heard calculus instructors curve grades at the end of the term because the material is so difficult. In each case, Abe is offering new observations and providing alternative explanations that can help Travis reframe the situation from an impossible one to a manageable one.

> **reframing**
> *offering ideas, observations, information, and alternative explanations that might help your partner understand the situation in a different light.*

5. **Giving advice.** At times, we can comfort people by **giving advice**—presenting relevant suggestions and proposals that a person can use to

> **giving advice**
> *presenting relevant suggestions and proposals that a person can use to satisfactorily resolve a situation.*

satisfactorily resolve a situation. Unfortunately, we often rush to give advice before we really understand the problem. Advice should not be given until our supportive intentions have been understood, we have attended to our partner's face needs, and we have sustained an other-centered interaction for some time. Only when your partner has had time to understand and make his or her own sense out of what has happened should you offer advice to help with unresolved issues. Before giving advice, always ask permission and acknowledge that your advice is only one suggestion of many that might work. Present the potential risks or costs associated with your advice, and let your partner know that it's OK if he or she chooses to ignore what you have said.

Gender and Cultural Considerations in Comforting

It is popularly thought that men and women differ in the value they place on emotional support, with women expecting, needing, and providing more. However, Burleson (2003, p. 572) reports that a growing body of research finds that both men and women of various ages place a high value on emotional support from their partners in a variety of relationships (siblings, same-sex friendships, opposite-sex friendships, and romantic relationships). Studies also find that men and women have similar ideas about what messages do a better or worse job of reducing emotional distress. Both men and women find that messages encouraging them to explore and elaborate on their feelings provide the most comfort. Research has also found that men are less likely to use other-centered messages when comforting.

Researchers have also examined cultural differences in comforting. Burleson (p. 574) reports that members of all social groups find solace strategies, especially other-centered messages, the most sensitive and comforting way to provide emotional support. Burleson has identified these cultural differences:

1. European Americans, more than other American ethnic groups, believe that openly discussing feelings will help a person feel better.

2. Americans are more sensitive to other-centered messages than are Chinese.

3. Both Chinese and Americans view avoidance strategies as less appropriate than approach strategies, but Chinese see avoidance as more appropriate than Americans do.

4. Married Chinese and married Americans both view the emotional support provided by their spouse to be the most important type of social support they receive.

5. African Americans place lower value on partner emotional support skills than do European or Asian Americans. This was especially true for African American women.

Overall, it appears that we are more alike than different concerning our desire to be supported by our partners and the types of messages we find to be emotionally comforting.

Figure 7.2 summarizes how good listeners and poor listeners deal with the five aspects of listening: attending, understanding, remembering, evaluating, and responding supportively.

	Good Listeners	Bad Listeners
ATTENDING	Attend to important information	May not hear what a person is saying
	Ready themselves physically and mentally	Fidget in their chairs, look out the window, and let their minds wander
	Listen objectively regardless of emotional involvement	Visibly react to emotional language
	Listen differently depending on situations	Listen the same way regardless of the type of material
UNDERSTANDING	Assign appropriate meaning to what is said	Hear what is said but are either unable to understand or assign different meaning to the words
	Seek out apparent purpose, main points, and supporting information	Ignore the way information is organized
	Ask mental questions to anticipate information	Fail to anticipate coming information
	Silently paraphrase to solidify understanding	Seldom or never mentally review information
	Seek out subtle meanings based on nonverbal cues	Ignore nonverbal cues
REMEMBERING	Retain information	Interpret message accurately but forget it
	Repeat key information	Assume they will remember
	Mentally create mnemonics for lists of words and ideas	Seldom single out any information as especially important
	Take notes	Rely on memory alone
EVALUATING	Listen critically	Hear and understand but are unable to weigh and consider it
	Separate facts from inferences	Don't differentiate between facts and inferences
	Evaluate inferences	Accept information at face value
RESPONDING SUPPORTIVELY	Provide supportive comforting statements	Pass off joy or hurt; change the subject
	Give alternative interpretations	Pass off hurt; change the subject

Figure 7.2
A summary of the five aspects of listening

Conversation and Analysis

Use your ThomsonNOW for *Communicate!* to access the video clip of Damien and Chris's conversation. As you watch the interaction, analyze how well Damien uses the skills of active listening and how well his responses demonstrate effective support and comforting. You can respond to this and other analysis questions by clicking on "Analysis" in the menu bar at the top of the screen. When you've answered all the questions, click "Done" to compare your answers to those provided by the authors.

Here is a transcript of the conversation. You can also find a copy of this transcript online, which allows you to take notes as you watch the video. Use your ThomsonNOW for *Communicate!* to access **Skill Learning Activity 7.7.** When you have finished viewing the video and taking notes, click on "Authors' Model Analysis" to compare your notes to the detailed conversational analysis provided by the authors.

Damien and Chris work in a small shop selling shirts and gifts. Usually they get along well, but lately Chris has seemed standoffish. Damien decides to talk with Chris to see if anything is wrong. Damien approaches Chris in the break room.

Conversation

DAMIEN: Chris, you've been kind of quiet lately, man. What's been going on?

CHRIS: Nothing.

DAMIEN: Come on, man, what's going on?

CHRIS: Just life. [*shrugs*] I'm just kind of down right now.

DAMIEN: Well, what am I here for? I thought we were friends.

CHRIS [*he thinks about it and decides to talk about it*]: Well, Carl's been on my case the last few weeks.

DAMIEN: Why? Did you do something?

CHRIS: Oh, he says that I'm sloppy when I restock and that I'm not always "polite" to our customers. You know, just 'cuz I don't smile all the time. I mean, what does he want—little Mary Sunshine?

DAMIEN: So you're angry with the boss.

CHRIS: Yeah, I guess . . . no, no, not so angry; I'm just frustrated. I come in to work every day, and I try to do my job, and I don't complain. You know, I'm sick and tired of getting stuck back there in the stock room reorga-

Jason Harris/© Thomson Higher Education

nizing everything. It's not like they're paying us big bucks here. And Carl shouldn't expect us to be charming with everybody who walks through that door. I mean, half of the people who walk through that door are, well, they're totally rude and act like jerks.

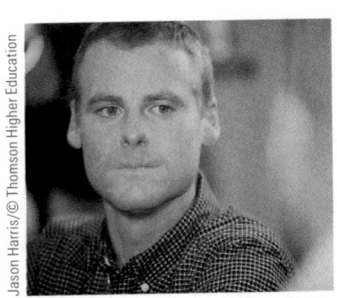

DAMIEN: Yeah, I feel like you on that. Some of those people shouldn't be allowed out in public. What is Carl saying about how you're dealing with the customers?

CHRIS: Oh, he just says that I've changed and that I'm not being "nice." I mean, he used to call me his top guy.

DAMIEN: I mean, you know how Carl is. He's a fanatic about customer service. You know how, when we first started, he drilled us about being polite and smiling and being courteous at all times. So maybe when he says "you're not being nice," he just means that you're not doing it the way you used to. I mean, I've noticed a change. I mean, you're just not yourself lately. Is anything going on outside of work?

CHRIS: You could say that. Sarah and I just bought a house, so money's been a bit tight. Now, she wants to quit her job and start a family, and I'm not sure we can afford it. On top of it all, my kid sister shows up a few weeks ago on our doorstep, pregnant, and so she's living with us, so yeah, it is a bit overwhelming. And I'm a bit worried that Carl's going to fire me.

DAMIEN: Wow, that is a lot of stuff! I can understand why you're down, but did Carl really threaten to fire you?

CHRIS: No, no, but I'm not perfect, and he could use my "attitude" as an excuse to fire me.

DAMIEN: Well, did you think about telling him what's been going on? And maybe, you know, he'll understand and cut you some slack.

CHRIS: Or he could see that I really have changed and he'd can me.

DAMIEN: OK, well, just tell me this. Do you like working here?

CHRIS: Yeah, of course I do.

DAMIEN: OK, well, then, you've just got to tough it out. I mean, you've just got to use the game face on these people. You used to be the best at doing that. So you're just gonna have to get back to being a salesman, and leave everything else behind.

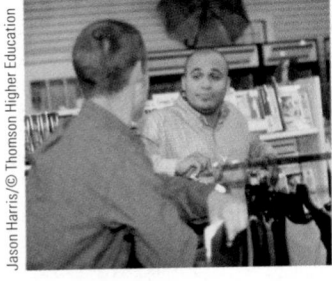

CHRIS: I guess I never realized how much my problems were affecting my work. I thought Carl was just out to get me, but now you're noticing something too, then maybe I have changed. Thanks, thanks for talking this out.

What Would You Do?

J aneen always disliked talking on the telephone—she thought it was an impersonal form of communication. Thus, college was a wonderful respite. When friends called her, instead of staying on the phone she could quickly run over to their dorm or meet them at a coffeehouse.

One day during reading period before exams, Janeen received a phone call from Barbara, an out-of-town friend. Before she was able to dismiss the call with her stock excuses, she found herself bombarded with information about old high school friends and their whereabouts. Not wanting to disappoint Barbara, who seemed eager to talk, Janeen tucked her phone under her chin and began straightening her room, answering Barbara with the occasional "uh-huh," "hmm," or "wow, that's cool!" As the "conversation" progressed, Janeen began reading through her mail and then her notes from class. After a few minutes, she realized there was silence on the other end of the line. Suddenly very ashamed, she said, "I'm sorry, what did you say? The phone . . . uh there was just a lot of static."

Barbara replied with obvious hurt in her voice, "I'm sorry I bothered you, you must be terribly busy."

Embarrassed, Janeen muttered, "I'm just really stressed, you know, with exams coming up and everything. I guess I wasn't listening very well; you didn't seem to be saying anything really important. I'm sorry. What were you saying?"

"Nothing 'important'," Barbara answered. "I was just trying to figure out a way to tell you. I know that you were friends with my brother Billy, and you see, we just found out yesterday that he's terminal with a rare form of leukemia. But you're right; it obviously isn't really important." With that, she hung up.

1. How ethical was Janeen's means of dealing with her dilemma of not wanting to talk on the phone but not wanting to hurt Barbara's feelings?

2. Identify ways in which both Janeen and Barbara could have used better and perhaps more ethical interpersonal communication skills. Rewrite the scenario incorporating these changes.

Summary

Listening is the complex process that encompasses attending, understanding, remembering, evaluating, and responding with support and comfort.

Attending is the process of selecting and focusing on specific stimuli from the countless ones that we receive. We can be more effective in attending if we (1) get ready both physically and mentally, (2) make the shift from speaker to listener complete (don't rehearse), (3) hear a person out before responding, and (4) observe nonverbal clues.

Understanding is the process of decoding a message so that the meaning accurately reflects that intended by the speaker. Empathizing, which is identifying with or vicariously experiencing the feelings of another, can increase understanding. We can also increase understanding by asking questions to clarify and get details and by paraphrasing the speaker's content and feelings.

Remembering is the process of retaining information so it can be recalled when it is needed. By repeating information, using mnemonics, and taking notes, we can increase the likelihood that we will remember what we hear.

Critical analysis is the process of evaluating what has been said to determine its truthfulness. Critical analysis is especially important when a speaker is asking you to believe, act on, or support what is being said. One important skill of critical analysis is to separate statements of fact from inferences. Statements of fact should be analyzed to see if they are true. Inferences should be tested to see if they are valid. Three questions can help us to test inferences: (1) What facts support this inference? (2) Is the information really central to the inference? (3) Are there other facts that would contradict the inference?

Responding with support and comfort helps people feel better about themselves and their behavior. Effective support messages are those that aim to help, accept others, demonstrate concern, show one's willingness to listen and be an ally, acknowledge and validate the speaker's feelings, and encourage elaboration. When we give comfort, we should use messages that clarify our intentions, practice politeness, are other-centered, reframe the situation, and offer advice on issues the speaker cannot seem to resolve.

Thomson NOW!

Communicate! Online

N ow that you have read Chapter 7, use your ThomsonNOW for *Communicate!* for quick access to the electronic resources that accompany this text. Your ThomsonNOW gives you access to the video of the conversation between Damien and Chris on pages 162–163, the Web Resources and Skill Learning Activities featured in this chapter, InfoTrac College Edition, and online study aids such as a digital glossary and review quizzes.

Your *Communicate!* ThomsonNOW is an online study system that helps you identify concepts you don't fully understand, allowing you to put your study time to the best use. Using chapter-by-chapter diagnostic pre-tests, the system creates a personalized study plan for each chapter. Each plan directs you to specific resources designed to improve your understanding, including pages from the text in e-book format. Chapter post-tests give you an opportunity to measure how much you've learned and let you know if you are ready for graded quizzes and exams.

Key Terms

Go to your ThomsonNOW for *Communicate!* to access your online glossary for Chapter 7. Print a copy of the glossary for this chapter and test yourself with the electronic flash cards or complete the crossword puzzle to help you master these key terms:

attending (146)
buffering (158)
clarify supportive intentions (158)
comfort (155)
content paraphrase (150)
critical analysis (154)
empathic responsiveness (147)
empathy (147)

factual statements (154)
feelings paraphrase (150)
giving advice (159)
inferences (154)
listening (146)
mnemonic device (152)
negative face needs (158)
other-centered messages (159)
paraphrasing (150)

perspective taking (148)
positive face needs (158)
question (148)
reframing (159)
remembering (150)
supportive messages (155)
sympathetic responsiveness (148)
understanding (147)

Review Quiz

Test your knowledge of the concepts in this chapter by taking the online review quiz for Chapter 7. Go to your ThomsonNOW for *Communicate!* to access the quiz. When you have completed the quiz, submit it for scoring.

Skill Learning Activities

Complete the Observe & Analyze, Test Your Competence, Skill Building, and Conversation and Analysis activities for Chapter 7 online at your ThomsonNOW for *Communicate!*. You can submit your Observe & Analyze answers to your instructor, compare your Test Your Competence and Skill Building answers to those provided by the authors, and do both for the Conversation and Analysis activity.

7.1: Observe & Analyze: Empathizing Effectively (150)
7.2: Skill Building: Questions and Paraphrases (151)
7.3: Test Your Competence: Creating Mnemonics (152)
7.4: Test Your Competence: Listening to Remember (153)
7.5: Test Your Competence: Evaluating Inferences (154)
7.6: Observe & Analyze: Critically Analyzing the Use of Facts and Inferences in the Media (154)
7.7: Conversation and Analysis: Damien and Chris (162)

Web Resources

Go to your ThomsonNOW for *Communicate!* to access the Web Resources for this chapter.
7.1: Listening Inventory (146)
7.2: Listening and Empathy Responding (148)
7.3: Mnemonics (152)

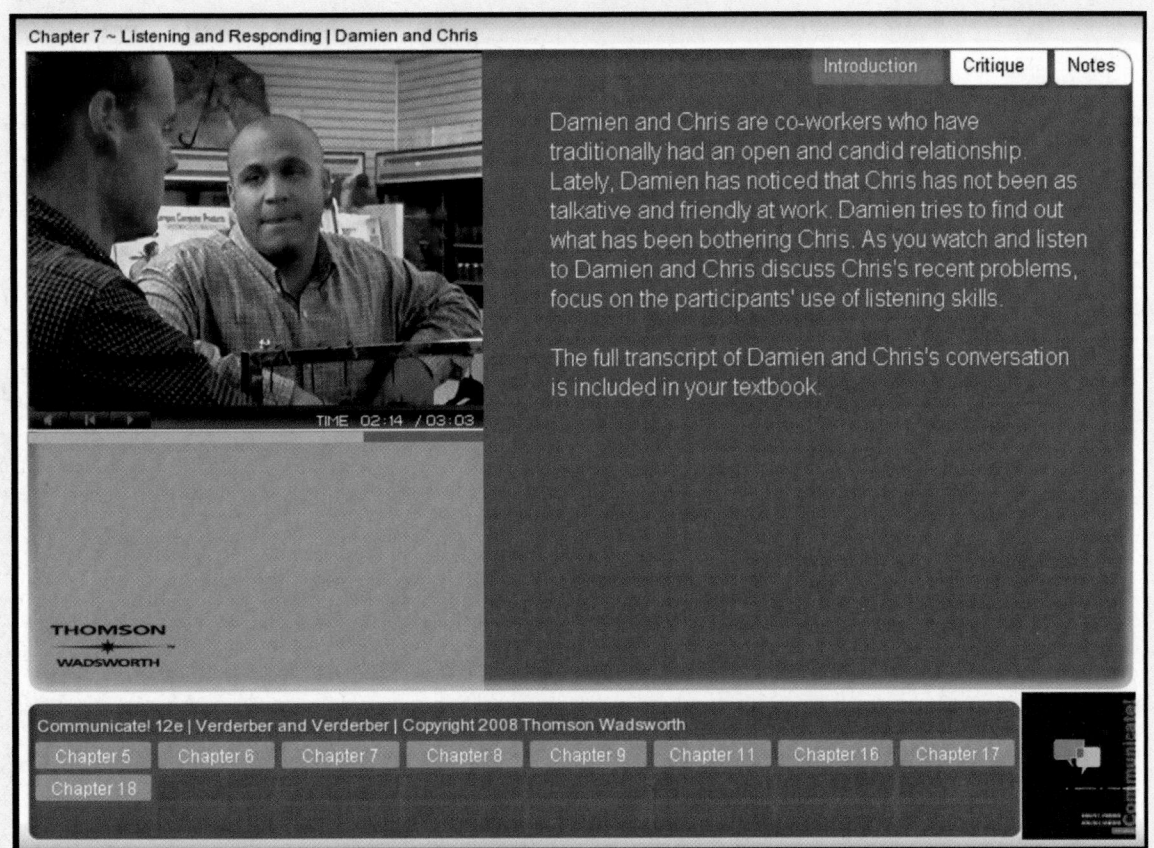

Introduction Critique Notes

Damien and Chris are co-workers who have traditionally had an open and candid relationship. Lately, Damien has noticed that Chris has not been as talkative and friendly at work. Damien tries to find out what has been bothering Chris. As you watch and listen to Damien and Chris discuss Chris's recent problems, focus on the participants' use of listening skills.

The full transcript of Damien and Chris's conversation is included in your textbook.

TIME 02:14 / 03:03

THOMSON
WADSWORTH

Communicate! 12e | Verderber and Verderber | Copyright 2008 Thomson Wadsworth

Chapter 5 Chapter 6 Chapter 7 Chapter 8 Chapter 9 Chapter 11 Chapter 16 Chapter 17
Chapter 18

Rob Nelson/Stockphoto.com

After you have read this chapter, you should be able to answer these questions:

- What is self-disclosure?
- What are the guidelines for effective disclosure?
- When and how does one describe feelings?
- What are the differences between displaying feelings and describing feelings?
- What can you do to improve how you give praise and constructive criticism?
- What is assertiveness?
- How does assertiveness differ from passive or aggressive behavior?
- How can you assert yourself appropriately?
- What are five conflict management styles and when is each style appropriate?

8

Developing Intimacy in Relationships: Self-Disclosure, Feedback, and Conflict Resolution

"Chuck, when that interviewer at the grocery store asked you whether you'd rather have rice than potatoes, you said 'Yes'! We've been married more than 20 years, and I'm just now learning that you like rice more than potatoes."

"Well, I'm sorry, Susan," Chuck said sheepishly.

"Chuck," Susan asks, "are there other things that you like or don't like that you haven't told me about during these more than 20 years I've been your wife?"

"Well, probably."

"Why aren't you telling me about these things?"

"Well, I don't know. I guess I didn't think they were all that important."

"Not important? Chuck, we have potatoes almost every night that I cook. And frankly, I hate potatoes. I wouldn't care if I never saw a potato again. Now I find out you like rice better!"

"Sue, why didn't you ever tell me that you don't like potatoes?"

"Well I, uh, uh . . ."

P oor Chuck—poor Susan—all those years! Although this opening story seems a bit silly, every day in your new and ongoing relationships you make decisions about the information you will share with your partners and how you will handle issues on which you disagree. The decisions that you make will affect the degree of intimacy and satisfaction you experience in your relationships. It is normal to sometimes feel that you want to be open and share with someone, yet feel at other times that you want to maintain your privacy. It is normal to sometimes feel a need to connect with someone, and at other times to feel the need to be independent. It is normal to sometimes want to have your partner act in predictable ways and at other times wish that your partner would do something to surprise you. These seemingly opposing forces (openness–closedness, autonomy–connection, and novelty–predictability) that you feel are called **relational dialectics** and they naturally occur in all interpersonal relationships. How we choose to deal with them causes changes in our relationship. Think of these tensions as a pendulum making a wide swing. When a relationship moves toward too much openness, too much connection, or too much predictability, it will naturally swing back toward its opposite of closedness, independence, or novelty.

In this chapter, we will explore the interpersonal processes that affect the ebb and flow of our relational dialectics. We begin by describing how self-disclosure and personal feedback affect the level of openness–closedness in a relationship. Then we explain how assertiveness helps us to maintain our autonomy. Finally, we discuss various styles of conflict management that we can use as we manage the tension that arises from these natural relationship dialectics.

relational dialectics
seemingly opposing forces (openness–closedness, autonomy–connection, and novelty–predictability) that occur in all interpersonal relationships.

Self-Disclosure and Privacy

As we saw in Chapter 6, we develop and grow our relationships through self-disclosure. Self-disclosure leads to openness and intimacy in our relationships. **Self-disclosure** is the process of revealing your biographical data, personal experiences, ideas, and feelings to someone else. Statements such as "I was 5′ 6″ in seventh grade" provide biographical information—facts about you as an individual. "I don't think prisons ever really rehabilitate criminals" discloses a personal idea. "I get scared whenever I have to make a speech" discloses feelings. Biographical disclosures may be the easiest to make, and some biographical information is public. Most of us find it more difficult to talk about our personal ideas and feelings (Rosenfeld, 2000, p. 6).

self-disclosure
sharing biographical data, personal experiences, ideas, and feelings.

Guidelines for Appropriate Self-Disclosure

We know that self-disclosure increases the intimacy of a relationship. But at the same time, it's risky. So we sometimes choose to avoid disclosure rather than risk personal or relationship consequences (Affifi and Guerrero, 2000, p. 179). The following guidelines can help you manage the dialectical tensions surrounding openness and closedness in your decisions about making a self-disclosure.

1. **Self-disclose the kind of information you want others to disclose to you.** When people are getting to know others, they begin by sharing information that they perceive to be low risk. This is information usually shared freely among people with that type of relationship in that culture and might include information about hobbies, sports, school, and views of current events. One way to determine what information is appropriate to disclose is to ask yourself whether you would feel comfortable having the person disclose that kind of information to you.

2. **Self-disclose more intimate information only when the disclosure represents an acceptable risk.** There is always some risk that disclosure will distress or alarm your partner and damage your relationship, but the better you know your partner, the more likely it is that a difficult disclosure will be well received. Incidentally, this guideline explains why people sometimes engage in inappropriate intimate self-disclosure with bartenders or with people they meet in travel. They perceive the disclosures as safe (representing reasonable risk) because the person either does not know them or is in no position to use the information against them. Some people who are extremely shy find it very difficult to self-disclose. For some good advice for those who are extremely reluctant to disclose, use your ThomsonNOW for *Communicate!* to access **Web Resource 8.1: Self-Disclosure and Shyness**.

3. **Continue self-disclosure only if it is reciprocated.** Research suggests that people expect a kind of equity in self-disclosure (Derlega et al., 1993, p. 33). When it is apparent that self-disclosure is not being returned, you should consider limiting the amount of disclosure you make. Someone's choice not to reciprocate indicates that the person does not yet feel comfortable with this level of self-disclosure. If the response you receive to your self-disclosure implies that it was inappropriate, try to find out why so that you may avoid this problem in the future.

4. **Self-disclose at deeper levels gradually.** Because receiving self-disclosure can be as threatening as giving it, most people who receive it become uncomfortable when the level of disclosure exceeds their expectations. As a relationship develops, the depth of disclosure should gradually increase. So we disclose biographical and demographic information early in a relationship and more closely held, personal information later, in a more developed relationship (Dindia, Fitzpatrick, & Kenny, 1997, p. 408).

5. **Reserve intimate or very personal self-disclosure for ongoing relationships.** Disclosures about intimate matters are appropriate in close, well-established relationships. When people disclose very personal information to acquaintances or business associates, they are not only taking a risk of being exposed; the disclosure may also threaten their partner. Making intimate disclosures before a bond of trust is established risks

DIVERSE VOICES

Long Overdue

by Naomi Shihab Nye

Poets like Naomi Shihab Nye devote their lives to using words to communicate their feelings and ideas, yet when Shihab Nye, whose father was Palestinian, encountered anti-Arab prejudice in the past, she was unable to disclose her Arab roots and to respond. In the excerpt that follows, Shihab Nye explores her silence.

The words we didn't say. How many times? Stones stuck in the throat. Endlessly revised silence. What was wrong with me? How could I, a person whose entire vocation has been dedicated one way or another to the use of words, lose words completely when I needed them? Where does vocal paralysis come from? Why does regret have such a long life span? My favorite poet William Stafford used to say, "Think of something you said. Now write what you *wish you* had said."

But I am always thinking of the times I said nothing.

In England, attending a play by myself, I was happy when the elderly woman next to me began speaking at intermission. Our arms had been touching lightly on the armrest between our seats.

"Smashingly talented," she said of Ben Kingsley, whose brilliant monologue we'd been watching. "I don't know how he does it—transporting us so effortlessly; he's a genius. Not many in the world like him." I agreed. But then she sighed and made an odd turn. "You know what's wrong with the world today? It's Arabs. I blame it all on the Arabs. Most world problems can really be traced to them."

My blood froze. Why was she saying this? The play wasn't about Arabs. Ben Kingsley was hardly your blue-blooded Englishman, either, so what brought it up? Nothing terrible about Arabs had happened lately in the news. I wasn't wearing a *kef"fiyeh* [traditional Arab headdress] around my neck.

But my mouth would not open.

"Why *did so* many of them come to England?" she continued, muttering as if she were sharing a confidence. "A ruination, that's what it is."

It struck me that she might be a landlady having trouble with tenants. I tried and tried to part my lips. Where is the end of the tangled thread? How will we roll it into a ball if we can't find an end?

She chatted on about something less consequential, never seeming to mind our utterly one-sided conversation, till the lights went down. Of course, I couldn't concentrate on the rest of the play. My precious ticket felt wasted. I twisted my icy hands together while my cheeks burned.

Even worse, she and I rode the same train afterwards. I had plenty of time to respond, to find a vocabulary for prejudice and fear. The dark night buildings flew by. I could have said, "Madam, I am half Arab. I pray your heart grows larger someday." I could have sent her off, stunned and embarrassed, into the dark.

My father would say, "People like that can't be embarrassed."

But what would he say back to her?

Oh I was ashamed for my silence and I have carried that shame across oceans, through the summer when it never rained, in my secret pocket, till now. I will never feel better about it. Like my reckless angry last words to the one who took his own life.

Years later, my son and I were sitting on an American island with a dear friend, the only African American living among 80 or so residents. A brilliant artist and poet in his seventies, he has made a beautiful lifetime of painting picture books, celebrating expression, encouraging the human spirit, reciting poems of other African American heroes, delighting children and adults alike.

We had spent a peaceful day riding bicycles, visiting the few students at the schoolhouse, picking up rounded stones on the beach, digging peat moss in the woods. We had sung hymns together in our resonant little church. Our friend had purchased a live lobster down at the dock for supper. My son and I were sad when it seemed to be knocking on the lid of the pot of boiling water. "Let me out." We vowed quietly to one another never to eat a lobster again.

After dinner, a friend of our friend dropped in, returned to the island from her traveling life as an anthropologist. We asked if she had heard anything about the elections in Israel—that was the day Shimon Peres and Benjamin Netanyahu vied for prime minister and we had been unable to pick up a final tally on the radio.

She thought Netanyahu had won. The election was very close. But then she said, "Good thing! He'll put those Arabs in their places. Arabs want more than they deserve."

My face froze. Was it possible I had heard correctly? An anthropologist speaking. Not a teenager, not a blithering idiot. I didn't speak another word during her visit. I wanted to. I should have, but I couldn't. My plate littered with red shells.

After she left, my friend put his gentle hand on my shoulder. He said simply, "Now you know a little more what it feels like to be black."

So what happens to my words when the going gets rough? In a world where certain equalities for human beings seem long, long, long, overdue,

where is the magic sentence to act as a tool? Where is the hoe, the tiller, the rake?

Pontificating, proving, proselytizing leave me cold. So do endless political debates over coffee after dinner. I can't listen to talk radio, drowning in jabber.

The poetic impulse—to suggest, hint, shape a little picture, to find a story, metaphor, scene—abides as a kind of music inside. Nor can I forget the journalist in Dubai who called me *donkey* for talking about vegetables when there was injustice in the world.

I can talk about sumac, too. When a friend asks what's that purple spice in the little shake-up jar at the Persian restaurant, tears cloud my eyes.

Is it good for you?

Are vegetables, in some indelible way, smarter than we are? Are animals?

But then the headlines take the power. The fanatical behavior.

"Problem is, we can't hear the voices of the moderates," said the Israeli man, who assured me his house was built on a spot where Arabs had never lived. "Where are *they?* Why don't they speak *louder?*"

(They don't like to raise their voices.)

(Maybe they can't hear you either.)

Excerpt from Naomi Shihab Nye, "Long Overdue," Post Gibran: An Anthology of New Arab American Writing (Syracuse University Press, 2000), p. 127.

alienating the other person. Moreover, people are often embarrassed by and hostile toward others who try to saddle them with intimate information in an effort to establish a personal relationship where none exists.

In the Diverse Voices feature, "Long Overdue," Naomi Shihab Nye describes her experiences with anti-Arab prejudice. As you read this excerpt from an interview with Ms. Shihab Nye, first try to empathize with her frustration about Arab stereotypes and, second, consider her courage in disclosing information about herself and her feelings.

Managing Privacy

At times, a relationship can feel too intimate and you may become uncomfortable with the openness; at these times, you may want to reduce the intimacy by distancing yourself and refraining from disclosure. So, it is equally

▶ Speech Assignment: Communicate on Your Feet

Personal Narrative

Prepare a short speech in which you tell a story about something that has happened to you. (Your instructor will give you specific time parameters and other directions.) Your story might be humorous, serious, or somewhere in between. It might be about something that has recently happened to you or about an event from your past.

Make a list of stories you might tell. As you think about the stories on your list, use the self-disclosure guidelines in this chapter to determine whether the story is appropriate for a classroom setting. In addition, be sure to consider not only your own privacy, but also the privacy of others who are part of the story.

As you prepare your speech, think about how to tell the story so that your audience can easily follow what you are saying. We tell most stories in chronological order, introducing people in the story as they "make their appearances." You can help your audience follow your story if you can chunk it into two, three, or four sequential parts, similar to the chapters of a book. For example, if you are going to tell a story about a cake-baking disaster, you could divide your story into three parts: problems with ingredients, problems with mixing, and problems with baking. Sometimes, for dramatic effect, we can tell the end of the story first and then back up and fill in the beginning and the middle. This organizational pattern for a narrative was popularized by radio personality Paul Harvey, who usually ended his legendary narratives with, "And now you know the rest of the story."

Briefly introduce your story in a way that piques the interest of your audience members. End your speech by summarizing what you learned, gained, and so on, from the experience you related.

---

privacy
the right of an individual to keep biographical data, personal ideas, and feelings secret.

managing privacy
a conscious decision to avoid disclosure and to withhold information or feelings from a relational partner.

important to understand how to manage your privacy in both developing and ongoing relationships. **Privacy** is the right of an individual to keep biographical data, personal ideas, and feelings secret. **Managing privacy** is a conscious decision to avoid disclosure and to withhold information or feelings from a relational partner. You may chose privacy over self-disclosure for many legitimate reasons, including protecting your partner's or another person's feelings, avoiding unnecessary conflict, helping another save face, and protecting the relationship. So when Will, who knows that his partner, Celeste, has worried to the point of weight loss and insomnia over a minor unpaid bill, becomes aware that there is a slight chance that he may lose his job due to a merger, he may decide to keep this information to himself unless the rumor is confirmed. If he later finds out that he will be laid off, he will, of course, need to tell Celeste, but he may not tell her that he has suspected this would happen for some time.

What can you do when you don't want to disclose? First, you can change the subject. For example, if your partner makes a disclosure that seems to invite a parallel disclosure that you are uncomfortable making, just introduce a new topic. So if Pat says, "I got an 83 on the test, how about you?" and you don't want to share your score, you can simply reply, "Hey, that's a 'B'. Good going! Did you finish the homework for calculus?" Second, you can tell a white lie, which is a false or misleading statement that is acceptable to use when telling the truth would embarrass you or your partner and when the untruth you tell does not cause serious harm to either of you or to your relationship. So you might tell Pat, "Gosh, I'm not sure I remember; I got several tests back this week." Third, you can establish a boundary by telling the other person that you don't want to share the information and perhaps why you choose to keep it private. So you might say to Pat, "I know that everyone is different, but because I am so competitive, I've adopted the policy of not asking anyone about their grades and not telling them mine."

Cultural and Gender Differences

Some people, by virtue of their culture, gender, or family upbringing, may readily self-disclose; others may have distinct privacy rules and customs. People from formal cultures, like Germany or Japan, value privacy and are less likely to disclose personal information. The United States is considered an informal culture (Samovar, Porter, & McDaniel, 2007), so most Americans tend to disclose information about themselves.

Particularly in the beginning stages of a cross-cultural friendship, cultural differences can easily lead to misperceptions and discomfort. For instance, an American student may perceive an exchange student from China to be reserved and not interested in establishing a genuine friendship because the exchange student doesn't volunteer personal information. At the same time, the Chinese exchange student may be feeling embarrassed by the American's personal disclosures. When we are aware of cultural differences, we can vary our level of disclosure so that it is appropriate for our partner.

© Jack Hollingsworth/CORBIS

Across cultures, when relationships become more intimate, self-disclosure increases.

Regardless of these cultural differences, however, Gudykunst and Kim (2003) have discovered that, across cultures, as relationships become more intimate, self-disclosure increases. In addition, they found that the more partners disclosed to each other, the more they were attracted to each other and the less uncertain they felt about each other (p. 329).

Differences in learned patterns of self-disclosure can create misunderstandings between men and women, especially in intimate relationships. In *You Just Don't Understand,* Deborah Tannen (1990, p. 48) argues that in their disclosure patterns, men are more likely to engage in **report-talk** (sharing information, displaying knowledge, negotiating, and preserving independence), whereas women engage in **rapport-talk** (sharing experiences and stories to establish bonds with others). When men and women fail to recognize these differences in disclosure patterns, the stage is set for misunderstandings about whether or not they are being truly open and intimate with each other.

report-talk
a way to share information, display knowledge, negotiate, and preserve independence.

rapport-talk
a way to share experiences and establish bonds with others.

Disclosing Feelings

At the heart of intimate self-disclosure is sharing our personal emotions, which is a risky business. Why? When we share our feelings, we usually give the other person potent knowledge about us that he or she might use to harm us. So all of us have to decide whether and how we disclose our feelings. Obviously, one option in managing our privacy is to withhold our emotions. If we decide to disclose our feelings, we can either display them or describe them.

Masking Feelings

We mask our feelings by concealing the verbal and nonverbal cues that would enable our partners to understand what we are really feeling. The straight-faced poker player who develops the neutral look that is impossible to decipher has become a master of masking feelings. Habitually masking your feelings leads to a variety of physical and psychological problems, such as heart disease and anxiety, and can prevent you from experiencing openness in your relationships. At times, masking your feelings is appropriate such as when a situation or relationship is inconsequential or when disclosing your feelings would pose an unreasonable risk to your physical or emotional safety. For example, it may be appropriate to mask your anger when a stranger cuts in line ahead of you at the theater concession stand, especially if the stranger appears to be menacing.

Displaying Feelings

We display our feelings when we express them through facial expressions, body responses, and verbal outbursts. Cheering over a great play at a sporting event, howling when you bang your head against the car doorjamb, and patting a coworker on the back for doing something well are all displays of feelings. Displaying feelings often serves as an escape valve for very strong emotions, so in some sense it is healthier to display feelings than to withhold them because we "get them out of our system." Unfortunately, although we may feel better, these displays usually stress our relational partners. Because most people are not able to interpret the emotional displays of others with consistent accuracy, misinterpretation of feelings often results. Displays of feelings harm relationships when negative feelings such as anger, disgust, or hatred are displayed in ways that frighten or threaten others. In addition, displays of feelings can damage our relationships and cause stress for our relationship partners. At times, displaying our feelings can rise to the level of abuse, both verbal and physical. Rather than masking or displaying our emotions, we can use the self-disclosure skill of describing feelings to help us share our feelings with others in an appropriate manner.

Describing Feelings

Describing feelings is the skill of naming the emotions you are feeling without judging them. When we describe our feelings, we teach others how to treat us by explaining how we are affected by what has happened. This knowledge gives our relational partners information they can use to help us deal with our emotions. For example, if you tell Paul that you enjoy his visits, your description of how you feel should encourage him to visit you again. Likewise, when you tell Gloria that you are annoyed when she borrows your MP3 player without asking, she is more likely to ask the next time. Describing your feelings allows you to exercise a measure of control over others' behavior simply by making them aware of the effects their actions have on you.

Many times, people think they are describing their feelings when they are actually displaying their feelings or evaluating the other person's behavior. For instance, an outburst like "Who the hell asked you for your opinion?" is a display of feelings, not a description. Simply beginning a sentence with "I feel . . ." may not guarantee that you are describing your feelings. In many cases, these statements can end up evaluating, blaming, or scapegoating someone or something. For example, "I feel like you don't respect me" actually blames the speaker. It doesn't let the speaker know how you feel about what happened. You might have felt hurt, betrayed, or angry. But you haven't disclosed this.

Sometimes we can't describe our emotions because we don't have an active vocabulary that allows us to name or accurately describe what we are feeling. What we are feeling may be similar to anger, but are we annoyed,

describing feelings
the skill of naming the emotions you are feeling without judging them.

Describing feelings is difficult for many people because it makes them vulnerable. Can you recall a situation in which you masked your feelings because you didn't trust others? Was your fear justified?

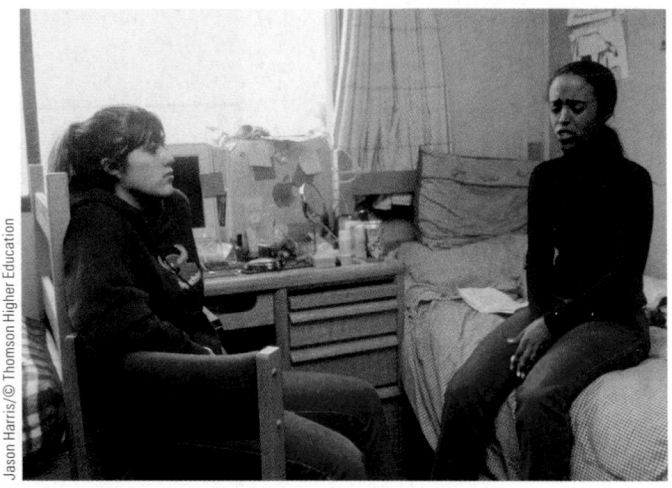

Jason Harris/© Thomson Higher Education

Words Related to *Angry*

annoyed	enraged	incensed	infuriated
irate	livid	mad	outraged

Words Related to *Loving*

affectionate	amorous	aroused	caring
fervent	heavenly	passionate	tender

Words Related to *Embarrassed*

flustered	humiliated	mortified	overwhelmed
rattled	shamefaced	sheepish	uncomfortable

Words Related to *Surprised*

astonished	astounded	baffled	jolted
mystified	shocked	startled	stunned

Words Related to *Fearful*

afraid	anxious	apprehensive	frightened
nervous	scared	terrified	worried

Words Related to *Disgusted*

aghast	appalled	dismayed	horror-struck
nauseated	repulsed	revolted	sickened

Words Related to *Hurt*

abused	damaged	forsaken	hassled
mistreated	offended	pained	wounded

Words Related to *Happy*

cheerful	contented	delighted	ecstatic
elated	glad	joyous	pleased

Words Related to *Lonely*

abandoned	alone	deserted	desolate
forlorn	isolated	lonesome	lost

Words Related to *Sad*

blue	depressed	downcast	gloomy
low	miserable	morose	sorrowful

Words Related to *Energetic*

animated	bouncy	brisk	lively
peppy	spirited	sprightly	vigorous

Figure 8.1
The vocabulary of emotions

betrayed, cheated, crushed, disturbed, furious, outraged, or shocked? Each of these words more richly describes a feeling that might less precisely be labeled anger. Figure 8.1 provides a short vocabulary of common emotions.

To describe your feelings: (1) Identify the behavior that has triggered the feeling. The feeling results from some specific behavior—what someone has said or done to or about you. (2) Identify the specific emotion you are experiencing as a result of the behavior. The vocabulary of emotions provided in Figure 8.1 can help you develop your ability to select specific words to describe your feelings. (3) Frame your response as an "I" statement: "I feel *happy, sad, irritated, vibrant.*" "I" statements help neutralize the impact of an emotional description because they do not blame the other or evaluate the other's behavior. Instead, a first-person message accu-

Communication Skill   **Describing Feelings**

Skill	Use	Procedure	Example
Putting an emotional state into words.	For self-disclosure; to teach people how to treat you.	1. Identify the behavior that has triggered the feeling. 2. Identify the specific emotion you are experiencing as a result of the behavior. Anger? Joy? Be specific. 3. Frame your response as an "I" statement. "I feel _____." 4. Verbalize the specific feeling.	"I just heard I didn't get the job, and I feel cheated and bitter" or "Because of the way you defended me when I was being belittled by Leah, I feel both grateful and humbled."

Skill Building   **Identifying Descriptions of Feelings**

For each of these statements, determine if the message is a description of feelings. If it is, place a "D" next to it. If you determine that the message is not a description of feelings, supply a message that provides a description of feelings.

1. That was a great movie!

2. I was really cheered by the flowers.

3. I feel that you are not respecting my rights.

4. Yuck!

5. Damn—I screwed that up again. I feel like an idiot.

6. I feel certain I got the job because I was the most qualified person.

7. Congratulations, I feel happy for you.

8. When Pam's around, I feel like a third wheel.

9. I'm ecstatic about winning the award.

10. I'm sick and tired of you.

Thomson NOW! You can complete this activity online and compare your answers to the authors'. Use your Thomson-NOW for *Communicate!* to access **Skill Learning Activity 8.3.**

---

rately conveys what you are expressing and why. (4) Verbalize the specific feeling.

Here are two examples of describing feelings. Notice that the first one begins with the trigger, and the second one begins with the feeling—either order is acceptable: (1) "Thank you for your compliment [trigger]; I [the person having the feeling] feel gratified [the specific feeling] that you noticed the effort I made." (2) "I [the person having the feeling] feel very resentful [the specific feeling] when you criticize my cooking on days I've worked as many hours as you have [trigger]."

To begin with, you may find it easier to describe positive feelings: "As a result of your taking me to the movie, I really feel cheered up" or "When you offered to help me with the housework, I really felt relieved." As you become comfortable describing positive feelings, you can move to describing negative feelings caused by environmental factors: "It's cold and cloudy; I feel gloomy" or "When there's a thunderstorm, I get jumpy." Finally, you can risk describing the difficult emotions you feel resulting from what people have said or done: "When you use a sarcastic tone while you are saying that what I did pleased you, I really feel confused."

To complete an activity that will help you build a vocabulary you can use to describe your emotions, go to your ThomsonNOW for *Communicate!* to access **Skill Learning Activity 8.2: Building Your Vocabulary of Emotions**. When you're done with the activity, compare your answer to the authors'.

Giving Personal Feedback

Sometimes in our interactions and relationships, it is appropriate to comment on another's message or behavior. When personal feedback is conveyed with sensitivity, it can help the other person to develop a more accurate self-concept, and it can increase the openness in the relationship. There are three skills that we use to give personal feedback: describing behavior, praising the positive behaviors of others, and constructively criticizing negative behaviors of others.

Describing Behavior

Effective praising and critiquing are both based on being descriptive rather than evaluative. Just as we must learn to describe our feelings as part of effective self-disclosure, so we must learn to describe the specific behavior of others if we are to give effective feedback. Unfortunately, people are quick to share generalized conclusions and evaluations. "You're so mean," "She's a tease," "You're a real friend," and countless statements like these are attempts to provide feedback but are stated as evaluative and vague.

describing behavior
accurately recounting the specific behaviors of another without commenting on their appropriateness.

Describing behavior is accurately recounting the specific behaviors of another without commenting on their appropriateness. When we describe behavior, we hold ourselves accountable for our observations and conclusions. To describe behavior, we move backward through the perceptual process by identifying the specific behaviors that have led to our generalized perception. What led you to conclude someone was "mean"? Was it something the person said? Did? If so, what? What did the person do or say that led you to conclude that he or she is a "real friend"? Once you have identified the specific behaviors, actions, or messages that led to your conclusion, you can share that information as feedback. For example, "Georgio, you called me a liar in front of the team, and you know I have no way to prove that I told the truth." "Shana, you came to my graduation even though it was on your twenty-first birthday." "You stayed and comforted me when Tyrone left, and you even volunteered to stay with my son so I could job hunt. You're a real friend."

Praising

Praise is describing the specific positive behaviors or accomplishments of another and the effect that behavior has on others. Too often, we fail to acknowledge the positive and helpful things people say and do. Yet our view of who we are—our identity as well as our behavior—is shaped by how others respond to us. Praise can be used to reinforce positive behavior and to help another develop a positive self-concept.

Praise is not the same as flattery. When we flatter someone, we use insincere compliments to ingratiate ourselves to that person. When we praise, our compliments are sincere. We express only admiration that we genuinely feel.

For praise to be effective, we need to focus the praise on the specific behavior and accomplishments and word the message according to the significance or value of the accomplishment or behavior. If your sister, who tends to be forgetful, remembers your birthday, that is a behavior that you will want to praise so that it is reinforced. But saying, "You're so wonderful, you're on top of everything" reinforces nothing because it is an overly general statement that does not identify a particular behavior or accomplishment. Simply saying something like, "Thanks for the birthday card; I really appreciate it" would be appropriate. The response acknowledges the accomplishment by describing the specific behavior and the positive feeling of gratitude that the behavior has caused. Although effective praise can enhance self-esteem, unnecessary praise can actually lower self-esteem. Check out an interesting article about praise and self-esteem in children, "Do You Praise Your Child Too Much?," available through InfoTrac College Edition. Use your ThomsonNOW for *Communicate!* to access **Web Resource 8.2: Too Much Praise?**

Praise, when appropriate, doesn't cost much, and it is usually valued and appreciated. Praise provides feedback and builds esteem; it can also deepen our relationship with that person because it increases the openness of the relationship. To increase your effectiveness in using praise, follow these steps: (1) identify the specific behavior or accomplishment that you want to reinforce; (2) describe the specific behavior or accomplishment; (3) describe any positive feelings or outcomes that you or others experienced as a result of the behavior or accomplishment; and (4) phrase the response so that the level of praise appropriately reflects the significance of the behavior or accomplishment. Let's look at two more examples.

> **Behavior:** Sonya takes responsibility for selecting and buying a group wedding present for a friend. The gift is a big hit.
>
> **Praise:** "Sonya, the present you chose for Stevie was really thoughtful. Not only did it fit our price range, but Stevie really liked it."
>
> **Accomplishment:** Cole has just received a letter inviting him to a reception at which he is to receive a scholarship award given for academic accomplishments and community service work.

praise
describing the specific positive behaviors or accomplishments of another and the effect that behavior has on others.

Praise: "Congratulations, Cole. I'm proud of you. It's really great to see that the effort you put into studying as well as the time and energy you have devoted to the Second Harvest Food Program and Big Brothers is being recognized and valued."

Giving Constructive Criticism

constructive criticism
describing specific behaviors of another that hurt the person or that person's relationships with others.

Research on reinforcement theory has found that people learn faster and better through positive rewards such as praise. Nevertheless, there are times when you need to give personal feedback to address negative behaviors or actions. **Constructive criticism** is describing specific behaviors of another that hurt the person or that person's relationships with others. Although the word *criticize* can mean judgment, constructive criticism does not condemn or judge but is based on empathy and a sincere desire to help someone understand the impact of his or her behavior. Use the following guidelines when giving constructive criticism.

1. **Ask the person's permission before giving criticism.** Before you give constructive criticism, you should make sure the person wants to hear what you have to say. A person who has agreed to hear constructive criticism is likely to be more receptive to it than is someone who is not accorded respect by being asked.

2. **Describe the behavior by accurately recounting precisely what was said or done without labeling the behavior good or bad, right or wrong.** By describing behavior, you lay an informative base for the feedback and increase the chances that the person will listen receptively. Feedback that is preceded with detailed description is less likely to be met defensively. Your description shows that you are criticizing the behavior rather than attacking the person, and it points the way to a solu-

Learning to give constructive criticism can help you avoid being met with a defensive reaction when you describe a person's negative behavior.

Jason Harris//© Thomson Higher Education

tion. For example, if DeShawn asks, "What did you think of the visuals I used when I delivered my report?" replying, "They weren't very effective" would be general and evaluative. Replying "Well, the type on the first two was small, and I had trouble reading them" is descriptive. Notice this constructive criticism does not attack DeShawn's competence. Instead, it points out a problem and in so doing enables DeShawn to see how to improve.

3. **Preface constructive criticism with an affirming statement.** Remember, by its nature even constructive criticism threatens the needs all of us have to be liked and admired. So, prefacing constructive criticism with statements that validate your respect or admiration of the other is important. One way to do this is to offer praise before criticism. In our example, you could begin your feedback to DeShawn by saying, "First, the charts and graphs were useful, and the color really helped us to see the problems. Second, the type size on the first two slides was small, and I had trouble reading them." Here the praise is relevant and significant. If you cannot preface feedback with significant praise, don't try. Prefacing feedback with empty praise will not help the person accept your feedback.

4. **When appropriate, suggest how the person can change the behavior.** Because the focus of constructive criticism is helping, it is appropriate to provide the person with your suggestions that might lead to positive change. In responding to DeShawn's request for feedback, you might also add, "When I make slides, I generally try to use 18-point font or larger. You might want to give that a try." By including a positive suggestion, you not only help the person by providing honest information, you also show that your intentions are positive.

5. **Consider how the feedback will affect your relationship.** Although appropriate personal feedback generally deepens a relationship, there are times when, by avoiding feedback, we may actually strengthen the relationship. For example, studies show that one of the most common problems in relationships is expressing complaints about one's partner too freely (Petronio, 2002). So before you offer constructive criticism, consider the context of your relationship. If you are overly free in your criticism, you risk having your partner become defensive or distant.

Assertiveness

A second dialectical tension in relationships is the tension we experience between wanting to be autonomous or independent and our need to be connected. At times, our desire for connectedness pushes us to subordinate our needs and opinions to the needs and opinions of our partner. At other times, our desire for autonomy pushes us to stand up for what we want and think. As we deal with this dialectical tension, we may find ourselves behaving passively, aggressively, or assertively.

OBSERVE & ANALYZE

Journal Activity

Praising and Criticizing

Think of someone you need to praise and someone to whom you would like to give constructive criticism. Prepare feedback for each person. Use the following steps:

1. Begin by writing a sentence that identifies your general impression of each person.

2. For each person, recall and write down the specific behaviors, actions, and messages that led to your impression.

3. Identify all the consequences that have resulted from the way this person has acted or spoken.

4. If you have any advice that seems appropriate to give to this person, record it.

5. Write a short feedback message for each person that follows the guidelines for effective praise or criticism.

In the next day or two, have a feedback conversation with at least one of these people and use your preparation to help you deliver the feedback. Then write a paragraph describing what happened and how well the feedback was received. Analyze why you believe the feedback was received as it was.

Thomson NOW! You can complete this activity online, download a preparation worksheet, and, if requested, e-mail it to your instructor. Use your ThomsonNOW for *Communicate!* to access **Skill Learning Activity 8.4.**

▶ Speech Assignment: Communicate on Your Feet

Giving Constructive Speech Criticism

When asked by your instructor, give praise and constructive criticism to one of your classmates who has given a personal narrative speech. Here are some guidelines for giving constructive speech criticism.

Praise What Was Done Well

One goal of post-speech feedback is to praise efforts at meeting the particular speech criteria. Always begin with positive feedback, because people are likely to continue doing things they are praised for. Be sure to make your comments as specific as you can. For example, instead of saying, "Jackie told a great story," you might say, "Jackie's use of language was particularly good; she did an excellent job using vivid and descriptive words that made her story come alive." General criteria that can be used as a starting point to evaluate any speech include the following:

- **Content of the speech:** Does the speaker seem to have expertise in the subject areas? Are visual aids appropriate and well used? Does the speaker establish common ground and adapt the content to the audience's interests, knowledge, and attitudes?

- **Organization of the speech:** Does the introduction of the speech get attention, build, and lead into the main topic of the speech? Are the main ideas of the speech clearly stated and meaningful? Do transitions lead smoothly from one point to another? Does the conclusion end the speech on a high note?

- **Language of the speech:** Is the language clear, vivid, emphatic, and appropriate?

- **Delivery of the speech:** Does the speaker sound enthusiastic? Show sufficient vocal expressiveness? Look at the audience? Have good posture and sufficient poise? Is the presentation spontaneous and fluent? Was the speaker's pronunciation and articulation acceptable?

You'll learn more about the appropriate criteria for various kinds of speeches in Chapters 12–17.

Identify What Could Have Been Done Better

The second goal of post-speech feedback is to show ways in which a speaker could have done better, regardless of how well she or he exhibited various speaking skills—even an "A" speech can be improved. (Notice we don't say to identify what was "bad" about a speech.) As with positive feedback, it is useful to phrase advice for improvement very specifically. Although you might start by saying, "I think Ernesto could have done even better transitioning from one part of his story to another," continue with a statement such as "I particularly liked the way he said, 'Now that I've told you how we came to be stranded in New York with no luggage and only six dollars between us, let me tell you how we managed to get home.' I would like to have heard more of those kinds of statements in the speeches." This specific, constructive phrasing shows speakers how they can do even better in their next speeches.

Passive, Aggressive, and Assertive Behavior

passive behavior
not expressing personal preferences or defending our rights because we fear the cost and are insecure in the relationships, have very low self-esteem, or value the other person above ourself.

We behave **passively** when we do not express our personal preferences or defend our rights because we value our connection with the other person more than we value our independence and we fear that we will lose our connection if we stand up for ourselves. We behave passively when we submit to other people's demands, even when doing so is inconvenient, against our best interests, or when it violates our rights. For example, Aaron and Katie routinely go to the gym at 10 a.m. Saturday mornings, but Aaron's Friday work schedule has changed and he doesn't get home until 3 a.m. on

Saturday morning. Aaron behaves passively if he doesn't say anything to Katie but drags himself out of bed even though he'd much rather sleep.

We behave **aggressively** when we forcefully make claims for our preferences, feelings, needs, or rights with little or no regard for the situation or for the feelings or rights of our partner. People can behave aggressively when they perceive themselves to be powerful, do not value the other person, lack emotional control, or feel defensive. Although aggressive behavior may stem from the need to establish more independence in a relationship, it also weakens feelings of connection and damages relationships. Research shows that people who receive aggressive messages from their partner are likely to feel hurt by them regardless of their relationship (Martin, Anderson, & Horvath, 1996, p. 24). Suppose that, without letting her know of his schedule change, Aaron has continued to meet Katie at the gym. If Katie suggests they meet next week at 8 a.m. instead of 10 a.m., Aaron may explode and aggressively reply, "No way! In fact, I don't care if I ever work out on Saturday again!" Katie, who has no context for understanding this aggressive outburst, may be startled, hurt, and confused.

Assertive behavior is expressing your personal preferences and defending your personal rights while respecting the preferences and rights of others. Assertiveness is an effective way of establishing our independence while continuing to nurture the relationship because our assertive messages teach our partners how to treat us. When we assert our needs and preferences effectively, we provide our partners with the honest and truthful information they need to understand and meet our needs. When Aaron's schedule changed, he could have behaved assertively and called Katie, explained his situation, and negotiated a more convenient time for working out together.

Assertive messages balance our rights and needs with the rights and needs of others. For a review of the characteristics of assertive behavior, see Figure 8.2.

aggressive behavior
belligerently or violently confronting another with your preferences, feelings, needs, or rights with little regard for the situation or for the feelings or rights of others.

assertive behavior
expressing your personal preferences and defending your personal rights while respecting the preferences and rights of others.

Own your feelings	Assertive individuals acknowledge that the thoughts and feelings expressed are theirs.
Avoid confrontational language	Assertive individuals do not use threats, evaluations, or dogmatic language.
Use specific statements directed to the behaviors at hand	Instead of focusing on extraneous issues, assertive individuals use descriptive statements that focus on the issue that is most relevant.
Maintain eye contact and firm body position	Assertive individuals look people in the eye rather than shifting gaze, looking at the floor, swaying back and forth, hunching over, or using other signs that may be perceived as indecisive or lacking conviction.
Maintain a firm but pleasant tone of voice	Assertive individuals speak firmly but at a normal pitch, volume, and rate.
Avoid hemming and hawing	Assertive individuals avoid vocalized pauses and other signs of indecisiveness.

Figure 8.2
Characteristics of assertive behavior

Here are some useful guidelines for practicing assertive behavior: (1) identify what you are thinking or feeling; (2) analyze the cause of these feelings; (3) identify what your real preferences and rights are; and (4) use describing feelings and describing behavior skills to make "I" statements that explain your position politely. For help in practicing a difficult assertive behavior, saying no, use your ThomsonNOW for *Communicate!* to access **Web Resource 8.3: How to Say No**.

Cultural Variations in Passive, Aggressive, and Assertive Behavior

Assertiveness is valued and practiced in Western cultures. Whereas North American culture is known for its assertive communication style, Asian and South American cultures value accord and harmony (Samovar, Porter, & McDaniel, 2007). In fact, in collectivist societies typical of Asia and South America, there is "a style of communication in which respecting the relationship through communication is more important than the information exchanged" (Jandt, 2001, p. 37). Jandt goes on to explain that these societies use group harmony, avoidance of loss of face to others and oneself, and a modest presentation of oneself as means of respecting the relationship. "One does not say what one actually thinks when it might hurt others in the group" (p. 37).

On the other hand, in Latin and Hispanic societies, men, especially, are frequently taught to exercise a form of self-expression that goes far beyond the guidelines presented here for assertive behavior. In these societies, the concept of "machismo" guides male behavior. Thus, the standard of assertiveness considered appropriate in the dominant American culture can seem inappropriate to people whose cultural frame of reference leads them to perceive it as either aggressive or weak.

Thus, when we use assertiveness—as with any other skill—we need to be aware that no single standard of behavior ensures that we will achieve our goals. Although what is labeled appropriate behavior varies across cultures, the results of passive and aggressive behaviors seem universal. Passive behavior can cause resentment and aggressive behavior leads to fear and misunderstanding. When talking with people whose culture, background, or lifestyle differs from your own, you may need to observe their behavior and their responses to your statements before you can be sure about the kinds of behavior that are likely to communicate your intentions effectively.

Managing Conflict in Relationships

When two people have an honest relationship, it is inevitable that there will be times when one person's attempt to satisfy his or her own needs will conflict with the other person's desires. When this happens, the partners experience conflict. **Interpersonal conflict** exists when the needs or

interpersonal conflict *when the needs or ideas of one person are at odds or in opposition to the needs or ideas of another.*

Communication Skill   Assertiveness

Skill	Use	Procedure	Example
Standing up for yourself and doing so in interpersonally effective ways that describe your feelings honestly and exercise your personal rights while respecting the rights of others.	To show clearly what you think or feel.	1. Identify what you are thinking or feeling. 2. Analyze the cause of these feelings. 3. Identify what your real preferences and rights are. 4. Use describing feelings and describing behavior skills to make "I" statements that politely explain your position.	When Gavin believes he is being unjustly charged, he says, "I have never been charged for a refill on iced tea before—has there been a change in policy?"

Skill Building   Assertive Messages

For each of the following situations, write an assertive response.

1. You come back to your dorm, apartment, or house to finish a paper that is due tomorrow, only to find that someone else is using your computer.
   Assertive response:

2. You work part time at a clothing store. Just as your shift is ending, your manager says to you, "I'd like you to work overtime, if you would. Martin's supposed to replace you, but he just called and can't get here for at least an hour." You have tickets to a concert that starts in an hour.
   Assertive response:

3. During a phone call with your elderly grandmother, she announces, "Your Great Aunt Margie called, and I told her you'd be happy to take us grocery shopping and out to lunch on Sunday." You were planning to spend Sunday working on your résumé for an interview on Monday.
   Assertive response:

4. You and your friend made a date to go dancing, an activity you really enjoy. When you meet, your friend says, "I don't feel like dancing tonight. Let's go to Joey's party instead."
   Assertive response:

5. You're riding in a car with a group of friends on the way to a party when the driver begins to clown around by swerving the car back and forth, speeding up to tailgate the car in front, and honking his horn. You believe this driving is dangerous, and you're becoming scared.
   Assertive response:

 You can complete this activity online and compare your responses to the authors'. Use your Thomson-NOW for *Communicate!* to access **Skill Learning Activity 8.6**.

ideas of one person are at odds or in opposition to the needs or ideas of another. In these conflict situations, participants have choices about how they act and how they communicate with each other.

Many people view conflict as a sign of a bad relationship, but the reality is that conflicts occur in all relationships. Although cultures differ in how they view conflict (for example, Asian cultures see it as dysfunctional), whether conflict hurts or strengthens a relationship depends on how we deal with it. In this section, we discuss five styles people use to manage conflict and how you can skillfully initiate and respond to conflict in your relationships.

Think about the last time you experienced a conflict. How did you react? Did you avoid it? Give in? Force the other person to accept your will? Did you compromise? Or did the two of you use a problem-solving approach. When faced with a conflict, you can withdraw, accommodate, force, compromise, or collaborate (Lulofs & Cahn, 2000, pp. 101–102).

withdrawing
managing conflict by physically or psychologically removing yourself.

One of the most common and easiest ways to deal with conflict is withdrawing or avoiding the conflict. **Withdrawing** involves physically or psychologically removing yourself from the conflict. You withdraw physically by leaving the site. For instance, imagine Eduardo and Justina get into an argument about their financial situation. Eduardo may withdraw physically by saying, "I don't want to talk about this" and walk out the door. Psychological withdrawal occurs when you simply ignore what the other person is saying. So, when Justina begins to talk about their financial situation, Eduardo may ignore her and act as though she has not spoken. When you repeatedly use withdrawing, you risk damaging your relationship. First, in terms of the dialectical tension in the relationship, withdrawing signals closedness rather than openness and autonomy rather than connection. Further, withdrawing doesn't eliminate the source of the conflict and it often increases the tension. In many cases, not confronting the problem when it occurs only makes it more difficult to deal with in the long run. Nevertheless, as a temporary strategy, withdrawing allows tempers to cool and may be appropriate when neither an issue nor a relationship is important.

accommodating
managing conflict by satisfying others' needs or accepting others' ideas while neglecting our own.

A second style of managing conflict is **accommodating,** which means satisfying others' needs or accepting others' ideas while neglecting your own. So people who adopt the accommodating style of conflict will use passive behavior. For instance, during a discussion of their upcoming vacation, Mariana and Juan disagree in their thinking about whether to invite friends to join them. Juan uses accommodation when Mariana says, "I think it would be fun to go with another couple, don't you?" and he replies, "OK, whatever you want."

Accommodating can result in poor communication because important facts, arguments, and positions are not voiced. There are situations, of course, in which it is appropriate and effective to accommodate. When the issue is not important to you, but the relationship is, accommodating is the preferred style. Hal and Yvonne are trying to decide where to go for dinner. Hal says, "I really have a craving for some Thai food tonight." Yvonne, who prefers pizza, says, "OK, that will be fine." Yvonne's interest in pizza was not very strong, and because Hal really seemed excited by Thai food, Yvonne accommodated.

forcing
managing conflict by satisfying your own needs or advancing your own ideas, with no concern for the needs or ideas of the other and no concern for the harm done to the relationship.

A third style of dealing with conflict is forcing or competing. **Forcing** means satisfying your own needs or advancing your own ideas with no concern for the needs or ideas of the other and no concern for the harm done

©1995 Baby Blues Partnership. Distributed by King Features Syndicate. Reprinted with special permission of King Features Syndicate, Inc.

to the relationship. Forcing may use aggressive behavior such as physical threats, verbal attacks, coercion, or manipulation. If you use forcing in a conflict and your partner avoids or accommodates, the conflict seems to subside. If, however, your partner answers your forcing style with a forcing style, the conflict escalates.

Although forcing may result in a person getting her or his own way, it usually hurts a relationship, at least in the short term. There are times, however, when forcing is an effective means to resolve conflict. In emergencies, when quick and decisive action must be taken to ensure safety or minimize harm, forcing is useful. When an issue is critical to your own or the other's welfare and you know you are right, you may find forcing necessary. Finally, if you are interacting with someone who will take advantage of you if you do not force the issue, this style is appropriate. For example, David knows that, statistically speaking, the likelihood of death or serious injury increases dramatically if one does not wear a helmet when riding a motorcycle. So he insists that his sister wear one when she rides with him, even though she complains bitterly about wearing one.

A fourth way to manage conflict is through **compromising,** which involves giving up part of what each wants, to provide at least some satisfaction for both parties. Under this approach, both people have to give up part of what they really want or believe, or they have to trade one thing they want to get something else. For example, if Heather and Paul are working together on a class project and need to meet outside of class but both have busy schedules, they may compromise on a time to meet.

Although compromising is a popular and effective style, there are drawbacks associated with it. One drawback is that the quality of a decision is affected if one of the parties "trades away" a better solution to find a compromise. Compromising is appropriate when the issue is moderately important, when there are time constraints, and when attempts at forcing or collaborating have not been successful.

A fifth style of dealing with conflict is through problem-solving discussion, or collaboration. When you **collaborate,** you both try to fully address the needs and issues of each of you and arrive at a solution that is mutually satisfying. In this approach, both of you view the disagreement as a

compromising
managing conflict by giving up part of what you want, to provide at least some satisfaction for both parties.

collaborating
managing conflict by fully addressing the needs and issues of each party and arriving at a solution that is mutually satisfying.

problem to be solved, so you discuss the issues, describe your feelings, and identify the characteristics of an effective solution. With collaboration, both people's needs are met and both sides feel that they have been heard. For example, if Juan and Mariana decide to collaborate on their conflict about asking friends to join them on vacation, Mariana may explain to Juan how she thinks that, by vacationing with friends, they can share expenses and lower their costs. Juan may describe his desire to have "alone time" with Mariana. As they explore what each wants from the vacation, they may arrive at a plan that meets both of their needs. So, they may end up vacationing alone, but spending several nights camping to lower their expenses. You can read more about managing conflict in a collaborative way at your ThomsonNOW for *Communicate!* Access **Web Resource 8.4: Skills for Collaborative Conflict**.

Conversation and Analysis

Thomson NOW!

Use your ThomsonNOW for *Communicate!* to access the video clip of Trevor and Meg's conversation. As you watch Trevor and Meg discuss the future of their relationship, focus on how effectively they are communicating. How do Trevor and Meg disclose their feelings? Note how effective each is at owning feelings and opinions. How well do Trevor and Meg use praise and constructive criticism? Notice how each demonstrates the characteristics of assertive behavior. What really is Meg's fear? You can respond to these analysis questions by clicking on "Analysis" in the menu bar at the top of the screen. When you've answered all the questions, click "Done" to compare your answers to those provided by the authors.

Here is a transcript of the conversation. You can also find a copy of this transcript online, which enables you to take notes as you watch the video. Use your ThomsonNOW for *Communicate!* to access **Skill Learning Activity 8.8**. When you have finished viewing the video and taking notes, click on "Authors' Model Analysis" to compare your notes to the detailed conversational analysis provided by the authors.

Trevor and Meg have been going together for the last several months of their senior year at college. Now that graduation is approaching, they are trying to figure out what to do about their relationship. They sit and talk.

Jason Harris/© Thomson Higher Education

Conversation

TREVOR: Meg, I think it's time we talk about making plans for the future. After all, we'll be graduating next month.

MEG: Trevor, you know how uncomfortable I feel about making any long-range plans at this time. We still need to know a lot more about each other before we even think about getting engaged.

What Would You Do?

Ronaldo sat in the study hall cramming for a final examination when two of his classmates, Chauncey and Doug, walked up to his table.

"Studying hard, huh?" Chauncey asked.

"Yeah. I'm stressing hard over this final," said Ronaldo. "What about you guys?"

"Hardly studying," said Chauncey.

Doug laughed.

Ronaldo looked at the two and saw that they both seemed relaxed and confident. "Something's not right with this picture," he said. "You're not going to tell me you guys are ready for this thing, are you?"

"Yep," said Chauncey.

Doug nodded.

"I don't get it," said Ronaldo. "You mean you've already gone back and studied everything we've covered this semester?"

"Hey, bright boy, you only need to study what's actually on the test," said Chauncey.

"And how would you know that when McAllister didn't even give us a study sheet to help us know

what would be on the test?" asked Ronaldo. He was beginning to put the puzzle together.

Doug placed his hand on Chauncey's arm. "Don't tell him anything else, man," he said.

"No, it's all right. Ronaldo's cool," said Chauncey. "He knows how to keep a secret. Don't you?"

"I guess," Ronaldo said uneasily.

"It's like this," said Chauncey. "Doug's little brother is a super geek with computers. He hacked into McAllister's system and downloaded a copy of the final exam. You interested in getting a head start?"

1. Assuming that Ronaldo declines Chauncey's offer to cheat, what are the remaining ethical issues he faces? Which would be more ethically compromising: letting Chauncey and Doug get away with cheating, or betraying their trust by notifying the professor about their actions?

2. When, if ever, is it ethically acceptable to divulge information that you have sworn not to share with others?

TREVOR: Why? We've both said we love each other, haven't we? [*Meg nods*] So why's this too soon? What else do we need to know?

MEG: For starters, I'll be going to law school this fall, and this year is going to be difficult. And, you haven't gotten a job yet.

TREVOR: Come on, Meg. You're going to law school in the city, so I'll have a degree in business, so I can probably get a job most anywhere.

MEG: But Trevor, that's just my point. I know I'll be starting law school; I've always wanted to be a lawyer. And you don't really have any idea what you want to do. And that bothers me. I can't be worrying about you and your career when I'm going to need to focus on my classes.

TREVOR: But I told you, I can get a job anywhere.

MEG: Yes, Trevor, but you need more than a job. You need to figure out what kind of job really turns you on, or else you risk waking up one day and regretting your life. And, I don't want to be there when that happens.

I watched my dad go through a midlife crisis, and he ended up walking out on us.

TREVOR: I'm not your dad, Meg. I won't leave you. And don't worry about me; I'll find a job.

MEG: Really? You knew I was going to law school in the city for over a month, but you still haven't even begun a job search. Trevor, right now is the time when people are hiring, and you haven't even done your résumé. The longer you wait, the more difficult your search is going to be.

TREVOR: Come on, Meg. You've already said I'm irresistible. What company wouldn't want me?

MEG: I'm serious, Trevor. Look, I've got a scholarship to law school, but it's only going to pay half of my expenses. I'll be taking a loan to get enough money to pay the rest and to have money to live on. I won't have the money or the time to be very supportive of you if you haven't found work. I need the security of knowing that you've got a job and that you are saving money.

TREVOR: Well, they say that "two can live as cheaply as one." I was thinking that once you got settled, I'd move in and that will save us a lot of money.

MEG: Whoa, Trevor. You know how I feel about that. I do love you, and I hope that we have a future together. But living together this year is not an option. I think we need at least a year of living on our own to get ourselves settled and make sure that we really are compatible. After all, we come from totally different backgrounds. I practically raised myself, and I've paid my own bills since I was 18, while you've been lucky enough to have parents who footed your bills. There have been several times when we've talked about important issues and the differences between us have been obvious, and they worry me.

TREVOR: You mean when I was joking around about our different taste in cars?

MEG: No, Trevor, not cars; that's minor. But we also have greatly different feelings about money and family. You've told me that once you get married you want to start a family immediately. As I see it, I've got a three-year commitment to law school, then seven to 10 years of hard work to make partner at a good firm. So I'm not sure when I want to start a family. But I know it won't be for at least six years.

TREVOR: So, what are you saying, Meg? Is it over? "Thanks for the good time, Trevor, but you're not in my plans?"

MEG: Please don't be sarcastic. I'm not trying to hurt you. It makes me happy to think that we'll spend the rest of our lives together. But I'm worried about several things, so I'm just not ready to commit to that now. Let's just take a year, get settled, and see what happens. I'll love it if you do get a job near where I'm in school. That way we can have time to sort through some of the issues between us.

TREVOR: You mean if you can fit me into your schedule? Meg, if we love each other now, aren't we still going to love each other next year? If we wait until we have everything settled, we might never get married; there'll always be something. After all, we are two different people. We're never going to agree on everything!

MEG: Are you saying that as unsettled as our lives are right now, we can shoulder the additional stress of planning for a marriage?

TREVOR: No, what I'm saying is that we live together this year, see how it goes, then if it isn't working, we don't have to get married.

Summary

In relationships, seemingly opposing forces of openness–closedness, autonomy–connection, and novelty–predictability naturally occur. Called relational dialectics, these opposites create tension, which must be managed in all interpersonal relationships. Communication through self-disclosure, feedback, assertiveness, and conflict management can assist in managing the dialectical tensions in relationships.

Self-disclosure reveals information about ourselves that is unknown to others. Guidelines can help us decide when self-disclosure is appropriate. Sometimes we have legitimate reasons for managing our privacy instead of disclosing information. Disclosing feelings can be difficult. We can deal with our feelings by withholding them, displaying them, or skillfully describing them. Instead of owning our own feelings and ideas, we often avoid disclosure by making generalized statements.

Personal feedback builds relationships by describing, not evaluating, behavior and its effects. Positive feedback is accomplished through praise. Negative feedback can be delivered effectively through constructive criticism.

Assertiveness is the skill of standing up for ourselves in interpersonally effective ways. Passive people are often unhappy as a result of not stating their needs; aggressive people get their ideas and feelings heard but may create other problems through their aggressiveness.

We cope with conflicts in a variety of ways: withdrawing, accommodating, forcing, compromising, and collaborating. Although there are positive and negative outcomes of each style, when we are concerned about the long-term relationship and the effectiveness of a solution, collaborating is often most appropriate.

Thomson™
NOW!

Communicate! Online

Now that you have read Chapter 8, use your ThomsonNOW for *Communicate!* for quick access to the electronic resources that accompany this text. Your ThomsonNOW gives you access to the video of the conversation between Trevor and Meg on pages 190–193, the Web Resources and Skill Learning Activities featured in this chapter, InfoTrac College Edition, and online study aids such as a digital glossary and review quizzes.

Your *Communicate!* ThomsonNOW is an online study system that helps you identify concepts you don't fully understand, allowing you to put your study time to the best use. Using chapter-by-chapter diagnostic pre-tests, the system creates a personalized study plan for each chapter. Each plan directs you to specific resources designed to improve your understanding, including pages from the text in e-book format. Chapter post-tests give you an opportunity to measure how much you've learned and let you know if you are ready for graded quizzes and exams.

Key Terms

Go to your ThomsonNOW for *Communicate!* to access your online glossary for Chapter 8. Print a copy of the glossary for this chapter and test yourself with the electronic flash cards or complete the crossword puzzle to help you master these key terms:

accommodating (188)	describing feelings (177)	rapport-talk (176)
aggressive behavior (184)	forcing (188)	relational dialectics (170)
assertive behavior (184)	interpersonal conflict (187)	report-talk (176)
collaborating (189)	managing privacy (174)	self-disclosure (170)
compromising (188)	passive behavior (184)	withdrawing (187)
constructive criticism (181)	praise (180)	
describing behavior (180)	privacy (174)	

Review Quiz

Test your knowledge of the concepts in this chapter by taking the online review quiz for Chapter 8. Go to your ThomsonNOW for *Communicate!* to access the quiz. When you have completed the quiz, submit it for scoring.

Skill Learning Activities

Complete the Observe & Analyze, Test Your Competence, Skill Building, and Conversation and Analysis activities for Chapter 8 online at your ThomsonNOW for *Communicate!*. You can submit your Observe & Analyze answers to your instructor, compare your Test Your Competence and Skill Building answers to those provided by the authors, and do both for the Conversation and Analysis activity.

8.1: Observe & Analyze: Self-Disclosure and Popular Media (175)
8.2: Test Your Competence: Building Your Vocabulary of Emotions (182)

Web Resources

Go to your ThomsonNOW for *Communicate!* to access the Web Resources for this chapter.

OBJECTIVES

After you have read this chapter, you should be able to answer these questions:

- What is an interview?
- What types of questions are used in an interview?
- What are the characteristics of open and closed, primary and secondary, and neutral and leading questions?
- How do you prepare for and conduct an information interview?
- How do you conduct a job interview?
- How do you present yourself successfully in a job interview?
- How do you participate in a media interview?

9
Interviewing

Terrence, the manager at Qwik In and Out, a convenience store and gas station, needed a new night cashier and was interviewing applicants. His first candidate arrived on time, and after taking a tour around the store, they retired to Terrence's office for the interview.

Terrence began, "Take a seat. What did you say your name was again?"

"Bobby. And, um, . . . I'm not sure where you want me to sit."

"Oh, well, just sit on that box over there. Sorry for the mess, but, you know, I've had a lot to do. So, Bobby, you want to work here at Qwik In and Out?"

"Yeah."

"Well, you understand that you will be working alone at night, right?"

"Yeah."

"So, it says on your application that you went to Highlands High School. Is that right?"

"Uh-huh."

"And now you're a student at CSCTU?"

"Yeah."

"Will school interfere with your work schedule?"

"Nope."

"Is there anything else I should know?"

"No."

"Well, I've got several other people to talk to, and I'll let you know by Monday what I decide."

"Okay."

After Bobby left the store, Terrence turned to Mary, the day cashier, and said, "Boy, that guy was sure a loser. He just wasn't at all prepared for the interview. I sure hope the next guy's better."

hat do you think about Terrence's assessment of Bobby? What do you think about the job Terrence did in conducting the interview? Interviewing is a powerful method you can use to collect or present firsthand information that may be unavailable elsewhere. So, it is an important communication skill to master. An **interview** is a planned, structured conversation in which one person asks questions and another person answers them. Unlike most interpersonal communication, interview participants usually prepare for the interview conversation.

We begin this chapter by describing interview planning, especially how you can construct good interview questions. Then we explain how you can prepare for and conduct an interview where the goal is to gather information. Next we discuss employment interviews from the perspective of both the interviewer and the interviewee. Finally, we provide information on how you can prepare for and participate in media interviews.

interview
a planned, structured conversation in which one person asks questions and another person answers them.

Questions Used in Interviewing

The success of any interview depends on preparing a list of good questions. You may want to ask questions about (1) behaviors (what a person has done or is doing), (2) demographics (such as age, education), (3) opinions or values, (4) knowledge (facts), (5) experiences, and (6) feelings. But regardless of content, your interview question list is likely to have a mix of open-ended and closed questions, which may be phrased neutrally or may be leading. Some of your questions will be primary and others secondary or follow-up questions.

Open versus Closed Questions

open questions
broad-based probes that call on the interviewee to provide perspective, ideas, information, feelings, or opinions as he or she answers the question.

Open questions are broad-based probes that call on the interviewee to provide perspective, ideas, information, feelings, or opinions as he or she answers the question. For example, in a job interview you might be asked, "What one accomplishment has best prepared you for this job?" In a customer service interview, a representative might ask, "What seems to be the problem?" or "Can you tell me the steps you took when you first set this product up?" Interviewers ask open questions to encourage the person to talk, allowing the interviewer an opportunity to listen and observe. Open questions take time to answer and give respondents more control, which means that interviewers can lose sight of their original purpose if they are not careful (Tengler & Jablin, 1983).

closed questions
narrowly focused questions that require the respondent to give very brief (one- or two-word) answers.

By contrast, **closed questions** are narrowly focused and require the respondent to give very brief (one- or two-word) answers. Closed questions range from those that can be answered "yes" or "no," such as "Have you had a course in marketing?" to those that require only a short answer, such as "Where did you buy the product?" By asking closed questions, interviewers can control the interview and obtain specific information quickly. The answers to closed questions cannot reveal the nuances behind responses, nor are they likely to capture the complexity of the story. Effective interview conversations contain a combination of open and closed questions. With this in mind, look again at the opening interview. What kinds of questions did Terrence ask Bobby. How did this affect what happened?

For an activity that will help you practice identifying and creating open and closed questions, go to your ThomsonNOW for *Communicate!* to access **Skill Learning Activity 9.1: Open and Closed Questions**.

Neutral versus Leading Questions

Open and closed questions may be either neutral or leading. **Neutral questions** do not direct a person's answer. "What can you tell me about your work with Habitat for Humanity?" or "What symptoms did you experience?" are both neutral questions. The neutral question gives the respondent free rein to answer the question without any knowledge of what the interviewer thinks or believes.

neutral questions
questions that do not direct a person's answer.

By contrast, **leading questions** guide respondents toward providing certain types of information and imply that the interviewer prefers one answer over another. "What do you like about working for Habitat for Humanity?" steers the respondent to describe only the positive aspects of the work. "Was this as painful as a migraine?" directs the answer by providing the standard for comparison. In most types of interviews, neutral questions are preferred. In the opening interview, which of Terrence's questions were neutral, and which were leading?

leading questions
questions that guide respondents toward providing certain types of information and imply that the interviewer prefers one answer over another.

Primary versus Secondary Questions

Primary questions are the lead-in questions that you use to introduce one of the major topics of the interview conversation. When planning interview questions, you should carefully choose the major topics you want to cover and then prepare at least one primary question for each topic. **Secondary or follow-up questions** are designed to probe the answers given to primary questions. When you expect a specific answer, you can preplan your secondary questions. Usually, however, your secondary questions will be spontaneous and you will construct them in response to an answer to a primary question. Some follow-up questions encourage the person to continue ("And then?" or "Is there more?"); some probe into what the person has said ("What does 'frequently' mean?" or "What were you thinking at the time?"); and some probe the feelings of the person ("How did it feel to get the prize?" or "Did it last longer than 15 minutes?"). The major purpose of follow-up questions is to encourage the person to expand on an answer that seems incomplete or vague. Sometimes the person may not understand how much detail you are looking for, and occasionally he or she may be purposely evasive. Notice that Terrence didn't really probe Bobby's answers.

primary questions
lead-in questions that introduce one of the major topics of the interview conversation.

secondary or follow-up questions
questions designed to probe the answers given to primary questions.

Interviewing for Information

Interviewing can be a valuable method for obtaining information on nearly any topic. Lawyers and police interview witnesses to establish facts; health care providers interview patients to obtain medical histories before making diagnoses; reporters interview sources for their stories; social workers and sales representatives interview clients; managers interview current and perspective employees; and students interview experts to obtain information for papers. Your interviews are more likely to achieve the desired result if they are carefully planned. Planning includes clearly defining the purpose of the interview, selecting the person (people) to interview, planning the interview protocol, and conducting the interview.

Defining the Purpose of the Interview

Informative interviews require a clear, identified purpose that can be summarized in one sentence. Without such a statement of purpose, your questions will probably have no direction, and the information derived from the interview may not fit together well. Your purpose may be to obtain expert information, investigate a complaint, get the story of someone's experience, or evaluate someone. Suppose you wanted to learn about the commercial food service business. Possible specific purposes would be:

1. To find out what criteria were used for selecting a commercial food service provider for this college.

2. To learn the most efficient means of food distribution in a dining hall.

3. To understand how dietitians create cost-effective menus that provide good nutrition.

Each of these topics covers an entirely different aspect of food service and will direct you toward who to interview and the types of questions to ask.

Selecting the Best Person to Interview

In some situations, it is obvious who you should interview. At other times, locating the right person to interview can be a challenge, especially when you need expert answers. You may have to do research before you can identify the right people. Suppose your purpose is to learn how dietitians create cost-effective menus that provide good nutrition. You might begin by asking one of the food service workers at the campus dining hall for the name of the food service manager. Or you could find the manager by calling the student center. In any case, the manager could give you the name and phone number (or e-mail address) of the dietitian. Once you have identified the person or people to be interviewed, you should contact them to make an appointment. Be sure to clearly state the purpose of the interview, how the interview information will be used, and how long you expect the

© Dana White/PhotoEdit

Focus groups are marketing interviews with a group of consumers. What adjustments do you think an interviewer must make in a group, versus a one-on-one, interview?

interview to take. When setting a time and date, be flexible by suggesting several dates and time ranges.

You don't want to bother your interviewee with information you can get elsewhere. So to prepare appropriate questions, you will need to do some research on the topic. If, for instance, you are going to interview a dietitian, you will want to find out what a dietitian is and does. If your purpose is to understand how nutritious, cost-effective menus are planned in an institutional setting, you can acquaint yourself with the current FDA nutritional standards and search for articles on cost factors in commercial food service operations. Interviewees will be more likely to enjoy talking with you if you're well informed, and familiarity with your subject will also enable you to ask better questions.

Developing the Interview Protocol

The heart of the interview plan is the **interview protocol,** an ordered list of questions that you have selected to meet the specific purpose of the interview. Preparation of the interview protocol begins by listing the topic areas to be covered in the interview. Once topics are listed, they need to be prioritized for importance. Figure 9.1 presents a list of topics for the interview with the dietitian.

For each topic, a list of questions should be generated. Questions should be revised until they are a mixture of open and closed questions that are phrased neutrally. Figure 9.2 shows some questions that could be asked about the topic "Determining Portion Costs."

interview protocol
an ordered list of questions that have been selected to meet the specific purpose of the interview.

Figure 9.1
Topics for an interview with
the dietitian

- Demographic information
- Determining portion costs
- Understanding student food preferences
- Deciding on menus

Figure 9.2
Questions to determine
portion costs

- Do you know the cost of each portion of all items?
- How are portion costs determined?
- Do you have a budget for each meal plan serving?
- Suppose you'd planned a menu and it turned out to be more expensive than you anticipated; what would happen?
- How important is portion control?
- What are some of the less expensive foods you use that are both nutritious and tasty?

Once a complete question list has been generated, you will need to estimate how long it will take to ask and answer all of the questions. A rule of thumb is to allow four minutes for each open-ended question and one minute for each close-ended question. If your realistic guess exceeds the time you have allotted for the interview, cull your questions by eliminating some from each topic list and by severely trimming those from less important topics.

The final step in creating the interview protocol is to develop a sequence for the questions. Your initial questions should be short and designed to get the interviewee involved in the conversation. In general, these opening questions should ask for facts. It is better to leave more complex or controversial questions until later, after you have established rapport. Answering fact questions can be boring for the interviewee, so you might consider spreading these throughout the interview. It is usually easier for people to talk about things in the present than it is for them to remember things in the past or to hypothesize about the future, so begin by asking about current practices or events, then work backward or forward. Be sure to place topics of great importance early in the interview, so you will have plenty of time for follow-up questions.

When you have finalized your interview protocol, reproduce it, leaving enough space between your questions for you to take complete notes of the answers.

Conducting the Interview

By applying the interpersonal skills we have discussed in this book, you'll find that you can turn your careful planning into an excellent interview.

First, of course, you will want to be courteous during the interview. Start by thanking the person for taking the time to talk to you. Remember, although the interviewee may enjoy talking about the subject, may be flattered, and may wish to share knowledge, that person has nothing to gain from the interview. Encourage the person to speak freely. Most of all, respect what the person says regardless of what you may think of the answers.

Second, listen carefully. At key places in the interview, you should paraphrase what the person has said to assure yourself that you really understand him or her.

Third, keep the interview moving. You do not want to rush the person, but you do want to get your questions answered during the allotted time.

Fourth, make sure that your nonverbal reactions—your facial expressions and your gestures—are in keeping with the tone you want to communicate. Maintain good eye contact with the person. Nod to show understanding, and smile occasionally to maintain the friendliness of the interview. How you look and act is likely to determine whether the person will warm up to you and give you an informative interview.

Finally, if you are going to publish the substance of the interview, be sure to get written permission for exact quotes; as a courtesy, offer to let the person see a copy of the article (or at least tell the person exactly when it will be published). Under some circumstances, you may want to show the interviewee a draft of your report about the interview before it goes into print, if only to allow him or her to double-check the accuracy of direct quotations. If so, provide a draft well before the deadline, to give the person the opportunity to read it and to give you time to deal with any suggestions. At times, you may wish to conduct an electronic interview by using e-mail. To read some useful tips for these types of interviews, access **Web Resource 9.1: E-mail Interviews** through your ThomsonNOW for *Communicate!*

Conducting Employment Interviews

Almost all organizations use interviewing as part of their hiring process. Employment interviews help organizations assess which applicants have the knowledge, experience, and skills to do a job and which applicants will "fit" into the organization's culture. Interviews allow organizations to evaluate personal characteristics (such as ambition, energy, and enthusiasm) and interpersonal skills (such as conversing and listening) that cannot be judged from a résumé.

Historically, most employment interviewing was done by human resource professionals or managers, but today organizations are using coworkers as interviewers. You may have already helped to conduct employment interviews, or you may be asked to do so in the near future.

Preparing for the Interview

As with information interviews, your preparation begins by doing research. In the case of employment interviewing, this means becoming familiar with the knowledge, skills, and aptitudes that someone must have to be successful in the job. It also means studying the résumés, references, and, if available, the test scores for each person you will interview.

In most employment interviewing situations, you will be seeing several candidates. You will want to make sure that all applicants are asked the same (or very similar) questions and that the questions selected allow applicants to disclose information you will need to know to make an informed hiring decision. To accomplish this, you will want to use a highly structured to moderately structured interview. This means that you will prepare a general interview protocol to use with all interviewees. Your protocol should have questions designed to probe the interviewees' knowledge, skills, and experiences that are relevant to the job. For potential queries, access **Web Resource 9.2: 109 Typical Job Interview Questions** through your ThomsonNOW for *Communicate!*

It is important that you avoid questions that violate fair employment practice legislation. The Equal Opportunity Commission has detailed guidelines that spell out what questions are unlawful. To read a generalized discussion of the types of questions that should not be asked in interviews, access **Web Resource 9.3: Discrimination Laws and Interviewing** through your ThomsonNOW for *Communicate!*

Conducting the Interview

A well-planned employment interview is carefully orchestrated. It has an introduction designed to establish rapport and help the interviewee relax. As the interviewer, you should warmly greet the applicant by name, shake hands, and introduce yourself. If you will be taking notes or recording the interview, you should explain that to the candidate. During the early part of the interview, you will want to establish rapport with the applicant. If the applicant is extremely nervous, you may want to ask a couple of "warm-up" questions designed to put the applicant at ease. If the applicant seems comfortable, you may move directly into the body of the interview, using the interview protocol.

In the body, or main part of the interview, candidates are carefully questioned to determine whether their knowledge, skills, experiences, personal characteristics, and interpersonal style fit with the demands of the job and with the organizational culture. During this period it is important for you, the interviewer, to keep the interview moving. You will want to give applicants sufficient time to answer your questions, but you don't want to waste time by allowing applicants to over-answer questions. One way to help applicants understand the scope of the interview is to preview each of the topic areas to be covered and the time you expect to spend in this conversation.

As you ask the questions, strive to sound spontaneous and to speak in a voice that is easily heard. Be sensitive to the nonverbal messages you are sending. Be careful that you are not "leading" applicants through nonverbal cues. Use follow-up questions to probe answers that are vague. Remember, your goal is to understand the applicant.

As the interview comes to an end, tell the applicant what will happen next. Explain how and approximately when the hiring decision will be made, and how the applicant will be notified. Unless you are the person with hiring authority, remain neutral about the candidate. You don't want to mislead the candidate with false hope or discouragement.

Interviewing to Get a Job

Being able to present yourself successfully in a job interview is an essential skill that you may engage in repeatedly during the course of a career. In this section, we present strategies for writing a cover letter, preparing a résumé, and participating in a job interview.

Jason Harris/©Thomson Higher Education

Getting the Interview

Because interviewing is time consuming, most organizations do not interview all the people who apply for a job. Rather, they use a variety of screening devices to eliminate people who don't meet their qualifications. Chief among these are evaluating the qualifications presented on the résumé and in the cover letter. The goal of your résumé with cover letter "is to communicate your qualifications in writing and sell yourself to prospective employers" (Kaplan, 2002, p. 6).

It all begins with research To write an effective cover letter and résumé that highlight your qualifications for a particular job, you need to know something about the job requirements and about the company. The career center advisers at your college or university can assist you with your research. You may also access **Web Resource 9.4: Research before You Write** through your ThomsonNOW for *Communicate!* This resource links you to additional sources of information on various companies.

Write an effective cover letter A **cover letter** is a short, well-written letter expressing your interest in a particular job. In a cover letter, it is important to focus on the employer's needs, and not your own needs. The letter should capture the reader's attention, demonstrate your qualifications, and request an interview. To learn more about how to write effective cover letters, read "Quick, Take Cover," available through InfoTrac College Edition— access **Web Resource 9.5: Quick Take Cover** through your ThomsonNOW for *Communicate!* You can also access **Web Resource 9.6: Cover**

Early in the interview, the interviewer should establish rapport. In addition to a welcoming greeting, what other methods have interviewers used to put you at ease?

Thomson
NOW!

cover letter
a short, well-written letter expressing your interest in a particular job.

Letter Don'ts to find a list of several cover letter faux pas that you will want to avoid.

résumé
a written summary of your skills and accomplishments.

Prepare a professional résumé The **résumé** is a summary of your skills and accomplishments and is your "silent sales representative" (Stewart & Cash, 2000, p. 274). Although there is no universal format for résumé writing, there is some agreement on what should be included. The following information should be included:

1. **Contact information:** Information including your name, addresses (current and permanent), telephone numbers, and e-mail address.

2. **Career objective:** A one-sentence objective focusing on your job search goals. To read more about formulating career objective statements, access **Web Resource 9.7: What Is Your Objective?** through your ThomsonNOW for *Communicate!*

3. **Employment history:** List of your paid and unpaid experiences, beginning with the most recent. List the name and address of the organization, your employment dates, your title, key duties, and noteworthy accomplishments.

4. **Education:** List the names and addresses of the schools you have attended (including specialized military schools), the degrees or certificates earned (or expected), and the dates of attendance and graduation. Also list academic honors received with degrees or certificates.

5. **Relevant professional affiliations:** List the names of the organizations, dates of membership, and any offices held.

6. **Military background:** List branch and dates of service, last rank held, significant commendations, and discharge status.

7. **Special skills:** List language fluencies, technical expertise, computer expertise, multimedia competencies, and so forth.

8. **Community service:** List significant involvement in community service organizations, clubs, and other volunteer efforts.

9. **References:** List or have available the names, addresses, e-mail addresses, and phone numbers of at least three people who will speak well of your ability, your work product, and your character.

Prepare your résumé so that it is easy to read, highlights your accomplishments, and is short. To read about—and avoid—the top 20 résumé pet peeves identified by 2,500 recruiters, access **Web Resource 9.8: Résumé Pet Peeves** through your ThomsonNOW for *Communicate!* And to practice writing a résumé for a position you think you'd enjoy, access **Web Resource 9.9: Résumé Builder** and complete **Skill Learning Activity 9.4: Résumé and Cover Letter.**

Figure 9.3 and Figure 9.4 display a sample cover letter and a sample résumé for a recent college graduate.

2326 Tower Place
Cincinnati, OH 45220
April 8, 2006

Mr. Kyle Jones
Acme Marketing Research Associates
P.O. Box 482
Cincinnati, OH 45201

Dear Mr. Jones:

I am applying for the position of first-year associate at Acme
Marketing Research Associates, which I learned about through the
Office of Career Counseling at the University of Cincinnati. I am
a senior mathematics major at the University of Cincinnati who
is interested in pursuing a career in marketing research. I am
highly motivated, eager to learn, and I enjoy working with all
types of people. I am excited by the prospect of working for a
firm like Acme Marketing Research Associates, where I can apply my leadership and problem-solving skills in a professional
setting.

As a mathematics major, I have developed the analytical proficiency that is necessary for working through complex problems. My
courses in statistics have especially prepared me for data analysis, and my more theoretical courses have taught me how to construct an effective argument. My leadership training and experiences have given me the ability to work effectively in groups and
have taught me the benefits of both individual and group problem
solving. My work on the Strategic Planning Committee has given me
an introduction to market analysis by teaching me skills associated with strategic planning. Finally, from my theatrical experience, I have gained the poise to make presentations in front
of small and large groups alike. I believe these experiences and
others have shaped who I am and have helped me to develop many of
the skills necessary to be successful. I am interested in learning more and continuing to grow.

I look forward to having the opportunity to interview with you in
the future. I have enclosed my résumé with my school address and
phone number. Thank you for your consideration. I hope to hear
from you soon.

Sincerely,

Elisa C. Vardin

Figure 9.3
Sample cover letter

Elisa C. Vardin

2326 Tower Avenue
Cincinnati, Ohio 45220
Phone: (513) 861-2497
E-mail: ElisVardin@UC.edu

PROFESSIONAL OBJECTIVE

To use my intellectual abilities, quantitative capabilities, communication skills, and proven leadership to further the mission of a high-integrity marketing research organization.

EDUCATIONAL BACKGROUND

UNIVERSITY OF CINCINNATI, Cincinnati, OH, B.A. in Mathematics June 2006. GPA 3.36. Dean's List.

NATIONAL THEATER INSTITUTE at the Eugene O'Neill Theater Center, Waterford, CT. Fall 2005. Acting, Voice, Movement, Directing, and Playwriting.

WORK AND OTHER BUSINESS-RELATED EXPERIENCE

REYNOLDS & DEWITT, Cincinnati, OH. Summer 2005. Intern at Brokerage/ Investment Management Firm. Provided administrative support. Created new databases, performance comparisons, and fact sheets in Excel and Word files.

MUMMERS THEATRE GUILD, University of Cincinnati, Spring 2002–Spring 2006. Treasurer. Responsible for all financial/accounting functions for this undergraduate theater community.

SUMMERBRIDGE CINCINNATI, Cincinnati Country Day School, Cincinnati, OH. Summer 2004. Teacher in program for "at-risk" junior high students. Taught seventh-grade mathematics, sixth- and seventh-grade speech communication, sign language; academic advisor; club leader. Organized five-hour diversity workshop and three-hour tension-reduction workshop for staff.

STRATEGIC PLANNING COMMITTEE, Summit Country Day School, Cincinnati, OH. Fall 2001–2002. One of two student members. Worked with the Board of Directors developing the first Strategic Plan for a 1,000-student independent school (pre-K through 12).

AYF INTERNATIONAL LEADERSHIP CONFERENCE, Miniwanca Conference Center, Shelby, MI. Summer 2000–2002. Participant in international student conference sponsored by American Youth Foundation.

PERSONAL
Musical Theater: lifetime involvement, including leads and choreography for several shows. A cappella singing group, 2002–2005; Director 2003–2004. Swing Club 2004–2006, President and teacher of student dance club. Junior high youth group leader, 2002. Math tutor, 2003. Aerobics instructor, 2005–2006. University of Cincinnati Choral Society, 2002–2006. American Sign Language instructor, Winter 2004, 2005.

TECHNICAL SKILLS AND TRAINING: SAS, SPSS, EXCEL, ACCESS, WORD. Univariate and Multivariate Statistics (2 courses), Regression Analysis (2 courses).

REFERENCES: Available on request.

Figure 9.4
Sample résumé

Electronic cover letters and résumés **Electronic cover letters and résumés** are sent online. Electronic résumés have become quite popular with employers and job seekers. For example, from 1995 to 1999 the number of résumés that were received electronically by Microsoft increased from 5 percent to 50 percent (Criscito, 2000, p. 2). Employers like electronic résumés because they can sift through large numbers, looking only for particular qualifications or characteristics. Candidates like electronic résumés because they can send essentially the same materials online, saving time and money. Your electronic résumé is the same résumé that you will send to employers and take to your interview, only you will need to alter the format so it is easy to post to the web (Dikel, 2006).

For more information about adapting your résumé to make it Internet-ready, access **Web Resource 9.10: Internet-Ready Résumés** through your ThomsonNOW for *Communicate!*

electronic cover letters
and résumés
these contain the same information as traditional cover letters and résumés but are sent online.

Preparing to Be Interviewed

Although the résumé and cover letter make you an attractive candidate for an employer, it is your behavior at the interview that will solidify your chances of receiving an offer. The following guidelines will help you prepare for the interview.

1. **Do your homework.** If you haven't yet done extensive research on the position and the company, do so before you go to the interview. Be sure you know the company's products and services, areas of operation, ownership, and financial health. Nothing puts off interviewers more than applicants who arrive at an interview knowing little about the company. Today, most medium and large organizations have a web presence so you can easily begin your research by looking online.

2. **Based on your research, prepare a list of questions about the organization and the job.** The employment interview should be a two-way street, where you size up the company as they are sizing you up. So you will probably have a number of specific questions to ask the interviewer. For example, "Can you describe a typical workday for the person in this position?" or "What is the biggest challenge in this job?" Make a list of your questions and take it with you to the interview.

3. **Rehearse the interview.** Several days before the interview, spend time outlining the job requirements and how your knowledge, skills, and experiences meet those requirements. Practice answering questions commonly asked in interviews, such as those listed in Figure 9.5 or those presented in **Web Resource 9.2: 109 Typical Job Interview Questions**. To sharpen your interviewing skills, answer sample questions, and receive help to improve your answers, access **Web Resource 9.11: Virtual Interview** through your ThomsonNOW for *Communicate!*

■ In what ways does your transcript reflect your ability?
■ Can you give an example of how you work under pressure?
■ What are your major strengths? Weaknesses?
■ Can you give an example of when you were a leader and what happened?
■ What have you done that shows your creativity?
■ What kind of position are you looking for?

Figure 9.5
Frequently asked interview questions

4. **Dress appropriately.** You want to make a good first impression, so it is important to be well groomed and neatly dressed. Although "casual" or "business casual" is common in many workplaces, some organizations still expect employees to be more formally dressed. If you don't know the dress code for the organization, call the Human Resources department and ask.

5. **Plan to arrive on time.** The interview is the organization's first exposure to your work behavior, so you don't want to be late. Find out how long it will take you to travel by making a dry run several days before. Plan to arrive 10 or 15 minutes before your appointment.

6. **Bring supplies.** Gather and bring extra copies of your résumé, cover letter, and references as well as the list of questions you plan to ask. You will also want to have paper and a pen so that you can make notes.

Behavior during the Interview

Interviewing is a crucial step in obtaining a job. Use these guidelines to help you put your best foot forward.

1. **Use active listening.** When we are anxious, we sometimes have trouble listening well. Work on attending, understanding, and remembering what is asked. Remember that the interviewer will be aware of your nonverbal behavior, so be sure to make and keep eye contact as you listen.

2. **Think before answering.** If you have prepared for the interview, you want to make sure that as you answer the questions posed, you also tell your story. So take a moment to consider how your answer will portray your skills and experiences. "Tell me about yourself" is not an invitation to give the interviewer your life history. Rather, you can focus your answer on presenting your experiences and qualifications that are related to the job.

3. **Be enthusiastic.** If you come across as bored or disinterested, the interviewer is likely to conclude that you would be an unmotivated employee.

4. **Ask questions.** As the interview is winding down, be sure to ask the questions you prepared that have not already been answered. You may

---

OBSERVE & ANALYZE

Journal Activity

Thinking Like an Interviewer

Read the sample résumé depicted in Figure 9.4 or find another sample résumé more to your interest online by using your ThomsonNOW for *Communicate!* to access **Web Resource 9.12: Sample Résumés Online**. Analyze the résumé based on the position for which it was written and on the candidate's education, experience, and skills. Write 10 primary questions you would ask the job candidate if you were going to interview him or her for the position.

Thomson™ NOW! You can complete this activity online and, if requested, e-mail it to your instructor. Use your ThomsonNOW for *Communicate!* to access **Skill Learning Activity 9.5**.

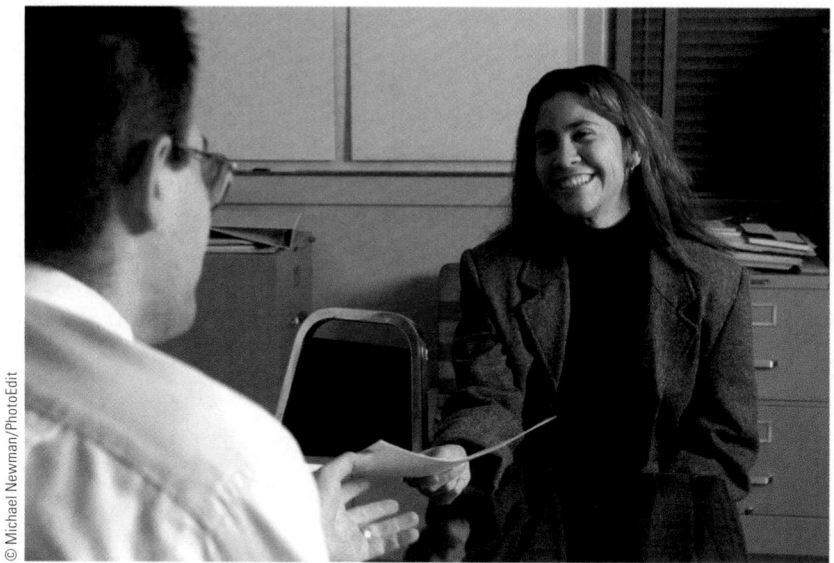
© Michael Newman/PhotoEdit

Active listening and enthusiasm are key to being an effective interviewee. What behaviors demonstrate enthusiasm in an interview?

also want to ask how well the interviewer believes your qualifications match the position, and what your strengths are.

5. **Avoid discussing salary and benefits.** The time to discuss salary is when you are offered the job. If the interviewer tries to pin you down, simply say something like, "I'm really more interested in talking about how my experiences map onto your needs and would like to defer talking about salary until we know we have a match." Similarly, discussions of benefits are best held until an offer is made.

Conversation and Analysis

Use your ThomsonNOW for *Communicate!* to access the video clip of El-liott Miller's job interview at Community Savings and Loan. As you watch the video, notice how well both Karen Bourne and Elliott Miller follow the guidelines for effective interviews. You can record your observations and respond to other analysis questions by clicking on "Analysis" in the menu bar at the top of the screen. When you've answered all the questions, click "Done" to compare your answers to those provided by the authors.

A transcript of the conversation is printed here. You can also find a copy of this transcript online, which allows you to take notes as you watch the video. Use your ThomsonNOW for *Communicate!* to access **Skill Learning**

Thomson
NOW!

Activity 9.6. When you have finished viewing the video and taking notes, click on "Authors' Model Analysis" to compare your notes to the detailed conversational analysis provided by the authors.

Elliott Miller is a second-semester senior who has double-majored in business and communication. Today he is interviewing with Community Savings and Loan, which is recruiting managerial trainees. Elliott has dressed carefully. He has on his good charcoal suit, a light blue shirt, a conservative necktie, and wingtips. At 10 a.m. sharp he knocks on the office door of Karen Bourne, the person with whom he has an interview. She is in her mid-thirties and dressed in a conservative navy blue suit. She opens the door and offers her hand to Elliott.

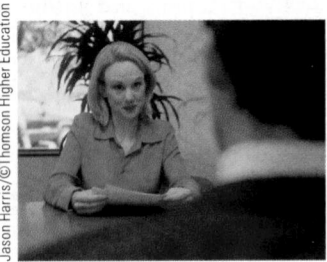

Conversation

BOURNE: Mr. Miller, I see you're right on time. That's a good start. [*They shake hands.*]

MILLER: Thank you for inviting me to interview today.

BOURNE: Sit down. [*He sits in the chair in front of her desk; she sits behind the desk.*] So you're about to finish college are you? I remember that time in my own life—exciting and scary!

MILLER: It's definitely both for me. I'm particularly excited about the job here at Community Savings and Loan.

BOURNE [*Smiles*]: Then there's a mutual interest. We had a lot of applications, but we're interviewing only eight of them. What I'd like to do is get a sense of your interests and tell you about our managerial trainee program here, so that we can see if the fit between us is as good as it looks on paper. Sound good to you?

MILLER: Great.

BOURNE: Let me start by telling you about a rather common problem we've had with our past managerial trainees. Many of them run into a problem—something they have trouble learning or doing right. That's normal enough—we expect that. But a lot of trainees seem to get derailed when that happens. Instead of finding another way to approach the problem, they get discouraged and give up. So I'm very interested in hearing what you've done when you've encountered problems or roadblocks in your life.

MILLER: Well, I can remember one time when I hit a real roadblock. I was taking an advanced chemistry course, and I just couldn't seem to understand the material. I failed the first exam, even though I'd studied hard.

BOURNE: Good example of a problem. What did you do?

MILLER: I started going to all the tutorial sessions that grad assistants offer. That helped a little, but I still wasn't getting the material the way I should. So I organized a study team and offered to pay for pizzas so that students who were on top of the class would have a reason to come.

BOURNE [*Nodding with admiration*]: That shows a lot of initiative and creativity. Did the study team work?

MILLER [*Smiling*]: It sure did. I wound up getting a B in the course, and so did several other members of the study team who had been in the same boat I was in early in the semester.

BOURNE: So you don't mind asking for help if you need it?

MILLER: I'd rather do that than flounder, but I'm usually pretty able to operate independently.

BOURNE: So you prefer working on your own to working with others?

MILLER: That depends on the situation or project. If I have all that I need to do something on my own, I'm comfortable working solo. But there are other cases in which I don't have everything I need to do something well—maybe I don't have experience in some aspect of the job or I don't have a particular skill or I don't understand some perspectives on the issues. In cases like that, I think teams are more effective than individuals.

BOURNE: Good. Banking management requires the ability to be self-initiating and also the ability to work with others. Let me ask another question. As I was looking over your transcript and résumé, I noticed that you changed your major several times. Does that indicate you have difficulty making a commitment and sticking with it?

Jason Harris/©Thomson Higher Education

MILLER: I guess you could think that, but it really shows that I was willing to explore a lot of alternatives before making a firm commitment.

BOURNE: But don't you think that you wasted a lot of time and courses getting to that commitment?

MILLER: I don't think so. I learned something in all of the courses I took. For instance, when I was a philosophy major, I learned about logical thinking and careful reasoning. That's going to be useful to me in management. When I was majoring in English, I learned how to write well and how to read others' writing critically. That's going to serve me well in management too.

BOURNE: So what led you to your final decision to double-major in business and communication? That's kind of an unusual combination.

MILLER: It seems a very natural one to me. I wanted to learn about business because I want to be a manager in an organization. I need to know how organizations work, and I need to understand different management philosophies and styles. At the same time, managers work with people, and that means I have to have strong communication skills.

Interview Follow-Up

When the interview is complete, there are several important steps to follow:

1. **Write a thank-you note.** It is appropriate to write a short note thanking the interviewer for the experience and re-expressing your interest in the job. For tips on writing thank-you notes, access **Web Resource 9.13: Notable Notes** through your ThomsonNOW for *Communicate!*

2. **Self-assess your performance.** Take time to critique your performance. How well did you do? What can you do better next time?

3. **Contact the interviewer for feedback.** If you don't get the job, you might call the interviewer and ask for feedback. Be sure to be polite and to indicate that you are only calling to get some help on your interviewing skills. Actively listen to the feedback, using questions and paraphrases to clarify what is being said. Be sure to thank the interviewer for helping you.

To practice what you've learned about job interviews in this chapter, use your ThomsonNOW for *Communicate!* to complete **Skill Learning Activity 9.7: Mock Interview.** In this activity, you will work with a partner to prepare and participate in two interviews, one in which you will use your partner's ad, résumé, and cover letter to prepare and interview your partner for a job, and the other in which your partner will use the material you supply to interview you for a job.

Media Interviews

Today we live in a media-saturated environment where any individual may be approached by a newsperson and asked to participate in an on-air interview. For example, we have a friend who became the object of media interest when the city council in his town refused to grant him a zoning variance so he could complete building a new home on his property. In the course of three days, his "story" became front-page news in his town and reports about his situation made the local radio and TV news shows. You might be asked for an interview when you attend public meetings, and at the mall, or within the context of your work or community service. For example, you may be asked to share your knowledge of your organization's programs, events, or activities. Because media interviews are likely to be edited in some way before they are aired and because they are reaching a wider audience, there are specific strategies you should use as you prepare for and participate in a media interview.

Before the Interview

The members of the media work under very tight deadlines, so it is crucial that you respond immediately to media requests for an interview. When people are insensitive to media deadlines, they can end up looking like they have purposefully evaded the interview and have something to hide. When you speak with the media representative, clarify what the focus of the interview will be and how the information will be presented. At times, the entire interview will be presented; however, it is more likely that the information from the interview will be edited or paraphrased, and all of your comments will not necessarily be reported.

As you prepare for the interview, identify three or four **talking points,** that is, the central ideas you will present as you answer the questions asked during a media interview. For example, before our friend was interviewed by the local TV news anchor, he knew that he wanted to emphasize that he was a victim of others' mistakes: (1) he had hired a licensed architect to draw the plans, (2) the city inspectors had repeatedly approved earlier stages of the building process, (3) the city planning commission had voted unanimously to grant him the variance, and (4) he would be out half the cost of the house if he were forced to tear it down and rebuild. Consider how you will tailor your information to the specific audience in terms they can understand. Consider how you will respond to tough or hostile questions.

talking points
the three or four central ideas you will present as you answer the questions that are asked during a media interview.

During the Interview

Media interviews call for a combination of interviewing, nonverbal communication, and public speaking skills (Boyd, 1999). There are many strategies to be followed during a media interview:

1. Present appropriate nonverbal cues. Inexperienced interviewees can often look or sound tense or stiff. By standing up during a phone interview, your voice will sound more energetic and authoritative. With on-camera interviews, when checking your notes, move your eyes but not your head. Keep a small smile when listening. Look at the interviewer, not into the camera.

2. Make clear and concise statements. It is important to speak slowly, to articulate clearly, and to avoid technical terms or jargon. Remember that the audience is not familiar with your area of expertise.

3. Realize that you are always "on the record." So, nothing should be said as an aside or confidentially to a reporter. Do not say anything that you would not want quoted. If you do not know an answer, do not speculate, but indicate that the question is outside of your area of expertise. Do not ramble during the interviewer's periods of silence. Do not allow yourself to be rushed into an answer.

4. Learn how to bridge. Media consultant Joanna Krotz (2006) defines a **bridge** as a transition you create so that you can move from the inter-

bridge
a transition you create in a media interview so that you can move from the interviewer's subject to the message you want to communicate.

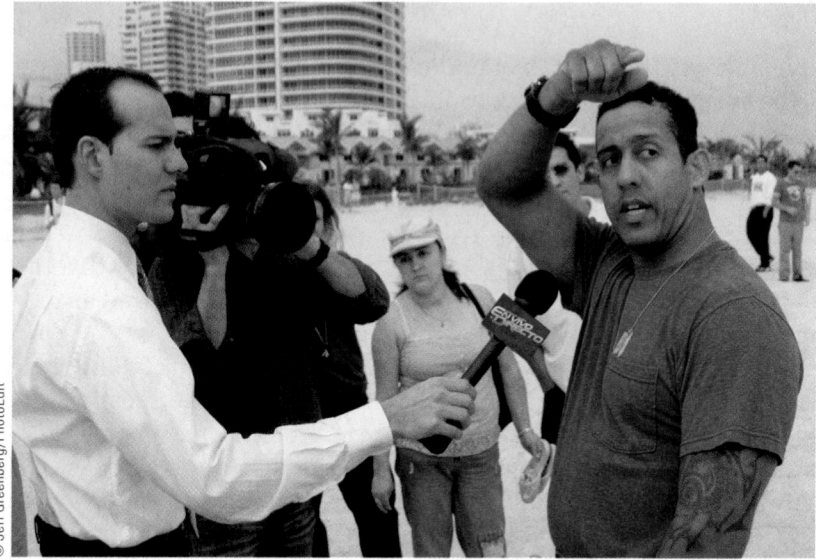

© Jeff Greenberg/PhotoEdit

It's more common than many of us think to be in a position to be interviewed by the media. By following a few simple guidelines, even the most novice interviewee can give a successful media interview.

viewer's subject to the message you want to communicate. To do this, you first answer the direct question and then use phrases such as "what's important to remember, however . . . ," "let me put that in perspective . . . ," or "it's also important to know . . ."

With careful preparation, specific communication strategies during the interview, and practice, one can skillfully deliver a message in any media interview format.

Summary

Interviewing can be a productive way to obtain information from an expert for a paper, an article, or a speech.

The key skill of interviewing is using questions effectively. Open questions allow for flexible responses; closed questions require very brief answers. Primary questions stimulate response; follow-up questions ask for additional information. Neutral questions allow the respondent free choice; leading questions require the person to answer in a particular way.

When you are interviewing for information, you will want to define the purpose, select the best person to interview, develop a protocol, and conduct the interview according to the protocol.

Job interviews are a specific type of communication setting, with particular demands for both interviewer and interviewee.

When you are interviewing prospective applicants for a job, structure your interview carefully to elicit maximal information about the candi-

What Would You Do?

en shifted in his chair as Ms. Goldsmith, his interviewer, looked over his résumé. "I have to tell you that you have considerably more experience than the average applicant we usually get coming straight out of college," Ms. Goldsmith said. "Let's see, you've managed a hardware store, been a bookkeeper for a chain of three restaurants, and were the number one salesman for six straight months at a cell phone store."

"That's right," Ken said. "My family has always stressed the value of hard work, so I have worked a full-time job every summer since I entered junior high school, right through my last year of college. During the school year, I usually worked four to six hours a day after class."

"Very impressive," Ms. Goldsmith said. "And still you managed to get excellent grades and do a considerable amount of volunteer work in your spare time. What's your secret?"

"Secret?" said Ken nervously. "There's no secret—just a lot of hard work."

"Yes, I see that," said Ms. Goldsmith. "What I mean is that there are only 24 hours in a day and you obviously had a lot on your plate each day, especially for someone so young. How did you manage to do it?"

Ken thought for a moment before answering. "I only need five hours of sleep a day." He could feel Ms. Goldsmith's eyes scrutinizing his face. He hadn't exactly lied on his résumé—just exaggerated a little bit. He had, in fact, helped his father run the family hardware store for a number of years. He had helped his aunt, from time to time, keep track of her restaurant's receipts. He had also spent one summer selling cell phones for his cousin. Of course, his family always required him to do his schoolwork first before they let him help at the store, so Ken often had little time to help at all, but there was no reason Ms. Goldsmith needed to know that.

"And you can provide references for these jobs?" Ms. Goldsmith asked.

"I have them with me right here," said Ken, pulling a typed page from his briefcase and handing it across the desk.

1. Are the exaggerated claims Ken made in his résumé ethical? Do the ethics of his actions change at all if he has references (family members) who will vouch for his claims?

2. Many people justify exaggerating or even lying on their résumés by saying that everybody does it and then rationalizing that, if they don't do it too, they will be handicapping their chances to get a good job. If the consequences of acting ethically diminish your economic prospects, are you justified in bending the rules? Explain your answer. If you think bending the rules is acceptable in such circumstances, how far can you bend them before you cross the line into unacceptable behavior?

date. Before the interview starts, become familiar with the data contained in the interviewee's application form, résumé, letters of recommendation, and test scores, if available. Be careful how you present yourself, do not waste time, do not ask questions that violate fair employment practice legislation, and give the applicant an opportunity to ask questions. At the end of the interview, explain to the applicant what will happen next in the process.

To get an interview, begin by taking the time to learn about the company and prepare an appropriate cover letter and résumé that are designed to motivate an employer to interview you. Electronic letters and résumés have become popular and need special preparation. For the interview itself, you should dress appropriately, be prompt, be alert, look directly at the interviewer, give yourself time to think before answering difficult questions, ask intelligent questions about the company and the job, and show enthusiasm for the position.

To participate in media interviews, prepare by understanding the focus and format of the interview and considering the few main points you want to convey. During the media interview, you should present appropriate nonverbal cues, make clear and concise statements, realize everything you say is on the record, and learn to use bridges as transitions to your message.

Thomson™
NOW!

Communicate! Online

Now that you have read Chapter 9, use your ThomsonNOW for *Communicate!* for quick access to the electronic resources that accompany this text. Your ThomsonNOW gives you access to the video of Elliott Miller's interview on pages 212–214, the Web Resources and Skill Learning Activities featured in this chapter, InfoTrac College Edition, and online study aids such as a digital glossary and review quizzes.

Your *Communicate!* ThomsonNOW is an online study system that helps you identify concepts you don't fully understand, allowing you to put your study time to the best use. Using chapter-by-chapter diagnostic pre-tests, the system creates a personalized study plan for each chapter. Each plan directs you to specific resources designed to improve your understanding, including pages from the text in e-book format. Chapter post-tests give you an opportunity to measure how much you've learned and let you know if you are ready for graded quizzes and exams.

Key Terms

Go to your ThomsonNOW for *Communicate!* to access your online glossary for Chapter 9. Print a copy of the glossary for this chapter and test yourself with the electronic flash cards or complete the crossword puzzle to help you master these key terms:

bridge (215)
closed questions (198)
cover letter (205)
electronic cover letters and
    résumés (209)

interview (198)
interview protocol (201)
leading questions (199)
neutral questions (199)
open questions (198)

primary questions (199)
résumé (206)
secondary or follow-up
    questions (199)
talking points (215)

Review Quiz

Test your knowledge of the concepts in this chapter by taking the online review quiz for Chapter 9. Go to your ThomsonNOW for *Communicate!* to access the quiz. When you have completed the quiz, submit it for scoring.

Skill Learning Activities

Complete the Observe & Analyze, Test Your Competence, and Conversation and Analysis activities for Chapter 9 online at your ThomsonNOW for *Communicate!*. You can submit your Observe & Analyze answers to your instructor, compare your Test Your Competence answers to those provided by the authors, and do both for the Conversation and Analysis activity.

Web Resources

Go to your ThomsonNOW for *Communicate!* to access the Web Resources for this chapter.

QUINTESSENTIAL CAREERS
Your Job Search Starts Here

QUINTCAREERS.COM

| I am a... | **Student** | **Job-Seeker** | **Career-Changer** | **Coach-Counselor** | **Other Visitor** |

Job-Hunting Tools:
- Search for Jobs
- Post Your Resume

Career Tools:
- Career Resources
- Career Articles
- Career Tutorials
- College Planning
- Free Career Newsletter
- Job/Career Bookstore
- Job-Search Samples
- Search this Site

Other Navigation:
- QuintCareers.com Home
- About QuintCareers.com
- The Career Doctor
- Employer Resources

The 109 Typical Job Interview Questions

These 109 questions include both traditional and behavioral interview questions. For more information about types of interview questions, go to our Interviewing Resources section of Quintessential Careers.

1. How would you describe yourself?

2. What specific goals, including those related to your occupation, have you established for your life?

3. How has your college experience prepared you for a business career?

4. Please describe the ideal job for you following graduation.

5. What influenced you to choose this career?

6. At what point did you choose this career?

7. What specific goals have you established for your career?

8. What will it take to attain your goals, and what steps have you taken toward attaining

PART II Interpersonal Communication | Self-Review

Interpersonal Communication from Chapters 5 through 9

What kind of an interpersonal communicator are you? This analysis looks at specific behaviors that are characteristic of effective interpersonal communicators. On the line provided for each statement, indicate the response that best captures your behavior: 1, almost always; 2, often; 3, occasionally; 4, rarely; 5, never.

_____ When I communicate with a person from another culture, I make an effort to keep an open mind and accept ambiguity in our interactions. (Ch. 5)

_____ When engaging in intercultural communication, I listen carefully to what the other person is saying and adjust my communication to that person and our situation. (Ch. 5)

_____ I make an effort to spend time with my friends, I share my feelings with them, and I provide them with comfort and support when they are feeling vulnerable. (Ch. 6)

_____ I maintain intimacy in my closest relationships by being dependable and responsive. (Ch. 6)

_____ I listen attentively, regardless of my interest in the person or the ideas. (Ch. 7)

_____ When I'm not sure whether I understand, I seek clarification. (Ch. 7)

_____ When a person describes an unfortunate experience, I am able to provide appropriate comfort. (Ch. 7)

_____ I describe objectively to others my negative feelings about their behavior toward me without withholding or blowing up. (Ch. 8)

_____ I am quick to praise people for doing things well. (Ch. 8)

_____ I criticize people for their mistakes only when they ask for criticism. (Ch. 8)

_____ When I find myself in conflict with another person, I am able to discuss the issue openly without withdrawing or appearing competitive or aggressive. (Ch. 8)

_____ I have an up-to-date résumé ready for immediate use. (Ch. 9)

_____ I present myself well when I am being interviewed. (Ch. 9)

Based on your responses, select the interpersonal communication behavior that you would most like to change. Write a communication improvement plan similar to the sample goal statement in Chapter 1 (page 22). If you would like verification of your self-review before you write a contract, have a friend or a coworker complete this same analysis for you.

Thomson NOW! You can complete this self-review online and, if requested, e-mail it to your instructor. Access Part II Self-Review at the ThomsonNOW for *Communicate!* under the chapter resources for Chapter 9.

OBJECTIVES

After you have read this chapter, you should be able to answer these questions:

- What characterizes effective groups?
- How can group discussion lead to improving group goal statements?
- What is the optimum size and composition of a group?
- What factors affect cohesiveness in groups?
- How do groups form, maintain, and change their norms?
- What is synergy and how does it affect a group?
- What issues of the environment facilitate good communication in face-to-face and virtual groups?
- What are the stages of group development?
- What are the steps of the problem-solving method?

10
Participating in Group Communication

Members of the Alpha Production Team at Meyer Foods were gathered to review their hiring policies. At the beginning of the meeting, Kareem, the team facilitator, began, "You know why I called you together. Each production team has been asked to review its hiring practices. So, let's get started." After a few seconds of silence, Kareem said, "Drew, what have you been thinking?"

"Well, I don't know," Drew replied, "I haven't really given it much thought." (There were nods of agreement all around the table.)

"Well," Jeremy said, "I'm not sure I even remember what our current policies are."

"But when I sent you the e-mail notice of the meeting, I attached a preliminary analysis of our practices and some questions I hoped each of us would think about before this meeting," Kareem replied.

"Oh, is that what that was?" Byron said. "I read the part about the meeting, but I guess I didn't get back to look at the attachment."

Kareem said, "I think the CEO is looking for some specific recommendations from us."

"Anything you think would be appropriate would be OK with me," Dawn added.

"Well, how about each of us trying to come up with some ideas for next time?" Kareem suggested. "Meeting adjourned."

As the group dispersed, Kareem overheard Drew whisper to Dawn, "These meetings sure are a waste of time, aren't they?"

P erhaps you have been part of a work group at school, at work, or in a volunteer organization. If so, the opening dialogue probably sounds familiar. When group meetings are ineffective, it is easy to point the finger at the leader; often, however, as is the case with this group, the responsibility for the "waste of time" or other ineffectiveness lies not with one person but with the complex nature of communication in a group setting. Because most of us spend some of our time interacting in groups, we need to learn how group process works and how to participate in ways that maximize group effectiveness.

In this chapter, we examine the characteristics of effective work groups, the stages of group development, and the problem-solving process in groups.

Characteristics of Effective Work Groups

work group
a collection of three or more people who must interact and influence each other to solve problems and to accomplish a common purpose.

A **work group** is a collection of three or more people who must interact and influence each other to solve problems and to accomplish a common purpose. Effective work groups have clearly defined goals, an optimum number of diverse members, cohesiveness, norms, a good working environment, and synergy. Let's consider each of these.

Clearly Defined Goals

group goal
a future state of affairs desired by enough members of the group to motivate the group to work toward its achievement.

An effective work group has clearly defined group goals. A **group goal** is a future state of affairs desired by enough members of the group to motivate the group to work toward its achievement (Johnson & Johnson, 2003, p. 73). Goals become clearer to members, and members become more committed to goals, when they are discussed. To read about various methods that can be used to arrive at group goals, use your ThomsonNOW for *Communicate!* to access **Web Resource 10.1: Setting Group Goals**. Through goal discussions, members are able to make sure goal statements are specific, consistent, challenging, and acceptable.

specific goal
a precisely stated, measurable, and behavioral goal.

First, goal statements must be specific. A **specific goal** is precisely stated, measurable, and behavioral. For example, the crew at a local fast food restaurant that began with the goal of "increasing profitability of the store" made the goal more specific and meaningful by revising the goal statement to read: "During the next quarter, the second shift night crew will increase the profitability of the store by reducing food costs on their shift by 1 percent through reducing the amount of food thrown away due to precooking."

consistent goals
complementary goals; achieving one goal does not prevent the achievement of another.

Second, goal statements must be consistent. **Consistent goals** are complementary; that is, achieving one goal does not prevent the achievement of another. To meet the consistency test, the team will have to believe that reducing the amount of precooking will not interfere with maintaining their current level of service. If they do not believe that these two goals can be accomplished simultaneously, they will need to reformulate the goals so that they are compatible.

Third, goal statements must be challenging. **Challenging goals** require hard work and team effort; they motivate group members to do things beyond what they might normally accomplish. The crew determined that a goal of 1 percent was a significant challenge.

Fourth, goal statements must be acceptable. **Acceptable goals** are seen as meaningful by team members and are goals to which members feel personally committed. People support things that they help to create. So group members who participate in setting their own goals are likely to exert high effort to see that the goals are achieved. Likewise, a group member who does not believe a goal is reasonable or just is likely to be unmotivated or to resist working toward accomplishing the goal. Because the members of the crew helped to formulate the profitability goal, they are more likely to work to achieve it.

challenging goals
goals that require hard work and team effort; they motivate group members to do things beyond what they might normally accomplish.

acceptable goals
goals to which members feel personally committed.

Optimum Number of Diverse Members

Effective groups are composed of enough diverse members to ensure good interaction but not so many members that discussion is stifled. In general, as the size of a group grows, so does the complexity it must manage. Bostrom (1970) noted that the addition of one member to a group has a geometric effect on the number of relationships. When only Jeff and Sue are in a group, there is only one relationship to manage. But when a third person, Bryan, joins them, the group now has four relationships to manage (Jeff–Sue; Bryan–Jeff; Bryan–Sue; Bryan–Sue–Jeff). As groups grow in size and complexity, the opportunities for each member to participate drop. People tend to be more satisfied in groups in which they can actively participate (Bonito, 2000). When many people cannot or will not contribute, the resulting decision is seldom a product of the group's collective thought (Beebe et al., 1994, p. 125).

So what is the right size for a group? It depends. In general, research shows that the best size for a group is the smallest number of people capable of effectively achieving the goal (Sundstrom et al., 1990). For many situations, this might mean as few as three to five people. As the size of the group increases, the time spent discussing and deciding also increases. This argues for very small groups because they will be able to make decisions more quickly. However, as the goals, problems, and issues become complex, it is unlikely that very small groups will have the diversity of information, knowledge, and skills needed to make high-quality decisions. For many situations, then, a group of five to seven or more might be desirable.

More important than having a certain number of people in a group is having the right combination of people in the group. Notice the heading of this section was "optimum number of *diverse* members." To meet this test, it is usually better to have a heterogeneous group rather than a homogeneous group. A **homogeneous group** is one in which members have a great deal of similarity. By contrast, a **heterogeneous group** is one in which various demographics, levels of knowledge, attitudes, and interests are represented. For example, a group composed of seven nurses who are all young, white females would be considered a homogeneous group; a group composed of nurses, doctors, nutritionists, and physical therapists who differ in age, race, and sex would be considered a heterogeneous group.

Effective groups are likely to be composed of people who bring different but relevant knowledge and skills into the group discussion (Valacich et al., 1994). In homogeneous groups, members are likely to know the same things, come at the problem from the same perspective, and, consequently, be likely to overlook some important information or take shortcuts in the problem-solving process. In contrast, groups composed of heterogeneous members are more likely to have diverse information, perspectives, and values, and, consequently, discuss issues more thoroughly before reaching a decision. A heterogeneous medical group described above would probably make a more comprehensive decision about a patient's care than the homogeneous group of nurses who were all similar demographically.

homogeneous group
group in which members have a great deal of similarity.

heterogeneous group
group in which various demographics, levels of knowledge, attitudes, and interests are represented.

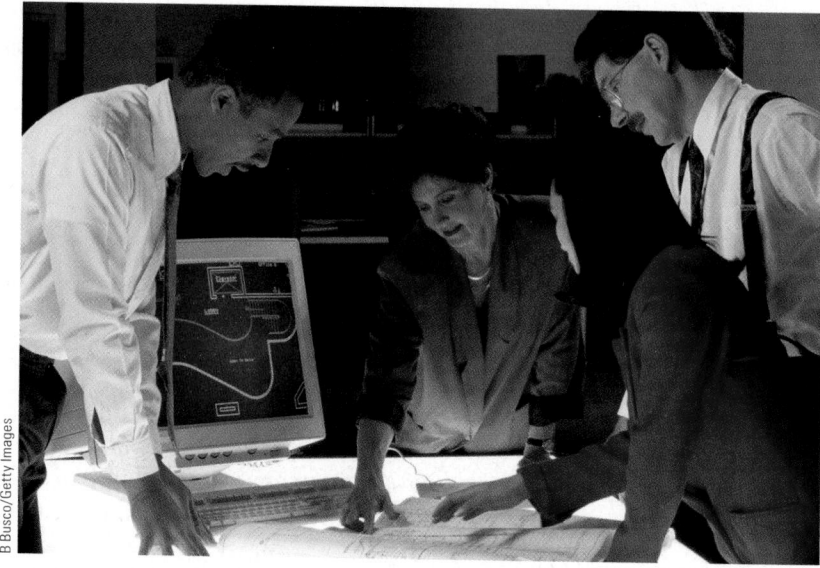

As groups become more diverse, achieving cohesiveness becomes more difficult. How can a group develop cohesiveness so that it can benefit from diversity?

B Busco/Getty Images

Cohesiveness

Effective work group are also cohesive. **Cohesiveness** is the degree of attraction members have to each other and to the group's goal. In a highly cohesive group, members genuinely like and respect each other, work cooperatively to reach the group's goals, and generally perform better than noncohesive groups (Evans & Dion, 1991). In contrast, a group that is not cohesive may have members who are indifferent toward or dislike each other, have little interest in what the group is trying to accomplish, and may even work in ways that prevent the group from being successful.

Research (Balgopal, Ephross, & Vassil, 1986; Widmer & Williams, 1991; Wilson, 2005) has shown that several factors lead to developing cohesiveness in groups: attractiveness of the group's purpose, voluntary membership, feeling of freedom to share opinions, members reinforcing each other, and progress and celebration of accomplishments.

1. **Attractiveness of the group's purpose.** Social or community groups, for example, build cohesiveness out of friendship or devotion to service. In a decision-making group, attractiveness is likely to be related to how important the task is to members. If Daniel is part of a campus group raising money for needy children, the cohesiveness of the group will depend, in part, on how motivated the group is to complete the task.

2. **Voluntary membership.** When we are forming groups, we should give people some control over joining. Even at work, group effectiveness may be enhanced if employees have some choice regarding team projects. Likewise, Daniel's group is likely to develop cohesiveness more easily if members are volunteering rather than being required to work on a fundraising project.

   If group members are appointed, or if they have some discomfort in working together, a group may benefit from **team-building activities** designed to help the group work better together (Midura & Glover, 2005). Often, this means having the group meet someplace outside of its normal setting, where members can engage in activities designed to help them recognize each other's strengths, share in group successes, and develop rituals. As group members learn to be more comfortable with each other socially, they are also likely to become more comfortable in the group setting.

3. **Feeling of freedom to share opinions.** Feeling comfortable in disagreeing with the ideas and positions of others is an important aspect of group cohesion. If Daniel's fundraising group members are comfortable sharing contrasting ideas without fear of being chastised, they are likely to develop better group cohesiveness. Moreover, group members should feel free to converse about their goals very soon after the group is formed. During this discussion, individual members should be encouraged to express their ideas about group goals and to hear the ideas of others. Through this discussion process, the group can clarify goals and build group commitment.

cohesiveness
the degree of attraction members have to each other and to the group's goal.

team-building activities
activities designed to help the group work better together.

Journal Activity

Cohesiveness in Homogeneous versus Heterogeneous Groups

Identify two groups (for example, a sports team, study group, fraternal or community group, or work team) to which you belong; one should have members you consider to be homogeneous, and the other, members you consider to be heterogeneous.

Analyze the demographic differences in each group. When you have completed this analysis, write a paragraph that discusses cohesiveness in each group. How cohesive is each group? Are both groups equally cohesive? Was it easier or more difficult to establish cohesiveness in a particular group? What real or potential pitfalls result from the level of cohesiveness in each group?

You can use your Student Workbook to complete this activity, or you can complete it online, download a demographic analysis worksheet to help you complete it, and, if requested, e-mail it to your instructor. Use your ThomsonNOW for *Communicate!* to access **Skill Learning Activity 10.1.**

norms
expectations for the way group members will behave while in the group.

ground rules
prescribed behaviors designed to help the group meet its goals and conduct its conversations.

4. **Members reinforcing each other.** A group will be more cohesive if members feel that others are listening to them and that their ideas count. Groups that provide support, encouragement, and positive feedback will become highly cohesive. No one wants to offer a suggestion in a group and have it be ignored. Even if the group decides not to pursue the idea, the careful consideration of each suggestion will send a reinforcing message that group members respect each other.

5. **Progress and celebration of accomplishments.** Groups should be encouraged to set subgoals that can be achieved early. Groups that feel good about the progress they are accomplishing develop a sense of unity. Once early subgoals are accomplished, the group can celebrate these achievements. Celebrations of early achievements cause members to more closely identify with the group and to see it as a "winner" (Renz & Greg, 2000, p. 54).

Keep in mind that the more heterogeneous the group, the more difficult it is to build cohesiveness. We know that heterogeneous groups generally arrive at better decisions, so we need to structure group conversations that can develop cohesiveness in all types of groups. This is why team-building activities, freedom to express controversial ideas, members reinforcing each other, and progress and celebration of achievements are so important with heterogeneous groups.

In addition, members should be taught to communicate in ways that foster supportive patterns of cooperative interaction. Groups become cohesive when individual members feel valued and respected. By using the skills of active listening, empathizing, describing, and collaborative conflict management, you can help heterogeneous groups become cohesive.

Productive Norms

Norms are expectations for the way group members will behave while in the group. Effective groups develop norms that support goal achievement (Shimanoff, 1992) and cohesiveness (Shaw, 1981). Norms begin to be developed early in the life of the group. Norms grow, change, and solidify as people get to know each other better. Group members usually comply with norms and are sanctioned by the group when they do not.

Norms can be developed through formal discussions or informal group processes (Johnson & Johnson, 2003, p. 27). Some groups choose to formulate explicit **ground rules,** prescribed behaviors designed to help the group meet its goals and conduct its conversations. These may include sticking to the agenda, refraining from interrupting others, making brief comments rather than lengthy monologues, actively listening to others, expecting everyone to participate, focusing arguments on issues rather than personalities, and sharing decision making. To read a list of group norms that contribute to group effectiveness, use your ThomsonNOW for *Communicate!* to access **Web Resource 10.2: Setting Group Norms.**

In most groups, however, norms evolve informally. When we become part of a new group, we try to act in ways that were considered appropriate in other groups in which we have participated. If the other members of our new group behave in ways that are consistent with our interpretation of the rules for behavior, an informal norm is established. For example, suppose Daniel and two other group members show up late for a meeting. If the group has already begun discussion and the latecomers are greeted with cold looks, showing that other members of this group do not abide by being late, then this group will develop an on-time norm. A group may never discuss informal norms that develop, but all veteran group members understand what they are and behave in line with the expectations of these informally established norms.

When group members violate a group norm, they are usually sanctioned. The severity of the sanction depends on the importance of the norm that was violated, the extent of the violation, and the status of the person who violated the norm. Violating a norm that is central to a group's performance or cohesiveness will generally receive a harsher sanction than will violating a norm that is less central. Minor violations of norms, or violation of a norm by a newcomer, or violations of norms that are frequently violated will generally receive more lenient sanctions. Group members who have achieved higher status in the group (for example, those with unique skills and abilities needed by the group) receive more lenient sanctions or escape sanctioning.

Some norms turn out to be counterproductive. For example, at the beginning of the first meeting of a work group, suppose a few folks cut up, tell jokes and stories, and generally ignore attempts by others to begin more serious discussion. If the group seems to encourage or does not effectively sanction this behavior, then this dallying behavior will become a group norm. As a result, the group may become so involved in these behaviors that work toward the group's goals is delayed, set aside, or perhaps even forgotten. If counterproductive behavior such as this continues for several meetings and becomes a norm, it will be very difficult to change.

What can a group member do to try to change a norm? Renz and Greg (2000) suggest that you can help your group change a counterproductive norm by (1) observing the norm and its outcome, (2) describing the results of the norm to the group, and (3) soliciting opinions of other members of the group (p. 52). For instance, you might observe whether every meeting begins late, note how long dallying tends to continue, determine whether discussion is productive, and judge whether extra meetings are necessary. Then you could start the next meeting by reporting the results of your observations and asking for reaction from group members.

Although norms are important mechanisms for guiding group behavior, social norms also influence our behavior in other, less structured group settings. Social norm theory has been used to guide recent successful alcohol, tobacco, and violence interventions on college campuses. To read more about such interventions, use your ThomsonNOW for *Communicate!* to access **Web Resource 10.3: Social Norm Interventions**.

Synergy

synergy
a commonality of purpose and a complementariness of each other's efforts that produces a group outcome greater than an individual outcome.

The old saying "two heads are better than one" captures an important characteristic of effective groups. **Synergy** is the multiplying force created by having a common purpose and complementariness of each others' efforts; it results in a group outcome that is more than what we would expect the individuals in the group to be capable of producing (Henman, 2003). When a group has synergy, the whole is more than the sum of its parts. For instance, a synergistic symphony orchestra may be able to outplay an orchestra that has more talented members. And the sports record books are replete with "no-name teams" that have won major championships over more talented rivals. An effectively functioning group can develop a collective intelligence and a dynamic energy that translate into an outcome that exceeds what even a highly talented individual could produce. When group members bring diversity and differing perspectives to a clearly defined and accepted group goal, and they develop cohesiveness and positive norms, the group is well on its way toward achieving synergy.

Appropriate Environment

face-to-face meeting
a meeting in which all members come together in one physical location to make a decision or solve a problem.

virtual meeting
a meeting in which people in various locations use technology to work together on a decision or problem.

The environment for group meetings may be **face-to-face,** where all members come together in one physical location to make a decision or solve a problem, or it may be **virtual,** where people in various locations use technology to work together on a decision or problem. In either case, there are issues you need to consider in order to create an environment conducive to effective communication.

Face-to-face meetings When your group meets face-to-face on an ongoing basis, it will want to choose a location that is convenient for its members, is an appropriate size for the group, has comfortable seating and temperature, and allows everyone to see and hear everyone else.

The physical setting can affect both group interaction and decision making (Figure 10.1). Seating can be too formal. When seating approximates a board of directors style, as illustrated in Figure 10.1a, where people sit indicates their status. In this style, a dominant–submissive pattern emerges that can inhibit group interaction. People who sit at the head of the table are likely to be looked to for leadership and are seen as having more influence than those members who sit on the side. People who sit across the table from each other interact with each other more frequently, but they also find themselves disagreeing with each other more often than they disagree with others at the table.

Figure 10.1
Which group members do you think will be able to arrive at a decision easily? Why or why not?

Excessively informal seating can also inhibit interaction. For instance, in Figure 10.1b, the three people sitting on the couch form their own little group; the two people seated next to each other form another group; and two members have placed themselves out of the main flow. In arrangements such as these, people are more likely to communicate with the people adjacent to them than with others. In such settings, it is more difficult to make eye contact with every group member. Johnson and Johnson (2003) maintain that "easy eye contact among members enhances the frequency of interaction, friendliness, cooperation, and liking for the group and its work" (p. 171).

The circle, generally considered the ideal arrangement for group discussions and problem solving, is depicted in Figure 10.1c. Circle configurations increase participant motivation to speak because sight lines are better for everyone and everyone appears to have equal status. When the location of the group meeting does not have a round table, the group may be better off without a table or with an arrangement that approximates a circle using square tables, as shown in Figure 10.1d.

Virtual meetings In virtual meetings, technologies such as e-mail, teleconferencing, and videoconferencing allow members who are dispersed geographically to communicate as a group. Awareness of several issues related to virtual meetings can improve the effectiveness of your group communication in mediated formats.

In group discussions via e-mail Listervs, members post comments for others to read at a later time and ideas are shared without interruption. Individual comments can be saved for everyone to read at a later point in time. Because it takes time to type comments, some discussion may be reduced in e-mail formats. However, e-mail discussions encourage equal participation and are less influenced by a member's status or dominance. They are also convenient because they allow members to participate on their own schedule and pace (Patton & Downs, 2003).

E-mail discussions are most productive when a discussion leader posts one question or decision at a time, with a deadline for response. Each person's comments should go to all members of the discussion group and a member should read all previous comments before posting a comment. The discussion leader should summarize responses or point out emerging differences of opinion periodically and then close the discussion by posting the decision reached by the deadline.

Teleconferencing is a form of meeting that allows geographically separated participants to enter a discussion in real time via speaker telephones. In a teleconference, you can hear but not see the other participants. Therefore, it is important to announce your name and location before making a comment so that listeners can recognize you. Because of the absence of nonverbal cues that signal turn-taking, you may have trouble avoiding interruptions. Announcing your name before making a remark also signals your intent to take a speaking turn. A skilled teleconference moderator can help overcome these obstacles by calling on members by name.

In videoconferencing, which is the most sophisticated of virtual meeting formats, all members of your group can see and hear all other members, even though they may be at different physical locations. Videoconferencing relies on expensive technology involving cameras, monitors, and microphones that must be available at the locations of all members, so it is usually reserved for meetings in which it is critical to approximate face-to-face interaction. Although you can see and hear other participants in videoconferences, there is no direct eye contact. Some of the nonverbal information available in face-to-face settings (such as to whom comments are directed) is not available. In addition, some people may feel self-conscious about maintaining an "on-screen image" and not react as they might in a face-to-face setting (Jones, Oyung, & Pace, 2005). But all three of these mediated forms of virtual meetings can save travel time and expense in conducting group communication when members are located around the globe. The issues of group goals, cohesiveness, and norms discussed so far apply to both virtual group discussions and face-to-face group discussions.

Stages of Group Development

Although some groups are brought together on a one-time-only basis to make a quick decision, most work groups convene regularly to consider a variety of issues. Once assembled, these typical work groups tend to move through stages of development. Although numerous models have been proposed to describe the stages of group development, Tuckman's (1965) model has been widely accepted because it identifies the central issues facing a group at each stage in its development. Tuckman named these stages forming, storming, norming, performing, and adjourning. Research by Wheelen and Hochberger (1996) has confirmed that groups can be observed moving through each of these stages. In this section, we describe each of the stages of group development and discuss the nature of communication during each phase.

Forming

Forming is the initial stage of group development during which people come to feel valued and accepted so that they identify with the group. At the beginning of any group, individual members will experience feelings of discomfort caused by the uncertainty they are facing in this new social situation. To explore the specific anxieties raised in a new group situation, use your ThomsonNOW for *Communicate!* to access **Web Resource 10.4: Forming Fears and Uncertainty**.

forming
the initial stage of group development during which people come to feel valued and accepted so that they identify with the group.

Politeness and tentativeness on the part of members may characterize group interactions as members try to understand the task before them, become acquainted with others, understand how the group will work, and find their place in the group. During forming, there may be awkward silences because people may feel unsure about how to act. Any real disagreements between people often remain unacknowledged because members strive to be seen as flexible. During this stage, if the group has formally appointed group leaders, group members depend on them for clues as to how they should behave. Members work to fit in and to be seen as likable.

Anderson (1988) suggests that during forming, we should express positive attitudes and feelings while refraining from abrasive or disagreeable comments; we should make appropriately benign self-disclosures and wait to see if they are reciprocated; and we should try to be friendly, open, and interested in others. So active listening and empathizing skills should be used to become better acquainted with other members of the group. Members should smile, nod, and maintain good eye contact, to make conversations a bit more relaxed.

Storming

Storming is the stage of group development during which the group clarifies its goals and determines the roles each member will have in the group power structure. The stress and strain that arise when groups begin to make

storming
the stage of group development during which the group clarifies its goals and determines the roles each member will have in the group power structure.

decisions are a natural result of the conflicting ideas, opinions, and personalities that begin to emerge during decision making. There may be underlying or expressed tension as members struggle to determine each other's
status and role in the group. In the forming stage, members are concerned
about fitting in, whereas in the storming stage, members are concerned
about expressing their ideas and opinions and finding their place. One
or more members may begin to question or challenge the formal leader's
position on issues. In groups that do not have formally appointed leaders,
two or more members may vie for informal leadership of the group. During
this phase, the overpoliteness exhibited during forming may be replaced
by snide comments, sarcastic remarks, or pointedly aggressive exchanges
between some members. While storming, members may take sides, forming
cliques and coalitions.

Storming, if controlled, is an important stage in a group's development.
During periods of storming, the group is confronted with alternative ideas,
opinions, and ways of viewing issues. Although storming will occur in all
groups, some groups will manage it better than others. When storming in a
group is severe, it can threaten the group's survival. When a group does not
storm, it may experience **groupthink,** a deterioration of mental efficiency,
reality testing, and moral judgment that results from in-group pressure
(Janis, 1982, p. 9). To avoid groupthink, we should encourage constructive
disagreement, self-monitor what we say to avoid name-calling and using in-
flammatory language, and use the active listening skills discussed earlier
with emphasis on paraphrasing and honest questioning (Anderson, 1988).
To read a comprehensive article on groupthink, use your ThomsonNOW for
Communicate! to access **Web Resource 10.5: Groupthink.**

groupthink
*a deterioration of mental
efficiency, reality testing, and
moral judgment that results
from in-group pressure.*

Thomson
NOW!

Norming

Norming is the stage of group development during which the group solidifies its rules for behavior, especially those that relate to how conflict will be
managed. As the group successfully completes a storming phase, it moves
into a phase where members begin to apply more pressure on each other to
conform. During this phase, the norms or standards of the group become
clear. Members for the most part comply with norms, although those who
have achieved higher status or power may continue to occasionally deviate
from them. Members who do not comply with norms are sanctioned.

During norming, competent communicators pay attention to the norms
that are developing. Then, they adapt their communication styles to the
norms of the group. Members increasingly go along with stated and un-
stated expectations and all aspects of the group function fairly smoothly.
When communicators who are monitoring norm development determine
that a norm is too rigid, too elastic, or in other ways counterproductive, they
initiate a group discussion about their observations. As you would expect,
these conversations are best received when the person initiating them uses
the skills of describing behavior, using specific and concrete language.

norming
*the stage of group develop-
ment during which the group
solidifies its rules for behavior, especially those that
relate to how conflict will
be managed.*

Performing

Performing is the stage of group development when the skills, knowledge, and abilities of all members are combined to overcome obstacles and meet goals successfully. Through each of the stages, groups are working to accomplish their goals. Once members have formed social bonds, settled power issues, and developed their norms, however, they "get in the groove," becoming more effective at creative problem solving and task performance. During this stage, conversations are focused on problem solving and sharing task-related information, with little energy directed to relationship building. Members who spend the group's time in chitchat not only detract from the effectiveness of the group but risk being perceived as unprepared or lazy. Performing is the most important stage of group development. This is the stage in which members freely share information, solicit ideas from others, and work to solve problems. This is the most productive stage of the group as members jointly arrive at an outcome.

performing
the stage of group development when the skills, knowledge, and abilities of all members are combined to overcome obstacles and meet goals successfully.

Adjourning

Adjourning is the stage of group development in which members assign meaning to what they have done and determine how to end or maintain interpersonal relations they have developed. Some groups are brought together for a finite time period, whereas for other groups work is continuous. Regardless of whether a group is short term or ongoing, all groups experience endings. A short-term project team will face adjourning when it has completed its work within the time period specified for its existence.

adjourning
the stage of group development in which members assign meaning to what they have done and determine how to end or maintain interpersonal relations they have developed.

Ongoing groups also experience endings. When the team has reached a particular goal, finished a specific project, or lost members to reassignments or resignations, it will confront the same developmental challenges faced by short-term groups in this phase.

Keyton's (1993) study of the adjourning phase of group development points to two challenges that groups face during this phase. First, groups need to construct meaning from their shared experience by evaluating and reflecting on the experience. They may discuss what led to their successes or failures, recall events and share memories of stressful times, and celebrate accomplishments. Second, members will need to find ways to sever or maintain interpersonal relationships that have developed during the group's life together. During this phase, people in the group may explore ways to maintain contact with those they have particularly enjoyed working with. They may continue the relationship on a purely social level or plan to undertake additional work together.

Keyton thinks it is especially important for groups to have a termination ritual, which can range from an informal debriefing session to formalized celebrations with group members and their friends, family, and colleagues. Whatever form the ritual takes, Keyton believes such a ritual "affects how

Journal Activity

Stages of Group Development

Think of a group to which you have belonged for less than one quarter, semester, or term (if you have an assigned group in this course, use that group). Now, write a paragraph that begins by identifying the stage of development the group is currently in and then describe how this group transitioned through each of the previous stages of group development. What event(s) do you recall as turning points, marking the group's movement from one stage to another? Has the group become "stuck" in a stage, or has it developed smoothly? What factors contributed to that? What can you do to help this group succeed in the stage that it is in and transition to the next stage?

You can use your Student Workbook to complete this activity, or you can complete it online and, if requested, e-mail it to your instructor. Use your ThomsonNOW for *Communicate!* to access **Skill Learning Activity 10.2.**

they [members] will interpret what they have experienced and what expectations they will take with them to similar situations" (p. 98).

The phases of group development explain the work that groups must do to aid the social and emotional development of the group. How the group develops through these phases is important to how effectively it works. But achieving group goals is also the result of how well the group uses the problem-solving process. We now turn our attention to understanding the problem-solving process and the communication skills that provide the focus for the performing stage of group development.

Problem Solving in Groups

Research shows that groups follow many different approaches to problem solving. Some groups move linearly through a series of steps to reach consensus, and some move in a spiral pattern in which they refine, accept, reject, modify, and combine ideas as they go along. Whether groups move in something approximating an orderly pattern or go in fits and starts, those groups that arrive at high-quality decisions are likely to accomplish certain tasks during their deliberations. These tasks include identifying a specific problem, analyzing the problem, arriving at criteria that an effective solution must meet, identifying possible alternative solutions to the problem, comparing the alternatives to the criteria, and determining the best solution or combination of solutions.

Defining the Problem

Much wheel-spinning takes place during the early stages of group discussion because the specific goal may not be understood by all group members. It is the duty of the person, agency, or parent group that forms a particular work group to give the group a charge, such as "work out a new way of selecting people for merit pay increases." However, rarely will the charge be stated in such a way that the group does not need to do some clarification of its own. Even when the charge seems clear, effective groups will want to make sure they are focusing on the real problem and not just symptoms of the problem. Let's look again at the charge "work out a new way of selecting people for merit pay increases." What is wrong with this as a problem definition? "Work out a new way of selecting" is too general to be meaningful. A clearer question would be "What are the most important criteria for selecting people for merit pay increases?"

Even when a group is given a well-defined charge, it will need to gather information before it can accurately define the specific problem. Accurately defining the problem requires the group to understand the background, history, and status of the problem. This means collecting and understanding a variety of information. Some groups, however, rush through defining the problem and end up working to solve symptoms, not root causes. To read an article suggesting that later stages of problem solving move more quickly if the group has thoroughly studied, discussed, and agreed on the problem, use your ThomsonNOW for *Communicate!* to access **Web Resource 10.6: What's Your Problem?**

Thomson
NOW!

It helps if the group formally states the problem in writing. This written statement can help the group avoid being sidetracked by tangential or unrelated issues. Unless the group can agree on a formal definition of the problem, there is little likelihood of the group's being able to work together toward a solution.

Effective problem definitions have these four characteristics.

1. **They are stated as questions.** Problem-solving groups begin from the assumption that solutions are not yet known, so problems should be stated as questions to be answered. For example, the merit pay committee might define the problem it will solve as follows: What are the most important criteria for determining merit pay increases? Phrasing the group's problem as a question furthers the spirit of inquiry.

2. **They contain only one central idea.** If the charge includes two questions—"Should the college abolish its foreign language and physical education requirements?"—the group should break it down into two separate questions: Should the college abolish its foreign language requirement? Should the college abolish its physical education requirement?

3. **They use specific and precise language to describe the problem.** For instance, the problem definition "What should the department do about courses that aren't getting the job done?" may be well intentioned, and participants may have at least some idea about their goal, but such vague wording as "getting the job done" can lead to problems later. Notice how this revision makes the intent much clearer: "What should the department do about courses that receive low scores on student evaluations?"

4. **They can be identified as a question of fact, value, or policy.** How we organize our problem-solving discussion will depend on the kind of question we are addressing: a question of fact, value, or policy.

Questions of fact are concerned with discovering what is true or to what extent something is true. Implied in such questions is the possibility of determining truth through the process of examining facts by way of directly observed, spoken, or recorded evidence. For instance, "Did Smith steal equipment from the warehouse?" "Did Mary's sales report follow the written guidelines for sales reports?" and "Do the data from our experiment support our hypothesis?" are all questions of fact. The group will discuss the validity of the evidence it has to determine what is true.

Questions of value concern subjective judgments of what is right, moral, good, or just. Questions of value can be recognized because they often contain evaluative words such as *good, reliable, effective,* or *worthy.* For instance, the program development team for a TV sitcom aimed at young teens may discuss: "Is the level of violence in the scripts we have devel-

questions of fact
questions concerned with discovering what is true or to what extent something is true.

questions of value
questions that concern subjective judgments of what is right, moral, good, or just.

oped appropriate for programs designed to appeal to children?" or "Is the proposed series of ads too sexually provocative?" Although we can establish criteria for "too sexually provocative" and "effectively" and measure material against those criteria, the criteria we choose and the evidence we accept depend on our judgment. A different group of people using different values might come to a different decision.

questions of policy
questions that concern what courses of action should be taken or what rules should be adopted to solve a problem.

Questions of policy concern what courses of action should be taken or what rules should be adopted to solve a problem. "Should the university offer online degrees?" and "Where should the new landfill be built?" are both questions of policy. The inclusion of the word *should* in questions of policy makes them the easiest to recognize and the easiest to phrase of all problem statements.

Thomson
NOW!

To complete an activity that will help you distinguish among questions of fact, value, and policy, use your ThomsonNOW for *Communicate!* to access **Skill Learning Activity 10.3: Stating Problems**.

Analyzing the Problem

Analysis of a problem entails finding out as much as possible about the problem and determining the criteria that must be met to find an acceptable solution. Three types of information can be helpful in analyzing problems. Most groups begin by sharing the information individual members have acquired through their experience. This is a good starting place, but groups that limit their information gathering to the existing knowledge of members often make decisions based on incomplete or faulty information.

A second source of information that should be examined includes published materials available through libraries, electronic databases, and the Internet. From these sources, a group can access information about the problem that has been collected, analyzed, and interpreted by others. Just because information is published, however, does not mean that it is accurate or valid. Accuracy and validity are especially an issue when the information comes from an Internet source, and the group will also have to evaluate the relevance and usefulness of the information.

A third source of information about a problem can be gathered from other people. At times, the group may want to interview experts for their ideas about a problem or conduct a survey to gather information from a particular target group.

Once group members have gathered information, it must be shared with other members. It is important for group members to share new information to fulfill the ethical responsibility that comes with group discussion. A study by Dennis (1996) shows that groups tend to spend more time discussing information common to group members if those with information don't work to get the information heard. The tendency to discuss common information while ignoring unique information leads to less effective decisions. To overcome this, groups need to ask each member to discuss the information he or she has uncovered that seems to contradict his or her personal beliefs about the issue. When addressing a complex issue, separate information sharing from decision making by holding separate meetings spaced far enough apart to enable members to think through their information.

Determining Solution Criteria

Once a group understands the nature of the problem, it is in a position to determine what tests a solution must pass to solve the problem. The criteria become the decisive factors in determining whether a particular solution will solve the problem. The criteria that are selected should be ones that the information gathered has suggested are critical to successfully solving the problem.

The criteria that the group decides on will be used to screen alternative solutions. Solutions that do not meet the test of all criteria are eliminated from further consideration. For example, a local citizens' committee is charged with selecting a site for a new county jail. The group arrives at the following phrasing for the problem: "Where should the new jail be located?" After the group agrees on this wording, they can then ask the question, "What are the criteria for a good site for a new jail?"

In that discussion, suppose members contribute information related to the county's budget, the need for inmates to maintain family contact, concerns about proximity to schools and parks, and space needs. After considering this kind of information, the group might then select the following criteria for selecting a site:

- Maximum cost of $1 million for purchasing the land.
- A location no more than three blocks from public transportation.
- A location that is one mile or more from any school, day care center, playground, or youth center.
- A lot size of at least 10 acres.

Kathryn Young and her colleagues (2000) suggest that when groups discuss and decide on criteria before they think about specific solutions, they increase their ability to avoid becoming polarized and are more likely to come to a decision that all members can accept.

Identifying Possible Solutions

For most policy questions, many solutions are possible. The trick is to tap the creative thinking of group members so that many ideas are generated. At this stage of discussion, the goal is not to worry about whether a particular solution fits all the criteria, but to come up with a large list of ideas.

One way to identify potential solutions is to brainstorm for ideas. **Brainstorming** is an uncritical, nonevaluative process of generating associated ideas. It involves verbalizing your ideas as they come to mind without stopping to evaluate their merits. Members are encouraged, however, to build

brainstorming
an uncritical, nonevaluative process of generating associated ideas.

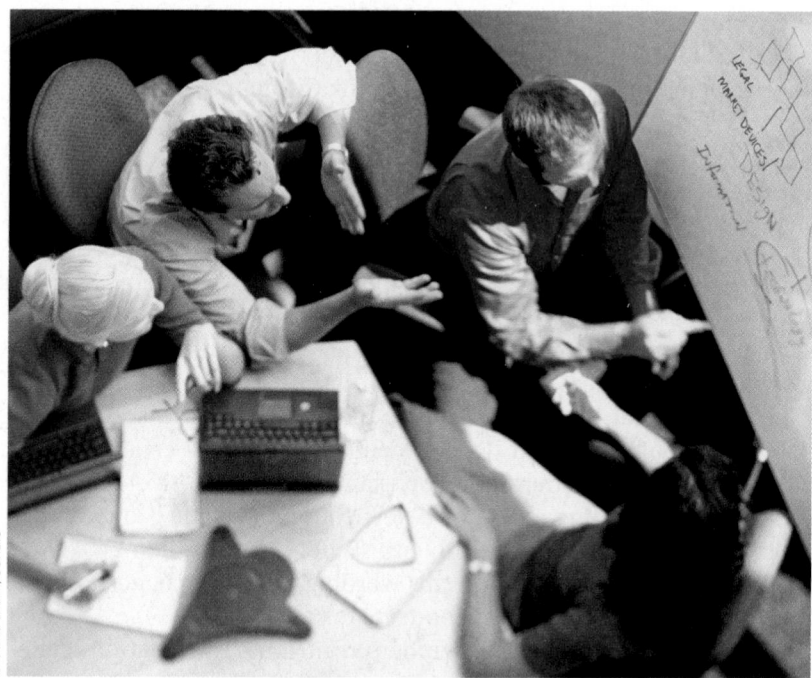

© Steve Chenn/CORBIS

How does building on the ideas of others during brainstorming help generate new ideas?

on the ideas presented by others. For a more detailed discussion of the brainstorming process, use your ThomsonNOW for *Communicate!* to access **Web Resource 10.7: Rules for Brainstorming**. In a 10- or 15-minute brainstorming session, a group may come up with 20 or more possible solutions, depending on the nature of the problem. For instance, the group working on the jail site question might mention 10 or more in just a few minutes of brainstorming, such as sites that individual members have thought of or have heard others mention.

Evaluating Solutions

Once the group has a list of possible solutions, it needs to compare each solution alternative to the criteria that it developed. During this phase, the group must determine whether each criterion is equally important or whether certain criteria should be given more weight in evaluating alternative solutions. Whether a group weighs certain criteria more heavily or not, it should use a process that ensures that each alternative solution is thoroughly assessed against all criteria.

Research by Randy Hirokawa (1987) confirmed that high-quality decisions are made by groups that are "careful, thoughtful, and systematic" in evaluating their options (p. 10). In another study, Hirokawa (1988) noted that it is common for groups to begin by eliminating solutions that clearly do not meet important criteria and then to compare the positive features of solutions that remain. You can read more about his work in the Spotlight on Scholars feature in this chapter.

Communication Skill Brainstorming

Skill	Use	Procedure	Example
An uncritical, nonevaluative process of generating associated ideas.	To generate a list of potential solutions to a problem.	1. Verbalize ideas as they come to mind. 2. Refrain from evaluating the merits of ideas. 3. Encourage outrageous and unique ideas. 4. Build on or modify the ideas of others. 5. Use extended effort to generate more ideas. 6. Record the ideas.	Problem: "What should we do to raise money to help a child who needs a liver transplant?" Ideas: sell cookies, sell candy, sell wrapping paper; wrap packages at a mall for donations; find corporate sponsors; have a corporate golf outing, a youth golf outing, a tennis tournament, a bowling tournament, a paintball tournament; auction donated paintings; or do odd jobs for money.

Deciding

A group brought together for problem solving may or may not be responsible for making the actual decision, but it is responsible for presenting its recommendation. **Decision making** is the process of choosing among alternatives. The following five methods differ in the extent to which they require all members to agree with the decision and the amount of time it takes to reach a decision.

decision making
the process of choosing among alternatives.

1. **The expert opinion method.** Once the group has eliminated alternatives that do not meet the criteria, the group asks the member with the most expertise to select the final choice. This method is quick, and it is useful when one member is much more knowledgeable about the issues or has a greater stake in implementation of the decision.

2. **The average group opinion method.** When using this approach, each member of the group ranks the alternatives that meet all the criteria. These rankings are then averaged, and the alternative receiving the highest average ranking becomes the choice. This method is useful for routine decisions or when a decision needs to be made quickly. It can also be used as an intermediate straw poll to enable the group to eliminate low-scoring alternatives before moving to a different process for making the final decision.

3. **The majority rule method.** When using this method, the group votes on each alternative, and the one that receives the majority of votes (50 percent +1) is selected. Although this method is considered democratic, it can create problems for implementation. If the majority voting

P rior to becoming the Dean of the College of Arts and Sciences at the University of Hawaii at Hilo, Randy Hirokawa devoted his academic career to the study of communication, specializing in small group communication and decision-making effectiveness. His interest in this area began while he was a graduate student at the University of Washington. At the time, he was taking a course on organizational behavior in the business school. As part of a unit on organizational decision making, he and his classmates read a case study in which B.F. Goodrich Tire Company employees made a series of bad decisions involving the design of a brake system for a U.S. Navy jet fighter. In the field tests, the brakes failed so miserably that a test pilot was almost killed and a Congressional committee was convened to investigate the problem. As the class discussed the case study, one of Hirokawa's classmates commented that the problem "stemmed from poor communication." The professor then turned to Hirokawa and asked him, as the communication expert in the class, what he knew about the role communication plays in organizational decision-making effectiveness. At the time, he had no answer for the question, but it piqued his curiosity and provided him with a guiding question for his dissertation and later research.

Hirokawa's work in small group communication and decision-making effectiveness ultimately led him and a colleague, Dr. Dennis Gouran, to develop the "functional perspective." This theory holds that communication facilitates or impedes a group's efforts to reach a good decision by affecting the group's ability to perform essential decision-making functions, including understanding problems, identifying the full range of choices available to the group, and recognizing the positive and negative aspects of alternative choices. In short, the functional perspective suggests that the quality of a group decision is greatly influenced by the way group members talk about the essential issues and questions surrounding the decision task. For example, if a group misconstrues a problem it faces, it is likely to make a bad decision.

Hirokawa began to develop his ideas about the functional perspective while preparing and evaluating a study he did for his dissertation. In that study, he gave groups the same decision-making task and had experts evaluate their decisions. He then divided the groups into two categories—those who made good decisions and those who made bad decisions—and measured and compared different aspects of their communication to see which communication aspects were associated with good decision making and which were associated with bad decision making. Following that initial study, Hirokawa and Dr. Gouran wrote an article that introduced the terminology, concepts, and general framework for the "functional perspective." Later, he and Dr. Gouran began testing different aspects of the theoretical framework in laboratory and case studies. With each new study's findings, Hirokawa and Dr. Gouran modified and adjusted the theory to what it is today.

Although Hirokawa has plenty of empirical evidence to validate the "functional perspective," his own professional experiences also provide ample anecdotal support for the theory. By now, he has been on enough university committees to recognize how aspects of the "functional perspective" influence the outcomes of the committees' decisions. Hirokawa feels that any students with experience in small group activities can probably provide their own anecdotal support for this theory, too.

For more information about Randy Hirokawa, log on to http://www.uhh.hawaii.edu/academics/cas/AbouttheDean.php.

© University of Hawaii at Hilo Photo Service

Communication Skill   Problem Solving in Groups

Skill	Use	Procedure	Example
Using a systematic, six-step process to work out difficulties or resolve issues.	A guide for groups to follow in arriving at conclusions to fact or value questions.	1. Define the problem in specific and precise language as a question of fact, value, or policy containing one central idea. The question is: "What textbook should we adopt for the required Human Communication course?" 2. Analyze the problem using the experiences of group members, information obtained from public sources, and through interviews with other knowledgeable people. 3. Determine the solution criteria. 4. Identify possible solutions through brainstorming. 5. Evaluate the solutions by comparing them to the criteria. 6. Decide using expert opinion, average group opinion, majority, unanimity, or consensus method.	The question is: "What textbook should we adopt for the required Human Communication course?" Members who have taught the course before recount their experiences with various texts. We read the publishers' information packets, and we talk to the sales reps. The criteria we will use are coverage, writing style, web support, and cost. We identify six books that might work. We compare the books to each other using our criteria. We adopt a consensus method for deciding.

Skill Building   The Problem-Solving Process

Describe how you would use the six steps in the problem-solving process to arrive at a solution to the following situation.

Your manager at work has decided that you and your coworkers should determine whether it is time to upgrade your company-supplied mobile phone hardware and service. If you decide to upgrade, you are sup-

posed to do the research and choose the equipment and service provider.

Thomson NOW! You can complete this activity online and compare your answers to the authors'. Use your ThomsonNOW for *Communicate!* to access **Skill Learning Activity 10.4**.

DIVERSE VOICES

The Group: A Japanese Context

by Delores Cathcart and Robert Cathcart

One of Japan's most prominent national characteristics is the individual's sense of the group. Loyalty to the group and a willingness to submit to its demands are key virtues in Japanese society.

This dependency and the interdependency of all members of a group is reinforced by the concept of *on*. A Japanese is expected to feel an indebtedness to those others in the group who provide security, care, and support. This indebtedness creates obligation and when combined with dependency is called *on*. *On* functions as a means of linking all persons in the group in an unending chain because obligation is never satisfied, but continues throughout life. *On* is fostered by a system known as the *oyabun-kobun* relationship. Traditionally the *oyabun* is a father, boss, or patron who protects and provides for a son, employee, or student in return for his or her service and loyalty. This is not a one-way dependency. Each boss or group leader recognizes his own dependency on those below. Without their undivided loyalty he or she could not function. *Oyabun* are also acutely aware of this double dimension because of having had to serve a long period of *kobun* on the way up the hierarchy to the position at the top. All had *oyabun* who protected and assisted them, much like a father, and now each must do the same for their *kobun*. *Oyabun* have one or more *kobun* whom they look after much as if they were children. The more loyal and devoted the "children" the more successful the "father."

This relationship is useful in modern life where large companies assume the role of superfamily and become involved in every aspect of their workers' lives. Bosses are *oyabun* and employees are *kobun* . . .

This uniquely Japanese way of viewing relationships creates a distinctive style of decision making known as *consensus decision*. The Japanese devotion to consensus building seems difficult for most

Westerners to grasp but loses some of its mystery when looked at as a solution to representing every member of the group. In a system that operates on *oyabun-kobun* relationships nothing is decided without concern for how the outcome will affect all. Ideas and plans are circulated up and down the company hierarchy until everyone has had a chance to react. This reactive process is not to exert pressure, but to make certain that all matters affecting the particular groups and the company are taken into consideration. Much time is spent assessing the mood of everyone involved and only after all the ramifications of how the decision will affect each group can there be a quiet assent. A group within the company may approve a decision that is not directly in its interest (or even causes it difficulties) because its members know they are not ignored, their feelings have been expressed and they can be assured that what is good for the company will ultimately be good for them. For this reason consensus decisions cannot be hurried along without chancing a slight or oversight that will cause future problems.

The process of consensus building in order to make decisions is a time-consuming one, not only because everyone must be considered, but also because the Japanese avoid verbalizing objections or doubts in order to preserve group harmony. The advice, often found in American group literature, that group communication should be characterized by open and candid statements expressing individual personal feelings, wishes, and dislikes, is the antithesis of the Japanese consensus process. No opposing speeches are made to argue alternate ideas; no conferences are held to debate issues. Instead, the process of assessing the feelings and mood of each work group proceeds slowly until there exists a climate of agreement. This process is possible because of the tight relationships that allow bosses and workers to know each other intimately and to know the group so well that needs and desires are easy to assess.

Excerpted from Delores Cathcart and Robert Cathcart, "The Group: A Japanese Context." In Intercultural Communication: A Reader, *8th ed., Larry A. Samovar and Richard E. Porter, eds. (Belmont, CA: Wadsworth, 1997), pp. 329–339. Reprinted by permission of the author.*

for an alternative is slight, there may be nearly as many members who do not support the choice as there are those that do. If these minority members object strongly to the choice, they may sabotage implementation of the solution either through active or passive means.

4. **The unanimous decision method.** In this method, the group must continue deliberation until every member of the group believes the same solution is the best. As you would expect, it is very difficult to arrive at truly unanimous decisions, and to do so takes a lot of time. When a group reaches unanimity, however, it can expect that each member of the group will be fully committed to selling the decision to others and to helping implement the decision.

5. **The consensus method.** This method is an alternative to the unanimous decision method. In consensus, the group continues deliberation until all members of the group find an acceptable variation—one they can support and are committed to helping implement. Members of a consensus group may believe that there is a better solution than the one that has been chosen, but they feel they can support and help implement the one they have agreed to. Although easier to achieve than reaching unanimity, arriving at consensus is still difficult. Although the majority rule method is widely used, selecting the consensus method is a wise investment if the group needs everyone's support to implement the decision successfully.

To read a complete comparison of the advantages and disadvantages of various decision-making methods, use your ThomsonNOW for *Communicate!* to access **Web Resource 10.8: Decision-Making Methods**.

In the United States, the majority rule method is the one under which many groups function. In Japan, the dominant decision-making method is the consensus method. This method is described in the Diverse Voices selection in this chapter.

OBSERVE & ANALYZE

Journal Activity

How Does Your Group Solve Problems?

Analyze a situation in which a group to which you belong attempted to solve a problem. Write a paragraph in which you answer the following questions. Did the group use all six of the problem-solving steps listed here? If not, which steps did the group overlook? Were there any steps the group should have placed more emphasis on? Was the group successful or not in its efforts to solve the problem? Explain why you think this was or was not the case.

You can use your Student Workbook to complete this activity, or you can complete it online, and, if requested, e-mail it to your instructor. Use your ThomsonNOW for *Communicate!* to access **Skill Learning Activity 10.5**.

Summary

Effective groups meet several criteria: They develop clearly defined goals, have an optimum number of diverse members, work to develop cohesiveness, establish norms, create appropriate environments in face-to-face and virtual meetings, and achieve synergy.

What Would You Do?

The Community Service and Outreach committee of Students in Communication was meeting to determine what cause should benefit from their annual fund-raising talent contest.

"So," said Mark, "does anyone have any ideas about whose cause we should sponsor?"

"Well," replied Glenna, "I think we should give it to a group that's doing literacy work."

"Sounds good to me," replied Mark.

"My aunt works at the Boardman Center as the literacy coordinator, so why don't we just adopt them?" asked Glenna.

"Gee, I don't know much about the group," said Reed.

"Come on, you know, they help people learn how to read," replied Glenna sarcastically.

"Well, I was kind of hoping we'd take a look at sponsoring the local Teen Runaway Center," offered Angelo.

"Listen, if your aunt works at the Boardman Center," commented Leticia, "let's go with it."

"Right," said Pablo, "that's good enough for me."

"Yeah," replied Heather, "let's do it and get out of here."

"I hear what you're saying, Heather," Mark responded, "I've got plenty of other stuff to do."

"No disrespect meant to Glenna, but wasn't the Boardman Center in the news because of questionable use of funds?" countered Angelo. "Do we really know enough about them?"

"OK," said Mark, "enough discussion. I've got to get to class. All in favor of the literacy program at the Boardman Center indicate by saying 'aye.' I think we've got a majority. Sorry, Angelo—you can't win them all."

"I wish all meetings went this smoothly," Heather said to Glenna as they left the room. "I mean, that was really a good meeting."

1. What did the group really know about the Boardman Center? Is it good group discussion practice to rely on a passing comment of one member?

2. Regardless of whether the meeting went smoothly, is there any ethical problem with this process? Explain.

Once groups have assembled, they tend to move through five stages of development: forming, getting people to feel valued and accepted so that they identify with the group; storming, clarifying goals while determining the role each member will have in the group power structure; norming, solidifying rules for behavior; performing, overcoming obstacles and meeting goals successfully; and adjourning, assigning meaning to what they have done and determining how to end or maintain interpersonal relations they have developed.

Once the group has reached the performing stage, they begin to move through a series of steps of problem solving, including defining the problem as a question of fact, value, or policy; analyzing the problem; determining solution criteria; identifying possible solutions; evaluating solutions; and deciding.

Thomson™ NOW!

Communicate! Online

ow that you have read Chapter 10, use your ThomsonNOW for *Communicate!* for quick access to the electronic resources that accompany this text. Your ThomsonNOW gives you access to the Web Resources and Skill Learning Activities featured in this chapter, InfoTrac College Edition, and online study aids such as a digital glossary and review quizzes.

Your *Communicate!* ThomsonNOW is an online study system that helps you identify concepts you don't fully understand, allowing you to put your study time to the best use. Using chapter-by-chapter diagnostic pre-tests, the system creates a personalized study plan for each chapter. Each plan directs you to specific resources designed to improve your understanding, including pages from the text in e-book format. Chapter post-tests give you an opportunity to measure how much you've learned and let you know if you are ready for graded quizzes and exams.

Key Terms

Go to your ThomsonNOW for *Communicate!* to access your online glossary for Chapter 10. Print a copy of the glossary for this chapter and test yourself with the electronic flash cards or complete the crossword puzzle to help you master these key terms:

acceptable goals (225)	ground rules (228)	questions of policy (238)
adjourning (235)	group goal (224)	questions of value (237)
brainstorming (239)	groupthink (234)	specific goal (224)
challenging goals (225)	heterogeneous group (226)	storming (233)
cohesiveness (227)	homogeneous group (226)	synergy (230)
consistent goals (224)	norming (234)	team-building activities (227)
decision making (241)	norms (228)	virtual meeting (230)
face-to-face meeting (230)	performing (235)	work group (224)
forming (233)	questions of fact (237)	

Review Quiz

Test your knowledge of the concepts in this chapter by taking the online review quiz for Chapter 10. Go to your ThomsonNOW for *Communicate!* to access the quiz. When you have completed the quiz, submit it for scoring.

Skill Learning Activities

Complete the Observe & Analyze, Test Your Competence, and Skill Building activities for Chapter 10 online at your ThomsonNOW for *Communicate!*. You can submit your Observe & Analyze answers to your instructor, and compare your Test Your Competence and Skill Building answers to those provided by the authors.

Web Resources

Go to your ThomsonNOW for *Communicate!* to access the Web Resources for this chapter.

Harry Sieplinga/HMS Images/Getty Images

11

Member Roles and Leadership in Groups

"Well, because we're all here, let's get started. The first item on the agenda is to review the three bids we got for landscaping services. Dontonio, will you be the note taker?"

"Sure, Ray, no problem."

"Okay. Sarella, we know that you have studied the bids. So why don't you start us out by summarizing what you found?"

"Well, only three of the six companies submitted detailed bids with all the information we wanted. It looks like they all will provide the same basic services and on the same schedules. Two of the bids came in at about the same amount, but the other one is much higher. The two lower bids were from Wildflowers and from J&M."

"Well, I've never heard of Wildflowers, but my brother-in-law used J&M for a while and dropped them because they ran over his flowers with their big riding mowers. I don't think we want to use them."

"Hey, Jose, be careful, my boyfriend works for J&M, and he wouldn't like you picking on him like that."

"Judith, I don't think Jose meant his comment as a personal attack on your boyfriend. I think he was just telling us something he had heard."

"Yeah, you're right, Shawn. It's a good thing we have you to keep us from getting into a fight here."

O ur beginning conversation is typical of interactions in groups. If you listened closely, you could hear that the members of this group were not only discussing the topic, but were acting in the ways expected of them by others in the group. Our goal in this chapter is to explain how members of groups take on specific roles that help or detract from the effectiveness of the group. We describe the types of roles members assume, and the responsibilities that group members have during meetings. Then we discuss group leadership, including understanding its functions, identifying several leadership roles, describing how members gain and maintain leadership, and the responsibilities of meeting leaders. Finally, we discuss ways to evaluate group effectiveness.

Members' Roles

role
a specific pattern of behavior that one group member performs based on the expectations of other members.

A **role** is a specific pattern of behavior that one group member performs based on the expectations of other members. The roles that group members play depend on their personalities and the requirements or needs of the group. Three common types of roles are task-related, maintenance, and self-centered roles.

Task-Related Roles

task-related roles
specific patterns of behavior that directly help the group accomplish its goals.

Task-related roles require specific patterns of behavior that directly help the group accomplish its goals. Task roles include initiator, information or opinion giver, information or opinion seeker, analyzer, and orienter.

initiator
a group member who gets the discussion started or moves it in a new direction.

Initiator You play the **initiator** role when your comment gets the discussion started or moves it in a new direction. You would be performing the initiating role by suggesting, "Let's begin by looking at the current problems in our inventory control system." Or by saying, "Perhaps we should move on to a discussion of quality concerns we have related to our vendors and suppliers."

information or opinion giver
a group member who provides content for the discussion.

Information or opinion giver You play the **information or opinion giver** role when you provide content for the discussion. People who perform these roles well are those who have expertise or who are well informed on the content of the task and share what they know with the group. An example of this role performance is "In my experience, telling a customer that it's against company policy just makes them angrier, so I don't think that is what we want to say in this situation."

information or opinion seeker
a group member who probes others for their factual ideas and opinions.

Information or opinion seeker You play the **information or opinion seeker** role when you ask questions that probe others for their ideas and opinions. Typical comments by those performing these roles include remarks such as, "Before going further, what information do we have about how raising dues is likely to affect membership?" Or, "How do members of the group feel about this idea?"

Analyzer In the **analyzer** role, you probe the content, reasoning, and evidence of members during discussion. To make good decisions, group members must critically examine ideas or suggestions provided by members and also the facts and data gathered by the group. A member would be performing this role by saying, "We need to be sure the numbers we have here on annual enrollment in our program are consistent with monthly totals."

analyzer
a group member who probes the content, reasoning, and evidence of members during discussion.

Orienter The **orienter** indicates to the group that it is off track, and summarizes points of agreement and disagreement among members. It's easy for a group to get so involved in a discussion that it loses track of the "big picture" or goes off on many tangents and wastes time with irrelevant issues. Thus, it is important that someone in the group monitors the group process. A member would be performing an orienting role by making a comment such as, "We might want to finish our listing of fund-raising sources before we move to talking about hiring a fund-raising consultant," or "We seem to be coming back again and again to the basic disagreement between having customer support functions at each location or consolidating them centrally. Is that the point we're stuck on right now?"

orienter
a group member who indicates to the group that it is off track or summarizes points of agreement and disagreement among members.

Maintenance Roles

Maintenance roles require specific patterns of behavior that help the group develop and maintain good member relationships, group cohesiveness, and effective levels of conflict. Members who play maintenance roles are likely to be gatekeepers, encouragers, and harmonizers.

maintenance roles
patterns of behavior that help the group develop and maintain good member relationships, group cohesiveness, and effective levels of conflict.

Gatekeeper As the **gatekeeper,** you ensure that everyone has an opportunity to speak and be heard. In some group discussions, certain people may talk more than their fair share while others remain silent, contributing little or nothing. By performing the gatekeeping role, you help to create more balanced participation among members so that the group can benefit from a variety of viewpoints and information sources. An example of gatekeeping is: "Let me interrupt you, Doug. We haven't heard from Juanita, and she seems to have something she wants to say."

gatekeeper
a group member who ensures that everyone has an opportunity to speak and be heard.

Encourager You are the **encourager** when your messages provide support for the contributions of other team members. Participants in a group discussion need to have their ideas acknowledged and supported from time to time. Otherwise, they are unsure if they are being heard and their ideas are being taken seriously. Examples of encouraging include: "That was a really good suggestion that Kent just made because it deals exactly with the problem we have in meeting client specifications." Or, "I think we should keep in mind Miranda's point about maintaining requirements until

encourager
a group member who provides support for the contributions of other team members.

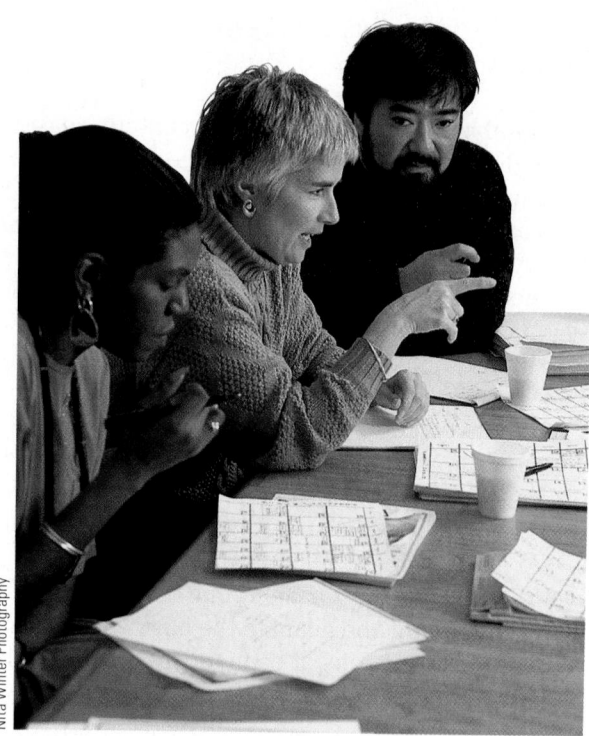

Nita Winter Photography

Some members provide information to the group, others help maintain harmonious relations among group members, and still others help the group stay on track. When you are part of a problem-solving group, which roles do you usually assume?

the next quarter. She made some good observations about the dangers of moving too quickly."

harmonizer
a group member who helps the group relieve tension and manage conflict.

Harmonizer You act as the **harmonizer** when you help the group relieve tension and manage conflict. It is inevitable that team decision making will become stressful at times, and conflicts may emerge. A member who acts as a harmonizer may temporarily relieve the tension by saying something witty or may help the group effectively deal with an emerging conflict. Examples of harmonizing behavior include: "The task of planning this product launch reminds me of dealing with Godzilla. Anyone see that movie?" Or, "We seem to be at odds around the issue of partnering with other schools. It seems that Elana and Nils strongly represent alternate perspectives. Before we get too polarized around these two options, maybe we should look at a range of possibilities."

Self-Centered Roles

self-centered roles
patterns of behavior that focus attention on individuals' needs and goals at the expense of the group.

Self-centered roles reflect specific patterns of behavior that focus attention on individuals' needs and goals at the expense of the group. Task-related and maintenance roles must be played for groups to be effective, but self-centered roles detract from group effectiveness. Members who play self-centered roles are likely to be aggressors, jokers, withdrawers, or blockers.

Aggressors **Aggressors** seek to enhance their own status by criticizing almost everything or blaming others when things get rough and by deflating the ego or status of others. Aggressors should be confronted and encouraged to assume a more positive role. They should be asked if they are aware of their actions and the effect their behavior is having on the group.

aggressor
a group member who seeks to enhance his or her own status by criticizing almost everything or blaming others when things get rough and by deflating the ego or status of others.

Jokers **Jokers** attempt to draw attention to themselves by clowning, mimicking, or generally making a joke of everything. Unlike tension relievers, the joker is not focused on helping the group relieve stress or tension. Rather, a joker disrupts work when the group is trying to focus on the task. Jokers should also be confronted; they should be encouraged to use their abilities when the group needs a break, but to refrain from disrupting the group when it is being productive.

joker
a group member who attempts to draw attention to himself or herself by clowning, mimicking, or generally making a joke of everything.

Withdrawers **Withdrawers** seek to meet their own goals at the expense of group goals by not participating in the discussion or the work of the group. Sometimes, withdrawers play their role by physically missing meetings or not participating in virtual meetings. At other times, withdrawers are present but remain silent in discussion or refuse to take responsibility for doing work. When a person has assumed this role, the group needs to find out why the person is choosing not to participate and find ways to get the member either involved in the group or removed from the group.

withdrawer
a group member who meets his or her own goals at the expense of group goals by not participating in the discussion or the work of the group.

Blockers **Blockers** routinely reject others' views and stubbornly disagree with emerging group decisions. They may hold out as a lone voice refusing to go along with the rest of the group. They may attempt to sabotage a group decision on which they do not agree. If a member has had ample opportunity to express his or her views and the rest of the group has genuinely listened to and considered those views, then the group must proceed without the blocker. The group should acknowledge and respect a member's right to disagree, but should assert the group's right to proceed with its work.

blocker
a group member who routinely rejects others' views and stubbornly disagrees with emerging group decisions.

Normal Distribution of Roles

What proportion of time in a "normal" group should be devoted to the various roles described in this section? According to Robert Bales (1971), a leading researcher in group interaction processes, 40 to 60 percent of discussion time is spent giving and asking for information and opinion; 8 to 15 percent of discussion time is spent on disagreement, tension, or unfriendliness; and 16 to 26 percent of discussion time is characterized by agreement or friendliness (positive maintenance functions). We can apply two norms as guidelines for effective group functioning: (1) approximately half of all discussion time should be devoted to information sharing, and (2) group agreement time should far outweigh group disagreement time.

To complete a survey that will help you find out the combination of roles you are most likely to play in a team or group, use your ThomsonNOW for *Communicate!* to access **Web Resource 11.1: Identifying Your Team Player Style**. How are you likely to contribute to group or team effectiveness? To complete an activity that will help you practice identifying characteristics of group member roles, access **Skill Learning Activity 11.1: Identifying Roles**.

Member Responsibilities in Group Meetings

Although members specialize in particular roles during group meetings, members of effective groups also assume common responsibilities for making their meetings successful. Here are some guidelines to help group members prepare for, participate in, and follow up on a meeting in order to increase its effectiveness.

Preparing

Too often, people think of meetings as a "happening" that requires attendance but no particular preparation. People often arrive at a meeting unprepared, even though they are carrying packets of material that they received before the meeting. The reality is that meetings should not be treated as impromptu events, but as carefully planned interactions that pool information from well-prepared individuals. Here are some important steps to take before attending a meeting.

1. **Study the agenda.** Consider the purpose of the meeting and determine what you need to do to be prepared. The agenda is an outline for your preparation.

2. **Study the minutes.** If this is one in a series of meetings, study the minutes and your own notes from the previous meetings. Because each meeting is not a separate event, what happened at one meeting should provide the basis for preparation for the next meeting.

3. **Prepare for your contributions.** Read the material distributed before the meeting and do your own research to become better informed about items on the agenda. If no material is provided, you should identify the issues and learn what you need to know to be a productive member of the group. Bring any materials you have uncovered that will help the group accomplish the agenda. If appropriate, discuss the agenda with

others who will not be attending the meeting and solicit their ideas concerning issues to be discussed in the meeting.

4. **Prepare to play a major role.** Consider which roles you are assigned or which you are interested in playing. What do you need to do to play those roles to the best of your ability?

5. **List questions.** Make a list of questions related to agenda items that you would like to have answered during the meeting.

Participating

Be involved in the meeting with the expectation that you will be a full participant. If there are five people in the group, all five should be participating.

1. **Listen attentively.** Concentrate on what others are saying so that you can use your material to complement, supplement, or counter what has been presented.

2. **Stay focused.** In a group setting, it is easy to get the discussion going in nonproductive directions. Keep your comments focused on the specific agenda item under discussion. If others have gotten off the subject, do what you can to get people back on track.

3. **Ask questions.** "Honest" questions that have answers you do not already know help to stimulate discussion and build ideas.

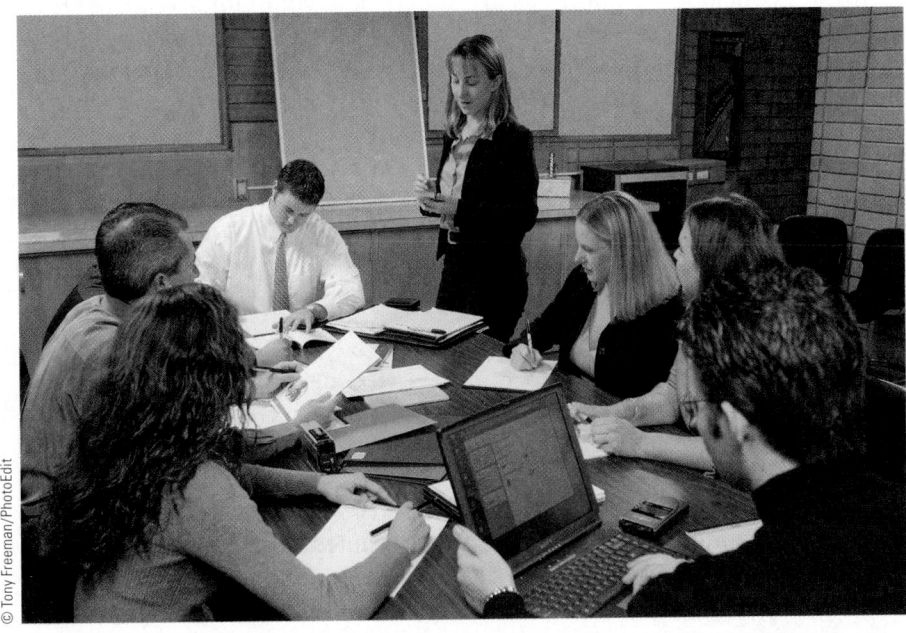

© Tony Freeman/PhotoEdit

Some people wait until the last minute to prepare for meetings. Do you find it annoying to attend meetings where people come unprepared to participate?

4. **Take notes.** Even if someone else is responsible for providing the official minutes, you will need notes that help you follow the line of development. Also, these notes will help you remember what has been said and any responsibilities you have agreed to take on. For useful tips on how to take minutes in meetings, use your ThomsonNOW for *Communicate!* to access **Web Resource 11.2: Taking Notes**.

5. **Play devil's advocate.** When you think an idea has not been fully discussed or tested, be willing to voice disagreement or encourage further discussion.

6. **Monitor your contributions.** Especially when people are well prepared, they have a tendency to dominate discussion. Make sure that you are neither dominating the discussion nor abdicating your responsibility to share insights and opinions. If you are a person who finds it difficult to participate in meetings, use your ThomsonNOW for *Communicate!* to access **Web Resource 11.3: Assert Yourself in Meetings**, which discusses useful steps for speaking out in meetings.

Following Up

When meetings end, too often people leave and forget about what took place until the next meeting. But what happens in one meeting provides a basis for what happens in the next; be prepared to move forward at the next meeting.

1. **Review and summarize your notes.** Try to do this shortly after the meeting has concluded, while ideas are still fresh in your mind. Make notes of what needs to be discussed next time. For a detailed discussion of how to process your meeting notes, use your ThomsonNOW for *Communicate!* to access **Web Resource 11.4: Dealing with Your Notes**.

2. **Evaluate your effectiveness.** How effective were you in helping the group move toward achieving its goals? Where were you strong? Where were you weak? What should you do next time that you did not do in this meeting?

3. **Review decisions.** Make note of what your role was in making decisions. Did you do all that you could have done?

4. **Communicate progress.** Inform others who need to know about information conveyed and decisions that were made in the meeting.

5. **Follow up.** Make sure you complete all assignments you received in the meeting.

6. **Review minutes.** Compare the official minutes of the meeting to your own notes, and report any significant discrepancies that you find.

Leadership

Although performance of all task, maintenance, and procedural roles helps groups to accomplish their goals, good leadership is also necessary to accomplish group goals. Scholars have offered numerous definitions of leadership, but common to most definitions is the notion that **leadership** is a process of influencing members to accomplish group goals (Shaw, 1981, p. 317). In this section, we will discuss various perspectives of leadership, types of leaders, and ways of becoming informal leaders.

leadership
is a process of influencing members to accomplish group goals.

Perspectives of Leadership

There are various ways to think about leadership. Each perspective focuses on different aspects of leadership, but taken together, these perspectives provide insight into characteristics and behaviors that can help you become an effective leader. The various perspectives emphasize different aspects such as leadership traits, situations, functions, and transformations.

Leadership traits This approach examines personality characteristics or traits that are associated with effective leaders. It is believed that certain leadership traits or abilities can reside within a person and are universal and constant. Some studies have shown that leaders typically possess achievement orientation, adaptability, energy, responsibility, self-confidence, intelligence, verbal communication ability, sociability, persistence, and innovativeness (Bass, 1981; Baker, 1990; Stogdill, 1981). To be an effective leader, you might think about some of the leadership traits you possess and be sure to demonstrate them in group decision-making situations.

Situational leadership This approach says that leadership depends on the situation. Unlike the trait approach, this view says there is no one style of effective leadership. Rather, effective leadership is a match between what a situation calls for and how a person behaves. Some situations, like an emergency, may call for a strong, task-oriented leader to be very directive and take charge. Another situation, like a decision-making team of very technically skilled people, may call for a nondirective leader who emphasizes maintenance behaviors and a sharing of information. To employ situational leadership, it is important to analyze what behaviors are needed in a group discussion, to employ those behaviors, and to monitor outcomes to see if alternative behaviors might be demonstrated.

Functional leadership The functional perspective suggests that leadership involves acting in a way that helps the group achieve its goals. It might mean that the leader performs certain task or maintenance roles that are not being handled by other members. Or it may involve the leader

OBSERVE & ANALYZE

Journal Activity

Member Meeting Responsibilities

Recall the last time you attended a small group problem-solving meeting. On a scale of 1 to 5 (1 = not at all, 2 = poorly, 3 = somewhat, 4 = well done, 5 = to the best of my ability) rate yourself on how well you carried out each of the preparation, participation, and follow-up guidelines. Analyze your responses and determine how effectively you participated in that meeting. What do you need to work on to become a more valuable member of a problem-solving group? Why? Write a paragraph in which you describe what you have learned.

You can use your Student Workbook to complete this activity, or you can complete it online, download a check sheet to help you complete it, and, if requested, Thomson e-mail it to your NOW! instructor. Use your ThomsonNOW for *Communicate!* to access **Skill Learning Activity 11.2.**

performing separate functions such as preparing the agenda, scheduling meetings, making assignments, and distributing minutes. Later in this chapter, we will discuss leader roles before, during, and after group meetings. As a functional leader, you will pay close attention to what group roles are needed for task accomplishment and be sure to perform many of those functions.

Transformational leadership This approach emphasizes being a visionary, helping the group to set goals and motivating, if not inspiring, the group to achieve its goals (Wilson, 2005). Transformational leaders are creative, charismatic, and inspire others (Barge, 1994). Famous leaders such as Gandhi or Martin Luther King would be considered transformational leaders. To engage in this leadership approach, you will want to focus on the big picture, help the group to see things in a novel way, and energetically promote the group's goals.

Types of Leaders

formal leader
an assigned, appointed, or elected leader who is given legitimate power to influence others.

informal leaders
members of the group whose authority to influence stems from the power they gain through their interactions in the group.

A group will often have more than one leader. Many groups have a designated **formal leader,** an assigned, appointed, or elected leader who is given legitimate power to influence others. During its work life, a group may have only one formal leader, but several people may play leadership roles. **Informal leaders** are members of the group whose authority to influence stems from the power they gain through their interactions in the group. Informal leaders do not have legitimate power; rather, their influence comes from their expertise or the extent that other group members like and respect them.

How Members Gain and Maintain Informal Leadership

According to research by Ernest Bormann (1990), leaders emerge through a two-step elimination process. During the first step of the process, members form crude impressions about each other based on early interactions. During this phase, members who do not demonstrate the commitment or skillfulness necessary to fulfill leadership roles are eliminated. Group members less likely to emerge as leaders include those who do not participate (either due to shyness or indifference); those who are overly strong and bossy in their opinions and positions; those who are perceived to be uninformed, less intelligent, or unskilled; and those with irritating interpersonal styles.

During the second phase, those who are still acceptable to the group may vie for leadership. Sometimes one contender will become an informal leader because the group faces a crisis that this member recognizes and is better able to help the group remedy than others are. At other times, a contender may become an informal leader because one or more members of the group have come to trust this person and openly support that person as a leader. To explore seven principles that are useful for maintaining leadership during difficult challenges, read "Leadership Principles for Tough Times," available through InfoTrac College Edition. Use your ThomsonNOW for *Communicate!* to access **Web Resource 11.5: Leadership Principles**.

In some groups, most members will eventually recognize one or more informal leaders. For example, one leader might be particularly attuned to group relationships and may help to keep conflict at healthy levels. The other leader may be skilled at keeping the group on track and moving through the agenda during meetings. Students are often interested in how they can show leadership in a group. Because leadership is demonstrated through communication behaviors, following these recommendations can help you emerge as a leader.

1. **Actively participate in discussions.** When members do not participate, others may view them as disinterested or uninformed. Indicate your interest and commitment to the group by participating in the group's discussions.

2. **Come to group meetings prepared.** Uninformed members rarely achieve leadership, whereas those who demonstrate expertise often emerge as leaders.

3. **Actively listen to the ideas and opinions of others.** Because leadership requires analyzing what a group needs, the leader must understand the ideas and needs of members. When you actively listen, you also demonstrate your willingness to consider a point of view different from your own.

4. **Avoid stating overly strong opinions.** When other members of the group perceive that someone is strongly opinionated or inflexible, they are less likely to accept that person as a leader.

5. **Stimulate creative and critical thinking.** When members bring original ideas and insights to a group or when they help the group to examine reasoning and evidence before making decisions, they increase their likelihood of emerging as leaders.

6. **Actively manage meaning.** People who offer vision or a perspective on the task at hand will often emerge as a leader. If you have a mental map or framework that can move the group to see things a certain way, offer it.

Gender and Leadership

In her book on communication, gender, and culture, Julia Wood (2007) explains that leadership, especially in workplaces, is often linked with stereotypically masculine styles of communicating, including independence, competitiveness, assertiveness, and confidence rather than stereotypically feminine styles of communication such as cooperation, collaboration, attentiveness, supportiveness, inclusion, and deference. If masculine behaviors

---

OBSERVE & ANALYZE

Journal Activity

Emerging Informal Leadership in CBS's *Survivor* Series

Watch an early episode of one of the popular CBS *Survivor* series (for example, Amazon or Outback). Select one tribe and identify the dominant roles that each member of the group seems to play in that episode. Who is vying for informal leadership? How are they trying to gain or maintain their leadership? What do you think will happen to each leader candidate?

Thomson NOW! Use your Thomson-NOW for *Communicate!* to access **Skill Learning Activity 11.3**, which provides a link to the website for each *Survivor* series. Use the "episode" recap on the website for the group you chose, to see how well your predictions held up. Write a short essay describing what you have learned. You can complete this activity online and, if requested, e-mail it to your instructor.

DIVERSE VOICES

How Carly Lost Her Gender Groove (And Will She Get It Back?)

by Maureen Dowd

Maureen Dowd is an author and celebrated columnist for The New York Times. *In her column of October 11, 2006, she wrote about the state of women in positions of power, focusing on Carly Fiorina, former CEO (1999–2005) and Chairman of the Board (2000–2005) of Hewlett-Packard. Fiorina's experiences in the male-dominated world of high-tech business highlights the differences between the leadership styles of men and women.*

Carly Fiorina prided herself on being adept at succeeding in a man's world without whining about sexism.

In her new memoir, *Tough Choices,* the expelled CEO of Hewlett-Packard—the first female head of a Fortune 20 company—describes how she insisted on going along to a business meeting at a Washington strip club when she started out as an ambitious young woman at AT&T.

"I was scared to death," she writes, adding that she wore her most conservative dress-for-success business suit and little bow tie, carried her briefcase like "a shield of honor," and repeated the mantra, "I am a professional woman," even when her cabdriver asked her if she was the new act for the club, where babes in see-through negligees danced on tables.

"In a show of empathy that brings tears to my eyes still," she recounts, "each woman who approached the table would look the situation over and say: 'Sorry, gentlemen. Not till the lady leaves.'"

On her first day at HP, she proclaimed, "The glass ceiling doesn't exist." But she now concedes that the glass trapdoor might.

"I think somehow men understand other men's need for respect differently than they understand it for a woman," Ms. Fiorina told Lesley Stahl on *60 Minutes.*

The male-dominated board's handling of her exit was "heartless in some ways and disrespectful in other ways," she said. "Maybe they took great pleasure in seeing me beat up publicly for weeks and weeks."

Other controlling blondes, like Hillary Clinton, Martha Stewart, and Tina Brown, were slapped back after great success (in a trend that *The Times*'s Alessandra Stanley dubbed blondenfreude), and Ms. Fiorina now thinks she was victimized by gender.

"In the chat rooms around Silicon Valley, from the time I arrived until long after I left HP, I was routinely referred to as either a 'bimbo' or a 'bitch,'" she writes. "Too soft or too hard, and presumptuous, besides." She adds: "I watched with interest as male CEOs fired people and were hailed as 'decisive.' I was labeled 'vindictive.'"

She reels off things that offended her: The editor of *Business Week* asked her if she was wearing an Armani suit. She felt adjectives such as "flashy," "glamorous," and "diamond studded" were meant to make her seem superficial. (Who doesn't like being called glamorous?) Stories referred to her by her first name. There was "painful commentary" that she'd chosen not to have children because she was "too ambitious."

"When I finally reached the top, after striving my entire career to be judged by results and accomplishments," she concludes, "the coverage of my gender, my appearance, and the perceptions of my personality would vastly outweigh anything else."

One of her foes was Tom Perkins, the 74-year-old rich venture capitalist on the HP board who also tangled with Patricia Dunn, the former board chairwoman. Being married to the romance novelist Danielle Steel and writing his own steamy novel, *Sex and the Single Zillionaire,* did not improve Mr. Perkins's skills in dealing with women, it seems.

With several of the few high-profile women at the top tanking, it's interesting to note that Columbia Business School has introduced a new program that teaches the importance of a more empathetic and sensitive leadership style in globalized business, as opposed to the command-and-control style that has dominated the White House and Pentagon for, lo, these many messed up years.

Students learn how to read facial expressions, body language, and posture, and get coaching on their brain's "mirror neurons"—how what they're thinking and feeling can affect others.

"This less autocratic leadership style draws on capabilities in which women are as good as men," says Michael Morris, a professor of psychology and management who is running the business school's new program.

Daniel Goleman, whose new book *Social Intelligence* is being taught in the program, points out that "while women are, in general, better at reading emotions, men tend to be better at managing them during a crisis. Women tend to be more sophisticated in reading social interactions but also tend to ruminate more when things go wrong."

And that can lead to score-settling memoirs—Ms. Fiorina fillets both her male tormentors on the "dysfunctional" board and Ms. Dunn—and to the sort of awful judgment and sneaky behavior that Ms. Dunn exhibited.

Neenu Sharma, an MBA student in the new Columbia program, says the moral of the story is that leadership works best with both sexes involved. "You need the woman there to know what's actually going on, but you need the man there to deal with the critical emotions at the time."

Excerpted from Maureen Dowd, "How Carly Lost Her Gender Groove (And Will She Get It Back?)," The New York Times, October 11, 2006. Copyright © 2006 by The New York Times Co. Reprinted by permission.

are equated with leadership, then women who communicate in more feminine ways may not be recognized as leaders. Yet, research does not support the position that only masculine styles of communicating contribute to effective leadership. Effective leadership depends on both the task-oriented behaviors associated with masculinity and the maintenance or people-related behaviors associated with femininity. Some situations call for a directive, take-charge style of leadership, while other situations call for cooperative leadership, which motivates and empowers others. A good leader should be able to demonstrate a full range of behaviors (Claes, 2002).

Another complicating factor of gendered leadership is the persistent research finding that leadership behaviors are evaluated differently based on the sex of the person using the behavior (Valian, 1998; Rhode, 2003). The same behavior may be perceived differently, depending on whether it is performed by a woman or a man. For example, a group member says, "I think we are repeating the same points here. Let's move on to the next agenda item." If the speaker is a woman, the comment may be seen as bossy or dominating. If a man makes the same comment, he may be seen as helpful and skilled in task-oriented roles. Because of gender expectations that women should be friendly, accommodating, and supportive, women who do not behave this way may be perceived negatively. Ironically, though, because assertive, directive, and competitive behaviors are associated with masculinity, sometimes when women use these behaviors, they are judged as behaving in too masculine a fashion. Similarly, if a man reacts emotionally in a leadership role, he may be perceived as weak or lacking credibility rather than being valued for an honest reaction. An emotional reaction from a female leader would likely be regarded as appropriate or typical.

So leaders should be aware that their behaviors will be judged, in part, through a gendered lens. This knowledge may help in understanding why group members sometimes react to leaders in the ways that they do. Some flexibility in communicating in both stereotypically masculine and feminine ways is necessary for all leaders.

Leading Group Meetings

In addition to performing task and maintenance roles in a decision-making meeting, there are duties to be completed before the meeting begins. By performing these jobs before leading a meeting, you can make sure that meeting time is spent productively and little time is wasted. When running a meeting, you should complete these five tasks.

Before the Meeting

1. **Define and communicate the meeting purpose.** It can be frustrating to be expected to attend a meeting for which you do not know the purpose. Participants in a meeting can prepare beforehand if they know the specific purpose of the meeting. They can also bring necessary materials to the meeting. For example, if the upcoming meeting of teachers involves curriculum planning, the purpose should be defined even more clearly. The memo announcing the meeting might say: "We will examine our existing curriculum goals and course topics as they relate to state curriculum requirements in the area of science."

2. **List specific outcomes that should be produced from the meeting.** Even with a clearly stated meeting goal, participants may not know what tasks should be accomplished or what decisions should be made during the meeting. Listing specific outcomes keeps the meeting focused on clear goals and serves to keep the group on track. For example, the meeting leader might specify, "By the end of the meeting we should have a written statement of eleventh- and twelfth-grade science goals that meet state requirements."

3. **Communicate a starting and ending time for the meeting and stick to it.** To use time efficiently and to be fair to those members who arrive on time, meetings should begin promptly. By waiting for latecomers, meeting leaders enable members to be late in the future because they know that the meeting will be delayed until everyone arrives. Likewise, in the workplace, people have very busy schedules and need to know when a meeting will end. The meeting leader should closely monitor time during the meeting to make sure it ends on time.

March 1, 2004

To: Campus computer discussion group
From: Janelle Smith
Re: Agenda for discussion group meeting

Date: March 8, 2004
Place: Student Union, Conference Room A
Time: 3:00 p.m. to 4:30 p.m. (Please be prompt.)

Meeting Objectives
1. We will familiarize ourselves with each of three courses that have been proposed for Internet-based delivery next semester.
2. We will evaluate each course against the criteria we developed last month.
3. We will use a consensus decision process to determine which of the three courses to offer.

Agenda for Group Discussion

Review of Philosophy 141   3:00–3:15
   Report by Justin on Philosophy 141 proposal
   Committee questions
   Comparison of PHIL 141 to criteria

Review of Art History 336   3:15–3:30
   Report by Marique on Art History 336 proposal
   Committee questions
   Comparison of ARTH 336 to criteria

Review of Communication 235   3:30–3:45
   Report by Kathryn on Communication 235
   Committee questions
   Comparison of COMM 235 to criteria

Consensus Building Discussion and Decision   3:45–4:15
   Which proposals fit the criteria?
   Are there non-criteria-related factors to consider?
   Which proposal is more acceptable to all members?

Discussion of next steps and task assignments.   4:15–4:25

Set date of next meeting.   4:25–4:30

Figure 11.1
Agenda for Internet course committee

4. **Send out a detailed agenda.** The agenda should include the date, time, and location of the meeting, and the topics to be discussed, with an approximate amount of time allocated to each agenda item; see Figure 11.1. This schedule of topics and times will allow the discussion to proceed efficiently and will keep the group discussion focused on concrete items. This agenda is useful also for participants who cannot attend the entire meeting or guests who need not be present for the whole meeting. With prior knowledge of which agenda items will be discussed when, meeting participants can attend at the crucial point in time. For other ideas about agenda preparation, use your ThomsonNOW for *Communicate!* to access **Web Resource 11.6: Scripting the Agenda**.

Thomson NOW!

5. **Make physical or technology arrangements.** This may include reserving a meeting room, arranging for a particular seating format, and ordering meeting supplies or food. Or for a virtual meeting, arrangements

may include working with technical support to plan for audio- or video-conferencing equipment and informing remote locations of their technical requirements.

During the Meeting

1. **Review and modify the agenda.** Begin the meeting by reviewing the agenda and modifying it based on members' suggestions. Because things can change between when an agenda is distributed and when the meeting is held, reviewing the agenda ensures that the group is working on items that are still important and relevant. Reviewing the agenda also gives members a chance to control what is to be discussed.

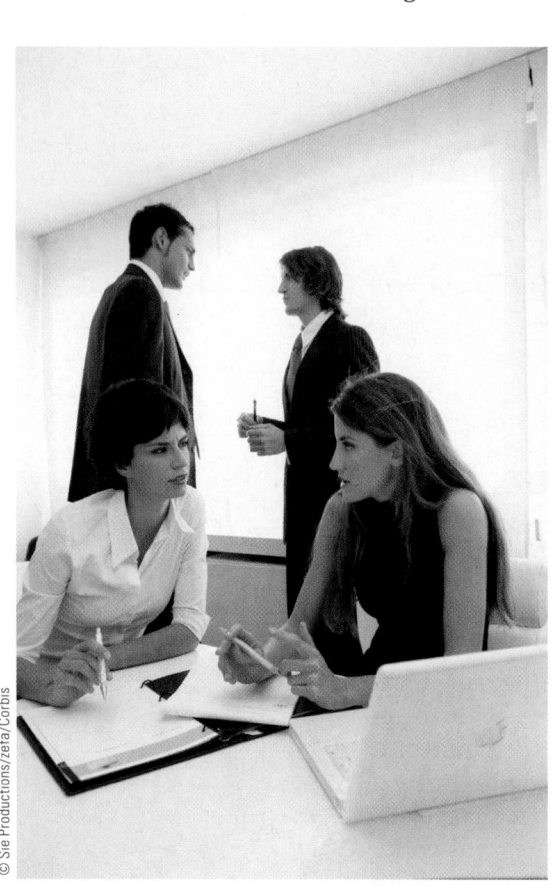

2. **Monitor roles members assume and consciously play roles that are unfilled by others.** The role of the leader during a discussion is to provide the task or maintenance roles that the group lacks. Leaders need to maintain awareness of what specific roles are needed by the group at a specific time. For example, if the leader notices that some people are talking more than their fair share and that no one else is trying to draw out quieter members, the leader should assume the gatekeeper role and ask reluctant members to comment on the discussion.

3. **Monitor the agenda and time so that the group stays on schedule.** It is easy for a group to get bogged down in a discussion or to go off on tangents. Although another group member may serve as the orienter, it is the leader's responsibility to make sure that the group stays on track with the agenda.

4. **Monitor conflicts and intervene as needed.** A healthy level of conflict should be encouraged in the group so that issues are fully examined. But if the conflict level becomes dysfunctional, the leader may need to perform a harmonizing role so that relationships are not unduly strained.

5. **Periodically check to see if the group is ready to make a decision.** The leader of the group should listen for agreement and move the group into its formal decision process when the leader senses that discussion is no longer adding insight.

6. **Implement the group's decision rules.** The leader is responsible for overseeing that the decision-making rule the group has agreed to is used. If the group is deciding by consensus, the leader must make sure that all members feel that the chosen alternative is one that they can support. If the group is deciding by majority rule, the leader calls for the vote and tallies the results.

Effective leaders hold informal conversations after the meeting to repair damaged relationships. Is this easy for you to do?

© Sie Productions/zefa/Corbis

7. **Before ending the meeting, summarize decisions and assignments.** To bring closure to the meeting and to make sure that each member is clear about what has been accomplished, the leader should summarize what has happened in the meeting. The leader also should reiterate task assignments made during the meeting and review what is left to accomplish or decide.

8. **Ask the group to decide if and when another meeting is needed.** Ongoing groups should be careful not to meet just for the sake of meeting. Leaders should clarify with members when, and if, future meetings are necessary. The overall purposes of future meetings will dictate the agenda that will need to be prepared.

Meeting Follow-Up

1. **Review the meeting outcomes and process.** A good leader learns how to be more effective by reflecting on and analyzing how well the previous meeting went. Leaders need to think about whether the meeting accomplished its goals and whether group cohesion was improved or damaged in the process.

2. **Prepare and distribute a summary of meeting outcomes.** Although some groups have a member who serves as the note taker and who distributes minutes, many groups rely on their leaders to do this. A written record of what was agreed to, accomplished, and next steps serve to remind group members of the work they have to do. If the group has a recorder, the leader should check to make sure that minutes are distributed in a timely manner.

3. **Repair damaged relationships through informal conversations.** If the debate during the meeting has been heated, it is likely that some people have damaged their relationships with others or left the meeting angry or hurt. Leaders can help repair relationships by seeking out these participants and talking with them. Through empathetic listening, leaders can soothe hurt feelings and spark a recommitment to the group.

4. **Follow up with members to see how they are progressing on items assigned to them.** When participants have been assigned specific task responsibilities, the leader should check with them to see if they have encountered any problems in completing those tasks.

Conversation and Analysis

Use your ThomsonNOW for *Communicate!* to access the video clip of the Student Government Financial Committee meeting. As you watch the conversation, observe the group's dynamics. Is their goal clear? Do they have sufficient diversity in their membership? What stage of group development do they appear to be in? Are they using the problem-solving method? What roles are being played by each member? Do they appear to be prepared for the meeting? You can answer these and other analysis questions by clicking on "Analysis" in the menu bar at the top of the screen. When you've answered all the questions, click "Done" to compare your answers to those provided by the authors.

Here is a transcript of the conversation. You can also find a copy of this transcript online, which allows you to take notes as you watch the video. Use your ThomsonNOW for *Communicate!* to access **Skill Learning Activity 11.5**. When you have finished viewing the video and taking notes, click on "Authors' Model Analysis" to compare your notes to the detailed conversational analysis provided by the authors.

As members of the Student Government Financial Committee, Davinia, Joyce, Thomas, and Pat make decisions on how much funding, if any, to give to various student groups that request support from the funds collected from student fees. They are meeting for the first time in a campus cafeteria.

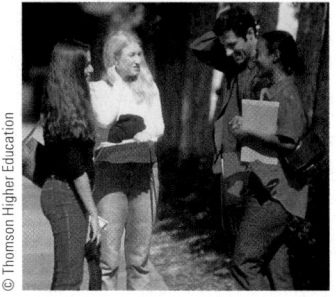

© Thomson Higher Education

Conversation

THOMAS: Well, we've got 23 applications for funding and a total of $19,000 that we can distribute.

DAVINIA: Maybe we should start by listing how much each of the 23 groups wants.

JOYCE: It might be better to start by determining the criteria that we will use to decide if groups get any funding from student fees.

DAVINIA: Yeah, right. We should set up our criteria before we look at applications.

THOMAS: Sounds good to me. Pat, what do you think?

PAT: I'm on board. Let's set up criteria first and then review the applications against those.

JOYCE: OK, we might start by looking at the criteria used last year by the Financial Committee. Does anyone have a copy of those?

THOMAS: I do. [*He passes out copies to the other three people.*] They had three criteria: service to a significant number of students, compliance with the college's nondiscrimination policies, and educational benefit.

DAVINIA: What counts as "educational benefit"? Did last year's committee specify that?

JOYCE: Good question. Thomas, you were on the committee last year. Do you remember what they counted as educational benefit?

THOMAS: The main thing I remember is that it was distinguished from artistic benefit—like a concert or art exhibit or something like that.

PAT: But can't art be educational?

DAVINIA: Yeah, I think so. Thomas, Joyce, do you?

THOMAS: I guess, but it's like art's primary purpose isn't to educate.

JOYCE: I agree. It's kind of hard to put into words, but I think educational benefit has more to do with information and the mind, and art has more to do with the soul. Does that sound too hokey? [*Laughter*]

PAT: OK, so we want to say that we don't distribute funds to any hokey groups, right? [*More laughter*]

© Thomson Higher Education

DAVINIA: It's not like we're against art or anything. It's just that the funding we can distribute is for educational benefit, right? [*Everyone nods.*]

JOYCE: OK, let's move on to another criterion. What is the significant number of students?

THOMAS: Last year we said that the proposals for using money had to be of potential interest to at least 20 percent of students to get funding. How does that sound to you?

PAT: Sounds OK as long as we remember that something can be of potential interest to students who aren't members of specific groups. Like, for instance, I might want to attend a program on Native American customs even though I'm not a Native American. See what I mean?

DAVINIA: Good point—we don't want to define student interest as student identity or anything like that. [*Nods of agreement*]

THOMAS: OK, so are we agreed that 20 percent is about right with the understanding that the 20 percent can include students who aren't in a group applying for funding? [*Nods*] OK, then, do we need to discuss the criterion of compliance with the college's policies on nondiscrimination?

Evaluating Group Effectiveness

There is an old saying that goes, "A camel is a horse built by a committee." Although this saying is humorous, for some groups it is also true. If we are to avoid ending up with camels when we want horses, we need to understand how to assess a group's effectiveness and how to improve group processes based on those evaluations. Groups can be evaluated on the quality of the decision, the quality of role taking, and the quality of leadership.

The Decision

That a group meets to discuss an issue does not necessarily mean that it will arrive at a decision. As foolish as it may seem, some groups thrash away for hours, only to adjourn without having reached a conclusion. Of course, some groups discuss such serious problems that a decision cannot be made without several meetings. In such cases, it is important that

Rate the group as a whole on each of the following questions using this scale: 1 = always, 2 = often, 3 = sometimes, 4 = rarely, 5 = never.

Group Characteristics

_____ 1. Did the group have a clearly defined goal to which most members were committed?

_____ 2. Did the group's size fit the tasks required to meet its goals?

_____ 3. Was group member diversity sufficient to ensure that important viewpoints were expressed?

_____ 4. Did group cohesiveness aid in task accomplishment?

_____ 5. Did group norms help accomplish goals and maintain relationships?

_____ 6. Was the physical setting conducive to accomplishing the work?

Member Relationships

_____ 1. Did members feel valued and respected by others?

_____ 2. Were members comfortable interacting with others?

_____ 3. Did members balance speaking time so that all members participated?

_____ 4. Were conflicts seen as positive experiences?

_____ 5. Did members like and enjoy each other?

Group Problem Solving

_____ 1. Did the group take time to define its problem?

_____ 2. Was high-quality information presented to help the group understand the problem?

_____ 3. Did the group develop criteria before suggesting solutions?

_____ 4. Were the criteria discussed sufficiently and based on all of the information available?

_____ 5. Did the group use effective brainstorming techniques to develop a comprehensive list of creative solution alternatives?

_____ 6. Did the group fairly and thoroughly compare each alternative to all solution criteria?

_____ 7. Did the group follow its decision rules in choosing among alternatives that met the criteria?

_____ 8. Did the group arrive at a decision that members agreed to support?

Figure 11.2
Group Effectiveness
Rating Sheet

the group adjourn with a clear understanding of what the next step will be. When a group "finishes" its work without arriving at some decision, however, the result is likely to be frustration and disillusionment. The Group Effectiveness Rating Sheet in Figure 11.2 provides one method for evaluating the quality of a group's decision based on three major aspects of groups: group characteristics, member relationships, and problem-solving ability. You can download and print a copy of the Group Effectiveness Rating Sheet by accessing **Skill Learning Activity 11.6: Consulting on Meeting Effectiveness** through your ThomsonNOW for *Communicate!* This activity will allow you to take on the role of a consultant, to practice evaluating the strengths and weaknesses of a group.

Individual Participation and Role Behavior

Although a group will struggle without leadership, it may not be able to function at all without members who are willing and able to meet the task and maintenance functions for the group. The Participation and Role Be-

Name of Participant: _____

For each characteristic listed below, rate the participant on a scale of 1 to 5: 1 = excellent, 2 = good, 3 = average, 4 = fair, 5 = poor.

Meeting Behavior

_____ 1. Prepared and knowledgeable
_____ 2. Contributed ideas and opinions
_____ 3. Actively listened to the ideas of others
_____ 4. Politely voiced disagreement
_____ 5. Completed between-meeting assigned tasks

Performance of Task-Oriented Roles

_____ 1. Acted as initiator
_____ 2. Acted as information or opinion giver
_____ 3. Acted as information or opinion seeker
_____ 4. Acted as analyzer
_____ 5. Acted as orienter

Performance of Maintenance Roles

_____ 1. Acted as gatekeeper
_____ 2. Acted as encourager
_____ 3. Acted as harmonizer

Avoidance of Self-Centered Roles

_____ 1. Avoided acting as aggressor
_____ 2. Avoided acting as joker
_____ 3. Avoided acting as withdrawer
_____ 4. Avoided acting as blocker

Qualitative Analysis

Based on the quantitative analysis above, write a two- to five-paragraph analysis of the person's participation. Be sure to give specific examples of the person's behavior to back up your conclusions.

Figure 11.3
Participation and Role Behavior Rating Sheet

havior Rating Sheet in Figure 11.3 provides one method for evaluating the behavior and role taking of each participant. You can download and print a copy of the Participation and Role Behavior Rating Sheet by accessing **Skill Learning Activity 11.7.**

Leadership

Some group discussions are leaderless, although no discussion should be without leadership. If there is an appointed leader—and most groups have one—evaluation can focus on that individual. If the group is truly leaderless, the evaluation should consider attempts at leadership by various members or focus on the apparent leader who emerges from the group. The Leader Behavior Rating Sheet in Figure 11.4 provides one method for evaluating the behavior and role taking of the meeting leader. You can download and print a copy of the Leader Behavior Rating Sheet by accessing **Skill Learning Activity 11.8.**

Was there a formal group leader? Yes _____ No _____
If yes, name this person: _____
Who were the informal leaders of the group?
a. _____
b. _____
c. _____
Which of these leaders was most influential in helping the group meet its goals?
_____

Rate this leader on each of the following questions using a scale of 1 to 5: 1 = always,
2 = often, 3 = sometimes, 4 = rarely, 5 = never.
_____ 1. Demonstrated commitment to the group and its goals.
_____ 2. Actively listened to ideas and opinions of others.
_____ 3. Adapted his or her behavior to the immediate needs of the group.
_____ 4. Avoided stating overly strong opinions.
_____ 5. Managed meaning for the group by framing issues and ideas.
_____ 6. Was prepared for all meetings.
_____ 7. Kept the group on task and on schedule.
_____ 8. Made sure that conflicts were handled effectively.
_____ 9. Implemented the group's decision rules effectively.
_____10. Worked to repair damaged relationships.
_____11. Followed up after meetings to see how members were progressing on
           assignments.

Figure 11.4
Leader behavior rating sheet

What Would You Do?

A QUESTION OF ETHICS

You know, Sue, we're going to be in deep trouble if the group doesn't support McGowan's resolution about dues reform."

"Well, we'll just have to see to it that all the arguments in favor of that resolution are heard, but in the end it's the group's decision."

"That's very democratic of you, Sue, but you know that if it doesn't pass, you're likely to be out on your tail."

"That may be, Heather, but I don't see what I can do about it."

"You don't want to see. First, right now the group respects you. If you would just apply a little pressure on a couple of the members, you'd get what you want."

"What do you mean?"

"Look, this is a good cause. You've got something on just about every member of the group. Take a couple of members aside and let them know that this is payoff time. I think you'll see that some key folks will see it your way."

1. Should Sue follow Heather's advice? Why or why not?

2. Is it appropriate to use personal influence to affect the outcome of group decisions? If you answered yes, at what point does the use of personal influence cross the line from ethical to unethical behavior? If you answered no, explain why personal influence shouldn't be one of the many factors groups consider when making decisions?

Summary

When individuals interact in groups, they assume roles. A role is a specific pattern of behavior that a member of the group performs based on the expectations of other members.

There are three types of roles: task-oriented roles, maintenance roles, and self-centered roles. Members select the roles they will play based on how roles fit with their personality, what is required of them by virtue of a position they hold, and what roles the group needs to have assumed that are not being played by other members. One role that is of particular importance to effective group functioning is the leadership role.

Leadership is the process of influencing members to accomplish goals. Leadership is viewed through various perspectives including traits, situations, functions, and transformations. Groups may have a single leader, but more commonly leadership is shared among group members. Groups may have both formal and informal leaders. Formal leaders have formal authority given to them either by some entity outside of the group or by the group members themselves. Informal leaders emerge during a two-stage process. Individuals who want to become recognized as informal leaders in a group should come to group meetings prepared, actively participate in discussions, actively listen to others, avoid appearing bossy or stating overly strong opinions, and manage the meaning for other participants by framing.

Using the forms provided, you can evaluate groups on the quality of the decision, the quality of note taking, and the quality of leadership.

Thomson™
NOW!

Communicate! Online

Now that you have read Chapter 11, use your ThomsonNOW for *Communicate!* for quick access to the electronic resources that accompany this text. Your ThomsonNOW gives you access to the video of the Student Government Financial Committee on pages 268–269, the Web Resources and Skill Learning Activities featured in this chapter, InfoTrac College Edition, and online study aids such as a digital glossary and review quizzes.

Your *Communicate!* ThomsonNOW is an online study system that helps you identify concepts you don't fully understand, allowing you to put your study time to the best use. Using chapter-by-chapter diagnostic pre-tests, the system creates a personalized study plan for each chapter. Each plan directs you to specific resources designed to improve your understanding, including pages from the text in e-book format. Chapter post-tests give you an opportunity to measure how much you've learned and let you know if you are ready for graded quizzes and exams.

Key Terms

Go to your ThomsonNOW for *Communicate!* to access your online glossary for Chapter 11. Print a copy of the glossary for this chapter and test yourself with the electronic flash cards or complete the crossword puzzle to help you master these key terms:

aggressor (255)
analyzer (253)
blocker (255)
encourager (253)
formal leader (260)
gatekeeper (253)
harmonizer (254)

informal leader (260)
information or opinion
 giver (252)
information or opinion
 seeker (252)
initiator (252)
joker (255)

leadership (259)
maintenance roles (253)
orienter (253)
role (252)
self-centered roles (254)
task-related roles (252)
withdrawer (255)

Review Quiz

Test your knowledge of the concepts in this chapter by taking the online review quiz for Chapter 11. Go to your ThomsonNOW for *Communicate!* to access the quiz. When you have completed the quiz, submit it for scoring.

Skill Learning Activities

Complete the Observe & Analyze, Test Your Competence, and Conversation and Analysis activities for Chapter 11 online at your ThomsonNOW for *Communicate!*. You can submit your Observe & Analyze answers to your instructor, compare your Test Your Competence answers to those provided by the authors, and do both for the Conversation and Analysis activity.

11.1: Test Your Competence: Identifying Roles (256)

11.2: Observe & Analyze: Member Meeting Responsibilities (259)

11.3: Observe & Analyze: Emerging Informal Leadership in CBS's *Survivor* Series (261)

11.4: Observe & Analyze: Media Depictions of Women Leaders (264)

11.5: Conversation and Analysis: Group Communication (268)

11.6: Test Your Competence: Consulting on Meeting Effectiveness (270)

11.7: Participation and Role Behavior Rating Sheet (271)

11.8: Leader Behavior Rating Sheet (271)

Web Resources

Go to your ThomsonNOW for *Communicate!* to access the Web Resources for this chapter.

11.1: Identifying Your Team Player Style (256)

11.2: Taking Notes (258)

11.3: Assert Yourself in Meetings (258)

11.4: Dealing with Your Notes (258)

11.5: Leadership Principles (261)

11.6: Scripting the Agenda (265)

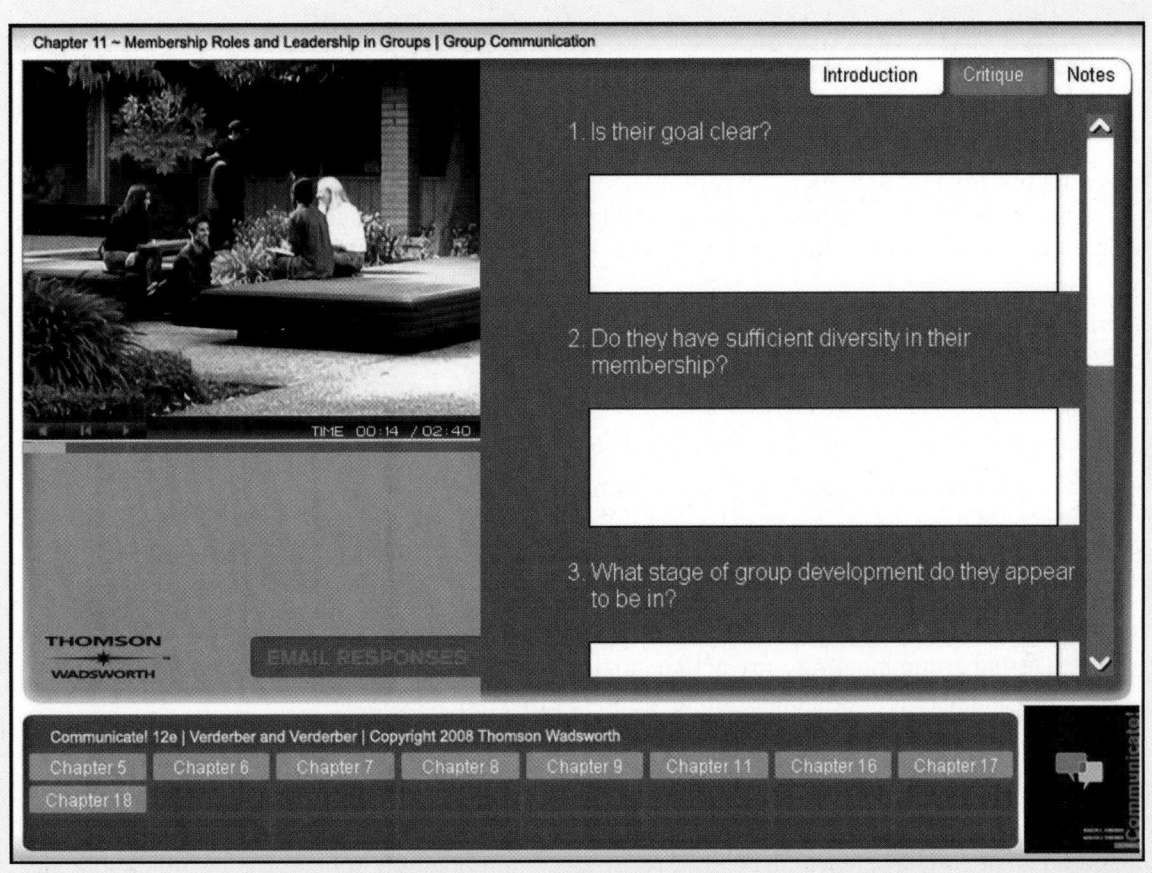

Group Communication from Chapters 10 and 11

How effective are you at working in problem-solving groups? The following statements can help you evaluate your effectiveness in group settings. Use this scale to assess the frequency with which you perform each behavior: 1 = always; 2 = often; 3 = sometimes; 4 = rarely; 5 = never.

_____   I enjoy working with others to accomplish goals. (Ch. 10)

_____   I actively listen and keep an open mind during problem-solving discussions. (Ch. 10)

_____   I adapt my behavior to the norms of the group. (Ch. 10)

_____   I am comfortable with conflict. (Ch. 10)

_____   I avoid performing self-centered roles in the group. (Ch. 11)

_____   I am equally adept at performing task-oriented and maintenance roles in the group. (Ch. 11)

_____   I come to group meetings prepared. (Ch. 11)

_____   During group meetings, my active participation makes positive contributions to goal accomplishment and maintaining good relationships. (Ch. 11)

_____   After meetings, I complete tasks I have been assigned and review meeting notes and minutes. (Ch. 11)

To verify this self-analysis, have a friend or fellow group member complete this review for you. Based on what you have learned, select the group communication behavior you would most like to improve. Write a communication improvement plan similar to the sample goal statement in Chapter 1 (page 22).

Thomson NOW!   You can complete this Self-Review online and, if requested, e-mail it to your instructor. Use your ThomsonNOW for *Communicate!* to access Part III Self-Review under the chapter resources for Chapter 11.

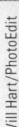
© Will Hart/PhotoEdit

After you have read this chapter, you should be able to answer these questions:

- How do you identify topics?
- How do you compile audience data?
- How do you predict level of audience interest in, knowledge of, and attitude toward a topic?
- How do you test your speech goal?
- What sources of information are commonly used in preparing speeches and how can you find them?
- How can you evaluate information sources?
- What types of information are useful for developing speeches?
- What is the difference between fact and opinion statements?
- Why should you use the note card system for recording information items?
- What should be included on a note card?
- How do you verbally cite the sources of the information items you use in a speech?

12

Developing Your Topic and Doing Your Research

Donna Montez is a marine biologist. She knows that her audience wants to hear her talk about marine biology, but she doesn't know what aspect of the topic she should focus on.

Romeo Brown has been invited to speak to a student assembly at the inner-city middle school he attended. He really wants them to understand what they need to do now to have a shot at going to college. However, he's not sure how to organize his thoughts.

Dan Wong is taking a required public speaking class. His first speech is scheduled for two weeks from tomorrow. As of today, he doesn't have the foggiest idea what he is going to talk about and he's scared to death.

Do any of these situations seem familiar? Do you identify with Dan? You may be taking this course as part of a graduation requirement and the thought of giving a speech can be overwhelming. However, developing public speaking skills is important. Why? Because when you are able to express your ideas to an audience, you are empowered. In a public forum, an effective speaker can stimulate and influence the thinking of others in ways that can improve their lives and the lives of those around them. In the workplace, effective public speaking skills are essential to advancement. From presenting oral reports and proposals, to responding to questions or training other workers, management-level and professional employees spend much of their work lives in activities that include or draw on public speaking skills.

Luckily, public speaking skills are not inborn; they are learned. So in the chapters that follow, we will be explaining how you can improve your public speaking through careful preparation. In chapters 12 through 15, you will learn a simple five-step process that will enable you to quickly and successfully prepare for the speeches you give. These steps are: (1) determine a specific speech goal that is adapted to the audience and occasion; (2) gather and evaluate material for use in the speech; (3) organize and develop the material in a way that is best suited to the audience and speech goal; (4) adapt the material to the needs of the specific audience; and (5) practice presenting the speech. In the final two chapters we go beyond this basic process and explain how to develop and organize informative and persuasive speeches.

In real-life settings, people are invited to speak because they have expertise in a particular subject or have some relationship to the audience. Nevertheless, expert speakers will still use the five action steps as they prepare their speeches.

In this chapter, we explain how to complete the first and second action steps: identifying a specific speech goal that meets the needs of the audience and occasion, and gathering and evaluating material for use in the speech.

Action Step 1: Determine a Specific Speech Goal That Is Adapted to the Audience and Occasion

To prepare an appropriate specific goal for your speech, you must first identify topics you'd be interested in speaking about, analyze your audience and setting, and then select your topic.

Identify Topics

What do you know? What has interested you enough so that you have gained some expertise? Our speech topics should come from subject areas in which we already have some knowledge and interest. What is the difference between subject and topic? A **subject** is a broad area of expertise, such as movies, cognitive psychology, computer technology, or the Middle East. A **topic** is a specific aspect of a subject. It is narrow and focused, allowing a speaker to state a main idea and thoroughly explain, support, or defend it in the space of a speech. So, if your broad area of expertise is movies, you might feel qualified to speak on a variety of topics such as how the Academy Awards nomination process works; the relationships between movie producers, directors, and distributors; and how technology is changing movie production.

subject
a broad area of knowledge.

topic
some specific aspect of a subject.

List Subjects

You can identify potential subjects for your speeches by simply listing those areas that (1) are important to you and (2) you know something about. These areas will probably include your vocation or area of formal study (major, prospective profession, or current job), your hobbies or leisure activities, and special interests (social, economic, educational, or political concerns). So, if retailing is your actual or prospective career, skateboarding is your favorite activity, and problems of illiteracy, substance abuse, and immigration are your special concerns, then these are subject areas from which you can identify topics for your speeches.

At this point, it is tempting to think, "Why not just talk on a subject that I know an audience wants to hear?" But in reality, all subject areas can interest an audience when speakers use their expertise or insight to enlighten the audience on a particular subject.

Figure 12.1 contains examples of subjects that students in two classes at the University of Cincinnati listed under (1) major or vocational interest, (2) hobby or activity, and (3) issue or concern.

Major or Vocational Interest	Hobby or Activity	Issue or Concern
communication	soccer	crime
disc jockey	weight lifting	governmental ethics
marketing	music	environment
public relations	travel	media impact on
society elementary school teaching	photography	censorship
sales	mountain biking	same-sex marriage
reporting	hiking	taxes
hotel management	volleyball	presidential politics
physics	tennis	cloning
fashion design	tracing your family tree	global warming
law	backpacking	child abuse
human resources	horseback riding	road rage
computer programming	sailing	illiteracy
nurse	swimming	effects of smoking
doctor	magic	women's rights
politics	gambling	abortion

Figure 12.1
Student subject lists

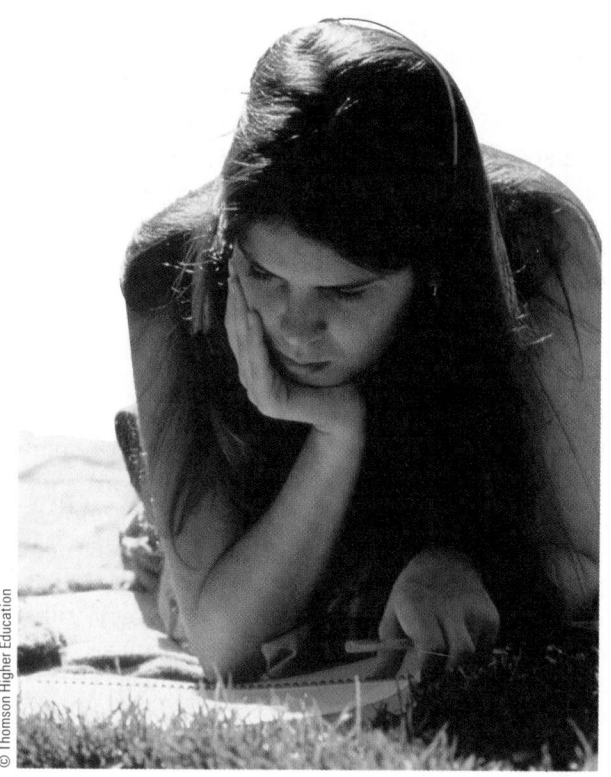

© Thomson Higher Education

When you brainstorm, you will come up with many topics from one subject. Try it!

Brainstorm for Topic Ideas

brainstorming
an uncritical, nonevaluative process of generating associated ideas.

Because a topic is a specific aspect of a subject, from one subject you can identify many topics. A quick way to identify numerous topics is through **brainstorming**—an uncritical, nonevaluative process of generating associated ideas. Concerning the subject of tennis, for example, a person who plays tennis may brainstorm a list that includes the types of serves, net play, the types of courts, player rating systems, and equipment improvements. Once you have lists of topic ideas, you will be able to develop speeches you might give on that subject for this course and other occasions. You can create a list of potential topics by completing Action Step 1.a: Brainstorm for Topics. For more ideas on how to use brainstorming for developing topics, go to your ThomsonNOW for *Communicate!* to access **Web Resource 12.1: Brainstorming**. This resource was written for students taking a composition course, but the ideas apply to preparing a speech.

Thomson
NOW!

Action Step 1.a

Brainstorm for Topics

1. Divide a sheet of paper into three columns. Label column 1 with your major or vocation, such as "Art History," label column 2 with a hobby or an activity, such as "Chess," and label column 3 with a concern or an issue, such as "Water Pollution."

2. Working on one subject column at a time, quickly brainstorm a list of at least 15 related topics for each column.

3. Place a check mark next to the three topics in each list that you would most enjoy speaking about.

4. Keep these lists for future use in choosing a topic for an assigned speech.

Thomson™ NOW! You can go online to print out a worksheet that will help you complete this Action Step. Use your ThomsonNOW for *Communicate!* to access **Skill Learning Activity 12.1.**

Analyze the Audience

Because speeches are given for a particular audience, before you can finally decide on a topic you need to identify your prospective audience. An **audience analysis** is a study of the intended audience for your speech. This information will help you select one topic from your list that is appropriate for most audience members. You will also use your audience analysis in **audience adaptation,** the process of tailoring your information to the specific speech audience. To read an interesting article on the importance of careful audience analysis, use your ThomsonNOW for *Communicate!* to access **Web Resource 12.2: Defining Your Audience.**

audience analysis
the study of the intended audience for your speech.

audience adaptation
the active process of developing a strategy for tailoring your information to the specific speech audience.

Identify Audience Analysis Information Needs

Audience analysis begins by gathering information that will allow you to know how audience members are alike and different from you and from each other. You will want to gather data that help you understand basic audience characteristics or demographics. Figure 12.2 presents a list of questions you can use to obtain necessary demographic information.

You will also want to collect subject-related audience data, including: how knowledgeable audience members are in your subject area, their initial level of interest in the subject, their attitude toward the subject, and their attitude toward you as a speaker. Once you determine what your audience

Age: Average age and age range?

Educational level: Percentage with high school, college, or postgraduate education?

Gender: Percentages of men and women?

Occupation: Single (or dominant) occupation or industry or diverse occupations and industries?

Socioeconomic background: percentage lower, medium, upper income?

Ethnicity: Dominant culture of group if any? Other co-cultures represented?

Religion: Religions represented? Is one preponderant?

Community: Single neighborhood, city, state, country? Or mixed?

Language: Common spoken language? Other first languages shared by a significant minority?

Figure 12.2
Demographic audience analysis questions

already knows about your subject, you can eliminate familiar topics that might bore them and choose a topic that will present them with new information and new insights. When you understand the initial level of interest that audience members have regarding your subject, you can choose a topic that builds on that interest, or you will need to adapt your material so that it captures their interest. Understanding your audience's attitude toward your subject is especially important when you want to influence their beliefs or move them to action. Because there is a limit to how persuasive any one speech can be, knowing your audience members' attitudes toward your subject will enable you to choose a topic that affects your audience's position without alienating them.

Gather Audience Data

There are four main methods you can use to gather the information you need for an audience analysis:

1. **Conduct a Survey:** Although it is not always feasible, the most direct and most accurate way to collect audience data is to survey the audience. A **survey** is a questionnaire designed to gather information from people. Some surveys are done as interviews; others are written forms that are completed by audience members. Survey questions or items can be: two-sided items (respondents choose between two answers), multiple response items (respondents choose between several items), scaled items (respondents choose between levels of intensity in a response), or open-ended items (respondents reply in any way they see fit). Figure 12.3 gives examples of each type of questions.

survey
a questionnaire designed to gather information from people.

2. **Informally Observe:** If the members of the audience are people whom we know, such as classmates or coworkers, we can learn a lot about them by just watching. For instance, after a couple of classes, we can determine the approximate average age of the class members, the ratio of men to women, and the general cultural makeup. As we listen to

Two-sided question

Are you _____ a man _____ a woman?

Question with multiple responses

Which is the highest educational level you have completed? _____ less than high school _____ high school _____ attended college _____ associate's degree _____ bachelor's degree _____ master's degree _____ doctorate degree _____ postdoctorate

Scaled items

How much do you know about Islam? _____ not much _____ a little _____ some _____ quite a lot _____ detailed knowledge

Open-ended item

What do you think about labor unions?

Figure 12.3
Sample survey questions

Action Step 1.b

Analyze Your Audience

1. Decide on the audience characteristics (demographics and subject-specific information that you need in order to choose a topic and adapt to your audience).

2. Choose a method for gathering audience information.

3. Collect the data.

   Thomson NOW! You can print out a worksheet that will help you complete this step. Just use your ThomsonNOW for *Communicate!* to access **Skill Learning Activity 12.2**. Save your completed worksheet so you can use the information to guide you as you choose your topic. You will also refer to it as you complete other steps of the speech planning process.

classmates talk, we learn about their knowledge of, and interest in, certain issues.

3. **Question a Representative:** When we are invited to make a speech, we can ask the contact person for audience information. You should specifically ask for data that are somewhat important for you as you choose a topic or work to adapt your material. For example, if your subject is ethanol, you would want to know if the audience members have a basic understanding of chemistry.

4. **Make Educated Guesses:** If you can't get information in any other way, you can make informed guesses based on indirect data such as the general profile of people in a certain community or the kinds of people likely to attend the event or occasion.

Analyze the Setting

setting
the occasion and location for your speech.

The location and occasion make up the speech **setting.** Answers to several questions about the setting should also guide your topic selection and other parts of your speech planning.

1. **What are the special expectations for the speech?** Every speaking occasion is surrounded by expectations. At an Episcopalian Sunday service, for example, the congregation expects the minister's sermon to have a religious theme. Likewise, at a national sales meeting, the field representatives expect to hear about new products. For your classroom speeches, a major expectation is that your speech will meet the assignment.

How do the setting and the occasion dictate what a speaker will talk about at a graduation ceremony?

© Bob Daemmrich/PhotoEdit

2. **What is the appropriate length for the speech?** The time limit for classroom speeches is usually quite short, so you will want to choose a topic that is narrow enough to be accomplished in the brief time allowed. For example, "Two Major Causes of Environmental Degradation" could be presented as a 10-minute speech, but "A History of Human Impact on the Environment" could not. Speakers who speak for more or less time than they have been scheduled can seriously interfere with the program of an event and lose the respect of both their hosts and their audience.

3. **How large will the audience be?** Although audience size may not directly affect the topic you select, it will affect how you adapt your material and how you present the speech. For example, if the audience is small (up to about 50), you can talk without a microphone and move about if you choose to do so. For larger audiences, you will have a microphone that may limit your range of movement.

4. **Where will the speech be given?** Rooms vary in size, shape, lighting, and seating arrangements. Some are a single level, some have stages or platforms, and some have tiered seating. The space affects the speech. For example, in a long narrow room, you may have to speak loudly to be heard in the back row. The brightness of the room and the availability of shades may affect what kinds of visual aids you can use. So you will want to know and consider the layout of the room as you plan your speech. At times, you might request that the room be changed or rearranged so that the space is better suited to your needs.

5. **What equipment is necessary to give the speech?** Would you like to use a microphone, podium, flip chart, overhead or slide projector and

Action Step 1.c

Understand the Speech Setting

Hold a conversation with the person who arranged for you to speak and get answers to the following questions:

1. What are the special expectations for the speech? _____

2. What is the appropriate length for the speech? _____

3. How large will the audience be? _____

4. Where will the speech be given? _____

5. What equipment is necessary to give the speech? _____

> **Thomson NOW!** Write a short paragraph mentioning which aspects of the setting are most important for you to consider in speech preparation and why. You can complete this activity online, print it out, and, if requested, e-mail it to your instructor. Use your ThomsonNOW for *Communicate!* to access **Skill Learning Activity 12.3.**

screen, or a hookup for your laptop computer during your speech? If so, you need to check with your host to make sure that the equipment can be made available to you. In some cases, the unavailability of equipment may limit your topic choice. Regardless of what arrangements have been made, however, experienced speakers expect that something may go wrong and are always prepared with alternative plans. For example, although computer-mediated visual aids can be very effective, there are often technological glitches that interfere with their use, so many speakers prepare overheads of key presentation slides and bring them along as backup.

Select a Topic

Armed with your topic lists and the information you have collected on your audience and setting, you are ready to select an appropriate topic. Are there some topics on your list that are too simple or too difficult for this audience? Eliminate them. Are some topics likely to bore the audience and you can't think of any way to peek their interest. Eliminate them. How does the audience's demographic profile mesh with each topic? Are some ill suited to this demographic profile? Eliminate them. At the end of this process you should have several topics that would be appropriate for your audience.

Now consider the setting. Are some of the remaining topics inappropriate for the expectations of the audience or too broad for the time allocated, or do they require equipment that is unavailable to you in this setting? If so, eliminate them.

Action Step 1.d

Select a Topic

Use your responses to Action Steps 1.a, 1.b, and 1.c to complete this step.

1. Write each of the topics that you checked in Action Step 1.a on the lines below:

_____ _____ _____

_____ _____ _____

_____

2. Using the information you compiled in Action Step 1.b, the audience analysis, compare each topic to your audience profile. Draw a line through those topics that seem less appropriate.

3. Using the information you compiled in Action Step 1.c, your analysis of the setting, compare the remaining topics to the requirements of the setting. Eliminate those topics that seem less suited to the setting.

4. From the topics that remain, choose the one that you would find most enjoyable to present. Circle that topic.

Thomson NOW! You can go online to complete this activity and print out a worksheet that will help you select your topic. Use your ThomsonNOW for *Communicate!* to access **Skill Learning Activity 12.5.**

From the topics that still remain after considering the audience and the setting, you should choose the one that you would find most enjoyable to share with the audience as your speech topic.

Write a Speech Goal

With a speech topic established, you are now ready to identify the general goal of your speech and to write a specific goal statement that specifies what you hope your audience will gain as a result of listening to you.

Identify Your General Goal

general speech goal
the intent of your speech.

The **general goal** of a speech indicates the type of audience response that is expected if the speech is successful. Speeches intend to entertain, inform, or persuade. If they are effective, then audience members are amused, enlightened, or convinced. Although any speech may have elements of each type of goal, overall, only one of these is the primary aim of the speaker. For example, the general goal of Conan Obrien's opening monologue is to entertain, even though it may include controversial topical material presented in a way that is clearly supportive of one side. Likewise, a politician's stock stump campaign speech has the general goal of persuading the audience to vote for the candidate, even though it contains material that informs the audience about the issues and may use humor to belittle the platform of the rival.

In this book, we focus on speeches that have goals to inform and to persuade; these are the kinds of speeches that you are most likely to be asked to present in academic, professional, and community settings.

Phrase a Specific Goal Statement

The **specific goal,** or specific purpose of your speech, is a single statement that identifies the exact response you want from the audience as a result of listening to this speech. A specific goal statement for an informative speech usually specifies whether you want the audience to learn about, understand, or appreciate the topic. "I would like the audience to understand the four major criteria used for evaluating a diamond" is a goal statement for an informative speech. A specific goal statement for a persuasive speech specifies whether you want the audience to accept the belief that you are presenting: "I want my audience to believe that the militarization of space is wrong," or to act a certain way: "I want my audience to donate money to the United Way." Figure 12.4 gives further examples of informative and persuasive speech goals.

To create a well-worded specific goal statement, we should follow these guidelines:

1. Write a first draft of your speech goal, using a complete sentence that specifies the type of response you want from the audience. Julia, who has been concerned with and is knowledgeable about the subject of illiteracy, drafts the following statement of her general speech goal: "I want my audience to be informed about the effects of illiteracy." Julia's draft is a complete sentence, and it specifies the response she wants from the audience: to understand the effects of illiteracy. Her phrasing tells us that she is planning to give an informative speech.

specific speech goal
a single statement of the exact response the speaker wants from the audience.

Informative Goals

Increasing understanding: I want my audience to understand the three basic forms of a mystery story.
Increasing knowledge: I want my audience to learn how to light a fire without a match.
Increasing appreciation: I want my audience to appreciate the intricacies of spider-web designs.

Persuasive Goals

Reinforce belief: I want my audience to maintain its belief in drug-free sports.
Change belief: I want my audience to believe that SUVs are environmentally destructive.
Motivation to act: I want my audience to join Amnesty International.

Figure 12.4
Informative and persuasive speech goals

2. Revise the draft statement until it focuses on the particular audience reaction that is desired. The draft, "I want my audience to understand illiteracy," was a good start, but it is an extremely broad statement. Just what is it about illiteracy that Julia wants the audience to understand? She narrows the statement to read, "I want my audience to understand three effects of illiteracy." This version is more specific than her first draft, but it still does not clearly capture her intention, so she revises it further to read, "I would like the audience to understand three effects of illiteracy in the workplace." Now the goal is limited not only by Julia's focus on the specific number of effects, but also by her focus on a specific situation. If Julia wanted to persuade her audience, her specific goal might be worded: "I want my audience to believe that illiteracy is a major problem."

3. **Make sure that the goal statement contains only one central idea.** Suppose Julia had written the following specific goal statement: "I want the audience to understand the nature of illiteracy and innumeracy." This would need to be revised because it includes two distinct ideas: understanding the nature of illiteracy and understanding the nature of

Action Step 1.e

Write a Specific Goal

Type of speech? _____

1. Write a draft of your general speech goal, using a complete sentence that specifies the type of response you want from the audience:

2. Does it focus on the particular response that you want from your audience? Revise it to be more precise.

3. Review the specific goal statement. If it contains more than one idea, select one and redraft your specific goal statement.

4. Test the infinitive phrase. Does the infinitive phrase express the specific audience reaction desired? If not, revise the infinitive phrase.

Write your final wording of the specific goal:

_____

_____

_____

_____

You can complete this activity online with Speech Builder Express, a speech organization and development program that will help you complete some of the action steps in this book to develop your speech. See the inside back cover of this book for instructions on how to access Speech Builder Express.

Communication Skill | Crafting a Specific Speech Goal That Meets Audience Needs

Skill	Use	Procedure	Example
The process of identifying a speech purpose that draws on the speaker's knowledge and interests and is adapted to a specific audience and setting.	To identify a speaking goal where speaker interest and expertise, audience needs and interests, and setting overlap.	1. Identify topics within subject areas in which you have interest and expertise. 2. Analyze your audience's demographic characteristics, interests, and attitudes toward your subject. 3. Understand the occasion and the location for the speech. 4. Select a topic that will meet the interests and needs of your audience and setting. 5. Write a specific speech goal that clearly states the exact response you want from your audience.	Ken first writes, "I want my audience to know what to look for in buying a dog." As he revises, he writes, "I want my audience to understand four important considerations in buying the perfect dog." Once Ken has a goal with a single focus and a clearly specified, desired audience reaction, he tests his first version by writing two differently worded versions.

innumeracy. Although these problems may be related, because both make it difficult for people to function in society, the root causes of illiteracy and innumeracy are different. As a result, it would be difficult for a speaker to adequately address both within one speech. So Julia needs to realize that this statement really includes two topic ideas and she needs to choose between them. If your goal statement includes the word "and," you may have more than one idea and will need to narrow your focus.

Action Step 2: Gather and Evaluate Material to Use in the Speech

To select and then use the most effective information to support your speech, you must be able to locate and evaluate appropriate sources of information, identify and select the information most relevant to your speech, draw information from multiple cultural perspectives, and then record the information in a way that will help you prepare for and present your speech.

Locate and Evaluate Information Sources

How can you quickly find the best information related to your specific speech goal? It depends. Speakers usually start by assessing their own knowledge, experience, and personal observations. Then they move on to secondary resources (many of which are available at the library) and electronically search for relevant books, articles, general references, and websites. Occasionally, when other resources do not have the information needed, speakers may have to conduct their own studies by surveying people, reading original documents, interviewing experts, or experimenting.

Personal Knowledge, Experience, and Observation

If you have chosen to speak on a topic you know something about, you are likely to have material that you can use as examples and personal experiences in your speech. For instance, musicians have special knowledge about music and instruments, entrepreneurs know about starting up their own businesses, and marine biologists have knowledge about marine reserves. So Erin, a skilled rock climber, can draw material from her own knowledge and experience for her speech on "Rappelling Down a Mountain."

For many topics, the knowledge you've gained from experience can be supplemented with careful observation. If, for instance, you are planning to talk about how a small claims court works or how churches help the homeless find shelter and job training, you can learn more about each of these by attending small claims sessions or visiting a church's outreach center. By focusing attention on specific behaviors and taking notes of your observations, you will have a record of specifics that you can use in your speech.

Secondary Research

secondary research
the process of locating information about your topic that has been discovered by other people.

Secondary research is the process of locating information about your topic that has been discovered by other people. Libraries house various sources of secondary research. Most libraries store information about their holdings in electronic databases. Users retrieve the information at computer terminals in the library or over the Internet. If you don't know how to access your school's library resources online, you can call the help desk at your library. If you have difficulty using library search tools, you can probably take a short seminar offered at your library or you can ask a research librarian for help. Secondary resources include the following types of materials.

Books If your topic has been around for at least six months, there are likely to be books written about it. To find them, you can do a key word search of the online library book catalog.

periodicals
magazines and journals that appear at fixed intervals.

Articles Articles, which may contain more current or highly specialized information on your topic than a book would, are published in **periodicals**— magazines and journals that appear at fixed periods. Today, most libraries subscribe to electronic databases that index periodical articles. Check with your librarian to learn what electronic indexes your college or university subscribes to.

Newspapers Newspaper articles are excellent sources of facts about and interpretations of both contemporary and historical issues. Three electronic newspaper indexes that are most useful if they are available to you are (1) *National Newspaper Index,* which indexes five major newspapers: the *New York Times,* the *Wall Street Journal,* the *Christian Science Monitor,* the *Washington Post,* and the *Los Angeles Times;* (2) *Newsbank,* which provides not only the indexes but also the text of articles from more than 450 U.S. and Canadian newspapers; and (3) InfoTrac College Edition's *National Newspaper Index.*

Statistical sources Statistical sources present numerical information on a wide variety of subjects. When you need facts about demography, continents, heads of state, weather, or similar subjects, access one of the many single-volume sources that report such data. Two of the most popular sources in this category are *The Statistical Abstract of the United States* (now available online), which provides reference material for numerical information and various aspects of American life, and *The World Almanac and Book of Facts.* For links to web-based statistical sources, consult **Web Resource 12.3: Statistics Online** through your ThomsonNOW for *Communicate!.*

Biographical references When you need accounts of a person's life, from thumbnail sketches to reasonably complete essays, you can turn to one of the many biographical references that are available. In addition to full-length books and encyclopedia entries, consult such books as *Who's Who in America* and *International Who's Who.* Your library may also carry *Contemporary Black Biography, Dictionary of Hispanic Biography, Native American Women, Who's Who of American Women, Who's Who Among Asian Americans,* and many more. For links to web-based collections of bibliographical references, consult **Web Resource 12.4: Online Biographical References** through your ThomsonNOW for *Communicate!.*

Books of quotations A good quotation can be especially provocative as well as informative, and there are times when you want to use a quotation from a respected person. For links to web-based collections of quotations, consult **Web Resource 12.5: Quotations Online** through your Thomson-NOW for *Communicate!.*

Government documents If your topic is related to public policy, government documents may provide you with useful information. For Internet links to several frequently used U.S. federal government documents, consult **Web Resource 12.6: Government Publications Online** through your

© Frank Pedrick/The Image Works

Have you ever taken a class at your library on online research? If not, consider doing so. You can save yourself lots of time and locate great sources of useful information.

ThomsonNOW for *Communicate!*. Similar documents for other countries, states, and cities may be found by using a search engine.

Internet-based resources   In addition to printed resources (which may be accessed online) there are electronic journals (not available in print), hosted websites, newsgroups (bulletin boards), personal web pages, and blogs that exist in cyberspace and may have information you can use in your speech.

Primary Research

primary research
the process of conducting your own study to acquire information for your speech.

Primary research is the process of conducting your own study to acquire information for your speech. It should be the option of last resort in satisfying your information needs because it is much more labor intensive and time consuming than secondary research, and in the professional world, it is much more costly. If, after making an exhaustive search of secondary sources, you cannot locate the information you need, you might consider getting it through one of the following primary research methods.

Surveying

You can gather information directly from a group of people through the use of a questionnaire. If you decide to conduct your own survey, consult **Web Resource 12.7 Conducting Surveys**, which you can access through your ThomsonNOW for *Communicate!*. This resource will provide you with important tips for collecting good information.

Interviewing

You can locate someone who is an acknowledged expert on your topic and ask for their opinions on your topic.

Examining Artifacts or Original Documents

Although the information you need may not have been published, it may exist in an original unpublished source (anything from ancient manuscripts to company files) or there may be an object that you can view to get the information you need.

Experimenting

You can design a study to test a hypothesis that you have. Then, based on your analysis, you can report the results in your speech.

Evaluate Sources

Information sources vary in the accuracy, reliability, and validity of the information they present. So before you use the information from a source in your speech, you will want to evaluate it. Three criteria you can use are:

1. **Authority.** The first test of a resource is the expertise of its author and/or the reputation of the publishing or sponsoring organization. When an author is listed, you can check the author's credentials through biographical references or by seeing if the author has a home page listing professional qualifications. Use the electronic periodical indexes or check the Library of Congress to see what else the author has published in the field (see *Using Cyber Resources*, 2000).

   On the Internet, you will find information that is anonymous or credited to someone whose background is not clear. In these cases, your ability to trust the information depends on evaluating the qualifications of the sponsoring organization. On the Internet, URLs ending in ".gov" (governmental), ".edu" (educational), and ".org" are noncommercial sites with institutional publishers. The URL ".com" indicates that the sponsor is a for-profit organization. If you do not know whether you can trust the sources, then do not use the information.

2. **Objectivity.** Although all authors have a viewpoint, you will want to be wary of information that is overly slanted. Documents that have been created under the sponsorship of some business, government, or public interest groups should be carefully scrutinized for obvious biases or good "public relations" fronts. To evaluate the potential biases in articles and books, read the preface or identify the thesis statement. These often reveal the author's point of view. When evaluating a website with which you are unfamiliar, look for the purpose of the website. Most home pages contain a purpose or mission statement that can help you understand why the site was created. Armed with this information, you are in a better position to recognize the biases that may be contained in the information. Remember, at some level all web pages can be seen as "infomer-

Journal Activity

Evaluating Online Sources

The Internet can be a gold mine for a researcher, but the challenge can be knowing the fool's gold from the real thing. Pick a subject at random and search the Internet for information on it. Find five reliable and five unreliable online sources on your subject, explaining your rationale for your evaluation of each source.

Thomson™ You can complete ░NOW! this activity online and, if requested, e-mail it to your instructor. Use your Thomson-NOW for *Communicate!* to access **Skill Learning Activity 12.7**.

Action Step 2.a

Locate and Evaluate Information Sources

The goal of this activity is to help you compile a list of potential sources for your speech.

1. Identify gaps in your current knowledge that you would like to fill.

2. Identify a person, an event, or a process that you could observe to broaden your personal knowledge base.

3. Brainstorm a list of key words that are related to your speech goal.

4. Working with paper or electronic versions of your library's card catalog, periodical indexes (including InfoTrac College Edition), and general references discussed in this chapter, find and list specific resources that appear to provide information for your speech.

5. Using a search engine, identify Internet sponsored and personal websites that may be sources of information for your speech.

6. Identify a person you could interview for additional information for this speech.

7. Skim the resources you have identified to decide which are likely to be most useful.

8. Evaluate each resource to determine how much faith you can place in the information.

Thomson™ You can complete this activity online, print it out, and, if requested, e-mail it to ░NOW! your instructor. Use your ThomsonNOW for *Communicate!* to access **Skill Learning Activity 12.8**.

cials," so always be concerned with who created this information and why (Kapoun, 2000).

3. **Currency.** In general, newer information is more accurate than older. So when evaluating your sources, be sure to consult the latest information you can find. One of the reasons for using web-based sources is that they can provide more up-to-date information than printed sources (Munger et al., 2000). But just because a source is found online does not mean that the information is timely. To determine how current the information is, you will need to find out when the book was published, the article was written, the study was conducted, or the article was placed on the web or revised. Web page dates are usually listed at the end of the article. If there are no dates listed, you have no way of judging how current the information is.

Web Resource 12.8: Analyzing Information Sources discusses additional criteria you can use to evaluate your sources.

Identify and Select Relevant Information

The information that you find in your sources may include factual statements, expert opinions, and elaborations.

Factual Statements

Factual statements are those that can be verified. "A recent study confirmed that preschoolers watch an average of 28 hours of television a week," and "Johannes Gutenberg invented printing from movable type in the 1400s" are both statements of fact that can be verified. One way to verify whether the information is factual is to check it against material from other sources on the same subject. Never use any information that is not carefully documented unless you have corroborating sources. Factual statements may be statistics or examples.

factual statements statements that can be verified.

1. **Statistics** are numerical facts. "Only five out of every ten local citizens voted in the last election" or "The cost of living rose 0.6 percent in January of 2006," can provide impressive support for a point, but when they are poorly used in the speech, they may be boring and, in some instances, downright deceiving. So you should:
   - Use only statistics that you can verify to be reliable. Taking statistics from only the most reliable sources and double-checking any startling statistics with another source will guard against the use of faulty statistics.
   - Use only recent statistics so your audience will not be misled.
   - Use statistics comparatively. One number does not reveal much, but when compared with another number, it can show growth, decline, gain, loss, and so on.

statistics numerical facts.

- Use statistics sparingly. A few pertinent numbers are far more effective than a battery of statistics.

examples
specific instances that illustrate or explain a general factual statement.

2. **Examples.** Specific instances that illustrate or explain a general factual statement are **examples.** Examples are useful because they provide concrete detail that makes a general statement more meaningful to the audience. One or two short examples like the following are often enough to help make a generalization meaningful: "One way a company increases its power is to buy out another company. Recently, K-Mart bought out Sears and thereby became a much larger company with many more products and outlets." "Professional billiard players practice many long hours every day. Jennifer Lee practices as many as 10 hours a day when she is not in a tournament."

Expert Opinions

expert opinions
interpretations and judgments made by authorities in a particular subject area.

expert
a person who has mastered a specific subject, usually through long-term study.

Expert opinions are interpretations and judgments made by an authority in a particular subject area. At times, they augment facts by helping to interpret what they mean or put them in proper perspective. "Watching 28 hours of television a week is far too much for young children, but may be OK for adults," and "The invention of printing from movable type was for all intents and purposes the start of mass communication" are opinions. Whether they are expert opinions depends on who made the statements. An **expert** is a person who has mastered a specific subject, usually through long-term study and who is recognized by other people in the field as being a knowledgeable and trustworthy authority.

Elaborations

Both factual information and expert opinions can be elaborated upon through anecdotes and narratives, comparisons and contrasts, or quotable explanations and opinions.

anecdotes
brief, often amusing stories.

narratives
accounts, personal experiences, tales, or lengthier stories.

1. **Anecdotes and narratives. Anecdotes** are brief, often amusing stories; **narratives** are accounts, personal experiences, tales, or lengthier stories. Because holding audience interest is important in a speech and because audience attention is likely to be captured by a story, anecdotes and narratives are worth looking for, creating, and using. The key to using stories is to make sure that the point of the story directly states or reinforces the point you make in your speech. Good stories and narratives may be humorous, sentimental, suspenseful, or dramatic.

comparisons
illuminate a point by showing similarities.

contrasts
highlight differences.

2. **Comparisons and contrasts.** One of the best ways to give meaning to new ideas or facts is through comparison and contrast. **Comparisons** illuminate a point by showing similarities, whereas **contrasts** highlight differences. Although comparisons and contrasts may be literal, like

comparing and contrasting the murder rates in different countries or during different eras, they may also be figurative such as:

- In short, living without health insurance is as much of a risk as having uncontrolled diabetes or driving without a safety belt (Nelson, 2006, p. 24). *(comparison)*
- If this morning you had bacon and eggs for breakfast, I think it illustrates the difference. The eggs represented "participation" on the part of the chicken. The bacon represented "total commitment" on the part of the pig! (Durst, 1989, p. 325). *(contrast)*

3. **Quotations.** At times, the information you find will be so well stated that you might want to directly quote it in your speech. Because the audience is interested in listening to your ideas and arguments, you should avoid using too lengthy or too many quotations. But when you find that an author or expert has worded an idea especially well, you may want to directly quote it and then verbally acknowledge the person who said or wrote it. Using quotations or close paraphrases without acknowledging the source is **plagiarism,** the unethical act of representing another person's work as your own.

plagiarism
the unethical act of representing a published author's work as your own.

Draw Information from Multiple Cultural Perspectives

How facts are perceived and what opinions are held often are influenced by a person's cultural background. Therefore, it is important to draw your information from culturally diverse perspectives by seeking sources that have differing cultural orientations and by interviewing experts with diverse cultural backgrounds. For example, when Carrie was preparing for her speech on proficiency testing in grade schools, she purposefully searched for articles written by noted Hispanic, Asian, African American, and European American authors. In addition, she interviewed two local school superintendents—one from an urban district and one from a suburban district. Because she consciously worked to develop diverse sources of information, Carrie felt more confident that her speech would more accurately reflect all sides of the debate on proficiency testing.

Dr. Molefi Kete Asante, an internationally renowned scholar, believes that limiting our research by only considering the viewpoints of those who

Spotlight on Scholars	Molefi Kete Asante	Professor of Africology, Temple University, on the Language of Prejudice and Racism

Molefi Kete Asante is an activist scholar who believes it is not enough to know; one must act to humanize the world. Over his career, Asante has sought to understand what he studied, and also to use that knowledge to help people discover how to exert their power.

In 1968, at the age of 26, Asante completed his Ph.D. in Speech Communication from UCLA. As a graduate student, Asante studied language and the rhetoric of agitation, and in his dissertation, he analyzed the speeches of one of the most zealous agitators during the American Revolution, Samuel Adams. During the late 1960s, however, Asante focused his attention on another revolution occurring in the United States that he found more compelling. Demonstrating his insatiable appetite for intellectual work, at the same time that he was working on his dissertation he also wrote *The Rhetoric of Black Revolution,* published in 1969.

Courtesy Molefi Kete Asante

As a scholar grounded in communication and the rhetoric of agitation, Asante began to notice how racism and communication were intertwined. As his thinking evolved, he began to formulate the theory that racism in our culture is embedded in our language system.

According to Asante, racism stems from a thought system that values a particular race over another. As a phenomenon of language, racism is demonstrated by what people say about others and how they justify their personal attitudes and beliefs. What Asante discovered is that our language reflects the "knowledge system" we are taught. In the United States and much of the world, this knowledge system reflected a European rather than a multicultural view of human events and achievements. As a result of the focus of these studies, we "learn" that nothing substantial or important originated from anywhere else. Thus,

we come to value the music, literature, rituals, opinions, and values of Europeans over those of other cultural groups. Because racism comes from valuing a particular race above another, Asante reasons, it was inevitable that mono-ethnic, Eurocentric approaches to education would result in our developing racist thoughts and a racist language structure that reifies those thoughts.

To combat racism and racist language, Asante believes that we must first enlarge our knowledge base to accurately reflect the contributions that have been made by other racial and cultural groups. For example, history should be taught from multiple perspectives, and literature, art, and music studies should be drawn from a body that includes the work of various racial and ethnic groups. When people learn that all racial and cultural groups have made significant contributions to the development of humankind and all have differing views about historical events and aesthetics about art, they will be less prone to view themselves as superior or inferior to others.

Asante's influence has been widespread. He is currently Professor of African American Studies at Temple University, where he established the first Ph.D. program in African American Studies. He is internationally known for his work on Afrocentricity and African culture. He has published over 60 books and 300 journal articles. One of his most recent books, *Race, Rhetoric, and Identity: The Architecton of Soul* explores the many ways in which modes of communication in American culture create a dehumanizing African American identity. Although he is widely recognized for his scholarship, Asante says, "Working with students is the centerpiece of what I do." For a list of some of Asante's major publications, see the References at the end of the book.

are like us promotes racism that is then transmitted as we speak. The Spotlight on Scholars box in this chapter features his work.

Record Information

As you find facts, opinions, and elaborations that you want to use in your speech, you need to record information accurately and keep a careful account of your sources so they can be cited appropriately.

Prepare Note Cards

How should you keep track of the information you plan to use? Although it may seem easier to record all material from one source on a single sheet of paper (or to photocopy source material), sorting and arranging material is much easier when each item is recorded separately. So it is wise to record information on note cards, which allow you to easily find, arrange, and rearrange each item of information as you prepare your speech.

A note card should be prepared for each factual statement, expert opinion, or elaboration that you find. To prepare a note card, begin by identifying a key word or category heading that captures the main idea of this piece of information and identifies the subcategory to which the information belongs. Next, record the specific fact, opinion, or elaboration statement. Any part of the information item that is quoted directly from the source should be enclosed with quotation marks. Finally, record the information you will need to complete the bibliographic citation for your source list.

The exact bibliographic citation you will record depends on the type of source the information came from and the style sheet (MLA, APA, etc.) you are using. Generally for a book, you will record the names of authors, title of the book, the place of publication and the publisher, the date of publication, and the page or pages from which the information is taken. For a periodical or newspaper, you will record the name of the author (if given), the title of the article, the name of the publication, volume and issue number, the date, and the page number from which the information is taken. For online sources, include the URL for the website, the heading under which you found the information, and the time and date that you accessed the site. Be sure to record enough source information so that you can relocate the material if you need to. Figure 12.5 provides a sample note card.

The number of sources and note cards that you will need depends, in part, on the type of speech you are giving and your own expertise. For a narrative/personal experience, you obviously will be the main, if not the only, source. For informative reports and persuasive speeches, however, speakers ordinarily draw from multiple sources. For a five-minute speech on bird flu in which you plan to talk about causes, symptoms, and means of transmission, you might have two or more note cards under each heading. Moreover, the note cards should come from a number of different sources.

Topic: Bird Flu

Heading: Mortality Rate

From 2003 until August 14, 2006 there have been 139 laboratory confirmed deaths worldwide from avian flu.

Google: Bird Flu.

"Cumulative Number of Confirmed Human Cases of Avian Influenza A/(H5N1) Reported to WHO, August 14, 2006." World Health Organization. http://www.who.int/csr/disease/avian_influenza/country/cases_table_2006_08_14/en/index.html
Accessed 7:21 p.m. EDT August 14, 2006.

Figure 12.5
A sample note card

Action Step 2.b

Prepare Note Cards: Record Facts, Opinions, and Elaborations

The goal of this step is to review the source material you identified in Action Step 2.a and to record specific items of information that you might wish to use in your speech.

1. Carefully read all print and electronic sources (including website material) that you have identified and evaluated as appropriate sources for your speech. Review your notes and tapes from all interviews and observations.

2. As you read an item (fact, opinion, example, illustration, statistic, anecdote, narrative, comparison/contrast, quotation, definition, or description) that you think might be useful in your speech, record the item on a note card or on the appropriate electronic note card form available on the website. If you are using an article that appeared in a periodical source but that you read online, use the periodical note card form.

Thomson NOW! Go to your ThomsonNOW for *Communicate!* to access **Skill Learning Activity 12.9**. There you can view samples of note cards prepared by another student, use online forms to prepare your own note cards, print them out to use as you prepare your speech, and, if requested, e-mail them to your instructor.

Selecting and using information from several sources allows you to develop an original approach to your topic, insures a broader research base, makes it more likely that you will uncover the various opinions related to your topic, and reduces the likelihood that you will plagiarize the ideas of another.

Citing Sources in Speeches

In your speeches, as in any communication in which you use ideas that are not your own, you need to acknowledge the sources of your ideas and statements. Specifically mentioning your sources helps the audience evaluate

"Thomas Friedman, noted international editor for the *New York Times,* stated in his book *The Lexis and the Olive Tree.* . ."

"In an interview with *New Republic* magazine, Governor Arnold Schwarzenegger stated . . . "

"According to an article about the 9/11 Commission Report in last week's *Newsweek* magazine . . . "

"In the latest Gallup poll cited in the February 10 issue of *Newsweek* . . . "

"But to get a complete picture we have to look at the statistics. According to the 2006 Statistical Abstract, the level of production for the European Economic Community rose from . . . "

"In a speech on business ethics delivered to the Public Relations Society of America last November, Preston Townly, CEO of the Conference Board, said . . . "

Figure 12.6
Appropriate speech source citations

the content and also adds to your credibility. In addition, citing sources will give concrete evidence of the depth of your research. Failure to cite sources, especially when you are presenting information that is meant to substantiate a controversial point, is unethical.

In a written report, ideas taken from other sources are credited in footnotes; in a speech, these notations must be included in your verbal statement of the material. Although you do not want to clutter your speech with long bibliographical citations, be sure to mention the sources of your most important information. Figure 12.6 gives several examples of appropriate source citations.

Summary

Five simple action steps can help you to prepare effective speeches: (1) determine a specific speech goal that is adapted to the audience and occasion; (2) gather and evaluate material to use in the speech; (3) organize and develop the material in a way that is suited to the audience and occasion; (4) adapt the material to fit the needs of the specific audience; and (5) practice presenting the speech.

Action Step 2.c

Citing Sources

On the back of each note card, write a short phrase that you can use in your speech as a verbal source citation for the material on this note card.

What Would You Do?

When Mr. Allen gave the class its final public speaking assignment, Alessandra decided that she would deliver a speech on the limited educational opportunities for women in the developing world. This topic was close to her heart, as her mother had struggled for years to improve education for women in her native country of Eritrea before immigrating to the United States. Moreover, Alessandra had already done quite a bit of reading on the topic in the past.

As chance would have it, Alessandra came down with the flu the week before her speech was due and was flat on her back for four days before she finally recovered. Because she was so far behind in her studies, Alessandra didn't begin working on her speech until the afternoon before it was due. Still, by midnight, she had completed what she felt was a strong draft.

The next morning she cleaned up a few typos and errors in her outline and then practiced delivering it the next two hours. Just before leaving for school, she read the instructions one last time to double check that she had done everything correctly. Were her eyes playing tricks on her? The speech needed to be supported by no fewer than *five* published sources, yet she had cited only four.

How could she have overlooked this detail? Alessandra thought frantically. She could ask for an extension, but she had too much other schoolwork to do in the coming days and needed to complete this project now. She could leave her speech as it was, but Mr. Allen was a stickler for little details and he'd certainly lower her grade over the missing source.

Alessandra had, of course, read other books on her topic in the past, even if she hadn't cited them in her speech. While she couldn't remember the specific details of these books, she recalled their general message well enough. That was the solution! She would write a few quotations from one of the books based on her memory, drop them into her speech—she knew just the spot—and then update her references with credit information pulled from the Internet.

In less than a half an hour, Alessandra completed her emergency revisions to her speech and was on her way to class.

1. While blatantly fabricating information from a source is clearly unethical, what about when someone like Alessandra writes quotations based on her memory of earlier reading?

2. What ethical obligations does Alessandra have to her sources?

To accomplish the first action step, determining a specific speech goal, you begin by identifying a topic through listing subjects you are interested in and know something about. Then for each subject, you brainstorm for topic ideas. To select an appropriate topic, you need to gather and analyze data about your audience members' information needs. Data should include demographic- and subject-related specifics. You can gather the data by conducting a survey, informally observing, questioning an audience representative, or by making educated guesses. When selecting a topic, you will also want to understand the setting in which you will be speaking and the occasion. Based on your audience and setting analyses, you can eliminate topics that would be inappropriate and then select your personal favorite from among the topics that remain. Once you have a topic, you can move to identify whether your general goal is to entertain, inform, or persuade. Finally, you can develop a specific goal—a single statement that identifies the exact response you want from your audience.

The second action step of the speech preparation process is to gather and evaluate material to use in your speech. The three general sources for information include (1) your personal knowledge, experiences, and observations; (2) secondary source research; and (3) primary source research. If you are an expert on your topic, you may already have most of the information you will need to use in your speech. But most of the time you will also need to do secondary research and find resources like books, articles, newspaper accounts, statistics, biographical information, quotations, government documents, and Internet-based information on your topic. In rare instances, you may need to conduct primary research to get the information you need by surveying, interviewing, examining artifacts or original documents, or conducting experiments. Before you use information that you find, you will want to evaluate it by testing its authority (expertise of the author and reputation of the publication), objectivity, and currency (newness). The information you find will include factual statements (statistics and examples), expert opinions, and elaborations (anecdotes and narratives, comparisons and contrasts, and quotations). As you look at information, you will want to draw from multiple cultural perspectives so that you accurately reflect what is known about your topic. As you review your sources, you will want to record the information you find on note cards. Each note card should contain only one factual statement, opinion, or elaboration so that you can easily access, sort, and arrange the source material as you prepare the speech. Besides noting the information, you will want to identify it with a key word or category so you can group it with others that are similar. You will also want to note the appropriate bibliographic information so that you can relocate the source if you need to prepare your source list. Finally, on the back of each note card, you should write a short statement citing the source of this fact, opinion, or elaboration that you can use in your speech.

Thomson NOW!

Communicate! Online

Now that you have read Chapter 12, use your ThomsonNOW for *Communicate!* for quick access to the electronic resources that accompany this text. Your ThomsonNOW gives you access to the Web Resources and Skill Learning Activities featured in this chapter, Speech Builder Express, InfoTrac College Edition, and online study aids such as a digital glossary and review quizzes.

Your *Communicate!* ThomsonNOW is an online study system that helps you identify concepts you don't fully understand, allowing you to put your study time to the best use. Using chapter-by-chapter diagnostic pre-tests, the system creates a personalized study plan for each chapter. Each plan directs you to specific resources designed to improve your understanding, including pages from the text in e-book format. Chapter post-tests give you an opportunity to measure how much you've learned and let you know if you are ready for graded quizzes and exams.

Key Terms

Go to your ThomsonNOW for *Communicate!* to access your online glossary for Chapter 12. Print a copy of the glossary for this chapter and test yourself with the electronic flash cards or complete the crossword puzzle to help you master these key terms:

anecdotes (298)
audience adaptation (283)
audience analysis (283)
brainstorming (282)
comparisons (298)
contrasts (298)
examples (298)
expert (298)

expert opinions (298)
factual statements (297)
general speech goal (288)
narratives (298)
periodicals (292)
plagiarism (299)
primary research (294)
secondary research (292)

setting (286)
specific speech goal (289)
statistics (297)
subject (281)
survey (284)
topic (281)

Review Quiz

Test your knowledge of the concepts in this chapter by taking the online review quiz for Chapter 12. Go to your ThomsonNOW for *Communicate!* to access the quiz. When you have completed the quiz, submit it for scoring.

Skill Learning Activities

Complete the Observe & Analyze and Action Step activities for Chapter 12 online at your ThomsonNOW for *Communicate!*. You can submit your Observe & Analyze and Action Step answers to your instructor.

12.1: Action Step 1.a: Brainstorm for Topics (283)

12.2: Action Step 1.b: Analyze Your Audience (285)

12.3: Action Step 1.c: Understand the Speech Setting (287)

12.4: Observe & Analyze: Audience and Setting (287)

12.5: Action Step 1.d: Select a Topic (288)

12.6: Observe & Analyze: Recognizing a Specific Goal (290)

12.7: Observe & Analyze: Evaluating Online Sources (296)

12.8: Action Step 2.a: Locate and Evaluate Information Sources (296)

12.9: Action Step 2.b: Prepare Note Cards: Record Facts, Opinions, and Elaborations (302)

Web Resources

Go to your ThomsonNOW for *Communicate!* to access the Web Resources for this chapter.

OBJECTIVES

After you have read this chapter, you should be able to answer these questions:

■ How do you determine the main points of your speech?

■ How do you construct a thesis statement for your speech?

■ How can you word the main points in your speech?

■ How can you determine which and what kind of supporting material you can use?

■ How can you create effective transitions?

■ What are the goals of an effective speech introduction?

■ What are common types of speech introductions?

■ What are the goals of an effective speech conclusion?

■ What are the common types of speech conclusions?

■ What is a speech outline?

■ How do you prepare a well-written speech outline?

13
Organizing Your Speech

"Troy, Mareka gave an awesome speech on recycling paper. I didn't realize the efforts that other universities are making to help the environment and I haven't heard so many powerful stories in a long time."

"Yeah, Brett, I agree; the stories were interesting. But, you know, I had a hard time following the talk. I couldn't really get a hold of what the main ideas were. Did you?"

"Well, she was talking about recycling and stuff, . . . but, now that you mention it, I'm not sure what she really wanted us to think or do about it. I mean, it was really interesting, but kind of confusing too."

T roy and Brett's experience is not that unusual; we often hear speeches that are packed with interesting information and delivered in ways that hold our attention, but when we reflect on what was said, we find it difficult to state what the speaker's main ideas were, or even what the overall goal of the speech was. Although every speech should have an introduction, a body, and a conclusion, not all speeches that have these components are well organized. So, we listen to a speech and find that even though we have been entertained for the moment, the speaker's words have no lasting impact on us. Well-constructed speeches have impact. When we have finished listening to a speech, we must remember not only the opening joke, or a random story, but we must also remember to think about the main ideas that the speaker presented. In this chapter, we describe the third of the five action steps: Organize and develop speech material to meet the needs of your particular audience. As you follow these steps, you will find that you are able to prepare a speech that will not only maintain your audience's interest, but will help your audience understand and remember what you have said.

Action Step 3: Organize and Develop Speech Material to Meet the Needs of Your Particular Audience

organizing
the process of selecting and arranging the main ideas and supporting material to be presented in the speech in a manner that makes it easy for the audience to understand.

Organizing, the process of selecting and structuring ideas you will present in your speech, is guided by your audience analysis. During organizing you (1) develop a thesis statement for the speech tailored to the information needs or persuasive disposition of your audience; (2) select and tailor the speech's main ideas and supporting materials so they are adapted to your audience; (3) choose an organizational pattern appropriate to the flow of your ideas; (4) create transitional statements to link main ideas; (5) create an introduction and conclusion to open and close your speech; and (6) prepare a formal sentence outline of the speech so you can check the soundness of the structure and logical flow of your ideas.

Developing the Body of the Speech

Once you have analyzed the audience, developed a speech goal, and assembled a body of information on your topic, you are ready to craft the body of your speech by (a) determining the main points; (b) writing a thesis statement; (c) outlining the body of the speech; (d) selecting and ordering supporting material (examples, statistics, illustrations, quotations, and so on) that elaborates on or supports each of your main points; and (e) preparing sectional transitions.

Determining Main Points

The **main points** of a speech are complete sentence statements of the two to five central ideas that you want to present in your speech. You will want to limit the number of main points in your speech so your audience members can keep track of your ideas and so you can develop each idea with an appropriate amount of supporting material. Usually, the difference between a 5-minute speech and a 25-minute speech with the same speech goal will not be the number of main ideas that are presented, but rather, the extent to which each main point is developed.

With some topics and goals, determining the main points is easy. Erin, who plays Division I volleyball for her college, doesn't need to do much research for her speech on how to spike a volleyball. And because she will be speaking to a group of volleyball players, it was easy for her to group the actions into three steps: the proper approach, a powerful swing, and effective follow-through.

But for other topics and goals, determining main points is more difficult. For example Emming wants to speak on choosing a credit card. His specific goal statement is: "I want the audience to understand the criteria for choosing a credit card." As he did his research, he uncovered numerous interesting facts related to the topic, but he has had trouble figuring out how to group these ideas. When you find yourself in Emming's shoes, you will need to do further work to determine the main ideas you want to present.

How can you proceed? First, begin by listing the ideas that you have found that relate to your specific goal. Like Emming, you may be able to list as many as nine or more. Second, eliminate ideas that your audience analysis suggests that this audience already understands. Third, check to see if some of the ideas can be grouped together under a broader concept. Fourth, eliminate ideas for which you do not have strong support in the sources you consulted. Fifth, eliminate any ideas that might be too complicated for this audience to comprehend in the time you have to explain them. Finally, from the ideas that remain, choose three to five that are the most important for your audience to understand if you are to accomplish your specific speech goal.

Let's look at how Emming used these steps to identify the main points for his speech on criteria for choosing a credit card. To begin with, Emming had some thoughts about possible main ideas for the speech, but it wasn't until he completed most of his research, sorted through what he had collected, and thought about it, that he was able to choose his main points. First, he listed ideas (in this case nine) that were discussed in the research materials he had found about choosing a credit card:

what is a credit card

interest rates

main points
complete sentence representations of the main ideas used in your thesis statement.

credit ratings

convenience

discounts

annual fee

institutional reputation

frequent flyer points

rebates

Second, Emming eliminated the idea "what is a credit card" because he knew that his audience already understood this. This left him with eight ideas—far too many for his first speech. Third, Emming noticed that several of the ideas seemed to be related. "Discounts," "frequent flyer points," and "rebates" are all types of incentives that card companies offer to entice people to choose their card. So Emming grouped these three ideas together under the single heading of "incentives." Fourth, Emming noticed that he had uncovered considerable information on interest rates, credit ratings, discounts, annual fees, rebates, and frequent flyer points, but had very little information on convenience or institutional reputation, so he crossed out these ideas.

Finally, Emming considered each of the six remaining ideas in light of the five-minute time requirement he faced. He decided to cross out "credit ratings" because, although people's credit ratings influence the types of cards and interest rates for which they might qualify, Emming believed that he could not adequately explain this idea in the short time available. In fact, he believed that explaining how a credit rating was made to this audience might take longer than five minutes and wasn't really as basic as some of the other ideas he had listed. When he was finished with his analysis and synthesis, his list looked like this:

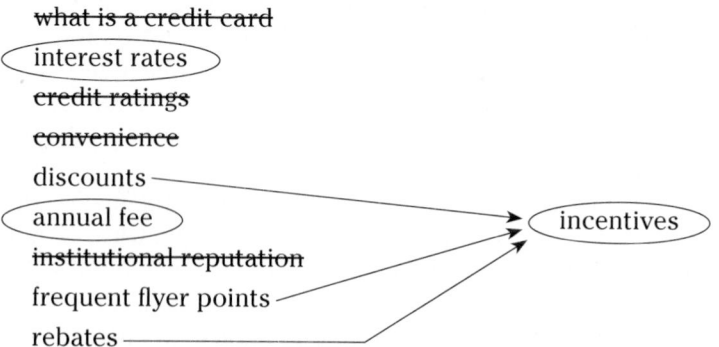

This process left Emming with three broad-based points that he could develop in his speech: interest rates, annual fee, and incentives. So, if you find that you want to talk about a topic that includes numerous forms, types, categories, and so on, follow Emming's steps to reduce the number of your main points to between two and five.

Action Step 3.a

Determining Main Points

The goal of this activity is to help you determine three to five main ideas or main points that you will present in your speech.

1. List all of the ideas you have found that relate to the specific goal of your speech.

2. If there are more than five:
   a. Draw a line through each of the ideas that you believe the audience already understands, or that you have no supporting information for, or that just seem too complicated for the time allowed.
   b. Look for and combine ideas that can be grouped together under a larger heading.

3. From those ideas that remain, choose the two to five that you think will make the best main points for your audience.

Thomson NOW! You can complete this activity online with Speech Builder Express, view a student sample of this activity, and, if requested, e-mail your completed activity to your instructor. Use your ThomsonNOW for *Communicate!* to access **Skill Learning Activity 13.1.**

Writing a Thesis Statement

A **thesis statement** is a sentence that states the specific goal and the main points of the speech. Thus, your thesis statement provides a blueprint from which you will organize the body of your speech.

> **thesis statement**
> *a sentence that identifies the topic of your speech and the main ideas you will present.*

Now let's consider how you arrive at this thesis statement. Recall that Emming determined three main ideas that he wanted to talk about in his speech on choosing a credit card: interest rates, annual fee, and incentives. Based on his specific goal and the main points he had determined, Emming was able to write the thesis statement: "Three criteria you should use to find the most suitable credit card are level of real interest rate, annual fee, and advertised incentives." For a more thorough discussion of how to write an analytical, expository, or persuasive thesis statement, use your ThomsonNOW for *Communicate!* to access **Web Resource 13.1: Writing Different Types of Thesis Statements**.

Thomson NOW!

Outlining the Body of the Speech

Once you have a thesis statement, you can begin to outline your speech. A **speech outline** is a sentence representation of the hierarchical and sequential relationships between the ideas presented in the speech. Your outline may have three hierarchical levels of information: main points (noted by

> **speech outline**
> *a sentence representation of the hierarchical and sequential relationships between the ideas presented in a speech.*

Action Step 3.b

Writing a Thesis Statement

The goal of this activity is to use your specific goal statement and the main points you have identified to develop a well-worded thesis statement for your speech.

1. Write the specific goal you developed in Chapter 12 with Action Step 1.e.

2. List the main points you determined in Action Step 3.a.

3. Now write a complete sentence that combines your specific goal with your main point ideas.

Thomson NOW! You can complete this activity online with Speech Builder Express, view a student sample of this activity, and, if requested, e-mail your completed activity to your instructor. Use your ThomsonNOW to access **Skill Learning Activity 13.2.**

OBSERVE & ANALYZE

Journal Activity

Identifying Thesis Statements

Access the American Rhetoric Online Speech Bank. Select five speeches and listen to the audio recordings or read the printed transcript of each speech. As you listen to or read the speeches, identify and write down the thesis statements in each. Not all speeches necessarily have explicit thesis statements, but all speeches have an implied thesis or purpose. If you feel any one of the speeches you have selected does not contain an explicit thesis, identify its implied thesis or purpose.

You can use your Student Workbook to complete this activity, or you can complete it online and, if requested, e-mail it to your instructor. Use your ThomsonNOW for *Communicate!* to access **Skill Learning Activity 13.3.**

---

the use of Roman numerals), subpoints that support a main point (noted by the use of capital letters), and sometimes sub-subpoints to support subpoints (noted by Arabic numbers). Figure 13.1 provides the general form of how the speech outline system looks.

You will want to write your main points and subpoints in complete sentences, to clarify the relationships between main points and subpoints. Once you have worded each main point and determined its relevant subpoints, you will choose a pattern of organization that fits your thesis. The sequential order in which you will present your main points will depend on the pattern of organization that you choose.

Wording main points Recall that Emming determined that interest rates, annual fee, and advertised inducements are the three major criteria for finding a suitable credit card and his thesis statement was: Three criteria that you can use to find a suitable credit card are level of real interest rate, annual fee, and advertised incentives. So Emming might write a first draft of the main points of his speech like this:

I. Examining the interest rate is one criterion that you can use to find a credit card that is suitable for where you are in life.

II. Another criterion that you can use to make sure you find a credit card that is suitable for where you are in life is to examine the annual fee.

III. Finding a credit card can also depend on weighing the advertised incentives, which is the third criterion that you will want to use to be sure that it is suitable for where you are in life.

Study these statements. Do they seem a bit vague? Sometimes, the first draft of a main point is well expressed and doesn't need additional work.

I. Main point one
  A. Subpoint A for main point one
    1. Sub-subpoint one for subpoint A of main point one
    2. Sub-subpoint two for subpoint A of main point one
  B. Subpoint B of main point one
    1. Sub-subpoint one for subpoint B of main point one
    2. Sub-subpoint two for subpoint B of main point one

II. Main point two
  A. Subpoint A for main point two
    1. Sub-subpoint one for subpoint A of main point two
    2. Sub-subpoint two for subpoint A of main point two
  B. Subpoint B of main point two
    1. Sub-subpoint one for subpoint B of main point two
    2. Sub-subpoint two for subpoint B of main point two
    3. Sub-subpoint three for subpoint B of main point two
  C. Subpoint C of main point two
    1. Sub-subpoint one for subpoint C of main point two
    2. Sub-subpoint two for subpoint C of main point two
    3. Sub-subpoint three for subpoint C of main point two

III. Main point three
  A. Subpoint A for main point three
    1. Sub-subpoint one for subpoint A of main point three
    2. Sub-subpoint two for subpoint A of main point three
  B. Subpoint B of main point three
    . . . and so on.

Figure 13.1
General form for a speech outline

More often, however, we find that our first attempt doesn't quite capture what we want to say. So we need to rework the statements to make them clearer. Testing our main points with two questions can help us as we revise.

1. *Does the main point statement specify how it is related to the goal?* Based on this question, Emming revised his main points like this:

   I. A low interest rate is one criterion that you can use to select a credit card that is suitable for where you are in life.

   II. Another criterion that you can use to make sure you find a credit card that is suitable for where you are in life is to look for a card with no annual fee or a very low one.

   III. Finding a credit card can also depend on weighing the value of the advertised incentives against the increased annual cost or interest rate, which is the third criterion that you will want to use to be sure that it is suitable for where you are in life.

2. *Are the main points parallel in structure?* Main points are **parallel** to each other when their wording follows the same structural pattern, often

parallel
wording in more than one sentence that follows the same structural pattern, often using the same introductory words.

using the same introductory words. Parallel structure helps the audience recognize main points by recalling a pattern in the wording. Based on this, Emming revised his main points to make them parallel:

   I. **The first criterion for choosing a credit card is to select a card with a relatively low interest rate.**

   II. **A second criterion for choosing a credit card is to select a card with no annual fee or a low annual fee.**

   III. **A third criterion for choosing a credit card is to weigh the value of the advertised incentives against the increased annual cost or interest rate.**

Selecting an organizational pattern for main points A speech can be organized in many different ways. Your objective is to find or create the structure that will help the audience make the most sense of the material. The speech pattern you select will guide the order in which you present your main points. Although speeches may follow many types of organization, there are three fundamental patterns for beginning speakers to learn: time, or sequential, order; topic order; and logical reasons order.

time, or sequential, order
organizing the main points by a chronological sequence, or by steps in a process.

1. *Time, or sequential, order.* **Time, or sequential, order** arranges main points by a chronological sequence or by steps in a process. Thus, when you are explaining how to do something, how to make something, how something works, or how something happened, you will want to use time order. Erin's speech on how to spike a volleyball is an example of time order (good approach, powerful swing, good follow-through). As the example below illustrates, the sequence of main points is as important for audiences to remember as the ideas of the main points.

   Thesis Statement: The four steps involved in developing a personal network are to analyze your current networking potential, to position yourself in places for opportunity, to advertise yourself, and to follow up on contacts.

   I. **First, analyze your current networking potential.**

   II. **Second, position yourself in places for opportunity.**

   III. **Third, advertise yourself.**

   IV. **Fourth, follow up on contacts.**

   Although the use of "first," "second," and so on, is not a requirement when using a time order, their inclusion serves as markers that help audience members understand the importance of sequence.

topic order
organizing the main points of the speech by categories or divisions of a subject.

2. *Topic order.* **Topic order** arranges the main points of the speech by categories or divisions of a subject. This is a common way of ordering main points because nearly any subject may be subdivided or categorized in many different ways. The order of the topics may go from general to specific, least important to most important, or some other logical sequence.

In the following example, the topics are presented in the order that the speaker believes is most suitable for the audience and speech goal, with the most important point presented last and the second most important point presented first.

Thesis Statement: Three proven methods for ridding our bodies of harmful toxins are reducing animal foods, hydrating, and eating natural whole foods.

   I. One proven method for ridding our bodies of harmful toxins is reducing our intake of animal products.

   II. A second proven method for ridding our bodies of harmful toxins is eating more natural whole foods.

   III. A third proven method for ridding our bodies of harmful toxins is keeping well hydrated.

3. *Logical reasons order.* **Logical reasons order** is used when the main points are the rationale or proof that support the thesis. For example:

   Thesis Statement: Donating to the United Way is appropriate because your one donation covers many charities, you can stipulate which specific charities you wish to support, and a high percentage of your donation goes to charities.

   I. When you donate to the United Way, your one donation covers many charities.

   II. When you donate to the United Way, you can stipulate which charities you wish to support.

   III. When you donate to the United Way, you know that a high percentage of your donation will go directly to the charities you've selected.

logical reasons order *emphasizes when the main points provide proof supporting the thesis statement.*

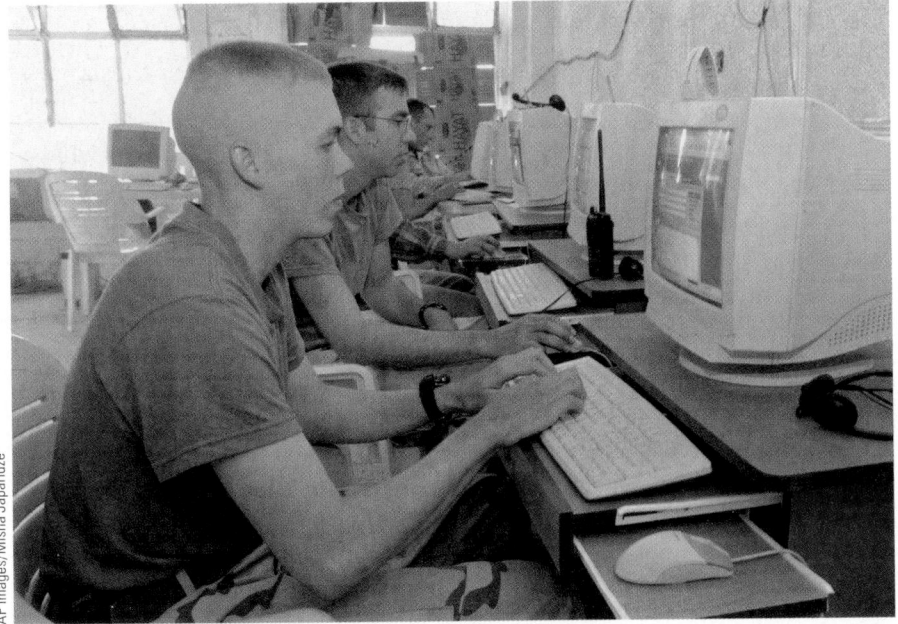

AP Images/Misha Japaridze

If you were giving a speech on the phenomenon of soldiers creating blogs about their combat experiences, what organizational pattern do you think would best suit your speech?

OBSERVE & ANALYZE

Journal Activity

Identifying Main Points

Choose one of the speeches you listened to or read in Skill Learning Activity 13.3. Listen to or read it again, but this time identify and write down the main points in each. What type of organizational pattern is the speaker using in the speech?

You can use your Student Workbook to complete this activity, or you can complete it online and, if requested, e-mail it to your instructor. Use your ThomsonNOW for *Communicate!* to access **Skill Learning Activity 13.4.**

Although these three organizational patterns are the most basic ones, in Chapters 16 and 17 you will be introduced to several other patterns that are appropriate for informative and persuasive speaking.

Selecting and outlining supporting material Although the main points provide the basic structure or skeleton of your speech, whether your audience understands, believes, or appreciates what you have to say usually depends on supporting material—information used to develop main points. You can identify supporting material by sorting the note cards you have prepared during your research into piles that correspond to each of your main points. The goal is to see what information you have that can help you develop each point. When Emming did this, he discovered that for his first point on choosing a credit card with a low interest rate, he had the following support:

- Most "Zero Percent" cards carry an average of 8 percent after a specified period.
- Some cards carry as much as 21 percent after the first year.
- Some cards offer a "grace period" before interest charges kick in.

Action Step 3.c

Organizing and Outlining the Main Points of Your Speech

The goal of this activity is to help you phrase and order your main points.

1. Write your thesis statement (Action Step 3.b).

2. Underline the two to five main points determined for your thesis statement.

3. For each underlined item, write one sentence that summarizes what you want your audience to know about that idea.

4. Review the main points as a group.
   a. Is the relationship of each main point statement to the goal statement clearly specified? If not, revise.
   b. Are the main points parallel in structure? If not, revise.

5. Choose an organizational pattern for your main points and write them in this order. Place a "I." before the main point you will make first, a "II." before your second point, and so on.

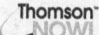 You can complete this activity online using Speech Builder Express, view a student sample of this activity, and, if requested, e-mail your completed activity to your instructor. Use your ThomsonNOW for *Communicate!* to access **Skill Learning Activity 13.5.**

- Department store interest rates are often higher than bank rates.
- Variable rate means that the interest rate can change from month to month.
- Fixed rate means the interest rate will stay the same.
- Many companies offer "Zero Percent" for up to 12 months.
- Some companies offer "Zero Percent" for a few months.

Once you have listed each of the supporting items, look for relationships between them that will allow you to group ideas under a broader heading and eliminate ideas that don't really belong. Then select the ideas that best support the main idea and develop them into complete sentences. When Emming did this, he came up with two statements that grouped the information he had found in support of his first main point. These two became his subpoints. He also had material that supported each subpoint. So he expanded his outline to include this material.

Action Step 3.d

Selecting and Outlining Supporting Material

The goal of this activity is to help you develop and outline your supporting material. Complete the following steps for each of your main points.

1. List the main point.

2. Using your note cards, list the key information related to that main point that you uncovered during your research.

3. Analyze that information by crossing out information that seems less relevant or doesn't fit.

4. Look for information that seems related and can be grouped under a broader heading.

5. Try to group information until you have between two and five supporting points.

6. Write the supporting subpoints in full sentences.

7. Write the supporting sub-subpoints in full sentences.

8. Repeat this process for all main points.

9. Write an outline using Roman numerals for main points, capital letters for supporting points, and Arabic numbers for material related to supporting points.

Thomson NOW! You can complete this activity online using Speech Builder Express and, if requested, e-mail your completed activity to your instructor. Use your ThomsonNOW for *Communicate!* to access **Skill Learning Activity 13.6**.

Here is Emming's outline:

I. The first criterion for choosing a credit card is to select a card with a lower interest rate.
   A. Interest rates are the percentages that a company charges you to carry a balance on your card past the due date.
      1. Most credit cards carry an average of 8 percent.
      2. Some cards carry as much as 21 percent.
      3. Many companies quote low rates (0%–3%) for a specific period.
   B. Interest rates can be variable or fixed.
      1. A variable rate means that the percent charged can vary from month to month.
      2. A fixed rate means that the rate will stay the same.

The outline includes supporting points of a speech, but it does not include all the development. For instance, Emming might use personal experiences, examples, illustrations, anecdotes, statistics, and quotations to elaborate on a main point or subpoint. But these are not detailed on the outline. Emming will choose these developmental materials later as he considers how to verbally and visually adapt to his audience. We will consider this in the next chapter.

transitions
words, phrases, or sentences that show the relationship between or bridge ideas.

Section transitions mentally prepare the audience to move to the next main idea.

Preparing section transitions Once you have outlined your main points, subpoints, and potential supporting material, you will want to consider how you will move smoothly from one main point to another. **Transitions** are words, phrases, or sentences that show the relationship between or bridge two ideas. Transitions act like tour guides leading the audience from point to point through the speech. Section transitions are complete sentences that show the relationship between or bridge major parts of the speech. They may summarize what has just been said or preview the next main idea. For example, suppose Kenneth has just finished the introduction of his speech on antiquing tables and is now ready to launch into his main points. Before stating his first main point he might say, "Antiquing a table is a process that has four steps. Now let's consider the first one." When his listeners hear this transition, they are signaled to mentally prepare to listen to and remember the first main point. When he finishes his first main point, he will use another section transition to signal that he is finished speaking about step one and is moving on to discuss step two: "Now that we see what is involved in cleaning the table, we can move on to the second step."

You might be thinking that this sounds repetitive or patronizing, but section transitions are important for two reasons. First, they help the audience follow the organization of ideas in the speech. If every member of the audience were able to pay complete attention to every word, then perhaps section transitions would not be needed. But as people's attention rises and falls during a speech, they often find themselves wondering where they are. Section transitions give us a mental jolt and say, "Pay attention."

Second, section transitions are important in helping us retain information. We may well remember something that was said once in a speech, but our retention is likely to increase markedly if we hear something more than once. Good transitions are important in writing, but they are even more important in speaking. If listeners get lost or think they have missed something, they cannot check back as they can with writing.

In a speech, if we forecast main points, then state each main point, and use transitions between each point, audiences are more likely to follow and remember the organization.

On your speech outline, section transitions are written in parentheses and at the junctures of the speech.

Creating the Introduction

Now that the body of the speech has been developed, you can decide how to begin your speech. Because the introduction establishes your relationship with your audience, you will want to develop two or three different introductions and then select the one that seems best for this particular audience. Although your introduction may be very short, it should gain audience attention and motivate audience members to listen to all that you have to say. An introduction is generally about 10 percent of the length of the entire speech, so for a five-minute speech (approximately 750 words), an introduction of 60 to 85 words is appropriate. A common problem for beginning speakers is to plan an introduction that is too time consuming, which causes them to deliver a speech that is too long.

Action Step 3.e

Preparing Section Transitions

The goal of this exercise is to help you prepare section transitions. Section transitions appear as parenthetical statements before or after each main point. Using complete sentences:

1. Write a transition from your first main point to your second.

2. Write a transition from each of your remaining main points to the one after it.

3. Add these transitional statements to your outline.

Thomson NOW! You can complete this activity online with Speech Builder Express, view a student sample of this activity, and, if requested, e-mail your completed activity to your instructor. Use your ThomsonNOW for *Communicate!* to access **Skill Learning Activity 13.8.**

Goals of the Introduction

An introduction should get audience's attention and introduce the thesis. In addition, effective introductions also begin to establish speaker credibility, set the tone for the speech, and create a bond of goodwill between the speaker and the audience.

Getting attention An audience's physical presence does not guarantee that audience members will actually listen to your speech. Your first goal, then, is to create an opening that will win your listeners' attention by arousing their curiosity and motivating them to continue listening. In the next section of this chapter, we discuss six types of attention-getting devices you can use to get the audience's attention and also to stimulate their interest in what you have to say.

Stating the thesis Because audiences want to know what the speech is going to be about, it's important to state your thesis, which will introduce them to the main points of your speech. For his speech about romantic love, after Miguel gained the audience's attention, he introduced his thesis, "In the next five minutes, I'd like to explain to you that romantic love consists of three elements: passion, intimacy, and commitment." Stating main points in the introduction is necessary unless you have some special reason for not revealing the details of the thesis. For instance, after getting the attention of his audience Miguel might say, "In the next five minutes, I'd like to explain the three aspects of romantic love," a statement that specifies the number of main points, but leaves stating specifics for transition statements immediately preceding main points. Now let's consider three other goals you might have for your introduction.

Establishing your credibility If someone hasn't formally introduced you before you speak, the audience members are going to wonder who you are and why they should pay attention to what you have to say. So another goal of the introduction may be to begin to build your credibility. For instance, it would be natural for an audience to question Miguel's qualifications for speaking on the topic of romantic love. So after his attention-getting statement he might say, "I became interested in this topic last semester, when I took an interdisciplinary seminar on romantic love, and I am now doing an independent research project on commitment in relationships."

Setting a tone The introductory remarks may also reflect the emotional tone that is appropriate for the topic. A humorous opening will signal a lighthearted tone; a serious opening signals a more thoughtful or somber tone. For instance, a speaker who starts with a rib-tickling, ribald story is putting the audience in a lighthearted, devil-may-care mood. If that speaker then says, "Now let's turn to the subject of abortion (or nuclear war, or global warming)," the audience will be confused by the preliminary introduction that signaled a far different type of subject.

Creating a bond of goodwill In your first few words, you may also establish how an audience will feel about you as a person. If you're enthusiastic, warm, and friendly and give a sense that what you're going to talk about is in the audience's best interest, it will make them feel more comfortable about spending time listening to you.

For longer speeches, you will have more time to accomplish all five goals in the introduction. But for shorter speeches, like those that you are likely to be giving in class, you will first focus on getting attention and stating the thesis; then you will use very brief comments to try to build your credibility, establish an appropriate tone, and develop goodwill.

Methods of Attention Gaining

The ways to gain your audience's attention as you begin a speech are limited only by your imagination. In this section, we describe six common methods you can use to get and excite your audience's interest in your topic: startling statements, rhetorical questions, personal references, quotations, stories, and suspense.

Startling statement A startling statement grabs your listeners' attention by shocking them in some way. Because of the shock of what has been said, audience members stop what they were doing or thinking about and focus on the speaker. The following example illustrates the attention-getting effect of a startling statement:

> By 2030—less than [25] years from now—the world's energy needs will be almost 50 percent greater than they were last year. That is a startling statistic, especially when you consider that 80 percent of that growth will come from one subset—developing countries.
>
> Developing countries in Asia alone will see energy demand increase by over 150 percent in the period from 2000 to 2030. This growing demand for energy reflects a growing demand worldwide [because] of a higher standard of living. Meeting [the demand] will require massive investment, access to resources, and a continued focus on technology (Tillerson, 2006, p. 441).

In less than a minute, this 95-word introduction grabs attention and leads into the speech.

Cathy copyright 1983 Cathy Guisewite. Reprinted with permission of Universal Press Syndicate. All rights reserved.

rhetorical question
*a question seeking a mental
rather than a vocal response.*

Rhetorical question Asking a **rhetorical question**—a question seeking a mental rather than a vocal response—is another appropriate opening for a short speech. Notice how a student began her speech on counterfeiting with these three short, rhetorical questions:

> **What would you do with this 20-dollar bill if I gave it to you? Take your friend to a movie? Treat yourself to a pizza and drinks? Well, if you did either of these things, you could get in big trouble—this bill is counterfeit!**
>
> **Today I want to explain the extent of counterfeiting in America and what our government is doing to curb it.**

This short opening that can be stated in less than 30 seconds gets attention and leads into the speech.

Personal reference A statement that can personalize the topic for audience members will quickly establish how the topic is in the individual's self-interest. In addition to getting attention, a personal reference can be especially effective at engaging listeners as active participants in a speech. A personal reference opening, like this one on exercise, may be suitable for a speech of any length:

> **Say, were you panting when you got to the top of those four flights of stairs this morning? I'll bet there were a few of you who vowed you're never going to take a class on the top floor of this building again.**
> **But did you ever stop to think that maybe the problem isn't that this class is on the top floor? It just might be that you are not getting enough exercise.**
>
> **Today I want to talk with you about how you can build an exercise program that will get you and keep you in shape, yet will only cost you three hours a week, and not one red cent!**

This 112-word opening, which can be presented in less than a minute, not only gets attention, but also personalizes the topic in a way that helps motivate listeners to pay attention.

Quotation A particularly vivid or thought-provoking quotation makes an excellent introduction to a speech of any length, especially if you can use your imagination to relate the quotation to your topic. For instance, in his introduction, notice how Thomas "Byron" Thames, M.D., Member, Board of Directors, AARP, uses a quotation to get the attention of his audience:

> **W. C. Fields was fond of saying, "There comes a time in a man's life when he must take the bull by the horns and face the situation." Well, ladies and gentlemen, the time has come for those of us with a stake in our nation's health care system to "take the bull by the horns and face the situation" regarding today's out-of-control health care costs (Thames, 2006, p. 315).**

A good quotation not only gets attention; it also motivates the audience to listen carefully to what the speaker is going to talk about.

Action Step $\overline{3.f}$

Writing Speech Introductions

The goal of this activity is to create choices for how you will begin your speech.

1. For the speech body you outlined earlier, write three different introductions using a startling statement, rhetorical question, personal reference, quotation, story, or suspense, that you believe meet the goals of effective introductions and that you believe would set an appropriate tone for your speech goal and audience.

2. Of the three you drafted, which do you believe is the best? Why?

3. Next, plan how you will introduce your thesis statement.

4. Develop a very short statement that will establish your credibility.

5. Consider how you might establish goodwill during the introduction.

6. Write that introduction in outline form.

Thomson NOW! You can complete this activity online with Speech Builder Express, view a student sample of this activity, and, if requested, e-mail your completed activity to your instructor. Use you ThomsonNOW for *Communicate!* to access **Skill Learning Activity 13.9**.

Stories A story is an account of something that has happened. Most people enjoy a well-told story. So, if you have uncovered an interesting story in your research that is related to the goal of the speech, consider using it for your introduction.

Unfortunately, many stories are lengthy and can take more time to tell than is appropriate for the length of your speech, so only use a story if you can abbreviate it to fit your speech length. Notice how the following story captures attention and leads into the topic of the speech, balancing stakeholder interests.

> A tightrope walker announced that he was going to walk across Niagara Falls. To everyone's amazement, he made it safely across, and everybody cheered. "Who believes I can ride a bicycle across?" and they all said "Don't do it, you'll fall!" But he got on his bicycle and made it safely across. "Who believes I can push a full wheelbarrow across?" Well, by this time the crowd had seen enough to make real believers of them, and they all shouted, "We do! We do!" At that he said, "Okay . . . Who wants to be the first to get in?"
>
> Well, that's how many investors feel about companies who have adopted the philosophy that balancing the interests of all stakeholders is the true route to maximum value. They go from skeptics to believers—but are very reluctant to get in that wheelbarrow.

> **What I would like to do this afternoon is share with you Eastman's philosophy [about] practice, and then I'll give you some results (Deavenport, 1995, p. 49).**

Suspense An introduction that is worded so that what is described remains uncertain or mysterious will excite the audience. When you begin your speech in a way that gets the audience to thinking, "What is she leading up to?" you have created suspense. The suspenseful opening is especially valuable when the topic is one that an audience does not already have an interest in hearing. Consider the attention-getting value of this introduction:

> **It costs the United States more than $116 billion per year. It has cost the loss of more jobs than a recession. It accounts for nearly 100,000 deaths a year. I'm not talking about cocaine abuse—the problem is alcoholism. Today I want to show you how we can avoid this inhumane killer by abstaining from it.**

Notice that by putting the problem "alcoholism" at the end, the speaker encourages the audience to try to anticipate the answer. And because the audience may well be thinking "narcotics," the revelation that the answer is alcoholism is likely to be much more effective.

Preparing the Conclusion

Shakespeare said, "All's well that ends well." A strong conclusion will summarize the main ideas and will leave the audience with a vivid impression of what they have learned. Even though the conclusion will be a relatively short part of the speech—seldom more than 5 percent (35 to 40 words for a five-minute speech)—it is important that your conclusion be carefully planned.

Just as with your speech introduction, you should prepare two or three conclusions and then choose the one you believe will be the most effective with your audience.

Summary of Main Points

Any effective speech conclusion is likely to include a summary of the main points. In very short speeches, a summary may be the only conclusion that is necessary. Thus, a short, appropriate ending for an informative speech on how to improve your grades might be: "So I hope you now understand that three techniques in helping you improve your grades are to attend classes regularly, to develop a positive attitude toward the course, and to study systematically." Likewise, a short ending for a persuasive speech on why you should lift weights might be: "So, remember that three major reasons why you should consider lifting weights are to improve your appearance, to improve your health, and to accomplish both with a minimum of effort."

Leaving Vivid Impressions

Although summaries achieve the first goal of an effective conclusion, a speaker may need to develop additional material designed to achieve the second goal: leaving the audience with a vivid impression. Vivid impressions can be created in variety of ways. Their purpose is to give the audience one memorable image that serves as an emotional summary of the speech. The following represent two ways to create vivid impressions.

Story For longer informative or persuasive speeches, speakers may also look for stories or other types of material that can further reinforce the message of the speech. Here we will give you one example of such a story. In his speech on corporate responsibility in the Hispanic business community, Solomon D. Trujillo (2002, p. 406) ends with a story that dramatizes the importance of acting now:

> **In closing, there's an old tale called "The Four Elements" from the Hispanic Southwest by my friend Rudolfo Anaya that captures my message.**
>
> **In the beginning, there were four elements on this earth, as well as in man. These basic elements in man and earth were Water, Fire, Wind and Honor. When the work of the creation was completed, the elements decided to separate, with each one seeking its own way. Water spoke first and said: "If you should ever need me, look for me under the earth and in the oceans." Fire then said: "If you should need me you will find me in steel and in the power of the sun." Wind whispered: "If you should need me, I will be in the heavens among the clouds." Honor, the**

When you end your speech with an emotional conclusion, you really drive your point home. Can you recall conclusions from speeches you have heard? Were they emotional?

Action Step 3.9

Creating Speech Conclusions

The goal of this activity is to help you create choices for how you will conclude your speech.

1. For the speech body you outlined earlier, write three different conclusions: summary, story, and appeal to action (or emotional impact) that review important points you want the audience to remember and leave the audience with vivid imagery or an emotional appeal.

2. Which do you believe is the best? Why?

3. Write that conclusion in outline form.

Thomson NOW! You can complete this activity online with Speech Builder Express, view a student sample of this activity, and, if requested, e-mail your completed activity to your instructor. Use you ThomsonNOW for *Communicate!* to access **Skill Learning Activity 13.11**.

bond of life, said: "If you lose me, don't look for me again—you will not find me."

So it is for corporate responsibility. Once lost, honor cannot be replaced. It is the right thing to do . . . it is right for business . . . it is inseparable in our interdependent world. Let's act now to bring Hispanic issues to the forefront of America's agenda.

Appeal to Action The appeal to action is a common way to end a persuasive speech. The **appeal** describes the behavior that you want your listeners to follow after they have heard your arguments. Notice how Llewellyn H. Rockwell, Jr. concludes his speech on Iraq and the Democratic Empire (2006, p. 302) with a strong appeal to action:

appeal
describes the behavior you want your listeners to follow after they have heard your arguments.

In the first, by the Left and the Democrats, we are asked to think of the state as an expansive Good Samaritan who clothes, feeds, and heals people at home and abroad, but fail to notice that this Samaritan ends up not helping people but enslaving its clients. In the second, as offered by the Right and the Republicans, we are asked to think of the state as an expansive Solomon with all power to right a wrong and bring justice and faith to all peoples at home and abroad. They completely fail to notice that Solomon ends up behaving more like Caesar Augustus and his successors. Are you independent minded? Reject these two false alternatives. Do you love freedom? Embrace peace. Do you love peace? Embrace private property. Do you love and defend civilization? Defend and protect us against all uses of Power, the evil against which we must proceed ever more boldly.

By their nature, appeals are most relevant for persuasive speeches, especially when the goal is to motivate an audience to act.

Listing Sources

Regardless of the type or length of speech, you'll want to prepare a list of the sources you are going to use in the speech. Although you may be required to prepare this list for the speeches you give in this course and other courses you take, in real settings, this list will enable you to direct audience members to the specific source of the information you have used, and will allow you to quickly find the information at a later date. The two standard methods of organizing source lists are (1) alphabetically by author's last name or (2) by content category, with items listed alphabetically by author within each category. For speeches with a short list, the first method is efficient. But for long speeches with a lengthy source list, it is helpful to group sources by content categories.

There are many formal bibliographic style formats you can use in citing sources (for example, MLA, APA, Chicago, CBE). And the "correct" form differs by professional or academic discipline. Check to see if your instructor has a preference about which style you use in class.

Regardless of the particular style, however, the specific information you need to record differs depending on whether the source is a book, a periodical, a newspaper, or an Internet source or website. The elements that are essential to all are author, title of article, title of publication, date of publication, and page numbers. Figure 13.2 gives examples of Modern Language Association (MLA) citations for the most commonly used sources.

Action Step 3.h

Compiling a List of Sources

The goal of this activity is to help you record the list of sources you used in the speech.

1. Review your note cards, separating those with information you have used in your speech from those you have not.

2. List the sources of information used in the speech by copying the bibliographic information recorded on the note card.

3. For short lists, organize your list alphabetically by the last name of the first author. Be sure to follow the form shown in Figure 13.2. If you did not record some of the bibliographic information on your note card, you will need to revisit the library, database, and so on, to find it.

Thomson NOW! You can complete the activity online with Speech Builder Express, view a student sample of this activity, and, if requested, e-mail your completed activity to your instructor. Use your ThomsonNOW for *Communicate!* to access **Skill Learning Activity 13.12.**

Book

Shell G. Richard. *Bargaining for Advantage: Negotiation Strategies for Reasonable People.* New York: Penguin Books, 2006.

Edited Book

Jens Lautrup Norguard. "Intercultural Alternatives: Critical Perspectives on Intercultural Encounters in Theory and Practice." *Intercultural Ethics.* Eds. Maribel Blaseo and Jan Gustafsson. New York: Mc-Graw Hill, 2004. 193–214.

Magazine

Poniewozik, James. "How to Create a Heavenly Host." *Time* 21 June 2006: 63.

Academic Journal

Barge, J. Kevin. "Reflexivity and Managerial Practice." *Communication Monographs* 71:1 (Mar. 2004): 70–96.

Newspaper

Bergin, Kathy. "A New Orleans Revival Plan." *The Chicago Tribune* 31 May 2006: A3.

Electronic Article

Friedman, Thomas L. "Connect the Dots." *New York Times* 25 Sept. 2003. http://www.nytimes.com/2003/09/25/opinion/25FRIED.html.

Electronic Site

Osterweil, Neil and Michael Smith. "Does Stress Cause Breast Cancer?" *WEB M.D.Health* 24 Sept. 2003. http://my.webmd.com/contents/article/74/89170.htm?z=3734_00000_1000_ts_01.

Observation

Schoenling Brewery. Spent an hour on the floor observing the use of various machines in the total process and employees' responsibilities at each stage. 22 April 2006.

Interviews

Mueller, Bruno. Personal interview with diamond cutter at Fegel's Jewelry. 19 March 2006.

Figure 13.2
Examples of the MLA citation form for speech sources

To view examples of common citations styled with the APA (American Psychological Association), *Chicago Manual of Style,* and AMA (American Medical Association) styles, use your ThomsonNOW for *Communicate!* to access **Web Resource 13.2: Citation Styles.**

Action Step 3.h helps you compile a list of sources used in your speech. Figure 13.3 gives an example of this activity completed by a student in this course.

Compiling a List of Sources

Dixon, Dougal, *The Practical Geologist.* (New York: Simon & Schuster, 1992.)
Farver, John, Professor of Geology. Personal interview. June 23, 2006.
Klein, Cornelius. *Manual of Mineralogy,* 2nd ed. (New York: John Wiley & Sons, 1993.)
Montgomery, Carla W. *Fundamentals of Geology,* 3rd ed. (Dubuque, IA: Wm. C. Brown, 1997.)

Figure 13.3
Student response to Action Step 3.h

Communication Skill   Organizing the Speech

Skill

The process of identifying main points, constructing a thesis statement, outlining the body of the speech, developing section transitions, creating an introduction, crafting a conclusion, and cataloguing a list of sources.

Use

To create a hierarchy and sequence of ideas that help a particular audience to easily understand the speaker's ideas and the goal of the speech.

Procedure

1. Identify your main ideas.
2. Write a thesis statement.
3. Outline the body of the speech by carefully wording main points, selecting an organizational pattern, selecting and organizing support, and preparing section transitions.
4. Create introductions and select the best one.
5. Create conclusions and select the best one.
6. List sources.

Example

The three aspects of romantic love are passion, intimacy, and commitment.

  I. Passion is the first aspect of romantic love to develop.
  II. Intimacy is the second.
  III. Commitment is the third.

Example for "passion":
A. Passion is a compelling feeling of love.
B. (Focus on function.)
C. (Discuss maintenance.)

Transition from I to II: Although passion is essential to a relationship, passion without intimacy is just sex.

Possible introduction: What does it mean to say "I'm in love"? And how can you know whether what you are experiencing is not just a crush?

Possible conclusion: Developing romantic love involves passion, intimacy, and commitment.

Sample entry: Strenberg, Robert J. and Michael L. Barnes, eds. *The Psychology of Love.* New Haven, CT: Yale University Press, 1988.

Reviewing the Outline

Now that you have created all of the parts of the outline, it is time to put them together in complete outline form and edit them to make sure the outline is well organized and well worded. Use this checklist to complete the final review of the outline before you move into adaptation and rehearsal.

1. *Have I used a standard set of symbols to indicate structure?* Main points are indicated by Roman numerals, major subdivisions by capital letters, minor subheadings by Arabic numerals, and further subdivisions by lowercase letters.

2. *Have I written main points and major subdivisions as complete sentences?* Complete sentences help you to see (1) whether each main point actually develops your speech goal and (2) whether the wording makes your intended point. Unless the key ideas are written out in full, it will be difficult to follow the next guidelines.

3. *Do main points and major subdivisions each contain a single idea?* This guideline ensures that the development of each part of the speech will be relevant to the point. Thus, rather than

   I. The park is beautiful and easy to get to.

   divide the sentence so that both parts are separate:

   I. The park is beautiful.
   II. The park is easy to get to.

   The two-point example sorts out distinct ideas so that the speaker can line up supporting material with confidence that the audience will see and understand its relationship to the main points.

4. *Does each major subdivision relate to or support its major point?* This principle, called subordination, insures that you don't wander off point and confuse your audience. For example:

   I. Proper equipment is necessary for successful play.
      A. Good gym shoes are needed for maneuverability.
      B. Padded gloves will help protect your hands.
      C. A lively ball provides sufficient bounce.
      D. And a good attitude doesn't hurt.

   Notice that the main point deals with equipment. A, B, and C (shoes, gloves, and ball) all relate to the main point. But D, attitude, is not equipment and should appear somewhere else, if at all.

5. *Are potential subdivision elaborations indicated?* Recall that it is the subdivision elaborations that help to build the speech. Because you don't know how long it might take you to discuss these elaborations, it is a good idea to include more than you are likely to use. During rehearsals, you may discuss each a different way.

6. *Does the outline include no more than one-third the total number of words anticipated in the speech?* An outline is only a skeleton of the speech—not a complete manuscript with letters and numbers attached. The outline should be short enough to allow you to experiment with different methods of development during practice periods and to adapt to audience reaction during the speech itself. An easy way to judge whether your outline is about the right length is to estimate the number of words that you are likely to be able to speak during the actual speech and compare this to the number of words in the outline (counting only the words in the outline minus speech goal, thesis statement, headings, and list of sources). Because approximate figures are all you need, to compute the approximate maximum words for your outline, start by assuming a speaking rate of 160 words per minute. (Last term, the speaking rate for the majority of speakers in my class was 140 to 180 words per minute.) Thus, using the average of 160 words per minute, a three- to five-minute speech would contain roughly 480 to 800 words, and the outline should be 160 to 300 words. An 8- to 10-minute speech, roughly 1,280 to 1,600 words, should have an outline of approximately 426 to 533 words.

Now that we have considered the various parts of an outline, let us put them together for a final look. The outline in Figure 13.4 illustrates the prin-

What Would You Do?

A QUESTION OF ETHICS

As Marna and Gloria were eating lunch together, Marna happened to ask Gloria, "How are you doing in Woodward's speech class?"

"Not bad," Gloria replied. "I'm working on this speech about product development. I think it will be really informative, but I'm having a little trouble with the opening. I just can't seem to get a good idea for getting started."

"Why not start with a story—that always worked for me in class."

"Thanks, Marna; I'll think on it."

The next day when Marna ran into Gloria again, she asked, "How's that introduction going?"

"Great. I've prepared a great story about Mary Kay—you know, the cosmetics woman? I'm going to tell about how she was terrible in school and no one thought she'd amount to anything. But she loved dabbling with cosmetics so much that she decided to start her own business—and the rest is history."

"That's a great story. I really like that part about being terrible in school. Was she really that bad?"

"I really don't know—the material I read didn't really focus on that part of her life. But I thought that angle would get people listening right away. And after all, I did it that way because you suggested starting with a story."

"Yes, but . . . "

"Listen, she did start the business. So what if the story isn't quite right? It makes the point I want to make—if people are creative and have a strong work ethic, they can make it big."

1. What are the ethical issues here?

2. Is anyone really hurt by Gloria's opening the speech with this story?

3. What are the speaker's ethical responsibilities?

OUTLINE

Specific Goal: I would like the audience to understand the major criteria for finding a suitable credit card.

Introduction

I. How many of you have been hounded by credit card vendors outside the Student Union?

II. Today I want to share with you three criteria you need to consider carefully before you decide on a particular credit card.

Thesis Statement: Three criteria that will enable audience members to find the credit card that is most suitable for them are level of real interest rate, annual fee, and advertised incentives.

Body

I. The first criterion for choosing a credit card is to select a card with a lower interest rate.

  A. Interest rates are the percentages that a company charges you to carry a balance on your card past the due date.
    1. Most credit cards carry an average of 8%.
    2. Some cards carry an average of as much as 21%.
    3. Many companies offer 0 interest rates for up to 12 months.
    4. Other companies offer 0 interest rates for a few months.
  B. Interest rates can be variable or fixed.
    1. Variable rates mean that the rate will change from month to month.
    2. Fixed rates mean that the rate will stay the same.

(Now that we have considered interest rates, let's look at the next criterion.)

II. A second criterion for choosing a suitable credit card is to select a card with no or a low annual fee.
  A. The annual fee is the cost the company charges you for extending you credit.
  B. The charges vary widely.
    1. Some cards advertise no annual fee.
    2. Most companies charge fees that average around 25 dollars.

(After you have considered interest and fees, you can weigh the benefits that the company promises you.)

ANALYSIS

Write your specific goal at the top of the page. Refer to the goal to test whether everything in the outline is relevant.

The heading *Introduction* sets the section apart as a separate unit. The introduction attempts to (1) get attention and (2) lead into the body of the speech as well as establish credibility, set a tone, and gain goodwill.

The thesis statement states the elements that are suggested in the specific goal. In the speech, the thesis serves as a forecast of the main points.

The heading *Body* sets this section apart as a separate unit. In this example, main point I begins a topical pattern of main points. It is stated as a complete sentence.

The two main subdivisions designated by A and B indicate the equal weight of these points. The second-level subdivisions— designated by 1, 2, and 3 for the major subpoint A, and 1 and 2 for the major subpoint B—give the necessary information for understanding the subpoints.

The number of major and second-level subpoints is at the discretion of the speaker. After the first two levels of subordination, words and phrases may be used in place of complete sentences for elaboration.

This transition reminds listeners of the first main point and forecasts the second.

Main point II, continuing the topical pattern, is a complete meaningful statement paralleling the wording of main point I. Furthermore, notice that each main point considers only one major idea.

This transition summarizes the first two criteria and forecasts the third.

Figure 13.4
Sample complete outline

OUTLINE

III. A third criterion for choosing a credit card is to weigh the incentives.
   A. Incentives are extras that you get for using a particular card.
      1. Some companies promise rebates.
      2. Some companies promise frequent flyer miles.
      3. Some companies promise discounts on "a wide variety of items."
   B. Incentives don't outweigh other criteria.

Conclusion

I. So, getting the credit card that's right for you may be the answer to your dreams.
II. But only if you exercise care in examining interest rates, annual fee, and perks.

Sources

Bankrate Monitor, http://www.Bankrate.com

"Congratulations, Grads—You're Bankrupt: Marketing Blitz Buries Kids in Plastic Debt," *Business Week*, May 21, 2001, p. 48

Hennefriend, Bill, *Office Pro*, October 2004, Vol. 64, pp. 17–20.

"Protect Your Credit Card," *Kiplinger's*, December 2004, p. 88.

Rose, Sarah, "Prepping for College Credit," *Money*, September 1998, pp. 156–157.

ANALYSIS

Main point III, continuing the topical pattern, is a complete meaningful statement paralleling the wording of main points I and II.

Throughout the outline, notice that main points and subpoints are factual statements. The speaker adds examples, experiences, and other developmental material during practice sessions.

The heading *Conclusion* sets this section apart as a separate unit. The content of the conclusion is intended to summarize the main ideas and leave the speech on a high note.

A list of sources should always be a part of the speech outline. The sources should show where the factual material of the speech came from. The list of sources is not a total of all sources available—only those that were used, directly or indirectly. Each of the sources is shown in proper form.

Figure 13.4
(*continued*)

ciples in practice. The commentary to the right of the outline relates each part of the outline to the guidelines we have discussed.

Summary

Organizing is the process of selecting and structuring ideas you will present in your speech; it is guided by your audience analysis. Once you have analyzed your audience, created a speech goal, and assembled a body of information on your topic, you are ready to identify the main ideas you wish to present in your speech and to craft them into a well-phrased thesis statement.

Once you have identified a thesis, you will prepare the body of the speech. The body of the speech is hierarchically ordered through the use of main points and subpoints. Once identified, main points and their related subpoints are written in complete sentences, which should be checked to make sure that they are clear, parallel in structure, meaningful, and limited in number to five or less. The sequential relationship between main point ideas and among subpoint ideas depends on the organizational pattern that is chosen. The three most basic organizational patterns are time, topic, and logical reasons order. You will want to choose an organizational pattern that best helps your audience understand and remember your main points. Main point sentences are written in outline form using the organizational pattern selected.

Subpoints support a main point with definitions, examples, statistics, personal experiences, stories, quotations, and so on. These subpoints also appear in the outline below the main point to which they belong. An organizational pattern will also be chosen for each set of subpoints.

Once the outline of the body is complete, transitions between the introduction and the body, between main points within the body, and between the body and the conclusion need to be devised so that the audience can easily follow the speech and identify each main point.

The organization process is completed by creating (1) an introduction that gets audience attention, introduces the thesis, establishes credibility, sets the tone for the speech, and creates goodwill; (2) a conclusion that summarizes the main points, and (3) a list of sources compiled from the bibliographic information recorded on research note cards.

The complete draft outline should be reviewed as revised to make sure that you have used a standard set of symbols, used complete sentences for main points and major subdivisions, limited each point to a single idea, related minor points to major points, and made sure the outline length is no more than one-third the number of words of the final speech.

Communicate! Online

Now that you have read Chapter 13, use your ThomsonNOW for *Communicate!* for quick access to the electronic resources that accompany this text. Your ThomsonNOW gives you access to the Web Resources and Skill Learning Activities featured in this chapter, InfoTrac College Edition, and online study aids such as a digital glossary and review quizzes.

Your *Communicate!* ThomsonNOW is an online study system that helps you identify concepts you don't fully understand, allowing you to put your study time to the best use. Using chapter-by-chapter diagnostic pre-tests, the system creates a personalized study plan for each chapter. Each plan directs you to specific resources designed to improve your understanding, including pages from the text in e-book format. Chapter post-tests give you an opportunity to measure how much you've learned and let you know if you are ready for graded quizzes and exams.

Key Terms

Go to your ThomsonNOW for *Communicate!* to access your online glossary for Chapter 13. Print a copy of the glossary for this chapter and test yourself with the electronic flash cards or complete the crossword puzzle to help you master these key terms:

appeal (328)	parallel structure (315)	time order (316)
logical reasons order (317)	rhetorical question (324)	topic order (316)
main points (311)	speech outline (313)	transitions (320)
organizing (310)	thesis statement (313)	

Review Quiz

Test your knowledge of the concepts in this chapter by taking the online review quiz for Chapter 13. Go to your ThomsonNOW for *Communicate!* to access the quiz. When you have completed the quiz, submit it for scoring.

Skill Learning Activities

Complete the Observe & Analyze and Action Step activities for Chapter 13 online at your ThomsonNOW for *Communicate!*. You can submit your Observe & Analyze and Action Step answers to your instructor.

13.1: Action Step 3.a: Determining Main Points (313)

13.2: Action Step 3.b: Writing a Thesis Statement (314)

13.3: Observe & Analyze: Identifying Thesis Statements (314)

13.4: Observe & Analyze: Identifying Main Points (318)

13.5: Action Step 3.c: Organizing and Outlining the Main Points of Your Speech (318)

13.6: Action Step 3.d: Selecting and Outlining Supporting Material (319)

13.7: Observe & Analyze: Identifying Supporting Materials (321)

13.8: Action Step 3.e: Preparing Section Transitions (321)

13.9: Action Step 3.f: Writing Speech Introductions (325)

13.10: Observe & Analyze: Identifying Transition Statements, Introductions, and Conclusions (327)

13.11: Action Step 3.g: Creating Speech Conclusions (328)

13.12: Action Step 3.h: Compiling a List of Sources (329)

Web Resources

Go to your ThomsonNOW for *Communicate!* to access the Web Resources for this chapter.

13.1: Writing Different Types of Thesis Statements (313)

13.2: Citation Styles (330)

the Hustle.

OBJECTIVES

After you have read this chapter, you should be able to answer these questions:

- What can you do to develop common ground?
- What can you do to create or build audience interest?
- What can you do to adapt to your audience's knowledge and sophistication?
- What can you do to build the audience's perception of you as a speaker?
- What can you do to reinforce or change an audience's attitude toward your topic?
- What criteria do you use to select and construct visual aids?
- What do you include in an audience adaptation strategy?

14

Adapting Verbally and Visually

Nathan had asked his friend George to listen to one of his speech rehearsals. As he finished the final sentence of the speech, "So, watching violence on TV does affect children in at least two ways—it desensitizes them to real violence, and it also influences them to behave more aggressively," he asked George, "So, what do you think?"

"You're giving the speech to your classmates, right?"

"Yeah."

"And they're mostly mass media majors?"

"Uh-huh."

"Well, it was a good speech, but I didn't hear anything that showed that you had media majors in mind."

audience adaptation
the process of customizing your speech material to your specific audience.

Nathan may have chosen his topic and main points with his audience in mind, but as he prepared, he had forgotten that an effective speech is one that is adapted to the specific audience. You will recall that in Chapter 12, we defined **audience adaptation** as the process of customizing your speech to your specific audience. We explained that audience adaptation depends on audience analysis, and so Action Step 1.b asked you to prepare an audience analysis. You used the results of your audience analysis for identifying your topic, deciding on a specific purpose, and selecting main points. Now you are going to learn how to use your audience analysis as you develop that speech. In this chapter, we will look at the fourth Action Step: Adapt the verbal and visual material to the needs of your specific audience. You will use your knowledge of your audience as you consider what specific verbal material you will present and how you will represent that material visually.

Action Step 4: Adapt the Verbal and Visual Material to the Needs of Your Specific Audience

The skill of adapting involves both verbally adapting and visually adapting by preparing visual aids that facilitate audience understanding.

Adapting to Your Audience Verbally

As you are choosing the supporting material for your speech, you will want to select material that demonstrates how this speech (1) is relevant to the audience, (2) helps the audience to comprehend the information, (3) establishes common ground between you and the audience, (4) enhances your credibility and the credibility of the material you are presenting, (5) is appropriate for the audience's initial attitudes, (6) is culturally sensitive to the diversity in the audience.

Relevance

relevance
adapting the information in the speech so that audience members view it as important to them.

As you work to adapt your speech to your audience, your first challenge will be to demonstrate **relevance** in the speech so that audience members view the speech goal as important to them. Listeners pay attention to and are interested in ideas when they have a personal impact (speak to the question, "What does this have to do with me?") and are bored when they don't see how what is being said relates to them. You can help the audience perceive your speech as relevant by including supporting material that is timely, proximate, and has a personal impact.

timely
showing how information is useful now or in the near future.

Establish timeliness Listeners are more likely to be interested in information they perceive as **timely**—they want to know how they can use the information *now*. In a speech on "The criteria for evaluating the quality of diamonds," presented to a college-aged audience, the introduction below ties the topic to an issue that is timely for most members and therefore piques their interest.

> **Most of us have dreamed about shopping for that special diamond that will seal our relationship to our beloved for all time. Well, the day when that becomes a reality is closer each day and I wonder if you're really ready to make such a big decision. No, I'm not talking about the emotional commitment. I'm talking about making the financial investment that a diamond represents. Well today, I'm going to help you out by explaining criteria for evaluating the quality of diamonds.**

Establish proximity Your listeners are more likely to be interested in information that has **proximity,** a relationship to their personal "space." Psychologically, we pay more attention to information that affects our "territory" than to information that we perceive as remote. So your audience is likely to be more attentive to information when it is related to them, their families, their neighborhoods, and/or their city, state, or country. You have probably heard speakers say something like this: "Let me bring this closer to home by showing you . . ." and then make their point by using a local example. As you review the supporting material you have collected during your research, you will want to look for statistics and examples that have proximity for your audience. For example, if you give a speech on the difficulties the EPA is having cleaning up Super Fund sites, you will want to find and use statistics and other material showing what is being done at Super Fund sites in your area.

proximity
a relationship to personal space.

Demonstrate personal impact When you present information on a topic that can have a serious physical, economic, or psychological impact on audience members, they will be interested in what you have to say. For

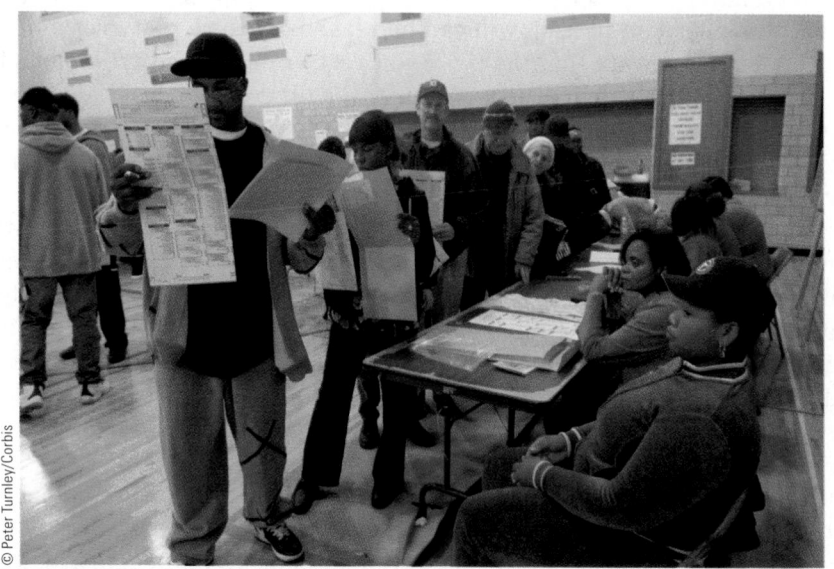

© Peter Turnley/Corbis

What points would you make in a speech on local, state, and federal elections to make the topic relevant for your classmates?

example, notice how your classmates' attention picks up when your instructor says that what is said next "will definitely be on the test." Your instructor understands that this economic impact (not paying attention can "cost") is enough to refocus most students' attention on what is being said.

As you prepare your speech, you will want to incorporate ideas that create personal impact for your audience. In a speech about toxic waste, you might show a serious physical impact by providing statistics on the effects of toxic waste on the health of people in your state. You may be able to demonstrate serious economic impact by citing the cost to the taxpayers of a recent toxic waste cleanup in your city. Or you might be able to illustrate a serious psychological impact by finding and recounting the stresses faced by one family (that is demographically similar to the audience) with a long-term toxic waste problem in their neighborhood.

Information Comprehension

Although your audience analysis helped you select a topic that was appropriate for your audience's current knowledge level, you will still need to adapt the information you present so that audience members can easily follow what you are saying and remember it when you are through. Six techniques that can aid you are (1) orienting or refamiliarizing the audience with basic information, (2) defining key terms, (3) creating vivid examples to illustrate new concepts, (4) personalizing information, (5) comparing unfamiliar ideas with those the audience recognizes, and (6) using multiple methods of development.

Orient the audience When listeners become confused or have forgotten basic information, they lose interest or do not understand what is being said. So you will want to quickly review the basic ideas that are critical to understanding the speech. For example, if your speech concerns U.S. military involvement in Iraq, you can be reasonably sure that everyone in your audience is aware that the U.S. and Great Britain were participants in the coalition, but many may not remember the other countries that participated. So before launching into the roles of various countries, remind your listeners by listing the nations that have provided troops, and where they have been stationed.

There may be, however, some audience members who do not need the reminder, so to avoid offending them by appearing to talk down at them and to save face for those who need the reminder, you should acknowledge that they probably already remember the information. Phrases such as: "As you will remember . . . ," "As we all probably learned in high school . . . ," and "As we have come to find out . . ." are ways of prefacing reviews so that they are not offensive.

Define key terms Words have many meanings, so you ensure audience members' comprehension of ideas by defining the key terms that may be unfamiliar to them or are critical to understanding your speech. This becomes especially important when you are using familiar words whose commonly accepted meanings have been altered. For instance, in a speech on the four major problems faced by functionally illiterate people in the workplace, it will be important to your audience to understand what you mean by "functionally illiterate." So early in the speech, you can offer your definition. "By 'functionally illiterate,' I mean people who have trouble accomplishing simple reading and writing tasks."

Illustrate new concepts with vivid examples Vivid examples help audience members understand and remember abstract, complex, and novel material. From one vivid example, we are better able to understand a more complicated concept. So as you prepare your speech, you will want to adapt by choosing real or hypothetical examples and illustrations to help your audience understand the new information you present. For example, in the definition we used above, the description "having trouble accomplishing simple reading and writing tasks" can be made more vivid when accompanied by the following example: "For instance, a functionally illiterate person could not read and understand the directions on a prescription label that states: 'Take three times a day with a glass of water. Do not take on an empty stomach.'"

Personalize information We **personalize** information by presenting it in a frame of reference that is familiar to the audience. Devon, a student at the University of California, is preparing to give a speech on how the Japanese economy affects U.S. markets at the student chapter of the American Marketing Association. He wants to help his audience understand geographic data about Japan. He could just quote the following statistics from the 2001 World Almanac:

personalize
presenting information in a frame of reference that is familiar to the audience.

> **Japan is small and densely populated. The nation's 126 million people live in a land area of 146,000 square miles, giving them a population density of 867 persons per square mile.**

Although this would provide the necessary information, it is not adapted to an audience consisting of college students in California, a large state in the United States. Devon can easily adapt the information to the audience by putting it in terms that are familiar to this student audience.

> **Japan is a small, densely populated nation. Its population of 126 million is less than half that of the *United States*. Yet the Japanese are crowded into a land area of only 146,000 square miles—roughly the same size as *California*. In fact, Japan packs 867 persons into every square mile of land, whereas in the *United States* we average about 74 persons per square mile. Overall, then, Japan is about 12 times as crowded as the *USA*.**

In order for Devon to personalize the information above, he had to find the statistics on the U.S. and California. If Devon were speaking to an audience from another state of the country, he could adapt to them by substituting information from that state.

Compare unknown ideas with familiar ones An easy way to adapt your material to your audience is to compare your new ideas with ones the audience already understands. For example, if I want an audience of Generation Xers to feel the excitement that was generated when telegrams were first introduced, I might compare it to the change that was experienced when e-mail became widely available. In the speech on functional illiteracy, if you want the audience of literates to sense what functionally illiterate people experience, you might compare it to the experience of surviving in a country where one is not fluent in the language.

Use multiple methods for developing criteria People vary in how they learn, so you will want to develop your ideas in different ways. Some people learn best with detailed explanations, some need precise definitions or vivid examples, others learn through statistics, and still others will benefit from a well-designed visual aid.

Let's look at how you might use multiple methods to develop an idea. Suppose the point you are trying to make is: "For the large numbers of Americans who are functionally illiterate, understanding simple directions can be a problem." Here's an example that develops this idea:

> **For instance, a person who is functionally illiterate might not be able to read or understand a label that states: "Take three times a day after eating."**

Now look at how much richer the meaning becomes when we build the statement by adding statistics and additional examples:

> **A significant number of Americans are functionally illiterate. That is, about 35 million people or about 20 percent of the adult population have serious difficulties with common reading tasks. They cannot read well enough to understand how to prepare a dish from a recipe, how to assemble a simple toy from the printed instructions, or which bus to catch to go across town from the signs at the bus stop. Many functionally illiterate people don't read well enough to follow the directions on a prescription that reads: "Take three times a day after eating."**

Common Ground

Each person in the audience is unique, with differing knowledge, attitudes, philosophies, experiences, and ways of perceiving the world. They may or may not know others in the audience. So it is easy for them to assume that they have nothing in common with you or with other audience members. Yet when you speak, you will be giving one message to that diverse group. **Common ground** is the background, knowledge, attitudes, experiences, and philosophies that are shared by audience members and the speaker. Effective speakers use the audience analysis to identify areas of similarity; then they use the adaptation techniques of using personal pronouns, asking rhetorical questions, and drawing on common experiences to create common ground.

common ground
the background, knowledge, attitudes, experiences, and philosophies that are shared by audience members and the speaker.

Use personal pronouns The simplest way of establishing common ground is to use **personal pronouns:** "we," "us," and "our," so speakers can acknowledge commonalities between themselves and members of the audience. For example, in a speech given to an audience whose members are known to be sympathetic to legislation limiting violence in children's programming on TV, notice the effect of using a personal pronoun:

> **I know that most *people* are worried about the effects that violence on TV is having on young children.**

> **I know that most of *us* worry about the effects that violence on TV is having on young children.**

By using "us" instead of "most people," the speaker includes the audience members and this gives them a "stake" in listening to what is to follow.

Ask rhetorical questions A **rhetorical question** is one whose answers are obvious to audience members and to which they are not really expected to reply. Rhetorical questions create common ground by alluding to information that is shared by audience members and the speaker. They are often used in the introduction to a speech, but can also be effective as transitions and in other parts of the speech. For instance, notice how this transition, phrased as a rhetorical question, creates common ground:

> **When you have watched a particularly violent TV program, have you ever asked yourself, "Did they really need to be this graphic to make the point"?**

Rhetorical questions are meant to have only one answer that highlights similarities between audience members and leads them to be more interested in the content that follows.

personal pronouns
"we," "us," and "our" pronouns that refer directly to members of the audience.

rhetorical questions
questions phrased to stimulate a mental response rather than an actual spoken response on the part of the audience.

© Ken James/Corbis

In what ways do you think the speaker in this situation could create common ground with the audience?

credibility
the level of trust that an audience has or will have in the speaker.

Draw from common experiences You can develop common ground by selecting and presenting personal experiences, examples, and illustrations that embody what you and the audience have in common. For instance, in a speech about the effects of television violence, you might allude to a common viewing experience:

> **Remember how sometimes at a key moment when you're watching a really frightening scene in a movie, you may quickly shut your eyes? I remember doing that over and over again. I vividly remember slamming my eyes shut during the snake scenes in *Indiana Jones.***

To be able to create material that draws on common experiences, you must study the audience analysis to understand how you and audience members are similar in the exposure you have had to the topic or in other areas that you can then compare to your topic.

Adapting your information so that it speaks directly to your specific audience, creating common ground, takes time and thought. But well-adapted speeches never leave an audience wondering, "What does this have to do with me?" Joan Gorham, the subject of this chapter's Spotlight on Scholars, has conducted many research projects that show the effect of adaptation, or what she calls "immediacy," on building attention and ensuring audience retention of information.

Speaker Credibility

Credibility is the confidence that an audience places in the truthfulness of what a speaker says. There are several theories of how speakers develop credibility. You can read a summary of these by accessing **Web Resource 14.1: Holistic Theory of Speaker Credibility**.

Some famous people are widely known as experts in a particular area and have proven to be trustworthy and likeable. When these people give a speech, they don't have to adapt their remarks to establish their credibility. However, for most of us, even though we may be given a formal introduction that attempts to acquaint the audience with our credentials and character prior to our speech, we will still need to adapt our remarks in the speech so that we can build audience confidence in the truthfulness of what we are saying. Three adaptation techniques that can affect how credible we are perceived are demonstrating knowledge and expertise, establishing trustworthiness, and displaying personableness.

knowledge and expertise
how well you convince your audience that you are qualified to speak on the topic.

Demonstrate knowledge and expertise When the audience perceives you to be a knowledgeable expert, it will perceive you as credible. Their assessment of your **knowledge and expertise** depends on how well you convince them that you are qualified to speak on this topic. You can demonstrate your knowledge and expertise through direct and indirect means.

You directly establish expertise when you disclose your experiences with your topic including formal education, special study, demonstrated

Spotlight on Scholars	Joan Gorham	**Professor of Communication Studies and Associate Dean of Academic Affairs, Eberly College of Arts and Sciences, West Virginia University, on Immediacy**

Joan Gorham began her professional career as a high school teacher, so it is not surprising that her research has focused on "immediacy," the use of communicative behaviors to enhance the physical and psychological closeness between teacher and student in the effort to improve student learning. Her first major work on the role of implicit communication in teaching was her dissertation at Northern Illinois University, in which she contrasted how a teacher's nonverbal messages affected learners.

When Gorham accepted a position at West Virginia University, she began building on research by Jan Andersen, James McCroskey, Virginia Richmond, and others on the subject of immediacy. Although she had not intended to focus her lifetime research on immediacy, Gorham explained, "The research just grew out of itself. As I reported the data from one study, I found myself with many unanswered questions that motivated me to initiate new studies on different facets of the subject."

Courtesy Joan Gorham

Taken together, Gorham's studies are helping teachers to understand how their communication behavior affects their relationship with their students and learning outcomes. Some of the early research on immediacy suggested that improved learning outcomes were just a perception. That is, students reported that they learned more from more immediate teachers, but these studies had not documented actual learning gains. As Gorham refined her research methods, she began to see results that supported the hypothesis that immediacy is directly correlated with learning.

Because the learning process consists of arousal, attention, and recall, Gorham believes teachers who demonstrate appropriate immediacy are more likely to stimulate their students to pay attention and are also more likely to increase the students' interest and motivation. As a result, students more easily understand and ultimately remember the information being presented.

From a practical sense, then, what specific behaviors must teachers use to increase their immediacy? From Gorham's studies, we learn that teachers gain immediacy, in part, through such nonverbal behaviors as using gestures, looking directly at students, smiling, moving around the classroom, and using variety in their vocal expressions. Moreover, Gorham's studies have shown that teachers gain immediacy through such verbal behaviors as using personal examples, relating personal experiences, using humor, using personal pronouns, addressing students by name, conversing with students outside of class, praising students' work, and soliciting students' perceptions about assignments.

Gorham believes teachers can modify their own behavior and work toward incorporating the methods that lead to appropriate levels of immediacy. High-immediacy teachers are rated by students as higher in extroversion, composure, competence, and character than are low-immediacy teachers. They are rated as more similar to their students in attitude, but more expert than non-immediate teachers. Students report being significantly more likely to engage in behaviors recommended by teachers who use immediacy behaviors. Thus, learning the appropriate degree of immediacy between teachers and students becomes an important goal in the teaching–learning process.

Thomson NOW! *For titles of several of her research publications, see the reference list at the end of this book. For more information about Gorham and her work, use your ThomsonNOW for* Communicate! *to access* **Web Resource 14.2: Dr. Joan Gorham**.

skill, and your "track record." Audience members will also assess your expertise through indirect means such as how prepared you seem and how much you demonstrate your firsthand involvement by using personal examples and illustrations. Audiences have an almost instinctive sense of when a speaker is "winging it," and most audiences distrust a speaker who does not appear to have command of the material. Speakers who are overly dependent on their notes or who "hem and haw," fumbling to find ways to express their ideas, undermine the confidence of the audience. When your ideas are easy to follow and are clearly expressed, audience members perceive you to be more credible.

Similarly, when the audience hears a speech in which the ideas are developed through specific statistics, high-quality examples, illustrations, and the personal experiences of the speaker, they are likely to view the speaker as credible. Recall how impressed you are with instructors who always seem to have two or three perfect examples and illustrations and who are able to recall statistics without looking at their notes. Compare this to your experiences with instructors who seem tied to the textbook and don't appear to know much about the subject beyond their prepared lecture. In which instance do you perceive the instructor to be more knowledgeable?

Therefore, as you prepare, you will want to adapt want you say so that you directly and indirectly demonstrate your expertise and knowledge.

trustworthiness
both character and apparent motives for speaking.

Why is Rudy Guiliani considered trustworthy?

Establish trustworthiness Your **trustworthiness** is the extent to which the audience can believe that what you say is accurate, true, and in their best interests. The more your audience sees you as trustworthy, the more credible you will be. People assess others' trustworthiness by judging their character and their motives. So you can establish yourself as trustworthy by following ethical standards and by honestly explaining what is motivating you to speak.

As you plan your speech, you need to consider how to demonstrate your character: that you are honest, industrious, dependable, and a morally strong person. For example, when you credit the source of your information as you speak, you confirm that the information is true—that you are not making it up—and you signal your honesty by not taking credit for someone else's ideas. Similarly, if you present the arguments evenly on both sides of an issue, instead of just the side you favor, audience members will see you as fair-minded.

How trustworthy you seem to be will also depend on how the audience views your motives. If people believe that what you are saying is self-serving rather than in their interest, they will be suspicious and view you as less trustworthy. Early in your speech, then, it is important to show how audience members will benefit from what you are saying. For example, in his speech on toxic waste, Brandon might describe how one community's ignorance of the dangers of toxic waste disposal allowed a toxic waste dump to be located in their community, with subsequent serious health issues. He can then share his motive by saying something like: "My hope is that this speech will give you the information you need to thoughtfully participate in decisions like these that may face your community."

By adapting your material so that it highlights your strong character and pure motives, you can establish your trustworthiness.

Display personableness We have more confidence in people that we like. **Personableness** is the extent to which you project an agreeable or pleasing personality. The more your listeners like you, the more likely they are to believe what you tell them. We quickly decide how much we like a new person based on our first impressions of them. As a speaker who is trying to build credibility with an audience, you should look for ways to adapt your personal style to one that will help the audience like you and perceive you as credible.

Besides dressing in a way that is appropriate for the audience and occasion, you can increase the chance that the audience will like you by smiling at individual audience members before beginning your remarks and by looking at individuals as you speak, acknowledging them with a quick nod. You can also demonstrate personableness by using humor, especially self-deprecating remarks.

*personableness
the extent to which you project an agreeable or pleasing personality.*

Initial Audience Attitudes

Initial audience attitudes are predispositions for or against a topic, usually expressed as an opinion. Meeting initial audience attitudes means framing a speech in a way that takes into account how much the audience knows and their attitude toward the topic. As part of your audience analysis, you identified the initial attitude that you expected most of your audience members to have toward your topic. During your speech preparation, you will be challenged to adapt the material you plan to present so that it takes this attitude into account.

Although adapting to listeners' attitudes is obviously important for persuasive speeches, it is also important for informative speeches. For example, although a speech on refinishing wood furniture is meant to be informative, you may face an audience whose initial attitude is that refinishing furniture is difficult and complicated, or you may face an audience of young homeowners who are addicted to HGTV and who are really looking forward to your talk. Although the process you describe in both instances would be the same, how you approached explaining the steps in furniture refinishing would need to take the audience's initial disposition into account. Suppose

*initial audience attitudes
predispositions for or against a topic, usually expressed as an opinion.*

you know that you have an audience of young, new-home owners and have found out through a simple show of hand that most of them enjoy watching HGTV. Then you will want to play upon their interest as you speak, or refer to some of the most popular shows on HGTV. If, however, you have an audience that initially views refinishing furniture as complicated and boring, then you will need to adjust what you say to develop their interest and convince them that the process is simpler than they initially thought. In Chapter 17, "Persuasive Speaking," we will examine strategies for dealing with listeners' attitudes in depth.

Language and Cultural Differences

Western Europeans' speaking traditions inform the approach to public speaking we discuss in this book. However, public speaking is a social and cultural act so, as you would expect, public speaking practices and their perceived effectiveness vary. As they prepare and present speeches, speakers from various cultures and subcultures draw on the traditions of their speech communities. Speakers who address audiences comprising people from ethnic and language groups different from their own face two additional challenges of adaptation: being understood when speaking in a second language and having limited common experiences on which to establish common ground.

Overcome linguistic problems When the first language spoken by the audience is different from that of the speaker, who is trying to speak their language, audience members often cannot understand what the speaker is saying due to mispronunciations, accents, vocabulary mistakes, and idiomatic speech meaning. Fear of making these mistakes can make second-language speakers self-conscious. But most audience members are more tolerant of mistakes made by second-language speakers than they are of those made by native speakers. Likewise, most audience members will work hard to understand a second-language speaker.

Nevertheless, when you are speaking in a second language, you have the additional responsibility to make your speech as understandable as possible. You can help your audience by speaking more slowly and articulating as clearly as you can. By slowing your speaking rate, you give yourself additional time to pronounce seemingly awkward sounds and choose words whose meanings you know. You also give your audience members additional time to "adjust their ear" so that they can more easily process what you are saying.

One of the best ways to improve when you are giving a speech in a second language is to practice the speech in front of friends and associates who are native speakers. These "trial audience members" should be instructed to take note of words and phrases that are mispronounced or misused. Then they can work with you to correct the pronunciation or to choose other words that better express your idea. Also, keep in mind that the more you practice speaking the language, the more comfortable you will become with the language and with your ability to relate to the audience members.

Choose culturally sensitive material Although overcoming linguistic problems can seem daunting, those whose cultural background differs significantly from that of their audience members also face the challenge of having few common experiences from which to draw. Much of our success in adapting to the audience hinges on establishing common ground and drawing on common experiences. But when we are speaking to audiences who are vastly different from us, we must learn as much as we can about the culture of our audience so that we can develop the material in a way that is meaningful to them. This may mean conducting additional library research to find statistics, examples, and so on that are meaningful to the

Action Step 4.a

Adapting to Your Audience Verbally

The goal of this activity is to help you plan how you will verbally adapt your material to the specific audience.

Write your thesis statement: _____

Review the audience analysis that you completed in Action Steps 1.b and 1.c. As you review the speech outline that you completed in Action Steps 3.a–3.h, plan the supporting material you will use to verbally adapt to your audience by answering the following questions:

1. How can I adapt this material so that it is relevant to this audience by showing that it is timely, proximate, and has a personal impact on them?

2. How can I make this material easier for the audience to comprehend by orienting them, defining key terms, using vivid examples, personalizing the information, comparing unknowns with what is known, and using diverse methods of development?

3. How can I establish common ground by using personal pronouns, asking rhetorical questions, and drawing from common experiences?

4. How can I establish my credibility by demonstrating my knowledge and expertise, my trustworthiness, and my personableness?

5. How can I adapt to the language and cultural differences that exist between me and the audience?

Thomson NOW! You can complete this activity online, view another student's sample of this activity, and, if requested, e-mail your completed activity to your instructor. Use your ThomsonNOW for *Communicate!* to access **Skill Learning Activity 14.2**.

DIVERSE VOICES

Public Speaking Patterns in Kenya

by Ann Neville Miller

One of the major differences in adapting to different groups is understanding their expectations and their reactions to your words. In this excerpt, Ann Neville Miller describes the different purposes of public speaking in Kenya and how those purposes influence how Kenyan speakers adapt their words to the expectations of their audiences.

uch public speaking in the United States is informative or persuasive in purpose; ceremonial occasions for public speaking are less common. This is due, in part, to the stress that mainstream U.S. culture places on informality. The average Kenyan, in contrast, will give far more ceremonial speeches in life than any other kind of speech. These may be speeches of greeting, introduction, tribute, and thanks, among others. Life events, both major and minor, are marked by ceremonies, and ceremonies occasion multiple public speeches.

This means that, unlike the majority of people in the United States, who report that they fear speaking in public, possibly even more than they fear death (Bruskin Report, 1973; McCroskey, 1993; Richmond & McCroskey, 1995), for most Kenyans, public speaking is an unavoidable responsibility. For example, when a Kenyan attends a church service or other event away from home, he or she will often be asked to stand up and give an impromptu word of greeting to the assembly. In more remote areas, where literacy rates are low and there is little access to electronic media, this word of greeting also can serve an informative purpose because the one who has traveled often brings news of the outside world. The "harambee," a kind of community fund-raising event peculiar to Kenya, is characterized by the presence of both a guest of honor and various dignitaries of a stature appropriate to the specific occasion, all of whom are likely at some point to address the gathering. Weddings and funerals overflow with ceremonial speeches; virtually any relative, friend, or business associate of the newly married or deceased may give advice

or pay tribute. Older members of the bride's family, for example, may remind her how important it is to feed her husband well, or warn the groom that in their family men are expected never to abuse their wives, but to settle marital disputes with patience. Even the woman selected to cut the cake expects to give a brief word of exhortation before performing her duty. The free dispensing of advice, a hallmark of Kenyan wedding celebrations, would be out of place at most receptions in the United States, where the focus of speeches is normally more on remembrances and well-wishing.

In fact, when it comes to marriage, speech making begins long before the actual wedding day, at bridal negotiations where up to 40 or 50 people from the two families attempt to settle on a bride price. At these negotiations especially, but also in other ceremonial speeches, "deep" language replete with proverbs and metaphors is expected. The family of the man may explain that their son has seen a beautiful flower, or a lovely she-goat, or some other item in the compound of the family of the young lady and that they would like to obtain it for their son. In a negotiation of this type that the author recently attended, the speaker for the bride's relatives explained that the family would require 20 goats as a major portion of the bride price. Because both parties were urban dwellers and would have no space to keep that many animals, the groom's family conferred with each other and determined that the bride's family really wanted cash. They settled on what they considered to be a reasonable price per goat, multiplied it by 20, and presented the total amount through a designated spokesperson to the representative of the bride.

The original speaker from the bride's family looked at the money and observed dryly that goats in the groom's area were considerably thinner than those the bride's family were accustomed to! This type of indirect communication, the subtlety of which affords immense satisfaction and sometimes amusement to both speaker and listener, is a form of the high-context communication described by [Edward T.] Hall. A full appreciation of the speech requires extensive knowledge of shared experiences and traditions.

Excerpted from Ann Neville Miller, "Public Speaking Patterns in Kenya." In Larry A. Samovar, Richard E. Porter, Edwin R. McDaniel, eds., Intercultural Communication: A Reader *(11th ed., pp. 238–245). Belmont, CA: Wadsworth, 2006.*

audience. Or it may require us to elaborate on ideas that would be self-explanatory in our own culture. For example, suppose that Maria, a Mexican American exchange student, was giving a personal narrative speech on the *quinceanera* party she had when she turned 15 for her speech class at Yeshiva University in Israel. Because students in Israel have no experience with the Mexican coming-of-age tradition of *quinceanera* parties, they would have trouble understanding the significance of this event unless Maria was able to use her knowledge of the Bar Mitzvah and Bat Mitzvah coming-of-age ritual celebrations in Jewish culture and relate it to those.

In the Diverse Voices feature, Ann Neville Miller provides us with insights into public speaking practices in Kenya and how Kenyans must adapt their speeches to appeal to their audiences' shared experiences and knowledge.

Adapting to Audiences Visually

As you adapt your speech to the specific needs of your audience, consider what visual material will help audience members understand and remember the material you present.

A **visual aid** is a form of speech development that allows the audience to see as well as hear information. You'll want to consider using visual aids; they enable you to adapt to an audience's level of knowledge because they can clarify and dramatize your verbal message. Visual aids also help audiences retain the information over long periods because people will be able to remember more when they use both their eyes and their ears rather than their ears alone.

visual aid
a form of speech development that allows the audience to see as well as to hear information.

Types of Visual Aids

Before you can choose visual aids to use for a specific speech, you need to recognize the various types of visual aids from which you can choose. Visual aids range from those that are simple to use and readily available from an existing source, to those that require practice to use effectively and must be custom produced for your specific speech. In this section, we describe the types of visual aids that you can consider using as you prepare your speech.

object
a three-dimensional representation of an idea you are communicating.

Objects An **object** is a three-dimensional representation of an idea you are communicating. Objects make good visual aids (1) if they are large enough to be seen by all audience members, and (2) when they are small enough to carry to the site of the speech. A volleyball or a braided rug are objects that would be appropriate in size for most classroom-sized audiences. A cell phone might be OK if the goal was simply to show a phone, but might be too small if the speaker wanted to demonstrate how to key in certain specialized functions.

On occasion, *you* can be an effective visual aid object. For instance, through descriptive gestures, you can show the height of a tennis net; through your posture and movement, you can show the motions involved in the butterfly swimming stroke; and through your attire you can illustrate the native dress of a different country.

Models When an object is too large to bring to the speech site or too small to be seen (like the cell phone), a three-dimensional model is appropriate. In a speech on the physics of bridge construction, a scale model of a suspension bridge would be an effective visual aid. Likewise, in a speech on genetic engineering, a model of the DNA double helix might help the audience understand what happens during these microscopic procedures.

Still photographs If an exact reproduction of material is needed, enlarged still photographs are excellent visual aids. In a speech on "smart weapons," enlarged before-and-after photos of target sites would be effective in helping the audience understand the pinpoint accuracy of these weapons.

Slides Like photographs, slides allow you to present an exact visual image to the audience. The advantage of slides over photographs is that the size of the image can be manipulated on-site so that they are easy for all audience members to see. In addition, if more than one image is to be shown, slides eliminate the awkwardness associated with manually changing photographs. The remote-control device allows you to smoothly move from one image to the next and to talk about each image as long as you would like. One drawback to using slides, however, is that in most cases the room must be darkened for the slides to be viewed. In this situation, it is easy for the slides to become the focal point for the audience. Many novice speakers are tempted to look and talk to the slides rather than to the audience. Moreover, to use slides, you must bring a projector to class with you.

Slides and photos used in PowerPoint presentations get and hold attention and can be seen by the entire audience.

Film and video clips You can use short clips from films and videos to demonstrate processes or to expose audiences to important people. But because effective clips generally run one to three minutes, for most classroom speeches they are ineffective and inappropriate because they dominate the speech and the speaker. In longer speeches when clips are used, speakers must ensure that the equipment needed is available and operative. This means performing a dry run on-site with the equipment prior to beginning the speech.

Simple drawings Simple drawings are easy to prepare. If you can use a compass, a straightedge, and a measure, you can draw well enough for the purposes of most speeches. For instance, if you are making the point that water-skiers must hold their arms straight, with the back straight and knees bent slightly, a stick figure (see Figure 14.1) will illustrate the point. Stick figures may not be as aesthetically pleasing as professional drawings or photographs, but to demonstrate a certain concept they can be quite effective. In fact, elaborate, detailed drawings may not be worth the time and effort and actual photographs may be so detailed that they obscure the point you wish to make.

Figure 14.1
Sample drawing

Once a drawing is prepared, it can be scanned and used as part of a PowerPoint presentation, or as an overhead, or the drawing can be used freestanding if it is enlarged and prepared on poster board or foamcore. Obviously, you will want to prepare drawings that are easily seen by all audience members. Drawings should be prepared on poster board or foamcore so that they remain rigid and are easy to display.

Maps Like drawings, maps are relatively easy to prepare. Simple maps allow you to orient audiences to landmarks (mountains, rivers, and lakes), states, cities, land routes, weather systems, and so on. Commercial maps are available, but simple maps are relatively easy to prepare and can be customized so that audience members are not confused by visual information that is irrelevant to your purposes. Like drawings, maps can be used as part of PowerPoint presentations, as overheads, or as freestanding items. Figure 14.2 is a good example of a map that focuses on weather systems.

charts
graphic representations that present information in easily interpreted formats.

word charts
used to preview, review, or highlight important ideas covered in a speech.

flow charts
use symbols and connecting lines to diagram the progressions through a complicated process.

Charts A **chart** is a graphic representation that distills a lot of information and presents it to an audience in an easily interpreted visual format. Word charts and flow charts are the most common.

A **word chart** is used to preview, review, or highlight important ideas covered in a speech. In a speech on Islam, a speaker might make a word chart that lists the five pillars of Islam, as shown in Figure 14.3. An outline of speech main points can become a word chart.

A **flow chart** uses symbols and connecting lines to diagram the progressions through a complicated process. Organizational charts are a common type of flow chart that shows the flow of authority and chain of command

Figure 14.2
Sample map

Five Pillars of Islam
1. Shahadah—Witness to Faith
2. Salat—Prayer
3. Sawm—Fasting
4. Zakat—Almsgiving
5. Hajj—Pilgrimate

Figure 14.3
Sample word chart

Figure 14.4
Sample organizational chart

in an organization. The chart in Figure 14.4 illustrates the organization of a student union board.

In a PowerPoint presentation, you can design the chart so that each part is displayed as you talk about it. If overheads are used, multiple overheads can be "stacked" so that each overhead adds information that appears on the screen. You can also create the same effect by using a large newsprint pad with a series of charts in which additional information is added on succeeding pages. Then mount the pad on an easel and, as you are talking, flip the pages to reveal more information as you discuss it.

Graphs A **graph** is a diagram that presents numerical information. Bar graphs, line graphs, and pie graphs are the most common forms of graphs.

A **bar graph** is a chart that presents information using a series of vertical or horizontal bars. It can show relationships between two or more variables at the same time or at various times on one or more dimensions. For instance, in a speech on fluctuations of economy, the bar graph in Figure 14.5 shows the actual (and estimated) increases for clothing exports from China from 1998 to 2005.

A **line graph** is a chart that represents the changes in one or more variables over time through use of a line or series of lines. In a speech on the population of the United States, for example, the line graph in Figure 14.6 helps by showing the population increase, in millions, from 1810 to 2000.

A **pie graph** is a chart that shows the relationships among parts of a single unit. In a speech on comparative family net worth, a pie graph such as the one in Figure 14.7 could be used to show the percentage of U.S. households that have achieved various levels of net worth.

graph
a chart that compares information.

bar graphs
charts that present information using a series of vertical or horizontal bars.

line graphs
charts that indicate changes in one or more variables over time.

pie graphs
charts that help audiences visualize the relationships among parts of a single unit.

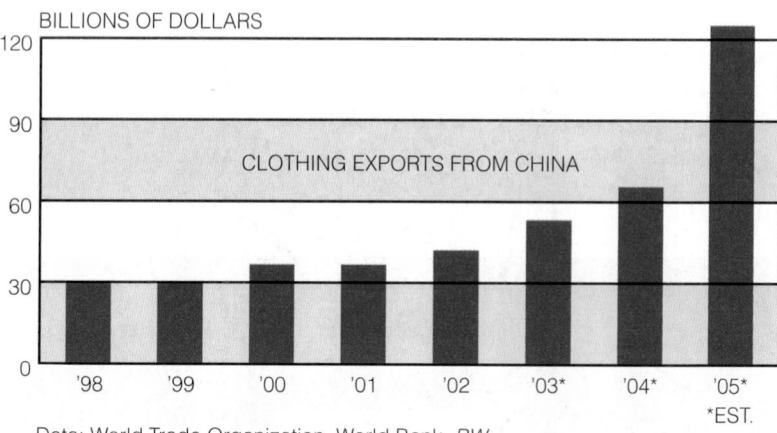

Figure 14.5
Sample bar graph

Data: World Trade Organization, World Bank, *BW.*

SOURCE: *Business Week,* December 15, 2003.

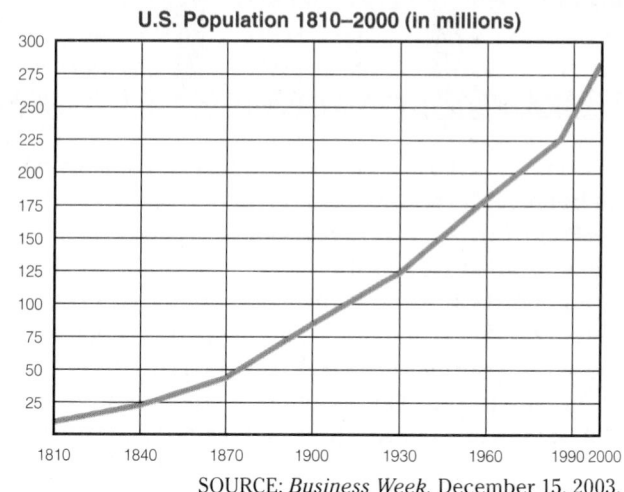

Figure 14.6
Sample line graph

SOURCE: *Business Week,* December 15, 2003.

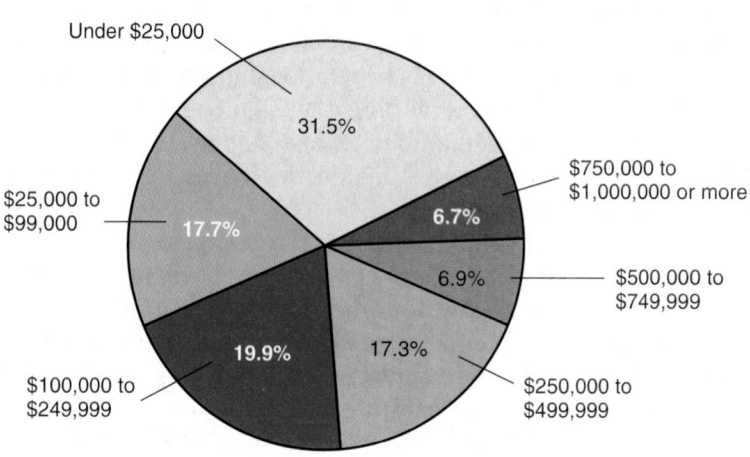

Figure 14.7
Sample pie graph

SOURCE: *Money,* December 2003, p. 99.

Most spreadsheet computer programs allow you to prepare colorful graphs easily and to compare the data arrayed as a bar, line, or pie graph. This allows you to choose which display you think will be most effective for your presentation. If you prepare your graphs on the computer, you will be able to insert them into a PowerPoint slide or print them onto an overhead.

When choosing or preparing graphs, make sure that labels are large enough to be read easily by audience members.

Methods for Displaying Visual Aids

Once you have decided on the specific visual aids for your speech, you will need to choose the method you will use to display them. There are trade-offs to be considered when choosing a method. Methods for displaying visual aids vary in the type of preparation they require, the amount of specialized training needed to use them effectively, and the professionalism they convey. Some methods, such as writing on a chalkboard, require little advanced preparation. Other methods, such as computer-generated presentation aids, can require extensive preparation. Similarly, it's easy to use an object or a flip chart, but you will need training to properly set up and run a slide or PowerPoint presentation. Finally, the quality of your visual presentation will affect your perceived credibility. A well-run, computer-generated presentation is impressive, but technical difficulties can make you look ill prepared. Hand-prepared charts and graphs that are hastily or sloppily developed mark you as an amateur, whereas professional-looking visual aids enhance your credibility. Speakers can choose from the following methods.

Computer-mediated presentations Today, in many educational and professional settings, audiences expect speakers to use computer-mediated visual aids. PowerPoint, Adobe Persuasion, and Lotus Freelance are popular presentation software. Using these programs, you can create your visual aids on your computer, download them to a disk or CD-ROM, and then use them on a computer/projector or monitor system at your speech site. Additionally, through the Internet you can find, download, and store your own library of images. Presentation software typically allows you to insert an image from your library into your presentation. Using a computer scanner, you can also digitize a photograph from a book or magazine and transfer it to your computer library.

The visuals you create can be displayed directly onto a screen or TV monitor as a computer "slide show," and they also can be used to create slides, overhead transparencies, or handouts. Visual aids developed with presentation software give a very polished look to your speech and allow you to develop complex multimedia presentations.

Today, most colleges and universities offer classes in developing and using presentation software and have dedicated classrooms or portable

Roger Persson/© Thomson Higher Education

Presentation software can be used for preparing and presenting visual aids. Although visual aids are useful, verbal adaptation is vital to effective communication.

roll-around carts that house the equipment needed to present computer-mediated visuals.

Preparing visual aids with presentation software is time consuming. Smoothly presenting a computerized visual presentation takes practice. But if you start simply, over time you will become more adept at creating professional-quality visuals. Well-developed and well-presented computer-mediated visual aids greatly enhance audience perceptions of speaker credibility. *Caution:* computer-mediated presentations can be addicting. Many novices overuse them, so instead of having visual aids (visuals that "aid" the speaker's ideas), the visuals become the show and the speaker is relegated to the role of projectionist (Ayres, 1991, pp. 73–79).

Overhead transparencies An easy way to display drawings, charts, and graphs is to transfer them to an acetate film and project them onto a screen via an overhead projector. With a master copy of the visual, you can make an overhead transparency using a copy machine, thermograph, color lift, or if the master is a computer document, with a computer printer. Overheads are easy and inexpensive to make, and the equipment needed to project overheads is easy to operate and likely to be available at most speech sites. Overheads work well in nearly any setting, and unlike other types of projections, they don't require dimming the lights in the room. Moreover, overheads can be useful for demonstrating a process because it is possible to write, trace, or draw on the transparency while you are talking. The size at which an overhead is projected can also be adjusted to the size of the room so that all audience members can see the image.

Flip charts A **flip chart,** a large pad of paper mounted on an easel, can be an effective method for presenting visual aids. Flip charts (and easels) are available in many sizes. For a presentation to four or five people, a small tabletop version works well; for a larger audience, a larger sized pad (30″ × 40″) is needed.

Flip charts are prepared before the speech; you use colorful markers to record the information. At times, a speaker may record some of the information before the speech begins and then add information while speaking.

When preparing flip charts, leave several pages between each visual on the pad. If you discover a mistake or decide to revise, you can tear out that sheet without disturbing the order of other visuals you may have prepared. After you have the visuals, tear out all but one sheet between each chart. This blank sheet serves as both a transition page and a cover sheet. Because you want your audience to focus on your words and not on visual material that is no longer being discussed, you can flip to the empty page while you are talking about material not covered by charts. Also, the empty page between charts ensures that heavy lines or colors from the next chart will not show through.

For flip charts to be effective, information that is handwritten or drawn must be neat and appropriately sized. Flip chart visuals that are not neatly done detract from speaker credibility. Flip charts can comfortably be used with smaller audiences (less than 100 people), but are not appropriate for larger settings. It is especially important when creating flip charts to make sure that the information is written large enough to be comfortably seen by all audience members.

Poster boards The easiest method for displaying simple drawings, charts, maps, and graphs is by preparing them on stiff cardboard or foam-core. Then the visual can be placed on an easel or in a chalk tray when it is referred to during the speech. Like flip charts, poster boards must be neat and appropriately sized. They are also limited in their use to smaller audiences.

Chalkboard Because the chalkboard is a staple in every college classroom, many novice (and ill-prepared) speakers rely on this method for displaying their visual aids. Unfortunately, the chalkboard is easy to misuse and to overuse. Moreover, chalkboards are not suitable for depicting complex material. So writing on a chalkboard is appropriate to use for very short items of information that can be written in a few seconds. Nevertheless, being able to use a chalkboard effectively should be a part of any speaker's repertoire.

Chalkboards should be written on prior to speaking or during a break in speaking. Otherwise, the visual is likely to either be illegible or partly obscured by your body as you write. Or you may end up talking to the board instead of to the audience. If you need to draw or write on the board

flip chart
a large pad of paper mounted on an easel; it can be an effective method for presenting visual aids.

while you are talking, you should practice doing it. If you are right-handed, stand to the right of what you are drawing. Try to face at least part of the audience while you work. Although it may seem awkward at first, your effort will allow you to maintain contact with your audience and will allow the audience to see what you are doing while you are doing it.

"Chalk talks" are easiest to prepare, but they are the most likely to result in damage to speaker credibility. It is the rare individual who can develop well-crafted visual aids on a chalkboard. More often, chalkboard visuals signal a lack of preparation.

Handouts At times, it may be useful for each member of the audience to have a personal copy of the visual aid. In these situations, you can prepare handouts: material printed or drawn on sheets of paper. On the plus side, you can prepare handouts quickly, and all the people in the audience can have their own professional-quality material to refer to and take with them from the speech. On the minus side is the distraction of distributing handouts and the potential for losing audience members' attention when you want them to be looking at you. Before you decide to use handouts, carefully consider why a handout is superior to other methods. If you decide on handouts, you may want to distribute them at the end of the speech.

Criteria for Choosing Visual Aids

Now that you understand the various types of visual aids and the methods you can use to display them, you have to decide what content needs to be depicted and the best way to do this. In this section, we focus on some of the key questions you need to answer to help you make visual aid choices.

1. **What are the most important ideas the audience needs to understand and remember?** These ideas are ones you may want to enhance with visual aids. Visual aids are likely to be remembered. So, you will want to make sure that what you present visually is what you want your audience to remember.

2. **Are there ideas that are complex or difficult to explain verbally but would be easy for members to understand visually?** The old saying that one picture is worth a thousand words is true. At times, we can help our audience by providing a visual explanation. Demonstrating the correct way to hold a golf club is much easier and clearer than simply describing the positioning of each hand and finger.

3. **How many visual aids are appropriate?** Unless you are doing a slide show in which the total focus of the speech is on visual images, the number of visual aids you use should be limited. For the most part, you want the focus of the audience to be on you, the speaker. You want to use visual aids when their use will hold attention, exemplify an idea, or help the audience remember. For each of these goals, the more visual aids used, the less value they will contribute. For a five-minute speech,

using three visual aids at crucial times will get attention, exemplify, and stimulate recall far better than using six or eight.

There is another reason for keeping the visual aids to a small number. A couple of well-crafted visual aids could maximize the power of your statements, whereas several poorly executed or poorly used visual aids could actually detract from the power of your words.

4. **How large is the audience?** The kinds of visual aids that will work for a small group of 20 or less differ from the kinds that will work for an audience of 100 or more. For an audience of 20 or less, as in most of your classroom speeches, you can show relatively small objects and use relatively small models and everyone will be able to see. For larger audiences, you'll want projections that can be seen from 100 or 200 feet away with ease.

5. **Is necessary equipment readily available?** At times, you may be speaking in an environment that is not equipped for certain visual displays. At many colleges and universities, most rooms are equipped with only a chalkboard, an overhead projector, and electrical outlets. If you want to use other equipment, you will have to bring it yourself or reserve it through the appropriate university media office. Be prepared! When you have scheduled equipment from an outside source, you need to prepare yourself for the possibility that the equipment may not arrive on time or may not work the way you thought it did. Call ahead, get to your speaking location early, and have an alternative visual aid to use, just in case.

6. **Is the time involved in making or getting the visual aid and/or equipment cost effective?** Visual aids are supplements. Their goal is to accent what you are doing verbally. If you believe that a particular visual aid will help you better achieve your goal, then the time spent is well worth it.

You'll notice that most of the visual aids we've discussed can be obtained or prepared relatively easily. But because some procedures are more complicated, we might find ourselves getting lost in making some of them. Visual aids definitely make a speech more interesting and engaging. However, I've found that the best advice is to keep it simple.

Use the following guidelines when choosing visual aids:

- Take a few minutes to consider your visual aid strategy. Where would some kind of visual aid make the most sense? What kind of visual aid is most appropriate?
- Adapt your visuals to your situation, speech topic, and audience needs.
- Choose visuals with which you are both comfortable and competent.
- Check out the audiovisual resources of the speaking site before you start preparing your visual aids.

Action Step 4.b

Adapting to Your Audience Visually

The goal of this activity is to help you decide which visual aids you will use in your speech.

1. Identify the key ideas in your speech that you could emphasize with a visual presentation to increase audience interest, understanding, or retention.

2. For each idea you have identified, list the type of visual presentation you think would be most appropriate to develop and use.

3. For each idea you plan to present visually, decide on the method or aid you will use to present it.

4. Write a brief paragraph describing why you chose the types of visual aids and methods that you did. Be sure to consider how your choices will affect your preparation time and the audience's perception of your credibility.

Thomson NOW! You can use your student workbook or Speech Builder Express to complete this activity, or you can complete it online, download a Visual Aids Planning Chart to keep track of your decisions, view a student sample of this activity, and, if requested, e-mail your work to your instructor. Use your ThomsonNOW for *Communicate!* to access **Skill Learning Activity 14.3**.

■ Be discriminating in the number of visual aids you use and the key points that they support.

For a thorough discussion of the methods and guidelines for using visual aids, use your ThomsonNOW for *Communicate!* to access **Web Resource 14.3: Visual Aids**.

Principles for Designing Effective Visual Aids

However simple you may think your visual aids will be, you still have to carefully design them. The visual aids that you are most likely to design for a classroom presentation are charts, graphs, diagrams, and drawings written on poster board or flip charts or projected on screens using overheads or slides. In this section, we will suggest eight principles for designing effective visual aids. Then, we'll look at several examples that illustrate these principles.

1. *Use a print or type size that can be seen easily by your entire audience.* If you're designing a hand-drawn poster board, check your lettering for size by moving as far away from the visual aid you've created as the farthest person in your audience will be sitting. If you can read the lettering and see the details from that distance, then both are large enough; if not, draw another sample and check it for size.

36 Major Headings

24 Subheads

18 Text material

Figure 14.8
Visual aid print sizes

When you project a typeface from an overhead onto a screen, the lettering on the screen will be much larger than the lettering on the overhead itself. So, what's a good rule of thumb for overhead lettering? Try 36-point type for major headings, 24-point for subheadings, and 18-point for text. Figure 14.8 shows how these sizes look on paper. The 36-point type will project to about two to three inches on the screen; 24-point will project to about one to two inches; 18-point will project to about one inch. Most presentational software will prompt you if you have chosen a font size that is too small.

2. *Use a typeface that is easy to read and pleasing to the eye.* Modern software packages, such as Microsoft Word, come with a variety of typefaces (fonts). Yet only a few of them will work well in projections. In general, avoid fonts that have heavy serifs or curlicues. Figure 14.9 shows a sample of four standard typefaces in regular and boldface 18-point size. Most other typefaces are designed for special situations.

Arial	Selecting Typefaces **Selecting Typefaces**
Times	Selecting Typefaces **Selecting Typefaces**
Lucida Sans	Selecting Typefaces **Selecting Typefaces**
Garamond	Selecting Typefaces **Selecting Typefaces**

Figure 14.9
Typefaces in 18-point regular and bold face

Figure 14.10
All capitals versus upper- and lowercase

CARAT—THE WEIGHT OF A DIAMOND
Carat—The Weight of a Diamond

Which of these typefaces seem easiest to read and most pleasing to your eye? Perhaps you'll decide that you'd like to use one typeface for the heading and another for the text. In general, you will not want to use more than two typefaces—headings in one, text in another. You want the typefaces to call attention to the material, not to themselves.

3. *Use upper- and lowercase type.* The combination of upper- and lowercase is easier to read. Some people think that printing in all capital letters creates emphasis. Although that may be true in some instances, ideas printed in all capital letters are more difficult to read—even when the ideas are written in short phrases (see Figure 14.10).

4. *Limit the lines of type to six or less.* You don't want the audience to spend a long time reading your visual aid—you want them listening to you. Limit the total number of lines to six or fewer and write points as phrases rather than as complete sentences. The visual aid is a reinforcement and summary of what you say, not the exact words you say. You don't want the audience to have to spend more than six or eight seconds "getting" your visual aid.

5. *Include only items of information that you will emphasize in your speech.* We often get ideas for visual aids from other sources, and the tendency is to include all the material that was original. But for speech purposes, keep the aid as simple as possible. Include only the key information and eliminate anything that distracts or takes emphasis away from the point you want to make.

Because the tendency to clutter is likely to present a special problem on graphs, let's consider two graphs that show college enrollment by age of students (Figure 14.11), based on figures reported in *The Chronicle of Higher Education.* The graph on the left shows all 11 age cat-

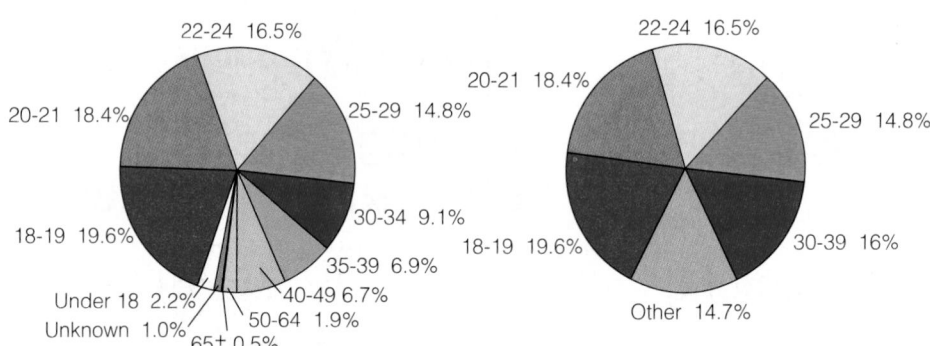

Figure 14.11
Comparative graphs

egories mentioned; the graph on the right simplifies this information by combining age ranges with small percentages. The graph on the right is not only easier to read, but it also emphasizes the highest percentage classifications.

6. *Make sure information is laid out in a way that is aesthetically pleasing.* Layout involves leaving white space around the whole message, indenting subordinate ideas, and using different type sizes as well as different treatments, such as bolding and underlining.

7. *Add pictures or clip art where appropriate to add interest.* If you are working with computer graphics, consider adding clip art. Most computer graphics packages have a wide variety of clip art that you can import to your document. You can also buy relatively inexpensive software packages that contain thousands of clip art images. A relevant piece of clip art can make the image look more professional and more dramatic. Be careful, though; clip art can be overdone. Don't let your message be overpowered by unnecessary pictures.

8. *Use color strategically.* Although black and white can work well for your visual aids, you should consider using color. Color can be used strategically to emphasize points. Use the following suggestions when incorporating color in your graphics.

- Use color to show similarities and differences between ideas.
- Use the same color background for each visual. Avoid dark backgrounds.
- Use bright colors, such as red, to highlight important information.
- Use black or deep blue for lettering, especially on flip charts.
- When using yellow or orange for lettering, outline the letters with a darker color because unless outlined, they can't be seen well from distance.
- Use no more than four colors; two or three are even better.
- When you want to get into more complex color usage, use a color wheel to select harmonizing colors.
- Don't crowd. Let the background color separate lettering and clip art.
- Always make a quick template before you prepare your visual aids. Pretend you are your audience. Sit as far away as they will be sitting, and evaluate the colors you have chosen for their readability and appeal.

Let's see if we can put all of these principles to work. Figure 14.12 contains a lot of important information that the speaker has presented, but notice how unpleasant this is to the eye. As you can see, this visual aid ignores all principles. However, with some thoughtful simplification, this speaker could produce the visual aid shown in Figure 14.13, which

OBSERVE & ANALYZE

Journal Activity

Evaluating Visual Aids

Analyze speeches or other public presentations such as lectures, articles, essays, newscasts, infomercials, and so on that you can find on campus, in print, online, or via television. Evaluate the use of at least one item from each of the following visuals aids: (1) objects, (2) models, (3) photographs, (4) slides, (5) film/video clip, (6) drawings, (7) maps, (8) charts, and (9) graphs. How effectively does the speaker or author use each item to illustrate or support his or her speech or presentation? Are there other ways the speaker might have used the visual aid more effectively? Would a different type of visual aid have conveyed the presentation's message more clearly?

Thomson You can complete NOW! this activity online and, if requested, e-mail it to your instructor. Use your Thomson-NOW for *Communicate!* to access **Skill Learning Activity 14.4.**

I WANT YOU TO REMEMBER THE THREE R'S OF RECYCLING

Reduce the amount of waste people produce like overpacking or using material that won't recycle.

Reuse by relying on cloth towels rather than paper towels, earthenware dishes rather than paper or plastic plates, and glass bottles rather than aluminum cans.

Recycle by collecting recyclable products, sorting them appropriately, and getting them to the appropriate recycling agency.

Figure 14.12
A cluttered and cumbersome visual aid

Remember the three R's of recycling

Reduce waste

Reuse
 cloth towels
 dishes
 glass bottles

Recycle
 collect
 sort
 deliver

Figure 14.13
A simple but effective visual aid

What Would You Do?

endra, I heard you telling Jim about the speech you're giving tomorrow. You think it's a winner, huh?"

"You got that right, Omar. I'm going to have Bardston eating out of the palm of my hand."

"You sound confident."

"This time I have reason to be. See, Professor Bardston's been talking about the importance of audience adaptation. These last two weeks that's all we've heard—adaptation, adaptation."

"What does she mean?"

"Talking about something in a way that really relates to people personally."

"OK—so how are you going to do that?"

"Well, you see, I'm giving this speech on abortion. Now here's the kick. Bardston let it slip that she's a supporter of Right to Life. So what I'm going to do is give this informative speech on the Right to Life movement. But I'm going to discuss the major beliefs of the movement in a way that'll get her to think that I'm a supporter. I'm going to mention aspects of the movement that I know she'll like."

"But I've heard you talk about how you're pro-choice."

"I am—all the way. But by keeping the information positive, she'll think I'm a supporter. It isn't as if I'm going to be telling any lies or anything."

1. In a speech, is it ethical to adapt in a way that resonates with your audience but isn't in keeping with what you really believe?

2. Could Kendra have achieved her goal using a different method? How?

---

sharpens the focus by emphasizing the key words (reduce, reuse, recycle), highlighting the major details, and adding clip art for a professional touch.

Now that you have created a plan for using visual aids in your speech and understand the principles for creating high-quality visual aids, you are in a position to visually adapt your speech to your particular audience. In the next chapter we describe a process for practicing your speech. You will want to have your visual aids ready to use during your practice sessions.

Summary

Audience adaptation is the process of customizing your speech to your specific audience. You need to consider both how to adapt your supporting material as you present it, and you need to consider how to adapt by using visual aids to help the audience understand and remember what you are saying.

First, you adapt to the audience verbally by (1) demonstrating relevance through showing how the information you are presenting is timely, proximate, and has personal impact on the audience; (2) ensuring that your material is easily comprehended by the audience. You accomplish this by orienting your audience, defining key terms, illustrating new concepts with vivid examples, personalizing the information to your audience, comparing unknown ideas with those your audience is familiar with, and by using multiple methods for developing your point; (3) establishing common ground by using personal pronouns, asking rhetorical questions, and drawing from common experiences; (4) demonstrating credibility through showing your knowledge and expertise, establishing your trustworthiness, and displaying personableness; and (5) adapting to language and cultural differences through overcoming linguistic problems and choosing culturally sensitive material.

Second, you adapt to audiences by developing and using appropriate visual aids. The most common types of visual aids are objects, models, photographs, slides, film and video clips, simple drawings, maps, charts, and graphs. There are various methods speakers can use to display visual aids, including computer-mediated presentation, overhead transparencies, flip charts, poster boards, chalkboards, and handouts. As you plan the visual aids you will use with a speech, consider the time and cost of preparation, the impact on audience understanding and memory, and the effect on speaker credibility. To design effective visual aids: (1) use printing or type size that can be seen easily by your entire audience; (2) use a typeface that is easy to read and pleasing to the eye; (3) use upper- and lowercase type; (4) limit the lines of type to six or less; (5) include only items of information that you will emphasize in your speech; (6) make sure information is laid out in a way that is aesthetically pleasing; (7) add clip art where appropriate; and (8) use color strategically.

Thomson NOW!

Communicate! Online

Now that you have read Chapter 14, use your ThomsonNOW for *Communicate!* for quick access to the electronic resources that accompany this text. Your ThomsonNOW gives you access to the Web Resources and Skill Learning Activities featured in this chapter, InfoTrac College Edition, and online study aids such as a digital glossary and review quizzes.

Your *Communicate!* ThomsonNOW is an online study system that helps you identify concepts you don't fully understand, allowing you to put your study time to the best use. Using chapter-by-chapter diagnostic pre-tests, the system creates a personalized study plan for each chapter. Each plan directs you to specific resources designed to improve your understanding, including pages from the text in e-book format. Chapter post-tests give you an opportunity to measure how much you've learned and let you know if you are ready for graded quizzes and exams.

Key Terms

Go to your ThomsonNOW for *Communicate!* to access your online glossary for Chapter 14. Print a copy of the glossary for this chapter and test yourself with the electronic flash cards or complete the crossword puzzle to help you master these key terms:

audience adaptation (342)	initial audience attitudes (351)	pie graph (359)
bar graphs (359)	knowledge and expertise (348)	proximity (343)
charts (358)		relevance (342)
common ground (346)	line graphs (359)	rhetorical questions (347)
credibility (348)	objects (356)	timely (342)
flip chart (363)	personal pronouns (347)	trustworthiness (350)
flow charts (358)	personableness (351)	visual aid (355)
graph (359)	personalize (345)	word charts (358)

Review Quiz

Test your knowledge of the concepts in this chapter by taking the online review quiz for Chapter 14. Go to your ThomsonNOW for *Communicate!* to access the quiz. When you have completed the quiz, submit it for scoring.

Skill Learning Activities

Complete the Observe & Analyze and Action Step activities for Chapter 14 online at your ThomsonNOW for *Communicate!*. You can submit your Observe & Analyze and Action Step answers to your instructor.

14.1: Observe & Analyze: Creating Common Ground (348)

14.2: Action Step 4.a: Adapting to Your Audience Verbally (353)

14.3: Action Step 4.b: Adapting to Your Audience Visually (366)

14.4: Observe & Analyze: Evaluating Visual Aids (369)

Web Resources

Go to your ThomsonNOW for *Communicate!* to access the Web Resources for this chapter.

14.1: Holistic Theory of Speaker Credibility (348)

14.2: Dr. Joan Gorham (349)

14.3: Visual Aids (366)

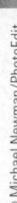

OBJECTIVES

After you have read this chapter, you should be able to answer these questions:

- What is public speaking apprehension?
- What are the symptoms and causes of public speaking apprehension?
- What techniques can be used for reducing speaking apprehension?
- What is extemporaneous speaking?
- How can you use your voice, articulation, bodily action, and enthusiasm to create a conversational quality to your speech delivery?
- What are the three most common types of speech delivery?
- How can you schedule and conduct your practice sessions so that you are prepared to deliver your speech?
- What are speaking notes and how should you prepare and use them?
- What are the key guidelines for using visual aids effectively during the speech?
- What are the three primary goals to achieve during practice sessions?
- By what criteria is an effective speech measured?

15
Overcoming Speech Apprehension by Practicing Delivery

When Gwen finished speaking, virtually everyone in the audience reacted by applauding, smiling, and saying to people around them, "That was a great speech."

Miguel turned to his friend Justin and said, "I can see why people are excited; the information was good and easy to follow. I thought it was excellent."

Justin replied, "Miguel, I've heard many speeches that had excellent information and were well organized, but what made this speech so good was her presentation. She talked with us, developed ideas fully, and most of all, used her voice and body motions in ways that helped her get her point across—and she wasn't nervous at all!"

A s Justin and his classmates have recognized, the difference between a good speech and a great speech is often how well it is delivered. Although delivery can't compensate for a poorly researched, poorly organized, or poorly developed speech, it can take a well-researched, well-organized, and well-developed speech and make it a powerful vehicle for accomplishing your speech goal. Although some people seem to be naturally fluent and comfortable speaking to a group, most of us are a bit frightened about the prospect and not really comfortable with our abilities to effectively present our ideas.

Action Step 5: Practice Your Speech Wording and Delivery

In this chapter, we're going to explain the fifth action step: *Practice your speech.* We begin by discussing stage fright or public speaking apprehension, which most of us face. Then we will explain the physical elements of effective delivery and the characteristics that are the hallmark of a conversational delivery style. Next, we describe three modes of speech delivery that someone might use to deliver a speech. Then we introduce you to a speech practice process designed to make your rehearsal sessions productive. Finally we explain criteria you can use to evaluate your speeches and others you might hear and, as an example, we apply the criteria to a sample student speech.

Public Speaking Apprehension

People probably have feared speaking in public since they first began doing it. So if you're a bit unnerved, you are in good company. And those of us who teach others to speak have been concerned with helping students like you overcome their fears almost as long. **Public speaking apprehension,** a type of communication anxiety (or nervousness), is the level of fear you experience when anticipating or actually speaking to an audience. Much of what we know about fear of speaking comes from the research of James McCroskey and his colleagues. The Spotlight on Scholars provides a short re-cap of his work.

public speaking apprehension
a type of communication anxiety (or nervousness), is the level of fear you experience when anticipating or actually speaking to an audience.

Almost all of us have some level of public speaking apprehension, but about 15 percent of the U.S. population experiences high levels of apprehension (Richmond & McCroskey, 1995, p. 98). Today, we benefit from the results of a significant amount of research that has studied public speaking apprehension and methods for helping us overcome it.

Symptoms and Causes

The signs of pubic speaking apprehension vary from individual to individual, and symptoms range from mild to debilitating. Symptoms include physical, emotional, and cognitive reactions. Physical signs may be stomach

Spotlight on Scholars

James McCroskey

Professor and Former Chair of the Department of Communication at West Virginia University, on Communication Apprehension

J im McCroskey's academic interest had been in public speaking and debate, so it was somewhat by chance that he became involved in the study of what was to become a focus of his lifelong scholarship. One day, McCroskey got a call from a therapist at the West Virginia University's Psychology Center who was concerned about a student who was suicidal and kept repeating, "I just can't face giving my speech." The thought that some people's fear of speaking in public was so profound that they considered suicide preferable to speaking was so compelling to McCroskey that he began an in-depth study of what he eventually called "communication apprehension."

Although a lot had been written about what was then called "stage fright," McCroskey found that there was no agreement about its causes and no way to go about measuring it. Since that time, McCroskey has made a significant contribution to our understanding of communication apprehension and ways of measuring it. When instruments for measuring a variable are developed, they must be both valid and reliable—*valid* in that the instrument must be proved to measure apprehension and not other related things, and *reliable* so that people with similar amounts of apprehension will score the same and that people who are measured more than once will receive a similar score. McCroskey and his colleagues' work culminated in what is considered the primary measure of communication apprehension, the Personal Report of Communication Apprehension (PRCA). McCroskey first published this self-report instrument in 1970. Since then, there have been several versions.

From the research that uses the PRCA, we have learned that 15 to 20 percent of the U.S. population experiences high levels of "trait" communication apprehension. "Trait apprehension" means that some people seem to be predisposed to be appre-

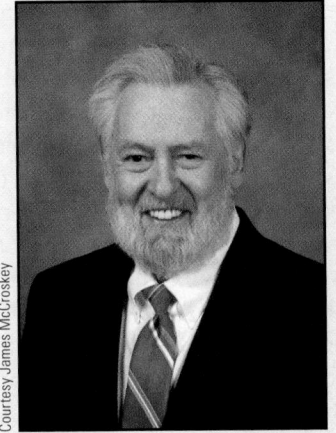

Courtesy James McCroskey

hensive and will show high levels of nervousness in all forms of speech including public speaking, interpersonal communication, and group communication. Likewise, we have learned that nearly everyone experiences times of high "state" communication apprehension. "State apprehension" means that under some circumstances, people will show high levels of nervousness in a single communication context such as public speaking.

What is next for McCroskey? Recently, he has begun to study genetic causes of apprehension. Although we can now identify those who suffer from communication apprehension and help them reduce their fears, there seem to be limits to how much reduction can take place for particular individuals. He believes genetic study is the wave of the future and may ultimately provide answers to dealing completely with communication apprehension.

Over the last 40 years, McCroskey has published more than 175 articles, 40 books, and 40 book chapters, and presented more than 250 convention papers. Currently, he teaches communication courses in instruction, organizational communication, interpersonal communication, nonverbal communication, and a graduate seminar.

As we might expect, McCroskey has received many awards for his scholarship, including the prestigious Robert J. Kibler Memorial Award of the National Communication Association and the Distinguished Research Award from the National Association of Teacher Educators. For a partial list of McCroskey's publications in communication apprehension, see the references at the end of this book.

McCroskey's scholarship—from identifying those with communication apprehension to finding ways to help people reduce their apprehension—has helped tremendous numbers of people become more competent communicators. For more information about McCroskey and his work, see http://www.jamescmccroskey.com/.

upset (or butterflies), flushed skin, sweating, shaking, light-headedness, rapid or heavy heartbeats, and verbal disfluencies including stuttering and vocalized pauses ("like," "you know," "ah," "um," and so on). Emotional symptoms include feeling anxious, worried, or upset. Symptoms can also include specific negative cognitions or thought patterns. For example, a highly apprehensive person might dwell on thoughts such as "I'm going to make a fool of myself," or "I just know that I'll blow it."

The level of public speaking apprehension we feel varies over the course of speaking. In an article written some years ago, researchers identified three phases of reaction that speakers proceed through: anticipation reaction, confrontation reaction, and adaptation reaction (Behnke & Carlile, 1971, p. 66). **Anticipation reaction** is the level of anxiety you experience prior to giving the speech, including the nervousness you feel while preparing and waiting to speak. Your **confrontation reaction** is the surge in your anxiety level that you feel as you begin your speech. This level begins to fall about a minute or so into your speech and will level off at your pre-speaking level about five minutes into your presentation. Your **adaptation reaction** is the gradual decline of your anxiety level that begins about one minute into the presentation and results in your anxiety level declining to its pre-speaking level in about five minutes.

The causes of public speaking apprehension are still being studied, but several sources have been suggested, including the idea that speaking apprehension may be inborn. Two other explanations for apprehension are negative reinforcement and underdeveloped skills.

Negative reinforcement concerns how others have responded to your public speaking endeavors in the past. If you experienced negative reactions, you will probably be more apprehensive about speaking in public than if you had been praised for your efforts (Motley, 1997, p. 2). But these feelings do not have to handicap future performances.

Underdeveloped skills (or "skill deficit" theory) was the earliest explanation for apprehension and continues to receive the attention of researchers. It suggests that many of us become apprehensive because we don't understand or perform the basic tasks associated with effective speech making. Luckily, in the past several chapters you have studied the Action Step process, which is designed to give you the skills you need to be successful.

Although knowing the skills of speech making is critical for reducing your apprehension, there are additional ways to manage and reduce your apprehension.

anticipation reaction
the level of anxiety you experience prior to giving the speech, including the nervousness you feel while preparing and waiting to speak.

confrontation reaction
the surge in your anxiety level that you feel as you begin your speech.

adaptation reaction
the gradual decline of your anxiety level that begins about one minute into the presentation and results in your anxiety level declining to its pre-speaking level in about five minutes.

Managing Your Apprehension

Many of us believe that we would be better off if we could be totally free from nervousness and apprehension. But based on years of study, Prof. Gerald Phillips has concluded that nervousness is not necessarily negative. He noted that "learning proceeds best when the organism is in a state of tension" (1977, p. 37). In fact, it helps to be a little nervous to do your best: If you are lackadaisical about giving a speech, you probably will not do a good job (Motley, 1997, p. 27).

Research also has confirmed that although most students in speaking courses experience apprehension, nearly all learn to cope with the nervousness (Phillips, 1977, p. 37). So how does this apply to you?

1. **Recognize that despite your apprehension, you can make it through your speech.** Very few people are so afflicted by public speaking apprehension that they are unable to function. You may not enjoy the "flutters" you experience, but you can still deliver an effective speech. In the years we've been teaching, we've only had two students who were so frightened that they were unable to give the speech. We have seen speakers forget some of what they planned to say, and some have strayed from their planned speech, but they all finished speaking. Moreover, we have had students who reported being scared stiff who actually gave excellent speeches.

2. **Realize that listeners may not perceive that you are anxious or nervous.** Some people increase their apprehension because they mistakenly think the audience will detect their fear. But the fact is that audience members are seldom aware of how nervous a person is. For instance, a classic study found that even speech instructors greatly underrate the amount of stage fright they believe a person has (Clevenger, 1959, p. 136).

3. **Understand that with careful preparation and rehearsal, apprehension will decrease.** If you follow the Speech Plan Action Steps that you have learned in this text, you will find yourself paying less attention to your apprehension as you become engrossed in the challenges of communicating with your particular audience. Moreover, by practicing for a speech, you'll reduce the anxiety you can expect to have if you are "winging it." A study by Kathleen Ellis reinforces previous research findings that students who believe they are competent speakers experience less public speaking apprehension than those who do not (Ellis, 1995, p. 73).

Techniques for Reducing Apprehension

Because there are multiple causes for our public speaking apprehension, there are multiple methods that can help us reduce our overall speech anxiety and also several specific techniques we can employ during a speech that are designed to control our nervousness in the moment.

1. **Visualization** is a method that reduces apprehension by helping you develop a mental picture of yourself giving a masterful speech. Joe Ayres and Theodore S. Hopf, two scholars who have conducted extensive research on visualization, have found that if people can visualize them-

visualization
a method that reduces apprehension by helping you develop a mental picture of yourself giving a masterful speech.

© Rick Rickman/NewSport/Corbis

Do you use positive self-talk to pump yourself up before you have an important event? Do the same before you speak. If you believe you can, you will.

selves going through an entire speech preparation and speech making process, they will have a much better chance of succeeding when they are speaking (1990, p. 77).

Visualization has been used extensively with athletes to improve sports performances. In a study of players trying to improve their foul-shooting percentages, players were divided into three groups. One group never practiced, another group practiced, and a third group visualized practicing. As we would expect, those who practiced improved far more than those who didn't. What seems amazing is that those who only visualized practicing improved almost as much as those who practiced (Scott 1997, p. 99). Imagine what happens when you visualize and also practice!

By visualizing the process of speech making, people seem to lower their general apprehension and they also report fewer negative thoughts when they actually speak (Ayres, Hopf, and Ayres, 1994, p. 256). So, you will want to use visualization activities as part of your speech preparation. One such activity is featured on your ThomsonNOW for *Communicate!*—access **Web Resource 15.1: Visualizing Your Success**. This audio feature will guide you through a visualization activity in which you will imagine your success at accomplishing the complete speech preparation and presentation process.

Thomson™
NOW!

systematic desensitization
a method that reduces apprehension by gradually having you visualize increasingly more frightening events.

2. **Systematic desensitization** is a method that reduces apprehension by gradually having you visualize increasingly more frightening events. The process involves consciously tensing and then relaxing muscle groups, to learn how to recognize the difference between the two states. Then, while in a relaxed state, you imagine yourself in successively more stressful situations—for example, researching a speech topic in the library, practicing the speech out loud to a roommate, and finally, giving

a speech. The ultimate goal of systematic desensitization is to have us transfer the calm feelings we attain while visualizing to the actual speaking event. Calmness on command—and it works.

3. **Public speaking skills training** is the systematic teaching of the skills associated with the processes involved in preparing and delivering an effective public speech, with the intention of improving speaking competence and thereby reducing public speaking apprehension.

Skills training is based on the assumption that some of our anxiety about speaking in public is due to our realization that we do not know how to be successful—that we lack the knowledge and behaviors to be effective. Therefore, if we learn the processes and behaviors associated with effective speech making, then we will be less anxious (Kelly, Phillips, & Keaen, 1995, pp. 11–13). Public speaking skills include those associated with the processes of goal analysis, audience and situation analysis, organization, delivery, and self-evaluation (ibid).

All three of the methods for reducing public speaking apprehension have been successful at helping people reduce their anxiety. Researchers are just beginning to conduct studies to identify which techniques are most appropriate for a particular person. A study conducted by Karen Kangas Dwyer suggests that the most effective program for combating apprehension is one that uses a variety of techniques, but individualizes these so that the techniques are used in an order that corresponds to the order in which the individual experiences apprehension (Dwyer, 2000). So, for example, when facing a speaking situation, if your immediate reaction is to think worrisome thoughts ("I don't know what I'm suppose to do," or "I'm going to make a fool out of myself"), which then lead you to feel nervous, you would be best served by first undergoing skills techniques. Another person who immediately feels the physical sensations (like nausea, rapid heartbeat, and so on) before thinking about the event would benefit from first learning systematic desensitization techniques; working with visualization or receiving skills training could follow. So to reduce your public speaking apprehension, you may need to use all three techniques, but use them in an order that matches the order in which you experience apprehension.

public speaking skills training
the systematic teaching of the skills associated with the processes involved in preparing and delivering an effective public speech, with the intention of improving speaking competence and thereby reducing public speaking apprehension.

OBSERVE & ANALYZE

Journal Activity

Controlling Nervousness

Interview one or two people who give frequent speeches (a minister, a politician, a lawyer, a businessperson, or a teacher). Ask what is likely to make them more or less nervous about giving the speech. Find out how they cope with their nervousness. Write a short paragraph summarizing what you have learned from the interviews. Then identify the behaviors used by those people that you believe might work for you.

Thomson NOW! You can complete this activity online and, if requested, e-mail it to your instructor. Use your Thomson-NOW for *Communicate!* to access **Skill Learning Activity 15.1**.

Elements of Delivery

The physical elements that affect the delivery of your speech are your voice, articulation, and bodily action.

Voice

Your voice is the vehicle that communicates the words of your speech to the audience. How you sound to your audience emphasizes, supplements, and, at times, even contradicts the meaning of the words you speak. As a result, the sound of your voice affects how successful you are in getting your ideas across. To use your voice well, it helps to understand how it works. The four major characteristics of voice are pitch, volume, rate, and quality. You can control these characteristics, to create vocal variety and emphasis that will help communicate your meaning effectively.

pitch
the scaled highness or lowness of the sound a voice makes.

Pitch refers to scaled highness or lowness of the sound a voice makes. Your voice is produced in the larynx by the vibration of your vocal folds. To feel this vibration, put your hand on your throat at the top of the Adam's apple and say "ah." Now, just as the pitch of a guitar string is changed by making it tighter or looser, so the pitch of your voice is changed by tightening and loosening the vocal folds. Natural pitch varies from person to person, but adult men generally have voices pitched lower than children and adult women. On average, people have a comfortable pitch range of more than an octave, which is eight full notes of a musical scale.

Most of us speak at a pitch range that is appropriate for us. Some people however, have pitch difficulties—that is, they have become accustomed to talking in tones that are either above or below their natural pitch. If you suspect that you have developed pitch difficulty, your instructor can refer you to a speech therapist who can help you readjust to your normal pitch. For most of us, when we speak, the question is not whether we have a satisfactory pitch range, but whether we are using our pitch range to help us communicate our thoughts.

volume
the degree of loudness of the tone you make as you normally exhale, your diaphragm relaxes, and air is expelled through the trachea.

Volume is the degree of loudness of the tone you make. As you normally exhale, your diaphragm relaxes, and air is expelled through the trachea. When you speak, you can increase the force of the expelled air on the vibrating vocal folds by contracting your abdominal muscles. This greater force behind the air you expel increases the volume of your tone.

To feel how these muscles work, place your hands on your sides with your fingers extended over the stomach. Say "ah" in a normal voice. Now say "ah" as loudly as you can. If you are making proper use of your muscles, you should feel an increase in stomach contractions as you increase volume. If you feel little or no stomach muscle contraction, you are probably trying to gain volume from the wrong source. This can result in tiredness, harshness, and lack of sufficient volume to be heard in a large room.

Regardless of your size, you can speak louder. If you are normally soft-spoken, you may have trouble talking loudly enough to be heard by an audience, so you will need to increase pressure from your abdominal area while you are talking.

rate
the speed at which you talk.

Rate is the speed at which you talk. In normal conversations, most people speak between 130 and 180 words per minute, but the rate that is best in a speech is determined by whether listeners can understand what you are saying. Usually, even a very fast rate of talking is acceptable if the ideas are not new and complex and when words are well articulated, with sufficient vocal variety and emphasis.

If you are told you speak too rapidly or too slowly, you may need to change your speaking rate. To do this, start by computing your speaking rate when reading written passages. First, read aloud for exactly three minutes. When you have finished, count the number of words you have read and divide by three to compute the number of words you read per minute. If you perceive that your reading rate significantly varied from the 130- to 180-word-per-minute range, then reread the same passage for another three-minute period, consciously decreasing or increasing the number of words you read. Again, count the words and divide by three.

At first, it may be difficult to change speed significantly, but with practice, you will see that you can read much more quickly or much more slowly when you want to. You may find that a different rate, whether faster or slower, will sound strange to you. To show improvement in your normal speaking, you have to learn to adjust your ear to a more appropriate rate of speed. If you practice daily, within a few weeks you should be able to accustom your ear to changes so that you can vary your rate with the type of material you read. As you gain confidence in your ability to alter your rate, you can practice with portions of speeches. You will talk more quickly when material is easy or when you are trying to create a mood of excitement; you will talk more slowly when the material is difficult or when you are trying to create a somber mood.

© 2004 by Sidney Harris

"LADIES AND GENTLEMEN... IS THAT MY VOICE?... I NEVER HEARD IT AMPLIFIED BEFORE. IT SOUNDS SO WEIRD. HELLO. HELLO. I CAN'T BELIEVE IT'S ME. WHAT A STRANGE SENSATION. ONE, TWO, THREE... HELLO. WOW..."

Quality is the tone, timbre, or sound of your voice. The best vocal quality is a clear and pleasant tone. Difficulties with quality include nasality ("talking through your nose" on vowel sounds), breathiness (too much escaping air during phonation), harshness (too much tension in the throat and chest), and hoarseness (a raspy sound). If you think your voice has one of these undesirable qualities, ask your instructor. If your instructor believes you need help, ask for a referral to a speech therapist, whose extensive knowledge of vocal anatomy and physiology can pinpoint your problem and help you correct it. (Many colleges have speech therapists on staff to work with students.)

quality
the tone, timbre, or sound of your voice.

Articulation

Articulation is using the tongue, palate, teeth, jaw movement, and lips to shape vocalized sounds that combine to produce a word. Articulation should not be confused with **pronunciation**—the form and accent of various syllables of a word. In the word "statistics," for instance, articulation refers to the shaping of the ten sounds (s-t-a-t-i-s-t-i-k-s); pronunciation refers to the grouping and accenting of the sounds (sta-tis'-tiks).

articulation
using the tongue, palate, teeth, jaw movement, and lips to shape vocalized sounds that combine to produce a word.

pronunciation
the form and accent of various syllables of a word.

Many speakers suffer from minor articulation problems such as adding a sound where none appears (ath**a**lete for athlete), leaving out a sound where one occurs (lib**a**ry for lib**r**ary), transposing sounds (rev**a**lent for rel**e**vant), and distorting sounds (tru**f** for tru**th**). Although some people have consistent articulation problems that require speech therapy (such as substituting *th* for *s* consistently in speech), most of us are guilty of habitual carelessness that is easily corrected.

Two of the most troublesome articulation problems for public speakers are slurring sounds (running sounds and words together) and leaving off word endings. Most spoken English contains some slurring of sounds. For instance, most English speakers are likely to say "tha-table," instead of "that table," because it is simply too difficult to make two *t* sounds in a row. But some people slur sounds and drop word endings to excess, making it difficult for listeners to understand. "Who ya gonna see?" for "Who are you going to see?" illustrates both of these errors.

If you have a mild case of "sluritis" caused by not taking time to form sounds clearly, you can make considerable improvement in articulation by taking 10 to 15 minutes three days a week to read passages aloud, and trying to overaccentuate each sound. Some teachers advocate "chewing" your words—that is, making sure that lips, jaw, and tongue move carefully for each sound you make. As with most other problems of delivery, to improve, speakers must work conscientiously for days, weeks, or months, depending on the severity of the problem.

Constant mispronunciation can give the impression that a speaker is unintelligent, so it is important to learn to articulate clearly. To complete an activity in which you can practice articulating difficult word combinations, use your ThomsonNOW for *Communicate!* to access **Skill Learning Activity 15.2: Articulation Practice**. In this activity, you will also access **Web Resource 15.2: Articulation Exercises**, where you will find a list of sentences that are difficult to articulate.

accent
the articulation, inflection, tone, and speech habits typical of the natives of a country, a region, or even a state or city.

A major concern of speakers from different cultures and different parts of the country is their **accent**—the articulation, inflection, tone, and speech habits typical of the natives of a country, a region, or even a state or city. Everyone speaks with some kind of an accent, because "accent" means any tone or inflection that differs from the way others speak. Natives of a particular city or region in the U.S. will speak with inflections and tones that they believe are "normal" for North American speech (for instance, people from the Northeast who drop the *r* sound (saying ca for car) or people from the South who "drawl." But when they visit a different city or region, they will be accused of having an "accent," because the people living in the city or region they visit hear inflections and tones that they perceive as *different* from their own speech.

When should people work to lessen or eliminate an accent? Only when the accent is so "heavy" or different from audience members that they have difficulty in communicating effectively, or if they expect to go into teaching, broadcasting, or other professions where an accent may have an adverse effect on their performance.

Bodily Action

When you deliver a speech, your meaning also depends on how your nonverbal bodily actions supplement the message of your voice. The nonverbal characteristics that affect your delivery are your facial expressions, gestures, movement, poise, and posture.

Facial expressions Your **facial expressions,** eye movement, and mouth movement convey your personableness. Audiences expect your expressions to vary and to be appropriate to what you are saying. Speakers who do not vary their facial expressions during their speech, but who wear deadpan expressions, perpetual grins, or scowls will be perceived by their audience as boring, insincere, or stern. Audiences respond positively to natural facial expressions that reflect what you are saying and how you feel about it.

facial expression
eye and mouth movement.

Gestures Your **gestures,** movements of your hands, arms, and fingers, describe and emphasize what you are saying. Some of us gesture a lot in our casual conversations, while others do not. If gesturing does not come easily to you, don't force yourself to gesture in a speech. Some people who normally use gestures find that, when giving a speech, they aren't able to gesture because they have clasped their hands behind their backs, put their hands in their pockets, or gripped the speaker's stand, and are unable to gracefully pry them free to gesture. As a result, they weirdly wiggle their elbows or appear stiff. To avoid this problem, when you practice and speak, leave your hands free so that they can be available to gesture as you normally do.

gestures
movements of your hands, arms, and fingers that describe and emphasize what you are saying.

Movement **Movement** refers to motion of the entire body. Some speakers stand perfectly still throughout an entire speech. Others are constantly on the move. In general, it is probably best to remain in one place unless you have some reason for moving. A little movement, however, adds action to a speech, so it may help hold attention. Ideally, movement should help to focus on a transition, emphasize an idea, or call attention to a particular aspect of a speech. Avoid such unmotivated movement as bobbing, weaving, shifting from foot to foot, or pacing from one side of the room to the other. At the beginning of your speech, stand up straight on both feet. If you find yourself in some peculiar posture during the course of the speech, return to the upright position, with your weight equally distributed on both feet.

movement
motion of the entire body.

Posture Your **posture** refers to the position or bearing of the body. In speeches, an upright stance and squared shoulders communicate a sense of poise to an audience. Speakers who slouch may give an unfavorable impression of themselves, including the impression of limited self-confidence and an uncaring attitude. As you practice, be aware of your posture and

posture
the position or bearing of the body.

You're Short, Besides!

by Dr. Sucheng Chan

Although nearly everyone shows nervousness at the thought of speaking in public, some people face more difficult situations than others. In this excerpt, Dr. Chan tells us about problems that, to many, would seem nearly impossible to surmount. Dr. Chan not only overcame apparent problems; she also used them as motivation to succeed.

1 was stricken simultaneously with pneumonia and polio at the age of four. Uncertain whether I had polio of the lungs, seven of the eight doctors who attended me—all practitioners of Western medicine—told my parents they should not feel optimistic about my survival. A Chinese fortune teller my mother consulted also gave a grim prognosis. All these pessimistic predictions notwithstanding, I hung onto life, if only by a thread. Being confined to bed was thus a mental agony as great as my physical pain. But I was determined to walk.

We left China as the Communist forces swept across the country in victory. We found an apartment in Hong Kong. After a year and a half in Hong Kong, we moved to Malaysia. The years in Malaysia were the happiest of my childhood even though I was consistently fending off children who ran after me calling, *"Baikah! Baikah!"* ("Cripple! Cripple!" in the Hokkien dialect commonly spoken in Malaysia). The taunts of children mattered little because I was a star pupil. I won one award after another for general scholarship as well as for art and public speaking. Whenever the school had important visitors, my teacher always called on me to recite in front of the class.

A significant event that marked me indelibly occurred when I was twelve. That year my school held a music recital and I was one of the students chosen to play the piano. I managed to get up the steps to the stage without any problem, but as I walked across the stage, I fell. Out of the audience, a voice said loudly and clearly, "Ayah! a *baikah* shouldn't be allowed to perform in public." I got up before anyone could get on stage to help me and, with tears streaming uncontrollably down my face, I rushed to the piano and began to play. That I managed to do so made me feel really strong. I never again feared ridicule.

Regardless of racial or cultural background, most handicapped people have to learn to find a balance between the desire to attain physical independence and the need to take care of ourselves by not overtaxing our bodies.

I've often wondered if I would have been a different person had I not been physically handicapped. I really don't know, though there is no question that being handicapped has marked me. But at the same time I usually do not *feel* handicapped—and consequently, I do not *act* handicapped. People are therefore less likely to treat me as a handicapped person. There is no doubt, however, that the lives of my parents, sister, husband, other family members, and some close friends have been affected by my physical condition. They have had to learn not to hide me away at home, not to feel embarrassed by how I look or react to people who say silly things to me, and not to resent me for the extra demands my condition makes on them. Perhaps the hardest thing for those who live with handicapped people is to know when and how to offer help.

So, has being physically handicapped been a handicap? It all depends on one's attitude. Some years ago, I told a friend that I had once said to an affirmative action compliance officer (somewhat sardonically since I do not believe in the head count approach to affirmative action) that the institution which employs me is triply lucky because it can count me as nonwhite, female, and handicapped. He responded, "Why don't you tell them to count you four times? . . . Remember, you're short, besides!"

Excerpted from Making Waves *by Asian Women United.*
© *1989 by Asian Women United. Reprinted by permission of the author.*

adjust it so that you remain upright, with your weight equally distributed on both feet. To read a thought-provoking discussion of how various body motions, including posture, affect audience attention during a speech, use your ThomsonNOW for *Communicate!* CD-ROM to access **Web Resource 15.3: Body Motions and Audience Attention**.

Poise **Poise** refers to assurance of manner. A poised speaker is able to avoid mannerisms that distract the audience, such as taking off or putting on glasses, jiggling pocket change, smacking the tongue, licking the lips, or scratching the nose, hand, or arm. As a general rule, anything that calls attention to itself is negative, and anything that helps reinforce an important idea is positive. Likewise, a poised speaker is able to control behaviors that accompany speech nervousness. Later in the chapter, we present several techniques you can use to reduce your nervousness.

poise
refers to assurance of manner.

Although all of these vocal characteristics and bodily actions may be difficult for speakers with specific handicaps to achieve, all speakers need to practice so that they are as effective at using their voice and body to create a conversational quality to their speaking as they can be. The Diverse Voices selection describes one woman's journey to build confidence and success.

Conversational Style

As you practice and deliver your speech, you will want to use your voice, articulation, and bodily action so that your presentation seems natural. A **conversational style** is an informal style of presenting a speech so that your audience feels you are talking with them, not at them. Five hallmarks of a conversational style are enthusiasm, vocal expressiveness, spontaneity, fluency, and eye contact.

conversational style
an informal style of presenting a speech so that your audience feels you are talking with them, not at them.

Enthusiasm

Enthusiasm is excitement or passion about your speech. If sounding enthusiastic does not come naturally to you, it will help if you have a topic that really excites you. Even normally enthusiastic people can have trouble sounding enthusiastic when they choose an uninspiring topic. Then, focus on how your listeners will benefit from what you have to say. If you are convinced that you have something worthwhile to communicate, you are likely to feel and show more enthusiasm.

enthusiasm
excitement or passion about your speech.

To validate the importance of enthusiasm, think of how your attitude toward a class differs depending on whether the professor's presentation says: "I'm really excited to be talking with you about geology (history, English lit)" or "I'd rather be anywhere than talking to you about this subject."

Time Life Pictures/Getty Image

No matter the topic of the speech, an enthusiastic speaker tends to hold an audience's attention and help them to remember his or her main points. What topic could you speak enthusiastically about?

A speaker who looks and sounds enthusiastic will be listened to, and that speaker's ideas will be remembered.

Vocal Expressiveness

vocal expressiveness
the contrasts in pitch, volume, rate, and quality that affect the meaning an audience gets from the sentences you speak.

Vocal expressiveness refers to the contrasts in pitch, volume, rate, and quality that affect the meaning an audience gets from the sentences you speak. Read the following sentence:

"We need to prosecute abusers."

What did the writer intend the focus of that sentence to be? Without hearing it spoken, it is difficult to say. Why? Because it is the vocal expressiveness that helps us understand meanings. Read the sentence aloud four times. Each time, **emphasize** (give a different shade of expressiveness to) a different word, and listen to how it changes the meaning. The first time, emphasize *We;* the second time, emphasize *need;* and so forth. Notice how each time you emphasize a different word, you subtly change the meaning of the sentence. The first time, the emphasis is on who should act. The second time, it is on the urgency and nonvoluntary nature of what is to be done. The third time, the emphasis is on what is to be done, and the final time the emphasis is on who needs to be acted upon. So, if you want to make sure that the audience understands your message, your voice must be expressive enough to delineate shades of meaning.

emphasis
giving different shades of expressiveness to words.

A total lack of vocal expressiveness produces a **monotone**—a voice in which the pitch, volume, and rate remain constant, with no word, idea, or sentence differing significantly from any other. Although few of us speak in a true monotone, many of us severely limit ourselves when we speak in public and use only two or three pitch levels and relatively unchang-

monotone
a voice in which the pitch, volume, and rate remain constant, with no word, idea, or sentence differing significantly from any other.

ing volume and rates. An actual or near monotone makes it difficult for an audience to maintain attention and can diminish the chances that your audience will understand what you are saying. So as you rehearse, you will want to work at developing vocal variety in what you are saying.

Spontaneity

Spontaneity is a naturalness that seems unrehearsed or memorized. A spontaneous speech delivery is fresh; it sounds as if the speaker is really thinking about both the ideas and the audience as he or she speaks. In contrast, labored speech sounds like a rote recitation and decreases the audience's attention to both speaker and speech.

Audiences often perceive a lack of spontaneity when speakers have memorized their speeches, because people who try to memorize often have to struggle so hard to remember the words that their delivery tends to become laborious. Although talented actors can make lines that they have spoken literally hundreds of times sound spontaneous and vocally expressive, most novice public speakers cannot.

How can you make your outlined and practiced speech still sound spontaneous? Learn the *ideas* of the speech instead of trying to memorize its words—you will maintain your spontaneity. Suppose someone asks you about the route you take on your drive to work. Because you are familiar with the route, you can present it spontaneously. You have never written out the route, nor have you memorized it—you simply know it. You develop spontaneity in public speaking by getting to know the ideas in your speech as well as you know the route you take to work. Study your outline and absorb the material you are going to present, and then enjoy talking with the audience about it.

spontaneity
a naturalness that seems unrehearsed or memorized.

Fluency

Effective delivery is also **fluent**—speech that flows easily, without hesitations and vocal interferences. Although most of us are occasionally guilty of using some vocal interferences such as *er, uh, well, OK, you know,* and *like.* These interferences become a problem when they are perceived by others as excessive and when they begin to call attention to themselves, thereby preventing listeners from concentrating on meaning.

fluency
speech that flows easily, without hesitations and vocal interferences.

Eye Contact

Eye contact is looking directly at the people to whom we are speaking. In speech making, it involves looking at people in all parts of an audience throughout a speech. As long as you are looking at someone (those in front of you, in the left rear of the room, in the right center of the room, and so on) and not at your notes or the ceiling, floor, or window, everyone in the audience will perceive you as having good eye contact with them.

eye contact
looking directly at the people to whom we are speaking.

Maintaining eye contact is important for several reasons.

1. **Maintaining eye contact helps audiences concentrate on the speech.** If speakers do not look at us while they talk, we are unlikely to maintain eye contact with them. This break in mutual eye contact often decreases concentration on the speaker's message.

2. **Maintaining eye contact increases the audience's confidence in you, the speaker.** Just as you are likely to be skeptical of people who do not look you in the eye as they converse, so too audiences will be skeptical of speakers who do not look at them. Eye contact is perceived as a sign of sincerity. Speakers who fail to maintain eye contact with audiences are perceived almost always as ill at ease and often as insincere or dishonest (Burgoon, et al., 1986).

3. **Maintaining eye contact helps you gain insight into the audience's reaction to the speech.** Because communication is two-way, your audience is speaking to you at the same time you are speaking to it. In conversation, the audience's response is likely to be both verbal and nonverbal; in public speaking, the audience's response is more likely to be shown by nonverbal cues alone. Audiences that pay attention are likely to look at you with varying amounts of intensity. Listeners who are bored yawn, look out the window, slouch in their chairs, and may even sleep. If audience members are confused, they will look puzzled; if they agree with what you say or understand it, they will nod their heads. By monitoring your audience's behavior, you can adjust by becoming more animated, offering additional examples, or moving more quickly through a point. If you are well prepared, you will be better equipped to make the adjustments and adapt to the needs of your audience.

One way of ensuring eye contact during your speech is to gaze at various groups of people in all parts of the audience throughout the speech. To establish effective eye contact, mentally divide your audience into small groups scattered around the room. Then, at random, talk for four to six seconds with each group. Eventually, you will find yourself going in a random pattern in which you look at all groups over a period of a few minutes. Using such a pattern helps you avoid spending a disproportionate amount of your time talking with those in front of you or in the center of the room.

Types of Delivery

Speeches vary in the amount of content preparation and the amount of practice that you do ahead of time. Each of these factors influences how a speech can be delivered. The three most common types of delivery are impromptu, scripted, and extemporaneous.

Impromptu Speeches

At times, you may be called on to speak "on the spot," with no notice or time to prepare. At a business meeting or in a class, you may be called upon to share what you know about a topic of interest. An **impromptu speech** is one that is delivered with only seconds or minutes of advance notice for preparation and is usually presented without referring to notes of any kind. You may have already been called on in this class to give an impromptu speech, so you know the pressure that comes with this type of speaking.

You can improve your impromptu performances by practicing mock impromptu speeches. For example, if you are taking a class in which the professor calls on students at random to answer questions, you can prepare by anticipating the questions that might be asked on the readings for the day and practice giving your answers. Over time, you will become more adept at organizing your answers and thinking on your feet.

impromptu speeches speeches that are delivered with only seconds or minutes of advance notice for preparation and usually presented without referring to notes of any kind.

Scripted Speeches

At the other extreme, there are situations in which you might carefully prepare a complete written manuscript of each word you will speak in your presentation. Then you will either memorize the text or read the text to the audience from a printed document or teleprompter. A **scripted speech** is one that is prepared by creating a complete written manuscript and delivered by rote memory or reading a written copy.

scripted speeches those that are prepared by creating a complete written manuscript and delivered by rote memory or by reading a written copy.

Obviously, effective scripted speeches take a great deal of time to prepare because both an outline and a word-for-word transcript must be prepared and perhaps memorized. When scripted speeches are memorized, you face the increased anxiety caused by fear of forgetting your lines. When you read a scripted speech, you must become adept at looking at the script with your peripheral vision so that you don't appear to be reading and can maintain eye contact with your audience.

Because of the time and skill required to effectively prepare and deliver a scripted speech, scripted speeches are usually reserved for important occasions that have grave consequences. Political speeches, keynote addresses at conventions, commencement addresses, and CEO remarks at annual stockholder meetings are examples of occasions when a scripted speech might be worth the effort.

Extemporaneous Speeches

Most speeches, whether at work, in the community, or in class, are delivered extemporaneously. An **extemporaneous speech** is researched and planned ahead of time, but the exact wording is not scripted and will vary from presentation to presentation. When speaking extemporaneously, you may refer to simple notes you have prepared to remind you of the ideas you want to present and the order in which you want to present them.

extemporaneous speeches speeches that are researched and planned ahead of time, although the exact wording is not scripted and will vary from presentation to presentation.

Extemporaneous speeches are the easiest to give effectively. Unlike impromptu speeches, when speaking extemporaneously, you are able to prepare your thoughts ahead of time, have notes to prompt you, and practice what you might actually say. Yet, unlike scripted speeches, extemporaneous speeches do not require as lengthy a preparation process to be effective. In the next section of this chapter, we describe how to rehearse successfully for an extemporaneous speech.

Rehearsal

rehearsing
practicing the presentation of your speech aloud.

Rehearsing is practicing the presentation of your speech aloud. In this section, we describe how to schedule your preparation and practice, prepare and use notes, and handle your visual aids, and we provide guidelines for effective rehearsal.

Scheduling and Conducting Rehearsal Sessions

Inexperienced speakers often believe they are ready to present the speech once they have finished their outline. But a speech that is not practiced is likely to be far less effective than it would have been had you given yourself sufficient practice time. In general, if you are not an experienced speaker, try to complete the outline at least two days before the speech is to be presented so that you have sufficient practice time to revise, evaluate, and mull over all aspects of the speech. Figure 15.1 provides a useful timetable for preparing a classroom speech.

Is it really necessary to practice a speech out loud? A study by Menzel and Carrell (1994) supports this notion and concludes that "The significance of rehearsing out loud probably reflects the fact that verbalization clarifies thought. As a result, oral rehearsal helps lead to success in the actual delivery of a speech" (p. 23).

Preparing Speaking Notes

speech notes
word or phrased outlines of your speech.

Prior to your first rehearsal session, prepare a draft of your speech notes. **Speech notes** are a word or phrase outline of your speech, including hard-to-remember information such as quotations and statistics designed to

7 days before	Select topic; begin research
6 days before	Continue research
5 days before	Outline body of speech
4 days before	Work on introduction and conclusion
3 days before	Finish outline; find additional material if needed; have all visual aids completed
2 days before	First rehearsal session
1 day before	Second rehearsal session
Due date	Give speech

Figure 15.1
Timetable for preparing a speech

help trigger memory. The best notes contain the fewest words possible written in lettering large enough to be seen instantly at a distance.

To develop your notes, begin by reducing your speech outline to an abbreviated outline of key phrases and words. Then, if you have details in the speech for which you must have a perfectly accurate representation—such as a specific example, a quotation, or a set of statistics—add these in the appropriate spot. Finally, indicate exactly where you plan to show visual aids.

Making speaking notes not only provides you with prompts when you are speaking, but also helps you cement the flow of the speech's ideas in your mind.

For a three- to five-minute speech, you will need only one or two 3 × 5-inch note cards to record your speaking notes. In longer speeches, you might need one card for the introduction, one for each main point, and one for the conclusion. If your speech contains a particularly important and long quotation or a complicated set of statistics, you can record this information in detail on separate cards. Figure 15.2 shows how Emming could represent his complete outline (shown on pages 334–335 of Chapter 13) on two 3 × 5 note cards.

Note Card 1

Intro

How many hounded by vendors?
Three criteria: 1 IR, 2 Fee, 3 Inducements

Body

1st C: Examine interest rates

IRs are % that a company charges to carry balance
■ Average of 8%
■ As much as 21%
■ Start as low as 0 to 8%—but contain restrictions
IR's variable or fixed
■ Variable—change month to month
■ Fixed—stay same
(Considered IRs: look at next criterion)

Note Card 2

2d C: Examine the annual fee—charges vary
■ Some, no annual fee
■ Most companies average around $25
(After considered interest and fees, weigh benefits)
3d C: Weigh inducements
■ Rebates
■ Freq flier miles
■ Discounts
Inducements not outweigh other factors

Conclusion

So, 3 criteria: IRs, annual fees, inducements

Figure 15.2
Note cards

During practice sessions, use the notes as you would in the speech. If you will use a podium, set the notes on the speaker's stand or, alternatively, hold them in one hand and refer to them only when needed. How important is it to construct good note cards? Speakers often find that the act of making a note card is so effective in helping cement ideas in the mind that during practice, or later during the speech itself, they do not need to use the notes at all.

Using Visual Aids during the Speech

Many speakers think that once they have prepared good visual aids, they will have no trouble using them in the speech. However, many speeches with good visual aids have become a shambles because the aids were not well handled. You can avoid problems by following these guidelines:

1. **Carefully plan when to use visual aids.** Indicate on your outline (and mark on your speaking notes) exactly when you will display each visual aid and when you will remove it. Practice introducing visual aids, handling them until you can use them comfortably and smoothly.

2. **Consider audience needs carefully.** As you practice, consider eliminating any visual aid that does not contribute substantially and directly to the audience's attention to, understanding of, or retention of the key ideas in the speech.

3. **Show a visual aid only when talking about it.** Because visual aids will draw audience attention, practice displaying them only when you are talking about them, and then remove visual aids from sight when they are no longer the focus of attention.

   A single visual aid may contain several bits of information. To keep audience attention where you want it, you can prepare the visual aid so that you only expose the portion of the visual aid that you are currently discussing.

4. **Describe specific aspects of the visual aid while showing it.** Practice helping your audience to understand the visual aid by verbally telling your audience what to look for, describing various parts, and interpreting figures, symbols, and percentages.

5. **Display visual aids so that everyone in the audience can see them.** It's frustrating not to be able to see a visual aid. So, if you hold the visual aid, practice positioning it away from your body and pointing it toward all parts of the audience. If you place your visual aid on a chalkboard or easel or mount it in some way, practice standing to one side and pointing with the arm nearest the visual aid. If it is necessary to roll or fold the visual aid, bring some transparent tape to mount it to the chalkboard or wall so that it does not unroll or wrinkle. If you are projecting your visual aid, try to practice in the space where you will give your speech so you will know how to position the equipment so that the image is the

What are the risks of using living things as visual aids?

appropriate size and in focus. If you cannot practice ahead of the date, be sure to arrive early enough on the day of the presentation to practice quickly with the equipment you will use.

6. **Talk to your audience, not to the visual aid.** Although you will want to acknowledge the visual aid by looking at it occasionally, it is important to keep your eye contact focused on your audience. When speakers become too engrossed in their visual aids, looking at the aid instead of at the audience, audience members can become bored. So as you practice, resist the urge to stare at your visual aid.

7. **Carefully consider the disadvantages of passing objects through the audience.** People look at, read, handle, and think about whatever they hold in their hands. While they are so occupied, they are not likely to be listening to you. So if you have a powerful and essential visual aid that must be passed, consider what you will do to maintain audience focus on what you are saying.

Practicing the Speech

Just as with any other activity, effective speech making requires practice, and the more you practice, the better your speech will be. During practice sessions, you have three major goals. First, you will practice wording your ideas so they are vivid and emphatic. Second, you will practice your speech by working with your voice and body so that your ideas are delivered with enthusiasm, appropriate emphasis, and spontaneity. Third, you will practice using visual aids. As part of each practice you will want to analyze how well it went and set goals for the next practice session. Let's look at how you can proceed through several practice rounds.

First practice Your initial rehearsal should include the following steps:

1. Audiotape your practice session. If you do not own a recorder, try to borrow one. You may also want to have a friend sit in on your practice.

2. Read through your complete sentence outline once or twice to refresh memory. Then put the outline out of sight and practice the speech using only the note cards you have prepared.

3. Make the practice as similar to the speech situation as possible, including using the visual aids you've prepared. Stand up and face your imaginary audience. Pretend that the chairs, lamps, books, and other objects in your practice room are people.

4. Write down the time that you begin.

5. Begin speaking. Regardless of what happens, keep going until you have presented your entire speech. If you goof, make a repair as you would have to do if you were actually delivering the speech to an audience.

6. Write down the time you finish. Compute the length of the speech for this first rehearsal.

Analysis Listen to the tape and look at your complete outline. How did it go? Did you leave out any key ideas? Did you talk too long on any one point and not long enough on another? Did you clarify each of your points? Did you adapt to your anticipated audience? (If you had a friend or relative listen to your practices, have him or her help with your analysis.) Were your note cards effective? How well did you do with your visual aids? Make any necessary changes before your second rehearsal.

Second practice Repeat the six steps outlined for the first rehearsal. By practicing a second time right after your analysis, you are more likely to make the kind of adjustments that begin to improve the speech.

Additional practices After you have completed one full rehearsal session, consisting of two practices and analysis, put the speech away until that night or the next day. Although you should rehearse the speech at least one more time, you will not benefit if you cram all the practices into one long rehearsal time. You may find that a final practice right before you go to bed will be very helpful; while you are sleeping, your subconscious will continue to work on the speech. As a result, you are likely to find

Action Step 5̄

Rehearsing Your Speech

The goal of this activity is to rehearse your speech, analyze it, and rehearse it again. One complete rehearsal includes a practice, an analysis, and a second practice.

1. Find a place where you can be alone to practice your speech. Follow the six points of the first practice as listed on p. 398.

2. Listen to the tape. Review your outline as you listen and then answer the following questions.

   Are you satisfied with how well:
   The introduction got attention and led into the speech? _____
   Main points were clearly stated? _____ And well developed? _____
   Material adapted to the audience? _____
   Section transitions were used? _____
   The conclusion summarized the main points? _____ Left the speech
      on a high note? _____
   Visual aids were used? _____
   Ideas were expressed vividly? _____ And emphatically? _____
   You maintained a conversational tone throughout? _____
   Sounded enthusiastic? _____ Sounded spontaneous? _____ Spoke
      fluently? _____

   List the three most important changes you will make in your next
   practice session:
   One: _____
   Two: _____
   Three: _____

3. Go through the six steps outlined for the first practice again. Then assess: Did you achieve the goals you set for the second practice? _____
   Reevaluate the speech using the checklist and continue to practice until you are satisfied with all parts of your presentation.

Thomson™
NOW! You can use your Student Workbook to complete this activity, or you can complete it online, print out copies of the Rehearsal Analysis Sheet, see a student sample of a practice round, and, if requested, e-mail your work to your instructor. Use your ThomsonNOW for *Communicate!* to access **Skill Learning Activity 15.4**.

significant improvement in your mastery of the speech when you practice again the next day.

How many times you practice depends on many variables, including your experience, your familiarity with the subject, and the length of your speech.

Criteria for Evaluating Speeches

In addition to learning to prepare and present speeches, you are learning to evaluate (critically analyze) the speeches you hear. From an educational standpoint, critical analysis of speeches provides the speaker with both an analysis of where the speech went right and where it went wrong, and it also gives you, the critic, insight into the methods that you want to incorporate or, perhaps, avoid in presenting your own speeches.

▶ Speech Assignment: Communicate on Your Feet

Presenting Your First Speech

1. Follow the speech plan action steps to prepare an informative or persuasive speech. The time and other parameters for this assignment will be announced by your instructor.

2. Criteria for evaluation include all the essentials of topic and purpose, content, organization, and presentation, but special emphasis will be placed on clarity of goal, clarity and appropriateness of main points, and delivery (items that are grouped under the boldface headings in the Speech Critique Checklist). As you practice your speech, you can use the checklist to ensure that you are meeting the basic criteria in your speech. In addition, you may want to refer to the sample student outline and speech that follow this assignment box.

3. Prior to presenting your speech, prepare a complete sentence outline and a written plan for adapting your speech to the audience.

If you have used Speech Builder Express to complete the action step activities online, you will be able to print out a copy of your completed outline. Your adaptation plan should describe how you plan to verbally and visually adapt your material to the audience, and should address how you will:

Indicate key aspects of audience to which you will need to adapt
Establish common ground
Build and maintain audience interest
Adjust to the audience's knowledge and sophistication
Build speaker credibility
Adapt to audiences' attitudes toward your speech goal
Adapt to audiences from different cultures and language communities (if relevant for you in this speech)
Use visual aids to enhance audience understanding and memory

If you completed the Action Step activities in Chapter 14, you can use them to form the basis of your written adaptation plan.

Although speech criticism is context specific (analyzing the effectiveness of an informative demonstration speech differs from analyzing the effectiveness of a persuasive action speech), in this section we look at criteria for evaluating public speaking in general. Classroom speeches are usually evaluated on the basis of how well the speaker has met specific criteria of effective speaking.

In Chapters 12 through 15, as you have been learning the Action Steps, you have also been learning the criteria by which speeches are measured. The critical assumption is that if a speech has good content that is well organized and adapted to the audience, and if it is delivered well, it is likely to achieve its goal. Thus, you can evaluate any speech by answering questions that relate to the basics of content, organization, and presentation. Figure 15.3 is a diagnostic speech checklist. You can use this checklist to analyze your first speech during your rehearsal period and to critique sample student speeches at the end of this chapter.

Thinking Critically about Speeches

Check all items that were accomplished effectively.

Content

_____ 1. Was the goal of the speech clear?
_____ 2. Did the speaker have high-quality information?
_____ 3. Did the speaker use a variety of kinds of developmental material?
_____ 4. Were visual aids appropriate and well used?
_____ 5. Did the speaker establish common ground and adapt the content to the audience's interests, knowledge, and attitudes?

Organization

_____ 6. Did the introduction gain attention and goodwill for the speaker, and did it lead into the speech?
_____ 7. Were the main points clear, parallel, and in meaningful complete sentences?
_____ 8. Did transitions lead smoothly from one point to another?
_____ 9. Did the conclusion tie the speech together?

Presentation

_____ 10. Was the language clear?
_____ 11. Was the language vivid?
_____ 12. Was the language emphatic?
_____ 13. Did the speaker sound enthusiastic?
_____ 14. Did the speaker show sufficient vocal expressiveness?
_____ 15. Was the presentation spontaneous?
_____ 16. Was the presentation fluent?
_____ 17. Did the speaker look at the audience?
_____ 18. Were the pronunciation and articulation acceptable?
_____ 19. Did the speaker have good posture?
_____ 20. Was speaker movement appropriate?
_____ 21. Did the speaker have sufficient poise?

Based on these criteria, evaluate the speech as (check one):
_____ excellent, _____ good, _____ satisfactory, _____ fair, _____ poor.

Figure 15.3
Speech critique checklist

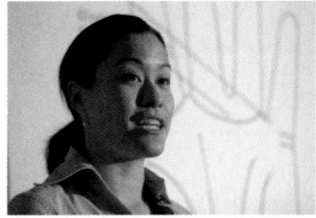

Sample Speech: Chinese Fortune Telling Adapted from a Speech by Chung-Yan Man, Collin County Community College*

1. Review the outline and adaptation plan developed by Chung-Yan Man in preparing his speech on Chinese fortune telling.
2. Then read the transcript of Chung-Yan's speech.
3. Use the Speech Critique Checklist from Figure 15.3 to help you evaluate this speech.

4. Use your ThomsonNOW for *Communicate!* to watch a video clip of a student presenting Chung-Yan's speech in class. (See the inside back cover of this book for how to access the speech videos through ThomsonNOW.)
5. Write a paragraph of feedback to Chung-Yan describing the strengths of his presentation and what he might do next time to be more effective.

You can use your Student Workbook to complete this activity, or you can use your ThomsonNOW for *Communicate!* to complete it online, print a copy of the Speech Critique Checklist, compare your feedback to that of the authors, and, if requested, e-mail your work to your instructor. Access **Skill Learning Activity 15.5**.

Adaptation Plan

1. **Key aspects of audience.** The majority of listeners are not familiar with Chinese culture and have had little exposure to Chinese mysticism.
2. **Establishing and maintaining common ground.** My main way of establishing common ground will be by using personal pronouns.
3. **Building and maintaining interest.** Because interest is not automatic, I will provide a variety of examples to pique audience interest.
4. **Audience knowledge and sophistication.** Because most of the class is not familiar with Chinese fortune telling, I will introduce them to the three most common forms of fortune telling. I believe that by repeating key points and by using a variety of examples, the audience will be more likely to retain the information.
5. **Building credibility.** Because I am Chinese, the audience will assume that I am familiar with the culture, and I will reinforce this as I speak.
6. **Audience attitudes.** The audience is likely to be curious but skeptical.
7. **Adapting to audiences from different cultures and language communities.** Because most audience members come from a different culture and

---

*Used with permission of Chung-Yan Man.

language community than I do and are unfamiliar with these practices, I will be careful to describe these techniques in everyday language.

8. **Using visual aids to enhance audience understanding and memory.** I will show an overhead transparency of the palm of a hand, a transparency of a face, and samples of the sticks used in joss stick fortune telling.

Speech Outline

General purpose: To inform.

Speech goal: I want my audience to appreciate three different kinds of Chinese fortune telling.

Introduction

I. Do you want to know what your future will be?
II. In general, people want to know the future, because knowledge of the future means control of the future.
III. As you know, I am from Hong Kong and I have experienced the mysterious and unique practice of fortune telling in the traditional Chinese culture.
IV. So, today I am going to going to talk about three different forms of Chinese fortune telling.

Body

I. One kind of Chinese fortune telling you may have heard of is palm reading.
   A. Palm reading, also termed palmistry, is the process of foretelling one's future by the imprints and marks on the palm.
      1. Palmistry is based upon the interpretation of the general characteristics of one's hands.
      2. Palmistry focuses on the study of lines, their patterns, and other formations and marks that appear on the palms and fingers. *(Overhead 1: Picture of palm with heart, head, and life lines labeled.)*
   B. Palmistry is divided into two subfields: the palm itself and the fingers.
      1. The three principle lines on your palm are heart, head, and life lines: if lines are deep, clear, and have no interruptions, it is a sign of a smooth and successful life.
      2. Fingers are also important in palm reading: length of the index and ring figure each indicates different beliefs.

Transition: So now that you have understood the basic ideas of palm reading, let us go on to a second kind of Chinese fortune telling, face reading.

II. The Chinese believe that the face can also be used to predict the future and fortune of an individual.
   A. Face reading is the Chinese art of predicting a person's future and fortunes by analyzing the different elements of his or her face. *(Overhead 2: Simple line drawing of a Chinese face.)*
      1. The major facial features that are used in developing the fortune are the nose, mouth, forehead, eyebrows, and eyes.
      2. The face shapes show basic constitution and attributes.
   B. Balance and proportion are important in face reading, as in paintings.

Transition: The final type of Chinese fortune telling uses joss sticks—you may be least familiar with this practice.

III. The oldest known method of fortune telling in the world is the use of fortune-telling sticks.
   A. It is to give an indication of the possibilities of the future instead of exactly what will happen.
   B. This method, which is part of religious practice, takes place in a temple.
      1. A believer selects numbered sticks from a bamboo case containing 78 sticks.
      2. Prayers burn joss sticks, then kneel before the main altar.

Conclusion

I. In conclusion, when people know more about Chinese fortune telling, they begin to understand that these methods are quite scientific and, to a certain extent, accurate.

II. So, I hope what you have learned today about palmistry, face reading, and joss sticks will give you an appreciation for Chinese culture and fortune-telling practices.

Works Cited

Bright, Maura. "Chinese Face Reading for Health Diagnosis and Self Knowledge." 2001. The Wholistic Research Company. 18 Oct. 2005. http://www.wholisticresearch.com/info/artshow.php3?artid=96.

Chan, King-Man Stephen. *Fortune Telling.* May. 2005. Chinese University of Hong Kong. 15 Oct. 2005. http://www.se.cuhk.edu.hk/~palm/chinese/fortune/ .

"Fortune Telling." *Chinese Customs.* 2003. British Born Chinese. 17 Oct. 2005. http://www.britishbornchinese.org.uk/pages/culture/customs/fortunetelling.html.

"Most Popular." *Wong Tai Sin Temple.* 18 Oct. 2005. Hong Kong Tourism Board. 18 Oct. 2005. http://www.discoverhongkong.com/eng/touring/popular/ta_popu_wong.jhtml.

"What is Palmistry?" 2004. *Palmistry.* 16 Oct. 2005. http://www.findyourfate.com/palmistry/palmistry.htm.

Speech and Analysis

Speech

Let me ask you a question: Do you want to know what your future will be? Don't all of us want to know? A lot of people want to know what the future will bring, because knowing it means that you can control the future. I am from Hong Kong, and in China we *can* tell the future. Well, actually, we can experience the mysterious and unique practice of fortune telling that is part of traditional Chinese culture. Today I am going to talk about three different kinds of Chinese fortune telling: the palm reading, the face reading, and the fortune-telling sticks.

One kind of Chinese fortune telling is palm reading. According to Stephen Chan in his web article "Fortune Telling," palm reading is the process of foretelling one's future by examining and interpreting the imprints, marks, and other general characteristics of one's hands. Palm reading, which is also known as palmistry, is divided into two subfields: the palm itself and each of the fingers. Take a look at your palm for a minute. The "What Is Palmistry?" page on FindYourFate .com tells us that the three principle lines on your palm are your heart, head, and life lines—the heart line is the long line up at the top of your palm; the head line is the line just below it that also runs across your palm; and the life line is the line running from the bottom of your palm and kind of arcing toward your thumb. If these lines are deep, clear, and have no breaks

Analysis

These opening rhetorical questions are designed to make the audience curious about the topic.

In this sentence, Chung-Yan establishes his credibility.

His thesis statement previews his three main points: the three types of Chinese fortune telling he will discuss.

His first main point focuses on the first type of fortune telling: palm reading.
Notice how he documents the definition.

He has two subpoints, which he quickly previews before explaining each.
Here he attempts to get the audience involved in identifying the nature of their own palm lines: the heart line, the head line, and the life line.

He encourages the audience to see whether these lines are deep, clear, or interruptions, it is a sign of a smooth and successful life. The length, shape, and spacing of the fingers are also important aspects of a palm reading. For example the lengths of the index and ring fingers indicate different aspects of your personality, such as whether or not you are a leader, artistic, or reckless in nature.

So now that you understand the basic ideas of palm reading, let's move on to a second kind of Chinese fortune telling, face reading. The Chinese believe that the face also can be used to predict the future and fortune of a person. In face reading, the fortune teller analyzes the different elements of a person's face. According to Maura Bright's web page, the major facial features used to determine a person's fortune are the nose, mouth, forehead, eyebrows, and eyes. The shape and condition of the face indicate a person's basic constitution, personality, and attributes. For example, a long, narrow face indicates that you are a leader and an organizer, whereas a short and square face means that you are practical and reliable. The balance and proportion of all your features are also important in face reading, just as they are in paintings.

Last but not least, the Chinese also use fortune-telling joss sticks. This is the oldest known method of fortune telling in the world. Joss sticks are a type of incense, and they are used to indicate the *possibilities* of the future, instead of exactly what will happen. This method of fortune telling, which is part of Chinese folk religious practice, takes place in a temple.

and without breaks or interruptions. But he doesn't really develop what "interruptions" might mean. The audience is left to guess.

He goes on to note the importance of the length, shape, and spacing of the fingers in palm reading. But again, he doesn't really develop the point.

Chung-Yan's transition signals that he will begin discussing a new type of fortune telling.

Again, he acknowledges the source of his information.

Chung-Yan gives a good example of how face shape is used to predict personal characteristics, but he doesn't explain how individual features or balance and proportion affect one's fortune.

Although better than no transition, this transition is trite and neither summarizes nor previews the main points.

Chung-Yan needed to clarify the difference between a "possibility" and an "exact future." An example would have helped.

As described on the "Most Popular" page of the Hong Kong Tourist Board's web site, a believer seeking his or her fortune lights a joss stick, kneels before a main altar and makes a wish, then selects a fortune stick from a bamboo case containing 78 numbered sticks. The fortune seeker exchanges the stick for a piece of paper with the same number on it, and his or her fortune is written on the paper.

Although he explains the process, this point would be made more meaningful with more detail. For example, what type of temple? Is the believer seeking an answer to a particular question, or is this a general fortune?

In conclusion, when people know more about Chinese fortune telling, they begin to understand that these methods are actually based in scientific fact and, to a certain extent, are accurate. I hope what you have learned today about palmistry, face reading, and joss sticks will give you an appreciation for Chinese culture and traditional fortune-telling practices.

In this conclusion, Chung-Yan claims that these practices are based on "scientific facts" and are "accurate." Yet nothing in the body of the speech supports this conclusion.

The speech has several strengths: it is well organized, has three distinct main points, uses several sources, and has clear transitions. But the material is covered very superficially. Chung-Yan might have given a better speech if he had limited his goal and only spoken about one type of Chinese fortune telling. Then he would have had time to elaborate so the audience would really understand.

Summary

Although speeches may be presented impromptu, by manuscript, or by memory, the material you have been reading is designed to help you present your speeches extemporaneously—that is, carefully prepared and practiced, but with the exact wording determined at the time of utterance.

Even though almost all of us experience public speaking apprehension, only 15 percent or less experience high levels of fear. The signs of speaking apprehension, or stage fright, vary from individual to individual. The causes of apprehension are still being studied—in fact, some speaking apprehension may be inborn. You can learn to manage it by recognizing that despite apprehension, you can make it through your speech by preparing carefully and rehearsing your speech.

What Would You Do?

Nalini sighed loudly as the club members of Toastmasters International took their seats. It was her first time meeting with the public speaking group, and she didn't want to be there, but her mom had insisted that she join the club in the hopes that it would help Nalini transfer from her community college to the state university. It wasn't that the idea of public speaking scared Nalini. She had already spent time in front of an audience as the lead singer of the defunct emo band, Deathstar. To Nalini's mind, public speaking was just another type of performance, like singing or acting, albeit a stuffy form better suited to middle-aged men and women than people her own age, a sentiment that explained why she wanted to be elsewhere at the moment.

After the club leader called the meeting to order, he asked each of the new members to stand, introduce themselves, and give a brief speech describing their background, aspirations, and reasons for joining the club. "Spare me," Nalini muttered loud enough for those next to her to hear. The club leader then called on a young woman to

Nalini's left, who rose and began to speak about her dream of becoming a lawyer and doing public advocacy work for the poor. After the young woman sat down, the club members applauded politely. Nalini whistled and clapped loudly and kept on clapping after the others had stopped.

The club leader, somewhat taken aback, called on Nalini next. She rose from her seat and introduced herself as the secret love child of a former president and a famous actress. Nalini then strung together a series of other fantastic lies about her past and her ambitions. She concluded her speech by saying that she had joined the club in the hopes that she could learn how to hypnotize audiences into obeying her commands. After Nalini sat, a few of the club members applauded quietly, while others cast glances at each other and the club leader.

1. Is mocking behavior in a formal public speaking setting, either by an audience member or a speaker, an ethical matter? Explain your answer.

2. What ethical obligations does an audience member have to a speaker? What about a speaker to his or her audience?

The major elements of speech delivery are voice (pitch, volume, rate, and quality), articulation (the shaping of sounds to produce words), and bodily action (facial expression, gestures, movement, and posture).

Effective speakers work to develop a conversational style, the major elements of which are enthusiasm, vocal expressiveness, spontaneity, fluency, and eye contact.

Three of the most common types of speech delivery are impromptu speaking (talking "on the spot"), scripted speeches (completely written manuscripts), and extemporaneous speaking (speeches that are researched, planned ahead, but not scripted).

Effective delivery also requires rehearsal. Experienced speakers schedule and conduct rehearsal sessions. Once outlines are complete, effective speakers usually rehearse at least twice, often using speech notes on cards that include key phrases and words.

In many cases, speakers may use visual aids to help audiences understand and remember the material. To be effective, visual aids need to be carefully planned, shown only when being talked about, and displayed so that all can see. Moreover, effective speakers talk to the audience, not the visual aid.

In addition to preparing and presenting, you are also learning to evaluate the speeches you hear, focusing on speech content, organization, presentation, and adaptation.

Thomson™ NOW!

Communicate! Online

Now that you have read Chapter 15, use your ThomsonNOW for *Communicate!* for quick access to the electronic resources that accompany this text. Your ThomsonNOW gives you access to the video of Chung-Yan's speech on Chinese fortune telling, the Web Resources and Skill Learning Activities featured in this chapter, InfoTrac College Edition, and online study aids such as a digital glossary and review quizzes.

Your *Communicate!* ThomsonNOW is an online study system that helps you identify concepts you don't fully understand, allowing you to put your study time to the best use. Using chapter-by-chapter diagnostic pre-tests, the system creates a personalized study plan for each chapter. Each plan directs you to specific resources designed to improve your understanding, including pages from the text in e-book format. Chapter post-tests give you an opportunity to measure how much you've learned and let you know if you are ready for graded quizzes and exams.

Key Terms

Go to your ThomsonNOW for *Communicate!* to access your online glossary for Chapter 15. Print a copy of the glossary for this chapter and test yourself with the electronic flash cards or complete the crossword puzzle to help you master these key terms:

accent (386)
adaptation reaction (380)
anticipation reaction (380)
articulation (385)
confrontation reaction (380)
conversational style (389)
emphasis (390)
enthusiasm (389)
extemporaneous speeches (393)
eye contact (391)
facial expression (387)
fluency (391)

gestures (387)
impromptu speeches (393)
monotone (390)
movement (387)
pitch (384)
poise (389)
posture (387)
pronunciation (385)
public speaking apprehension (378)
public speaking skills training (383)
rate (384)

rehearsing (394)
quality (385)
scripted speeches (393)
speech notes (394)
spontaneity (391)
systematic desensitization (382)
visualization (381)
vocal expressiveness (390)
volume (384)

Review Quiz

Test your knowledge of the concepts in this chapter by taking the online review quiz for Chapter 15. Go to your ThomsonNOW for *Communicate!* to access the quiz. When you have completed the quiz, submit it for scoring.

Skill Learning Activities

Complete the Observe & Analyze, Test Your Competence, and Speech and Analysis activities for Chapter 15 online at your ThomsonNOW for *Communicate!* You can submit your Observe & Analyze, Action Step, and Speech and Analysis answers to your instructor, and compare your Test Your Competence and Speech and Analysis answers to those provided by the authors.

15.1: Observe & Analyze: Controlling Nervousness (383)

15.2: Test Your Competence: Articulation Practice (386)

15.3: Observe & Analyze: Evaluating Speaker Vocal and Body Action Behaviors (392)

15.4: Action Step 5: Rehearsing Your Speech (399)

15.5: Speech and Analysis: Chinese Fortune Telling (402)

Web Resources

Go to your ThomsonNOW for *Communicate!* to access the Web Resources for this chapter.

15.1: Visualizing Your Success (382)

15.2: Articulation Exercises (386)

15.3: Body Motions and Audience Attention (389)

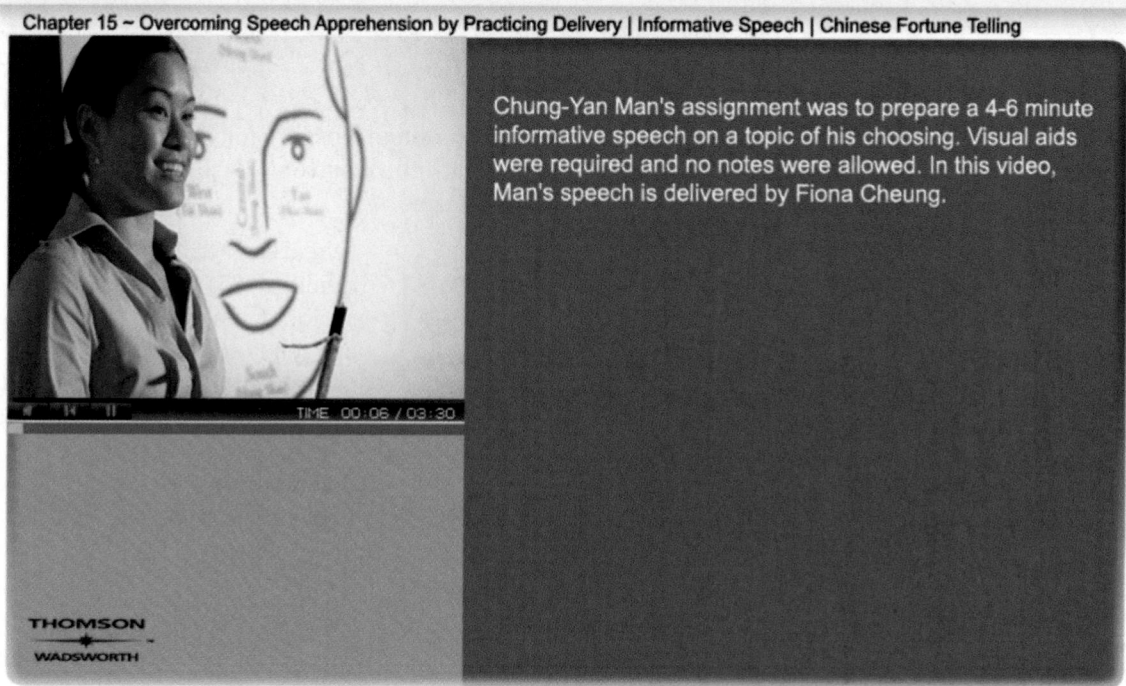

Chapter 15 ~ Overcoming Speech Apprehension by Practicing Delivery | Informative Speech | Chinese Fortune Telling

Chung-Yan Man's assignment was to prepare a 4-6 minute informative speech on a topic of his choosing. Visual aids were required and no notes were allowed. In this video, Man's speech is delivered by Fiona Cheung.

TIME 00:06 / 03:30

THOMSON
WADSWORTH

OBJECTIVES

After you have read this chapter, you should be able to answer these questions:

- What are the characteristics of informative speaking?
- What makes speeches intellectually stimulating?
- What makes speeches creative?
- What key techniques can you use to improve memory?
- What are the major methods of informing?
- What are the common informative frameworks?
- What are the major elements of process speeches?
- What are the major types of expository speeches?

16
Informative Speaking

For several months, a major architectural firm had been working on designs for the arts center to be built in the middle of downtown. Members of the city council, guests from various constituencies in the city, and a number of concerned citizens were taking seats as the long-anticipated presentation was about to begin. As Linda Garner, mayor and presiding officer of the city council, finished her introduction, Donald Harper, the principal architect of the project, walked to the microphone to begin his speech about the proposed design.

his is but one of many scenes played out every day when experts deliver speeches to help others understand complex information. In the last four chapters, we described the basic action steps that you will use to prepare any kind of speech. Now in this chapter, we go beyond the basics and focus on the characteristics of good informative speaking and the methods that you can use to develop an effective informative speech.

An **informative speech** is one that has a goal to explain or describe facts, truths, and principles in a way that stimulates interest, facilitates understanding, and increases likelihood that audiences will remember. In short, informative speeches are designed to educate an audience. Thus, most lectures that your instructors present in class are classified as informative speeches (although, as you are aware, they may range from excellent to poor in quality).

In the first section of this chapter, we focus on three distinguishing characteristic of informing. In the second section, we discuss five methods of informing. And in the final section, we discuss two common types of informative speeches and provide examples of each.

informative speech
a speech that has a goal to explain or describe facts, truths, and principles in a way that increases understanding.

Characteristics of Effective Informative Speaking

Effective informative speeches are intellectually stimulating, creative, and use emphasis to aid memory.

Intellectually Stimulating

intellectually stimulating
information that is new to audience members.

Information will be perceived by your audience to be **intellectually stimulating** when it is new to them and when it is explained in a way that peaks audience curiosity and excites their interest. When we say *new* information, we mean either that most of your audience is unfamiliar with what you present, or that the way you present the information provides your audience with new insights into a topic with which they are already familiar.

If your audience is unfamiliar with your topic, you should consider how you might tap the audience's natural curiosity. Imagine that you are an anthropology major who is interested in early human forms, not an interest that is widely shared by most members of your audience. You know that in 1991, a 5,300-year-old man, Ötzi, as he has become known, was found perfectly preserved in an ice field in the mountains between Austria and Italy. Even though it was big news at the time, it is unlikely that most of your audience knows much about this. You can draw on their natural curiosity, however, as you present "Unraveling the Mystery of the Iceman," in which you describe scientists' efforts to understand who Ötzi was and what happened to him (Ice Man, http://www.idgonsite.com/drdig/mummy/22.html).

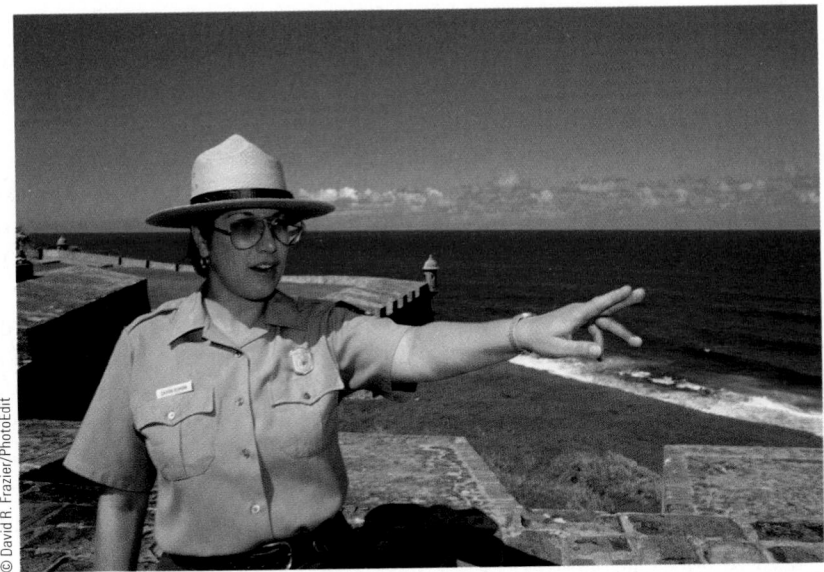

© David R. Frazier/PhotoEdit

Rangers, guides, and interpreters at parks and museums work to become experts so they can tailor their presentations to the needs of specific audiences. If you were listening to this ranger, what would you want to know?

If your audience is familiar with your topic, you will need to identify information that is new to them. Suppose you are a car buff and want to give a speech on SUVs. Because most of your audience is familiar with these cars and their drawbacks, what can you talk about that is likely to be intellectually stimulating to them? You and your audience are aware that SUVs are gas hogs, so you might find out the challenges that manufacturers face when they try to make them more fuel-efficient. As you can see, when your topic is one that the audience is familiar with, your challenge will be to find a new angle that will be intellectually stimulating to them. To do this, choose a goal and develop your speech to present information that challenges most members of your audience to think about what you are saying.

Creative

Information will be perceived by your audience to be **creative** when you use information in a way that yields different or original ideas and insights. You may never have considered yourself to be creative, but that may be because you have never worked to develop innovative ideas. Contrary to what you may think, creativity is not a gift that some have and some don't; rather, it is the result of hard work. Creativity comes from good research, time, and divergent thinking.

creative
using information in a way that yields different or original ideas and insights.

Creative informative speeches begin with good research. The more you learn about the topic, the more you will have to think about, and creatively develop. If all you know about your topic is enough information to fill the time you are allotted, you will be hard pressed to come up with novel ways to approach the information. Speakers who creatively present information do so because they have given themselves lots of material to work with.

For the creative process to work, you also have to give yourself time. So if you want to creatively present the material, you need to decide on your main points and major subpoints at least a couple of days before you speak. This will give you the time to create examples and illustrations, to develop ways of adapting your statistics to the audience, and so on. Rarely do creative ideas come when we are in a time crunch. Instead, they are likely to come when we least expect it, when we're driving our car, preparing for bed, or daydreaming. So the creative process depends on having time to mull over ideas.

divergent thinking
thinking that occurs when we contemplate something from a variety of different perspectives.

For the creative process to work, you have to think divergently. **Divergent thinking** occurs when we contemplate something from a variety of different perspectives. Each perspective may give us at least one new insight that can yield numerous ideas from which we can choose as we work to make our speech creative. Then, with numerous ideas to choose from, we can select the ones that are best suited to our particular audience. In the article "Thinking Like a Genius," available through InfoTrac College Edition, author Michael Michalko describes eight specific tactics that can be used to become better at divergent thinking. To read this article, use your ThomsonNOW for *Communicate!* to access **Web Resource 16.1: Thinking Like a Genius**. Let's look at how divergent thinking can help to identify different approaches to a topic. Suppose you want to give a speech on climatic variation in the United States, and in your research, you ran across the data shown in Figure 16.1.

By looking at the data from different perspectives, you can identify several possible lines of development for your speech. For instance, you might

City	Yearly Temperature (in degrees Fahrenheit)		Precipitation (in inches)	
	High	Low	July	Annual
Chicago	95	−21	3.7	35
Cincinnati	98	−7	3.3	39
Denver	104	−3	1.9	15
Los Angeles	104	40	trace	15
Miami	96	50	5.7	56
Minneapolis	95	−27	3.5	28
New Orleans	95	26	6.1	62
New York	98	−2	4.4	42
Phoenix	117	35	0.8	7
Portland, ME	94	−18	3.1	44
St. Louis	97	−9	3.9	37
San Francisco	94	35	trace	19
Seattle	94	23	0.9	38

Figure 16.1
Temperature and precipitation highs and lows in selected U.S. cities

notice that the yearly high temperatures vary less than the yearly low temperatures. Most people wouldn't understand why this is so and would be curious about this. Looking at the data from another perspective, you might spot that it hardly ever rains on the west coast in the summer. In fact, Seattle, a city that most of us consider to be rainy, is shown as receiving less than an inch of rain in July, which is three inches less than any eastern city and five inches less than Miami. Again, an explanation of this anomaly would interest most audience members. Looking at these data yet another way reveals that although most of us might think of July as a month that is relatively dry, cities in the Midwest and on the east coast get more than the average rainfall we would expect in July. Again, some audience members might find an explanation of this interesting.

Divergent thought can also help us to create alternative ways to make the same point. Again, using the information in Figure 16.1, we can quickly create two ways to support the point: "Yearly high temperatures in U.S. cities vary far less than yearly low temperatures."

Alternative A: **"Of the 13 cities in this table, 10 or 77 percent of them had yearly highs between 90 and 100 degrees. Four or 30 percent had yearly lows above freezing; two or 15 percent had yearly lows between zero and 32 degrees; and seven or 54 percent had low temperatures below zero."**

Alternative B: **"Cincinnati, Miami, Minneapolis, New York, and St. Louis, cities at different latitudes, all had yearly high temperatures of 95 to 98 degrees. In contrast, the lowest temperature for Miami was 50 degrees, while the lowest temperatures for Cincinnati, Minneapolis, New York, and St. Louis were −7, −27, −2, −9 degrees, respectively.**

If you'd like to use Figure 16.1 to further practice divergent thinking, access **Skill Learning Activity 16.1: Creating through Divergent Thinking** through your ThomsonNOW for *Communicate!*

Thomson
NOW!

Use Emphasis to Aid Memory

If your speech is really informative, your audience will hear a lot of new information but will need your help in remembering the most important. In addition to emphasizing the specific goal and making sure your main points are stated in parallel language, you can use visual aids, repetition, transitions, humor, and memory aids to further highlight important information that you want your audience to remember.

Visual aids When we can visualize what we are learning, we remember more than when we only hear. When listening to an informative speech, audiences are more likely to remember information that is presented with visual aids. So your visual aids should be used to emphasize what you want your audience to remember. When choosing your visual aids, be careful not to confuse your audience by presenting exciting visualizations of minor points or details that your audience needn't remember.

Repetition We remember information that is repeated. Think about it. In class, when you are taking notes, aren't you more likely to write down something that your instructor repeats? So, another easy way to help the audience remember something important is to repeat it. You can repeat the idea word-for-word ("The first dimension of romantic love is passion— that's passion.") or you can paraphrase the idea ("The first dimension of romantic love is passion. That is, it can't really be romantic love if there is no sexual attraction.). Be careful not to overdo repetition, because it can become boring and counterproductive if used as the sole way of reinforcing important information.

Transitions Effective transitions can help your audience members identify your organization pattern and differentiate between main ideas and subpoints. In your introduction, you can preview the structure so that audience members will know what to listen for. For example, toward the end of the introduction to a speech on romantic love, the speaker might preview what will be discussed:

> **Today, I'm going to explain the three characteristics of romantic love and five ways you can keep romantic love alive.**

Then, as the speaker moves from describing the characteristics to discussing the how-to's, the speaker might use a transition to summarize and orient the audience:

> **So, there are three characteristics of romantic love: passion, intimacy, and commitment. Now let's see how people keep love alive.**

Again, as the speaker moves into the conclusion, a good transition will remind the audience of the main ideas and signal that the speech is coming to a close:

> **Today, I've told you that romantic love is comprised of passion, intimacy, and commitment. You've also learned how engaging in small talk, being supportive, and openly sharing ideas and feelings, in addition to self-development and relationship rituals, can keep the romantic flame burning . . .**

Effective transitions emphasize your main ideas and help the audience to remember them.

Humor We remember things that are funny. So, effective speakers use humor to emphasize important ideas. For example, in a speech on reducing stress, one of the speaker's main points was "Keep things in perspective." To emphasize the point, he told the following story:

> **A problem that seems enormous at the moment can be perceived as less stressful when put in perspective. For instance, there was a man who went to the racetrack and in the first race bet two dollars on a horse that had the same name as the elementary school he had attended. The horse won and the man won 10 dollars. In each of the next several races, he**

continued with his "system"—betting on "Apple Pie," his favorite dessert, and "Kathie's Prize," his wife's name. And he kept on winning, each time betting all that he had made on the subsequent race. By the end of the sixth race, he had won 700 dollars. He was about to leave when he noticed that in the seventh race, "Seventh Veil" was scheduled to race from the number seven position, and was currently going off at odds of seven to one. Well, he couldn't resist. So he took the entire 700 dollars and bet it on the horse . . . who sure enough, came in seventh. When he got home his wife asked, "How did you do at the track today?" to which he calmly replied, "Not too bad; I lost two dollars." Now that's perspective!

Verbal memory aids You can emphasize ideas and help your audience remember them by using such verbal memory aids as mnemonics and acronyms.

Mnemonics is a system of improving memory by using formulas. For example, if you can word your main points so that a key word in each point starts with the same letter, then you can point out this mnemonic to your audience. For example, in an informative speech on diamonds, the four criteria for evaluating a diamond—weight, clarity, tint, and shape—might be recast into "the four C's" of carat, clarity, color, and cut.

Similarly you might develop an **acronym,** a word formed from the first letter of a series of words to emphasize the ideas. In a speech on effective goal setting, a speaker might say that "useful goals are **SMART**—**S**pecific, **M**easurable, **A**ction-Oriented, **R**easonable, and **T**ime Bound." Now that you understand the characteristics of effective informative speeches, let's look

mnemonics
a system of improving memory by using formulas.

acronyms
words formed from the first letter of a series of words.

© Reuters/CORBIS

How do mnemonic devices help audiences remember information?

at the different methods you can use to inform your audience about your topic.

Methods of Informing

We can inform through description, definition, comparison and contrast, narration, and demonstration. Let's look more closely at each of these patterns.

Description

Description is the informative method used to create an accurate, vivid, verbal picture of an object, geographic feature, setting, or image. If the thing that is to be described is simple and familiar (like a light bulb or a river), the description may not need to be detailed. But if the thing to be described is complex and unfamiliar (like a sextant or holograph), the description will need to be more exhaustive. Descriptions are, of course, easier if you have a visual aid, but verbal descriptions that are clear and vivid can create mental pictures that are equally informative. To describe something effectively, you can explain its size, shape, weight, color, composition, age, condition, and spatial organization. Although your description may focus on only a few of these features, each is helpful to consider as you create your description.

You can describe size subjectively as large or small and objectively by noting the specific numerical measures. For example, you can describe a book subjectively as large, or point out that it is 9 by 6 inches with 369 pages.

You can describe shape by reference to common geometric forms like round, triangular, oblong, spherical, conical, cylindrical, rectangular, and so on, or by reference to the shapes of well-known objects such as by saying, "the lower peninsula of Michigan can be described as a left-handed mitten." Shape is made more vivid by using adjectives, such as smooth, jagged, and so on.

You can describe weight subjectively as heavy or light and objectively by pounds and ounces or grams, kilograms, milligrams, or karats, and so on.

You can describe color by coupling a basic color with a common familiar object. For instance, instead of describing something as puce or ocher, you might do better by describing the object as "eggplant purple" or "clay pot orange."

You can describe the composition of something by indicating what it is actually made of, such as by saying the building was made of brick, concrete, wood, or siding. Or, an object may described as what it appears to be, such as by saying it looks "metallic," even if it is made of plastic rather than metal.

---

description
the informative method used to create an accurate, vivid, verbal picture of an object, geographic feature, setting, or image.

You can describe something by its age and by its condition. For example, describing a city as ancient and well kept gives rise to different mental pictures than does describing a city as old and war torn.

Finally, when you describe, you need to follow one spatial organization pattern going from top to bottom, left to right, outer to inner, and so on. A description of the Sistine Chapel might go from the floor to the ceiling, for example.

Definition

Definition is a method of informing that explains something by identifying its meaning. There are four ways that you can use to explain what something means.

First, you can define a word or idea by classifying it and differentiating it from similar ideas. For example, in a speech on vegetarianism, you might use information from the Vegan Society's website (http://www .vegansociety.com) to develop the following explanation of a "vegan." "A vegan is a vegetarian who is seeking a lifestyle free from animal products for the benefit of people, animals, and the environment. Vegans eat a plant-based diet free from all animal products including milk, eggs, and honey. Vegans also don't wear leather, wool, or silk and avoid other animal-based products."

Second, you can define a word by explaining its derivation or history. For instance, the word *vegan* is made up from the beginning and end of the word *VEGetariAN* and was coined in the U.K. in 1944 when the Vegan Society was founded. Offering this etymology will help your audience to remember the meaning of vegan.

Third, you can define a word by explaining its use or function. When you say, "A plane is a hand-powered tool that is used to smooth the edges of wooden board," you are defining this tool by indicating its use.

The fourth, and perhaps the quickest way you can define something, is by using a familiar synonym or antonym. A **synonym** is a word that has the same or similar meaning; an **antonym** is a word that is a direct opposition. So if you wanted to give a quick definition of a "vegan," you could use the word "vegetarian," a synonym.

Comparison and Contrast

Comparison and contrast is a method of informing that explains something by focusing on how it is similar and different from other things. For example, in a speech on vegans, you might want to tell your audience how vegans are similar and different from other types of vegetarians. You can point out that like all vegetarians, vegans don't eat meat, but that unlike semi-vegetarians, they also do not eat fish or poultry. Like lacto-vegetarians, vegans don't eat eggs, but unlike this group and the lacto-ovo vegetarians,

definition
a method of informing that explains something by identifying its meaning.

synonym
a word that has the same or similar meaning.

antonym
a word that is a direct opposition.

comparison and contrast
a method of informing that explains something by focusing on how it is similar and different from other things.

vegans also don't use dairy products. So of all vegetarians, vegans have the most restrictive diets.

As you will remember, comparisons and contrasts can be figurative or literal. So you can use metaphors and analogies in explaining your ideas as well as making actual comparisons.

Narration

narration
a method of informing that explains something by recounting events.

Narration is a method of informing that explains something by recounting events. Narration of autobiographical or biographical events as well as myths, stories, and other accounts can be effective ways to explain an idea. Narrations usually have four parts. First, the narration orients the listener to the event to be recounted by describing when and where the event took place and by introducing the important people or characters. Second, once listeners are oriented, the narration explains the sequence of events that led to a complication or problem, including details that enhance the development. Third, the narration discusses how the complication or problem affected the key people in the narrative. Finally, the narration recounts how the complication or problem was solved. The characteristics of a good narration include a strong "story line; use of descriptive language and detail that enhance the plot, people, setting, and events; effective use of dialogue; pacing that builds suspense; and a strong voice (Baerwald, http://ccweb .norshore.wednet.edu/writingcorner/narrative.html). The effectiveness of the narration will depend on how much your audience can identify with the key people in the story.

Narrations can be presented in a first-, second-, or third-person voice. When you use first person, you report what you have personally experienced or observed. "Let me tell you about the first time I tried to become a vegetarian . . ." might be the opening for a narrative story told in first person. When you use second person, you place your audience "at the scene" and use the pronouns "you" and "your." "Imagine that you have just gotten off the plane in Pakistan. You look at the signs, but can't read a thing. Which way is the terminal? . . ." When you use third person, you describe to your audience what has happened, is happening, or will happen to other people. "When the immigrants arrived at Ellis island, the first thing they saw was . . ."

Demonstration

demonstration
a method of informing that explains something by showing how something is done, by displaying the stages of a process, or by depicting how something works.

Demonstration is a method of informing that explains something by showing how something is done, by displaying the stages of a process, or by depicting how something works. Demonstrations range from very simple with a few easy-to-follow steps (like how to make an international phone call), to very complex (such as explaining how to make ethanol). Regardless of whether the topic is simple or complex, effective demonstrations require expertise, developing a hierarchy of steps, and using visual language and aids.

In a demonstration, your experience with what you are demonstrating is critical. Expertise gives you the necessary background to supplement bare-bones instructions with personal, lived experience. Why are TV cooking shows so popular? Because the chef doesn't just read the recipe and do what it says. Rather, while performing each step, the chef shares tips about what to do that won't be mentioned in any cookbook. It is the chef's experience that allows the chef to say that one egg will work as well as two, or that you can't substitute margarine for butter.

In a demonstration, you organize the steps into a time-ordered hierarchy so that your audience will be able to remember the sequence of actions accurately. Suppose that you want to demonstrate the steps in using a touch screen voting machine. If, rather than presenting 14 separate points, you group them under the four headings of I. Get ready to vote, II. Vote, III. Review your choices, and IV. Cast your ballot, chances are much higher that the audience will be able to remember most if not all the items in each of the four groups.

Although you could explain a process with only words, most demonstrations actually show the audience the process or parts of the process. If what you are explaining is relatively simple, you can demonstrate the entire process from start to finish. However if the process is lengthy or complex, you may choose to pre-prepare material so that although all stages in the process are shown, not every single step is completed as the audience watches.

Effective demonstrations require practice. Remember that under the pressure of speaking to an audience, even the simplest task can become difficult (did you ever try to thread a needle with 25 people watching you?). As you practice, you will want to consider the size of your audience and

A carefully prepared and well-organized demonstration can help listeners retain information. At times, it could save a life.

OBSERVE & ANALYZE

Journal Activity

Evaluating Demonstrations

Watch an informative speech involving a demonstration and evaluate how effectively the speaker performed the demonstration. (Do-it-yourself and home improvement TV programs, like those shown on the cable DIY and HGTV channels, often feature demonstrations.) Did the speaker perform a complete or modified demonstration? Did the speaker only use the tools, equipment, or other items needed to perform the demonstrated task, or did he or she also use other items such as visual aids? How effective was the demonstration overall? Were there any areas of the demonstration the speaker could have improved?

Thomson You can complete
NOW! this activity online and, if requested, e-mail it to your instructor. Use your Thomson-NOW for *Communicate!* to access **Skill Learning Activity 16.3**.

the configuration of the room. Be sure that all of the audience can actually see what you are doing. You may find that your demonstration takes longer than the time limit you have been given. In these cases, you might want to pre-prepare a step or two.

Common Types of Informative Speeches

Although you can give a speech that uses any of the methods of informing as the primary framework for organizing an informative speech, two of the most common informative speech types are process speeches and expository speeches.

Process Speeches

The goal of a process speech is to demonstrate how something is done or made, or how it works. Effective process speeches require you to carefully delineate the steps in the process and the order in which they occur. Then steps are grouped and concrete explanations for each step and substep are developed. Because it is based on demonstration, a process speech will likely use visual aids and/or full or modified demonstrations.

For example, Allie is a floral designer and has been asked by her former art teacher to speak on the basics of floral arrangement to a high school art class. The teacher has given her five minutes for her presentation. In preparing for the speech, Allie recognized that in five minutes she could not complete arranging one floral display of any size, let alone help students understand how to create various effects. So she opted to physically demonstrate only parts of the process and bring as additional visual aids, arrangements in various stages of completion. For example, the first step in floral arranging is to choose the right vase and frog. So she brought in vases and frogs of various sizes and shapes to display as she explained how to choose a vase and frog based on the types of flowers to be used and the visual effect that is desired. The second step is to prepare the basic triangle of blooms, so she began to demonstrate how to place the flowers she had brought to form one triangle. Rather than hurrying and trying to get everything perfect in the few seconds she had, however, she also brought out several other partially finished arrangements that were behind a draped table. These showed other carefully completed triangles that used other types of flowers. The third step was adding additional flowers and greenery to complete an arrangement and bring about various artistic effects. Again, Allie actually demonstrated how to place several blooms, and then, as she described them, she brought out several completed arrangements that illustrated various artistic effects. Even though Allie did not physically perform all of each step, her visual presentation was an excellent demonstration of floral arranging.

Although some process speeches require you to demonstrate, others are not suited to demonstrations, but use visual aids to help the audience

▶ Speech Assignment: Communicate on Your Feet

A Process Speech

1. Follow the speech plan Action Steps to prepare a process speech. Your instructor will announce the time limit and other parameters for this assignment.

2. Criteria for evaluation include all the general criteria of topic and purpose, content, organization, and presentation, but special emphasis will be placed on how intellectually stimulating the topic is made for the audience, how creatively ideas are presented, and how clearly the important information is emphasized.

3. Prior to presenting your speech, prepare a complete sentence outline and source list (bibliography) as well as a written plan for adapting your speech to the audience. If you have used Speech Builder Express to complete the action step activities online, you will be able to print out a copy of your completed outline and source list. Your adaptation plan should describe how you plan to verbally and visually adapt your material to the audience. It should also describe how you will address the issues listed in step 3 of the Communicate on Your Feet speech assignment for an expository speech on page 429.

"see" the steps in the process. In a speech on making iron, it wouldn't be practical to demonstrate the process; however, a speaker would be able to greatly enhance the verbal description by showing pictures or drawings of each stage.

In process speeches, the steps are the main points and the speech is organized in time order, so that earlier steps are discussed before later ones.

To see a sample process speech, "Flag Etiquette" by Cindy Gardner, use your ThomsonNOW to access the video resources for Chapter 16. In addition to watching this speech, you can also read Cindy's adaptation plan, outline, and manuscript and analyze them using the process speech evaluation form provided.

Expository Speeches

An **expository speech** is an informative presentation that provides carefully researched, in-depth knowledge about a complex topic. For example, "understanding the health care debate," "the origins and classification of nursery rhymes," "the sociobiological theory of child abuse," and "viewing gangsta rap as poetry" are all topics on which you could give an interesting expository speech. Lengthy expository speeches are known as lectures.

All expository speeches require that the speaker use an extensive research base for preparing the presentation, choose an organizational pattern that helps the audience understand the material that is discussed, and use a variety of the informative methods we just discussed to sustain the audience's attention and comprehension of the material presented.

expository speech
an informative presentation that provides carefully researched, in-depth knowledge about a complex topic.

Even college professors who are experts in their fields draw from a variety of source material when they prepare their lectures. You will want to acquire your information from reputable sources. Then as you are speaking, you will want to cite the sources for the information you present. In this way, you can establish the trustworthiness of the information you present and also strengthen your own credibility.

Expository speakers also must choose an organizational pattern that is best suited to the material they will present. Different types of expository speeches are suited to different organizational patterns, so it is up to the speaker to arrange the main points of the speech thoughtfully so they flow in a manner that aids audience understanding and memory.

Finally, a hallmark of effective expository speaking is that it uses various methods of informing for developing material. Within one speech, you may hear the speaker use descriptions, definitions, comparisons and contrasts, narration, and short demonstrations to develop the main points.

Expository speeches include those that explain a political, economic, social, religious, or ethical issue; those that explain events or forces of history; those that explain a theory, principle, or law; and those that explain a creative work.

Exposition of political, economic, social, or religious issues One type of expository speech you might give would help the audience understand the background or context of a political, economic, social, or religious issue. In such a speech, you would explain the forces that gave rise to the issue and are continuing to affect it. You may also present the various positions that are held about the issue and the reasoning behind these positions. Finally, you may discuss various ways that have been presented for the issue to be resolved.

The general goal of your speech is to inform, not to persuade. So you will want to evenly present all sides of controversial issues, without advocating which side is better. You will also want to make sure that the sources you are drawing from are respected experts and are objective in what they report. Finally, you will want to present complex issues in a straightforward manner that helps your audience understand, while not oversimplifying knotty issues.

For example, while researching a speech on drilling for oil and natural gas in Arctic National Wildlife Refuge (ANWR), you need to be careful to consult articles and experts on all sides of this controversial issue and fairly represent and incorporate their views in your outline. Because this is a very complex issue, you will want to discuss all important aspects of the controversy, including the ecological, economic, political (national, state, and local), and technological aspects. If time is limited, you may limit the discussion to just one or two of these aspects, but you should at least inform the audience of the other considerations that affect the issue.

Exposition of historical events and forces A second important type of expository speech is one that explains historical events or forces. History can be fascinating for its own sake, but when history is explained, we can see its relevance for what is happening today. As an expository speaker, you have a special obligation during your research to seek out stories and narratives that can enliven your speech. And you will want to consult sources that analyze the events you will describe so that you are able to describe the impact they had at the time they occurred and the meaning they have today. Although many of us know the historical fact that the United States developed the atomic bomb during World War II, an expository speech on the "Manhattan Project" (as it was known) that dramatizes the race to produce the bomb and also tells the stories of the main players, would add to our understanding of the inner workings of "secret," government-funded research projects and might also place modern arms races and the fear of nuclear proliferation in their proper historical context.

Exposition of a theory, principle, or law The way we live is affected by natural and man-made laws and principles, and is explained by various theories. Yet there are many theories, principles, and laws that we do not completely understand or we don't understand how they affect us. So an expository speech can inform us by explaining these important phenomena. As an expository speaker, you will be challenged to find material that explains the theory, law, or principle in language that is understandable to the audience. You will want to search for or create examples and illustrations that demystify esoteric or complicated terminology. Effective examples and comparing unfamiliar ideas with those that the audience already knows can help you explain the law. In a speech on the psychological principles of operant conditioning, a speaker could help the audience understand the difference between continuous reinforcement and intermittent reinforcement with the following explanation:

> When a behavior is reinforced continuously, each time the person performs the behavior they get the reward, but when the behavior is reinforced intermittently, the reward is not always given when the behavior is displayed. Behavior that is learned by continuous reinforcement disappears quickly when the reward no longer is provided, but behavior that is learned by intermittent reinforcement continues for long periods of time, even when not reinforced. Every day you can see the effects of how a behavior was conditioned. For example, take the behavior of putting a coin in the slot of a machine. If the machine was a vending machine, you expect to be rewarded every time you "play." And if the machine doesn't eject the item, you might wonder if the machine is out of order and "play" just one more coin or you might bang on the machine. In any case, you are unlikely to put in more than one more coin. But suppose the machine is a slot machine, or a machine that dispenses instant winner lottery tickets. Now how many coins will you "play" before you stop and conclude that the machine is "out of order"? Why the difference? Because you were conditioned to a vending machine on a continuous schedule, but a

slot machine or automatic lottery ticket dispenser "teaches" you on an intermittent schedule.

Exposition of creative work Probably every university in the country offers courses in art, theatre, music, literature, and film appreciation. The purpose of these courses is to explain the nature of the creative work and to give the student tools by which to recognize the style, historical period, and quality of a particular piece or group of pieces. Yet most of us know very little about how to understand a creative work, so presentations designed to explain creative works like poems, novels, songs, or even famous speeches can be very instructive for audience members.

When developing a speech that explains a creative work or body of work, you will want to find information on the work and the artist(s) who created the work(s). You will also want to find sources that educate you about the period in which this work was created and inform you about the criteria that critics use to evaluate works of this type. So, for example, if you wanted to give an expository speech on Fredrick Douglas's Fourth of July Oration given in Rochester, New York in 1852, you might need to orient your audience by first reminding them of who Douglas was. Then you would want to explain the traditional expectation that was set for Fourth of July speakers at this point in history. After this, you might want to summarize the speech and perhaps share a few memorable quotes. Finally, you would want to discuss how speech critics view the speech and why the speech is considered to be "great."

Figure 16.2 presents examples of topics for each of the four types of expository speeches.

Topic Ideas for Political, Economic, Social, or Religious Issues

The Bush doctrine of preemption	Stem cell research
Gay marriage	School vouchers
Mandatory sentencing	School uniforms
Home schooling	Immigration

Topic Ideas for Historical Events, Forces, and People

W. E. B. DuBois	Gandhi's leadership
The papacy	The colonization of Africa
Conquering Mt. Everest	The Vietnam War
The Balfour declaration	The Republic of Texas

Topic Ideas for Exposition of Theory, Principle, or Law

Monetary theory	Boyle's law
Number theory	Psychoanalytic theory
Global warming	Intelligent design
The normal distribution	Color theory

Topic Ideas for Expositions of Creative Work

Jazz	The films of Alfred Hitchcock
Impressionist painting	The love sonnets of Shakespeare
Salsa dancing	Kabuki theater
Inaugural addresses	Iconography

Figure 16.2
Examples of expository
speech topics

▶ Speech Assignment: Communicate on Your Feet

An Expository Speech

1. Follow the speech plan Action Steps to prepare a five- to eight-minute informative speech in which you present carefully researched, in-depth information about a complex topic. Your instructor will announce other parameters for this assignment.

2. Criteria for evaluation include all the general criteria of topic and purpose, content, organization, and presentation, but special emphasis will be placed on how intellectually stimulating the topic is made for the audience, how creatively ideas are presented, and how clearly the important information is emphasized. Use the Expository Speech Evaluation Checklist in Figure 16.3 to critique yourself as you practice your speech.

3. Prior to presenting your speech, prepare a complete-sentence outline, a source list (bibliography), and a written plan for adapting your speech to the audience. If you have used Speech Builder Express to complete the action step activities online, you will be able to print out a copy of your completed outline and source list. Your adaptation plan should describe how you plan to verbally and visually adapt your material to the audience and should address how you will:

- Establish common ground
- Build and maintain audience interest
- Adjust to the audience's knowledge and sophistication
- Build speaker credibility
- Adapt to the audience's attitudes toward your speech goal
- Adapt to audiences from different cultures and language communities (if relevant for you in this speech)
- Use visual aids to enhance audience understanding and memory

---

You can use this form to critique an expository speech that you hear in class. As you listen, outline the speech and identify which type of expository speech the speaker is giving. Then answer the questions that follow.

Type of Expository Speech

_____ Exposition of political, economic, social, or religious issue
_____ Exposition of historical events or forces
_____ Exposition of a theory, principle, or law
_____ Exposition of creative work

Primary Criteria

_____ 1. Was the specific goal of the speech to provide well-researched information on a complex topic?
_____ 2. Did the speaker effectively use a variety of methods to convey the information?
_____ 3. Did the speaker emphasize the main ideas and important supporting material?
_____ 4. Did the speaker use high-quality sources for the information presented?
_____ 5. Was the speech well organized, with clearly identifiable main points?
_____ 6. Did the speaker present in-depth, high-quality information?

General Criteria

_____ 1. Was the specific goal clear?
_____ 2. Was the introduction effective in creating interest and introducing the process to be explained?
_____ 3. Was the speech organized using time order?
_____ 4. Was the language clear, vivid, emphatic, and appropriate?
_____ 5. Was the conclusion effective in summarizing the steps?
_____ 6. Was the speech delivered enthusiastically, with vocal expressiveness, fluency, spontaneity, and directness?

Figure 16.3
Expository speech evaluation checklist

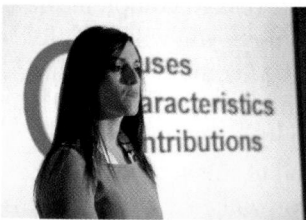

Sample Expository Speech: The Three C's of Down Syndrome Adapted from a Speech by Elizabeth Lopez, Collin County Community College*

This section presents a sample expository speech adaptation plan, outline, and transcript given by a student in an introductory speaking course.

1. Review the outline and adaptation plan developed by Elizabeth Lopez in preparing her speech on Down syndrome.

2. Then read the transcript of Elizabeth Lopez's speech.

3. Use the Expository Speech Evaluation Checklist from Figure 16.3 to help you evaluate this speech.

4. Use your ThomsonNOW for *Communicate!* to watch a video clip of Elizabeth presenting her speech in class. (See the inside back cover of this book for how to access the speech videos through ThomsonNOW.)

5. Write a paragraph of feedback to Elizabeth Lopez, describing the strengths of her presentation and what you think she might do next time to be more effective.

You can use your Student Workbook to complete this activity, or you can use your ThomsonNOW for *Communicate!* to complete it online, print a copy of the Expository Speech Evaluation Checklist, compare your feedback to that of the authors, and, if requested, e-mail your work to your instructor. Access **Skill Learning Activity 16.4**.

Adaptation Plan

1. **Key aspects of audience.** Because audience members have probably seen someone with Down syndrome but don't really know much about it, I will need to provide basic information.

2. **Establishing and maintaining common ground.** My main way of establishing common ground will be by using inclusive personal pronouns (we, us, our).

3. **Building and maintaining interest.** I will build interest by pointing out my personal relationship and interest in Down syndrome and through the use of examples.

4. **Audience knowledge and sophistication.** Because most of the class is not familiar with Down syndrome, I will provide as much explanatory information as I can.

---

*Used with permission of Elizabeth Lopez.

5. **Building credibility.** Early in the speech, I will demonstrate credibility by mentioning my volunteer experience, educational background, and most importantly, my daughter, who has Down syndrome.

6. **Audience attitudes.** I expect my audience to be curious about Down syndrome, but probably uncomfortable with the idea of interacting with people who have the syndrome. So, I will give them information to help them become more knowledgeable and, I hope, less fearful.

7. **Adapt to audiences from different cultures and language communities.** Although the audience is diverse and because Down syndrome occurs in all ethnic groups and in both sexes, I won't do anything specific to adapt.

8. **Use visual aids to enhance audience understanding and memory.** I will use several PowerPoint slides to highlight Down syndrome characteristics.

Speech Outline: The Three C's of Down Syndrome

General purpose: To inform

Speech goal: In this speech, I am going to familiarize the audience with the three C's of Down syndrome: its causes, its characteristics, and the contributions people with Down syndrome make.

Introduction

I. In our lifetime, we will encounter many people who, for a variety of reasons, are "different."

II. Today I want to speak to you about one of those differences—Down syndrome.

III. Why do I want to talk about this topic? Because I have a daughter who has Down syndrome.

IV. In this speech, I will discuss with you the three C's of Down syndrome. *(Slide 1: Causes, Characteristics, and Contributions)*

Body

I. To begin, let it be understood what causes Down syndrome.
   A. Although Down syndrome is a genetic condition, it is not hereditary.
      1. People with Down syndrome have 47 chromosomes instead of the normal 46 (www.nads.org).
      2. This extra chromosome is caused by a random error in cell division within chromosome 21 prior to conception. *(Slide 2: Chromosome 21)*
      3. Although individuals do not inherit the mutant chromosome 21, so neither parent is to blame, once a couple has a child with Down syndrome, the likelihood of reoccurrence with the same two parents is increased. *(Slide 3: Genetic but Not Inherited)*

B. There are approximately 350,000 people living in the U.S. with Down syndrome.

1. Down syndrome occurs in one of every 800 live births, and an unknown number of fetuses with Down syndrome are aborted each year.

2. Women over the age of 35 are most likely to produce chromosome 21–altered eggs, but most children with Down syndrome are born to younger mothers because younger women have a greater percentage of babies.

Transition: Now that you know what causes Down syndrome, I want to describe the key physical and mental differences that people with this syndrome have.

II. People with Down syndrome differ from others both physically and mentally.

A. People with Down syndrome look different, and this syndrome also can create a number of physical health problems. *(Slide 4: Characteristics: Physical and Health Differences)*

1. The major physical differences are facial, such as a flat face, slanted eyes, and a large tongue in conjunction with a small mouth, but people with Down syndrome also experience low muscle tone.

2. The major health concerns include heart defects, hearing loss, vision loss, and a weaker immune system.

B. Second, people with Down syndrome are also mentally different, experiencing developmental delays, cognitive impairments, and emotional precociousness. *(Slide 5: Characteristics)*

1. The delayed developmental characteristics of Down syndrome are speech, cognitive, and motor skills.

2. The cognitive developmental characteristics of children with Down syndrome are varied among children with Down syndrome.

3. People with Down syndrome are emotionally precocious.

Transition: Now that you understand what Down syndrome is and how people with the syndrome differ from others, I would like to explain the special and unique ways that people with Down syndrome contribute to others.

III. People with Down syndrome positively affect their families and communities. *(Slide 6: Contributions)*

A. What are the positive contributions people with Down syndrome make in families?

1. Families with a child who has Down syndrome often include a tighter marriage and more compassionate siblings.

2. Families with a child who has Down syndrome also tend to experience a higher degree of acceptance in their communities.

B. People with Down syndrome contribute to their communities.
   1. Children with Down syndrome who are mainstreamed in classrooms teach their peers to value differences.
   2. Many adults with Down syndrome in the workplace are role models of dedication and perseverance.

Conclusion

I. To review, now you know that Down syndrome is caused by a preconception change in chromosome 21 that causes people with Down syndrome to be physically and mentally different, and you also know that many people with Down syndrome make positive contributions to society.
II. So, the next time you encounter someone with Down syndrome, I hope you'll remember what you have learned so you can enjoy getting to know this person rather than being afraid.

Works Cited

Faragher, R. Down syndrome: it's a matter of quality of life. *Journal of Intellectual Disability Research,* October 2005, 49:761–765. *Academic Search Premier.* EBSCOE Host Research Databases. Collin County Community College District. Accessed October 7, 2005 at www.web27.epnet.com.

Helders, Paul. Children with Down syndrome. 2005: 141. *Academic Search Premier.* EBSCOE Host Research Databases. Collin County Community College District. Accessed October 7, 2005 at www.web27.epnet.com.

"Information and Resources," National Down Syndrome Society. Accessed October 7, 2005 at www.ndss.org.

National Association for Down syndrome. Accessed October 7, 2005 at www.nads.org.

Rietveld, Christine. Classroom learning experiences by new children with Down syndrome. *Journal of Intellectual and Developmental Disability,* September 2005, 30:127–138. *Academic Search Premier.* EBSCOE Host Research Databases. Collin County Community College District. Accessed October 7, 2005 at www.web27.epnet.com.

Speech and Analysis

Speech

In our lifetimes, we will encounter many people who, for a variety of reasons, are considered "different" by those who consider themselves "normal." Today I want to speak to you about one of those things that makes people seem different: Down syndrome. Why do I want to talk about this topic? In part, because I have volunteered with mentally disabled children for many

Analysis

Elizabeth opens with a statement about normal and different, then quickly introduces her topic.

She immediately establishes her credibility by showing that she has worked with children with Down

years, I am pursuing a professional career in special education, and I'd like to share with you what I've been learning. But, more importantly, I have a toddler daughter who has Down syndrome, and I've found from personal experience that when people know more about what makes my daughter different, they're more accepting of her and of people who are different in other ways.

In this speech, I'd like to share with you some basic information about this syndrome—I call them the three C's. First, I will discuss what causes Down syndrome. Then I will explain the typical characteristics that differentiate people with Down syndrome from others. Finally, I will describe the positive contributions that people with Down syndrome make in their families and communities.

To begin, let me explain what causes Down syndrome. Contrary to what some people believe, Down syndrome is not hereditary—it is a genetic condition. According to the website for the National Association for Down Syndrome, people with Down syndrome have 47 chromosomes instead of the normal 46. This extra chromosome is produced by a random error in cell division within chromosome 21 prior to conception. Because you don't inherit the mutant chromosome 21, neither parent is to "blame," so to speak, for producing a child with Down syndrome. However, once a couple has a child with Down syndrome, the likelihood that the same two parents could have another child with the same syndrome increases.

syndrome, and she also has a daughter who has the syndrome.

She concludes her introduction by using a mnemonic device, the three C's, to preview her main points.

Here, Elizabeth clearly explains that although Down syndrome is a genetic condition, it is not an inherited one. Her PowerPoint slide is simple and visually reinforces her point.

According to the National Down Syndrome Society website, there are approximately 350,000 people with Down syndrome in the United States. Down syndrome occurs in one of about every 800 live births, and an unknown number of fetuses with Down syndrome are aborted each year. Many of us have heard that older women are more likely to have babies with Down syndrome. It's true that women over the age of 35 are most likely to produce chromosome 21–altered eggs, but, really, most Down syndrome children are born to younger mothers because younger women have a greater percentage of babies.

Having established its genetic cause, Elizabeth elaborates and explains more about the prevalence of Down syndrome and which parents are likely to have children with Down syndrome.

Now that I've talked about what causes Down syndrome, let me describe the main physical and mental characteristics that differentiate people with Down syndrome from others. Of course, one of the first things people notice about people with Down syndrome is that they look different, but Down syndrome can also create a number of health problems. The major physical differences we notice first are facial characteristics, like a flat face, slanted eyes, and a large tongue in a small mouth, although not all people with the syndrome have all of these facial features. But people with Down syndrome also often experience low muscle tone and more problematic health concerns like heart defects, hearing loss, vision loss, and a weak immune system.

Here Elizabeth uses a good transition in which she reinforces two of her C's: causes and characteristics.

People with Down syndrome are also mentally different from the rest of us. According to R. Faragher in his article on Down syndrome in

Here Elizabeth cites one of the sources of her information.

the *Journal of Intellectual Disability Research,* they experience developmental delays, mostly affecting their speech, cognitive, and motor skills. The degree of delays in cognitive development varies quite a bit among children with Down syndrome. As Christine Rietveld explains in her article on Down syndrome in the *Journal of Intellectual and Developmental Disability,* some children with Down syndrome are able to be mainstreamed and attend public school with other children, some need to attend special education classes in mainstream schools, and others need more specialized programs outside of regular schools.

People with Down syndrome are also emotionally precocious, which means that they often seem emotionally mature for their age and have few inhibitions about expressing their emotions. If you have spent time with a child who has Down syndrome, you know what it means to be loved unconditionally.

Elizabeth could have developed this characteristic a bit more, perhaps by giving an example.

Now that you know a little more about what characterizes people with Down syndrome, I'd like to explain the special and unique ways that these people contribute to others. As many of us who live with people with Down syndrome know, there's no doubt that they have a positive effect on their families and communities. As R. Faragher explains, parents of a child with Down syndrome often have a very close, tightly knit marriage—they learn to come together in support of their child who has the syndrome and of their children who don't have Down syn-

Again, Elizabeth uses a transition that reinforces two of the C's that define her main points: characteristics and contributions.

Although Elizabeth begins by telling the audience that she has a child with Down syndrome, she misses the opportunity to personalize this point. She might have further developed it by giving personal examples of how her daughter has contributed to her family.

drome, and they learn to rely on each other more to raise a child with special needs. In addition, the siblings of children with Down syndrome are often more compassionate because they understand what it's like to be viewed as "different." Families with a child who has Down syndrome also often experience a higher degree of acceptance in their communities. It's easy for people to become fond of a child with Down syndrome because they tend to be happy, loving kids who express affection easily. And when people feel fond of a child with Down syndrome, they also feel protective and accepting of the child's family.

In turn, people with Down syndrome often make important contributions to their communities, just as many of us do. For example, such children who are mainstreamed in classrooms teach their peers to value differences and to develop compassion and empathy for people who are not necessarily like everyone else. As adults, many people with Down syndrome are role models of dedication and perseverance in the workplace— I'll bet at least a few of you have encountered a cheerful and professional person with Down syndrome who has helped you in a store or who works with you in an office setting.

Again, specific examples would have aided the development of her point.

In review, now you know that Down syndrome is caused by a change in chromosome 21 before conception, and that this results in people with Down syndrome having several different physical and mental characteristics. But you also know that people with

In this conclusion, she reviews the three C's of causes, characteristics, and contributions, helping us remember what her speech was about.

the syndrome often make positive contributions to their families and communities. So, the next time you encounter someone with Down syndrome, I hope you'll remember what you have learned and that you enjoy getting to know this person as a unique and interesting individual.

All in all, this is a well-presented, informative speech with sufficient documentation.

Summary

An informative speech is one that has a goal to explain or describe facts, truths, and principles in a way that stimulates interest, facilitates understanding, and increases likelihood that audiences will remember. In short, informative speeches are designed to educate an audience.

Effective informative speeches are intellectually stimulating, creative, and use emphasis to aid memory. Informative speeches will be perceived as intellectually stimulating when the information is new and when it is explained in a way that excites interest. Informative speeches are creative when they produce new or original ideas or insights. Informative speeches use emphasis to stimulate audience memory.

We can inform by describing something, defining it, comparing and contrasting it with other things, narrating stories about it, or demonstrating it.

What Would You Do?

fter class, as Gina and Paul were discussing what they intended to talk about in their process speeches, Paul said, "I think I'm going to talk about how to make a synthetic diamond."

Gina was impressed. "That sounds interesting. I didn't know you had expertise with that."

"I don't. But the way I see it, Professor Henderson will really be impressed with my speech because my topic will be so novel."

"Well, yeah," Gina replied, "but didn't he stress that for this speech we should choose a topic that was important to us and that we knew a lot about?"

"Sure," Paul said sarcastically, "he's going to be impressed if I talk about how to maintain a blog? Forget it. Just watch—everyone's going to think I make diamonds in my basement and I'm going to get a good grade."

1. Is Paul's plan unethical? Why?

2. What should Gina say to challenge Paul's last statement?

Two common forms of informative speeches are process speeches, in which the steps of something are shown, and expository speeches that are well-researched explanations of complex ideas. Expository speeches include those that explain political, economic, social, or religious issues; explain events or forces of history; explain a theory, principle, or law; and those that explain a creative work.

Thomson NOW!

Communicate! Online

Now that you have read Chapter 16, use your ThomsonNOW for *Communicate!* for quick access to the electronic resources that accompany this text. Your ThomsonNOW gives you access to the video of Elizabeth's speech on Down syndrome, the Web Resources and Skill Learning Activities featured in this chapter, InfoTrac College Edition, and online study aids such as a digital glossary and review quizzes.

Your *Communicate!* ThomsonNOW is an online study system that helps you identify concepts you don't fully understand, allowing you to put your study time to the best use. Using chapter-by-chapter diagnostic pre-tests, the system creates a personalized study plan for each chapter. Each plan directs you to specific resources designed to improve your understanding, including pages from the text in e-book format. Chapter post-tests give you an opportunity to measure how much you've learned and let you know if you are ready for graded quizzes and exams.

Key Terms

Go to your ThomsonNOW for *Communicate!* to access your online glossary for Chapter 16. Print a copy of the glossary for this chapter and test yourself with the electronic flash cards or complete the crossword puzzle to help you master these key terms:

acronyms (419)
antonym (421)
comparison and contrast (421)
creative (415)

definition (421)
demonstration (422)
description (420)
divergent thinking (416)
expository speech (425)

informative speech (414)
intellectually stimulating (414)
mnemonics (419)
narration (422)
synonym (421)

Review Quiz

Test your knowledge of the concepts in this chapter by taking the online review quiz for Chapter 16. Go to your ThomsonNOW for *Communicate!* to access the quiz. When you have completed the quiz, submit it for scoring.

Skill Learning Activities

Complete the Observe & Analyze, Test Your Competence, and Speech and Analysis activities for Chapter 16 online at your ThomsonNOW for *Communicate!* You can submit your Observe & Analyze, Action Step, and Speech and Analysis answers to your instructor, and compare your Test Your Competence and Speech and Analysis answers to those provided by the authors.

Web Resources

Go to your ThomsonNOW for *Communicate!* to access the Web Resources for this chapter.

OBJECTIVES

After you have read this chapter, you should be able to answer these questions:

- How do people listen to and evaluate persuasive messages?
- What are the different types of persuasive speaking goals or propositions?
- How does the audience's initial attitude toward your topic affect your proposition?
- What are good reasons?
- What kinds of evidence can you use to support reasons?
- What types of arguments can be created and how can each be tested?
- What are some common fallacies you should avoid when developing your reasons?
- How can you build goodwill so that your credibility is enhanced?
- What does it mean to motivate?
- How do incentives motivate?
- What are the common patterns used to organize persuasive speeches?

17

Persuasive Speaking

As members of the zoning commission walked out of the auditorium, Dan remarked, "Wow, after an hour and a half of dull speeches, I was about to go to sleep, but two minutes into Commissioner Kate Tucker's speech, I was wide awake."

"Me too," Lydia replied. "I mean, with each point she made I could see more people listening closely, nodding, and agreeing with what she had to say."

"Not only were her reasons easy for me to understand," agreed Stan, "but she had the facts to support each point. How could you not believe what she had to say? If only everyone who spoke tonight had been that good."

persuasive speech
a speech that has a goal to influence the beliefs or behavior of audience members.

A lthough it is easy to get excited about a powerful speech, real-life attempts to persuade others require the speaker to be knowledgeable about forming arguments and adapting them well to the needs of the audience. A **persuasive speech** is one that has a goal to influence the beliefs and/or behavior of audience members. It is, perhaps, the most demanding speech challenge. You will need to use all of the skills you have studied and developed so far. You will also need to build arguments that are convincing to your audience, use emotion to increase your audience's involvement with your topic, develop your credibility by demonstrating goodwill, use incentives to motivate your audience when you want them to take action, and choose an effective organizational strategy. In this chapter, you will learn how to prepare an effective persuasive speech. We begin by presenting a widely accepted theoretical model that explains how people process persuasive messages. Then, based on this model, we describe how you can meet the challenge of developing an effective persuasive speech.

How People Process Persuasive Messages: The Elaboration Likelihood Model (ELM)

Do you remember times when you listened carefully and thoughtfully to an idea someone was trying to convince you about? Do you remember consciously thinking over what had been said and making a deliberate decision? Do you remember other times when you only half-listened and made up your mind quickly based on your "gut" feeling about the truthfulness of what had been said? What determines how well we listen to and how carefully we evaluate the hundreds of persuasive messages we hear each day? Richard Petty and John Cacioppo developed a now widely accepted model that explains how likely people are to spend time evaluating information (such as the arguments they hear in a speech) in an *elaborate* way, using their critical thinking skills, rather than processing information in a simpler, less critical manner. Called the Elaboration Likelihood Model (ELM), this theory can be used by speakers to develop persuasive speeches that will be influential with audience members, regardless of how they process information.

The model suggests that people process information in one of two ways. One way is intense and more time consuming. People using this "central route" listen carefully, think about what is said, and may even mentally elaborate on the message. The second way, called the "peripheral route," is a shortcut that relies on simple cues such as a quick evaluation of the speaker's credibility, or a gut check on what the listener feels about the message.

According to the ELM model, the importance we attribute to an issue determines whether we use the central route or the peripheral route. When we feel involved in an issue, we are willing to expend the energy necessary for processing on the central route. When the issue is less important to us, we take the peripheral route. So, how closely your audience members will follow your arguments depends on how involved they feel with your topic. For example, if you have a serious chronic illness that is expensive to treat, you are more likely to pay attention to and evaluate for yourself any proposals to change your health care benefits. If you are healthy, you will probably quickly agree with suggestions from someone you perceive to be credible, or go along with a proposal that seems compassionate.

The ELM model also suggests that when we form attitudes as a result of central processing (critical thinking), we are less likely to change our minds than when our attitudes have been form based on peripheral cues. You can probably remember times when you were swayed at the moment by a powerful speaker, but later upon reflection, regretted your action and changed your mind. Likewise, based on information you have heard and spent time thinking about, you probably have some strongly held beliefs that are not easily changed.

When you prepare a persuasive speech, you will draw on the ELM model theory by developing your topic so that you increase the likelihood of your audience members feeling personally involved with the topic. You will want to develop sound reasons so that audience members who use the central, critical thinking approach to your speech will find your arguments convincing. For members who are less involved, you will want to appeal to their emotions and include information that enables them to see you as credible. In the Spotlight on Scholars, we feature Richard Petty, one of the

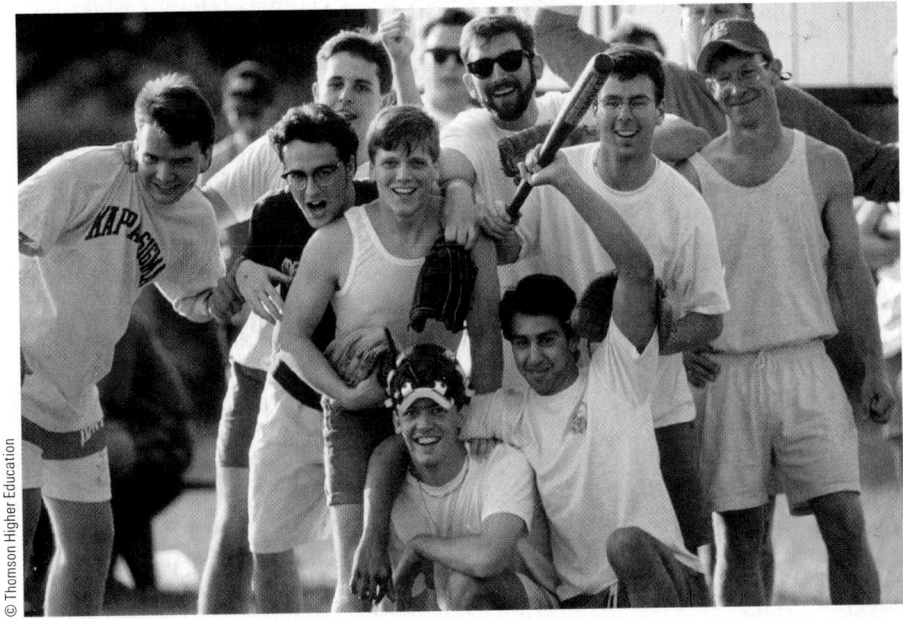

© Thomson Higher Education

What type of audience would this be for a speaker whose goal was to convince audience members to abstain from premarital sex? What led you to your conclusion?

| Spotlight on Scholars | Richard Petty | Professor of Psychology, the Ohio State University, on Attitude Change |

As an undergraduate political science major, Richard Petty got so interested in how people change their attitudes that he chose to minor in psychology; he wanted to take more courses in attitude change and learn empirical research methods. He then continued graduate work in psychology at the Ohio State University, focusing his studies on attitude change and persuasion. Like many scholars, the subject of his doctoral dissertation—attitude change induced by persuasive communications—laid the foundation for a career of research.

When Petty began his research, the psychological scholarship of the previous 40 years had been unable to demonstrate a relationship between people's attitudes and their behavior. Petty believed this was because some attitudes were consistently related to behavior, but other attitudes were not. The key was to understand how attitudes were formed and which processes led to strong rather than weak attitudes. Based on his work, Petty is now in the forefront of scholars who have demonstrated that attitude change and behavior are, in fact, related, but in a complex way.

During the last 20 years, Petty has published scores of research articles, on his own and with colleagues, on various aspects of attitude and persuasion to find out under what circumstances attitudes affect behavior. His work with various collaborators has been so successful that he has gained international acclaim. Many of his works have been published worldwide, and the theory of the Elaboration Likelihood Model (ELM) of persuasion that he developed in collaboration with John Cacioppo has become the most cited theoretical approach to attitude and persuasion.

In its most basic form, Petty and Cacioppo's theory states that attitude change is likely to occur from one of just two relatively distinct

Courtesy Richard Petty

"routes to persuasion." The first type, the central route, occurs as a result of a person's careful and thoughtful consideration of the true merits of the information presented in support of a claim. The second type, the peripheral route, occurs as a result of simple cues in the persuasion context (such as an attractive source) that induce change without necessitating scrutiny of the central merits of the claim. Following their initial speculation about these two routes to persuasion, Petty and Cacioppo developed, researched, and refined the theory supporting the ELM.

The ELM hypothesizes that what is persuasive to a person and how lasting any attitude change is likely to be are dependent on how motivated and able people are to assess the merits of a speaker, an issue, or a position. People who are highly motivated and skilled in critical thinking are likely to study available information about the claim. As a result, they are more likely to arrive at a reasoned attitude regarding the speaker's claim. For people who are less motivated or less able to analyze information related to the claim, attitude change can result from a number of processes that require fewer resources and do not require effortful evaluation of the relevant information. Consequently, their attitude changes are likely to be weaker in endurance and have less impact on behavior.

So what impact does Petty's research have on speakers who seek to persuade? First, speakers must recognize that audience attitude change is a result of persuasive techniques chosen by the speaker and also choices made by the audience regarding how deeply they wish to probe into speakers' claims. Using the ELM, speakers can better understand and predict the variables that will affect audience attitudes and the consequences of these attitudes. Thus, sound reasons and supporting evidence adapted to audience needs should account for attitude change when audience aptitude is great. In contrast, speakers' apparent credibility and emotional appeals should be more likely to account for change when listener thinking is superficial.

This complexity of attitude change suggests that a speaker must have the necessary information to form well-constructed arguments, and he or she must also have the artistic sense to understand important aspects of the audience (locus of belief, time constraints, interest, and so forth) and the artistic power to, as Aristotle once said, use available means of persuasion effectively.

For titles of several of his publications, see the references at the end of this book. For more information about Richard Petty and his work, go to http://www.psy.ohio-state .edu/petty/.

originators of the ELM model. In the rest of this chapter, we describe how you can adapt the speech plan action step process to help you accomplish the model's objectives.

Writing Persuasive Speech Goals as Propositions

A persuasive speech's specific goal is stated as a proposition. A **proposition** is a declarative sentence that clearly indicates the speaker's position on the topic. For example, "I want to convince my audience that smoking causes cancer." The goal of persuasive speech to get the audience to agree with what the speaker is advocating. The goal may focus on what the audience's attitude or belief should be or how the audience should act. Figure 17.1 provides examples of propositions aimed at changing an attitude or belief and propositions aimed at audience action.

proposition
a declarative sentence that clearly indicates the speaker's position on the topic.

Tailoring Your Proposition to Your Audience

As you consider your topic and the proposition you will argue, you'll want to understand the opinions your audience members currently have about your topic.

Audience member opinions about your speech topic can range from highly favorable to highly opposed and can be visualized as lying on a con-

Propositions of Attitude/Belief	Propositions of Action
I want my audience to believe that the city should build a downtown entertainment center.	I want my audience to vote for the tax levy to build a downtown entertainment center.
I want my audience to believe that more funding is needed for cancer research.	I want my audience to donate money to the American Cancer Society.
I want my audience to believe that recycling is necessary to reduce waste.	I want my audience to order and use the recycling bins available to them in their neighborhoods.

Figure 17.1
Examples of propositions of attitude/belief and action

Highly opposed	Opposed	Mildly opposed	Neither in favor nor opposed	Mildly in favor	In favor	Highly in favor
2	2	11	1	2	2	0

Figure 17.2
Sample opinion continuum

tinuum like the one pictured in Figure 17.2. Even though an audience will include individuals whose opinions fall nearly every point along the distribution, generally audience members' opinions tend to cluster in one area of the continuum. For instance, the opinions of the audience represented in Figure 17.2 cluster around "mildly opposed," even though a few people were more hostile and a few others had favorable opinions.

You will use the cluster point to classify your audience's initial attitude toward your topic as "opposed" (opposed to a particular belief or action or holding an opposite point of view), "no opinion" (uninformed, neutral, or apathetic), or "in favor" (already supportive of a particular belief or action) and you will consider this initial opinion as you develop your proposition and speech.

Opposed If your audience is very much opposed to your goal, it is unrealistic to believe that you will be able to change their attitude from "opposed" to "in favor" in only one short speech. So, you should consider a proposition that moves your audience in the direction that you would like, but does not expect them to make a complete change. For example, when you determine that your audience is likely to be totally opposed to the proposition: "I want to convince my audience that gay marriage should be legalized," you may rephrase your goal to: "I want to convince my audience to believe that committed gay couples should be able to have the same legal protection that is afforded to committed heterosexual couples through state-recognized marriage.

When you believe your listeners are only mildly opposed to your topic, you will need to understand their resistance and present arguments to overcome it. Your goal should be to provide them with strong reasons that support your position, including evidence that would counter other attitudes. Your proposition might be phrased: "I want to convince my audience that gay marriage will benefit society."

Neutral When you perceive that your audience is neutral, you need to consider whether they are uninformed, impartial, or apathetic about your topic. When they are **uninformed,** that is, they do not know enough about a topic to have formed an opinion, you will need to provide the basic arguments and information that they need to become informed. Make sure that each of your reasons is really well supported with good information. When your audience is **impartial,** that is, the audience knows the basics about your topic but still has no opinion, you will want to provide more elabo-

uninformed
not knowing enough about a topic to have formed an opinion.

impartial
knowing the basics about a topic but still having no opinion about it.

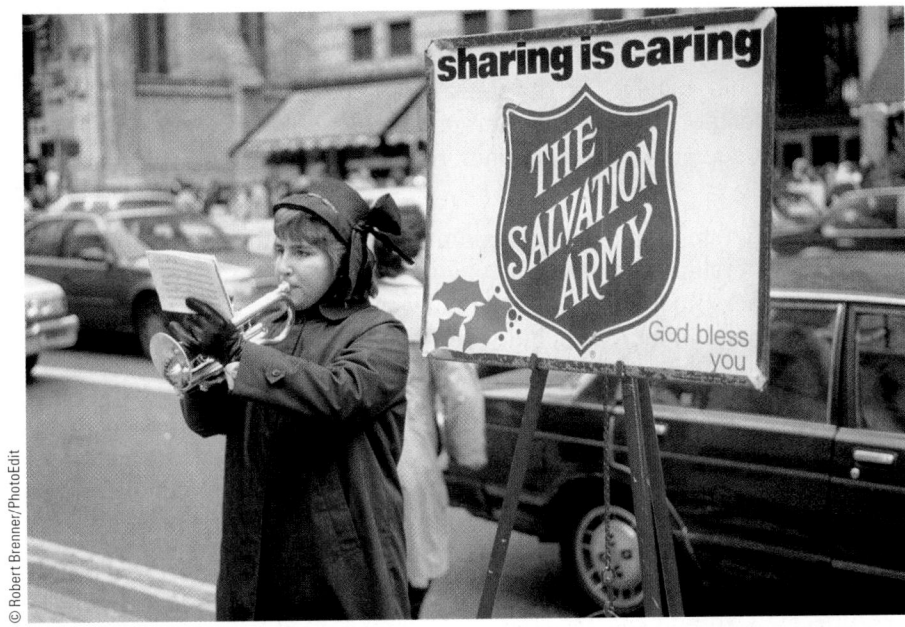

Is it more challenging to try to change the attitude of a hostile audience, or to persuade people who are neutral to give money to a cause?

rate or secondary arguments and more robust evidence. When audience members have no opinion because they are **apathetic,** you will need to find ways to personalize the topic for them so that they see how it relates to them or their needs.

apathetic
having no opinion because one is uninterested, unconcerned, or indifferent to a topic.

In favor When your audience is only mildly in favor of your proposal, your task is to reinforce and strengthen their beliefs. An audience whose beliefs favor your topic will still benefit from an elaboration of the reasons for holding these beliefs. The audience may also become further committed to the belief by hearing additional or new reasons and more recent evidence that supports it.

When your audience strongly agrees with your position, then you can consider a proposition that builds on that belief and moves the audience to act on it. So, for example if the topic is gay marriage, and your audience poll shows that most audience members strongly favor the idea, then your goal may be: "I want my audience members to walk in Saturday's march in support of gay marriage."

Developing Arguments That Support Your Proposition

Persuasive speeches are composed of reasons and evidence that are used to make arguments in support of the proposition. Once you have identified a proposition tailored to your audience, you will use the research you have acquired to help you choose the main points of the speech. In a persuasive speech, the main points are reasons that support the proposition; the supporting materials presented are evidence that buttress the reasons.

reasons
main point statements that summarize several related pieces of evidence and show why you should believe or do something.

Finding reasons to use as main points **Reasons** are main point statements that summarize several related pieces of evidence and show *why* you should believe or do something. For example, suppose your speech proposition is: "I want the audience to believe home ownership is good for a society." Based on your research, you develop six potential reasons:

I. Home ownership builds strong communities.
II. Home ownership reduces crime.
III. Home ownership increases individual wealth.
IV. Home ownership increases individual self-esteem.
V. Home ownership improves the value of a neighborhood.
VI. Home ownership is growing in the suburbs.

Once you have a list of reasons, you can weigh and evaluate each and choose the three or four that have the highest quality. You can judge the quality of each reason by asking the following questions:

1. **Is the reason directly related to proving the proposition?** Sometimes, we find information that can be summarized into a reason, but that reason doesn't directly argue the proposition. For instance, you may have uncovered a lot of research that supports the notion that "Home ownership is growing in the suburbs." Unfortunately, it isn't clear how the growth of home ownership in the suburbs benefits society as a whole. So when choosing a reason, eliminate those that are only tangentially related to your proposition.

2. **Do I have strong evidence to support a reason?** A reason may sound impressive, but in your research you may not have been able to find solid evidence that supports it. Because the audience will assess whether they accept your reason based on the evidence you present, eliminate reasons for which you do not have strong support. For example, the second reason, "Home ownership reduces crime," sounds like a good one; but if the only proof you have is an opinion that is expressed by one person whose expertise is questionable, or if, in your research, you discover that although crime is lower in areas with high home ownership, there is little evidence to suggest a cause-and-effect relationship, you should eliminate this reason from consideration.

3. **Will this reason be persuasive for this audience?** Suppose that you have a lot of factual evidence to support the reason, "Home ownership encourages self-esteem." This reason might be very persuasive to an audience of social workers, psychologists, and teachers, but less important to an audience of financial planners, bankers, and economists. So once you are convinced that your reasons are related to the proposition and have strong evidence to support them, choose to use as main points of your speech the three or four that you believe will be most persuasive for your particular audience.

Selecting evidence to support reasons Although a reason may seem self-explanatory, most audience members will not believe it unless they hear information that backs it up. As you researched, you may have discovered more evidence to support a reason than you will be able to use in the time allotted for your speech. So, you will have to select the pieces of evidence you will present. Both facts and opinions can serve as evidence.

Suppose that, in your speech to convince people that Alzheimer's research should be better funded, you want to use the reason "Alzheimer's disease is an increasing health problem in America." The following would be a factual statement that supports the reason: "According to a 2003 article in the *Archives of Neurology*, the number of Americans with Alzheimer's has more than doubled since 1980 and is expected to continue to grow, affecting between 11.3 and 16 million Americans by the year 2050."

Statements from people who are experts on a subject can also be used as evidence to support a reason. For example, the statement "According to the Surgeon General, 'By 2050, Alzheimer's disease may afflict 14 million people a year'" is an expert opinion.

Let's look at an example of how fact and opinion evidence can be used in combination to support a proposition.

Proposition: I want the audience to believe that television violence has a harmful effect on children.

Reason: Television violence desensitizes children to violence.

Support: "In Los Angeles, California, a survey of 50 children between the ages of 5 and 10 who had just watched an episode of *Teenage Mutant Ninja Turtles,* asked the children whether or not violence was acceptable. Thirty-nine of the 50, or about 80 percent of them responded, 'Yes, because it helps you to win fights' (facts). Regardless of the rationale that children express, the fact remains that viewing violence desensitizes children and this can lead to real violence. According to Kirsten Houston, a well-regarded scholar writing in the July 1997 issue of *Journal of Psychology,* "Repeated exposure to media violence is a major factor in the gradual desensitization of individuals to such scenes. This desensitization, in turn, weakens some viewers' psychological restraints on violent behavior" (opinion).

Regardless of whether the evidence is based on opinions or facts, you will want to use the best evidence you have found to support your point. You can use the answers to the following questions to help you select evidence that is likely to persuade your audience:

1. **Does the evidence come from a well-respected source?** This question involves both the people who offered the opinions or compiled the facts and the book, journal, or Internet sources in which they were reported. Just as some people's opinions are more reliable than others,

some printed and Internet sources are more reliable than others. Be especially careful of undocumented information. Eliminate evidence that comes from a questionable, unreliable, or biased source.

2. **Is the evidence recent; if not, is it still valid?** Things change, so information that was accurate for a particular time period may or may not be valid today. As you look at your evidence, consider when the evidence was gathered. Something that was true five years ago may not be true today. A trend that was forecast a year ago may have been revised since then. A statistic that was reported last week may be based on data that were collected three years ago. So whether it is a fact or an opinion, you want to choose evidence that is valid today. For example, the evidence "The total cost of caring for individuals with Alzheimer's is at least $100 billion according to the Alzheimer's Association and the National Institute on Aging," was cited in a 2003 NIH publication. But it is based on information from a study conducted using 1991 data that were updated to 1994 data before being published. As a result, we can expect that today, annual costs would be higher. If you choose to use this evidence, you should disclose the age of the data used in the study and indicate that today, the costs would be higher.

3. **Does the evidence really support the reason?** Just as reasons need to be relevant to the proposition, evidence needs to be relevant to the reason. Some of the evidence you have found may be only indirectly related to the reason and should be eliminated in favor of evidence that provides more central support.

4. **Will this evidence be persuasive for this audience?** Finally, just as when you select your reasons, you will want to choose evidence that your particular audience is likely to find persuasive. So, if you have your choice of two quotations from experts, you will want to use the one from the person your audience is likely to find more credible.

argument
the process of proving conclusions you have drawn from reasons and evidence.

Types and tests of arguments An **argument** is the logical relationship between the proposition and the reasons or between the reasons and the evidence. So far, we have concentrated on choosing propositions, reasons, and supporting evidence, but if your audience is not convinced that your evidence provides a convincing argument for your reason, they will not agree with it. And if your audience doesn't buy the argument form from your reasons, they will not support your proposition.

Several kinds of arguments links can be developed, as follows:

arguing by example
support a claim by providing one or more individual examples.

1. *Arguing by examples.* You are **arguing by example** when the reasons you offer are examples of the proposition or when the evidence you offer provides examples of the reason you state. For example, if you say, "Anyone who studies can get "A's," and offer as evidence: "Tom, Jane, and Josh studied and they all got 'A's,'" you would be making an argument by example. The general form of an argument by example is that "what is

true in some instances/examples is true in all instances." When arguing by example, you can make sure that your argument is valid by answering the following questions: "Were enough instances (examples) cited so that listeners understand that they are not isolated or handpicked examples? Were the instances typical and representative? Are the negative instances really atypical?" If the answer to any of these questions is "No," then consider making your argument in a different way.

2. *Arguing by analogy.* You are **arguing by analogy** when you support your reason with a single comparable example that is so significantly similar to the subject that it offers strong proof. For example, if you support your proposition that "the Cherry Fork Volunteer Fire Department should hold a raffle to raise money for three portable defibrillator units" by saying, "the Mack Volunteer Fire Department, which is similar to Cherry Fork, held a raffle and raised enough money for four units," you would be arguing by analogy. The general form of an argument by analogy is "What is true or will work in one set of circumstances is true or will work in a comparable set of circumstances." When arguing by analogy, make sure your argument is valid by answering these questions: "Are the subjects really comparable?" "Are the Cherry Fork and Mack Fire Departments really similar in all important ways?" If they are not, then your argument is not valid. "Are any of the ways that the subjects are dissimilar important to the conclusion?" If so, the reasoning is not sound.

arguing by analogy
support a claim with a single comparable example that is significantly similar to the subject of the claim.

arguing from causation
support a claim by citing events that have occurred to bring about the claim.

3. *Arguing from causation.* You are **arguing from causation** when you cite evidence that one or more events always or almost always brings about, leads to, creates, or prevents a predictable event or set of effects. If you support your proposition "The wheat crop will have a lower yield than last year" by saying, "We've had a very dry spring," you would be arguing from causation. Your argument can be boiled down to "The lack of sufficient rain causes a poor crop." The general form of a causal argument can be stated: If A, which is known to bring about B, has happened, then we can expect B to occur. To make sure your causal arguments are sound, you should answer the following questions: "Are the events alone enough to cause the stated effect?" "Do other events accompanying the events cited actually cause the effect?" "Is the relationship between causal

When the government makes manufacturers place warning labels on products, it is trying to influence consumers by reasoning from causation.

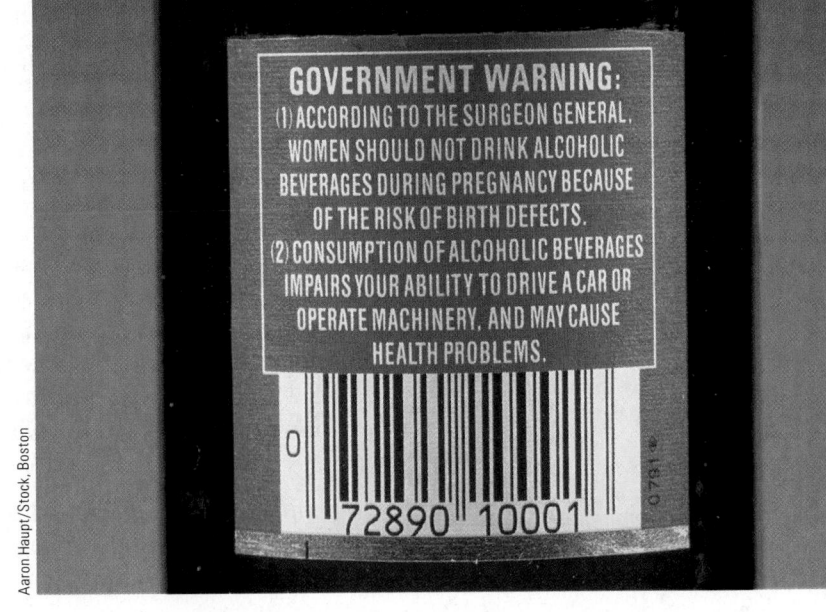

Aaron Haupt/Stock, Boston

GOVERNMENT WARNING: (1) ACCORDING TO THE SURGEON GENERAL, WOMEN SHOULD NOT DRINK ALCOHOLIC BEVERAGES DURING PREGNANCY BECAUSE OF THE RISK OF BIRTH DEFECTS. (2) CONSUMPTION OF ALCOHOLIC BEVERAGES IMPAIRS YOUR ABILITY TO DRIVE A CAR OR OPERATE MACHINERY, AND MAY CAUSE HEALTH PROBLEMS.

events and effect consistent?" If the answer to one of these questions is "No," the reasoning is not sound.

4. *Arguing by sign.* You are **arguing by sign** when you offer as a reason to support your proposition or as evidence to support your reason, that events have occurred that are outward signals of the truth of your proposition or reason. For example, you might support your point that the recession is worsening by noting that the local soup kitchens have experienced an increase in the number of people they are serving. Your argument would be "Longer lines at soup kitchens are a sign of the worsening recession." To test this kind of argument, you should ask, "Does the sign cited always or usually signal the conclusion drawn?" "Are a sufficient number of signs present?" and "Are contradictory signs also in evidence?"

Avoiding Fallacies of Reasoning

As you are developing your reasons and the arguments that you will make, you should check to make sure that your reasoning is appropriate for the particular situation. This will allow you to avoid fallacies or errors in your reasoning. Three common fallacies to avoid include:

1. *Hasty generalization.* A **hasty generalization** is a fallacy that presents a generalization that is either not supported with evidence or is supported with only one weak example. Because the supporting material that is cited should be representative of all the supporting material that could be cited, enough supporting material must be presented to satisfy the audience that the instances are not isolated or handpicked. Because you can find an example or statistic to support almost anything, avoiding hasty generalizations requires you to be confident that the instances you cite as support are typical and representative of your claim. For example, someone who argued, "All Akitas are vicious dogs," whose sole piece of evidence was "My neighbor had an Akita and it bit my best friend's sister," would be guilty of a hasty generalization. It is hasty to generalize about the temperament of a whole breed of dogs based on a single action of one dog.

2. *False cause.* A **false cause** occurs when the alleged cause fails to be related to, or to produce the effect. Just because two things happened one after the other, does not mean that the first necessarily caused the second. Just as people who blame monetary setbacks or illness on crossing paths with black cats, or broken mirrors, you need to be careful that you don't take coincidental events or signal events and present them as causal.

3. *Ad hominem argument.* An **ad hominem argument** supports a claim by attacking or praising the character of someone or something. Ad hominem literally means "to the man." For example, if Jamal's support for his

claim that his audience should buy an Apple computer was that Steve Jobs, the founder and current president of Apple Computer, is a genius, he would be making an ad hominem argument. Jobs's intelligence isn't really a reason to buy a particular brand of computer. Television commercials that feature celebrities using the product are often guilty of ad hominem reasoning.

Increasing Audience Involvement through Emotional Appeals

As you will recall, the ELM model suggests that people are more likely to listen to and think about information when they are involved in the topic. We are more likely to be involved in a topic when we have an emotional stake in it. As a speaker, if you can give your audience an emotional stake in what you are saying, they are more likely to listen to and think about your arguments. You can increase your audience members' involvement by evoking negative or positive emotions in your speeches (Nabi, 2002, p. 292).

Negative emotions are disquieting, so when people experience them, they look for ways to eliminate the discomfort. During your speech, you can arouse negative feelings in your audience so that they will listen to your proposition, which should provide a way for the audience to alleviate the discomfort. There are numerous negative emotions that you might tap; the five most common are fear, guilt, shame, anger, and sadness. Notice in the following statement how "fear" personalizes the statistics on heart disease and peaks your interest in listening to what the speaker has to say:

> **One out of every three Americans age 18 and older has high blood pressure. It is the primary cause of stroke, heart disease, heart failure, kidney disease, and blindness. It triples a person's chance of developing heart disease, and boosts the chance of stroke seven times and the chance of congestive heart failure six times. Look at the person on your right, look at the person on your left. If they don't get it, chances are, you will. Today, I'd like to convince you that you are at risk of developing high blood pressure.**

Positive emotional involvement can also lead audience members to more carefully consider your proposition and arguments. When you evoke positive emotions, audience members will look for ways to sustain or further enhance the feeling. Five of the most common emotions that you can evoke so that audience members listen to and process what you have to say include: happiness/joy, pride, relief, hope, and compassion. For example, notice how the speaker used the emotion of "pride" to peak interest in a speech designed to get the audience to sign up for an alternative spring break experience with Habitat for Humanity:

> **Imagine you are an Olympian who has won your event and now stands on the podium with a medal around your neck as they play your national**

OBSERVE & ANALYZE

Journal Activity

Giving Good Reasons and Evidence

The goal of this activity is to analyze reasons and evidence.

1. Use your ThomsonNOW for *Communicate!* to access **Web Resource 17.1: Maintaining the Faith** and read the speech "Terrorism and Islam: Maintaining Our Faith" by Mahathir Bin Mohamad, available through InfoTrac College Edition. Identify each of the main points or reasons the speaker offers in support of his thesis.

2. Are his reasons good? Are they supported? Relevant? Adapted to the audience?

3. Analyze his supporting evidence. Assess the quality, currency, and relevance to his reasons.

4. Identify two kinds of reasoning links that he uses, and then test them using the appropriate questions. Are the links you tested logical? Explain.

5. Are there any fallacies that you can detect in his argument? Explain.

Thomson NOW! You can complete this activity online and, if requested, e-mail it to your instructor. Use your ThomsonNOW for *Communicate!* to access **Skill Learning Activity 17.2.**

anthem. Imagine opening your mail and finding out that you have gotten into the number one ranking graduate program in the country. Now imagine that you are standing on the front porch of a brand new home that you have helped to build and are being hugged by the mother of four children who, thanks to your selfless work, will no longer have to share a one bedroom fifth floor walk up. Imagine the pride? How long has it been since you felt so good? Well folks, that's just what you'll experience and much more when you sign up to work with the Habitat for Humanity House being constructed in your community.

To read more about how to appeal to the various negative and positive emotions mentioned here, use your ThomsonNOW for *Communicate!* to access **Web Resource 17.2: Evoking Negative and Positive Emotions**.

Cueing Your Audience through Credibility: Demonstrating Goodwill

Even when you have tried to involve your audience in your topic, not everyone will choose to listen carefully and evaluate and elaborate on what you have said. Some will still choose to pay minimal attention to your arguments and instead will use simple cues and process your message. The most important cues that people use when they process information along the peripheral route is the credibility of the speaker. In Chapter 14, we discussed three speaker characteristics (expertise, trustworthiness, and personableness) that audience members pay attention to when evaluating credibility. A fourth characteristic, goodwill, is crucial to motivating uninvolved audience members to believe what the speaker is saying. **Goodwill** is the audience perception that the speaker understands, empathizes with, and is responsive to them. In other words, goodwill is the audience members' belief that the speaker's intentions toward them are for their good. Audience members who perceive the speaker as exhibiting goodwill toward them are more willing to believe what the speaker is saying.

You can demonstrate that you understand your audience by personalizing your information. Information you gleaned from your audience analysis can help you with this. For example, Meg, a union rep trying to convince the membership to accept a new contract change to health care benefits, might build goodwill by personalizing one aspect of the proposal:

> I know that about 40 percent of you have little use for eye care, which is part of the new package. But for the 60 percent of you who wear glasses or have dependents who wear glasses, this plan will not only pay for your annual eye exam, but it will also pay 30 percent of the cost of new glasses or 25 percent of the new cost of contact lenses. This will mean about $250 in your pocket each year and with less overtime predicted for this year, that's a real benefit.

Speakers demonstrate goodwill by showing that they understand their audience and also by empathizing with them. Empathizing requires you to go beyond understanding and to identify emotionally with audience mem-

goodwill
the audience perception that the speaker understands, empathizes with, and is responsive to them.

bers' views. This doesn't mean, however, that you accept their views as your own. It does mean that you acknowledge them as valid. Even when your speech is designed to change audience members' views, the sensitivity you show to their feelings will demonstrate goodwill. For example the union rep might demonstrate empathy by saying:

> **I can imagine what it will be like for some of you who, under this new plan, will go to the drugstore and find that there is now a high co-pay required for a drug you take that is no longer on the formulary. But I also guarantee that the plan formulary will have drugs that your doctor can prescribe that will be direct substitutes, or you will be able to appeal the co-pay.**

Finally, to demonstrate goodwill, you will want to show your responsiveness to the audience. **Being responsive** is showing care about the audience by acknowledging feedback from the audience, especially subtle negative cues. The union rep can demonstrate responsiveness by referencing feedback that the membership had provided earlier:

being responsive
showing care about the audience by acknowledging feedback from the audience, especially subtle negative cues.

> **Before we started negotiations, we surveyed you asking what changes you wanted to see in the health care program. Seventy-five percent of you said that your number one concern was keeping the office visit co-pay at $10, and in this contract we were able to do that.**

Or, if she notices that some members of the audience are looking disgusted and shaking their heads, she might respond:

> **I can see that some of you are disappointed with the increase in premiums. So am I. I wish we could have done better on this issue. But the fact is, health care costs have risen 15 percent nationwide this year, and our usage has exceeded this average.**

By establishing goodwill, you enhance your credibility with the audience, which is especially important for those audience members who are not personally involved with your topic.

Motivating Your Audience to Act through Incentives

When your speech proposition is aimed at influencing your audience members' attitudes or beliefs, you will use emotional appeals to encourage the audience to become involved with your topic. But when you want to influence your audience to act on what you have said, you will need to provide motivation by showing how what you are asking them to do will meet their needs. **Motivation,** "forces acting on or within an organism to initiate and direct behavior" (Petri, 1996, p. 3), is often a result of incentives that meet needs.

An **incentive** is a reward promised if a particular action is taken or goal is reached (Petri, 1996, p. 3). Incentives can be physical (food, shelter, money, sex), psychological (self-esteem, peace of mind), or social (acceptance, popularity, status) rewards.

motivation
forces acting on or within an organism to initiate and direct behavior.

incentive
a reward promised if a particular action is taken or goal is reached.

Incentives are only valuable to the extent that they can satisfy a need that is felt by the audience and their value must not be outweighed by costs associated with the action.

Using Incentives to Satisfy Unmet Needs

Incentives are more likely to motivate people when they satisfy a strong but unmet need. Various ways for categorizing needs have been developed to help us understand types of needs. One of the most widely recognized is Maslow's hierarchy of needs. Abraham Maslow divided people's needs into five categories, illustrated in Figure 17.3: (1) physiological needs, including food, drink, and life-sustaining temperature; (2) safety and security needs, including long-term survival and stability; (3) belongingness and love needs, including the need to identify with friends, loved ones, and family; (4) esteem needs—ego gratification including the quest for material goods, recognition, and power or influence; (5) cognitive needs; (6) aesthetic needs; and (7) self-actualization needs, including the need to develop one's self to realize one's full potential and engage in creative acts (Maslow, 1954, 80–92). Maslow believed that these needs were hierarchical; that is, that your "lower order" needs had to be met before you would be motivated by "higher order" needs. In theory, then, a person cannot be motivated to meet an esteem need of gaining recognition until basic physiological, safety, and belongingness and love needs have been met.

The hierarchical nature of needs is still debated because there is evidence that at times, some people will sacrifice lower order needs to satisfy higher order ones. Nevertheless, as a speaker, when you can tie the incentives that accompany your proposal with unmet audience needs,

Figure 17.3
Maslow's hierarchy of needs

you increase the likelihood that the audience will take the action you are proposing. Let's see how this could work in the volunteering for literacy speech with a college student audience. Suppose that, during the speech, you point out that people who volunteer 30 hours or more a year receive a recognition certificate and are invited to attend a private dinner with the stars of the hot band that will be headlining the big spring campus concert. After announcing this you add,

> **I know that although most of you care about literacy, you're thinking about what else you could do with that hour. But the really cool part of spending your time as a literacy volunteer is that you will feel good about yourself because you have improved someone's life, and you also will be able to list this service and recognition on your résumé. As a bonus, you'll get to brag to your friends about having dinner with several celebrities.**

In the first part of this short statement, you have enumerated three incentives that are tied to volunteering: a physical incentive (an award certificate), a psychological incentive of enhanced self-concept (I feel good about myself because I have helped someone else), and a social incentive (having dinner with an elite group and meeting celebrities). In the second part you have also tied each incentive to a need that it can satisfy. With enhanced résumés, people are more likely to get jobs that provide money for food and shelter. If by helping someone else, we feel better about ourselves, then we have met a self-actualization need. And by attending the private dinner, we might satisfy both esteem needs and belongingness needs.

Outweighing Costs

As you prepare your speech, you must be concerned with presenting the incentives that meet the needs of your audience, and you also need to understand the potential costs for audience members who act in line with your proposal. For example, in the literacy speech, one obvious cost is the hour of free time each week that might subtract from time audience members currently spend with their friends or family. This could create a potential deficit in their belongingness need. To address this concern, you might point out, "Now I know you might be concerned about the time this will take away from your friends or family, but relax. Your friends and family are likely to understand and admire you (esteem need substitute for belongingness). Also, at the Literacy Center, you're going to have time before the tutoring starts to meet other volunteers (belongingness) and they are some really cool people (esteem). I know a couple who just got engaged and they met through their volunteering (big-time belongingness)."

If, through your audience analysis, you discover that you cannot relate your proposition to meeting basic audience needs or if the analysis reveals that the costs associated with your proposition would outweigh the incentives, then you probably need to reconsider what you are asking the audience to do. For example, if you discover that most of your audience members are overcommitted and have little free time to take on volunteer activity, then it is probably unrealistic to think you will be able to convince them to volunteer an hour a week. So, you may need to modify your proposition and persuade them to donate a book or money to buy a book for the literacy library.

Finally, if your incentives are to motivate your audience, the audience must be convinced that there is a high likelihood that if they act as you suggest, they will receive the incentives. It is important, therefore, that you discuss only those incentives that you have strong reason to believe are closely tied to the action you are requesting and are received by almost all people who act in the recommended way. Although there is an annual award given to the literacy volunteer who has donated the most time that year, mentioning this in your speech is unlikely to motivate the audience because only one person receives it, and the cost is very high.

So when you want to move an audience to action, you need to understand their needs and explain the incentives they can receive by taking the action you suggest. You also need to make sure that the incentives you mention fulfill unmet needs in the audience.

Organizational Patterns for Persuasive Speeches

Having developed a proposition, selected evidence to support your reasons, identified ways to increase audience involvement through emotional appeals, determined how you will enhance your credibility by developing goodwill, and identified the incentives you will use to motivate your audience, you are ready to choose a pattern to organize your speech. The most common patterns for organizing persuasive speeches include statement of reasons, problem solution, comparative advantages, criteria satisfaction, and motivated sequence. In this section, we describe and illustrate these persuasive organizational patterns and identify the type of proposition for which they are most commonly used. So that you can contrast the patterns and better understand their use, we will illustrate each pattern by examining the same topic with slightly different propositions that use the same (or similar) reasons.

Statement of Reasons Pattern

statement of reasons pattern
a straightforward organization in which you present the best-supported reasons you can find.

The **statement of reasons** is a form of persuasive organization used for proving propositions of fact in which you present your best-supported reasons in a specific order, to increase the likelihood that the audience will accept your argument. For a speech with three reasons or more, place the strongest reason last because this is the reason you believe the audience will find most persuasive. Place the second strongest reason first because you want to start with a significant point. Place the other reasons in between.

> ***Proposition:*** I want my audience to believe that passing the proposed school tax levy is necessary.

  I. The income will enable the schools to restore vital programs. (second strongest)
 II. The income will enable the schools to give teachers the raises they need to keep up with the cost of living.
III. The income will allow the community to maintain local control and will save the district from state intervention. (strongest)

Comparative Advantages Pattern

The **comparative advantages pattern** is a form of persuasive organization used for arguing a proposition of value when the goal is to prove that something has more value than something else. A comparative advantages approach to a school tax proposition would look like this:

> ***Proposition:*** I want my audience to believe that passing the school tax levy is better than not passing it. (compares the value of change to the status quo)

  I. Income from a tax levy will enable schools to reintroduce important programs that had to be cut. (advantage 1)
 II. Income from a tax levy will enable schools to avoid a tentative strike by teachers who are underpaid. (advantage 2)
III. Income from a tax levy will enable us to retain local control of our schools, which will be lost to the state if additional local funding is not provided. (advantage 3)

comparative advantages pattern
an organization that allows you to place all the emphasis on the superiority of the proposed course of action.

Criteria Satisfaction

The **criteria satisfaction pattern** seeks audience agreement on criteria that should be considered when evaluating a particular idea and then shows how the proposition that the speaker is advocating satisfies the criteria. A criteria satisfaction pattern is especially useful when your audience is opposed to your proposition, because it approaches the proposition indirectly by first focusing on the criteria that the audience may agree with before introducing the specific solution. A criteria satisfaction organization for the school levy would look like this:

> ***Proposition:*** I want my audience to believe that passing a school levy is a good way to fund our schools.

  I. We can all agree that a good school funding method must meet three criteria:

criteria satisfaction pattern
an indirect organization that first seeks audience agreement on criteria that should be considered when they evaluate a particular proposition and then shows how the proposition satisfies those criteria.

A. A good funding method results in the reestablishment of programs that have been dropped due to budget constraints.
B. A good funding method results in fair pay for teachers.
C. A good funding method generates enough income to maintain local control, avoiding state intervention.
II. Passage of a local school tax levy is a good way to fund our schools.
A. A local levy will allow us to re-fund important programs.
B. A local levy will allow us to give teachers a raise.
C. A local levy will generate enough income to maintain local control and avoid state intervention.

Problem Solution Pattern

problem solution pattern
an organization that provides a framework for clarifying the nature of the problem and for illustrating why a given proposal is the best one.

The **problem solution pattern** is an organizational pattern that provides a framework for clarifying the nature of some problem and for illustrating why a given proposal is the best solution. This organization works well when the audience is neutral or only agrees that there is a problem but has no opinion about a particular solution. In a problem solution speech, the claim ("There is a problem that can be solved by X.") is supported by three reasons that take the general form: (1) There is a problem that requires action. (2) Proposal X will solve the problem. (3) Proposal X is the best solution to the problem, because it will lead to positive consequences and minimize or avoid negative ones. A problem solution organization for the school tax proposition might look like this:

> ***Proposition:*** The current fiscal crisis in the school district can be solved through a local tax levy.
> I. The current funding is insufficient and has resulted in program cuts, labor problems resulting from stagnant wages, and a threatened state take-over of local schools. (statement of problem)
> II. The proposed local tax levy is large enough to solve these problems. (solution)
> III. The proposed local tax levy is the best means of solving the funding crisis.

Motivated Sequence Pattern

motivated sequence pattern
an organization that combines the problem solution pattern with explicit appeals designed to motivate the audience to act.

The **motivated sequence pattern,** articulated by Allan Monroe, combines the problem solution pattern with explicit appeals designed to motivate the audience to act. The motivational sequence pattern is a five-point, unified sequence that replaces the normal introduction–body–conclusion model with (1) an attention step, (2) a need step that fully explains the nature of the problem, (3) a satisfaction step that explains how the proposal solves the problem in a satisfactory manner, (4) a visualization step that provides a personal application of the proposal, and (5) an action appeal step that

How would you apply each of the organizational patterns described in this chapter to a speech about rebuilding the wetlands of Louisiana to help reduce the effects of a large hurricane on New Orleans?

emphasizes the specific direction that listeners' action should take. A motivational pattern for the school tax levy proposition would look like this:

> ***Proposition:*** I want my audience to vote in favor of the school tax levy on the November ballot.

I. Comparisons of worldwide test scores in math and science have refocused our attention on education. (attention)

II. The shortage of money is resulting in cost-saving measures that compromise our ability to teach basic academic subjects well. (need, statement of problem)

III. The proposed increase is large enough to solve those problems in ways that allow for increased emphasis on academic need areas. (satisfaction, how the proposal solves the problem)

IV. Think of the contribution you will be making to the education of your future children and also to efforts to return our educational system to the world-class level it once held. (visualization of personal application)

V. Here are "Vote Yes" buttons that you can wear to show you are willing to support this much-needed tax levy. (action appeal showing specific direction)

Because motivational patterns are variations of problem solution patterns, the underlying assumption is similar: When the current means are not solving the problem, a new solution that does solve the problem should be adopted. To read a transcript of a speech that uses the motivated sequence pattern, use your ThomsonNOW for *Communicate!* to access **Web Resource 17.3: Motivated Sequence Speech**.

OBSERVE & ANALYZE

Journal Activity

Persuasive Organizational Methods

The goal of this activity is to analyze organizational patterns.

1. Use your ThomsonNOW for *Communicate!* to access **Web Resource 17.1: Maintaining the Faith** and read the speech "Terrorism and Islam: Maintaining Our Faith" by Mahathir Bin Mohamad, available through InfoTrac College Edition. Analyze the organizational methods Mahathir uses.

2. How well does his pattern fit the attitudes you believe his audience holds toward his position? Are there other patterns that might have served him better?

Thomson NOW! You can complete this activity online and, if requested, e-mail it to your instructor. Use your Thomson-NOW for *Communicate!* to access **Skill Learning Activity 17.4**.

You can use this form to critique a persuasive speech to convince that you hear in class. As you listen to the speaker, outline the speech, paying close attention to the reasoning process the speaker uses. Also note the claims and support used in the arguments and identify the types of warrants being used. Then answer the questions that follow.

Primary Criteria

_____ 1. Was the specific goal phrased as a proposition (were you clear about the position the speaker was taking on the issue)?
_____ 2. Did the proposition appear to be adapted to the initial attitude of most members of the audience?
_____ 3. Were emotional appeals used to involve the audience with the topic?
_____ 4. Were the reasons used in the speech
  _____ directly related to the proposition?
  _____ supported by strong evidence?
  _____ persuasive for the particular audience?
_____ 5. Was the evidence (support) used to back the reasons (claims)
  _____ from well-respected sources?
  _____ recent and/or still valid?
  _____ persuasive for this audience?
  _____ typical of all evidence that might have been used?
  _____ sufficient (enough evidence was cited)?
_____ 6. Could you identify the types of arguments that were used?
  _____ Did the speaker argue by example?   _____ If so, was it valid?
  _____ Did the speaker argue by analogy?   _____ If so, was it valid?
  _____ Did the speaker argue from causation?   _____ If so, was it valid?
  _____ Did the speaker argue by sign?   _____ If so, was it valid?
_____ 7. Could you identify any fallacies of reasoning in the speech?
  _____ hasty generalizations
  _____ arguing from false cause
  _____ ad hominem attacks
_____ 8. Did the speaker demonstrate goodwill?
_____ 9. If the speech called for the audience to take action,
  _____ did the speaker describe incentives and relate them to audience needs?
  _____ did the speaker acknowledge any costs associated with the action?
_____ 10. Did the speaker use an appropriate persuasive organizational pattern?
  _____ statement of reasons
  _____ problem solution
  _____ comparative advantages
  _____ criteria satisfaction
  _____ motivated sequence

General Criteria

_____ 1. Was the proposition clear? Could you tell the speaker's position on the issue?
_____ 2. Was the introduction effective in creating interest and involving the audience in the speech?
_____ 3. Was the speech organized using an appropriate persuasive pattern?
_____ 4. Was the language clear, vivid, emphatic, and appropriate?
_____ 5. Was the conclusion effective in summarizing what had been said and mobilizing the audience to act?
_____ 6. Was the speech delivered enthusiastically, with vocal expressiveness, fluency, spontaneity, and directness?
_____ 7. Did the speaker establish credibility?
  _____ expertise
  _____ personableness
  _____ trustworthiness

Overall evaluation of the speech (check one):
_____ excellent _____ good _____ average _____ fair _____ poor

Use the information from this checklist to support your evaluation.

Figure 17.4
Persuasive speech evaluation checklist

▶ Speech Assignment: Communicate on Your Feet

A Persuasive Speech

1. Follow the speech plan action steps to prepare a speech in which you change audience belief. Your instructor will announce the time limit and other parameters for this assignment.

2. Criteria for evaluation include all the general criteria of topic and purpose, content, organization, and presentation, but special emphasis will be placed on the primary persuasive criteria of how well the speech's specific goal was adapted to the audience's initial attitude toward the topic, the soundness of the reasons, the evidence cited in support of them, and the credibility of the arguments.

3. Use the Persuasive Speech Evaluation Checklist in Figure 17.4 to critique yourself as you practice your speech.

4. Prior to presenting your speech, prepare a complete sentence outline and source list (bibliography). If you have used Speech Builder Express to complete the action step activities online, you will be able to print out a copy of your completed outline and source list. Also prepare a written plan for adapting your speech to the audience. Your adaptation plan should address the following issues:

   - How does your goal adapt to whether your prevailing audience attitude is in favor, no opinion, or opposed?
   - What reasons will you use, and how will the organizational pattern you select fit your topic and audience?
   - How will you establish your credibility with this audience?
   - How will you motivate your audience?
   - How you will organize your reasons?

Sample Expository Speech: Don't Chat and Drive Adapted from a Speech by Cedrick McBeth, Collin County Community College*

This section presents a sample expository speech adaptation plan, outline, and transcript given by a student in an introductory speaking course.

1. Review the outline and adaptation plan developed by Cedrick McBeth in preparing his speech on cell phones and driving.
2. Then read the transcript of Cedrick McBeth's speech.
3. Use the Persuasive Speech Evaluation Checklist from Figure 17.4 to help you evaluate this speech.

---

*Used with permission of Cedrick McBeth.

Thomson
NOW!

4. Use your ThomsonNOW for *Communicate!* to watch a video clip of Cedrick presenting his speech in class. (See the inside back cover of this book for how to access the speech videos through ThomsonNOW.)

5. Write a paragraph of feedback to Cedrick McBeth describing the strengths of his presentation and what you think he might do next time to be more effective.

You can use your Student Workbook to complete this activity, or you can use your ThomsonNOW for *Communicate!* to complete it online, print a copy of the Persuasive Speech Evaluation Checklist, compare your feedback to that of the authors, and, if requested, e-mail your work to your instructor. Access **Skill Learning Activity 17.5**.

Adaptation Plan

1. **Key aspects of audience.** Although the majority of listeners are familiar with the problem of using cell phones while driving, I will present information and arguments to convince them to support legislation banning cell phone use while driving.

2. **Establishing and maintaining common ground.** My main way of establishing common ground will be by using the pronouns "we," "us," and so on.

3. **Building and maintaining interest.** I will use the Manocchio and Peña stories as well as startling statistics to create and maintain attention.

4. **Audience knowledge and sophistication.** Because most of the class is familiar with the general problem of driving while using cell phones, I will present specific statistics that underlie the problem.

5. **Building credibility.** Early in the speech, I will refer to the reading and research I have done on this issue.

6. **Audience attitudes.** Because my classmates are busy commuter students, I believe most own cell phones and use them while driving, so they will be slightly hostile to my proposition.

7. **Adapt to audiences from different cultures and language communities.** Although my audience members are demographically diverse, cell phones are used by most class members and issues are cross-cultural.

8. **Use visual aids to enhance audience understanding and memory.** I will start the speech with a cell phone in hand, as though I were talking and driving.

Speech Outline

Don't Chat and Drive

General purpose: To persuade

Speech goal (proposition): I want to persuade my classmates that cell phones should be prohibited from use while driving an automobile.

Introduction

 I. Alexander Manocchio is on trial for vehicular homicide.
 II. How many of us in this classroom generally talk on cell phones while driving a car? How many of us take into consideration the dangers of talking on our cell phones while driving a car?
 III. What I hope to convince you of today is that using a cell phone while driving an automobile should be prohibited.

Body

 I. First, let's see how great a problem cell phone use is while driving.
   A. Overall, cell phone usage has increased tremendously in the last 12 to 14 years.
     1. Statistics show that 168 million people used cell phones as of August 2004.
     2. Compare this figure to the approximately 4.3 million people who used cell phones in 1990.
   B. The jump in cell phone use has been accompanied by the jump in traffic accidents linked to cell phone use.
     1. In 2001, in Texas alone, there were 1,032 accidents with eight fatalities in which cell phone usage was considered a contributing factor.
     2. Regardless of the age or the driving experience of the driver, the risk of collision when using a cell phone is four times higher than when a cell phone is not used by the driver.
   C. Cell phone usage increases the likelihood of fatalities in accidents.
     1. The risk factor for driving while using a cell phone amounts to 6.4 fatalities per million drivers annually.
     2. The chance that a driver using a cell phone would kill a pedestrian or other motorists is 1.5 per 1 million people.
     3. Combining these figures with the 210 million licensed drivers in the U.S. amounts to a risk factor of roughly 1,660 fatalities per year involving cell phone–related accidents.

Transition: Now that we have established that a problem exists, let's look more closely at why cell phone use creates this problem.

 II. Using a cell phone while driving is distracting.
   A. First, when accessing or dialing a phone, the driver loses eye contact with the road.
   B. Second, while conversing, mental attention is split between conversation and the ever-changing road conditions.
 III. Here are the advantages to prohibiting the use of cell phones while driving.
   A. It would eliminate the sources of mental distraction.

B. It would eliminate one source of physical distraction.

C. It would decrease the number of accidents and fatalities.

Conclusion

I. I've shown you how the increased use of cell phones while driving has led to an increase in accidents and fatalities.

II. I've explained how cell phones distract drivers.

III. I've identified a policy that would reduce driver distractions and the accidents they cause.

IV. A quotation by Patricia Peña shows the effect that one cell phone call can have.

Work Cited

Cellular Telecommunications & Internet Association. November 1997. "An Investigation of the Safety Implications of Wireless Communications in Vehicles."

Dunn, Susan. 2004. "Two Good Reasons Not to Use Your Cell Phone in the Car." *USA Today.* (http://www.americaninsurancedepot.com/protectyourself/cellphones.htm)

Gebler, Dan. 2000. "Cell Phones and Automobiles." *Wireless Newsfactor.* (http://www.uvm.edu/~vlrs/doc/cell_phones.htm)

Greve, Frank. 2000. "Restricting Car Phones is a Difficult Sell in the US." *Philadelphia Inquirer.*

National Conference of State Legislatures. August 1999. "Cell Phones and Driving: 1999 State Legislative Update."

Speech and Analysis

Speech

On June 17, 2006, Alexander Manocchio reached for a ringing cell phone and killed Karyn Cordell and her unborn son. You see, Manocchio was driving a car at the time. Now two people are dead and Alexander's life is in a shambles, all because he answered a phone. Alexander faces two counts of vehicular homicide.

How many of us in this classroom are also guilty of putting lives at risk by talking on cell phones while driving a car? I'll bet almost all of us have done it and many of us do it everyday. But do we ever consider the dangers of

Analysis

Cedrick begins with an example that is designed to build our interest in the speech.

He then asks us to consider our behavior.

talking on our cell phones while driving a car? As I read the statistics and studied this situation, I became convinced that cell phone use while driving has become an unacceptable risk. Today, I hope to convince you that using a cell phone while driving an automobile should be illegal.

Let's begin by establishing that using a cell phone while you're driving has become a serious and growing problem. Overall, cell phone usage has increased tremendously in the last 12 to 14 years. According to the Cellular Telecommunications & Internet Association, as of August 2004, 168 million people used cell phones compared to only 4.3 million in 1990. That's a 390 percent increase. Not surprisingly, according to Vermont Legislative Research Shop, this jump in cell phone use has been accompanied by a jump in traffic accidents linked to cell phone use. According to a 2004 article in *USA Today* by Susan Dunn, in Texas alone during 2001, cell phone usage was considered a contributing factor in 1,032 accidents and resulted in eight fatalities. Regardless of the age or the driving experience of the driver, the risk of being in a collision when using a cell phone is four times higher than when not talking on the phone.

Cell phone usage also increases the likelihood of fatalities. An independent study done in 2002 by the Harvard Center for Risk Analysis found that driving while using a cell phone increases the risk to 6.4 fatalities per million drivers annually. The study also

Here Cedrick begins to establish his credibility.

He then states his goal: to convince you that using a cell phone while driving should be illegal.

Using a problem solution organizational pattern, he begins to establish the problem of using cell phones.

He then goes on to show the dramatic increase in the use of cell phones.

He then points out that this jump in use has also resulted in a jump in traffic accidents.

He then cites a source to show the results.

With his second point, he shows that the problem is not only the increase in accidents but also the increase in fatalities. Again, he uses statistics to support this claim.

Cedrick's language here is unclear. Although he speaks of "risk," he

found that the chance that a driver using a cell phone would kill a pedestrian or other motorists was 1.5 per 1 million people. Extrapolating from these figures, with 210 million licensed drivers in the U.S., this amounts to roughly 1,660 fatalities per year stemming from cell phone–related accidents.

So, I'm sure you'll agree that we have a problem. But how does using a cell phone while driving create accidents? Whether we realize it or not, no matter how experienced we are as drivers, we are distracted from paying attention to the road when we use a cell phone while driving. Think about it—when you access your phone or dial a number, you lose eye contact with the road. Even if you use a hands-free phone, your mental attention is split between your conversation and ever-changing road conditions. Being absorbed in a conversation affects your ability to concentrate on driving, which can jeopardize your safety and the safety of pedestrians and people in other cars.

Now let's consider a solution. To eliminate this problem, I recommend that we petition our congressional and state representatives to enact policies that prohibit the use of cell phones while driving a car. Drivers would be required to pull over to a safe place before making a call, and the policy would apply to drivers of all ages. The public would be informed of the policy via mainstream news sources. If this sort of policy were enacted, fewer people would use cell phones while they were driving, they would be less distracted, and the result

states raw numbers. Risk is usually stated as a percentage.

At this point, the audience may be losing interest as Cedrick uses one statistic after another, with no references to help ground them.

Notice how here as well as other places in the speech he uses the pronoun we to show that all of us can and may be involved.

Here Cedrick asks the audience members to personalize the process of using cell phones while driving.

Having established the problem, he now offers a solution to eliminate this problem.

His proposal is vague and perhaps a bit overambitious for a speech to a slightly hostile audience.

It might have been better to ask audience members to personally would be a decrease in the overall number of accidents and fatalities per year.

In conclusion, I've shown you today how the increased use of cell phones over the past several years has led to increased use of cell phones while driving, which in turn has led to an increase in car accidents and fatalities. I've also explained how cell phones distract drivers both physically—such as when they look for their phones and dial them—and mentally— such as when their conversation distracts them from their driving. And, finally, I've recommended that we ask the government to enact a policy that would greatly reduce the use of cell phones while driving and thus reduce driver distractions and the accidents they cause.

I began this speech by telling you of Alexander Manocchio, a cell phone user who killed a pregnant woman. I'd like to end by quoting a woman who lost her 2-year-old daughter because a man felt he could safely drive a car while talking on his cell phone:

"My name is Patricia Peña. On November 2, 1999, my 2-year-old daughter Morgan and I were on our way home, when our car was broadsided by another vehicle. Police reports proved that the crash was caused by a driver who was paying more attention to his cell phone than to the road and, as a result, ran a stop sign at 40 miles per hour. Morgan was rushed to the hospital, where she clung to life for the next 16 hours. But she never regained consciousness and was pronounced dead at 4:58 a.m. on November 3rd."

refrain from using cell phones while driving.

In this conclusion he reviews the main points of his speech to re-inforce audience memory of what he has said.

Again, notice how his entire speech is given in a way that shows that we are involved, and thus, when we are talking on a cell phone while driving, we need to consider either moving to the side of the road or stating that we should talk later.

He then ends with an emotional appeal, the words of a woman whose daughter died as a result of the driver paying more attention to a cell phone than to the road. Although relevant, the quote does not convey much emotion.

This is just one of many such accidents that have increased with the use of cell phones by drivers. I just pray this never happens to you or someone you love.

Overall, this is a good persuasive speech of reasons with well-documented use of statistics.

Summary

Persuasive speeches are designed to influence the beliefs and/or the behavior of audience members. They present logical reasons but must also present those reasons in a way that motivates the audience to listen and think about what the speaker is saying. The elaboration likelihood model (ELM) suggests that when people hear an argument, they can process it one of two ways. Either they can listen carefully, think about the information, and elaborate its implications for themselves; or they can make decisions about what they are hearing based on simple cues about the speaker's credibility. According to the model, people who feel personally involved with a proposition are more likely to process it carefully.

So in preparing a persuasive speech, the speaker must choose a proposition (goal) that takes into account the audience's initial attitude. An audience may be opposed to the proposition, neutral (because they are uninformed, impartial, or apathetic), or in favor.

The speaker must choose good reasons and sound evidence. Reasons are main point statements that support the proposition. Evidence is information (facts, opinions, and so on) selected to support reasons. Then the speaker needs to identify and test the forms of argument that will be used in supporting the proposition and in supporting each reason. Four of the most common types of arguments are: arguing by example, by analogy, from causation, and by sign. Speakers also need to check arguments so that they avoid three of the common fallacies that occur in reasoning: hasty generalizations, false cause, and ad hominem arguments.

Speakers can use emotional appeals to increase audience members' involvement with the proposition. Both appeals to negative and positive emotions can be effective.

When speakers want their audience to act, they should also consider what incentives the audience has for acting in accord with the speakers' propositions and how these incentives meet the needs of the audience. Audience needs include physiological, safety, belongingness, esteem, and self-actualization. Speakers should also consider whether the costs that audience members may experience would outweigh the incentives attached to the proposition.

The reasons that support a proposition can be organized following one of five patterns, which include: the statement of reasons pattern in which you present the best-supported reasons you can find; the comparative advantages pattern in which you show each of the advantages of your solution over others; the problem solution pattern in which you introduce the problem, offer a proposal to solve it, and show why it is the best solution; the criteria satisfaction pattern in which you present the criteria that a proposition needs to meet to be acceptable and then show how the speaker's proposition meets all the criteria; and the motivational pattern (used for propositions that influence the audience to take action), which replaces the normal model by including an attention step, a need step, a satisfaction step, a visualization step, and an appeal step.

Thomson
NOW!
Communicate! Online

N ow that you have read Chapter 17, use your ThomsonNOW for *Communicate!* for quick access to the electronic resources that accompany this text. Your ThomsonNOW gives you access to the video of Cedrick's speech on cell phones and driving, the Web Resources and Skill Learning Activities featured in this chapter, InfoTrac College Edition, and online study aids such as a digital glossary and review quizzes.

Your *Communicate!* ThomsonNOW is an online study system that helps you identify concepts you don't fully understand, allowing you to put your study time to the best use. Using chapter-by-chapter diagnostic pre-tests, the system creates a personalized study plan for each chapter. Each plan directs you to specific resources designed to improve your understanding, including pages from the text in e-book format. Chapter post-tests give you an opportunity to measure how much you've learned and let you know if you are ready for graded quizzes and exams.

Key Terms

Go to your ThomsonNOW for *Communicate!* to access your online glossary for Chapter 17. Print a copy of the glossary for this chapter and test yourself with the electronic flash cards or complete the crossword puzzle to help you master these key terms:

ad hominem argument (454)
apathetic (449)
arguing by analogy (453)
arguing by example (452)
arguing by sign (454)
arguing from causation (453)
argument (452)
being responsive (457)

comparative advantages pattern (461)
criteria satisfaction pattern (461)
false cause (454)
goodwill (456)
hasty generalization (454)
impartial (448)
incentive (457)

motivated sequence pattern (462)
motivation (457)
persuasive speech (444)
problem solution pattern (462)
proposition (447)
reasons (450)
statement of reasons (460)
uninformed (448)

Review Quiz

Test your knowledge of the concepts in this chapter by taking the online review quiz for Chapter 17. Go to your ThomsonNOW for *Communicate!* to access the quiz. When you have completed the quiz, submit it for scoring.

Skill Learning Activities

Complete the Observe & Analyze and Speech and Analysis activities for Chapter 17 online at your ThomsonNOW for *Communicate!* You can submit your Observe & Analyze and Speech and Analysis answers to your instructor, and compare your Speech and Analysis answers to those provided by the authors.

17.1: Observe & Analyze: A Specific Goal Statement in a Persuasive Speech (450)

17.2: Observe & Analyze: Giving Good Reasons and Evidence (455)

17.3: Observe & Analyze: Motivating Audiences (460)

17.4: Observe & Analyze: Persuasive Organizational Methods (464)

17.5: Speech and Analysis: Don't Chat and Drive (466)

Web Resources

Go to your ThomsonNOW for *Communicate!* to access the Web Resources for this chapter.

17.1: Maintaining the Faith (450)

17.2: Evoking Negative and Positive Emotions (456)

17.3: Motivated Sequence Speech (463)

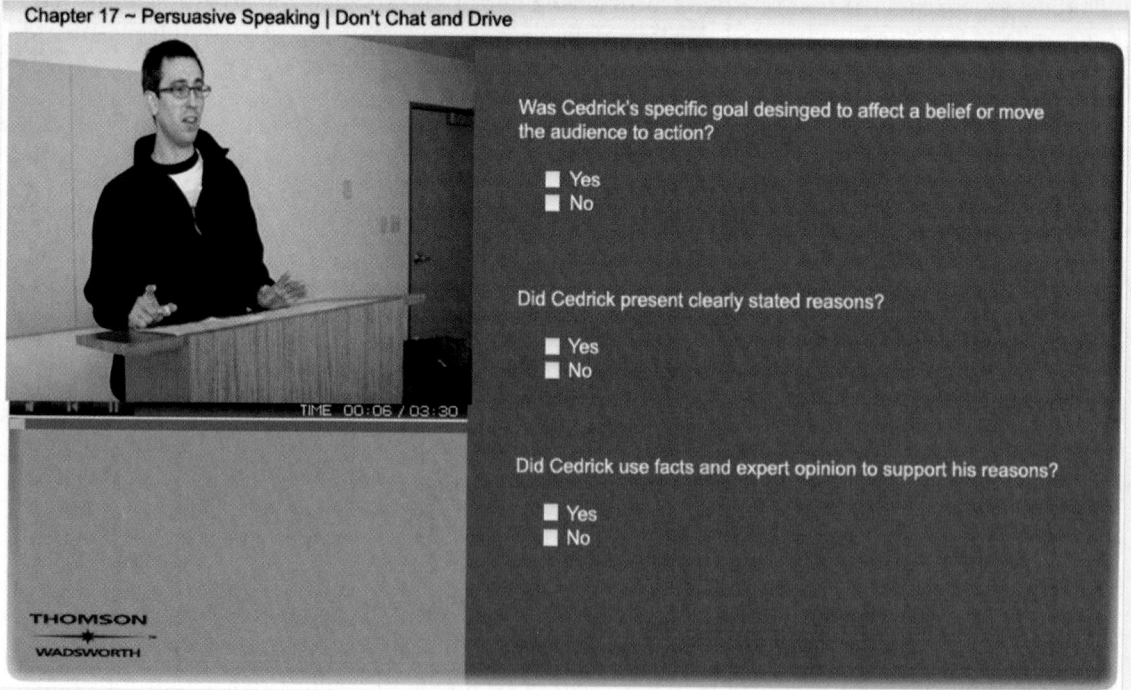

PART IV | **Public Speaking** | Self-Review

Public Speaking from Chapters 12 to 17

What kind of a public speaker are you? The following analysis looks at 11 specifics that are basic to a public-speaking profile. Use this scale to assess the frequency with which you perform each behavior: 1 = always; 2 = often; 3 = sometimes; 4 = rarely; 5 = never.

_____ When I am asked to speak, I am able to select a topic and determine a speech goal with confidence. (Ch. 12)

_____ When I speak, I use material from a variety of sources. (Ch. 12)

_____ In my preparation, I construct clear main points and organize them to follow some consistent pattern. (Ch. 13)

_____ In my preparation, I am careful to be sure that I have developed ideas to meet audience needs. (Ch. 14)

_____ When I speak, I sense that my audience perceives my language as clear and vivid. (Ch. 15)

_____ I look directly at members of my audience when I speak. (Ch. 15)

_____ My public-speaking voice shows variation in pitch, speed, and volume. (Ch. 15)

_____ When I speak, my bodily actions help supplement or reinforce my ideas; I feel and look involved. (Ch. 15)

_____ I have confidence in my ability to speak in public. (Ch. 15)

_____ When I give informative speeches, I am careful to use techniques designed to get audience attention, create audience understanding, and increase audience retention. (Ch. 16)

_____ When I give persuasive speeches, I am careful to use techniques designed to build my credibility, prove my reasons, and motivate my audience. (Ch. 17)

To verify this self-analysis, have a friend or fellow group member complete this review for you. Based on what you have learned, select the public-speaking behavior you would most like to improve. Write a communication improvement plan similar to the sample goal statement in Chapter 1 (page 22).

Thomson NOW! You can complete this Self-Review online and, if requested, e-mail it to your instructor. Use your ThomsonNOW for *Communicate!* to access Part IV Self-Review under the chapter resources for Chapter 17.

REFERENCES

Adler, R. B. (1977). *Confidence in communication: A guide to assertive and social skills.* New York: Holt, Rinehart & Winston.

Affifi, W. A., & Guerrero, L. K. (2000). Motivations underlying topic avoidance in close relationships. In S. Petronio (Ed.), *Balancing the secrets of private disclosures* (pp. 165–180). Mahwah, NJ: Erlbaum.

Ahladas, J. (1989, April 1). Global warming. *Vital Speeches of the Day,* 381–384.

Alberti, R. E., & Emmons, M. L. (1995). *Your perfect right: A guide to assertive living* (7th ed.). San Luis Obispo, CA: Impact.

Anderson, J. (1988). Communication competency in the small group. In R. Cathcart & L. Samovar (Eds.), *Small group communication: A reader.* Dubuque, IA: Wm. Brown.

Andersen, P. A., Hecht, M. L., Hoobler, G. D., & Smallwood, M. (2003). Nonverbal communication across cultures. In W. B. Gudykunst (Ed.), *Cross-cultural and intercultural communication.* Thousand Oaks, CA: Sage.

Anzaldúa, G. (1999). *Borderlands/LaFrontera: The New Mestiza.* San Francisco, CA: Aunt Lute Books.

Aron, A., Aron, E. N., Tudor, M., & Nelson, G. (2004). Close relationships as including other in the self. In H. T. Reis & C. E. Rusbult (Eds.), *Close relationships* (pp. 365–379). New York: Psychology Press.

Aronson, E. (1999). *The social animal.* New York: Worth.

Asante, M. K. (2002). *American history: A journey of liberation.* Maywood, NJ: Peoples Publishing Group, Inc.

Asante, M. K. (2002). *Culture and customs of Egypt.* Westport, CT: Greenwood Press.

Asante, M. K. (2003). *Afrocentricity: The theory of social change.* Chicago: African American Images.

Asante, M. K. (2003). *Erasing racism: The survival of the American nation.* Amherst, NY: Prometheus Books.

Axtell, R. E. (1991). *Gestures: The do's and taboos of body language around the world* (rev. ed.). New York: Wiley.

Ayres, J. (1991, June–December). Using visual aids to reduce speech anxiety. *Communication Research Reports,* 73–79.

Ayres, J., & Hopf, T. S. (1990, January). The long-term effect of visualization in the classroom: A brief research report. *Communication Education, 39,* 75–78.

Ayres, J., Hopf, T. S., & Ayres, D. M. (1994, July). An examination of whether imaging ability enhances the effectiveness of an intervention designed to reduce speech anxiety. *Communication Education, 43,* 252–258.

Bach, K., & Harnish, R. M. (1979). *Linguistic communication and speech acts.* Cambridge, MA: MIT Press.

Baeder, D. L. (1980, June 1). Chemical wastes. *Vital Speeches of the Day,* 496–500.

Baerwald, D. Narrative. Northshore School District, http://ccweb.norshore.wednet.edu/writingcorner/narrative.html.

Baker, D. C. (1990). A qualitative and quantitative analysis of verbal style and the elimination of potential leaders in small groups. *Small Group Research, 38,* 13–26.

Bales, R. F. (1971). *Personality and interpersonal behavior.* New York: Holt, Rinehart & Winston.

Balgopal, P. R., Ephross, P. H., & Vassil, T. V. (1986). Self help groups and professional helpers. *Small Group Research, 17,* 123–137.

Banks, M. A. (1997). *Web psychos, stalkers and pranksters.* Scottsdale, AZ: Coriolis Groups.

Barge, J. K. (1994). *Leadership: Communication skills for organizations and groups.* New York: St. Martin's.

Barnes, S. B. (2003). *Computer-mediated communication: Human-to-human communication across the Internet.* Boston, MA: Allyn & Bacon.

Baron, R. A., Bryne, D., & Brascombe, N. R. (2006). *Social psychology* (11th ed.). Boston: Allyn & Bacon.

Bass, B. M. (1981). Traits of leadership: A follow-up to 1970. In R. M. Stogdill (Ed.), *Handbook of Leadership* (pp. 73–96). New York: Free Press.

Baxter, L. (1982). Strategies for ending relationships: Two studies. *Western Journal of Speech Communication, 46,* 223–241.

Becherer, H. W. (2000, September 15). Enduring values for a secular age: Faith, hope and love. *Vital Speeches of the Day,* 732–744.

Beebe, M. B., Anthony, T., Salas, E., & Driskell, J. E. (1994). Group cohesiveness and quality of decision making. *Small Group Research, 25,* 189–204.

Behnke, R. R., & Carlile, L. W. (1971). Heart rate as an index of speech anxiety. *Speech Monographs, 38,* 66.

Berger, C. R., & Brada, J. J. (1982). *Language and social knowledge: Uncertainty in interpersonal relations.* London: Arnold.

Bigelow, J. D. (1999). The Web as an organizational behavior learning medium. *Journal of Management Education, 23,* 635–650.

Bommelje, R., Houston, J. M., & Smither, R. (2003). Personalty characteristics of effective listeners: A five factor perspective. *International Journal of Listening, 17,* 32–46.

Bonito, J. (2000). The effect of contributing substantively on perceptions of participation. *Small Group Research, 31,* 528–553.

Bonvillain, N. (2003). *Language, culture and communication: The meaning of messages.* (4th ed.). Upper Saddle River, NJ: Prentice-Hall.

Boon, S. D. (1994). Dispelling doubt and uncertainty: Trust in romantic relationships. In S. Duck (Ed.), *Dynamics of Relationships* (pp. 86–111). Thousand Oaks, CA: Sage.

Bormann, E. (1990). *Small group communication: Theory and practice.* New York: Harper & Row.

Bostrom, R. (1970). Patterns of communicative interaction in small groups. *Speech Monographs, 37,* 257–263.

Boyd, A. (1999). *How to handle media interviews.* London: Mercury.

Bright, William (2000). The sociolinguistics of the "S-word": "Squaw" in American placenames. Retrieved September 27, 2006, from www.ncidc.org/bright/Squaw_revised.doc.

Brown, P., & Levinson, S. (1987). *Politeness: Some universals in language usage.* Cambridge, U.K.: Cambridge University Press.

Brownell, J. (2002). *Listening: Attitudes, principles, and skills* (2nd ed.). Boston: Allyn & Bacon.

Burger, C. (2000, September 15). Sooner than you think. *Vital Speeches of the Day,* 710–712.

Burgoon, J. K., & Bacue, A. E. (2003). Nonverbal communication skills. In J. O. Greene & B. R. Burleson (Eds.), *Handbook of communication and social interaction skills* (pp. 179–220). Mahwah, NJ: Erlbaum.

Burgoon, J. K., Buller, D. B., & Woodall, W. G. (1989). *Nonverbal communication: The unspoken dialogue.* New York: Harper & Row.

Burgoon, J. K., & Burgoon, M. (2002). Expectancy theories. In W. P. Robinson & H. Giles (Eds.), *The new handbook of language and social psychology.* New York: Wiley.

Burgoon, J. K., Coker, D. A., & Coker, R. A. (1986). Communicative effects of gaze behavior: A test of two contrasting explanations. *Human Communication Research, 12,* 495–524.

Burgoon, J. K., Dunbar, N. E., & Segrin, C. (2002). Nonverbal influence. In J. P. Dillard & M. Pfau (Eds.), *The persuasion handbook: Developments in theory and practice.* Thousand Oaks, CA: Sage.

Burgoon, J. K., & Hoobler, G. D. (2002). Nonverbal signals. In M. L. Knapp & J. A. Daly (Eds.), *Handbook of interpersonal communication* (3rd ed., pp. 240–299). Thousand Oaks, CA: Sage.

Burke, K. (1968). *Language as symbolic action.* Berkeley: University of California Press.

Burleson, B. R. (2003). Emotional support skills. In J. O. Green & B. R. Burleson (Eds.), *Handbook of communication and social interaction skills* (pp. 551–594). Mahwah, NJ: Erlbaum.

Burleson, B. R., & Goldsmith, D. J. (1998). How the comforting process works: Alleviating emotional distress through conversationally induced reappraisals. In P. A. Andersen & L. K. Guerrero (Eds.), *Handbook of communication and emotion: Research, theory, applications, and contexts* (pp. 248–280). San Diego, CA: Academic Press.

Burleson, B. R., & MacGeorge, E. L. (2002). Supportive communication. In M. L. Knapp, J. A. Daly, & G. R. Miller (Eds.), *Handbook of interpersonal communication* (3rd ed., pp. 374–424). Thousand Oaks, CA: Sage.

Burleson, B. R., & Samter, W. (1990). Effects of cognitive complexity on the perceived importance of communication skills in friends. *Communication Research, 17,* 165–182.

Cahn, D. D. (1990). Intimates in conflict: A research review. In D. D. Cahn (Ed.), *Intimates in conflict: A communication perspective* (pp. 1–24). Hillsdale, NJ: Erlbaum.

Canary, D. J., & Hause, K. (1993). Is there any reason to research sex differences in communication? *Communication Quarterly, 41,* 129–144.

Canary, D. J., Cupach, W. R., & Messman, S. J. (1995). *Relationship conflict: Conflict in parent–child, friendship, and romantic relationships.* Thousand Oaks, CA: Sage.

Carlo-Casellas, I. R. (January 14, 2002). Marketing to US Hispanic Population Requires Analysis of Cultures, p. 9.

Cegala, D. J., & Sillars, A. L. (1989). Further examination of nonverbal manifestations of interaction involvement. *Communication Reports, 2,* 45.

Chen, G. M., & Starosta, W. J. (1998). *Foundations of intercultural communication.* Boston: Allyn & Bacon.

Chuang, R. (2004). An examination of Taoist and Buddhist perspectives on interpersonal conflict, emotions and adversities. In F. E. Jandt (Ed.), *Intercultural communication: A global reader* (pp. 38–50). Thousand Oaks, CA: Sage.

Claes, M. T. (2002). Women, men and management styles. In P. J. Dubeck & D. Dunn (Eds.), *Workplace/women's place: An anthology* (2nd ed., pp. 121–125). Los Angeles: Roxbury.

Cleveland, H. The limits to cultural diversity. In L. A. Samovar, R. E. Porter, & E. R. McDaniel (Eds.), *Intercultural communication: A reader* (11th ed., pp. 405–408). Belmont, CA: Thomson Wadsworth. Reprinted by permission of the World Future Society.

Clevenger, T., Jr. (1959, April). A synthesis of experimental research in stage fright. *Quarterly Journal of Speech, 45,* 134–145.

Cloven, D. H., & Roloff, M. E. (1991). Sense-making activities and interpersonal conflict: Communicative cures for the mulling blues. *Western Journal of Speech Communication, 55,* 134–158.

Cornog, M. W. (1998). *Merriam Webster's vocabulary builder.* Springfield, MA: Merriam Webster.

Criscito, P. (2000). *Résumés in cyberspace* (2nd ed.). Hauppauge, NY: Barron's Educational Series, Inc.

Crumlish, C. (1997). *The Internet for busy people* (2nd ed.). Berkeley, CA: Osborne/McGraw-Hill.

Cupach, W. R., & Canary, D. J. (1997). *Competence in interpersonal conflict.* New York: McGraw-Hill.

Cupach, W. R., & Metts, S. (1986). Accounts of relational disclosure: A comparison of marital and nonmarital relationships. *Communication Monographs, 53,* 319–321.

Dahl, S. (2004). Intercultural research: The current state of knowledge. Middlesex University Discussion Paper no. 26. Available at SSRN, http://SSRN.com/abstrate=658202.

Dale, P. (1999). *"Did you say something, Susan?" How any woman can gain confidence with assertive communication.* Secaucus, NJ: Carol.

Darling, A. L., & Dannels, D. P. (2003, January). Practicing engineers talk about the importance of talk: A report on the role of oral communication in the workplace. *Communication Education, 52,* 1–16.

Deaux, K., Dane, F. C., & Wrightsman, L. S. (1993). *Social psychology in the '90s* (6th ed.). Pacific Grove, CA: Brooks/Cole.

Deavenport, E. W. (1995, July 15). Walking the high wire: Balancing stakeholder interests. *Vital Speeches of the Day,* 595–597.

Demo, D. H. (1987). Family relations and the self-esteem of adolescents and their parents. *Journal of Marriage and the Family, 49,* 705–715.

Dennis, A. R. (1996). Information exchange and use in small group decision making. *Small Group Research, 27,* 532–550.

Derlega, V. J., Metts, S., Petronio, S., & Margulis, S. T. (1993). *Self-disclosure.* Newbury Park, CA: Sage.

Dikel, M. Prepare your resume for e-mailing or posting on the Internet. The Internet-ready resume. Retrieved 9/06/2006 from http://www.rileyguide.com/eresume.html.

Dindia, K. (2000a). Relational maintenance. In C. Hendrick & S. S. Hendrick (Eds.), *Close relationships: A sourcebook* (pp. 287–300). Thousand Oaks, CA: Sage.

Dindia, K. (2000b). Sex differences in self-disclosure, reciprocity of self-disclosure, and self-disclosure and liking: Three metaanalyses reviewed. In S. Petronio (Ed.), *Balancing the secrets of private disclosures* (pp. 21–36). Mahwah, NJ: Erlbaum.

Dindia, K., Fitzpatrick, M. A., & Kenny, D. A. (1997). Self-disclosure in spouse and stranger interaction: A social relations analysis. *Human Communication Research, 23,* 388–412.

Dindia, K., & Timmerman, L. (2003). Accomplishing romantic relationships. In J. O. Greene & B. R. Burleson (Eds.), *Handbook of communication and social interaction* (pp. 685–722). Mahwah, NJ: Erlbaum.

Donoghue, P. J., & Seigel, M. E. (2005). *Are you really listening?: Keys to successful communication.* Notre Dame, IN: Sorin Books.

Downey, G., Freitas, A. L., Michaelis, B., & Khouri, H. (2004). The self-fulfilling prophecy in close relationships: Rejection sensitivity and rejection by romantic partners. In H. T. Reis & C. E. Rusbult (Eds.), *Close relationships* (pp. 153–174). New York: Psychology Press.

Duck, S. (1987). How to lose friends without influencing people. In M. E. Roloff & G. R. Miller (Eds.), *Interpersonal processes: New directions in communication research.* Beverly Hills, CA: Sage.

Duck, S. (1998). *Human relationships* (3rd ed.). Thousand Oaks, CA: Sage.

Duck, S. (1999). *Relating to others.* Philadelphia: Open University Press.

DuFrene, D. D., & Lehman, C. M. (2002). Persuasive appeal for clean language. *Business Communication Quarterly, 65* (March), 48–56. [Available on InfoTrac College Edition]

Dunkel, P., & Pialorsi, F. (2005). *Advanced listening comprehension: Developing aural and notetaking skills.* Boston: Thomson Heinle.

Durst, G. M. (1989, March 1). The manager as a developer. *Vital Speeches of the Day,* 309–314.

Dwyer, K. K. (2000, January). The multidimensional model: Teaching students to self-manage high communication apprehension by self-selecting treatments. *Communication Education, 49,* 79.

Eggins, S., & Slade, D. (1997). *Analyzing casual conversation.* Washington, DC: Cassell.

Ekman, P. (1999). Facial expressions. In T. Dalgleish & M. Power (Eds.), *Handbook of cognition and emotions* (pp. 301–320). New York: John Wiley & Sons Ltd.

Ekman, P., & Friesen, W. V. (1969). The repertoire of nonverbal behavior: Categories, origins, usage, and coding. *Semiotica, I,* 49–98.

Ellis, K. (1995, January). Apprehension, self-perceived competency, and teacher immediacy in the laboratory-supported public speaking course: Trends and relationships. *Communication Education, 44,* 64–78.

Encyclopedia.com. (2002). [Online]. Available: www.encyclopedia.com

Estes, W. K. (1989). Learning theory. In A. Lesgold & R. Glaser (Eds.), *Foundations for a psychology of education* (pp. 1–49). Hillsdale, NJ: Erlbaum.

Ettinger, H. R. (2000, September 15). Shattering the glass floor: Women donors as leaders of fundamental change. *Vital Speeches of the Day,* 727–730.

Evans, C., & Dion, K. (1991). Group cohesion and performance: A meta-analysis. *Small Group Research, 22,* 175–186.

Fairhurst, G. T. (2001). Dualism in leadership. In F. M. Jablin & L. M. Putnam (Eds.), *The new handbook of organizational communication* (pp. 379–439). Thousand Oaks, CA: Sage.

Fairhurst, G. T., & Sarr, R. A. (1996). *The art of framing.* San Francisco: Jossey-Bass.

Flaherty, L. M., Pearce, K. J., & Rubin, R. B. (1998). Internet and face-to-face communication: Not functional alternatives. *Communication Quarterly, 46* (Summer), 250–268.

Floyd, K., & Morman, M. T. (1998). The measurement of affectionate communication. *Communication Quarterly, 46* (Spring), 144–162.

Ford, C. E., Fox, B. A., & Thompson, S. A. (2002). Introduction. In C. E. Ford, B. A. Fox, & S. A. Thompson (Eds.), *The language of turn and sequence* (pp. 3–13). New York: Oxford University Press.

Forgas, J. P. (1991). Affect and person perception. In J. P. Forgas (Ed.), *Emotion and social judgments* (pp. 387–406). New York: Pergamon Press.

Forgas, J. P. (2000). Feelings and thinking: Summary and integration. In J. P. Forgas (Ed.), *Feeling and thinking: The role of affect in social cognition* (pp. 387–406). New York: Cambridge University Press.

Gannon, M. J. (2001). *Understanding global culture* (3rd ed.). Thousand Oaks, CA: Sage.

Gentry, G. (1980). Group size and attitudes towards the simulation experience. *Simulation and Games, 11,* 451–460.

Geyer, G. A. (1999, September 15). Dressing in the name of respect. *Cincinnati Enquirer,* p. A12.

Globus, S. (2002, February 28). The good and bad and the Internet: Like it or not, life is happening more and more in cyberspace. *Current Health,* 13–17.

Gilbert, D., & Kahl, J. A. (1982). *The American class structure: A new synthesis.* Homewood, IL: Dorsey.

Gmelch, S. B. (1998). *Gender on campus: Issues for college women.* New Brunswick, NJ: Rutgers University Press.

Goldberg, B. (1999). *Overcoming high-tech anxiety: Thriving in a wired world.* San Francisco, CA: Jossey-Bass.

Goleman, D. (1998). *Working with emotional intelligence.* New York: Bantam Books.

Gordon, T. (1971). *The basic modules of the instructor outline for effectiveness training courses.* Pasadena, CA: Effectiveness Training Associates.

Gorham, J., & Christophel, D. M. (1995). A test–retest analysis of student motivation, teacher immediacy, and perceived sources of motivation and demotivation in college classes. *Communication Education, 44,* 292–307.

Gorham, J., Cohen, S. H., & Morris, T. L. (1997). Fashion in the classroom II: Instructor immediacy and attire. *Communication Research Reports, 14,* 11–24.

Gorham, J., Morris, T. L., & Tracy, L. (1999). Fashion in the classroom III: Effects of instructor attire and immediacy in natural classroom interactions. *Communication Quarterly, 47* (Summer), 281–299.

Gouran, D. S., & Hirokawa, R. Y. (1996). Functional theory and communication in decision-making groups: An expanded view. In R. Y. Hirokawa & M. S. Poole (Eds.), *Communication and group decision making* (2nd ed., pp. 55–80). Thousand Oaks, CA: Sage.

Grice, H. P. (1975). Logic and conversation. In P. Cole & J. L. Morgan (Eds.), *Syntax and semantics,* vol. 3: *Speech acts.* New York: Academic Press.

Griffiths, M. (1998). Internet addiction: Does it really exist? In J. Gackenbach (Ed.), *Psychology and the Internet: Intrapersonal, interpersonal, and transpersonal implications* (pp. 61–76). San Diego, CA: Academic Press.

Gudykunst, W. B., & Kim, Y. Y. (2003). *Communicating with strangers: An approach to intercultural communication* (4th ed.). Boston: Allyn & Bacon.

Gudykunst, W. B., & Matsumoto, Y. (1996). Cross-cultural variability of communication in personal relationships. In W. B. Gudykunst, S. Ting-Toomey, & T. Nishida (Eds.), *Communication in personal relationships across cultures* (pp. 19–56). Thousand Oaks, CA: Sage.

Guerrero, L. K., & Andersen, P. A. (2000). Cross-cultural variability of communication in personal relationships. In C. Hendrick & S. S. Hendrick (Eds.), *Close relationships: A sourcebook* (pp. 287–300). Thousand Oaks, CA: Sage.

Guidelines for meeting participants. (1998, Fall). Unpublished manuscript developed by students in BAD 305, Understanding behavior in organizations. Northern Kentucky University.

Hall, B. J. (2002). *Among cultures: The challenge of communication.* Belmont, CA: Wadsworth.

Hall, B.J. (2005). *Among cultures: The challenge of communication.* Belmont, CA: Thomson Learning.

Hall, E. T. (1976). *Beyond culture.* Garden City: NJ: Anchor Press.

Hall, E. T. (1959). *The silent language.* Greenwich, CT: Fawcett.

Hall, E. T. (1969). *The hidden dimension.* Garden City, NY: Doubleday.

Hall, J. A. (1998). How big are nonverbal sex differences? The case of smiling and sensitivity to nonverbal cues. In D. J. Canary & K. Dindia (Eds.), *Sex differences and similarities in communication: Critical essays and empirical investigations of sex and gender in interaction* (pp. 155–178). Mahwah, NJ: Erlbaum.

Hattie, J. (1992). *Self-concept.* Hillsdale, NJ: Erlbaum.

Haviland, W. A. (1993). *Cultural anthropology.* Fort Worth, TX: Harcourt, Brace, Jovanovich.

Hayes, J. (2002). *Interpersonal skills at work* (2nd ed.). New York: Routledge.

Henman, L. D. (2003). Groups as systems: A functional perspective. In R. Y. Hirokawa, R. S. Cathcart, L. A. Samovar, & L. D. Henman (Eds.), *Small group communication theory and practice: An anthology* (8th ed., pp. 3–7). Los Angeles: Roxbury.

Hensley, C. W. (1995, September 1). Speak with style and watch the impact: Make things happen. *Vital Speeches of the Day,* 703.

Hill, B., & Leeman, R. W. (1997). *The art and practice of argumentation and debate.* Mountain View, CA: Mayfield.

Hirokawa, R. Y. (1987). Why informed groups make faulty decisions. *Small Group Behavior, 18,* 3–29.

Hirokawa, R. Y. (1988). Group communication and decision-making performance: A continued test of the functional perspective. *Human Communication Research, 14,* 487–515.

Hofstede, G. (1997). *Cultures and organizations: Software of the mind.* New York: McGraw Hill.

Hofstede, G. (1980). *Culture's consequences.* Beverly Hills, CA: Sage.

Hofstede, G. (Ed.) (1998). *Masculinity and femininity: The taboo dimension of national cultures.* Thousand Oaks, CA: Sage.

Hofstede, G. (2000). The cultural relativity of the quality of life concept. In G. R. Weaver (Ed.), *Cultural communication and conflict: Readings in intercultural relations.* Boston: Allyn & Bacon.

Hollman, T. D. (1972). Employment interviewer's errors in processing positive and negative information. *Journal of Psychology, 56,* 130–134.

Holtgraves, T. (2002). *Language as social action: Social psychology and language use.* Mahwah, NJ: Erlbaum.

Hotz, R. L. (April 15, 1995). Official racial definitions have shifted sharply and often. *Los Angeles Times,* p. A14.

Howard, J. A. (2000, August 1). Principles in default: Rediscovered and reapplied. *Vital Speeches of the Day,* 618–619.

Humphrey, J. (1998, May 15). Executive eloquence: A seven-fold path to inspirational leadership. *Vital Speeches of the Day,* 470.

Hundt, R. E. (1995, September 1). Serving kids and the community: Do we want TV to help or hurt children? *Vital Speeches of the Day,* 675.

Ice Man, http://www.digonsite.com/drdig/mummy/22.html.

Jackson, R. L. II (Ed.) (2004). *African American communication and identities.* Thousand Oaks, CA: Sage.

Jandt, F. E. (2001). *Intercultural communication: An introduction* (3rd ed.). Thousand Oaks, CA: Sage.

Janis, I. L. (1982). *Groupthink: Psychological studies of policy decisions and fiascoes.* Boston: Houghton Mifflin.

Janis, I. L. (1989). *Crucial decisions: Leadership in policy making and crisis management.* New York: Free Press.

Jensen, A. D., & Chilberg, J. C. (1991). *Small group communication: Theory and application.* Belmont, CA: Wadsworth.

Johnson, D., & Johnson, F. (2003). *Joining together: Group theory and group skills* (8th ed.). Boston: Allyn & Bacon.

Jones, M. (2002). *Social psychology of prejudice.* Upper Saddle River, NJ: Prentice-Hall.

Jones, R., Oyung, R., & Pace, L. (2005). *Working virtually: Challenges of virtual teams.* Hershey, PA: IRM Press.

Jussim, L. J., McCauley, C. R., & Lee, Y.-T. (1995). Why study stereotype accuracy and inaccuracy? In Y.-T. Lee, L. J. Jussim, & C. R. McCauley (Eds.), *Stereotype accuracy: Toward appreciating group differences* (pp. 3–28). Washington, DC: American Psychological Association.

Kaplan, R. M. (2002). *How to say it in your job search: Choice words, phrases, sentences and paragraphs for résumés, cover letters and interviews.* Patamus, NJ: Prentice-Hall.

Kapoun, J. (2000, January 25). *Teaching undergraduates Web evaluation: A guide for library instruction* [Online]. Available: http://www.ala.org/acrl/undwebev.htm [Accessed October 17, 2001].

Katz, J. E., & Aspden, P. (2004). Social and public policy Internet research: Goals and achievements. www.communitytechnology.org/aspden.

Kelly, L., Phillips, G. M., & Keaen, J. A. (1995). *Teaching people to speak well: Training and remediation of communication reticence.* Cresskill, NJ: Hampton.

Kennedy C. W., & Camden, C. T. (1983). A new look at interruptions. *Western Journal of Speech Communication, 47,* 55.

Keyton, J. (1993). Group termination: Completing the study of group development. *Small Group Research, 24,* 84–100.

Kinesics. (2006, June 12). In *Wikipedia, The Free Encyclopedia.* Retrieved July 1, 2006, from http://en.wikipedia.org/w/index.php?title=Kinesics&oldid=58224782.

Klyukanov, I. E. (2005). *Principles of intercultural communication.* New York: Pearson.

Knapp, M. L., & Hall, J. A. (2006). *Nonverbal communication in human interaction* (5th ed.). Belmont, CA: Thomson Wadsworth.

Knapp, M. L. & Vangelisti, A. L. (2000). *Interpersonal communication and human relationships* (4th ed.). Boston: Allyn & Bacon.

Koehler, C. (1998, June 15). Mending the body by lending an ear: The healing power of listening. *Vital Speeches of the Day,* 543–544.

Koncz, A. (2006). Employers cite communication skills as key, but say many job seekers lack them. *Job Outlook 2006.* Bethlehem, PA: National Association of Colleges and Employers.

Kramer, J., & Kramarae, C. (1997). Gendered ethics on the Internet. In J. M. Makau & R. C. Arnett (Eds.), *Communication ethics in the age of diversity* (pp. 226–244). Chicago: University of Illinois Press.

Krotz, J. (2006). 6 tips for taking control in media interviews. www.microsoft.com/smallbuiness/resources/management/leadership_training_6 tips.

Kunkel, A. W., & Burleson, B. R. (1999). Assessing explanations for sex differences in emotional support: A test of the different cultures and skill specialization accounts. *Human Communication Research, 25,* 307–340.

Leary, M. R. (2002). When selves collide: The nature of the self and the dynamics of interpersonal relationships. In A. Tesser, D. A. Stapel, & J. V. Wood (Eds.), *Self and motivation: Emerging psychological perspectives* (pp. 119–145). Washington, DC: American Psychological Association.

Leathers, D. (1997). *Successful nonverbal communication: Principles and applications* (3rd ed.). Boston: Allyn & Bacon.

Lefton, L. A. (2001). *Interactive psychology online.* Boston: Allyn & Bacon.

Listening Factoid. (2003). [Online]. International Listening Association. Available: http://www.listen.org/pages/ factoids.html.

Littlejohn, S. W. (2002). *Theories of human communication* (7th ed.). Belmont, CA: Wadsworth.

Littlejohn, S. W., & Foss, K. A. (2005). *Theories of human communication.* Belmont, CA: Thomson Wadsworth.

Luckmann, J. (1999). *Transcultural communication in nursing.* New York: Delmar Publishers.

Luft, J. (1970). *Group processes: An introduction to group dynamics.* Palo Alto, CA: Mayfield.

Lulofs, R. S., & Cahn, D. D. (2000). *Conflict: From theory to action* (2nd ed.). Boston: Allyn & Bacon.

Martin, J. N., & Nakayama, T. K. (2000). *Intercultural communication in contexts* (2nd ed.). Mountain View, CA: Mayfield.

Martin, M. M., Anderson, C. M., & Horvath, C. L. (1996). Feelings about verbal aggression: Justifications for sending and hurt from receiving verbally aggressive messages. *Communication Research Reports, 13*(1), 19–26.

Maslow, A. H. (1954). *Motivation and personality.* New York: Harper & Row.

Masters, M. F., & Albright, R. R. (2002). *The complete guide to conflict resolution in the workplace.* New York: Amacom.

Mehrabian, A. (1972). *Nonverbal communication.* Chicago: Aldine.

McCroskey, J. C. (1970). Measures of communication-bound anxiety. *Speech Monographs* (November), 269–277.

McCroskey, J. C., & Beatty, M. J. (1998). Communication apprehension. In J. C. McCroskey, J. A. Daley, M. M. Martin, & M. J. Beatty (Eds.), *Communication and personality: Trait perspectives* (pp. 215–232). Cresshill, NJ: Hampton Press.

McCroskey, J. C., & McCroskey, L. L. (2002). Willingness to communicate and communication apprehension in the classroom. In J. L. Chesebro & J. C. McCroskey (Eds.), *Communication for teachers.* Boston: Allyn & Bacon.

McCroskey, J. C., & Neuliep, J. W. (1997). The development in intercultural and interethnic communication apprehension scales. *Communication Research Reports, 14,* 145–157.

McCroskey, J. C., & Tenin, J. J. (1999). Goodwill: A reexamination of the construct and its measurement. *Communication Monographs, 66,* 90–103.

McDaniel, E. R., Samovar, L. A., & Porter, R. E. (2006). Understanding intercultural communication: An overview. In L. A. Samovar, R. E. Porter, & E. R. McDaniel

(Eds.), *Intercultural communication: A reader* (11th ed., pp. 6–15). Belmont, CA: Thomson Wadsworth.

Menzel, K. E., & Carrell, L. J. (1994). The relationship between preparation and performance in public speaking. *Communication Education, 43,* 17–26.

Merriam-Webster's Collegiate Dictionary (2005). Springfield, MA: Merriam-Webster.

Michener, H. A., & DeLamater, J. D. (1999). *Social psychology* (4th ed.). Orlando, FL: Harcourt Brace.

Midura, D. W., & Glover, D. R. (2005). *Essentials of teambuilding.* Champaign, IL: Human Kinetics.

Miller, M. (1999). *The Lycos personal Internet guide.* Indianapolis, IN: Que Corporation.

Morse, S. (2001, January 1). The rap of change: A new generation of solutions. *Vital Speeches of the Day,* 186–189.

Motley, M. (1997). COM Therapy. In J. A. Daly, J. C. McCroskey, J. Ayres, T. Hopf, & D. M. Ayres (Eds.), *Avoiding communication: Shyness, reticence, and communication apprehension* (2nd ed., pp. 379–400). Cresskill, NJ: Hampton Press.

Mruk, C. (1999). *Self-esteem: Research, theory, and practice* (2nd ed.). New York: Springer.

Mulac, A. (1998). The gender-linked language effect: Do language differences really make a difference? In D. J. Canary & K. Dindia (Eds.), *Sex differences and similarities in communication: Critical essays and empirical investigations of sex and gender in interaction* (pp. 127–154). Mahwah, NJ: Erlbaum.

Munger, D., Anderson, D., Benjamin, B., Busiel, C., & Pardes-Holt, B. (2000). *Researching online* (3rd ed.). New York: Longman.

Nabi, Robin L. (2002). Discrete emotions and persuasion. In J. P. Dillard and M. Pfau (Eds.), *The persuasion handbook: Developments in theory and practice* (pp. 291–299). Thousand Oaks, CA: Sage.

Napier, R. W., & Gershenfeld, M. K. (1999). *Groups: Theory and experience* (6th ed.). Boston, MA: Houghton Mifflin Company.

Neuleip, J. W. (2006). *Intercultural communication: A contextual approach* (3rd ed.). Thousand Oaks, CA: Sage.

Nieto, S. (2000). *Affirming diversity: The sociological context of multicultural education* (3rd ed.). New York: Longman.

O'Connor, J. V. (2000). FAQs #1 Cuss Control Academy [Online]. Available: http://www.cusscontrol.com/faqs .html.

Ogden, C. K., & Richards, I. A. (1923). *The meaning of meaning.* London: Kegan, Paul, Trench, Trubner.

Okrent, D. (1999, May 10). Raising kids online: What can parents do? *Time,* pp. 38–43.

Omdahl, B. L. (1995). *Cognitive appraisal, emotion, and empathy.* Mahwah, NJ: Erlbaum.

Opheim, C. (2000, November 1). Making democracy work: Your responsibility to society. *Vital Speeches of the Day,* 60–61.

Patterson, B. R., Bettini, L., & Nussbaum, J. F. (1993). The meaning of friendship across the life-span: Two studies. *Communication Quarterly, 41,* 145.

Patterson, M. E., Danscreau, D. F., & Newbern, D. (1992). Effects of communication aids on cooperative teaching. *Journal of Educational Psychology, 84,* 453–461.

Patton, B. R., & Downs, T. M. (2003). *Decison-making group interaction* (4th ed.). Boston: Allyn & Bacon.

Pearson, J. C., West, R. L., & Turner, L. H. (1995). *Gender & communication* (3rd ed.). Dubuque, IA: Brown & Benchmark.

Petri, H. L. (1996). *Motivation: Theory, research, and applications* (4th ed.). Belmont, CA: Wadsworth.

Petronio, S. (2002). *Boundaries of privacy: Dialectics of disclosure.* Albany: State University of New York Press.

Petty, R. E., & Cacioppo, J. (1996). *Attitudes and persuasion: Classic and contemporary approaches.* Boulder, CO: Westview.

Petty, R. E., DeSteno, D., & Rucker, D. (2001). The role of affect in persuasion and attitude change. In J. Forgas (Ed.), *Handbook of affect and social cognition* (pp. 212–233). Mahwah, NJ: Erlbaum.

Petty, R. E., Wheeler, S. C., & Bizer, G. Y. (2000). Attitude functions and persuasion: An elaboration likelihood approach to matched versus mismatched messages. In G. R. Maio & J. M. Olson (Eds.), *Why we evaluate: Functions of attitudes* (pp. 133–162). Mahwah, NJ: Erlbaum.

Phillips, G. (1977). Rhetoritherapy versus the medical model: Dealing with reticence. *Communication Education, 26,* 34–43.

Preece, J. (2000). *Online communities.* New York: Wiley.

Rabby, M., & Walther, J. B. (2003). Computer mediated communication effects in relationship formation and maintenance. In D. J. Canary & M. Dainton (Eds.), *Maintaining relationships through communication* (pp. 141–162). Mahwah, NJ: Erlbaum.

Random House Dictionary of the English Language (2nd ed.). (1983). New York: Random House.

Rayner, S. G. (2001). Aspects of the self as learner: Perception, concept, and esteem. In R. J. Riding & S. G. Rayner (Eds.), *Self perception: International perspectives on individual differences,* vol. 2. Westport, CN: Ablex.

Reis, H. T. (1998). Gender differences in intimacy and related behaviors: Context and process. In D. J. Canary & K. Dindia (Eds.), *Sex differences and similarities in communication: Critical essays and empirical investigations of sex and gender in interaction* (pp. 203–232). Mahwah, NJ: Erlbaum.

Renz, M. A., & Greg, J. B. (2000). *Effective small group communication in theory and practice.* Boston: Allyn & Bacon.

Rhode, D. L. (Ed.) (2003). *The difference "difference" makes: Women and leadership.* Stanford, CA: Stanford Law and Politics.

Richmond, V. P., & McCroskey, J. C. (1995). *Communication: Apprehension, avoidance, and effectiveness* (4th ed.). Scottsdale, AZ: Gorsuch Scarisbrick.

Richmond, V. P., & McCroskey, J. C. (2000). *Communication: Apprehension, avoidance, and effectiveness* (5th ed.). Scottsdale, AZ: Gorsuch Scarisbrick.

Richmond, Y., & Gestrin, P. (1998). *Into Africa: Intercultural insights.* Yarmouth, ME: Intercultural Press.

Rockwell, Llewellyn B. (2006, March 1). Iraq and the democratic empire. *Vital Speeches of the Day,* 302.

Roloff, M. E., & Cloven, D. H. (1990). The chilling effect in interpersonal relationships: The reluctance to speak one's mind. In D. D. Cahn (Ed.), *Intimates in conflict: A communication perspective* (pp. 49–76). Hillsdale, NJ: Erlbaum.

Rosenfeld, L. B. (2000). Overview of the ways privacy, secrecy, and disclosure are balanced in today's society. In S. Petronio (Ed.), *Balancing the secrets of private disclosures* (pp. 3–18). Mahwah, NJ: Erlbaum.

Rothwell, J. D. (1998). *In mixed company* (3rd ed.). Fort Worth, TX: Harcourt Brace.

Rusbult, C. E., Olsen, N., Davis, J. L., & Hannon, P. A. (2004). Commitment and relationship maintenance mechanisms. In H. T. Reis & C. E. Rusbult (Eds.), *Key readings on close relationships* (pp. 287–304). Washington, DC: Taylor & Francis.

Samovar, L. A., & Porter, R. E. (2001). *Communication between cultures* (4th ed.). Belmont, CA: Wadsworth.

Samovar, L. A., Porter, R. E., & McDaniel, E. R. (2007). *Communication between cultures* (6th ed.). Belmont, CA: Thomson Wadsworth.

Samovar, L. A., Porter, R. E., & McDaniel, E. R. (Eds.) (2006). *Intercultural communication: A reader.* Belmont, CA: Thomson Learning.

Sampson, E. E. (1999). *Dealing with differences: An introduction to the social psychology of prejudice.* Fort Worth, TX: Harcourt Brace.

Samter, W. (2003). Friendship interaction skills across the lifespan. In J. O. Greene & B. R. Burleson (Eds.), *Handbook of communication and social interaction skills* (pp. 637–684). Mahwah, NJ: Erlbaum.

Schimanoff, S. B. (1980). *Communication rules: Theory and research.* Beverly Hills, CA: Sage.

Schmidt, W. V., & Conaway, R. N. (1999). *Results-oriented interviewing: Principles, practices, and procedures.* Boston: Allyn & Bacon.

Scott, P. (1997, January–February). Mind of a champion. *Natural Health, 27,* 99.

Shaw, M. E. (1981). *Group dynamics: The psychology of small group behavior* (3rd ed.). New York: McGraw-Hill.

Shimanoff, M. (1992). Group interaction and communication rules. In R. Cathcart & L. Samovar (Eds.), *Small group communication: A reader.* Dubuque, IA: Wm. Brown.

Spitzberg, B. H. (2000). A model of intercultural communication competence. In L. A. Samovar & R. E. Porter (Eds.), *Intercultural communication: A reader* (9th ed., pp. 375–387). Belmont, CA: Wadsworth.

Spitzberg, B. H. (2003). Methods of interpersonal skill assessment. In J. O. Greene & B. R. Burleson (Eds.), *Handbook of communication and social interaction skills* (pp. 93–134). Mahwah, NJ: Erlbaum.

Spitzberg, B. H., & Cupach, W. R. (2002). Interpersonal skills. In M. L. Knapp & J. A. Daly (Eds.), *Handbook of interpersonal communication* (pp. 564–611). Thousand Oaks, CA: Sage.

Stewart, C. J., & Cash, W. B. (2000). *Interviewing: Principles and practices* (9th ed.). Dubuque, IA: William C. Brown.

Stewart, L. P., Cooper, P. J., Stewart, A. D., & Friedley, S. A. (1998). *Communication and gender* (3rd ed.). Boston: Allyn & Bacon.

Stiff, J. B., Dillard, J. P., Somera, L., Kim, H., & Sleight, C. (1988). Empathy, communication and prosocial behavior. *Communication Monographs, 55,* 198–213.

Sundstrom, E., DeMeuse, K. P., & Futrell, D. (1990, February). Work teams: Applications and effectiveness. *American Psychologist,* 120–133.

Tannen, D. (2003). "Put that paper down and talk to me!": Rapport-talk and report-talk. In K. M. Galvin & P. J. Cooper (Eds.), *Making connections: Readings in relational communication* (3rd ed., pp. 91–102). Los Angeles: Roxbury.

Tannen, D. (1990). *You just don't understand.* New York: HarperCollins.

Tanno, D. V. (2001). Names, narratives, and the evolution of ethnic identity. In A. Gonzalez, M. Houston, & V. Chen (Eds.), *Our voices: Essays in cultural ethnicity and communication* (3rd ed., pp. 25–28). Los Angeles: Roxbury.

Taylor, D. A., & Altman, I. (1987). Communication in interpersonal relationships: Social penetration theory. In M. E. Roloff & G. R. Miller (Eds.), *Interpersonal processes: New directions in communication research* (pp. 257–277). Beverly Hills, CA: Sage.

Temple, L. E., & Loewen, K. R. (1993). Perceptions of power: First impressions of a woman wearing a jacket. *Perceptual and Motor Skills, 76,* 345.

Tengler, C. D., & Jablin, F. M. (1983). Effects of question type, orientation, and sequencing in the employment screening interview. *Communication Monographs, 50,* 261.

Terkel, S. N., & Duval, R. S. (Eds.) (1999). *Encyclopedia of ethics.* New York: Facts on File.

The World Almanac and Book of Facts. Mahwah, NJ: World Almanac Books, 2001.

Thames, T. B. (2006, March 1). Window of opportunity: The AARP perspective on reforming America's health care system. *Vital Speeches of the Day,* 315.

Thibaut, J. W., & Kelley, H. H. (1986). *The social psychology of groups* (reprint). New Brunswick, NJ: Transaction Books.

Thurlow, C., Lengel, L., & Tomic, A. (2004). *Computer mediated communication: Social interaction and the Internet.* Thousand Oaks, CA: Sage.

Tillerson, R. W. (2006, May 6). Economic and environmental solutions in the global energy system. *Vital Speeches of the Day,* 441.

Ting-Toomey, S. (1999). *Communicating across cultures.* New York: Guilford Press.

Ting-Toomey, S., Yee-Jung, K., Shapiro, R., Garcia, W., Wright, T., & Oetzel, J. G. (2000). Cultural/ethnic identity salience and conflict styles. *International Journal of Intercultural Relations, 23,* 47–81.

Toulmin, S. (1958). *The uses of argument.* Cambridge: Cambridge University Press.

Trachtenberg, S. J. (1986, August 15). Five ways in which thinking is dangerous. *Vital Speeches of the Day,* 653.

Tracy, K. (2002). *Everyday talk: Building and reflecting identities.* New York: Guilford Press.

Trompenaars, F., & Hampden-Turner, C. (2004). *Managing people across cultures.* Oxford: Capstone.

Trujillo, S. D. (2002, April 15). The Hispanic destiny: Corporate responsibility. *Vital Speeches of the Day,* 406.

Tuckman, B. W. (1965). Developmental sequence in small groups. *Psychological Bulletin, 6393,* 384–399.

Turk, D. R., & Monahan, J. L. (1999). "Here I go again": An examination of repetitive behaviors during interpersonal conflicts. *Southern Communication Journal, 64* (Spring), 232–244.

Turner, M. M., Mazur, M. A., Wendel, N., & Winslow, R. (2003). Relational ruin or social glue? The joint effect of relationship type and gossip valence on liking, trust, and expertise. *Communication Monographs, 70*(2), 129–141.

Tversky, B. (1997). Memory for pictures, maps, environments, and graphs. In D. G. Payne & F. G. Conrad (Eds.), *Intersections in basic and applied memory research* (pp. 257–277). Mahwah, NJ: Erlbaum.

Valacich, J. S., George, J. F., Nonamaker, J. F., Jr., & Vogel, D. R. (1994). Idea generation in computer based groups: A new ending to an old story. *Small Group Research, 25,* 83–104.

Valian, V. (1998). *Why so slow? The advancement of women.* Cambridge, MA: MIT Press.

Vangelisti, A. L. (2002). Interpersonal processes in romantic relationship. In M. L. Knapp & J. A. Daly (Eds.), *Handbook of interpersonal communication* (3rd ed., pp. 643–679). Thousand Oaks, CA: Sage.

Vegan Society's Web site, http://www.vegansociety.com.

Waldeck, J. H., Kearney, P., & Plax, T. G. (2001). Teacher e-mail message strategies and students' willingness to communicate. *Journal of Applied Communication Research, 29,* 54–70.

Walther, J. B. (1996). Computer-mediated communication: Impersonal, interpersonal and hyperpersonal interaction. *Western Journal of Communication, 57,* 381–398.

Walther, J. B., & Parks, M. R. (2002). Cues filtered out, cues filtered in: Computer-mediated communication and relationships. In M. C. Knapp & J. A. Daly (Eds.), *Handbook of interpersonal communication* (pp. 529–563). Thousand Oaks, CA: Sage.

Ward, C. C., & Tracy, T. J. G. (2004). Relation of shyness with aspects of online relationship involvement. *Journal of Social and Personal Relationships, 21,* 611–623.

Weaver, J. B. III, & Kirtley, M. B. (1995). Listening styles and empathy. *Southern Communication Journal, 60,* 131–140.

Weiten, W. (1998). *Psychology: Themes and variations* (4th ed.). Pacific Grove, CA: Brooks/Cole.

Wikipedia, http://en.wikipedia.org/wiki/kinesics, 2006.

Wheelen, S. A., & Hochberger, J. M. (1996). Validation studies of the group development questionnaire. *Small Group Research, 27*(1), 143–170.

Whetten, D. A., & Cameron, K. S. (2002). *Developing management skills* (5th ed.). Upper Saddle River, NJ: Prentice-Hall.

Widmer, W. N., & Williams, J. M. (1991). Predicting cohesion in a coacting sport. *Small Group Research, 22,* 548–570.

Williams, R. G., & Ware, J. E., Jr. (1976). Validity of student ratings of instruction under different incentive conditions: A further study of the Dr. Fox effect. *Journal of Educational Psychology, 68,* 48–56.

Wilson, G. L. (2005). *Groups in context: Leadership and participation in small groups* (7th ed.). New York: McGraw Hill.

Winstead, B. A., Derlega, V. J., & Rose, S. (1997). *Gender and close relationships.* Thousand Oaks, CA: Sage.

Wolvin, A., & Coakley, C. G. (1996*). Listening* (5th ed.). Dubuque, IA: Brown & Benchmark.

Wood, J. T. (2007). *Gendered lives: Communication, gender, and culture* (7th ed.). Belmont, CA: Wadsworth.

Wood, J. T., & Dindia, K. (1998). What's the difference? A dialogue about differences and similarities between women and men. In D. J. Canary & K. Dindia (Eds.), *Sex differences and similarities in communication: Critical essays and empirical investigations of sex and gender in interaction* (pp. 19–40). Mahwah, NJ: Erlbaum.

Wood, J. T., & Inman, C. (1993). In a different mode: Recognizing male modes of closeness. *Journal of Applied Communication Research, 21,* 279–295.

Wright, J. W. (2002). *New York Times Almanac.* New York: New York Times.

Young, K. S., Wood, J. T., Phillips, G. M., & Pederson, J. D. (2000). *Group discussion: A practical guide to participation and leadership* (3rd ed.). Prospect Heights, IL: Waveland Press.

Zempke, R., Raines, C., & Filipczak (2000). *Generations at work.* New York: Amacom.

INDEX

Italicized page numbers indicate materials in figures, graphs, or tables.